THE ROUTLEDGE HISTORY OF SOCIAL PROTEST IN POPULAR MUSIC

Edited by
Jonathan C. Friedman

Routledge
Taylor & Francis Group

NEW YORK AND LONDON

First published in paperback 2017

First published 2013
by Routledge
711 Third Avenue, New York, NY 10017

Simultaneously published in the UK
by Routledge
2 Park Square, Milton Park, Abingdon, Oxon OX14 4RN

Routledge is an imprint of the Taylor & Francis Group, an informa business

Library of Congress Cataloging in Publication Data
   The Routledge history of social protest in popular music /
   edited by Jonathan C. Friedman.
   pages cm
   1. Popular music—Political aspects. 2. Popular music—Social aspects.
   3. Protest songs—History and criticism.
   4. Protest movements—Songs and music.
   I. Friedman, Jonathan C., 1966– editor.
   ML3918.P67R68 2013
   781.64'1592—dc23
   2012046125

ISBN: 978–0–415–50952–7 (hbk)
ISBN: 978–1–138–21622–8 (pbk)
ISBN: 978–0–203–12488–8 (ebk)

Typeset in Baskerville MT
by Swales & Willis Ltd, Exeter, Devon
Printed at CPI on sustainably sourced paper

Senior editor: Constance Ditzel
Editorial assistant: Elysse Preposi
Production manager: Bonita Glanville-Morris
Senior marketing manager: Paul Myatovich
Project manager: Swales & Willis Ltd
Copy editor: Polly Morgan for Swales and Willis
Proofreader: Lizzie Kent
Cover designer: Jayne Varney

CONTENTS

CONTENTS

CONTRIBUTORS

Saheed Aderinto is an assistant professor of history at Western Carolina University. He received his Ph.D. in African history from the University of Texas at Austin, and his areas of expertise include gender and sexuality; nationalism and historiography; peace and conflict; and the African Diaspora. In addition to numerous journal articles, book chapters, encyclopedia entries, and book reviews, Dr. Aderinto is the co-author of *Nigeria, Nationalism, and Writing History* (University of Rochester Press, 2010). He is currently working on another monograph on the history of sexuality in Lagos, Nigeria.

Benjamin Bierman is a composer, trumpet player, educator, arranger, producer, and bandleader. His works have been performed by, among others, Cygnus Ensemble, Monica Harte, The Remarkable Theater Brigade, 60×60 Project, Anderson/Fader guitar duo, The New York Victorian Consort (he is their resident arranger), and the CUNY Graduate Center Contemporary Music Ensemble. Ben was the Composer-in-Residence for the Goliard Ensemble, and his orchestral work "Proximities" was conferred the status of special recognition by the Los Angeles Philharmonic in their Synergy Project competition. He is currently an assistant professor in the Department of Art and Music at John Jay College of Criminal Justice, City University of New York.

Anne-Kristin Borszik graduated as a sociologist from Freie Universität Berlin (Germany) in 2004, with a thesis on composition strategies, development discourses and listeners' preferences in "intervention music" from Guinea-Bissau. After having collaborated with a Portuguese NGO as project manager for São Tomé and Príncipe and Guinea-Bissau, she is, since 2007, the coordinator of a collaborative research project that analyzes strategies of conflict management in Guinea-Bissau. Within this project, she is also writing her Ph.D. entitled "There is No Justice in Guinea-Bissau: A Case Study of Institutions and Modes of Dispute Settlement."

Ingrid Bianca Byerly received her undergraduate education in her native country, South Africa, before doing graduate work in England and the United States. She received her Ph.D. from Duke University in ethnomusicology. Dr. Byerly is a senior lecturing fellow in cultural anthropology and music at Duke, and adjunct professor of music for the University of Virginia's Semester at Sea program, teaching courses in Global Music and the Politics of Music on their Round-the-World and Mediterranean voyages.

Elyse Carter Vosen is an assistant professor in the Department of Global, Cultural, and Language Studies at The College of St. Scholastica, where she teaches cultural studies, anthropology, and ethnomusicology, and directs the Oreck-Alpern Interreligious Forum. She has worked closely with members of the Anishinaabe communities in northern Minnesota and taught Ojibwe language for the past fourteen years. Her dissertation explored popular music and drum and dance performance as decolonizing forces in the lives of Anishinaabe young people and their communities.

John Cline is a Ph.D. graduate of the University of Texas at Austin's Department of American Studies. He has written extensively on both popular music and film, in both popular and academic settings. His work has been published in *The Oxford American* magazine, *The Los Angeles Review of Books*, *The Grove Dictionary of American Music*, and *The Oxford Handbook of Science Fiction*. With co-editor Robert G. Weiner, he published two books on "transgressive cinema" (*From the Arthouse to the Grindhouse* and *Cinema Inferno*) in 2010. John is currently working on two manuscripts: one about experimental music collectives, the other on Harry Belafonte's 1956 album, *Calypso*.

H. Louise Davis is currently assistant professor of American Studies and Director of the Bachelor of Integrative Studies Program at Miami University in Miami, Ohio. A specialist in ethical consumerism, social movements, and media and cultural studies, Professor Davis has published articles on representations of the African Madonna and Child icon and celebrity activism. She is currently working on a book-length exploration of an emerging transatlantic "culture of charity" that emerged out of Third World Aid campaigns of the mid-1980s.

Jacqueline Edmondson is associate dean for undergraduate and graduate studies and professor of education at the Pennsylvania State University. She has published a number of biographies for adolescent readers and is editor of *Music in American Life: The Songs, Stars, Styles and Stories That Shaped Our Culture* (Santa Barbara, CA: ABC-CLIO, forthcoming, 2013).

Jonathan C. Friedman is professor of history and Director of Holocaust and Genocide Studies at West Chester University, in West Chester, Pennsylvania. He is the author or editor of six books, including *The Routledge History of the Holocaust* (Routledge, 2011), *Rainbow Jews: Gay and Jewish Identity in the Performing Arts* (Lexington Books, 2007), and *The Lion and the Star: Gentile-Jewish Relations in Three Hessian Communities, 1919–1945* (University Press of Kentucky, 1998).

Scott Gac, author of *Singing for Freedom: The Hutchinson Family Singers and the Nineteenth-Century Culture of Antebellum Reform* (Yale University Press, 2007), is an associate professor of American studies and history at Trinity College in Hartford, Connecticut. He writes on nineteenth-century American entertainment, culture, and violence.

Stephen Gaunson is a cultural and film historian. He currently holds the position of teaching and research fellow in the School of Media and Communication at RMIT University. His research interests cover history films, adaptation, genre and representation. His new book, *The Ned Kelly Films*, is forthcoming from Intellect.

Travis A. Jackson is an ethnomusicologist and associate professor of music and the humanities at the University of Chicago whose work centers on jazz, rock, and recording technology. His theoretical interests include urban geography, race/culture and identity, ethnographic method, performance and aesthetics. He is author of *Blowin' the Blues Away: Performance and Meaning on the New York Jazz Scene* (California, forthcoming), as well as articles on topics ranging from the intersection of jazz and poetic performance to the interpretation of meaning in rock. His current work focuses on the affective attachment of musicians and listeners to recording labels.

Kile Jones holds a Master's in Theological Studies (M.T.S.) and a Master's in Sacred Theology (S.T.M.) from Boston University. He is working towards a Ph.D. in Religion, Ethics, and Society at Claremont Lincoln University. He has been published in *Free Inquiry*, *Philosophy Now*, *Zygon: Journal of Religion and Science*, and many others. He is the Founder/Editor-in-Chief of *The Claremont Journal of Religion*.

Stephen A. King is professor of communication studies at Delta State University, located in Cleveland, Mississippi. **P. Renee Foster** is an instructor of marketing at Delta State University. King and Foster have worked extensively on popular music and heritage tourism, publishing their work in journals including the *Journal of Nonprofit & Public Sector Marketing*. Foster served as a contributor to King's 2002 book, *Reggae, Rastafari, and the Reggae of Social Control* (University Press of Mississippi). King's second book, *I'm Feeling the Blues Right Now: Blues Tourism and the Mississippi Delta*, was published by the University Press of Mississippi in 2011. King's work has also been published in a variety of journals, including the *Southern Communication Journal*, *Popular Music and Society*, and *Caribbean Studies*, as well as edited books such as *The Resisting Muse: Popular Music and Social Protest* (Ashgate, 2006) and *Popular Music and Human Rights, Volume I* (Ashgate, 2011).

Robert J. Kodosky is an assistant professor of history at West Chester University, Pennsylvania. He is the author of *Psychological Operations American Style* (Lexington Books, 2007). He has contributed articles to the *Encyclopedia of Military Science*, *The Journal of Popular Culture*, the *Philadelphia Inquirer* and *Public History News*. He has reviewed numerous books for *History: Reviews of New Books* and *H-War*. He also coordinates Soldiers to Scholars (www.soldierstoscholars.com), an oral history project focused on military veterans returning from Iraq and Afghanistan.

Prakash Kona is a writer, teacher, and researcher, working as an associate professor in the department of English literature at The English and Foreign Languages University (EFLU) in Hyderabad, India. He is the author of *Nunc Stans* (Crossing Chaos Enigmatic Ink, Ontario, Canada, 2009), *Pearls of an Unstrung Necklace* (Fugue State Press, 2005), and *Streets That Smell of Dying Roses* (Fugue State Press, 2003).

Edward Macan is professor of music at College of the Redwoods in Eureka, California. He is the author of *Rocking the Classics: English Progressive Rock and the Counterculture* (Oxford, 1997), *Endless Enigma: A Musical Biography of Emerson, Lake and Palmer* (Open Court, 2006), and numerous articles on rock music subjects. He is currently writing a book that surveys the impact of pastoralism, medievalism, and orientalism on the music of Ralph Vaughan Williams, Gustav Holst, and subsequent British music.

Nandipha Malange is a graduate student at Nelson Mandela Metropolitan University in South Africa. Her research interests include Apartheid and post-Apartheid, as well as race and development in Southern Africa.

Mark Malisa teaches at the College of Saint Rose in Albany, New York. His research interests include African cultures and globalization.

Shayna Maskell is a Ph.D. candidate in American Studies at the University of Maryland, focusing on Washington, DC, punk rock from 1978 to 1983 through the lens of aesthetics and politics. She has been published in the *Journal of Popular Music Studies*, written a chapter on the Bonnaroo Music Festival in *Festivals and Fairs: American Culture, Sub-Culture and Counter-Culture*, and one on class and race in DC punk in *Punkademics*. In addition, she has presented papers on Patti Smith and music as a form of social change; Bad Brains and the Construction of Identity, Class and Race in DC Punk Rock; and the World Social Forum and Post-Colonialism.

Allan Moore is professor of popular music at the University of Surrey, U.K. Author of more than 100 articles and books on popular music, he is on the editorial board of the journal *Popular Music*, and was series editor for Ashgate's *Library of Essays on Popular Music*. His hermeneutic methodology for popular song, *Song Means*, was recently published by Ashgate. He is currently engaged on preparing a third edition of his *Rock: The Primary Text* and is also working on a critical history of the English folk-song tradition in the twentieth century.

Burton W. Peretti is professor of history at Western Connecticut State University. He is the author of *Lift Every Voice: The History of African American Music* (2009), *Night-*

club City: Politics and Amusement in Manhattan (2007), *Jazz in American Culture* (1997), *The Creation of Jazz: Music, Race, and Culture in Urban America* (1992), and numerous articles.

Anna G. Piotrowska received her Ph.D. in musicology in 2002 from Jagiellonian University, in Krakow, Poland, completing a dissertation entitled, *The Idea of National Music in the Works of American Composers in the First Half of the 20th Century*. She is currently an assistant professor in the Institute of Musicology at Jagiellonian University.

Dennis Rea is a Seattle-based musician and author whose book *Live at the Forbidden City: Musical Encounters in China and Taiwan* was published in 2006. He was a key participant in both the mainland Chinese and Taiwanese music scenes from 1989 to 1996. He currently performs with the acclaimed instrumental band Moraine, among many other involvements.

David Alexander Robinson is a lecturer of history and politics at Edith Cowan University, Western Australia, where he teaches courses on global history, war and conflict, human rights, and genocide. His eclectic research interests include African history, international relations, contemporary social movements, Marxist political economy, and Zizekian social theory. Amongst his ongoing research projects is a book on the politics and lyrical references of the radical rap-metal band Rage Against the Machine.

Ricardo Santhiago is a journalist and a historian. He is the co-coordinator of the Center for Studies in Music and Media (MusiMid) and an associated researcher at the University of São Paulo, Brazil. He holds a Master's in Social History from the same institution and is completing his doctoral dissertation on the development of oral history in Brazil. He has published numerous works, including the authored book *Solistas Dissonantes: História (Oral) de Cantoras Negras* (Letra e Voz, 2009) and the edited book *O Brasil dos Gilbertos: Notas Sobre o Pensamento (Musical) Brasileiro* (Letra e Voz, 2011, co-edited with Heloísa Valente).

James Smethurst is professor of Afro-American studies at the University of Massachusetts Amherst. Professor Smethurst is the author of numerous books, including *The New Red Negro: The Literary Left and African American Poetry, 1930–1946* (Oxford, 1999), *The Black Arts Movement: Literary Nationalism in the 1960s and 1970s* (University of North Carolina Press, 2005), and *The African American Roots of Modernism: Reconstruction to the Harlem Renaissance* (University of North Carolina Press, 2011). He is currently working on a history of the Black Arts Movement in the South and is co-editing *SOS? Calling All Black People: A Black Arts Reader*, with John Bracey and Sonia Sanchez.

Katherine L. Turner holds a Ph.D. in musicology from the University of Texas. Her areas of specialty include the musical cultures of early modern women and the politics of popular music in the first half of the twentieth century, especially music as part of the Long Civil Rights Movement. She has presented across the United States and internationally, and is currently editing a collection of essays on music and irony and working on a monograph on "Strange Fruit."

Robert G. Weiner is associate humanities librarian at Texas Tech University and liaison to the College of Visual and Performing Arts. He has been published in the *Routledge History of the Holocaust, The Gospel According to Superheroes, Undead in the West,* and *Too Bold for the Box Office.* He is the author of *Marvel Graphic Novels* and co-author of the *Grateful Dead and the Deadheads.* Weiner has edited or co-edited *Web Spinning Heroics, Perspectives on the Grateful Dead, The Storyteller Speaks: Rare and Different Fictions of the Grateful Dead, From the Arthouse to the Grindhouse, Cinema Inferno,* and numerous others books related to films, comics, music, and popular culture. He has also been published in *Shofar, West Texas Historical Association Yearbook, Texas Library Journal,* and the *Journal of Popular Culture.* He is on the editorial board of the *Journal of Graphic Novels and Comics* (also published by Routledge). He lives in Lubbock Texas with a group of magical creatures known as prairie dogs.

Gail Hilson Woldu, professor of music at Trinity College in Connecticut, is a music historian who has written extensively on American popular music and music in France between 1870 and 1930. Her most recent scholarship focuses on schools of music in France, composer Vincent d'Indy, and hip-hop culture. Two books are the result of this work: *The Words and Music of Ice Cube* (Praeger, 2008) and a translation with introduction and notes of *Vincent d'Indy's Cours de composition musicale* (University of Oklahoma Press, 2010). Professor Woldu is writing a book on the music of black American women. She holds degrees from Yale University (Ph.D.) and Goucher College (B.A.).

INTRODUCTION

What Is Social Protest Music? One Historian's Perspective

Jonathan C. Friedman

My parents tell the story that, sometime in 1969, when I was three years old, my grandparents took me shopping in Columbus, Ohio, and were mortified that, as we strolled down the aisles, I was singing at the top of my lungs the words from "Solidarity Forever" and Woody Guthrie's "Union Maid." These very sweet middle-American, Eisenhower Republicans (who today would have been regarded as socialists by many within the current Republican establishment), wondered what on earth my parents were teaching me. My father was hardly a leftie; he had just written an article on the problem of race for *The National Review*, and neither he nor my mother subscribed to the counter-culture. In fact, I don't think we even had a Beatles record in the house until I bought one in high school. Yet my parents loved folk music, and they owned a copy of the Almanac Singers' *Talking Union*, from 1941, which, along with other standard kids' fare from the time, I apparently devoured. The retention of such a song at the exclusion of newer protest music from the 1960s offered insight into my parents' "silent generation," and the song was perhaps the first glimpse into what would become (to my parents' dismay) a lifelong social commitment to "all-things-hippie" on my part.

Professionally, I followed in my father's footsteps and studied modern Jewish history and the Holocaust, eventually becoming a professor of Holocaust and Genocide Studies at West Chester University in Pennsylvania. While my first research projects were very much within the dominant modes of inquiry for someone in the field, I quickly moved beyond the boundaries of European history to merge my interests in social justice and musical performance in order to investigate protest on the Broadway stage and the intersection of gay and Jewish identity in the performing arts. Although some have regarded these cross-disciplinary and cross-thematic forays as either irrelevant or vanity projects, I see them as central to any study of persecution and how a victimized group can respond to such persecution, in this case through performance. Scholars of the Holocaust are keenly aware of the impact of popular culture on preserving historical memory. After *Schindler's List*, Steven Spielberg created the Survivors of the Shoah Foundation to collect the oral testimonies of thousands of Holocaust survivors. Just as dramatic, after the West German broadcast of the 1979 television miniseries, *The Holocaust*, public opinion moved in favor of a more thorough and collective soul-searching, and it may have helped to tip the balance in the German parliament towards removing the statute of limitations on Nazi war crimes.

Performance is clearly a potent medium for spreading and making accessible what otherwise might be problematic and unpopular. A song's poetry and music can change reality, maybe not by immediately resulting in changes in law, but by having a deeper impact on the society that makes laws. "We Shall Overcome" is perhaps nearly as emblematic of the civil rights movement as Martin Luther King's "I Have a Dream" speech.[1] The culture and musical expression of the antiwar movement of the 1960s are also nearly impossible to separate from a discussion of its politics. In the late 1980s, and especially in to the 1990s, a number of important protest pieces on Broadway, television, and film, raised awareness about AIDS and helped to cultivate greater sympathy and action on behalf of sufferers of the disease. In the end, I would argue that one cannot understate the impact of performance on both shifts in popular attitudes and the construction of the national imaginary. In the words of David Román, professor of English at the University of Southern California, performance allows for a "process of exchange—between artists and audiences, between the past and the present—where new societal formations emerge."[2]

The major objective of this volume is to analyze the trends, musical formats, and rhetorical devices used in popular music to illuminate the human condition. By comparing and contrasting musical offerings in a number of countries, and in different contexts from the nineteenth century until today, the book aims to be a sweeping introduction to the history of social protest music. Questions and themes which the volume will address include:

1 What is social protest music?
2 What has been the historical link between social protest and popular music, and how has this evolved over time?
3 What has been the impact of social protest music on society in general?
4 How has social protest music addressed issues of race, gender, and class?
5 What were the diverse forms of social protest music in the United States in the twentieth century? How or why did so much social protest come from this one setting?
6 What are the shared tropological characteristics of, and salient differences between, musical social protest forms in countries across the globe?
7 What are criteria for effective uses of music as a form of social protest?

This collection demonstrates the great diversity in form and content of popular music (rock and roll in particular) as a means of social protest over time, focusing largely on the American and British context but also including a scan across continents. The volume owes its theoretical framework to the work of scholars Reebee Garofalo, Ian Peddie, R. Serge Denisoff, Ron Eyerman, and Andrew Jamison. Denisoff, one of the first sociologists to examine critically the role of protest music, saw such songs as functions of a broader political movement. "Magnetic" songs, like "Give Peace a Chance," and "We Shall Overcome" attract people to movements and promote group solidarity.[3] "Rhetorical" songs (like Marvin Gaye's "What's Goin' On," and one of my personal favorites, Peter Gabriel's "Biko") are intended to change public opinion.[4] Eyerman and Jamison, in their groundbreaking work from 1998, *Music and Social Movements*, argued that Denisoff's view was too narrow, insisting that, "in social movements, musical and other kinds of cultural traditions are made and remade, and after movements fade away as political forces, the music remains as memory and as a potential way to inspire new waves of mobilization."[5] "What's Goin' On" illuminates this point, re-recorded in 2001 in multiple versions as an album to combat AIDS. The embrace by the gay rights movement in the 1970s of disco music and songs like Queen's "We Are the Champions," which were not intended as protest media, demonstrates how music can be reinvented and encoded with protest content over time.

By virtue of the history of rock music, the volume is primarily Anglo-American centered, but a focus on this realm from the 1950s onward alone would be too narrow. I began with the supposition that the book's temporal and spatial framework had to be broadened for it to have the greatest explanatory power. This entailed going back in time in United States history to show the various strands of musical protest in popular music that fed into rock and roll, and then expanding outward from the US to assess similar musical movements worldwide—and particularly the relationship between an external cultural force, like American rock, and indigenous pop music forms with protest content. Because of the historically significant impact of rock from the United Kingdom (from the "British Invasion" through punk and beyond), it is essential to include a number of distinct, stand-alone chapters here. To end the story in this way, though, would render voiceless the bulk of the world's population. In order to present a full picture in a way that is both specific (about social protest in rock and pop music) and broad in its application, I envisioned a volume in three parts—one dealing with the historical roots of pop music protest in the US in the nineteenth century through the 1960s; one dealing with protest in diverse forms of rock from the 1970s onward; and, finally, a part focusing on rock/pop, politics, and social criticism across continents.

Protest music continues to be a relevant mode of artist expression and, when music is overtly political, controversy usually lurks close behind. Neil Young's 2006 song, "Let's Impeach the President," slammed the US war in Iraq, and in 2010 songwriters Mexia and Raul Antonio Hernandez protested Arizona's controversial immigration law with "Todos Somos Arizona—We Are All Arizona." The assault on unions by Republican lawmakers, which began with a vengeance in Wisconsin in 2011, resulted in VO5's aptly titled "Cheddar Revolution." In May 2011, television personality Jon Stewart faced off against his conservative counterpart Bill O'Reilly over the issue of rapper Common's performance at the White House. Common has a song defending Joanne Chesimard, aka Assata Shakur, an African-American activist, former member of the Black Panthers, and convicted cop killer who escaped from prison in 1979 and has been living in Cuba ever since. During the interview, Stewart pointed to the hypocrisy of those on the right not decrying visits to the Bush White House by U2's Bono, whose song, "Native Son," about the Native American activist and convicted killer of two FBI agents, Leonard Peltier, could merit similar outrage.

Protest songs might not always be effective, nor may their impact be immediately felt, as Denisoff importantly reminds us.[6] Even Pete Seeger recognized his medium's limitations when he declared in 1968 that "No song I can sign will make Governor Wallace change his mind."[7] In 2012, the music accompanying the protests against union busting in Wisconsin did not help sway the voters of the state to recall their governor, and the "shock protest" against Vladimir Putin staged by the Russian feminist punk rock band Pussy Riot in Moscow's Cathedral of Christ the Savior in February 2012 resulted in two-year prison sentences for three of its members. Whatever the result of such public agitprop, it is clear that protest through song has become embedded in the DNA of our modern social and political fabric. The far more lasting significance of the musical canon of protest music is what it reveals about the human condition in the modern world of mass mobilization, mass politics, and mass media.

Notes

1 Dr. King declared that protest songs "serve to give unity to a movement." King, "Protest Movements: Class Consciousness and the Propaganda Song," *Sociological Quarterly*, Vol. 9 (Spring 1968): 228–247.

2 David Román, *Performance in America: Contemporary U.S. Culture and the Performing Arts* (Durham, North Carolina: Duke University Press, 2005), 1, 2.

3 Ron Eyerman and Andrew Jamison, *Music and Social Movements: Mobilizing Traditions in the 20th Century* (Cambridge: Cambridge University Press, 1998), 9. See also R. Serge Denisoff, *The Sounds of Social Change* (New York: Rand McNally, 1972), Reebee Garofalo, ed., *Rockin' the Boat: Mass Music and Mass Movements* (Cambridge, Massachusetts: South End Press, 1992), and Ian Peddie, *The Resisting Muse: Popular Music and Social Protest* (Burlington, Vermont: Ashgate Publishing, 2006).

4 Eyerman and Jamison, *Music and Social Movements*, 9.

5 Eyerman and Jamison, *Music and Social Movements*, 1, 2.

6 R. Serge Denisoff, "Protest Songs: Those on the Top Forty, and Those of the Streets," *American Quarterly*, Vol. 22, No. 4 (Winter 1970): 807–823.

7 Pete Seeger, "False from True," *Broadside*, Vol. 88 (January 1968), 1, as cited in Denisoff, "Protest Songs," 823.

Part I

HISTORICAL BEGINNINGS, WAR, AND CIVIL RIGHTS

1

SIGNIFYING FREEDOM

Protest in Nineteenth-Century African American Music

Burton W. Peretti

Figure 1.1 Slaves dance to music on a Southern plantation.

Two significant artifacts bracket the history of African American music in the nineteenth century: Richard Allen's *Collection of Spiritual Songs and Hymns* and James Weldon Johnson's and John Rosamond Johnson's song, *Lift Every Voice and Sing*.

In 1801, Allen, a former slave and a Methodist minister in Philadelphia, published his hymnal, the first ever compiled by an African American. Blending Allen's own verse with popular lyrics by Isaac Watts and other whites, the hymnal expressed the evangelical Christian dichotomy of good and evil. It did not, however, specifically mention slavery or emancipation. The *Collection* was a milestone in the founding of the African Methodist Episcopal (AME) Church. The AME Church was created by Allen and others in reaction to racial discrimination by white Methodists. In services, the hymnal was utilized in a culturally African American manner. Its contents were "lined out" by deacons, and congregants repeated the lines in response. Allen's hymnal inspired an urban form of the African tradition of call and response. Similarly, the hymns' images of sinners burning in hell and Christians finding salvation informed parishioners' views of slavery, which still flourished south of Pennsylvania. After 1810, Allen grew pessimistic about race relations and helped to plan efforts to colonize free blacks in West Africa. In these ways, the general sentiments of sin and salvation in the hymns took on political meaning within the AME.[1]

In 1900, James Weldon Johnson, principal of the Stanton School in Jacksonville, Florida, read his new poem "Lift Every Voice and Sing" at the school's annual Lincoln's Birthday celebration. Slavery now was extinct, and African American churches, schools, and other institutions had proliferated. "Lift Every Voice and Sing" indirectly paid tribute to Booker T. Washington, the guest of honor that day, whose national prominence was unprecedented among African Americans. Five years later, James's brother, John Rosamond Johnson, a successful songwriter and performer, set the poem to music. In 1919 the National Association for the Advancement of Colored People (NAACP) proclaimed the Johnsons' song "the Negro National Anthem."[2]

The differing circumstances surrounding Allen's hymnal and the Johnsons' anthem encapsulates a century of change for African Americans. As the 1800s dawned, slavery was the norm of black life. Allen witnessed the revolution in Haiti, but also the failure of revolts in the United States and the westward expansion of slavery. After Allen's death in 1831, though, political and military conflict led to the destruction of slavery and a new legal status for all black people. The Johnson brothers in 1900 enjoyed freedoms, wealth, and opportunities that Allen had never known. Nevertheless, despite these changes, the United States in 1900 remained discriminatory and lethally hostile to blacks. After the demise of Reconstruction, segregation, lynching, and unequal justice ruled the South, and discrimination and racism prevailed nationwide.

As a result, the anthem, like Allen's hymnal, became a coded statement of protest. The hymnal couched its concerns in the rhetoric of religion, while the Johnsons' song optimistically stressed social uplift. Black music throughout the 1800s generally is devoid of overt protest. The music cannot be said to illustrate the diverse and articulate activism of black abolitionists, officials, and community leaders in that century.[3] Instead of explicitly addressing grievances, music of the 1800s encoded and emboldened black political and social movements for equality.

Music, like religion, both supported and transcended daily struggle, offering less of a diary of protest than a rich cultural and emotional crucible in which the struggle was forged. The struggle altered black life profoundly. Shackles were broken, families migrated from plantations, urban black communities expanded, levels of education grew exponentially, and skilled black professionals multiplied. Music evolved in step with these revolutionary events, but also remained a repository of cultural memory. Still-popular spirituals evoked the miseries of slavery, but also reminded black listeners of the persistence of poverty, limited education, segregation, and backwards rural life as the twentieth century dawned. The double-faced nature of music, looking backward to lingering horrors and forward to a radically improved future, helped to make it a powerful presence in African American culture.

The AME church's story illustrates religion's central role in formulating an articulate black musical voice. As a young slave, Richard Allen became a Methodist because "the plain simple gospel suits best for any people." Like white Methodists, slaves and free blacks were stirred by the emotional immediacy of the hymns and their message of personal salvation. In Allen's Philadelphia church and in other AME parishes, loud and spirited singing predominated. Parishioners set hymn verses to well-known tunes, but also improvised their own melodies. White observers were struck by their spontaneous vocal response to the deacons' line readings. One noted a "quicker and more animated style of singing," while another was haunted by verses sung "in a loud, shrill monotone" and the "agonizing, heart-rending moaning" that concluded the readings. Men and women often took turns in singing the responses. Individual singers, moved by the worship, offered their own musical contributions. This emotionalism was the urban equivalent of the spiritual rapture experienced by blacks (as well as whites) in the southern rural revivals of the early 1800s.[4] In the North, Christianity inspired African Americans to condemn slavery on the basis of Christian values. The hymnal also abetted the rise of literacy among politically-minded African Americans.

The growth the AME church and its music took place within the context of increased white hostility and the expansion of slavery. Racist "scientific" theories of human difference undermined ideals of equality espoused by Enlightenment philosophers. Political parties and working men's associations empowered average white men to the detriment of nonwhites, whom they demonized as unworthy competitors. Slavery was abolished in the North, but black residents lost voting and civil rights and suffered from de facto segregation. In the South, the cotton boom expanded slavery. Prosperous planters no longer bothered to apologize for slavery as a necessary evil. Black leaders, such as Richard Allen, were moved to advocate African colonization, ostensibly to convert natives' souls, but mainly to create havens for refugees from American racism.

Positive developments also shaped black musical expression. Show business emerged as an industry, especially in the North, and talented performers found receptive black and white audiences. Small black economic elites of New York, Philadelphia, and other cities patronized classical performers such as the soprano Elizabeth Taylor Greenfield, the tenor Thomas Bowers, and the trumpet player and conductor Frank Johnson. The AME and other churches produced concerts of sacred music, and trained composers wrote classical works. During the 1820s, the African Grove Theater in Manhattan pioneered all-black musical theater that entertained patrons of both races.[5]

The black working class experience also proved significant. Competition for jobs turned northern cities into racial tinderboxes, which often exploded into riots. The southern migrant and civic activist David Walker attacked southern slavery in his *Appeal* (1829), but its ferocity resulted from the daily indignities Walker endured in Boston.[6] Black militancy was suppressed violently by working-class whites, and it was also symbolically neutralized by the latter's favorite theatrical genre, blackface minstrelsy. White minstrel performers' crude mimicking of mannerisms, language, and bodily movement ridiculed African Americans, but also paid a curious backhanded compliment to black music and dance. Working-class race relations would continue to shape popular music.

Since overt protest would have been fruitless, black performers instead exploited minstrelsy to advance their careers. The dancer William Henry Lane, who gained fame as Master Juba, was the sole African American performer to conquer the antebellum stage. The amazingly acrobatic Lane helped to invent modern tap dancing, and his high-stepping dance routine, known as "patting Juba," shaped black dance nationwide. Lane toured Europe and entertained royalty before his premature death in 1852.[7] Other dancers, musicians, and composers gained some renown, becoming pioneers in African American commercial music. Popular entertainment militated against social activism, but it provided black performers with unprecedented fame and visibility, and it gave them opportunities to communicate in code with a national audience.

In these same years, race relations were aggravated by growing disputes over slavery. Rebellions such as the Denmark Vesey conspiracy of 1822 and Nat Turner's insurrection in 1831 led white masters to fear slave religion. In these rebellions, plots were hatched during religious services and cited the crusading language of hymns and the Bible. Masters suspected that music served as a coded plotters' language. Among the dozens hanged with Denmark Vesey was a man falsely accused of sounding a trumpet to incite revolt. Nat Turner's preaching and reading of the Bible compelled fearful southerners to outlaw literacy, religious gatherings, and hymn singing among slaves.[8]

Slave music had faced repression for centuries. Caribbean masters regulated music-making beginning in the 1600s. After the Stono Rebellion of 1739, South Carolina prohibited slaves' use of "drums, horns, or other loud instruments, which may call together, or give sign or notice to one another of their wicked designs or purposes."[9] By the 1800s, all slave states had passed such laws. In the wake of Nat Turner's revolt and the rise of northern abolitionism, southern whites developed paranoia about slave insurrection that, itself, helped to precipitate the Civil War.

Little study of slave music was made before 1861. Nevertheless, eyewitness accounts document African American musical expression in the South. This testimony indicates that slave songs often expressed not rebellion, but simple endurance. People in bondage were forced to work without wages for six long days every week. Work songs alleviated some of the burden of their work in varied settings. At docks, slave stevedores bellowed out improvised verses while handling boat cargo. Most slaves were employed on cotton plantations, and accounts indicate that many of them were forced to sing against their will. Masters and overseers mistrusted silent workers and believed that singing improved their productivity and morale. Due to this coercion, "field hollers" and "shouts" did not merely assist repetitive physical work; they also expressed despair. As Frederick Douglass memorably wrote, "it is a great mistake to suppose [slaves] happy because they sing. The songs of the slave represent the sorrow, rather than the joys, of his heart; and he is relieved by them, only as an aching heart is relieved by tears."[10]

Though they might have resulted from coercion, field hollers and shouts diverted slaves from drudgery and stoked their creativity. Call and response was widely practiced; a work-gang leader sang lines of verse, and gang members improvised answers. Some field hollers revisited the plots of popular trickster tales—stories about Br'er Rabbit and other animals who outwitted powerful oppressors. Trickster tales might be called secular analogues to the coded messages of salvation found in hymns. Field hollers also made reference to biblical tales of liberation involving Moses, liberator of the Hebrews, and Christ the Savior. Other work songs, though, expressed a loss of hope, enumerating slaves' grievances against God and master. People sold "down the river" sang laments on the way to their new plantations. By telling it like it really was, though, such songs subverted whites' demands that slaves sing cheerfully. As a former slave insisted, these "sorrow songs" "can't be sung without a full heart and a troubled spirit."[11]

Seasonal events inspired work song genres such as the celebrated corn shucking songs. In December, slaves would gather to husk mountains of corn ears. White families picnicked on porches and listened to the corn shuckers, who "make the forest ring with their music." Verbally creative work leaders called out verses that described the event itself:

> All them pretty girls will be there …
> They will fix it for us rare …
> I know that supper will be big …
> I think I smell a fine roast pig …
> A supper is provided, so they said …
> I hope they'll have some nice wheat bread, / Shuck that corn before you eat.[12]

Such light-hearted lyrics suggest what the slaves probably sang to themselves when they did not work. During Sunday rest, dance tunes were as common as hymns—although devout masters often forbade dancing. Some owners, though, encouraged Sunday revels so that slaves might subsequently work harder. Some musicians could play the fiddle or banjo, while homemade instruments were constructed out of gourds, wood, animal guts, bones, and rocks. These revels borrowed white lyrics and dance steps, but also featured unmistakably African-derived movement, such as jerking, shuffling, or patting Juba, and African American musical elements such as call and response. The songs retold trickster stories and satirized masters' manners.[13]

Even well-intentioned white listeners invaded slaves' privacy on Sundays. Family and community life among slaves were permitted little sanctity. Enslaved blacks thus practiced caution. Expressions of rebellion and the desire for freedom were translated into coded trickster work songs and spirituals about Moses. This coding persisted long after slavery was abolished, and still influences African American music today.

Slaves' distinct skill at expressing multiple meanings in songs and stories has been labeled "signifying." Rooted deeply in the culture of the African Diaspora, "signifying" mystified antebellum whites. In 1838, for example, the actress Fanny Kemble was puzzled when slave rowers at her husband's Georgia plantation sang:

Jenny shake her toe at me, / Jenny gone away.
Hurrah! Miss Susy, oh! / Jenny gone away.

"What the obnoxious Jenny meant by shaking her toe, whether defiance or mere departure, I never could ascertain," Kemble wrote. "I have never yet heard the Negroes … sing any words that could be said to have any sense." Chadwick Hansen has since determined that the rowers actually said the word *to*, from the African Kikongo language, meaning "body part" or "buttocks." Jenny actually was not shaking her toe. Fanny Kemble reported the rowers' "satisfaction" as they conveyed this coded message with "a good deal of dramatic and musical effect."[14]

Slaves' work songs were rough analogues to the commercial music enjoyed by northern free blacks. These secular music genres, taken together, became the foundation of future black popular music. For white listeners, though, as well as for ministers and other black leaders, the most significant slave music was religious. In the 1860s, white authors first grouped sacred slave songs under the designation "spirituals." Spirituals poignantly expressed African Americans' emotional and sacred yearnings. Many of the songs featured borrowings from Baptist and Methodist hymnody. Spirituals combined hymn phrases with slaves' favorite parables and folk tales, and preachers often lined out the verses through call and response.[15]

Spirituals especially captivated elite white listeners. They jotted down the lyrics of spirituals, and a few even notated the tunes. Whites usually overheard the singing of spirituals while witnessing field labor, Sunday services, and slave holidays. Like work songs, many spirituals were "sorrow songs," biblical expressions of grief and longing that were relevant to slave life. The titles convey these sentiments: "Sometimes I Feel

Like a Motherless Child," "Trouble in Mind," "O Rocks, Don't Fall on Me," "And the Moon Will Turn to Blood," "I've Been Rebuked and I've Been Scorned," and "Let My People Go."

Early published collections represented spirituals as unadorned melodies, obscuring the fact that they were sung in many different ways. As even the collectors noted, slaves rarely sang in unison, but entered at different times to create a rich counterpoint. African heterophony, or multi-part singing, thus persisted in the South. Individual singers stretched syllables and embroidered the melodies, and clapping and vocal interjections enlivened the spiritual. "Jubilee" songs, the optimistic counterpart to sorrow spirituals, celebrated the Hebrew escape from bondage, the Resurrection, and other liberationist tales. "Swing Low, Sweet Chariot," "Roll, Jordan, Roll," "My Lord, What a Morning," and "Sabbath Has No End" were common jubilee spirituals.[16]

When slave religion was outlawed in the wake of the Turner rebellion, services went underground. As a result, most singing of spirituals was unheard by whites until the Civil War. Sunday services, baptisms, and even weddings and funerals transpired in forests and swamps far removed from the masters' homes. As former slaves later recounted, ring shouts often followed these clandestine Christian services. Dancing in a circle, in shuffling or in elaborate steps, participants took care not to cross their legs, as in secular dance. Since drums were outlawed, slaves used bones, wood, patting Juba (hands on the hips and thighs), and their shuffling feet to supply the rhythm. As at revival meetings, participants might be overcome by the spirit and fall unconscious.[17]

Spirituals, ring shouts, and coded songs mocking white masters expressed the discontent that led thousands to escape slavery via the Underground Railroad. In the North, former slaves such as Frederick Douglass and William Wells Brown told whites of the horrors of the "peculiar institution" and converted many to abolitionism. Douglass and Brown cited the spirituals as evidence of the slaves' Christian faith and humility. White abolitionists portrayed slaves even more sentimentally, describing them as powerless victims. This tendency obscured the variety and richness of slave music, at least until the Civil War opened up rural black life to more observation.

During the Civil War, as Union armies moved southward and plantation owners fled, slavery steadily eroded. It was in the black "contraband" camps, and the experimental free communities they originated, that most northern reformers were first exposed to slave music. A white observer in Louisiana was struck by the "melodic speech" he heard in a congregation, where a freed man's "voice rises and falls in the cadence of a rude song, the congregation accompanying his voice, the men in a groaning voice and the women and children in all sorts of wailings and whinings." In the Sea Islands of South Carolina and Georgia, Charlotte Forten, a black Philadelphia abolitionist, and the white Colonel Thomas Wentworth Higginson recorded "spirichels"–a local term for sacred songs that later took hold nationally. Higginson, commander of the first Union Army company of emancipated slaves, sketched his troops' musical activity one night in camp. "A feeble flute stir[red] somewhere in some tent …, a drum throb[bed] far away in another." A ring shout took place in "a regular native African hut … crammed with men, singing at the top of their voices, in one of their quaint, monotonous, endless, negro-Methodist chants" while "all keep steadily circling like dervishes." Higginson heard singers devise clever new lyrics for the tune "John Brown's Body."[18]

The announcement of the Emancipation Proclamation on New Year's Day 1863 was greeted as the long-awaited jubilee. On a South Carolina island, soldiers and local African Americans held a gala ceremony and feast. As Colonel Higginson waved an American flag, an elderly black man and two women began an impromptu rendition of "My Country, 'Tis of Thee." "Firmly and irrepressibly the quavering voices sang on, verse after verse; others of the colored people joined in." "I never saw anything so electric; … it seemed the choked voice of a race at last unloosed." Black singing greeted other Union advances as well. When General Sherman's soldiers captured Savannah, Georgia, black residents sang, "Glory be to God, we are free!" In 1865, the fall of the rebel capital inspired more musical celebrations. Men jailed in a Richmond, Virginia, auction pen, sang, "Slavery chain done broke at last … I's goin' to praise God till I die"; other black men soon set them free. Crowds of freed-people sang "Richmond town is burning down, High diddle diddle inctum inctum ah," and greeted Abraham Lincoln's brief visit with jubilee songs.[19]

Emancipation altered African American music in important ways. Four million freedpeople transformed their lives, reuniting their families, giving themselves new names, seeking jobs and schooling, and building communities. "We have progressed a century in a year," the black missionary Jonathan Gibbs exulted. New black churches proliferated and became community institutions. Ministers and Union Army veterans became model "race men"—principled and hard-working defenders of black people's new status. New laws, such activists argued, must provide African American men with paid work, property ownership, legal marriages and parent-hood, and the vote. (Black women did not benefit from such advocacy.) Their efforts helped to achieve the Fifteenth Amendment to the Constitution, intended to protect the black man's vote.[20]

Freedom gradually transformed black church music. Some congregations retained folk elements. In many AME and Methodist churches, Sunday gatherings began with a formal service in which an elder "deaconed" or line-read a hymn, and the congregation responded. As the white observer William Francis Allen noted, a ring shout might follow: "the benches are pushed back to the wall … old and young … all stand up in the middle of the floor, and … the 'sperichil' is struck up." However, some ministers, influenced, to some extent, by visiting northern white abolitionists, banned the ring shout. Believing that former slaves must be "lifted up" to the values of the genteel middle class, they instituted formal singing and a strict code of church behavior. In 1867, Allen observed that spirituals were "going out of use on the plantations" of the Sea Islands and being replaced by formal hymn singing. Harriet Beecher Stowe similarly regretted that black church singing was becoming "a closer imitation of white, genteel worship ... solemn, dull, and nasal."[21]

Spirituals were publicized nationally by white admirers, who transformed them for public consumption. In the manner of some postwar black church services, spirituals became more genteel and separate from their folk roots. In the Sea Islands, William Francis Allen, Lucy McKim Garrison, and Charles Pickward Ware compiled an extensive portfolio of slave songs, published in 1867 as *Slave Songs of the United States*. It was the first collection of its kind. Allen's preface differentiated slave songs from "spurious" minstrel tunes, and sought to locate their African qualities. He identified heterophony when he noted that "there is no singing in parts, as we understand it, and yet no two [people] appear to be singing the same thing." Allen also cautioned that, while the spirituals were "taken down by the editors from the lips of the colored people themselves," the transcriptions are "but a faint shadow of the original":

> The voices of the colored people have a peculiar quality that nothing can imitate; and the intonations and delicate variations of even one singer cannot be reproduced on paper. And I despair of conveying any notion of the effect of a number singing together.[22]

Slave Songs, as well as subsequent collections, such as Thomas P. Fenner's *Cabin and Plantation Songs* (1876), helped to adapt African American music to white middle-class tastes. White anthologists eagerly "cleaned up" the rhythm, harmony, and pitches in the process of notating them. This bowdlerizing made spirituals accessible to middle-class whites, who considered even the simplified printed versions to be exotic and fascinating. Fearful about the future of race relations after emancipation, white Americans embraced simplified black music as evidence that African Americans were well-mannered and unthreatening.

The Fisk University Jubilee Singers became famous in this context. Fisk, located in Nashville, struggled financially. In 1871, George L. White, Fisk's white treasurer, and Ella Sheppard, a student and former slave, transformed the glee club into a fundraising attraction. The nine-person choir (seven of them ex-slaves) sang in local churches and encountered white hostility. White then scheduled a tour of the North. Performing a classical repertoire, the Jubilee Singers became the first African American group to give formal concerts. Racism and poor ticket sales continued to bedevil them, though, until an audience of ministers in Oberlin, Ohio, cheered them. Prestigious invitations poured in, and the Singers appeared at Henry Ward Beecher's famed Brooklyn church and at the White House. Touring Europe, they sang before Queen Victoria. The Singers returned to Fisk with $50,000 in earnings.

Like the spirituals anthologists, the Jubilee Singers simplified slave songs. Their white arranger, Theodore Seward, set the tunes in European harmony and eliminated call and response, heterophony, and pentatonic scales. Songs in the Fisk catalog contained virtually no laments or protests. These arrangements, like others, aimed to "lift up" black music and align it with white middle-class values. The Singers' success bred imitators at other black colleges, as well as fraudulent "Fisk Jubilee Singers" that crisscrossed the nation. Fisk's ensemble, weary of touring, disbanded in 1878.[23]

These were also problematic years for African American churches. Observers noted that males, especially, were abandoning the pews, and that congregations increasingly were dominated by women. After about 1880, though, African American churches showed signs of revival. The Holiness or Sanctified movement brought millions back into the fold; the old spirituals were celebrated in new published collections; and the Fisk Jubilee Singers resumed touring.[24] African American culture was becoming increasingly secular, but black churches adapted, and their music remained vital.

In the secular realm, the dedication to cultural uplift reflected the high value that educated African Americans placed on classical music. Like their white counterparts, black elites viewed classical music as a vehicle for intellectual and spiritual self-cultivation. In the 1870s, black-run opera houses operated in Washington, D.C., and Brooklyn. For forty years Walter Craig led a popular high-society band in Manhattan. Elizabeth Taylor Greenfield and other antebellum African American concert singers had embarked on tours, and after the Civil War their examples were followed by Mamie Flowers, Ann and Emma Hyers, Sisieretta Jones, and Sidney Woodward.[25]

James Monroe Trotter expressed the ideal of cultural uplift through classical music in his book *Music and Some Highly Musical People* (1878), the first musical history of America ever published. An escaped slave, Union Army veteran, and Boston civil servant, Trotter promoted "the beauty, power, and uses of music" and chronicled the activities of black musicians nationwide. He briefly acknowledged that these musicians suffered from "color-prejudice, the extent of whose terrible, blighting power none can ever imagine that do not actually meet it." Some years later, elite African Americans and advocates of spirituals received endorsement from one of Europe's leading classical composers. In 1892, Antonin Dvořák became the director of the National Conservatory of Music in New York. African American students such as Will Marion Cook and Harry Burleigh performed spirituals for Dvořák, who told a reporter, "I am now satisfied that the future music of this country must be founded upon what are called negro melodies. These are the folk songs of America, and your composers must turn to them … In the negro melodies of America I discover all that is needed for a great and noble school of music."[26]

The effort to improve the lot of African Americans by lifting them up culturally faced many difficulties. Uplift, above all, was checked by persistent white racism.

When the euphoria surrounding emancipation had dissipated, American race relations regained its typically bleak appearance. Despite sacrifices in battle and constitutional gains, most African Americans found daily life after the war little changed from before. Radical Reconstruction was challenged by the Ku Klux Klan and other southern whites. Reconstruction policies did not provide economic independence to former slaves, and northern whites, distracted by other issues, withdrew their support. Poverty, illiteracy, and the indignity of sharecropping burdened most southern African Americans, and new segregation laws and restrictions on voting relegated them to second-class citizenship.

Black musicians suffered along with them. Racism dogged the Fisk Jubilee Singers even in the North, where white journalists called them "trained monkeys" who sang "with a wild darkey air." The Singers were banned from better hotels and forbidden from entering concert venues through the front door. Klan violence encouraged Fisk University to use the Singers' earnings to build the fortress-like Jubilee Hall. A leading black pianist, Thomas Greene Wiggins, suffered throughout his life from racism. At the age of eight, Wiggins, a self-taught, blind player with a staggering technique and memory, had been first exhibited in recital by his master, James Bethune, who advertised him as "Blind Tom Bethune." When Wiggins turned twenty-one, after emancipation, James Bethune persuaded the Georgia government to declare him insane and name Bethune as his guardian. Decades later, Wiggins was still touring, billed as "the last slave set free." Wiggins earned the Bethune family $750,000 during a half century of performing. (Another blind piano virtuoso, John William "Blind" Boone, enjoyed a profitable concert career thanks to a supportive black manager.)[27]

In such conditions, protest—musical and otherwise—was dangerous. Black professionals, such as musicians, inspired white envy, and mere survival might prove difficult. Successful black performers were targets of mob hatred. In 1900, the father of jazz clarinetist Big Eye Louis Nelson was among the African Americans killed in New Orleans by rioting whites. The same year, Manhattan's theater district was wracked by racial violence. George Walker, half of the famous stage team of Williams and Walker, was knocked unconscious and dragged down the street by whites, and was rescued from a likely death by policemen. The singer and songwriter Ernest Hogan also was injured in this riot.

Some performers transcended this racism, though, and turned music into a coded form of protest, in effect beating whites at their own game. Some achieved fame and fortune, and a few even managed to express themselves freely and honestly. During Reconstruction, musicians manipulated white expectations to achieve professional success. In this era, song lyrics often were racially offensive; black stage stereotypes were vicious caricatures; and African Americans' earnings were inferior to those of whites. These conditions exacted a psychological toll on black performers, but tough, ambitious, and talented individuals made the most of opportunities. In the 1870s and 1880s, they pioneered African American success in commercial music, blazing trails for future generations.

The first, and most problematic, genre in which musicians emerged was blackface minstrelsy. Like racism itself, minstrelsy survived the Civil War, but the war also fundamentally altered it. Its core audience now lay in the rural South, not northern cities, and shows now featured African American performers, who, like their white predecessors, covered their faces with burnt cork to become "black" in the minstrel manner. The original "Georgia Minstrels" troupe was created in 1865 by a white man who employed fifteen of his former slaves; its success inspired many other similarly named groups. Black minstrel comedians, such as Wallace King and Billy Kersands, gained wealth and fame, at the price of perpetuating stereotypes throughout their careers.[28]

The performer-songwriters James A. Bland, Sam Lucas, and Gussie Davis were luckier. Although they initially performed in blackface and wrote songs in the offensive "coon" genre, these men were educated musicians who earned success in Tin Pan Alley, New York City's songwriting industry. Bland, the composer of "Carry Me Back to Old Virginny," eventually moved to Europe, where he performed out of blackface. Lucas left minstrelsy for the theater, becoming the first African American actor to play the title role in *Uncle Tom's Cabin*. Davis operated his own minstrel troupe before moving to New York City. The ballad "In the Baggage Coach Ahead" was one of Tin Pan Alley's biggest hits, making Davis the most successful black songwriter.[29]

Always, though, performers had to contend with the crippling stereotypes of the day. Music and the theater romanticized the antebellum South. White Americans wary of intense industrialization, immigration, and labor conflict embraced nostalgic images of white "colonels" and "belles," faithful elderly slaves, and foolish "pickaninnies" and "coons." Such imagery reinforced southerners' pride in the Confederacy, reaffirmed white prejudices, and helped Yankees and Rebels heal their divisions. In the 1890s, some minstrel troupes joined large touring "spectacles," such as *The South before the War*, which reinforced this nostalgia. Other performing genres excluded blacks. Until 1910, when Bert Williams successfully integrated vaudeville, that thriving entertainment industry had been lily-white.[30]

African American performers especially achieved breakthroughs in genres that emerged during the 1890s. The Nineties have often been called a watershed in American culture, bringing movies, amusement parks, bicycles, chewing gum, and ragtime music to the fore. Leisure became less formal, allowing men and women to mix more. Ethnicities and races also increasingly interacted in entertainment venues. Music reflected the excitement and cultural change of the decade. Ragtime expressed the faster pace of city life and gave African American syncopation national exposure, but its heyday came after 1900. In the meantime, professional black performers found jobs in other genres. Hundreds were employed by Billy McClain, the white impresario of the nostalgic revues *The South before the War* and *Darkest America*. In 1890, the United States census enumerated 1,490 "Negro actors [and] showmen"; ten years later, 530 were counted in New York and Chicago alone. Entertainment trade papers, such as *The Freeman*, advertised job opportunities.[31]

Black dancers exploited whites' interest in the cakewalk. In city theaters, tuxedo- and gown-clad black dancers enacted this competition for a cake, accompanied by minstrel tunes. Allegedly originating among slaves in Florida, the cakewalk first fascinated white audiences at postwar minstrel shows. By the 1890s, cakewalks incorporated stylized "high stepping" and "strutting." Urbanization had diluted the plantation stereotype, allowing black dancers such as Dora Dean, Charles Johnson, Bob Cole, and Stella Wiley to perform in respectable clothing and for good pay. Significantly, white spectators copied their cakewalk steps. African American music and dance were beginning to define mainstream white leisure.[32]

Other breakthroughs were achieved. In May 1890, Edison Records released George W. Johnson's "The Whistling Coon," the first recording ever made by an African American. Recordings, though, earned little income or publicity for black performers. More important was the genesis of black musical theater in New York. In 1897, the cakewalk dancer Bob Cole helped to devise *A Trip to Coontown*, the first show created by African Americans to appear on Broadway. As its title suggests, this musical comedy evoked old stereotypes; even innovative young black musicians had to recycle traditional formulas to gain a foothold. *A Trip to Coontown*, though, did not feature blackface or minstrel dances. A hit, it toured America and was later revived in New York.[33]

In 1898, another unexpected hit arrived. The score of *Clorindy, or the Origins of the Cakewalk* was composed by Will Marion Cook. A product of the black elite, Cook had studied in Europe and with Dvořák in New York, but racism barred his success in classical music. *Clorindy* featured dialect songs such as "Darktown is Out Tonight" and "Who Dat Say Chicken in Dis Crowd?" but his sophisticated musical score belied old stereotypes, as did Cook's well-publicized leadership of the all-white pit orchestra. Performers in *Clorindy* included the comedian Ernest Hogan (billing himself as "the unbleached American") and the team of Bert Williams and George Walker. Williams and Walker had begun touring as "the Two Real Coons," but they now were leading "race men" among entertainers. In a protest against lynching, the two performers refused, whenever possible, to appear in the Jim Crow South.[34]

In the meantime, Bob Cole teamed with John Rosamond Johnson and James Weldon Johnson to produce a series of musical comedies that broke with old stereotypes. The shows contained songs written in a non-derogatory African American dialect. John Rosamond Johnson, a pianist, regularly appeared with Cole in a stage act, dressed in white tie and black tails. The Johnson brothers, natives of Jacksonville, Florida, were well-educated advocates of black civil rights. James Weldon Johnson— novelist, diplomat, and later the first black secretary of the NAACP—particularly embodied the post-Civil War generation's dual commitment to black artistic expression and racial equality.[35]

In 1900, as we have seen, James Weldon Johnson commemorated Lincoln's birthday with "Lift Every Voice and Sing," a song that blended his musical and political concerns. This "Negro National Anthem" was a fitting introduction to the new century, which W. E. B. Du Bois argued would be dedicated to solving "the problem of the color line."[36] As Du Bois also realized, African Americans taking part in the twentieth-century struggle for civil rights would rely, in part, upon a rich musical culture, closely allied with religion, as a foundation for expression and emotional fortitude. Music developed in the nineteenth century provided African Americans with a range of strategies and statements that taught reformers and revolutionaries how to speak, sing, and negotiate the racial landscape in pursuit of justice and equal rights.

Notes

1 Eileen Southern, *The Music of Black Americans*, 3rd ed. (New York: Norton, 1997), 75–86; Eileen Southern, "Afro-American Music," in H. Wiley Hitchcock and Stanley Sadie, eds., *The New Grove Dictionary of American Music* (New York: Grove's Dictionaries of Music, 1986), 1: 14; and Richard S. Newman, *Freedom's Prophet: Bishop Richard Allen, the AME Church, and the Black Founding Fathers* (New York: NYU Press, 2009), 222.

2 Rudolph Byrd, "Introduction," in Rudolph Byrd, ed., *The Essential Writings of James Weldon Johnson* (New York: Modern Library, 2008), xix–xx; James Weldon Johnson, *Along This Way: The Autobiography of James Weldon Johnson* (1933; New York: Da Capo, 2000), 155–156.

3 See, for example, Benjamin Quarles, *Black Abolitionists* (New York: Oxford University Press, 1969); Wilson Jeremiah Moses, *The Golden Age of Black Nationalism, 1850–1925*, 2nd ed. (New York: Oxford University Press, 1988); and Jinping Wu, *Frederick Douglass and the Black Liberation Movement: The North Star of American Blacks* (New York: Garland, 2000).

4 Southern, *Music of Black Americans*, 79–80; and Albert J. Raboteau, *Slave Religion: The "Invisible Institution" in the Antebellum South*, updated ed. (New York: Oxford University Press, 2004), 59–72.

5 Southern, *Music of Black Americans*, 103–110, 116–121.

6 David Walker, *Walker's Appeal, in Four Articles* (1829; Chapel Hill, North Carolina: University of North Carolina Press, 2011).

7 Tyler Anbinder, *Five Points* (New York: Plume, 2002), 172–174; and Southern, *Music of Black Americans*, 94–95.

8 Dena J. Epstein, *Sinful Tunes and Spirituals: Black Folk Music to the Civil War* (Urbana: University of Illinois Press, 2003), 195, 229.

9 Epstein, *Sinful Tunes and Spirituals*, 59.

10 Frederick Douglass, *Narrative of the Life of Frederick Douglass, an American Slave* (1845; New York: Barnes & Noble, 2005), 30; Epstein, *Sinful Tunes and Spirituals*, Chapter 9; and Southern, *Music of Black Americans*, 147–150.

11 Lawrence W. Levine, *Black Culture and Black Consciousness: Afro-American Folk Thought from*

Slavery to Freedom (New York: Oxford University Press, 1977), 102–120, 130–132; and Southern, *The Music of Black Americans*, 158–159, 166.

12 Mrs. R. H. Marshall, "A Negro Corn-shucking" (1852), quoted in Roger D. Abrahams, *Singing the Master: The Emergence of African-American Culture in the Plantation South* (New York: Pantheon, 1992), 229; and Southern, *Music of Black Americans*, 200–202.

13 Epstein, *Sinful Tunes and Spirituals*, Chapter 8, 155.

14 Henry Louis Gates, Jr., *The Signifying Monkey: A Theory of Afro-American Literary Criticism* (New York: Oxford University Press, 1988); Fanny Kemble, *Journal of a Residence on a Georgian Plantation in 1838–1839* (Athens: University of Georgia Press, 1984), 163; Chadwick Hansen, "Jenny's Toe Revisited: White Responses to Afro-American Shaking Dances," *American Music*, Vol. 5, No. 1 (Spring 1987): 1–19, and Mark Tucker, "On Toodle-oo, Todalo, and Jenny's Toe," *American Music*, Vol. 6, No. 1 (Spring 1988): 88–91.

15 Southern, *Music of Black Americans*, 143–150, 180–189; Levine, *Black Culture and Black Consciousness*, 25–34; and Epstein, *Sinful Tunes and Spirituals*, 217–228. A critique of the traditional historiography of spirituals is Ronald Radano, *Lying up a Nation: Race and Black Music* (Chicago: University of Chicago Press, 2003), 141–145.

16 Southern, *Music of Black Americans*, 187–188.

17 Southern, *Music of Black Americans*, 181–184; Levine, *Black Culture and Black Consciousness*, 37–38; and Epstein, *Sinful Tunes and Spirituals*, 278–287.

18 Jon Michael Spencer, *Sacred Symphony: The Chanted Sermon of the Black Preacher* (New York: Greenwood Press, 1988), 1; and Thomas W. Higginson, "December 3, 1862," in *Army Life in a Black Regiment* (Boston: Fields, Osgood, 1870), at www.gutenberg.org/ebooks/6764, accessed April 2012.

19 Higginson, "January 1, 1863 (evening)," in *Army Life in a Black Regiment*; and Leon F. Litwack, *Been in the Storm So Long: The Aftermath of Slavery* (New York: Knopf, 1980), 167–169.

20 Eric Foner, *Reconstruction: America's Unfinished Revolution, 1863–1877* (New York: Harper & Row, 1988), 102, Chapters 3, 8.

21 William Francis Allen, Charles Pickard Ware, and Lucy McKim Garrison, *Slave Songs of the United States* (1867; Bedford, Massachusetts: Applewood, 1996), viii, xx.

22 Allen et al., *Slave Songs of the United States*, iv–v.

23 Andrew Ward, *Dark Midnight When I Rise: The Story of the Fisk Jubilee Singers* (New York: HarperCollins, 2000).

24 Southern, *Music of Black Americans*, 262–263.

25 Southern, *Music of Black Americans*, 246–254, 299, and Thomas L. Riis, *Just before Jazz: Black Musical Theater in New York, 1890 to 1915* (Washington, D.C.: Smithsonian, 1989), Chapters 1–2.

26 James M. Trotter, *Music and Some Highly Musical People* (1878; New York: Johnson Reprint, 1968), 352; Joseph Horowitz, *Dvořák in America: In Search of the New World* (Chicago: Cricket Books, 2003), 72; and Antonin Dvořák, "Music in America," in *Harper's Weekly*, No. 14 (February 1895): 431–433.

27 *New York World* (1873), quoted in Llewellyn Smith and Andrew Ward, *The American Experience: Jubilee Singers*, www.pbs.org/wgbh/amex/singers/film-more/transcript.html (accessed April 2012); and Geneva H. Southall, *Blind Tom, the Black Pianist-Composer (1849–1908): Continually Enslaved* (Lanham, Maryland: Scarecrow Press, 1999).

28 Robert C. Toll, *Blacking Up: The Minstrel Show in Nineteenth-Century America* (New York: Oxford University Press, 1974), 219–229, 254–257.

29 Southern, *Music of Black Americans*, 237–244.

30 Camille F. Forbes, *Introducing Bert Williams: Burnt Cork, Broadway, and the Story of America's First Black Star* (New York: Basic Civitas, 2008), 53–57, 198–201.

31 Southern, *Music of Black Americans*, 235, 256–257.

32 Southern, *Music of Black Americans*, 316–317; and Riis, *Just before Jazz*, 78–82.

33 Riis, *Just before Jazz*, 75–79, 83–85; and Tim Brooks, *Lost Sounds: Blacks and the Birth of the Recording Industry, 1890–1919* (Urbana, Illinois: University of Illinois Press, 2005), 5–6, 26–30.

34 Riis, *Just before Jazz*, 79–81, 94–102; and Will Marion Cook, "Clorindy, the Origin of the Cakewalk," in *Theatre Arts*, Vol. 31 No. 9 (September 1947): 62.

35 Johnson, *Along This Way*, 156–159, 186–192; and Riis, *Just Before Jazz*, 61–71, 129–141.

36 W. E. B. Du Bois, *The Souls of Black Folk* (1903; New York: Modern Library, 2005), 9.

2

GOD, GARRISON, AND THE GROUND

The Hutchinson Family Singers and the Origins of Commercial Protest Music

Scott Gac

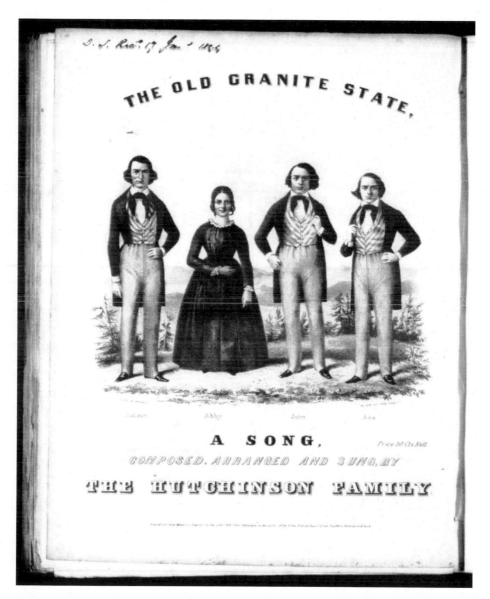

Figure 2.1 Cover of "The Old Granite State," by The Hutchinson Family.

"I am in the Minerva Rooms, on Broadway, in New York City, the commercial emporium of the Western continent," reported abolitionist Henry Wright in a letter from May 1848.

> I am sitting by a table, in front of a platform, on which sits Wm. L. Garrison, as President of the American Anti-Slavery Society, Francis Jackson, Wendell Phillips, and others. The hall is full, and we are in a most exciting and pleasant scene. I can term it nothing less than 'The Hutchinsons' Repentance.'

The celebrated music quartet, the Hutchinson Family Singers, was in trouble. Five years before, at a January 1843 antislavery meeting, the members of the group, a then unknown and unheralded band, embraced a public stance against the practice of American slavery. Their move hurtled the musicians into the spotlight, where through the composition and performance of abolitionist song, they developed the sound of the antislavery movement.[1]

Now, in the spring 1848, as Wright's report suggests, the protest singers were about to lose it all—the sheet music sales, sold-out shows in New York and Boston, and renown rarely matched in the history of American popular culture. A recent censure by the officials of the American Anti-Slavery Society stood in their way. The Hutchinsons had played a welcome song for Whig politician Henry Clay, whose gradualist stance on emancipation was hated by abolitionists like William Lloyd Garrison, Wendell Phillips, and Frederick Douglass. The musicians' singular act exposed the charged, changed, nature of the reform movement and threatened the social activist credentials that the Hutchinsons had worked hard to gain.

At the New York meeting, the quartet, true to form, surprised attendees when, during a lull, they struck "a violent abolition song, avowing revolution if there be not emancipation."[2] William Lloyd Garrison responded: "Do they wish us to take this as evidence of their repentance? Are they sorry for what they've done?" In the silence that followed, America's chief anti-slavery moralist added, "If they are sorry for the deed, we shall hear from them again."[3]

The group waited until the meeting's next day to announce their atonement. It was a performance that showed an "Anti-Slavery duty and testimony" that convinced Frederick Douglass of the "honor, integrity, and fidelity of the Hutchinsons."[4] Antislavery reformers were relieved by the reunion of the reform society and the songsters, whom they believed "with their voices of most extraordinary melody, have great power over men's heads and hearts, for good or evil." Henry Wright closed his 1848 dispatch confident that "Anti-slavery claims them for her own, and should and will, I trust, have them to be *all* her own."[5]

What was at stake, however, stood beyond the realm of protest song and social reform. In the 1840s, market forces wrought tensions that helped define many aspects of American life—in particular, the market shaped how American consumers interacted with a variety of cultural producers. There is no doubt that the Hutchinsons' antislavery crusade was central to the musicians' public and personal identities. But too much of a focus on the Hutchinson Family Singers' songs of protest clouds one of the most important functions of their social activism. Along with the Hutchinsons' espousal of nature and religion, their embrace of social reform helped listeners to see the musical act as one uncoupled from the gross Yankee materialism many feared rampant in the antebellum era. The support of the leaders of antislavery reform thus helped the Hutchinson Family Singers portray themselves as candid musicians—entertainers whose motivations embodied ideals nobler than profit. "They are not wandering, mercenary troubadours," Nathaniel Peabody Rogers explained, "who go about selling their strains for bread or brandy."[6] The sanction of the American Anti-Slavery Society was one of the three pillars of the Hutchinson Family Singers' public presentation; it protected them from the ironic scorn of many consumers, who cursed cultural productions undertaken solely for economic gain while purchasing tickets to the next event. It was the Hutchinsons' persona, crafted around God, Garrison, and the New Hampshire ground, that shielded the singers from such accusations, permitted them to sing for conscience and profit, and pushed listeners to welcome them as an authentic voice of social change.

As northern support for antislavery grew in the late 1840s, the goals for antislavery reform diffused. When Garrison and others had founded the American Anti-Slavery Society in 1833, they instilled in it the steadfast principles of moral suasion (changing peoples' hearts and minds rather than the political system) and immediatism (emancipation must happen now). But by the end of 1848, such an antislavery front had fractured. Stalwarts in the reform movement's political wing, which had started with the Liberty Party and continued in the Free Soil Party, now sought to curb slavery's expansion in the United States in the hope that the practice of slavery would someday die. The call to end slavery now (along with Garrison's more radical rhetoric on African American equality) held little widespread appeal as antislavery developed into a national political position. Many antislavery activists found themselves stretched thin amid the reform's irreconcilable poles.

As the popular voice of antislavery, the members of the Hutchinson Family Singers struggled to keep their socially conscious listeners content. During the presidential contest of 1844, the sheet music cover for the group's Liberty Party campaign song "Get Off the Track" depicted a train pulling the various antislavery factions—from Garrison's newspaper the *Liberator*, "Immediate Abolition," and the American Anti-Slavery Society, to the Liberty Party and Nathaniel Peabody Rogers's New Hampshire publication *The Herald of Freedom*—to victory. Such a harmonious vision, one that plunged a locomotive labeled for Henry Clay into a background ravine, proved to be a mirage.[7] As a result, the musicians who failed to keep everyone happy were in New York City in May 1848 to apologize to the American Anti-Slavery Society for their transgression: a salute to a gradual emancipationist and politician.

The Hutchinson musicians understood the importance of their ties to the American Anti-Slavery Society, an organization that shepherded them from the backwoods of New Hampshire to international fame. In the months following their New York penitence, though, the group's members hardly stayed true to the goals of Garrison's antislavery organization. Instead, they were swept by the strong political antislavery movement that took place in upstate New York, where the founders of the Free Soil Party held a well-attended meeting that settled on a platform that included, among other decrees, the non-extension of slavery into new territory. Many Free Soil adherents were more concerned with the effects of slavery on white workers than with black Americans or the callous practice of human bondage. As the politician, lawyer, and future Union Army general Benjamin Butler said in 1848: "Free labor cannot exist where slavery holds sway."[8] It was, some claim, a price that social reformers had to pay to reach a broad spectrum of Americans. The Free Soilers had launched a decidedly different version of antislavery from that of William Garrison and the American Anti-Slavery Society. Some of the Hutchinson clan attended the Free Soil convention. They composed new, festive, songs to embrace the latest political antislavery movement.[9]

In the upcoming years, Garrison, Douglass, and others battled with the members of the Hutchinson Family Singers over the group's ideals and reform commitment. The friction between the Hutchinson Family Singers and the American Anti-Slavery Society reflected the social and political realities of American reform in the 1840s and 1850s. Yet, even in the hubbub that led to the 1848 showdown with the American Anti-Slavery Society, the matter of materialism loomed. Critics characterized the welcome song for Henry Clay as transparent commercialism—"Anything to make money, now-a-days!" declared an editor in the *New Hampshire Gazette*.[10]

To the members of the Hutchinson Family Singers, such allegations were by now familiar. Throughout their career they navigated the line between music performance and profit. In 1844, for example, the musicians formed a communitarian society, comprised of their immediate relations, to quell family complaints over the singing troupe's sudden wealth. Asa Hutchinson understood the issue as one of personal and public import: "We cannot be so free to sing high and lofty sentiments to an audience when we feel bound to sing to their Pockets instead of their hearts."[11]

In May 1848, the Hutchinson Family Singers were one of the most renowned musical acts in the English-speaking world. They earned more than $1,000 a night for shows in New York and Boston—in an age when $500 represented a comfortable, respected, annual salary—regularly sold-out the largest urban venues at home and abroad, and sold thousands of copies of sheet music. They were also the voice of an antislavery culture that would culminate in *Uncle Tom's Cabin* (1852).

The celebrity of the Hutchinson Family Singers spawned a stream of family-singing imitators, from the Parker Family and Alleghenians to the New Hutchinson Family Singers, a second-rate act of the siblings' relatives formed in

1845–1846 when the real Hutchinson troupe was in Great Britain. The musicians in the Hutchinson Family Singers worried over such phenomena—and not because they might lose money to competition. They were concerned over their success. What did it mean that the group's sheet music – where the lithographed expressions of John, Judson, Asa, and Abby Hutchinson stared out from the covers – could be found in many northern parlors, while notes on the inner pages directed what was performed and heard? What did celebrity and wealth signal about the Hutchinsons as individuals and as a group? The quartet, and many of their listeners, wanted to know whether, as "advocates of human advancement," the Hutchinson Family Singers were a saleable curiosity or a valued addition to American life.[12]

The stardom and economic achievement of the protest musicians reveals the great change in New England and the North in the years before the Civil War. And, like many of their peers, the Hutchinsons looked upon one source of the change—the encroachment of market forces—with deep suspicion. Yet those same forces ensured that goods and information moved more quickly to a greater variety of places, more people lived and worked in urban settings, and that a stable, permanent, form of market exchange fostered leisure time for many middle and upper class Americans, who now could purchase for their families what they once had to make: in effect, the market revolution created the possibility for professional music performance. The books, meetings, museums, and music that filled Americans' lives helped proliferate cultural offerings on a scale previously unimagined. The accomplishment of the Hutchinson Family Singers, the first American music group to employ a message of social protest while earning a significant profit, was inextricably bound to these transformations.

To adequately come to terms with the Hutchinsons' career as social activists and musicians, one must move beyond their personal perseverance—which was legendary in the dismal times from 1840 to 1842, when it was easier for them to accumulate debt than applause—to appreciate how they navigated ties to the market as individuals and as public figures. Through an elaborate deployment of religion, reform, and nature in their personal and professional lives, the musicians of the Hutchinson Family Singers crafted an anti-market stance at the same time as they welcomed the market and earned impressive amounts of money.

Raised in a Baptist family in Milford, New Hampshire, a town on the state's southern border, John, Judson, Asa, and Abby Hutchinson were imbued with Christian ideals, not only at home, where events such as a harvest, birth, or death were explained through a religious framework, but in more communal spaces, such as school, where members of the quartet sat in a building that, for a while, served for both Baptist worship and public learning. Indeed, the teachers in Milford, John remembered years later, often "read the Bible and prayed" in class.[13] The Hutchinson youngsters were thus fully steeped in the ideals of the Second Great Awakening when a series of Baptist revivals hit Milford between 1829 and 1831. At that time, John, along with his brothers, Benjamin, Joshua, Caleb, and several others of the Hutchinson clan, officially declared their faith.

A religious revivalist upbringing marked John, Judson, Asa, and Abby as part of an American generation confident in the ideals of free will, the power to make oneself worthy of being saved, and human perfection, a notion that privileged inner truths over outer display. Throughout their lives, the musicians upheld feeling over thought, community over country, and Christian morals over material gain. In choosing a career in music, the Hutchinson siblings opted for a genre many believed genuinely expressed emotion, represented the character of the land in which the performers were raised, and presented, in its purest form, a divine communication.[14] John Sullivan Dwight said, "there is always a calm Sabbath of the soul in the complete enjoyment of true music, filling the breast with light and love," to which William Wetmore Story would add, "Music seems to contain every other art, but no other art wholly contains music." And many agreed with the *Godey's Magazine* editor who, in 1844, heard the Hutchinson Family Singers "and felt proud of the genius which the green hills of New Hampshire had inspired and nurtured."[15]

Such ideals, though, often stood at odds with the commercialization of early America and the quartet's goal of professional musicianship. Raised in a world all but void of a history of American popular musicians, especially those to combine social protest and public entertainment, it's not surprising that the Hutchinson Family Singers first struggled to reconcile personal ideals with their performance. Though the group faced little competition when on tour in 1841 and 1842 in rural New Hampshire and Massachusetts, they failed to distinguish themselves beyond a harmonious vocal blend. Indeed, their concert repertoire apparently relied solely on the popular tunes of others. The Hutchinsons failed to give the 1840s cultural consumer what was most sought: as was the case for those who went to Christian revivals, the concertgoer expected to gain understanding and, especially, a window into the self. Whether in religion, where God was found within, popular culture, where Ralph Emerson and others lectured on the individual's preeminence, or in politics, where in campaign after campaign candidates framed themselves as men of humble means remade through self-reliance, antebellum American culture exhibited an array of self-expression.

Two moves fostered a more personalized persona for the Hutchinson Family Singers: Abby Hutchinson joined her brothers on stage and, from the stage, the musicians started to declare their reform ideals. The motivation for the group's first change, the inclusion of Abby, was most likely undertaken to address both a musical and social concern. Abby's contralto singing added a higher-pitched voice that countered the trio's blend of two baritones and a bass. Most important, when combined with her stage presence, the twelve year-old completed, in sight and sound, the Hutchinson act as a *family*—and many of their fans agreed. At one of her first shows with the brothers, at Dartmouth College in July 1842, the singers noted of the audience, "all Gentlemen, No Ladies." The next night, John remembered years later, women "came out in number."[16] The Hutchinsons found a way to clear the moral hurdle that many musicians confronted. To be seen and heard as an ethical entertainment earned the sanction of the men of Hanover, New Hampshire, who clearly judged the songsters suitable for the entire household.

As a "nest of brothers with a sister in it," the Hutchinson Family Singers began to embrace a more intimate public persona.[17] Their adoption of a public antislavery position further articulated a distinctive identity for the performers. In the summer of 1842, Nathaniel Peabody Rogers, the William Lloyd Garrison of New Hampshire, prodded the Hutchinson Family Singers to craft an antislavery music. "They are abolitionists," Rogers said in his newspaper. "It need not affright them to have it announced."[18] Though the musicians were likely scared—such reform views, even in the antislavery stronghold of New England, were hotly contested, capable of eliciting an antiabolition response that ranged from noisy disturbance and arrest to violence—they opted to listen to him.

The group welcomed the new year, 1843, with some of their first public abolitionist offerings at an antislavery meeting in Milford, New Hampshire. On January 4th and 5th, activists gathered to honor Thomas Parnell Beach, a white protestor who had been jailed for his antislavery views. Recently released from prison, Beach entered Milford's Old Meeting House when suddenly, from the balcony or balcony stairs, the Hutchinson Family Singers "burst down upon" the assembly in song.[19] As unstaged as the music of the Hutchinsons appeared, clearly the singers were students of recent religious celebrations. In the revival tent, ministers read and anticipated the crowd's reactions to present a dramatic display founded on the appearance of spontaneity. The Hutchinson Family Singers, in their first foray into abolitionist entertainment, established a similar framework. Nathaniel Rogers was one of the first to note how carefully the group's "anti-slavery zeal" was linked to the "popular and striking music of Advent and Revival." Soon, their "practiced spontaneity" was, along with lyrical improvisation, an expected part of a Hutchinson Family Singers performance.[20]

The embrace of antislavery by the Hutchinsons brought about a swift change to the sound of antislavery reform. Earlier abolitionist music was based on the more staid Christian hymn tradition, which, according to the then famed church-tune composer Lowell Mason, should feature diatonic melody and harmony, present a limited range of notes (preferably no more than an octave), and move along a straightforward rhythm (no syncopation).[21] Antislavery music, such as Maria Weston Chapman's 1836 "Hark, Hark, it is the Trumpet Call" (also known as "Hymn No. 4,"), which is based on a Mason melody, embodies the genre.[22] The Hutchinson Family Singers moved antislavery music to the more frenetic sights and sounds of

Christian revivals, where songs looked to inspire an excess of movement and emotion. What the group's antislavery listeners heard and saw in a Hutchinson Family Singers performance, then, was often understood as more modern, progressive—the voice of a growing, younger generation.

The bond that John, Judson, Asa, and Abby forged with Christian revivalism and the antislavery movement created a powerful shield against accusations of market-based materialism. But it certainly did not, in and of itself, solve the issue. The ethics of the group were questioned not only by their critics, who assaulted them for making money from socially conscious song, but, thanks to the more conservative views of certain members of the antislavery movement, even sympathetic listeners voiced concern. "We are sorry to hear that the Hutchinson family of singers are expected to be there," said Lucretia Mott of an antislavery meeting in 1843. Disappointed that the American Anti-Slavery Society had stooped "to mere excitement to carry on the work," Mott grounded her complaint in Quaker ideology. "Music," she once wrote, "very wicked."[23]

While the Hutchinsons faced confrontation over the years, the benefits of their alliance with antislavery reformers and organizations is unquestioned. At the start of 1843, the Hutchinson Family Singers was a struggling act. By the fall, it had replaced the antislavery sensation of 1842—Frederick Douglass—as the latest, inspired reform offering. The antislavery movement, particularly the American Anti-Slavery Society and its subsidiaries, provided the Hutchinsons with a public platform, where they found not only eager listeners and consumers for their music, but an active network of newspapers, meetings, and celebrations that promoted the musicians as a unique antislavery creation.

Under the tutelage of American Anti-Slavery Society leaders such as Nathaniel Peabody Rogers, Frederick Douglass, and William Lloyd Garrison, the music quartet developed into a premier voice for the antislavery movement. The Hutchinsons crafted a style of social activism that was at once entertaining, socially uplifting, and on sale. As the first American musicians to combine impressive market success and social reform, the members of the group often downplayed their profit and highlighted their protest. In part, theirs was a response to that early American unease with the advance of market forces, which were framed as individualistic, immoral, and dangerous. They also faced the more timeless charge hurled at many a reformer through the ages: the selling of a reform-based ware, whether a newspaper, novel, or song, brings into question the sincerity of a reformer's commitment. To battle such notions, the Hutchinsons built their antislavery performance on Christian ideas and sounds; they also made overt displays of charity. John, Judson, Asa, and Abby donated to antislavery and temperance organizations, built spaces reserved for antislavery meetings and entertainment, and, in a move that reflected the economic and authoritative biases among black and white antislavery reformers, publicly passed the monies collected on their behalf to black antislavery advocates. At an 1843 reform meeting in Haverhill, Massachusetts, for example, the musicians turned over a collection's proceeds to George Latimer, the famed former fugitive slave, and Charles Lenox Remond, the respected black lecturer.[24]

When the sibling quartet added to their musical presentation of religion and reform a focus on nature, they completed a three-pronged approach that defended or downplayed their market success. The chorus of one of the group's most popular tunes announces: "We have come from the mountains, we have come from the mountains, we have come from the mountains of the Old Granite State."[25] The Hutchinsons used visions of the natural world in their shows and advertisements to craft a public persona seemingly free from wanton commerce. The song "Old Granite State," which contains expressions of antislavery reform and religious piety, explicitly linked the Hutchinson Family Singers to the most recognizable destination in their home state. White Mountain tourism boomed in the 1840s, becoming a near-national ritual for the genteel and the rugged alike.

That the musicians penned the song before having ever visited the mountains reveals an early navigation of the public/private divide in American popular culture. The use of nature, the White Mountains, though, tapped into a commercial strain then familiar to many American consumers. From guidebooks and promotional pamphlets to the painting of Thomas Cole and the writing of Henry David Thoreau, the marketing of nature was a shared antebellum American experience. In the "Old Granite State," the Hutchinson Family Singers tapped into this strain, which framed a particular, reverent view of nature—Americans were, in effect, trained to uncover a Romantic sublimity by the culture of nature in force at the time.

The New Hampshire origins of the group, which were promoted throughout the 1840s, spited the fact that the quartet spent most of their time on tour—in urban areas such as New York, Philadelphia, and London—and, by 1844, that the brothers had relocated to the Boston suburb of Lynn. On a personal and professional level, the continued identification with the Granite State allowed the musicians an anti-market stance that they believed was key to independence, health, and virtue. Milford, N.H., was removed from the city, away from a supposed source of commercial endeavor. John, Judson, Asa, and Abby heralded their parents' home to provide themselves and their listeners with a stable identity. The burgeoning industrial age in New England, after all, scared many, particularly in older generations, who were overwhelmed by the geographic mobility introduced by technology and the industrial economy.

Forever bonded to the Old Granite State, "the New Hampshire vocalists," as some papers took to calling them, and their musical ability were understood to have originated in the wilds of their home state.[26] Critics and audience members adapted a Romantic outlook that situated unique individuals as products of the natural world in which they were raised and as emblems of the land. Creative genius buttressed local and national concerns in this view—so Beethoven was seen as the product of fertile German land and an example of Germanic brilliance, and the Hutchinsons showcased the richness and depth of New Hampshire, New England, and, ultimately, America. Such a reputation remained when the group went abroad. Reports from Dublin in 1845 noted, "No man can listen to the Hutchinson family without feeling that America—Yankee America has a national music; and none without acknowledging that 'the family' are happy in their illustrations of the harmony of New England."[27] A writer for the *London Chronicle* asked, "why should not the children of the old granite state—for the Hutchinsons are from New Hampshire, which has given rise to the sobriquet—have music in their souls?"[28]

The New Hampshire farm of the Hutchinson family allowed the Hutchinson Family Singers to access a steady, rustic, personality that offered them the appearance of a crucial buffer from the growing world of antebellum American commerce. Their supporters' preferred to situate the musicians not as pioneers in a burgeoning economy of American entertainment, but as a troupe of farmers who happened to be musical. "The months of July and August they will spend with their parents," explained a letter to the *Albany Evening Journal*, "gathering up the harvest which they helped to sow in the spring time, and when they have completed this rural task, they will again sally forth to captivate the ears and win affections of all the true lovers of music."[29] The daily avocation of John, Judson, Asa, and Abby, wrote a fan in the *Connecticut Courant*, was as "tillers of the soil."[30] In fact, said the *Lynn Pioneer*, the Hutchinson Family Singers "prefer to spend the first months of summer on their fine farm on the banks of the Souhegan, to any professional honors which can possibly await them."[31]

The reality was far more complex. As young adults, the members of the Hutchinson Family Singers rejected the strenuous tedium of the preindustrial farm. While some of their older siblings opted to open hardware and grocery stores in places like Lynn and Boston, the members of the singing troupe expressed their preference for a modern urban America through employment in entertainment. But, to make money from music, they were forced, time and again, to acknowledge their agricultural roots. And, like many Americans in the pre-Civil War age, despite their professional choices, the musicians believed farm work to be redemptive. On tour, the brothers were like most musicians through the ages—they sometimes got thrills from goofing off, fighting, and acting rude. They were sure, though, that "if we had good hard farm work to do we should not be so earnest to be playing and making nonsensical remarks."[32] The musicians thus reconciled the mix of old and new ideologies with an acknowledgment of a personal want to farm, while never actually taking the steps to fully return to an agricultural life. In England, a homesick Asa would dream of his future "and the nice little farm that I will have where I will have sheep, cattle, hens and chickens, a donkey, a horse, a cat, a dog, a neat cottage, a garden, fruit trees, and everything to make a farmer happy." Back in the United States at his parents' farmstead, though, he would do no more than sow "some carrot seed in an onion bed. (*Onions* no go.)"[33]

Farm life tied together the three pillars of the Hutchinson Family Singers' public persona as moral, upright entertainment. As the antislavery movement moved toward a full acceptance of free labor ideology, which pushed ideas of social equality and social justice to the fringe of social activism, notions of freedom, free labor, and farming worked hand-in-hand. During a visit to the Florence community experiment in Northampton, Massachusetts, where the Hutchinsons sang and Frederick Douglass "preached" to the "community friends," the musicians toured the society's extensive farm—"They can and will make a home for the free, I hope," Asa said. And, on arrival at their parents' house after a string of concerts, one member of the troupe announced in their shared journal—"I love the free!"[34] Farm life thus served the Hutchinsons on a personal, political, and cultural level, working not only to buffer the negative effects of musical commercialism, but offering them a way to find meaning in their social activism: to espouse antislavery ideas framed them as proponents of a farm world in which they believed, in heart and soul. The siblings simply found the fame and recompense of professional musicianship more redemptive than back-breaking farm work. Their espousal of religion, antislavery, and the New Hampshire land crafted a potent identity that placed them in professional music for reasons other than profit. In the end, such a stance opened the way for the Hutchinson Family Singers to become one of the most successfully marketed identities of the 1840s and 1850s.

Historians have typically used two distinct explanations, the onset of religious revivalism or the market revolution, to account for the rise in social reform in the antebellum era. The example of the Hutchinson Family Singers illuminates that a much more intricate array of forces were in play. Using nature, religion, and social reform, the famed music act shunned market-based behavior while, at the same time, embraced the new world of entertainment opened by market forces. The rise of social reform movements such as antislavery thus appears less the product of a new, religious, outburst than the discovery of how such an outburst could be channeled into a commercial endeavor.

Notes

1 Henry C. Wright, "The Hutchinsons' Repentance," *Liberator*, 19 May 1848, 79.
2 "The New York Anniversaries," *New Hampshire Gazette and Republican Union*, 16 May 1848, 2.
3 Wright, "The Hutchinsons' Repentance," 79.
4 Frederick Douglass, "The Hutchinson Family," *The North Star*, 9 June 1848, 2.
5 Wright, "The Hutchinsons' Repentance," 79.
6 Nathaniel P. Rogers, "Anniversary of the Massachusetts A.S. Society in Faneuil Hall," *Liberator*, 24 Feb. 1843, 32. See also, Scott Gac, *Singing for Freedom: The Hutchinson Family Singers and the Nineteenth-Century Culture of Antebellum Reform* (New Haven: Yale University Press, 2007), 61–62.
7 "Get Off the Track!" (New York: Jesse Hutchinson, Jr., 1844).
8 Butler, quoted in Gac, *Singing*, 224.

9 *Buffalo Republic. Extra. Official Proceedings of the National Free Soil Convention, Assembled at Buffalo, N.Y., August 9 and 10th, 1848* (n.p., n.d.). See also, Gac, *Singing*, 222–223.

10 "The Hutchinson Family," *New Hampshire Gazette*, 18 April 1848, 2.

11 Entry on 9 Jan. 1844 in *Excelsior: Journals of the Hutchinson Family Singers, 1842–1846* (Stuyvesant, New York: Pendragon Press, 1989), 179–180; Gac, *Singing*, 184.

12 William Howitt, "The Hutchinson Family," *Portsmouth Journal*, 29 July 1848, 1.

13 Gac, *Singing*, 82–83, 102–103; John Wallace Hutchinson, *The Story of the Hutchinsons (Tribe of Jesse)*, ed., Charles E. Mann (Boston: Lee and Shepard, 1896), I: 14–15, 21.

14 Gac, *Singing*, 106–107, 97–99, 100–101; William Strauss and Neil Howe, *Generations: The History of America's Future, 1584 to 2069* (New York: Quill, 1991), 193–195.

15 John Sullivan Dwight, "The Religion of Music," *Dwight's Journal of Music*, 19 Sept. 1874, 310; "William Wetmore Story" in Irving Lowens, *Music and Musicians in Early America* (New York: W. W. Norton, 1964), 255; see also, Gac, "The Eternal Symphony Afloat: The Transcendentalists' Quest for a National Culture," *ATQ*, Vol. 16, No. 2 (2002): 153–156; "Editor's Book Table," *Godey's Magazine and Lady's Book* (March 1844): 150.

16 *Excelsior*, 15 July 1842, 13.

17 "A Famous Family of Singers," *The Dial*, 16 October 1896, 223.

18 Rogers, "The Hutchinson Singers" [from the *Herald of Freedom*, 11 August 1842]; *Liberator*, 30 December 1842, 208; Gac, *Singing*, 55.

19 Gac, *Singing*, 59.

20 Daniel W. Patterson, "Word, Song, and Motion: Instruments of Celebration Among Protestant Radicals in Early Nineteenth-Century America," in Victor Turner, ed., *Celebration: Studies in Festivity and Ritual* (Washington, D.C.: Smithsonian Institution Press, 1982), 220–230; Rogers, "Milford Convention," *Herald of Freedom*, 13 January 1843, 186; Gac, *Singing*, 108–109, 60.

21 Gac, *Singing*, 89.

22 Maria Weston Chapman, *Songs of the Free, and Hymns of Christian Freedom* (Boston: Isaac Knapp, 1836), 189–201.

23 Lucretia Mott, "Letter Dated 4th mo., 4th, 1843," in *James and Lucretia Mott: Life and Letters*, ed., Anna Davis Hallowell (Boston: Houghton, Mifflin, 1884) 241–242; Gac, *Singing*, 56–59.

24 Gac, *Singing*, 66.

25 The Hutchinson Family, "The Old Granite State" (Boston: Oliver Ditson, 1843).

26 "The Hutchinson Family," *Emancipator and Weekly Chronicle* [Boston], 20 August 1845, 68.

27 "The Hutchinsons and American Music," *The Sun* [Baltimore], 26 November 1845, 1.

28 "The Hutchinson Family," *London Chronicle*, 11 February 1846, in *Albany Evening Journal*, 23 March 1846, 2.

29 "Correspondence of the Evening Journal," *Albany Evening Journal*, 26 May 143, 2.

30 "The Hutchinson Family," *Connecticut Courant*, 2 August 1844, 126.

31 *Lynn Pioneer* in "The Hutchinson Family," *Newport Mercury* 18 April 1846, 2.

32 *Excelsior*, 8 January 1844, 177.

33 7 March 1846, 15 May 1844, *Excelsior*, 357, 277.

34 27 April 1844, 3 December 1842, *Excelsior*, 267–268, 89.

3

SOLIDARITY FOREVER

Music and the Labor Movement in the United States

Benjamin Bierman

Figure 3.1 A.K. Bierman leading a strike of faculty members at San Francisco College, 1969. Permission granted by the photographer, Phiz Mezey.

This essay examines the history of the relationship between music and labor in the United States during the first half of the twentieth century, an extremely active period for songs regarding the struggle for workers' rights. As an introduction, picture yourself doing some type of repetitive work, such as on an assembly line, running a textile loom, or, perhaps, in a coal mine. Then, imagine having the opportunity to sing with your colleagues as you work. It would lift your spirits and create a feeling of commonality and community. Your workplace and your job would become a shared social experience, rather than an isolated one, and potential tedium would be alleviated, with time moving more quickly.

Let us escalate this scenario. Imagine you are in the midst of a labor strike due to sub-standard wages, dangerous working conditions, and lack of benefits. A strike is dangerous, frightening, isolating, and financially precarious, and you only resort to it because you feel that you absolutely must—there is no other choice. You do not strike alone, however, because you feel safer with others sharing the burden, as well as sharing the potentially devastating effects, such as not having money to feed your family and losing your job. Your negotiating is stronger in numbers, and you might have, or be fighting for, union representation. Imagine yourself on the picket line. Again—and I say this from personal experience—this is a daunting activity and interaction. There is often an intense police presence, because the threat of violence is frequent, and emotions run very high on both sides. Some workers take on the vacated jobs during a strike—these workers are pejoratively referred to as "scabs"— and this causes another level of tension, again with the potential for violence, perhaps as they cross the picket line. This is no joking matter, as people's livelihoods on both sides are at stake. You and your fellow workers may be harboring years of resentment for what you feel is poor treatment or, perhaps, you are frustrated with what you believe is a poor and unfair wage; the organization you are striking against has its own perspective.

This is all to say that labor issues are fraught with intense emotions, and livelihoods are on the line. There are families to feed and rents to pay. So, you strike. You take a chance. Each striker is concerned about what will happen, but you all find some kind of solace and security in being in this situation with your fellow workers. On the picket line—not a fun activity in and of itself—the idea of fervently and joyfully singing songs to express yourselves, to help pass long tedious hours, perhaps in the heat or cold, to create community and solidarity, and even, perhaps, to allay your fears, is a wonderful and powerful thing. This can be seen in the faces of the strikers in the photograph that opens this chapter.

The striking professor at the front of the line happens to be my father, A. K. Bierman. I might very well have been on the picket line that day, as well. Look at the strikers' faces as they sing on the line. They are vigorous, determined, and even joyful; yet I know the pressures that they were all living under. They all lost income, and some lost their jobs. Certainly, the stress on my father, who was one of the leaders of this faculty strike at San Francisco State College (now San Francisco State University) in 1969, was intense for a wide range of reasons. Yet, there they are, walking the picket line and singing in a resolute and exuberant manner. Expressing your anger, frustrations, and goals through song is powerful, and the history of songs of labor and labor unions proves this.

Music connected to labor falls under the heading of protest music, but the amount of music in this genre, and its importance to the culture and heritage of the United States, puts it in a category of its own. In fact, songs revolving around the labor movement dominated much of the protest music genre in the first half of the twentieth century. Additionally, the ties between labor protest music and the civil rights movement and anti-Vietnam War protests, for example, are clear, and influence the Occupy movement even today.

There is a great deal of research on this topic, and it tends to be from at least some type of leftist perspective and generally focuses on the workers' point of view. There is good reason for this. Labor strikes and labor organizing have often been part of what is referred to as progressive politics, a term usually applied to left-leaning perspectives, so it appears to be primarily the province of left-oriented scholars, as opposed to those on the right. In this essay, I provide an overview of some of this research, as well as a consideration of important songs and artists, the context in which they were written, and how such songs and artists connected with the labor movement and radical politics. I examine two types of songs concerned with issues of labor and left-wing politics from the early twentieth century through the 1950s: music in a folk style, and works by art music composers.[1]

Early Songs of Labor

Although I begin in the early 1900s, it is important to understand that the tradition of protest music in the US goes back to the pre-Revolutionary War era. In the nineteenth century, songs about labor protests were common, and there is some important scholarship in this area. Clark D. Halker discusses labor publications and musicians in the late nineteenth century in his book, *For Democracy, Workers and God: Labor Song-Poems and Labor Protest 1865–1895*, and Philip S. Foner's *Labor Songs of the Nineteenth Century* is a compilation of songs on a wide range of social issues—and which are primarily set, as with many labor songs, to existing popular tunes—as well as songs related to early unions, such as the Knights of Labor and the American Federation of Labor (AFL).

Another union, the Industrial Workers of the World (IWW, or the Wobblies) is particularly crucial to the history of protest music in the early twentieth century. This important union, founded in 1905 and still extant today, was founded as an alternative to the AFL, with the goal of representing all workers, regardless of trade, in a struggle against the "employing class."[2]

Music was always crucial to the IWW, beginning with the need to compete with Salvation Army brass bands that were, at times, sent to drown out Wobbly speakers in the streets. In addition, their meetings were begun by singing, and "the IWW's use of music as a direct organizing arm inspired later song agitators by offering song as a front-line device for building morale, recruiting new members, and garnering publicity."[3] The songs also give a rich history of labor struggles, and David King Dunaway states that "the IWW probably employed the greatest range of different types of protest songs."[4] The importance of songs to the union manifested itself early, with the publication of the union's own songbook, the *Little Red Songbook*, in 1909. Since then, there have been numerous editions, including as recently as 2010.

The *Little Red Songbook* primarily included original songs, often set to hymns—such as those used by the competing Salvation Army bands—and popular tunes, which Richard Reuss states "were grounded firmly in real labor experiences in contrast to the verse of other radical groups before 1930."[5] The *Songbook* was the first publication to publish "Solidarity Forever," one of the most popular American union songs.[6] Other important contributors were T-Bone Slim (1880–1940) and Harry McClintock (1882–1957).[7] McClintock was a professional musician, and his "Hallelujah I'm a Bum," set to the hymn "Revive Us Again," was a well-known tune of the day.[8] By far the best-known songwriter in this collection, however, was Joe Hill (1879–1915), whose lyrics were also generally set to popular tunes or hymns. His notoriety stems largely from the circumstances surrounding his controversial murder conviction for the killing of a grocer, as well as his subsequent execution by a firing squad in 1915. There was an international furor surrounding the trial and his execution, and, ironically, Hill is best known for a song that he did not write, but that instead memorializes him, "I Dreamed I Saw Joe Hill Last Night."[9] "There is Power in the Union," set to the hymn "There is Power in The Blood," is an example of Joe Hill's work.[10]

As the Communist Party in America sought and gained influence in the area of workers' rights and social justice, the IWW faded from prominence through the 1920s. While the US struggled through fierce economic woes, culminating in the Great Depression, the Marxist vision of the Soviet Union offered an alternative economic and social approach, and appealed to many intellectuals and artists who were intent upon social change. Many artists were intent on employing their art, whether music, painting, writing, or dance, towards that end.

Communism in the United States

It is impossible to discuss early workers' songs of protest without reference to socialism and the Communist Party, as its history is intertwined with the labor movement in the US, particularly in the period between the 1920s and the 1940s. During the 1920s, in the early and tumultuous stages of the communist movement in the US, the concept of proletarian music—music of and for the working class—was not a priority. The predominant musical vehicle was the revolutionary chorus. The vast majority of members of the Communist Party were native speakers of other languages, and a number of these various ethnic groups, largely eastern European, each "developed its own chorus, orchestra, or other musical unit, and some developed several."[11] These choruses had both social and political functions and "occupied a position of central importance in the cultural life of the early communist movement and so influenced the direction of the movement's musical activity for a considerable period."[12]

The combination of the relative stability of the Communist Party during its Third Period (1928–1934), and the economic and social crises of the Depression, "broadened communism's appeal to the urban middle class, especially to intellectuals and artists."[13] From this came numerous cultural organizations, or clubs, whose goal was to create "proletarian art": art for the workers. There were clubs for actors, such as the New Theatre League, and writers had the John Reed Clubs. Out of the New York John Reed Club grew the Workers' Music League, whose primary goals were "the creation and performance of revolutionary music and ... a forum for discussion of how modern music could be used to further the workers' cause."[14] The Pierre Degeyter Club was one of a number of leftist musicians' organizations affiliated with the Workers' Music League, and out of the Degeyter Club came the Composers' Collective.[15]

The Composers' Collective

The Composers' Collective was formed in 1932, and its members included numerous important composers, many of who were European-trained and worked in a modernist art music medium, such as Charles Seeger, Henry Cowell, Wallingford Riegger, George Antheil, Elie Siegmeister, and Marc Blitzstein. There were few models available for marrying contemporary composition with radical politics, and Hanns Eisler, an Austrian-German composer who studied with Arnold Schoenberg and collaborated with Bertolt Brecht, had a powerful influence on these composers. The Collective composed and performed new works as well as more established material, all intended as revolutionary music, and was also interested in establishing methods for composing proletarian music. To this end, the Composers' Collective published a collection of their songs, the *Workers Songbook*, in 1934 and 1935.[16]

The first edition of the *Songbook* contained thirteen compositions by members of the Collective, including Charles Seeger and Elie Siegmeister (under the pseudonyms Carl Sands and L. E. Swift). Even at a cursory glance, much of the material is clearly for educated, or at least experienced, musicians, and frequently has challenging modernist elements that are problematic for untrained musicians. For two brief examples, Seeger's first song, "Mount the Barricades," is in the unusual time signature of 1/4, and Siegmeister's "The Scottsboro Boys Shall Not Die" has a piano accompaniment based largely on fourths harmonies, as opposed to more traditional triadic chords. It appears that their attempts at a straightforward presentation revolve around their approach to melody, as the accompaniments are particularly tricky, while the melodies are generally more straightforward. The complex approach to music carries over into the language employed in the *Songbook*, and gives insight into the Collective's overall approach.

In the Foreword they set out two types of revolutionary works: "popular bourgeois tunes to which revolutionary words have been set" and "original tunes by proletarian composers." While referring to "bourgeois music" as containing "defeatist melancholy, morbidity, hysteria, and triviality," they admit, "we shall have to use, for some time to come, the basic elements of the old idiom." They continue: "We can, however, and must subject these basic elements to revolutionary scrutiny with a view of finding which of them we cannot help but use, which must be discarded as unsuitable and which must be given a leftward turn that will yield us a recognizably revolutionary music for revolutionary words."[17]

Even the language they use seems to have the potential to alienate the workers that they are striving to unite, just as the modernist language of their music was somewhat off-putting and disconnected from the musical experience of most in the workers' movement. Consequently, workers did not effectively employ their compositions. The work of the Collective, however, represents an important movement of artists and intellectuals that felt impelled to engage and support the workers' struggle during the difficult days of the Depression while remaining true to their artistic principles as well as their commitment to leftist causes. While most members were not communists, many were at the very least sympathetic to the Communist Party line. There was a significant split in the group regarding approaches to the use of music in service of the workers' cause, however.

The *Workers Songbook* was not the only Communist Party music publication of the Workers' Music League, as the *Red Song Book* preceded it. The *Red Song Book* included folk-oriented material such as songs by Aunt Molly Jackson (1880–1960) and Ella May Wiggins (1900–1929), two activist folk artists whose songs were drawn from the southern folk tradition. Their songs stemmed from extremely contentious workers' strikes—the Harlan County, Kentucky, miners' strike of 1931–32, and the Gastonia, North Carolina, textile workers' strike of 1929, respectively—as opposed to the modernist compositional style of much of the *Workers Songbook*. Ray and Lida Auville, singer-songwriters in the folk tradition, also published workers' songs in *Songs of the American Worker*. In *The Worker Musician*, a monthly publication of the Workers' Music League, the *Red Song Book* and *Songs of the American Worker* were criticized for being overly simple. This set up a conflict between the Collective's art music perspective and the Communist Party's cultural critic, Mike Gold, who felt their attitude was elitist and lauded the Auvilles.

This split also reared its head with the performance of Aunt Molly Jackson at a Composers' Collective meeting. Jackson was a radical organizer for the National Miners' Union who adeptly and effectively set lyrics to traditional Appalachian tunes. After attending some Collective meetings which included debates over what it means to create a good workers' song, Jackson performed some of her material. Reuss states that Charles Seeger recalled the Collective's members "were more bewildered than inspired" by her performance, and that Aunt Molly Jackson was, in turn, unimpressed by the Collective's works. Her performance is referred to as an important turning point in the discussion of the respective efficacy, as workers' songs, of folk-style music versus art music.

The composers of the Collective responded to this controversy—art music versus folk and popular forms—in their own manner: they examined the communist movement's revamped stance on folk and popular styles as they began to assess their own frustrations with their art music approach to reaching the masses. Their frustration with the latter is shown by the fact that the many of the songs in the Collective's last songbook were set to well-known tunes. Reuss posits that their public split from the dogma of Hanns Eisler further exemplifies the Collective's members' separation from the party line. Along with these cultural workers' movement towards popular and folk materials, New Deal programs, such as the Works Progress Administration's Federal Music Project (of which Charles Seeger was assistant director), the work of folklorists such as John and Alan Lomax, and the work of Margaret Larkin and Mike Gold, who publicized and promoted activist artists working in a folk music idiom, propelled the movement away from the use of art music and in the direction of the use of folk-style material to promote workers' causes.[18]

Labor politics had its place on Broadway as well. As the Composers' Collective attempted to marry modernism with radical text, Marc Blitzstein (1905–1964), a member of the Collective, sought to do so through theatrical means. His 1937 musical *The Cradle Will Rock* owes much to the musical traditions of Hanns Eisler and Bertolt Brecht as well as to the American musical theater.[19] Blitzstein was also involved in another Broadway production that was union-oriented, *Pins and Needles*. While the actors were amateurs drawn from the International Ladies' Garment Workers' Union (ILGWU) Players, the production team consisted of theater professionals, including composer-lyricist Harold Rome, Blitzstein, and the writer Emmanuel Eisenberg. Trudi Wright states: "*Pins and Needles* offered these leftist writers a creative vehicle in which to give voice to their political and social opinions."[20] Its 1,108 performances make it the longest running musical of the Depression era.

As Charles Seeger's vision of class-conscious composers began to prevail over the more modernist approach—towards song and the proletariat—of other composers, such as Henry Cowell, the Collective withdrew from the Pierre Degeyter Club in 1935. Weismann stresses the relationship between Charles Seeger and Alan Lomax as crucial to protest music in general,[21] as well as to the folk music revival, as they "created a vision of using folk songs as a tool for radical change."[22] The Almanac Singers are an excellent representation of this tendency, and have strong familial ties to the Composers' Collective.

The Almanac Singers, People's Songs, Inc., People's Artists, and The Weavers

New York City was the hub of the music business in the United States, and it was there that the Almanac Singers (1941–1944) gradually came together, initially including Pete Seeger, Lee Hays, Millard Lampell, and John Peter Dawes. The Almanacs were a small and fluid group that wrote and performed folk-style music in support of unions, particularly those in the Congress of Industrial Organizations (CIO) as well as the Communist Party USA. The group soon grew to include, at various times, Woody Guthrie, Josh White, Sonny Terry, Brownie McGhee, Cisco Houston, and the composer Earl Robinson, as well as others, most of whom had some type of radical background.

They formed a collective, even in their loft-living arrangements. It was in this shared space that the concept of a "hootenanny" was born. Admission was charged to hear a concert with an informal and casual air, making the performance almost like a gathering, as opposed to a paid performance. Some members went on to commercial success. Seeger and Hays were members of The Weavers (discussed below), Burl Ives became a popular folk singer and actor; Josh White created a genre-crossing style that mixed the blues and folk music, Lead Belly's rough-hewn yet sophisticated guitar and vocal style made him popular, and Sonny Terry and Brownie McGhee became an in-demand duo with a refined country blues style.

This New York City-based aggregation of socially conscious, leftist, musicians was committed to the use of music as a political and organizing tool. They collected material from songbooks, but also traveled extensively collecting songs; this eventually led to the publication of the important song collection *Hard Hitting Songs for Hard-Hit People*, a collaboration between Pete Seeger, Woody Guthrie, and Alan Lomax. Seeger and Guthrie, both crucial musical figures in the leftist movement, were eventually at the center of the Almanacs.

Pete Seeger (1919) is the son of Charles Seeger, who, as we have seen, was a major figure both in the Composers' Collective and in the collection and preservation of folk material. Pete Seeger is a wonderful guitarist and banjo player, with a powerful, emotional, expressive, and distinctive voice. His presence on various political scenes throughout his life sets him apart from all others as the most important musical figure in protest music in the United States. While there were certainly many that set the stage for him, Seeger's importance to the left as musical support and inspiration for a variety of struggles, such as labor rights, civil rights, anti-war sentiment, and ecology, is unmatched.

Woody Guthrie (1912–1967) has a very different background from Seeger. Originally from Oklahoma, Guthrie was forced by the Great Depression and the Dust Bowl era to travel in search of work. These travels, along with the other "Okies" that traveled to California to find work, are frequent subjects of his songwriting. He became connected to the leftist community in southern California, and then went to New York where the burgeoning leftist music community quickly accepted him. The legend of the wandering hobo mixed with labor activist and singer-songwriter contrasts with more problematic aspects of his personality. He was a prolific writer of both prose and songs. Just a few of his well-known songs are "So Long, It's Been Good to Know Yuh," "Hobo's Lullaby," "Tom Joad," "Talking Dust

Bowl Blues," "Pastures of Plenty," "Union Maid," and the ubiquitous "This Land is Your Land," which has been employed by both the right and the left. Beginning in the late 1940s, as a result of Huntington's disease, an extremely debilitating genetic disorder that causes a loss of muscle coordination and cognitive and psychiatric disorders, Guthrie's life became increasingly difficult and isolated until his death in 1967.

The political climate in the late 1930s was extremely complicated and fraught. The country was in the midst of a depression, labor strife was high, and the relationship of the United States to struggles abroad was complicated, including for those involved with, or sympathetic to, the Communist Party. The Party was initially firmly anti-fascist, evidenced by its involvement in supporting the Republicans in the Spanish Civil War who opposed the Francisco Franco-led fascists. After Hitler's pact with Stalin in August 1939, however, the Communist Party of the United States (CPUSA) favored non-intervention in Europe and World War II.

To support the stance of CPUSA, and in response to an anticipated US involvement in the war, the Almanacs wrote and recorded six original songs for *The Death of John Doe* in 1941, which powerfully attacked Franklin Roosevelt and protested against intervention in the war. With the United States joining the war effort shortly thereafter, and Germany's invasion of the Soviet Union, the album's subject matter took on a particularly incendiary—some said treasonous—tone and was withdrawn. After Germany's invasion of the Soviet Union, the Almanacs could no longer sing anti-war material, and Pete Seeger's "Dear Mr. President," for the album *Dear Mr. President*, exemplifies the Almanacs' shift to a pro-war stance. The Almanacs combined this stance with their union sympathies, and began to write songs that depicted the working man's support for the war effort. As the war escalated, the Almanacs lost numerous personnel, with Seeger and Guthrie being drafted, and others involved in war relief work, and the Almanacs faded from sight.

In 1946, after World War II and out of the ashes of the Almanac Singers, Pete Seeger created a new organization, People's Songs, Inc., to advance the tradition of radical protest music. The Board of Directors resembled the Almanacs, with Woody Guthrie, Millard Lampell, Lee Hays, and Earl Robinson, as well as Alan Lomax (1915–2002) and the singer-songwriter Tom Glazer. Members also included non-folk-based artists such as Harold Rome (who worked on *The Cradle Shall Rock*) and E. Y. "Yip" Harburg, a successful Tin Pan Alley lyricist (he wrote the lyrics for "Brother, Can You Spare a Dime?" and "It's Only a Paper Moon"), in an attempt to be more broad-based, musically, than the Almanac Singers. Based in New York City, it eventually had branches in Los Angeles, San Francisco, and Chicago, as well as other cities. The organization published a monthly bulletin and educational pamphlets, booked musicians, and published *The People's Song Book*. They performed in concert halls, on picket lines, and at demonstrations, and were heavily involved in the Presidential campaign of Henry Wallace, who was running on the

Progressive Party ticket. The organization lasted until 1949, when it disbanded after having financial difficulty.

As the People's Songs organization was dissolving, Pete Seeger, Lee Hays, Ronnie Gilbert, and Fred Hellerman formed the quartet The Weavers. Following the demise of People's Songs, The Weavers were booked into the Village Vanguard, a Greenwich Village nightclub, and soon became a huge success, selling over four million records between 1950 and 1952. There are in essence two Weavers. Their live recordings, with Seeger on banjo and Hellerman on guitar, display their folk-style roots as they play original and traditional material. The other is in a much more commercial context, featuring orchestral and choral arrangements by Gordon Jenkins, an excellent arranger who wrote for Nat "King" Cole and Frank Sinatra, among others. All of the members sang, and The Weavers were known for their effective harmonies. They composed original material, and Hays and Seeger wrote numerous songs together, the most famous being "If I Had a Hammer (The Hammer Song)," one of the most known, popular, and effective songs of the period. An initial Weavers' recording of Lead Belly's "Goodnight Irene," and "Tzena Tzena," an Israeli popular song, reached numbers one and two on the *Billboard* charts. Originally a product of the left-wing movement, their popularity raised issues regarding their, perhaps—at times—reluctant, embrace of commercial success and its clash with their socialist ideology.

Seeger and Irwin Silber, along with others, had formed People's Artists to continue to provide support for radical causes through music. People's Artists initially booked The Weavers, but once they had professional management outside of the organization, because of the political climate and out of commercial considerations, The Weavers significantly softened their political stance, particularly in their recorded material, and distanced themselves from leftist politics. In 1950, People's Artists began to publish *Sing Out!*, a monthly magazine (it is still extant as a quarterly publication) with Irwin Silber as the editor. As the Communist Party declined, so did the work of musicians working for People's Artists. Between this and internal organizational strife, People's Artists was gradually dissolved so that, by 1957, its focus was solely on the publishing of *Sing Out!*

In addition, during this period, anti-communist sentiment was at its height and the House Un-American Activities Committee (HUAC) was active in the persecution of those perceived to be affiliated with the Communist Party. Eventually, hundreds of artists were boycotted as a result. A 1950 pamphlet, "Red Channels," was part of this effort. Many from the Almanac Singers, People's Songs, and People's Artists were on this list, including Pete Seeger, Alan Lomax, Burl Ives, Oscar Brand, Josh White, and Earl Robinson. Composer Aaron Copland, who was earlier associated with the Composers' Collective, was also on the list, as was composer-conductor Leonard Bernstein. The blacklists altered people's lives in a significant manner, and many had difficulty resuming their careers.[23]

There are clear connections between the Almanac Singers, People's Songs, Inc., People's Artists, and The Weavers, but they are all also closely associated with the Composers' Collective, as Pete Seeger's father, Charles Seeger, was a driving force in that organization. Given this, it is not surprising that they shared the goal of creating and promoting radical music designed to effect social change; in addition, they shared the debate about which types of musical styles were appropriate for this purpose. It is fascinating to see these shared principles and practices a generation removed, with the emphasis having shifted predominantly towards a folk-oriented style: the direction in which Charles and Ruth Crawford Seeger headed as the art music-oriented Collective disbanded. Clearly, the Seeger family influence has carried through, even to today's political movements—as evidenced by Pete Seeger and Arlo Guthrie (Woody Guthrie's son), marching with the Occupy Wall Street protesters in October 2011, as the crowd chanted and sang popular protest songs such as "We Shall Overcome" and "This Little Light of Mine."[24]

Conclusion

While these various organizations may not have directly achieved their goals of establishing a music that supported the struggle for workers' rights and engaging workers from the labor movement, a largely negative assessment seems misguided. The succession of the Composers' Collective, Almanac Singers, People's Songs, Inc., People's Artists, The Weavers, and the future success of many of their members—as well as their influence on the next generation of folk-style singers involved in music bent on social change, such as Bob Dylan, Phil Ochs, and Joan Baez—is a significant legacy. The path they set, and the ideological commitment that they exhibited, had a powerful effect on the notion of music as a vehicle for social change in the United States. It also influenced the direction of the music business, while raising the profile of folk music as an important American genre. Much of this can be attributed to the relationship of music to the labor movement throughout the first half of the twentieth century in the United States.

Notes

1 For this essay I particularly relied upon the following comprehensive sources, each with their own perspective: Richard A. Reuss with JoAnne C. Reuss, *American Folk Music and Left-Wing Politics, 1927–1957* (Lanham, Maryland: The Scarecrow Press, 2000); Ronald D. Cohen, *Work and Sing: A History of Occupational and Labor Union Songs in the United States* (Crocket, California: Carquinez Press, 2010); Dick Weissman, *Which Side Are You On? An Inside History of the Folk Music Revival in America* (New York: Continuum, 2005); David King Dunaway, "Music and Politics in the United States" *Folk Music Journal*, Vol. 5, No. 3 (1987); and R. Serge Denisoff, *Great Day Coming: Folk Music and the American Left* (Urbana, Illinois: University of Illinois Press, 1971). Cohen presents the history of song

and labor through comprehensive research regarding song collections, the collectors, and the artists. Weismann examines these topics in relation to the 1960s folk music revival in the United States. Reuss offers perhaps the most comprehensive examination of the relationship between folk music and left-wing politics. Denisoff examines the relationship between the communists and these artists and their music. Dunaway examines the topic in the context of politics and music in the history of the United States.

2 "Preamble to the IWW Constitution," http://www.iww.org/en/culture/official/preamble.shtml, accessed 1 June 2012.

3 Dunaway, "Music and Politics," 283.

4 Dunaway, "Music and Politics," 287.

5 Reuss, *American Folk Music and Left-Wing Politics*, 26.

6 For the lyrics to this song, see *Songs of the Workers to Fan the Flames of Discontent: The Little Red Songbook* (Limited Centenary Concert Edition. Philadelphia: Industrial Workers of the World, 2005), 4.

7 T-Bone Slim wrote "The Mysteries of a Hobo's Life," published in the 17th edition of *Little Red Songbook*, and McClintock's most well known song is perhaps "Big Rock Candy Mountain."

8 For the lyrics to this song, see *Little Red Songbook*, 12.

9 Lyrics by Alfred Hayes and composer Earl Robinson, written circa 1930.

10 For the lyrics to this song, see *Little Red Songbook*, 50.

11 *Little Red Songbook*, 41.

12 *Little Red Songbook*, 41.

13 *Little Red Songbook*, 43.

14 Barbara L. Tischler, "Modernists and Proletarian Music: The Composers' Collective of the Early 1930s," in David Castriota, ed., *Artistic Strategy and the Rhetoric of Power: Political Uses of Art from Antiquity to the Present* (Carbondale and Edwardsville: Southern Illinois University Press, 1986), 137.

15 In 1888, Pierre Degeyter, a French workers' chorus director, composed the music for "L'Internationale," a Eugène Pottier poem, creating one of the most widely known socialist songs.

16 A great deal of research has been done regarding the struggle of leftist modernist art music composers through the Workers' Music League and the Pierre Degeyter Club, as these composers attempted to unite their artistic desires with their political goals. Judith Tick examines it through Charles and Ruth Crawford Seeger (*Ruth Crawford Seeger: A Composer's Search for American Music* [New York: Oxford University Press, 1997, Chapter 12]), and Elizabeth B. Crist through composer Aaron Copland (*Music for the Common Man: Aaron Copland during the Depression and War* [New York: Oxford University Press, 2005, Chapter 1]). Barbara L. Tischler concentrates on the Composers' Collective itself ("Modernists and Proletarian Music: The Composers' Collective of the Early 1930s," in David Castriota, ed., *Artistic Strategy and the Rhetoric of Power: Political Uses of Art from Antiquity to the Present* [Carbondale and Edwardsville: Southern Illinois University Press, 1986]), and Ellie M. Hisama through a musicological and analytical examination of Ruth Crawford Seeger ("In Pursuit of a Proletarian Music: Ruth Crawford's "Sacco, Vanzetti," in Ray Allen and Ellie M. Hisama, eds., *Ruth Crawford Seeger's Worlds: Innovation and Tradition in*

Twentieth-Century American Music [Rochester: University of Rochester Press, 2007]). Melissa J. de Graaf discusses it through Ruth Crawford Seeger's involvement in the Composers' Forum and the Composers' Collective ("The Reception of an Ultramodernist: Ruth Crawford's 'Sacco, Vanzetti'," in *Ruth Crawford Seeger's Worlds*).

17 *Workers Songbook* (New York: Workers' Music League, 1934), 2.

18 Reuss, *American Folk Music and Left-Wing Politics*, 70.

19 Marc Blitzstein and *Cradle* are examined by Jonathan C. Friedman in this volume; Robert J. Dietz, "Marc Blitzstein and the 'Agit-Prop' theatre of the 1930s," *Anuario Interamericano de Investigacion Musical*, Vol. 6 [1970]: 51–66); John D. Shout, "The Musical Theater of Marc Blitzstein," *American Music*, Vol. 3, No. 4 [Winter 1985]: 413–428), and Carol Oja, "Marc Blitzstein's 'The Cradle Will Rock' and Mass-Song Style of the 1930s," *The Musical Quarterly*, Vol. 73, No. 4 [1989]: 445–475.

20 Trudi Wright, "Labor Takes the Stage: A Musical and Social Analysis of *Pins and Needles* (1937–1941)" (Ph.D. dissertation, University of Colorado, 2010), 6.

21 Charles Seeger went on to hold a number of governmental positions during which he supervised fieldwork throughout the Americas. These positions included Deputy Director of the Federal Music Project, part of Franklin D. Roosevelt's Works Progress Administration (WPA), and chief of the music division of the Pan-American Union. He was later extremely active as an ethnomusicologist and musicologist. Alan Lomax and his father, John, did extensive fieldwork, recording local folk material and "discovering" local artists. Among other activities, Lomax compiled and edited folk song collections, conducted oral histories, and was a researcher and author. The multifarious collections (recordings, photographs, videos, etc.) assembled by the Lomaxes are now housed in The Alan Lomax Collection at the American Folklife Center, The Library of Congress.

22 Weissman, *Which Side Are You On?*, 43.

23 My father, A. K. Bierman, was also a leader in the fight against HUAC in San Francisco in 1959–1960. For an account of this struggle, as well as his own account of the grassroots organizing campaign that culminated in "Black Friday," see http://www.notinkansas.us/#AKBierman.

24 Cristian Salazar and Karen Matthews, "Pete Seeger, Arlo Guthrie Occupy Wall Street, Perform," *Huffington Post*, 22 October 2011, http://www.huffingtonpost.com/2011/10/22/pete-seeger-arlo-guthrie-occupy-wall-street_n_1026299.html, accessed 13 June 2012.

4

SONIC OPPOSITION

Protesting Racial Violence before Civil Rights

Katherine L. Turner

Figure 4.1   Billie Holiday performing at Metropolitan Opera House.

> Shut up in ghettos, sneered at, beaten, enslaved,
> We always have answered our oppressors
> With brave singing, dancing, and laughing.[1]

Protesting and musicking are such natural companions that the association need only be whispered to be true. Nowhere is this more profound than in the music of the African-American community. The decades preceding the "freedom songs" of the 1960s were the fertile proving grounds of expression and sonic opposition. The black community had a rightful laundry list of grievances, some common to the human experience—romance gone bad, loneliness, and bad luck—others more particular to the economic and racial tides of the day, including poverty, unjust "Jim Crow" practices, and race-based violence. These themes could be overt within the lyrics but were often coded, the private property of those who truly understood. This essay addresses two types of popular song that helped build protest against Jim Crow violence in the first half of the twentieth century: the first is folksong, written/performed by and for the black community; the second, the more "studied" type of compositions, were collaborations between white and black creators/performers. These two types of music may have had different musical foundations, formal constructions and intended audiences, but their objective was the same: to articulate, crystalize and disseminate the message of dissent and solidarity.

In the wake of the abolition of slavery, a new series of humiliating subjugations, legalized discriminatory actions, and cultural practices took hold. "Jim Crow"—once a minstrel stereotype for the backwards, uneducated, slap-happy black—became the generic term for the social, employment, and legal suppression rampant in the South and increasingly present in the North. The blues, reflecting this linguistic trend, employed the term "Jim Crow" in every grammatical fashion: as nouns in Lead Belly's "Jim Crow Blues," and Big Bill Broonzy's lyric, "What you gonna do about the old Jim Crow?," a modifier: Josh White's "Jim Crow Train," and as a verb: Cow Cow Davenport's "Jim Crow Blues" opens with "I'm tired of being Jim Crowed." Such songs addressed specific ills and generic racist practices with a substrate apprehension for the ever-present threat of bodily harm faced by the individual singer and by the community at large.[2]

The most heinous of racial violence was the practice of lynching. The term has long been contested, and a fluid definition has led to varied statistics, but, generally speaking, it was an extra-judicial murder committed by a mob which believed it was acting justly. In most cases, the assailants faced no incrimination even when clearly identifiable as the perpetrators.[3] In practical terms, although no racial group was immune, lynchings of blacks by whites became spectacle events most prominent between Reconstruction and World War II. The Tuskegee Institute reports that 4,743 lynchings took place in America, 1882–1968.[4] Just over 70 percent of victims were black, 75 percent took place in the states of the former Confederacy, and almost all were men. The height was in 1892, which recorded 230 lynchings, including 161 blacks. The numbers did not settle below one per week until the 1920s, and all but disappeared post-war. Common offenses (although guilt was not a prerequisite) included murder followed by sexual assault, but "seeming uppity" or talking back to a white person was cause enough.[5] A victim might be taken from his home or even the jail, the law being unable or unwilling to intercede. He was likely beaten, shot, dragged, hanged and/or burned. His fingers and toes became collectable relics, his testicles might be detached, and he was often tortured alive before a crowd of men, women, and children, which often included people from miles away, even neighboring states. The remains served as the background for souvenir photograph/postcards; people from the crowd posed for such photos, and newspapers covered the largest such events, carrying the story around the world.

There was a significant anti-lynching movement that included a cross-section of Americans. The NAACP made it central to their mission; progressives and communists were some of the most dynamic activists; and religious groups, labor organizations, and women, especially (white) southern women, politically and socially campaigned to end the practice. While the NAACP represented the concerns of black Americans, most rural southern blacks were not members. Instead of letter writing or raising funds for legal defense, black folksong— especially the blues—emerged at least partly as a means of expressing individual and collective thoughts, feelings and objections about the treatment of their community.[6] Russell Ames, a white musicologist who collected and published research about black music in the US between the 1920 and 1950s, wrote about the importance of recognizing the value and artistic merit of black music:

> The seeming surface of the blues is one of lament and self-pity, now and then laced with irony. But much of this sentimental surface is protective, while the irony is an outcropping of the hard metal beneath. The deeper content of the blues has been stated by a blues singer, in the presence of Alan Lomax: "The blues is mostly revenge." And a friend answered: "That's right. Signifyin' and gettin' his revenge through song."[7]

The need to be "protective"—from white authorities, primarily—continues a long tradition of covert language and meaning, to be sure, but there can also be found a directness that stands as a bold challenge. Undertones of revenge are carefully constructed in many of the examples below. To be too bold would be a mistake, but some blues singers were intimating powerful questions, eliciting the responses and conveying the anger that was the catalyst for change.

More recently, Adam Gussow has written about the ways in which the African-American community addressed issues of violence and identity through the "blues subject" in *Seems like Murder Here: Southern Violence and the Blues.*[8] His conclusion is that two main types of violence appear in blues songs and autobiographies of early to mid-twentieth-century musicians: white-on-black racially-motivated events, namely lynching, and black-on-black violence, such as shootings, cuttings, and domestic violence.[9]

He is quick to note that white lynch mobs and references to the threat of racially-motivated violence are conspicuously absent from [recorded] blues songs.

Brutal, public, terrifying … Lynching was all these things. Yet lynching was also, according to blues scholars, a taboo subject in its own time, all but unaddressed by black blues singers—singers who were more than willing to speak back, overtly and covertly, to the other violent disciplines hemming them in. [Including] "hard times" and "bad luck" … economic inequality, chain gangs, high sheriffs, big cruel bossmen, and mean old railroad engineers are apostrophized in ways that can clearly be construed as racial protest.[10]

Gussow attributes this seemingly unusual omission to abject fear. He argues that the subconscious minds of blues singers instead defined their thoughts and feelings about lynchings through a series of codes employed in many blues lyrics:

The "loss" half of the love-and-loss dialectic articulated by blues song is a way of transcoding such tribulations and torments: the bluesman sings of romantic mistreatment as a way of signifying on and mourning the "sadder blues" of racial mistreatment.[11]

He posits that the blues itself may have emerged as a response to the culture of lynching as a means of catharsis and dissent; rather than becoming paralyzed by the terror, the blues became a creative outlet for blacks to emote in [relative] safety behind the language of everyday scenarios and concerns.[12] Regretfully, he seems to have found no stable pattern of widely understood codes or signifyin' as is the case with the spirituals of the slave days.[13] Through a series of examples spanning the 1890s to the 1960s, Gussow demonstrates how the blues can be traced to the culture of violence and its manifestations in the black community.[14] While his approach seeks to uncover underlying veiled references to violence, the following discussion seeks examples of blues songs that informed listeners about different means of protest: posing questions, asking the audience to evaluate their own feelings and actions, and putting events in the context of the growing protest movement.

The essential problems of the black community under Jim Crow coalesce in Big Bill Broonzy's "Black, Brown and White." In it he describes pervasive and familiar discrimination in living and working conditions; in one version he describes having helped build and fight for the country, but with no increase in respect. The refrain points to prejudice based on hue of blackness.[15] The clear message throughout is that his very dark skin put him at the end of the employment line, made him invisible to shop keepers, and that he would only be safe if he kept moving farther away. The tight rhyming pairs are quite effective in establishing the pungency of his argument. White is right, brown stays around, black gets back. The repetition of this third part is especially telling, with the same melodic ascension and strumming pattern. It is really quite catchy, as if he is hopping (or being pushed) backwards again and again.[16] The light-hearted, even humorous, tone belies the inclination to get as far away from trouble as possible; many towns put up literal markers at the city limits warning blacks to "get back," with signs reading "Nigger, don't let the sun go down on you here."[17] The implication was not just that there were no jobs or housing for blacks, but that the night was the hunting grounds of racist mobs. Is this what the boss, the barkeep, and the government employee, who spoke the lines of the refrain, were saying to him?

In singing this song, Big Bill Broonzy promoted the conversation of opposition. A first person narrative, as most blues songs were, he explicitly addresses his audience and engages them in the process of protest. He is at once describing to his audience the events in his life and, by example, serving as a point of information: this is the consequence of being as black as I am. This is a variant of the call-and-response technique that is central to the blues and African-American music in general, but here, instead of repeating or varying the line in AAB form, the call is left open-ended for the audience to complete.[18] He leaves his listener with a challenge about what he or she was going to do about Jim Crow. Big Bill recorded the song in 1951 as black communities and their supporters were gaining momentum that would become the civil rights activities of the 1950s and 1960s.[19]

Blues legend Lead Belly, known for performing blues and folk songs with a larger purpose and for working with ethnomusicologist Alan Lomax, made a similar plea in "Jim Crow Blues" for his listeners to become more active in confronting Jim Crow practices. According to the Tuskegee Archive, the states mentioned (one each on the western, northern and eastern borders of the Southern block) were three of the top eight in terms of lynching statistics and, in each state, more than 80 percent of the victims were black. Whereas Big Bill looked to individuals (*tell me brother*) to respond to him, Lead Belly promoted solidarity (everyone *get together*). Big Bill leaves the outcome open by asking what to do; Lead Belly declares a way forward.

These last two examples give advice to the listeners (like a blues Public Service Announcement). Sleepy John Estes sang about his real-life experience with the law and how he got out of trouble. He identifies his lawyer Mr. Clark (and how to find his offices "in town" and his residence near the lake on "70 Road"). On the one hand this is a swift recommendation— this man doesn't rob his clients and he will help— but it is also a means of reminding audience members that worse than the dreaded penitentiary is death by lynch mob. His subtle protest implies that his offense was such that the lawyer could prove him innocent in a courtroom, but that no offense was too slight for mob punishment. Even if African-Americans did escape the lynch mob, there was certainly no guarantee that the system of justice would be fair.

One of Lead Belly's most poignant songs was "Scottsboro Boys." The song was based on the trials of nine African-American males falsely accused of a variety of crimes including the sexual assault of two white women on a train. The case became a referendum on the failures of the justice system and systematic inequity towards blacks. There was no actual lynching in the Scottsboro case, although lynch mobs did threaten and attempt to harm the defendants and their supporters many times over the course of the trials, which lasted from their 1931 arrest through the next two decades, including re-hearings, paroles, dropped, and added charges.

In Lead Belly's 1938 live session, he sings the lyrics he was known for, including the refrain above, and also tells the tale of the contemporary political situation—how some of the boys had been released and some had not. The lyrics here strike the same themes as lynchings—blacks chased from their homes (in this case by the landlord). In Alabama, colored people have to watch their backs, and a white woman's lie in the Jim Crow South will kill "a thousand colored men." His message this time is to those blacks who live in the North; they should protest through song. The vaudevillian cadence on "sing," with its extended rhythmic value and melodic slide to tonic reminds the listener that what he was doing was a contribution to the fight against Jim Crow, one in which his audience, too, could participate. This pro-activity is echoed by Ethel Waters and quoted at the top of this essay: singing is bravery in the face of oppression.

Waters was a blues, pop, and jazz singer, as well as a star of stage and screen. She was not especially politically active, but her contribution to protesting racial violence was every bit as affecting and personal as if she had written the protest blues herself. Instead, her music is the first of three examples of "studied" music composed by someone other than the performer: "Supper Time," "Strange Fruit," and "And They Lynched Him on a Tree" were composed by professional or semi-professional composers, written and published as sheet music, performed by African-Americans for mixed audiences, and each was the product of bi-racial collaboration.

In 1933, Waters was part of the interracial cast in Moss Hart and Irving Berlin's *As Thousands Cheer*, a Broadway revue with biting political and social commentary. Each of twenty-one scenes was prefaced with a newspaper heading ranging from President Hoover leaving the White House to the foibles of the Rockefellers, society dinners to commercials that interrupted opera. Several of the songs became hits in their own right, outliving the one-year run of the musical—most notably, "Easter Parade." Although some serious subjects were broached, including Gandhi and Cuba, most of the hits were the similarly cheerful, upbeat, sort, rather than the close-to-home marked unpleasantness performed by Waters. Irving Berlin was a Jewish immigrant and, according to his biographer, had come a long way in his thinking about race relations.[20] "This was surely not the light, satirical fare Irving intended to include, but the songwriter's "Supper Time" demonstrated that a tragedy as well as a farce could inspire a hit song."[21] The song was a commercial success, both as part of the musical and for Ethel Waters; it became one of her signature songs.

The pulsing stream of media lambasting and satire of the first act is broken after intermission with scene two. Ushered in with the newspaper heading: "Unknown Negro Lynched by Frenzied Mob," the scene begins with Ethel Waters singing "Supper Time."[22] In context, the audience would readily have comprehended that, when she sang "I should set the table 'cause it's supper time. Somehow I'm not able 'cause that man o'mine ain't comin' home no more," she was lamenting the death of her husband at the hands of a lynch mob and bemoaning the effect it will have on her family. Out of context, it could be mistaken as a man who ran off abandoning his wife and children, a not unfamiliar topic in blues lyrics. It is certainly blues influenced, with the use of "black" dialect, melodic and harmonic gestures borrowed from the blues, and some textual repetition, but not in the form or the instrumentation (the full orchestra prelude and postlude give it away). The text is set conversationally, with long notes interspersed amongst short durations; most of the melodic and harmonic interest is found in the piano accompaniment, which seems a bit disjunctive from the tone of the vocal work.[23]

> She displayed her dramatic range in "Supper Time," the magnificently understated lament of the wife of the victim, who must tell her children that they will never see their father again. This was a tragic strain, to be sure, but by no means a protest song. Berlin had so personalized and muted the incendiary racial aspects of the event that what the song lost in bite it gained in universality.[24]

True, the text is not explicit: the word "lynching" is not in the lyrics, there is no gruesome description, no inkling of racial disparagement or so much as a veiled threat. However, I disagree with Berlin's biographer, in that the song in context pre-established the culture of racial violence. The images and stories of lynchings were inescapable, even in New York. Audience members would have been familiar with both the general concept of racial violence and the horrific specifics of the unsung event. The newspaper headline preceding the song would have placed those thoughts and images at the forefront of listeners' minds.

It seems incredulous that Berlin did not conceive this as a form of protest; Jews were among the most ardent supporters of the anti-lynching movement. Their own history with anti-Semitism led many to donate their time and money to ending the practice and supporting federal legislation.[25] He also knew his audience: the Broadway set was educated, liberal, and politically savvy. Berlin may not have been aiming for a grand political statement, but he was not avoiding one either.[26] The "personalization" of the event would only serve to highlight the injustice of lynching. Waters' performance forced audience members to sit across from her at the supper table as she mourned. The song had "universality" *because* it had "bite."

In her autobiography, Waters revealed that the song was more than just a stage performance. It was a meaningful way of seeking justice based on her personal experience with lynching.

> I sat and prayed with the family of that lynched boy while I was in Macon [Georgia]. But there was little I or anyone else could do for them. At least

so it seemed to me then. I never dreamed that some years later, in a gay and sparkling Broadway show, I would have the chance to tell the story of their misery and their impotence.[27]

"Supper Time" stood out amongst the songs of the musical of course, but it also stood out from the general category of "popular song." In 1933, there were few other songs that addressed lynching. There were blues songs, such as those discussed above, but these "race records" were mostly limited to the black community; there were songs by white folk singers such as Woody Guthrie but, again, there was not a great deal of cross-racial appeal.[28] "Supper Time," with its Broadway backing (not to mention the reputation of Irving Berlin), and its interpretation by a top African-American singer, gave the song a broad audience. Waters understood the incongruence of musical farce backing against musical truth, of fur coats paying to hear about the poverty-stricken and persecuted; she also knew the power her delivery could have. "If one song can tell the whole tragic history of a race, "Supper Time" was that song. In singing it I was telling my comfortable well-fed, well-dressed listeners about my people."[29]

A little over five years later, another black woman would sing on the same theme, with the same passion, a song again written by a Jewish man and again promoted to white, affluent New York audiences.

"Strange Fruit" was written in the late 1930s by Jewish schoolteacher Abel Meeropol under the pen name Lewis Allan. A twelve-line poem was his emotional and literary response to the culture of lynching; photographs and stories were in the New York newspapers and art galleries and a topic of conversation amongst his progressive social, political, and artistic groups.[30] He later set his gut-wrenching poem to music. A fairly minimalist tune, with almost no harmonic movement, it was performed a few times locally but became famous in 1939 when he gave it to Billie Holiday (1915–1959). At that moment she was the rising star of Greenwich Village's Café Society—a new type of nightclub that satirized the very (wealthy) clientele it served—and, for the first time, Holiday could socialize with an audience which notably included both white and black patrons.[31]

What must the audience have thought that first night? A beautiful, sultry, singer at the end of a set about lost love and upbeat "living life" numbers, then the lights are turned out—only a pinpoint of light on her face, the waiters stops serving, the audience frozen in their seats not daring to move—"Southern trees bear a strange fruit" quickly revealed to be a *black body* tortured and lynched by the *gallant* South and then left on display.

> It was like a bomb is dropped from some height. Before it can burst there's a slight split second. That's what happened the first time. Silence. Absolute silence. And then—boom! This big explosion. The audience really exploded to the point where they rose to applaud. It was a terrific thing.[32]

Holiday, like all African-American performers, had experienced castigation and discrimination on tour, in the recording industry, and at the hands of club owners, managers, and agents. "Strange Fruit" became a staple of her repertoire, her singular exemplar of opposition. She called it her "personal protest," and told people it reminded her of her father's death at the hands of hospitals that would not treat his pneumonia because he was black.[33] Under contract with Columbia records, which refused to record the song, she made it with Milt Gabler's Commodore Records. The B-side, "Fine and Mellow" became a jukebox favorite and "Strange Fruit" rose to 16th on the Billboard Charts despite being banned from airplay.[34]

Critics and fans alternately hailed and condemned the song and its performance. Audiences clamored for it, often calling for it mid-show, not realizing that she only sang it last, a habit she retained from the Café Society, where owner Barney Josephson wanted audiences to "remember every word."[35] Shock and revulsion turned to support for the anti-lynching movement that was actively campaigning for social change, the enforcement of state laws, and a federal statute. However, some thought it inappropriate for an evening of entertainment, and many blacks in the 1940s and 1950s did not want to be reminded of this horror, especially as lynchings had been on the decline for more than 20 years. Holiday continued to sing the song until her death in 1959 and, although often given sole credit for the song, it was an important part of folk singer/activist Josh White's repertoire in the 1940s and early 1950s. Every singer who presented it in public live or in recording claimed it proudly as outright protest and as something that brought a certain amount of backlash. Holiday often said the song made her a target: she was arrested for narcotics through a hail of bullets after singing it one night against the wishes of a Philadelphia theater's management, and Josh White suffered a beating at the hands of white servicemen who did not like that he was singing such things.[36] Perhaps singing it, despite the knowledge that doing so was a lynchable offense, was the ultimate form of protest. In 1999, the song's power as sonic efficacy was recognized by *Time* magazine as "the song of the century."[37]

Although the precise genre of "Strange Fruit" is up for contention—not blues, but not jazz, not a torch song nor Tin Pan Alley—it was a popular song, if for no other reason that it was sung and promoted by popular entertainers. This last example stretches the notion of "popular" because, strictly speaking, it was "classical." However, it was premiered alongside patriotic music and spirituals, and it actively engaged the audience in popular protest against racial violence. "And They Lynched Him on a Tree" began, like "Strange Fruit," as a poetic reaction to the culture of lynching. Alain Locke of the Harlem Renaissance, patron of the arts Charlotte Mason, and established society poet Katherine Garrison Chapin designed to have the latter's words set to music; the "Dean of Afro-American Composers" William Grant Still was quickly and enthusiastically enmeshed in the project.[38] Written as a "choral ballad" for contralto solo, male narrator, two choruses (one a "white mob," the other "black mourners," who all come together in the finale) and a chamber orchestra, it was premiered as part of the 1940 summer concert series at New York's Lewisohn Stadium. This was an outdoor venue that routinely presented a variety of musical styles and genres from European orchestral fare to popular music performed by the famous and not-so-famous.

The concert opened with the American-inspired "Largo" from Dvořák's "New World Symphony, Challenge 1940," a rousing flag-waver by Roy Harris, Still's "And They Lynched Him on a Tree," followed by Jaromir Weinberger's Variations and Fugue on "Under the Spreading Chestnut Tree," a recent work based on an English tune.[39] The second half of the program included famous singer Paul Robeson's "Ol' Man River," followed by Earl Robinson's "Ballad for Americans"; the concert concluded with a group of spirituals. Wayne Shirley notes that:

> [T]his was an excellent program on which to introduce "And They Lynched Him": Robeson and the "Ballad for Americans" ensured a large audience, one which would believe that a new work by an American composer could say something important to Americans.[40]

It also helped that Robeson and Robinson were known for their leftist politics, providing an audience base that was already disposed to anti-lynching sentiments.

Early in 1939, Locke introduced the idea to Still, describing it as "a powerful poem on lynching, really an epic indictment but by way of pure poetry not propaganda."[41] Still responded positively:

> For a long time I've wished to add my voice to those that are now protesting against lynching, but naturally I've been waiting for the proper vehicle to present itself. This seems to offer the right opportunity.[42]

Several final versions of the work exist; the discrepancy lies in the final lines, which were considered too controversial for the New York premier: "A long dark shadow will fall across your land!" was replaced, temporarily, with "And clear the shadow that falls across your land!"[43] The original is more foreboding, implying that the plague of racial violence is a permanent blight on the future. The revision, especially as sung by both choruses, is active in the present tense with a more positive sentiment. This version was seen as pro-American; Locke called it a "Ballad for Democracy."[44]

An interesting dichotomy emerges between the two types of lynching protest music presented here. On the one hand are blues songs reflecting the immediate concerns of the black community by those who had the most to lose in singing, veiled or not, words that protested the act of lynching and the threat of race-based violence. Such songs emerged organically from generations of hard work and hard living. They stemmed from African musical elements steeped in traditions, and evoked an "inside looking out perspective." On the other hand are songs progressed by the agendas of white activists with the collaboration of, or through the medium of, African-American performers. Their objective was the same—to end the heinous violence—but their approach, the "outside looking in," was ultimately to encourage white audiences to become involved in social or political protests.

It is perhaps ironic that most of these songs were created and/or recorded long after lynchings in America were on the decline. Of course, those who sang the songs had no way of knowing the practice would not make a comeback, and "lynching" became a metaphor for the wide variety of practices that continued—separate and unequal educational opportunities, unfair housing and hiring practices, voter suppression, abuse of peaceful protesters … issues that still exist. Perhaps that is why these songs still resonate today.

Notes

1 Ethel Waters and Charles Samuels, *His Eye Is on the Sparrow: An Autobiography* (New York: Da Capo Press), 93.

2 A rare blues with a lynching description is Lil' Son Jackson's 1960 ("Lil Son Jackson," Arhoolie F-1004) "Charley Cherry," with the lines, "Well now he arrested my brother, tied him to a tree. You could hear him crying "please don't murder me." For a variety of blues lyrics, see Eric Sackheim and Jonathan Shahn, *The Blues Line: Blues Lyrics from Leadbelly to Muddy Waters* (New York: Thunder's Mouth Press, 2004). Lead Belly in this chapter is spelled as two words, his own preferred spelling, rather than the more common one word, Leadbelly.

3 Christopher Waldrep, "War of Words: The Controversy over the Definition of Lynching, 1899–1940," *The Journal of Southern History*, Vol. 66, No. 1 (February 2000): 75–100.

4 Another source of lynching data online is the ongoing H.A.L. (Historical American Lynching) Data Collection Project; it contains cases that were not tabulated by Tuskegee, additional details (such as the occurrence of black mobs and the victims' offense). http://people.uncw.edu/hinese/HAL/HAL%20Web%20Page.htm

5 Dora Apel and Shawn Michelle Smith, *Lynching Photographs* (Berkeley: University of California Press, 2007), 18–23. See also Paula Giddings, *Ida: A Sword among Lions: Ida B. Wells and the Campaign against Lynching* (New York: Amistad Press, 2008); Glenda Elizabeth Gilmore, *Defying Dixie: The Radical Roots of Civil Rights, 1919–1950* (New York: W.W. Norton Co., 2008); Jennie Lightweis-Goff, *Blood at the Root: Lynching as American Cultural Nucleus* (Albany, New York: State University of New York Press, 2011); and James H. Madison, *Lynching in the Heartland: Race and Memory in America* (New York: Palgrave, 2001).

6 Karlos Hill, "Resisting Lynching: Black Grassroots Responses to Lynching in the Mississippi and Arkansas Deltas, 1882–1938" (Ph.D. diss., University of Illinois, Urbana-Champaign, 2009).

7 Russell Ames, "Protest and Irony in Negro Folksong," *Science and Society*, Vol. 14, No. 3 (Summer 1950): 203. The conversation by anonymous blues singers to Alan Lomax is quoted from the highly progressive magazine *The Nation* from 1917.

8 Adam *Gussow, Seems Like Murder Here: Southern Violence and the Blues (Chicago:* University of Chicago Press, 2002).

9 LeRoi Jones, *Blues People: The Negro Experience in White America and the Music that Developed from It* (New York: Morrow Quill Paperbacks, 1963); Angela Y. Davis, *Blues Legacies and Black Feminism: Gertruede "Ma" Rainey, Bessie Smith, and Billie Holiday* (New York: Pantheon Books, 1998); Mary Ellison, *Lyrical Protest: Black Music's Struggle against Discrimination* (New York: Praeger, 1989); and Paul Oliver, *Saints and Songsters: Vocal Traditions on Race Records* (Cambridge: Cambridge University Press, 1984).

10 Gussow, *Seems Like Murder*, 18.

11 Gussow, *Seems Like Murder*, 56.

12 Gussow, *Seems Like Murder*, 22.

13 See James H. Cone, *The Spirituals and the Blues: An Interpretation* (Maryknoll, New York: Orbis Books, 1991); John Lovell, *Black Song: The Forge and the Flame: The Story of How the Afro-American Spiritual Was Hammered Out* (New York: Macmillan, 1972); and Bernice Johnson Reagon, *If You Don't Go, Don't Hinder Me: The African American Sacred Song Tradition* (Lincoln, Nebraska: University of Nebraska Press, 2001).

14 His work is influential and certainly provides a fascinating interdisciplinary foundation for thought, even if his logic seems to point that any and every blues is really about violence.

15 Shade of skin color is not one of the most common blues themes, but it does occur; Blind Willie McTell's "Statesboro Blues" (1928) includes the lines, "Goin' up the country, Mama, don't you want to go? May take me a fair brown, may take me one or two more."

16 The oldest known "Jim Crow" reference is to the nineteenth-century minstrel character who danced in a hopping fashion, "Jump Jim Crow." See Sam Dennison, *Scandalize My Name: Black Imagery in American Popular Music* (New York and London: Garland Publishing, 1982), 45–48.

17 These so-called "sundown towns" were largely the suburbs around northern cities and apparently are still in existence today: James W. Loewen, *Sundown Towns: A Hidden Dimension of Segregation in America* (New York: New Press, 2005).

18 Jones, *Blues People*; and Ralph Ellison, *Richard Wright's Blues* (United States: s.n, 1945), *Shadow and Act* (New York: Random House, 1964), and, with Robert G. O'Meally, *Living with Music: Ralph Ellison's Jazz Writings* (New York: Modern Library, 2001).

19 Big Bill Broonzy, "Black, Brown and White," on *Big Bill Broonzy*, Black and Blue 33.012 (France), songs recorded between 1952 and 1955.

20 Laurence Bergreen, *As Thousands Cheer: The Life of Irving Berlin* (New York: Da Capo Press, 1996), 316–318.

21 Bergreen, *As Thousands Cheer*, 314.

22 Gerald Boardman, *A Chronicle of American Musical Theatre* (Oxford: Oxford University Press, 2011).

23 This is perhaps the only ironic or satirical element of the song.

24 Bergreen, *As Thousands Cheer*, 321.

25 For example, the Anti-Defamation League was founded to defend against anti-Semitism in 1913 after the brutal lynching of a Jewish man in Georgia; the ADL actively campaigned for political and social change across racial lines.

26 He was, in any case, very keen as to the financial success of his work.

27 Waters, *His Eye*, 160.

28 Mark Allan Jackson, "Dark Memory: a Look at Lynching in America through the Life, Times, and Songs of Woody Guthrie," *Popular Music & Society*, Vol. 28 No. 5 (2005): 663–675.

29 Waters, *His Eye*, xi.

30 Nancy Kovaleff Baker, "Abel Meeropol (a.k.a. Lewis Allan): Political Commentator and Social Conscience," *American Music*, Vol. 20, No. 1 (Spring, 2002): 25–79.

31 Holiday's (auto)biography, *Lady Sings the Blues*, written with William Dufty (New York: Doubleday Press, 1956). All of her later biographers note the significance of the song both to her as a performer and as an unparalleled moment of overt protest. See Donald Clarke, *Wishing on the Moon: The Life and Times of Billie Holiday* (New York: Viking Press, 1994) and Robert O'Meally, *Lady Day: The Many Faces of Billie Holiday* (New York: Arcade Publishing, 1991).

32 Barney Josephson and Terry Trilling-Josephson, *Café Society: The Wrong Place for the Right People* (Urbana, Illinois: University of Illinois Press, 2009), 48.

33 As with much of her autobiography, this story has a basis in truth but is exaggerated before the microphone. Holiday/Dufty, *Lady*, Chapter 9, "Café Society."

34 An interesting general readership booklet is David Margolick, *Strange Fruit: The Biography of a Song* (New York: Ecco Press, 2001).

35 Josephson, *Café Society*, 47.

36 Julia Blackburn, *With Billie* (New York: Pantheon Books, 2005), 110–111 contains excerpts from interviews she gave to *Down Beat* magazine. See also Elijah Wald, *Josh White: Society Blues* (Amherst, Massachusetts: University of Massachusetts Press, 2000), 110.

37 "The Best of the Century," *Time* magazine, December 31, 1999.

38 Wayne E. Shirley, "William Grant Still's Choral Ballad 'And They Lynched Him on a Tree,'" *American Music*, Vol. 12, No. 4 (Winter, 1994): 425–461.

39 Anne G. Gilchrist, "'Under the Spreading Chestnut Tree': The Adventures of a Tune," *The Musical Times*, Vol. 81, No. 1165 (March 1940): 112–113.

40 Shirley, "William Grant Still's Choral Ballad," 446.

41 Shirley, "William Grant Still's Choral Ballad," 429.

42 Shirley, "William Grant Still's Choral Ballad," 430.

43 Shirley, "William Grant Still's Choral Ballad," the appendix to which provides the full text of three versions: the original, the NY altered and the published vocal/piano score.

44 Shirley, "William Grant Still's Choral Ballad," 449.

5

JEWISH VOICES OF PROTEST ON BROADWAY

From *The Eternal Road* to *The Cradle Will Rock* and Beyond

Jonathan C. Friedman

Figure 5.1 Emily Watson and John Turturro in *Cradle Will Rock*, written and directed by Tim Robbins.

The performing arts have been an inextricable component in modern Jewish history. Not only has performance provided comfort for Jews in times of persecution and dislocation, but some of the defining features of the arts have been sculpted with Jewish chisels. One cannot conceive of the modern American theater, and especially musical theater, without the likes of Richard Rodgers, Lorenz Hart, Irving Berlin, or George Gershwin, and one cannot understate the cultural influence of musical theater as a genre.[1] As theater historian Andrea Most points out, "in the first three decades of the [twentieth] century, the musical theater *was* popular culture."[2] Jews have been drawn to cultural pursuits to a disproportionate degree in the modern world, for a variety of reasons, but, in the United States, musical theater was a forum to which Jews had unprecedented access, in part because Gentile playwrights regarded it as "low culture."[3]

The stage offered Jews both a mode of acculturation into American society, as well as nostalgia for the communities which they had left behind in Europe. Broadway has also afforded opportunities for Jewish producers, writers, and thespians to issue commentary on the difficulties of being an outsider and on the human condition in general. On these subjects, Jews have produced an extensive body of work, ranging in time from Gershwin's *Porgy and Bess* to Tony Kushner's *Caroline, or Change* and in degrees of intent from Rodgers and (non-Jewish) Oscar Hammerstein II's *Oklahoma* and *South Pacific* to Clifford Odets' *Waiting for Lefty* and *Awake and Sing!* Again, according to Andrea Most, "For all sorts of outsiders, the way to become American [has been] ... a Jewish way, and those who follow that path perform—wittingly or unwittingly—a Jewish story."[4] Following Most's theoretical lead, this essay evaluates the extent to which musical theater, as a Jewish construction, has been a forum of protest against social ills such as racism, anti-Semitism, and class and gender bias; in other words, the social reality of the outsider. The temporal context is essentially Broadway in the 1930s, a time when stage and protest were well-matched, and the specific exercise for this paper is a comparison of two protest plays from 1937, Max Reinhardt, Kurt Weill, and Franz Werfel's *The Eternal Road* and Marc Blitzstein's *The Cradle Will Rock*.

American musicals admittedly have an uneven track record when it comes to representing "the other." Minstrel shows of the nineteenth century all the way down to contemporary productions (such as *Thoroughly Modern Mille* and even *Miss Saigon*) have reinforced some of the ugliest stereotypes about minorities.[5] It is, for instance, difficult, if not downright painful, to watch *South Pacific* today without cringing at its abundant sexism and racism, despite its status as a musical in defense of racial tolerance. Jerome Kern and Oscar Hammerstein II's *Show Boat* from 1927 is also illustrative on this point. As the first plot-driven musical, the play was ground-breaking enough, but the fact that it featured an interracial marriage, a bi-racial character, and a mixed race cast was truly revolutionary, and yet the frequent use of the "n" word and dialogue for African-Americans constructed by white men have problematized the play's legacy.[6] Postmodern theories of language analysis offer ways to move past dismissals of productions like *South Pacific* and *Show Boat* by recognizing cultural constraints of discourse and the extent to which art can be reinvented over time.

Postmodernism's rejection of essentialism provides another level of complexity for this analysis. To ascribe either a universalizing or minoritizing thrust to Jewish protest would run afoul of the postmodern opposition to binary codes. In a postmodern framework, social protest, Jewish identity, and a specific Jewish voice of protest are all too variable and shifting to assign a unifying definition. And yet I am arguing in this essay that Jews did in fact encode specific Jewish content into their protest musicals. Who a Jew is, or was, is less important to me than uncovering Jewish tropes and subtext. That being the case, what are these Jewish tropes? What is their content? Curt Sach's criterion that Jewish music is anything "made by Jews, for Jews, as Jews" is too narrow, as is Stephen Whitfield's insistence that "The Jew in the pew is pivotal."[7] When Oscar Hammerstein II, an Episcopalian whose grandfather had been a German Jew, asked Jerome Kern, whose parents were also German Jews, what kind of music he would write for a show on Marco Polo, Kern allegedly responded: "It'll be good Jewish music."[8] But what did this mean? Kern rarely expounded on the subject.

I would argue that, in addition to American Jewry's rich spectrum of identity, from Orthodoxy to secular humanism, concepts like *tikkun* (healing) and *tzedakah* (charity) have become basic cultural codes. One would have to look no further than the montage of Jewish voices repeating the phrase *tikkun olam* (to heal the world) at the conclusion of the permanent exhibit in the Museum of Jewish Heritage in New York, to see just how important the notion of social justice is for American Jews. While I agree with Vincent Brooks that a defining element of Jewish identity and Jewish culture is "the increasing inability, yet persistent necessity, to define it," I see American Jewry's diversity, and diverse approaches to creating a more just world, as overarching features.[9] The memes and rhetorical devices with which Jewish artists have populated their works of art reflect this incredible diversity.

Context: Jewish Protest, Musical Protest

In the late nineteenth and early twentieth centuries, American Jews generally represented themselves as ordinary folk in Yiddish theater, and their approach to musical comedy was similarly slanted towards acculturation. As Jews encountered, in English-language theater, the persistence of representations that were often negative (overtly feminized Jewish men versus masculinized Jewish women), Jews sought avenues of acceptance, such as donning blackface.[10] Plays and musicals with Jewish content and characters actually increased in the 1920s, peaking, in many ways, with *The Jazz Singer* (1925), until the anti-Semitism of the 1930s resulted in a concerted effort to efface Jewish imagery from stage and screen. As Kara Manning describes, the mid-century works of writers like Clifford Odets, Arthur Miller, and S.N. Behrman became "Americanized." She asks, "what would the fate of *Death of a Salesman* have been if Miller had made American Everyman Willy Loman boldly Jewish? Would ... audiences of 1949 have cozied up to a play with frankly Jewish characters?"[11] The answer was obviously no, not in a country that produced such noted anti-Semites as Henry Ford, Father Charles Coughlin, and William Dudley Pelley, and whose public opinion polls, even after 1941, showed that nearly one out of every four Americans believed Jews to be "a menace."[12]

Accommodationism, rather than cultural assertion or protest might have typified the sensibility of Jewish theatrical production in general in the early decades of the twentieth century, but this was not the sole idiom of Jewish expression. Despite the drawdown in Jewish-specific content in the 1930s, there were watershed moments in musical theater in this period, during which Jews pushed boundaries of racial accept-ance, raised awareness of the suffering of the Jews in Europe, and engaged in blistering critiques of capitalism. One need look no further than *Show Boat* (1927), *Porgy and Bess* (1935), Marc Blitzstein's *The Cradle Will Rock* (1937), and the less well-known pageant by Max Reinhardt, Franz Werfel, and Kurt Weill, *The Eternal Road* (1937). To these one could add numerous smaller scale satires and "agitprop" productions.[13] In the 1930s, *Strike Up the Band*, George S. Kaufman's collaboration with co-religionists Mor-rie Ryskind and Ira and George Gershwin, was one of the first satirical musicals in the wake of the Depression, although it actually dates back to 1927, when, in its first unsuc-cessful incarnation, it depicted a U.S. war with Switzerland over cheese tariffs. (The revised version, which had a fair run of 191 shows in the winter and spring of 1930, featured a "Scrooge-like chocolate czar.") The team of Kaufman/Ryskind/Gersh-win had greater success with the 1931 musical, *Of Thee I Sing*, a send-up of American politics which won the Pulitzer Prize for best play and ran for 441 performances.[14] Perhaps more well-known is Irving Berlin and Moss Hart's 1933 revue *As Thousands Cheer*, which ran nearly as long as *Of Thee I Sing* and featured the Ethel Waters show-stopper, "Supper Time," a lament by an African-American woman over the lynching of her husband.

The relatively successful runs of the Kaufman and Berlin musicals aside, most social satire plays and musicals of the early to mid-1930s were box office failures. Bertolt Brecht's *Threepenny Opera* closed after twelve performances in April 1933. The first overt, left-wing musical revue, *Parade*, which featured police attacking poor people, unemployed college graduates, and a skit lampooning an American version of Hit-ler, was so relentlessly on the nose that it tanked after thirty-two performances in May 1935. The musical *Saluta*, which featured Milton Berle as a night club owner who goes to Italy to put on an anti-fascist opera, also bombed after thirty-nine per-formances.[15] Paul Green's *Hymn to the Rising Sun*, a tale of abuse in a southern prison camp, lasted ten shows in May 1937, while Lillian Hellman's class drama, *Days to Come*, ran for only seven in December 1936.[16] Even *Porgy and Bess* could not break even despite 124 shows and a tour.

Like *Show Boat*, *Porgy and Bess* has a problematic history, with depictions of Afri-can-Americans as physically deformed, immoral, drug-abusing, and murderous. At the same time, the show broke barriers when the cast protested segregation at the National Theatre in Washington, D.C., for its shows in 1936, leading to the first-ever integrated audience at the venue. Moreover, for the Broadway run's twenty African-

American principal actors and chorus members, the show provided, in the words of John Bush Jones, "steadier work for more black performers in the mid-1930s than did the total of short-lived black revues."[17] Related to the theme of this essay, Geoffrey Block points out that Gershwin grafted his Jewishness onto his interpretation of the African-American experience. "The strong kinship between these musically compatible traditions is evident in Sportin' Life's theme, which might be interpreted as a chromatic transformation of the Jewish blessing that precedes and follows the reading of the Torah."[18]

The fact that between 1935 and 1938 Broadway featured so many plays of social conscience without regard to their profitability is illustrative of the mentality and climate of the time. Legislation in Hitler's Third Reich had resulted in the effective de-emancipation of German Jews and, in the United States, racism in the deep South remained systemic and codified, and economic misery continued, lending increased urgency to protect worker rights through unions. Historian John Hunter, in describing the context for *The Cradle Will Rock*, goes further, declaring that unionism was "the really hot subject of 1937 ... Pitched battles between strikers and police in the months of May and June 1937 resulted in the killing of several strikers, both men and women."[19] The depression, unemployment, racism, and anti-Semitism were obvious fodder for dramatic commentary, and the boost to the arts in 1935 through federal legislation that created the Works Progress Administration (WPA), which provided federal funding for a number of public works projects, incentivized an outpouring of creative activity. The driving engine for theatrical work was the Federal Theatre Project (FTP), which went on to support over 12,000 actors across the county. Because of its initially free, and then inexpensive, ticket costs, the FTP was able to reach some 25 million people, many of whom had never been to the theater.[20] By the second half of the 1930s, due in no small part to the efforts of the Federal Theatre Project, New York's entertainment industry had rebounded from the wave of closings—thirty out of eighty live venues in the theater district—resulting from the Great Depression.

Social protest as performance was not the Federal Theatre's mandate or even primary agenda, but it promoted a number of such plays, including the previously mentioned *Hymn to the Rising Sun*, which FTP director Hallie Flanagan called "one of the most terrifying studies of inhumanity ever written."[21] The Federal Theatre began with the play *Triple Plowed Under*, which dealt with poverty among farmers, moved on to a critique of public schools in 1936's *Chalk Dust*, lent its support to *The Cradle Will Rock* in 1937, and tackled anti-Semitism by bringing émigré Friedrich Wolf's play *Professor Mamlock* to the Experimental Theater in April 1937. This play, one of over a dozen protest plays written by Jewish and non-Jewish refugees from Nazi Germany, centered on a Jewish doctor whose support for Germany blinded him to the reality of Hitler's regime.[22] After *Cradle*, perhaps the most significant activist play of the Federal Theatre Project was

Arthur Arent's *One Third of a Nation*, which took up President Franklin D. Roosevelt's plea on behalf of millions who were living without adequate housing, clothing, and food. The play premiered at the Adelphi Theatre in January 1938 and ran concurrently with *Cradle's* stint at the Windsor Theatre, outlasting it by several months.

The Eternal Road and The Cradle Will Rock

The Broadway plays and musicals of 1937 demonstrated a high level of quality and historical significance. The year began with shows like *Dr. Faustus* at Maxine Elliott's Theater, *Othello* at the New Amsterdam Theatre, and *You Can't Take It With You* at the Booth Theatre. It ended with Harold Rome's long-running protest revue, *Pins and Needles*, which featured a cast of mostly Jewish members of the International Ladies Garment Workers' Union and anti-Fascist protest music by a number of Jewish composers, including Arent and Blitzstein. (One of the production's later songs, "Mene, Mene, Tekel" used the Biblical tale of the demise of tyrannical king Balshazzar to make a similar point about Hitler's inevitable ruin.[23]) In 1937, theatergoers could have seen other socially conscious plays as well, such as *Tide Rising*, and John Howard Lawson's *Marching Song*, set in an abandoned factory. Or one could have paid between one dollar and a record 100 dollars (for loge seats) to sit through the five hour production of *The Eternal Road* at the Manhattan Opera House, which opened on January 7. Six months later, one could have made the 19-block trek from the blockaded Maxine Elliott Theater to the Venice Theater to take in Marc Blitzstein's Federal Theatre Project funded (and nearly cancelled) *Cradle Will Rock*, which went on to have its official run at the Windsor, where *Pins and Needles* ultimately ended up in 1939.

The Eternal Road was the most notable occasion in which Reinhardt, Werfel, and Weill joined together to issue a condemnation of the Nazi assault on the Jewish people. The opera centers on a congregation of Jews in an unspecified European country holed up in a synagogue awaiting an attack by a mob. To boost morale before the inevitable end, the congregants recount the biblical tales of Abraham, Moses, David, Ruth, and Solomon. From its hours-long duration to its nearly acre-sized stage and lengthy list of performers, including Broadway stars like Sam Jaffe, and future Hollywood names such as Sidney Lumet and Dick van Patten, *The Eternal Road* was a massive, expensive, and (perhaps unfairly) bloated undertaking. Producer Meyer Weisgal allegedly dubbed it one of the most brilliant money losers ever. Yet the opera remains of great interest to scholars on three levels: as a musical piece, as a rejoinder to Nazism, and as a revelation of the complexities of Jewish identity.

The Cradle Will Rock might not have been as expansive in its scope as *The Eternal Road* (with only sixty principals), but it certainly was in terms of its ideals. Structurally similar to *Road*, in that it is almost completely sung-through, *Cradle* relies on more popular musical genres to convey its pro-union message. (This is not to discount the often modern and popular musical forms that appear throughout *Road*.) Set in "Steel-town, USA," *Cradle* uses generic names for its characters to represent archetypes. Its hero is Larry Foreman, the unionizer; its villain, Mr. Mister, the town's wealthy businessman who controls everything—from the factory to the press and church. Other characters include Moll the prostitute, a contemptible priest (Reverend Salvation) and physician (Doctor Specialist), Mr. Mister's equally despicable family (Mrs. Mister, Junior and Sister Mister), sellout artists (Dauber and Yasha), and immigrants Gus and Sadie Polock. The drama begins with the arrest of the town's prominent citizens (who comprise an anti-union group known as the Liberty Committee), who are mistaken for pro-union picketers. While awaiting their release by Mr. Mister, the characters recount their tales and respective sins in a series of flashbacks. At the end, Mr. Mister tempts Larry with membership on the Liberty Committee, but he refuses, and the workers begin their uprising.

Both *Road* and *Cradle* suffered drama on and off the stage, and neither was a sure bet to open. Money ran out for *Road* at one point, and, during the construction of the massive stage at the Manhattan Opera House, the production team hit bedrock and then water, flooding the entire theater and forcing an abrupt halt to the rehearsals. Moreover, on *Road*'s opening night, just before curtain-time, fire-fighters converged on the theater and told producer Weisgal that the opera could not go on in the presence of lit candles and in the absence of a fire curtain. Weisgal was fortunate enough to enlist the help of Mayor Fiorello La Guardia to break the stand-off.[24] The story of what happened to *The Cradle Will Rock*, meanwhile, is now the stuff of legend—the feuds between director Orson Welles and producer John Houseman, the lockout and blockade of the Maxine Elliott Theater by WPA guards after the agency cut its funding (because of the play's content), the march to the Venice Theater for the counter-performance, and the actors, spurred by Olive Stanton's lead, singing from the audience and balconies against the wishes of the actors' union.

In terms of their content, reference points, and the motivations of their creators, *The Eternal Road* and *The Cradle Will Rock* seem to be thoroughly dissimilar. *Road* sought to raise public awareness about Hitler's persecution of German Jews, while *Cradle* was a union play in the context of battles between steelworkers and the police. *Road* was the creation of German-speaking Jewish émigrés, while *Cradle* was the product of a native-born son of Russian Jewish immigrants. *Road* was a pageant; *Cradle* was agitprop theater. The libretto of the *Eternal Road* owed its construction to Jewish liturgy and theology, while *Cradle*'s influences were the worker songs of the 1930s and Bertolt Brecht.[25] (Blitzstein's piece allegedly grew out of imagined conversations he was having between himself and the German playwright.) *Road*'s eschatology was often conflicted, as a product of its numerous creators, while *Cradle* had the benefit of a singular, unifying voice. *Road*'s producer Weisgal disliked Werfel's original ending, which featured a messiah appearing out of the ruins of the Temple, preferring, in the words of Werfel's wife, Alma, "a God of vengeance!"[26] A subplot involving an interfaith romance (between a young man and a generically dubbed "alien girl") also challenged prevailing Jewish attitudes at the time.[27] Either to mute Weisgal's criticisms or to soft-pedal the intermarriage angle, Werfel injected overtones of Zionism during both the story of David and the finale, which resolved the synagogue drama with the forced expulsion of the congregation.[28] With songs like "Joe Worker," and rhetoric about lockouts and machine gunned workers, *The Cradle Will Rock* demonstrates abundant utopianism as well, but it is a utopia of class, not religion or ethnicity.

Musically, though, the productions do not operate in disconnected universes.[29] Weill's opera blends not only disparate secular forms, from classical to modern to jazz, but also distinct Jewish melodies. According to writer David Schiff:

> [while] the music of the German synagogue echoed ... Schubert and the harmonies of Mendelssohn, [it] had its own historic integrity ... Although it never sounds Jewish ... [it] is in fact a musical reliquary for a vanished liturgical tradition. [Weill's] use of important German-Jewish melodies is pervasive and ... dramatically apt, with themes from the Shavuoth and Yom Kippur services matched to crucial events in the play.[30]

Jazz motifs are present in both *Road* and *Cradle*, and, while Blitzstein often had harsh things to say about Weill, even *The Eternal Road*, the songs in *Cradle* sound very much like the jazz inflected tunes of *Threepenny Opera*.[31] As Eric Gordon suggests, Blitzstein's attraction to *Kleinkunst*, or the minor arts of musical commentary, often meant utilizing a number of popular idioms, from cabaret songs to the Jewish *badkhen* or the wedding entertainers' tradition.[32]

Along this line of thought, both protest pieces share overt and covert infusions of motifs that reflect the historical experiences of Jews in the modern world. Both *Road* and *Cradle* negatively construct incarnations of the "modern Jew," with characters such as the Adversary, Rich Man, and Estranged One in the former, and Yasha the musician in the latter. The Rich Man represents the court Jew, blinded by a faith in material status and connections to the king, while the Estranged One symbolizes the assimilated Jew who laments his ethnic heritage.[33] The Adversary, meanwhile, offers comic relief through a cynical voice evocative of the "Evil Son" of Passover. In *Cradle*, the characters of Yasha the violinist and Dauber the painter prostitute their art to serve the interests of the Misters.[34] Blitzstein may have projected in Yasha his own fear of becoming a sell-out, and the theme of prostitution undergirds Blitzstein's sense of the workings of capitalism.

In both musicals, too, Jews are victims of physical assault, and, while the pogrom motif serves as an overt vehicle for the unfolding drama in *The Eternal Road*, it is interesting that Blitzstein employed a similar scenario of violence against the only Jewish couple in *The Cradle Will Rock*, Gus and Sadie Polock. Although the couple are identified as Poles, it is clear that both are Polish-Jewish immigrants, and they are targeted for murder by a hitman hired by Mr. Mister, not necessarily because of xenophobia or anti-Semitism, although these may have been unconscious motivations, but, rather, to intimidate other steelworkers like Gus.

The different discourses in the two plays are as much about personality as they are about the brand of Jewishness each artist brought to the table—from Reinhardt's *parvenu* sensibility, to Werfel's ambivalence and love affair with Catholic imagery, to Weill's and Blitzstein's socialism. In describing the project he was undertaking, Reinhardt mused that "whenever the Jews were in crisis, they returned to their holy books … and looked to the past to hope for the future." He added, to deflect charges that he was creating propaganda, that "the books of the Bible … are hallowed artwork of incomprehensible, mystical greatness."[35] And yet, Reinhardt's sense of himself as a Jew was cryptic and often contradictory. His son Gottfried claimed that his father resented "being made to belong to a 'people' whose existence he doubted. A nation of Jews in Palestine he thought a utopia bereft of any attraction for him."[36] In the same breath, Gottfried maintained that his father had a penchant for Eastern European Jews. "One can put it this way: If Jewishness must be emphasized (which he did not recommend, especially in politics), then let it be the genuine kind!"[37] Werfel and Weill held similarly complex, and often conflicting views of their Jewish identities. Werfel once maintained that he was a "Jew in the flesh and a Christian in spirit" and that he would be "happiest in a world that comes closest to the period of primitive Christianity."[38] His take on *The Eternal Road* also avoided a particular defense of Judaism: "All I have tried to do is to bring out the truth—the tolerance, the love, and by all means the culture that is in the Bible. We need more peace and friendship."[39] Weill, the son of a cantor, conceived the Jewish historical experience "primarily as a universal lesson, 'never to forget' the enormity of humankind's mindless capacity for cruelty … but also a remarkable resilience that enables survivors of good will to follow the dictates of their God-given creative potential."[40] At the same time, he had very mixed feelings about his Jewishness:

> I searched for a community, and I thought I found it in Jewish society, but I have grown to despise Jewish circles…What remains is only this: Very gradually, out of one's own human development, we must find our way back to our childhood faith.[41]

Of the four principals under discussion here, Blitzstein was the least overtly Jewish. According to biographer Eric Gordon, "The Blitzsteins ran a distinctly assimilationist household, more Russian than Jewish. If they knew Yiddish, they did not speak it at home. Inclined toward socialist ideas and decidedly unreligious, Mrs. Blitzstein did not bother to keep a kosher kitchen."[42] On his application to the Curtis School of Music, Blitzstein offered a window into his own complex identity, listing his race as Jewish and nationality as American, drawing a line through religion to indicate none.

Contemporary Jewish Voices

The heirs today of the likes of Marc Blitzstein are Tony Kushner (with his tripartite identity as a gay, Jewish, socialist) and even William Finn, Jewish playwrights who offer biting, often satirical, commentary on race and sexuality in productions such as *Angels in America*, *Caroline, or Change*, and the *Falsettoland* trilogy. The first part of Finn's *Falsettoland*, entitled *March of the Falsettos*, was truly revolutionary, as a musical about gay Jews coming out of the closet. Premiering in 1981, just as AIDS was beginning to surface, the musical showcased Jewish characters and holidays and the hilarious opening number, "Four Jews in a Room, Bitching." In 1990, Finn released the sequel to *March of the Falsettos*. Entitled *Falsettoland*, the musical developed its storyline around AIDS and deepened its Jewish focus by anchoring the climax around a *bar mitzvah*.[43] Three years after *Falsettoland*, Tony Kusher's epic two-part AIDS drama, *Angels in America*, opened at the Walter Kerr Theatre. *Rent*, Jonathan Larson's hugely successful rock musical about AIDS, debuted in 1996. Larson's death before the show's premiere cut short a promising career and eliminated a major, Jewish-influenced voice of protest from the Broadway stage.

In 2002, Kushner continued to press social issues with the release of the musical *Caroline, or Change*, about an African-American maid (Caroline) working for a Jewish family (the Gellmans) in Louisiana in the 1960s. The play served the dual purpose of political and social commentary about race, religion, class, and gender, as well as a fictionalized representation of Kushner's own childhood growing up in Louisiana. Like *The Eternal Road*, *Caroline* is replete with Jewish archetypes, although the Gellman family seems to be more of the adversary in the narrative; they have money, the wife is obsessed with money, the son is careless with it, and Caroline faces the dilemma about what to do about the loose change which the son, Noah, keeps leaving in his pants pockets. A Jewish setting, in particular a Chanukah party, provides the opportunity to ventilate Jewish attitudes towards practically everything—politics, religion, race, civil rights, the entire North–South divide, while revealing superficialities and hypocrisies along the way (all through words set to good old fashioned klezmer music). With its social commentary and conflation of popular music styles, from gospel, soul, rhythm and blues, jazz, rock, and even klezmer, *Caroline* operates in a textual and musicological world similar to that of *The Cradle Will Rock*.

The extent to which Jewish identity has informed any of the above-mentioned Jewish artists is difficult to quantify, and what constitutes Jewishness may be in this very incoherence or recognition of the messiness and contradictions of life; it may emerge, as well, as an overt expression of criticism—critique of the world, critique of the status of outsiders, lamentation about otherness. For Kushner and Finn, just as much as Reinhardt, Werfel, Weill, and Blitzstein, it has been the greatness of the art that matters most. At the same time, Jewishness has provided an operative framework for understanding what it means to be a minority. Quoting Kushner:

Growing up gay and Jewish in a small Southern town made my condition as an outsider very clear. Like most gay people, I encountered a lot of homophobia. Like most Jewish people in this culture, I come from a tradition of proud declaration of my identity. Being Jewish taught me how to be gay and being gay taught me how to be Jewish.[44]

For Finn:

[what is] best about being Jewish is that Judaism—unlike most other religions—cares more about the person than about the dogma ... I'm always most proud that the Jews take care of the individual at the expense of the many, so never for a moment did I feel that being gay was an affront to the religion.[45]

Broadly speaking, then, many of the narratives of protest in musical theater on Broadway, as competing and complex as they have been, share what Deb Margolin might call a Jewish "intonation."[46] With Jewish voices behind protest musicals such as *Prop 8*, which criticized California's gay marriage ban in 2008, the work of utilizing music and theater as a forum to criticize social wrongs through a Jewish prism clearly continues.

Notes

1 Stephen J. Whitfield, *In Search of American Jewish Culture* (Waltham, Massachusetts: Brandeis University Press, 1999), 60.

2 Andrea Most, *Making Americans: Jews and the Broadway Musical* (Cambridge, Massachusetts: Harvard University Press, 2004), 28.

3 See Jacob Katz, "German Culture and the Jews," in Jehuda Reinharz, ed., *The Jewish Response to German Culture: From the Enlightenment to the Second World War* (Hanover, New Hampshire: University Press of New England, 1985), 91, and Paul Buhle, *From the Lower East Side to Hollywood: Jews in American Popular Culture* (New York: Verso Books, 2004).

4 Most, *Making Americans*, 3.

5 Sylviane Gold, "On Broadway: Musical Theater has Tackled Racism for Decades, Albeit Covertly at Times," *Dance Magazine*, June 2005, at: http://findarticles.com/p/articles/mi_m1083/is_6_79/ai_n13817669/, 2, accessed 19 May 2011.

6 See Douglass Daniel, "They Just Keep Rolling Along: Images of Blacks in Film Versions of *Show Boat*," in the *Proceedings of the Annual Meeting of the Association for Education in Journalism and Mass Communication*, Chicago, 30 July to 2 August 1997.

7 Whitfield, *In Search of American Jewish Culture*, 19, 81, 241, and Sachs, "Opening Lecture to the First International Congress of Jewish Music in 1957," quoted by Bathja Bayer in her entry on "Music," in *Encyclopedia Judaica* (Jerusalem: Keter Publishing, 1972), 12: 555 both cited in Vincent Brook, "Introduction," *You Should See Yourself: Jewish Identity in Postmodern American Culture* (New Brunswick, New Jersey: Rutgers University Press, 2006), 5, 6.

8 Hugh Fordin, *Getting to Know Him: A Biography of Oscar Hammerstein* (New York: Random House, 1977), 125–126, Paul Zollo, "Sultans of Song, Part II," *Reform Judaism Online*, Vol. 31, No. 3, at http://www.reformjudaismmag.net/03spring/sultan.shtml, accessed on 20 May 2011, and Whitfield, *In Search of American Jewish Culture*, 61.

9 Brook, "Introduction," 6.

10 Most, *Making Americans*, 26.

11 Dennis Klein, "Angels in America as Jewish-American Drama," *Yiddish*, Vol. 12, No. 4 (2001): 41, Kara Manning, "Are We Not Jews? Such Questions May Still Confound, But Several New-Generation Theatre Writers Have Answers Ready." See the website: http://www.tcg.org/am_theatre/at_articles/AT_Volume_17/Nov00/at_web1100_jews.html, and Manning, "Are We Not Jews?" *American Theatre*, Vol. 17, No. 9 (November 2000): 24–28.

12 See http://www.holocaustchronicle.org/StaticPages/535.html.

13 John Bush Jones, *Our Musicals, Ourselves: A History of American Musical Theatre* (Waltham, Massachusetts: Brandeis, 2003), 101–103, and Eric Gordon, *Mark the Music: The Life and Work of Marc Blitzstein* (New York: St. Martin's, 1989), 134.

14 John Bush Jones, *Our Musicals Ourselves*, 90–101, and Deborah Bletstein, "Jewish Themes in Mainstream Broadway Musicals: 1920–1960" (Master's thesis, Jewish Theological Seminary, n.d., 15).

15 John Bush Jones, *Our Musicals, Ourselves*, 101.

16 See http://www.ibdb.com/production.php?id=9742 and http://www.ibdb.com/production.php?id=12243.

17 John Bush Jones, *Our Musicals, Ourselves*, 84, 85.

18 Geoffrey Block, *Enchanted Evenings: The Broadway Musical from Show Boat to Sondheim* (New York: Oxford University Press, 1997), 74.

19 John Hunter, "Marc Blitzstein's *The Cradle Will Rock*, as a Document of America, 1937," *American Quarterly*, Vol. 18, No. 2 (Summer 1966): 231.

20 John Bush Jones, *Our Musicals, Ourselves*, 103.

21 Hallie Flanagan, *Arena* (New York: Duell, Sloan, and Pearce, 1940), 200, as cited by John Hunter, "Marc Blitzstein's *The Cradle Will Rock*," 230.

22 Anat Feinberg, "Jewish Fate in German Drama," *Leo Baeck Institute Yearbook*, Vol. 29, No. 1 (1984): 60, 64, 57–71.

23 Some of the lyrics of this song are pretty awful. Consider this verse: "He was a tyrant took delight in … startin' wars and doin' fightin'… sons of Israel he called scamps … Sent them all to makin' bricks in concentration camps." Quoted in Bletstein, "Jewish Themes," 20.

24 Meyer Weisgal, … *So Far: An Autobiography* (New York: Random House, 1971), 133, and Atay Citron, "Pageantry and Theater in the Service of Jewish Nationalism in the United States, 1933–1946" (Ph.D. dissertation, New York University, 1989), 202.

25 Brecht dubbed *Cradle* a "folk" play. See Carol Oja, "Marc Blitzstein's *The Cradle Will Rock* and Mass-Song Style of the 1930s," *The Musical Quarterly*, Vol. 73, No. 4 (1989): 446; Bertolt Brecht, "Notes on the Folk Play," in John Willett, ed., *Brecht on Theatre* (New York: Hill and Wang, 1964), 153–157; and Robert J. Dietz, "Marc Blitzstein and the 'Agit-Prop' Theatre of the 1930s," *Anuario Interamericano de Investigacion Musical*, Vol. 6 (1970): 56.

26 Weisgal, … *So Far*, 120, and Alma Mahler, *Mein Leben* (Frankfurt: Fischer, 1960), 216.

27 Franz Werfel, *The Eternal Road: A Drama in Four Parts*, trans. Ludwig Lewisohn (New York: Viking Press, 1936), 93.

28 Werfel, *The Eternal Road*, 106, 144.

29 See Blitzstein, "Theatre-Music in Paris," *Modern Music* (March–April 1935): 128–134, and Blitzstein, "Notes for Lecture 5," as cited in Eric Gordon, *Mark the Music*, 20, 95.

30 David Schiff, "On the Road toward Hope: Kurt Weill's Celebration of the Jews," *New York Times*, 27 February 2000.

31 Of Weill, Blitzstein said in 1928: "He hasn't a thing to say in his music … entirely cerebral and uninspired …" Blitzstein, "Notes for Lecture 5," as cited by Eric Gordon, *Mark the Music*, 20. Blitzstein also described *The Eternal Road* as Weill's best though most uneven work. Blitzstein, "Theatre-Music in Paris," *Modern Music* (March–April 1935): 128–134, and Gordon, *Mark the Music*, 95.

32 Gordon, *Mark the Music*, 100.

33 Franz Werfel, *The Eternal Road*, 7.

34 Marc Blitzstein, *The Cradle Will Rock*, CD, track 20, "Art for Art's Sake," © 1999, Jay Productions.

35 Max Reinhardt, "Konzept für eine Rede," in Edda Fuhrich Leisler and Gisela Prossnitz, eds., *Max Reinhardt in Amerika* (Salzburg, Austria: O. Müller, 1976).

36 Gottfried Reinhardt, *The Genius: A Memoir of Max Reinhardt* (New York: Knopf, 1979), 244.

37 Gottfried Reinhardt, *The Genius*, 245.

38 Cited from Alma Mahler-Werfel's *Mein Leben* (Frankfurt am Main: Fischer, 1960), 220ff., and Peter Jungk, *Franz Werfel: A Life in Prague, Vienna, and Hollywood* (New York: Grove Weidenfeld, 1990), 129.

39 Victoria Powell, "Notes for public lectures on *The Eternal Road*," n.d., n.p., Weill-Lenya Research Center, New York City.

40 "*The Eternal Road* and Kurt Weill's German, Jewish, and American Identity: A Discussion with Kim H. Kowalke, Jürgen Schebera, Christian Kuhnt, and Alexander Ringer," *Theater*, Vol. 30, No. 3 (2000): 95.

41 Letter cited by Schebera in "*The Eternal Road* and Kurt Weill's German, Jewish, and American Identity," 89.

42 Gordon, *Mark the Music*, 4, 20.

43 William Finn, *The Marvin Songs: Three One-Act Musicals* (New York: Fireside Theater, n.d.), 182–184.

44 Kushner to *Minneapolis Star-Tribune*, as cited at http://gaytoday.badpuppy.com/garchive/quote/050498qu.htm. See also Rabbi Norman J. Cohen, "Wrestling with Angels," Interview with Tony Kushner, in *Tony Kushner: In Conversation*, ed. Robert Vorlicky (Ann Arbor, Michigan: University of Michigan Press, 1998), 217, 218.

45 E-Mail from William Finn to Jonathan Friedman, 14 April 2006.

46 Deb Margolin, "Oh Wholly Night and Other Jewish Solecisms" (1996), as cited by Kara Manning, "Are We Not Jews?" 24–28.

6

MUSICAL MÊLÉE
Twentieth-Century America's Contested Wartime Soundtrack

Robert J. Kodosky

Figure 6.1 Pete Seeger performing live on stage.

Popular music constitutes a powerful political force. A song's lyrics enable performers to "criticize, mobilize, express dissenting views, raise an issue, and spread counter-hegemonic discourses and ideas about rights and freedoms."[1] "Masters of War," a Bob Dylan song included on the iconic performer's second album, *The Freewheelin' Bob Dylan*, released by Columbia Records in 1963, exemplifies this ability. The song's lyrics condemn America's military-industrial complex. Dylan delivers them with a venomous sneer that packs "the baleful power of a witch's curse." Decades after its release, "Masters of War" "remains untameably over-the-top."[2] It is routinely covered in concert by Pearl Jam, a contemporary alternative rock band.

While popular music fosters subversion, it also enables oppression. It has "accompanied, and even been the instrument of, appalling acts of inhumanity and oppression."[3] During America's intervention in Vietnam, for example, Americans and Vietnamese employed music against one another as a weapon of psychological warfare. United States forces utilized songs such as Creedence Clearwater Revival's "Run through the Jungle," from the band's 1970 Fantasy Records release *Cosmo's Factory*, to "confuse and disorient the enemy." Meanwhile, Vietnamese communist prison officials acted "particularly cruel in playing Christmas carols during the holidays" in an effort to "manipulate the minds" of American prisoners that they deemed "most vulnerable."[4]

Popular music's political promise is substantial. Its direction, however, is hardly predetermined. It can help further the cause of war. It might also enhance the prospect for peace. It is a fiercely contested tool that represents an "important site of struggle for power."[5] This is rendered evident by exploring the relationship that evolved during the twentieth century between music and the American military. The United States military reflects its nation's early reliance on the militia. It makes use of citizen-soldiers, filling out its ranks during wartime and demobilizing for times of peace.[6]

As the United States assumed global preeminence during the twentieth century, it drafted citizens to serve as soldiers during both world wars, the Korean War and the Vietnam War. In each case, American officials justified the use of force as the means necessary to resist authoritarianism and to promote democracy. The irony of this situation escaped few soldiers. To secure the freedoms of others, their government required them to surrender theirs. As prominent civil rights attorney, Victor Rabinowitz, told *The New York Times* in 1969, "There's no question but what in the traditional sense soldiers have almost no civil liberties."[7]

Military service demands that conscripts set aside their individual liberties when they put on their uniforms. Citizen-soldiers must "adapt to communal arrangements for sleeping, eating, training, recreation and amusement," while also accepting the "disquieting possibilities of physical combat and injury or even loss of life."[8] It is a process that spawned a soundtrack, one that situated a contest between military officials and the rank and file that culminated while Americans waged war in Vietnam.

United States military officials have long connected the importance of music to morale. As early as the American Revolutionary War, Continental Army General George Washington observed that, "Nothing is more agreeable, and ornamental, than good music; every officer, for the credit of his corps, should take to provide it."[9] This notion became even more resolute over time. During World War II, the

European Theater of Operations Special and Morale Services' Guide, published by the United States Special Service Division in 1944, noted that music constitutes a "language that everyone speaks," and that the "soldier speaks it with gusto." In outlining strategies for commanders for "satisfying the soldier who likes to listen to music," the Special Service Division advised that "music is good morale ammunition."[10]

The struggle to control this ammunition, though, is a long one. In 1897, *The New York Times* reported that "These are trying times for conscientious musicians held to service in the army or navy of the United States and subject to the Articles of War." The paper informed its readers that the leader of a Marine Band played music "displeasing to a Lieutenant of the Marine Corps." The band leader "firmly refused" to alter the selection to "El Capitan" as ordered, and the Lieutenant had him placed under arrest. While *The New York Times* expressed its support for the jailed band leader, it opined that "an order that Sousa shall be played instead of Beethoven is a lawful order." Setting up as "musical authority against the military is," the newspaper suggested, "a hazardous enterprise."[11]

The United States entered World War I in April 1917. While it sought to "Make the World Safe for Democracy," the nation's military leaders discovered the need to provide soldiers with a "Will to Win." The program that they devised, in order to do so, paralleled the work carried out domestically by President Woodrow Wilson's Committee of Public Information (CPI): to create and sustain a nationalistic unity of ideals and purpose that was otherwise lacking.[12] Overwhelmed by the logistics of simply putting an army in the field, however, the Military Morale Section under the Military Intelligence Branch of the General Staff did not become operational until August 1918. As a result, the military relied heavily on the YMCA to entertain troops in France with "Y-Men" and "Y-Huts" near the front.

The Wilson administration turned to New York's Tin Pan Alley, a network of professional songwriters, for help. The group delivered a number of inspirational songs for soldiering that included George M. Cohan's "Over There" (1916), "Hunting the Hun" (1918) by Archie Gottler and Howard E. Rogers, and Arthur Lange and Andrew B. Sterling's "America Here's My Boy" (1917). Quickly written and recorded by popular musicians such as the Peerless Quartet, these songs accompanied the already existent patriotic anthems utilized by the government to promote wartime unity, such as "My Country 'Tis of Thee" and "The Star Spangled Banner." Tin Pan Alley songwriters responded to their nation's call, producing song after song, notable mainly for their "uninformed bravado."[13]

By war's end, General Peyton C. March, the head of the Morale Branch, who went on to become Chief of Staff, resolved to do things differently next time. Citing, in particular, the high percentage of "Y-Men" that contracted venereal disease, March called for change. He made clear that, in the event of another global conflict, he "would not have with the Army in the field any collateral welfare organizations."

Such work, he proclaimed, should be carried out "by the Army itself," enabling the military in the future to "avoid a number of things that are highly undesirable."[14]

Consequently, when America went to war once again in 1941, the military acted swiftly to centralize its efforts at bolstering soldier morale. It created the Special Services as part of the Morale Branch and designated Captain Howard C. Bronson as the Army's first Music Officer in June 1941. Bronson established a music program "predicated on a basic philosophy of morale building through soldier participation, emotional stability through self-entertainment, and a combat attitude through the use of music as a weapon."[15] The music program distributed song materials through a number of sources published by the Army, including *The Army Song Book* and *Hymns from Home*.

From World War I to World War II, military officials seized the conductor's wand and promoted traditional standards such as "Faith of Our Fathers," "America the Beautiful," "Battle Hymn of the Republic," and "God Bless America." They soon found it necessary to acknowledge, though, that, while "'the Army Song Book' and the training of Army song leaders did much to encourage group singing," the "men in the ranks wanted to sing the current song hits that they hear on the air."[16] This prompted monthly circulation of the *Army Hit Kit of Songs* beginning in March 1943, made possible by the cooperative Music Publishers' Protective Association.

According to the exhaustive study of popular music during World War II authored by John Bush Jones, the most successful hits of the era came "from the ranks of those touching on the emotions of GIs abroad."[17] Notable examples from prominent songwriters include "The Last Call for Love," penned by E. Y. Harburg, Burton Lane and Margery Cumming in 1942, and, from the same year, Paul Cunningham's "My Heart Belongs to America." Both songs "fused romantic love and love of country in a single number."[18] With the military assuming a more direct role in its distribution, American popular music during World War II fulfilled many of the same national needs that it addressed in World War I. It offered America's citizen-soldiers the "sentimental attractions of identification with the nation's cause," the "enhancement of self-identity as a warrior" and the "integrative rewards of fraternization."[19]

Despite the military's push of the patriotic, and its stress on the sentimental, during both world wars, American soldiers turned to singing different songs, ones that they perceived to reflect the reality of their experience, rather than the romantic ideals that popular music espoused. According to folklore scholars Gustave O. Arlt and Chandler Harris, "The songs which soldiers and sailors sing are rarely those printed in their official song books or those inspired by morale officers or song leaders." Officially disseminated songs, such as Gitz Rice's "Keep your head down, Allemand" (1918), Arlt and Harris suggest, succeeded "only in stimulating parodies on them." While no morale officer "ever looked with favor upon" the bawdy "Mademoiselle from Armentieres," it became the "unofficial anthem of the [American Expeditionary Force]."[20]

The more combat seasoned that they became, the more skepticism they expressed about the romantic depictions of war that popular songs provided them. Literary scholar Dorlea Rikard identifies this tendency as apparent in *Three Soldiers*, a work of war fiction, acclaimed for its realism, that John Dos Passos, a veteran of the U.S. Army Medical Corps, authored in 1920. Rikard points out that Dos Passos "laces his entire book with references to music," an affirmation of the importance of song to World War I soldiers. Soldiers resented the "Y-Men," however, for telling them what to sing. According to Rikard, Dos Passos portrays "Y-Men" as "shallowly patriotic and ineffective." Soldiers "do not regard them as comrades," and they "do not want to be told what to think (or what to sing) by the 'Y-Man.'"[21]

Soldiers located their own voices, ones that contested the dominant refrain of patriotic sentimentalism that echoed throughout the popular music that served the nation's agenda for war. To express their views, often antimilitarist and antiwar, soldiers utilized a familiar style, that of the occupational song. Steeped in ballads imported from the British Isles, along with the spirituals, field hollers and work songs adopted by slaves, folk music enabled expression for those oppressed. From rural communities to urban workspaces, by the beginning of the twentieth century, folk singing had become widespread. Song lyrics "were memorized and passed along orally" and set to accessible and well-known tunes. Often, words were "changed in the transmission to mirror the circumstances, such as occupation and social reality, of the singer."[22]

America's citizen-soldiers took the tradition of occupational song with them to the frontlines. It provided a "counterpoint to the content of popular music," and an outlet for "grumbling, discontent, fear, satire, derision and oppositional sentiments."[23] In the folk song tradition, soldiers used familiar tunes to insert new lyrics which typically went unattributed and remained subject to further revision. One example from World War I is "Joe Soap's Army," performed to "Onward Christian Soldiers." The song is skeptical about individual sacrifice and critical of military leadership. "Forward Joe Soap's Army/Marching without fear/With our old Commander/Safely in the rear/... But the men who really did the job/Are dead and in their grave."[24] In another parody, soldiers rewrote George M. Cohan's "Over There." They replaced the last line in the chorus, "And we won't come back 'til it's over over there" with "And we won't come back, we'll be buried over there."[25]

Some songs arrived to the front ready made. The Industrial Workers of the World (IWW), a radical labor organization that promoted the idea of "One Big Union," a single union to combat capitalism, galvanized American workers to action on the eve of World War I through the use of song. An IWW member, James H. Walsh, fostered the creation of the first *Little Red Songbook* in 1909. It contained simple, repetitive songs based on popular tunes that entertained, informed and struck at an emotional chord. The *Little Red Songbook* became "a particularly potent means of organizing, for the songs united workers who spoke different languages and came from different countries."[26]

Prior to the war, the IWW published annual editions of its songbook. The 8th edition, published in 1916, included John F. Kendrick's "Christians at War," a bitterly antiwar song that, like "Joe Soap's Army," is set to "Onward Christian Soldiers." It posits the war as a conflict waged by capitalists at the expense of the working class, and underscores the contradiction between Christianity's professed ideals with the eagerness of nation states to invoke the Divine while employing violent means."[27]

The songbooks published by the IWW inspired the next generation of folk singers on the eve of America's entry into World War II. In the spring of 1941, the Almanac Singers, a group of radical leftists that featured Pete Seeger, Lee Hays, Millard Lampell and Woody Guthrie, recorded *Songs for John Doe*. Issued in May by Keynote Records under the Almanac label, the album vehemently connects war and capitalism. "Billy Boy," set to the familiar "Oh where have you been, Billy Boy, Billy Boy?" suggests that an American entrance to war would serve only the interests of Chicago's anti-union Republic Steel.[28]

Songs for John Doe targeted the presidential administration of Franklin Delano Roosevelt, portraying the president as a warmonger. "Plow Under" draws an analogy between war and Roosevelt's New Deal program, the Agricultural Adjustment Act. The "Ballad of October 16" condemns Roosevelt's decision to support legislation for a military draft. When Roosevelt heard the recording, he "flew into a rage and wondered aloud if it was grounds for arrest."[29] Roosevelt need not have worried. On 22 June 1941 the Nazis shattered their pact with the communist Soviet Union and invaded it. Forced to choose, members of the Almanacs elected to defend communism over pacifism. "The Peace songs were out. Roosevelt was an ally again."[30] Woody Guthrie soon affixed to his guitar the slogan: "This Machine Kills Fascists."

Guthrie had company. According to John Bush Jones, "by the time the war ended, Tin Pan Alley and hillbilly writers had written a total of fifty-eight patriotic, 119 militant, and fifty-six Axis bashing songs." The "number of such songs by amateurs," he adds, "was likely somewhere in the thousands."[31] As during World War I, though, evidence suggests that such songs failed to resonate widely with those engaged in combat. World War II infantry veteran and eminent scholar Paul Fussell recalls popular songwriter Frank Loesser's "The Ballad of Rodger Young" (1945), an ode to a fallen soldier. Fussell labels the song "too embarrassing for either the troops or the more intelligent home folks to take to their hearts."[32]

Fussell concedes that, "Some, it is true, were singing 'Lili Marlene,'" but cites that others, "requiring a way to object to the war without openly do so," chose to sing other songs.[33] As occurred during World War I, soldiers turned to parody. They spoofed the show tune "People Will Say We're in Love" from the 1943 musical *Oklahoma!* by devising new lyrics. "Don't throw grenades at me/... Kraut-buddy don't you see/People will say I'm done in."[34] They also borrowed from the British, adopting as their own "I Don't Want to Be a Soldier," a song existent in the British Army since the Napoleonic Wars. "I don't want to be a soldier/I don't want to go to war."[35] Such songs offered soldiers the ability to contest the space dominated by the idealized and romantic portrayals of war that popular songwriters churned out. "Spots," a parody of "Casey Jones" that circulated among marines located little glory in dying for one's country, and the song's chorus, in particular, questions the value placed on individual life by the nation.[36]

The antiwar sentiments expressed by soldier songs remained within the ranks. As powerfully as they spoke to those who experienced the reality of combat, they sounded equally off key to the ears of Americans accustomed to more patriotic revelry. Soldiers understood this. They recognized that "optimistic publicity and euphemism had rendered their experience so falsely that it would never be readily communicable." World War II widened the gap between the ways in which America imagined war and the way that the nation's soldiers endured it. A "conspiracy of silence" had developed.[37] Patriotic sentimentalism and martial spirit drowned out all other voices.

This trend continued into the Cold War, a conflict that turned "hot" by the summer of 1950. Communist North Korea launched a military attack against American-aligned South Korea on 26 June. The United States received approval from the United Nations Security Council to intervene militarily, and hastily dispatched a force under the command of United States General Douglas MacArthur. Popular music responded immediately, in predictable fashion. Jimmie Osborne, self proclaimed as "The Kentucky Folk Singer," released "God, Please Protect America" on 26 July 1950. The song peaked at number nine on the *Billboard* charts and managed to make a "fairly significant impact," inspiring schoolchildren to sing along as they "marched and pretended to be soldiers during recess."[38]

Other patriotic songs followed, including "Korea, Here We Come," written and recorded by Harry Choates in 1951 and, from the same year, Jackie Doll and his Pickled Peppers' "When They Drop the Atomic Bomb." Whether these too became popular with schoolchildren is unknown, but soldiers favored other songs. This occurred despite the military's effort to bring popular patriotic songs to the troops by providing logistical support to the United Service Organizations (USO). A private, nonprofit organization founded in 1941, the USO partnered with the military to bring popular entertainment to the troops during World War II. Once war began in Korea, USO volunteers grew to number 113,394. They presented 5,422 performances during the war.[39]

As during World War II, entertainment officially sponsored by the military did little to discourage troops from singing out. The persona of "Sammy Hall" originated in Korea, enabling "the U.S. fighter pilot to vent his anger, frustration, and obscenity" in ways otherwise not possible.[40] Soldiers also borrowed oppositional songs from earlier wars that undermined popular hyperbole and hardly proved fit for schoolyard recess. "Fuck 'em all" is one example. "Fuck 'em all, fuck 'em all/The long, the short, the tall/... Fuck all the generals and above all fuck you!"[41]

The Korean War did little to lessen the gap between soldier songs and popular music. America's war in Vietnam did. By 1965, the television set had become a ubiquitous feature of American households. Increasingly, the device provided an important window on current events, and a crucial shaper of opinion. In 1960, it helped boost Senator John F. Kennedy, a Democrat from Massachusetts, to the presidency. Viewers gave Kennedy the nod after watching his performance against Republican Vice President Richard M. Nixon in the nation's first televised presidential debate.

Television news broadcasts soon expanded from 15 minutes to 30 minutes. Newly launched satellites enabled networks to broadcast from around the globe, including from the turbulent Republic of Vietnam (RVN) where, by the time of President Kennedy's assassination in November 1963, nearly 20,000 American advisers were stationed to prevent communist dominoes from falling. By this time, there existed over 50 million televisions in American households to deliver the day's news each evening.[42]

Viewers also turned to television for entertainment. By the early 1960s, rock and roll music was on the ropes. Its idols had departed. Elvis Presley was in the Army. Jerry Lee Lewis and Chuck Berry faced legal problems. Buddy Holly was dead. Folk music reemerged after enduring a difficult decade. In 1954, Woody Guthrie entered Brooklyn State Hospital, diagnosed with Huntington's disease. In 1955, Pete Seeger received a summons to appear before the House Un-American Activities Committee (HUAC) which found him in contempt. Seeger's conviction was not overturned until 1962.[43]

Seeger never stopped writing, though. Shortly after appearing before HUAC, he penned the lyrics to "Where Have All the Flowers Gone?" The song, made famous by the Kingston Trio in 1961, heralded the return of folk music. As Ron Eyerman explains:

> The success of the Kingston Trio in the late 1950s pointed to a factor that was of relatively little importance in the 1930s and 1940s: college students. Aside from the conservative political climate arising from the Cold War, perhaps the two greatest factors in shaping the field of culture in the 1950s were the new post-war prosperity and the concurrent expansion of higher education, both of which served to extend and redefine the nature of youth and leisure.[44]

In 1962, "Where Have All the Flowers Gone?" provided the foundation for the anti-war music of the Vietnam War era when performed by Peter, Paul, and Mary for their debut album. The record nested in the *Billboard* Top 100 for three years, "introducing millions" to Seeger's composition.[45] In 1963, they performed Bob Dylan's landmark spiritual "Blowin' in the Wind." That same year, Dylan and his singing partner Joan Baez participated in Martin Luther King, Jr.'s March on Washington, and the former released his antiwar song, "Masters of War," later appropriated by the anti-Vietnam movement. In August 1964, President Lyndon B. Johnson asked, and received permission from Congress, to escalate America's involvement in Vietnam.

One of the earliest responses in popular song to the war in Vietnam came from an American soldier. Staff Sergeant Barry Sadler, a member of an elite Army special force, the Green Berets, who had served in Vietnam as a medic, wrote "Ballad of the Green Berets" while recovering from a wound he suffered on patrol in 1965. The song became one of the biggest hits of the entire decade, after the RCA Victor Records label released it in 1966. With its overtly patriotic theme and its glorification of military sacrifice, RCA Victor dubbed it as the Vietnam War's national theme song. Many Green Berets, though, were "less than enthusiastic" about the song, calling it "too vainglorious."[46]

In Vietnam, Sadler's song provided the structure for numerous parodies. One criticized the Army Security Agency (ASA), the Army's signal intelligence branch: "Drunken soldiers, always high/We've been cleared and we're not queers/One hundred men we'll test today/But only three make the ASA."[47] Another lampooned military journalists, Public Information Officers (PIOs): "There he goes, the PIO/… And when he gets to the golden gate/St. Peter says, 'You've goofed up mate!'/So go to hell, in all your glory/When you get back, you can do your story."[48]

The sheer volume of oppositional songs powerfully struck United States Air Force Major General Edward Geary Lansdale. He detected in them a reality of the war's nature that eluded officials. Lansdale provided copies to President Lyndon Baines Johnson, United States Army General William Childs Westmoreland and United States Ambassador to Vietnam Henry Cabot Lodge "to impart a greater understanding of the political and psychological nature of the war to those making decisions." Unprecedented, the effort proved futile.[49] So, too, did the effort made to convince Americans that the war could be won. Television broadcast increasingly skeptical reports from Vietnam that placed official predictions about victory in doubt.[50]

An antiwar movement, unprecedented in scale, erupted. It drew inspiration from antiwar music that crossed all genres, from folk to Motown, including artists such as Phil Ochs ("Draft Dodger Rag," 1965, and "I Ain't Marching Anymore," also 1965), Tom Paxton ("Lyndon Johnson Told the Nation," 1965), Country Joe and the Fish ("I-Feel-Like-I'm-Fixin'-To-Die Rag, 1967), Creedence Clearwater Revival ("Fortunate Son," 1969), Edwin Starr ("War," 1969), the Plastic Ono Band ("Give Peace a Chance," 1969), Crosby, Stills, Nash, and Young ("Ohio," 1970), Marvin Gaye ("What's Going On," 1971), and Joan Baez ("Where Are You Now, My Son?" a 23-minute account of Baez' trip to Hanoi in 1972, during which she survived the eleven-day "Christmas" bombings of the city). Barry McGuire's version of P. F. Sloan's "Eve of Destruction" went to number one on the *Billboard* charts in

September 1965, although a number of radio stations banned it.[51] In September 1967, CBS censors axed Pete Seeger's anti-Vietnam song, "Waist Deep in the Big Muddy," from the Smothers Brothers Comedy Hour; only after its hosts protested did Seeger receive an invitation to perform the song on a later episode. A few weeks after the Seeger incident, Woody Guthrie's son, Arlo, released his 18-minute spoken blues classic, "Alice's Restaurant," which recounted Arlo's travails during his aborted conscription into the Army. (He was denied entry because he had a criminal record for littering.) In August 1968, Phil Ochs played "I Ain't Marching Anymore" as part of the protests outside the Democratic National Convention in Chicago. Although R. Serge Denisoff cautions that the impact of these artists should not be overstated,[52] they provided opponents of the war in Vietnam at home with a powerful soundtrack. They gave the soldiers in Vietnam one as well.

In January 1971, U.S. Air Force Sergeant Clyde David Delay, using the name of "Dave Rabbit," launched a pirate radio station in a Saigon brothel. For twenty-one days, Dave Rabbit and his partners, Nguyen, a Vietnamese woman employed by Armed Forces Vietnam Network and "Pete," Rabbit's roommate in the Air Force, broadcast programming that contrasted the "bullshit that was constantly cranking out on AFVN."[53] Moreover, F.T.A. (Free the Army/Fuck the Army) coffee houses had cropped up near army posts in the U.S. and in the Pacific. F.T.A. stage shows consisted of "political vaudeville" that featured antiwar music. The military resorted to heavy-handed efforts and bogus charges to close the coffee houses down.[54] For the first time, American soldiers expressing antiwar sentiments through opposi- tional songs received widespread affirmation of their views from songs popular back home.

Unable to separate its soldiers from the counterculture, military officials sought to exercise control by tapping it as a means to build morale and to boost recruiting. As early as 1964, the Armed Forces' *Song Folio* included songs from the Beatles, the Ani- mals, Jan and Dean and the Zombies, but steered well clear of any political expres- sion, such as "I'm Crying," and "Ride the Wild Surf." Special Services sought to tap into the popularity of folk music by publishing *Folk Festival*, which featured "Military Folk Music," "Folk Favorites," "International Folk Music," and "Christmas Folk Music." The "Folk Favorites" section included "On the First Thanksgiving Day," and "Wimoweh," among others just as innocuous. The publication also included "This Land Is Your Land" by Woody Guthrie, stripped of its "private property" verse that criticizes American capitalism.[55]

In Germany, where American troops remained stationed to prevent an ostensi- ble communist invasion of Europe, a thin line existed between the home front and military service. In November 1965, the Monks, a band comprised of five newly dis- charged American soldiers, began recording their revolutionary album *Black Monk Time*. The album opened with the band's theme song, "Monk Time." "You know we don't like the army/What army?/Who cares about the army?/Why do you kill all those kids in Vietnam/Mad Vietcong!/My brother died in Vietnam/Stop it/Stop it/I don't like it!"[56]

Special Services sought to bring this counterculture into the military fold by sponsoring its own shows for troops, "The Electric Army," in 1969, and "Experience '70" the following year. These productions generated enough enthusiasm among the troops for Special Services to roll out "The First Annual Original Magnificent Special Services Entertainment Showband Contest" in 1971. According to Ken Smith, entertainment director for the United States Army in Europe, the contest constituted a "modern approach to the former annual Special Services entertainment contest." He added, "This is apparently what the troops want and that's our function—to give 'em what they want."[57]

Lewis Hitt, the guitarist for East of Underground, one of the bands that competed, remembers, "It was understood that the path of least resistance was to let the soldiers express themselves."[58] The finals for the Army's "Battle of the Bands" contest took place at the BFV Sports Arena in Mannheim, Germany. Crowds numbered in the thousands for the two-day affair. It resulted in a tie between SOAP, from Hessen Support District, and East of Underground, from Sued Bayern. The winning bands received the opportunity to tour Europe under the auspices of Special Services, and to record an album at the Armed Forces Network studios in Frankfurt, Germany. The Army pressed and distributed the resulting double album to Army recruitment centers across the United States. It briefly used the recording as a recruiting tool until, presumably, somebody listened to the lyrics.

The whole episode—including the next year's follow up contest, which produced recordings from joint winners The Black Seeds and Sound Trek—remained largely forgotten, until archivist and collector Dante Carfagna found a copy of the original record in a thrift store in Kansas City in 1997.[59] The recordings have most recently been reissued as a box set collection of remastered compact discs by Now-Again Records in 2011, titled *East of Underground: Hell Below*. Of the show, Kurt Loder, then writing for *The Overseas Weekly*, reported that SOAP deviated from its officially approved set list to play an original song, set to the tune of John Lennon's "Working Class Hero." Loder wrote, "I don't know how much the powers-that-be dug this song." The song, entitled "Twenty Year Lifer," questioned the wisdom of making the military a career.[60]

Clearly, band members used their status as "show band" performers to push back against Army regulations. Loder observed in his piece that East of Underground's members dressed in "outlandish" costumes onstage that featured "coal black capes, medieval jerkins, long, flowing velvet robes and a variety of other freaky—and apparently expensive accoutrements."[61] The band's guitarist, Lewis Hitt, acknowledges that, "we might have gotten away with it a little bit." He recalls that the band's frontman, Austin Webb, wore an afro packed under his hat. At one point during the show, a General "came through and was kind of checking it out." When the General inquired about Webb's hair, the Special Services director "explained that it was a wig."[62]

Webb's hair represented the challenge facing the military. So, too, did his band's name, East of Underground, derived from the identification of its members with the underground movement back home. The military had attempted to rob the counterculture of its power by appropriating its form, not its substance. For the first time in the twentieth century, the military found it was lacking a viable pro-war culture that it could utilize to drown out dissent. Its attempt to resurrect the USO had failed. Soldiers booed the aging comedian Bob Hope at a 1970 USO show, prompting one of the Army's entertainment directors to question "whether Bob Hope appealed to soldiers as much as more modern entertainers."[63] The entertainment mattered less to soldiers than the war that its nation made them wage, even as it seemingly took little interest in addressing the injustices that they perceived back home.

East of Underground's recording reflects the marginalization its members felt, not only from the military, but from America. The band featured selections that addressed the racial disparity in the United States, from "Smiling Faces Sometimes" (1971) to "People Get Ready" (1965), both originally recorded by the Temptations. They showcased an incendiary cover of the Curtis Mayfield song, "Hell Below" (1970). These all constituted musical indictments of the American hypocrisy that they detected. In similar fashion, SOAP featured Neil Young's "Southern Man" (1970), while both The Black Seeds and Sound Trek played The O'Jays' "Backstabbers" (1972).

"Maybe we all mistrusted a lot of what was going on," Lewis Hitt suggests, "and we didn't like the war."[64] Army Entertainment would never be the same. The military made certain of that. Following the war in Vietnam, the military reclaimed the musical terrain. It revised regulations to stipulate that performances "deliver messages of pride, inspiration, team spirit, cohesiveness and common goodwill." Moreover, it requires that all band members appear in uniform.[65]

Notes

1 Thierry Côté, "Popular Musicians and Their Songs as Threats to National Security: A World Perspective," *The Journal of Popular Culture*, Vol. 44 (2011): 735.

2 Dorian Lynskey, *33 Revolutions Per Minute: A History of Protest Songs, from Billie Holiday to Green Day* (New York: HarperCollins, 2011), 57.

3 Martin Cloonan and Bruce Johnson, "Killing Me Softly With His Song: An Initial Investigation into the Use of Popular Music as a Tool of Oppression," *Popular Music*, Vol. 21 (2002): 27.

4 Lee Andresen, *Battle Notes: Music of the Vietnam War*, 2nd edition (Superior, Wisconsin: Savage Press, 2003), 184–185.

5 Côté, "Popular Musicians," 741.

6 See Allan R. Millett and Peter Maslowski, *For the Common Defense: A Military History of the United States of America* (New York and London: The Free Press, 1984).

7 Robert Sherrill, "Must the Citizen Give Up His Civil Liberties When He Joins the Army?" *The New York Times*, 18 May 1969, 25.

8 Les Cleveland, "Singing Warriors: Popular Songs in Wartime," *The Journal of Popular Culture*, Vol. 28 (1994): 155.

9 Field Manual 12–50, *U.S. Army Bands* (Washington, D.C.: Department of the Army, Headquarters, 2010), 1–2.

10 *ETOUSA Special Morale and Services Guide*, Special Services Division, May 1944, Combined Arms Research Library Digital Library (CARLDL, hereafter), at: http://cgsc.cdmhost.com/cdm/singleitem/collection/p4013coll8/id/2458/rec/1630, 30, accessed 25 May 2012.

11 "Discipline and Music," *The New York Times*, 2 June 1897, 6.

12 Thomas M. Camfield, "Will to Win—The U.S. Army Troop Morale Program of World War I," *Military Affairs*, 41 (October 1977): 125.

13 Dorlea Rikard, "Patriotism, Propaganda, Parody, and Protest: The Music of Three American Wars," *War, Literature & The Arts*, 16 (2004): 130.

14 George Plank, "A Survey of the U.S. Army Entertainment Program in Europe During the Early 1980s with a Study of Its Origins in American History" (Master's thesis, 1988), 22.

15 M. Claude Rosenberry, "The Army Music Program," *Music Educator's Journal*, Vol. 30 (April 1944): 18.

16 Rosenberry, "The Army Music Program," 18.

17 John Bush Jones, *The Songs that Fought the War: Popular Music and the Home Front, 1939–1945* (Lebanon, New Hampshire: Brandeis University Press, 2006), 236.

18 Jones, *The Songs that Fought the War*, 243.

19 Cleveland, "Singing Warriors," 168.

20 Gustave O. Arlt and Chandler Harris, "Songs of the Services," *California Folklore Quarterly*, Vol. 3 (January 1944): 36.

21 Rikard, "Patriotism," 131.

22 Lawrence J. Epstein, *Political Folk Music in America from Its Origins to Bob Dylan* (Jefferson, North Carolina and London: McFarland & Company, 2010), 10.

23 Cleveland, "Singing Soldiers," 157.

24 Max Arthur, *When This Bloody War Is Over: Soldiers' Songs of the First World War* (London: Piatkus, 2001), 127.

25 Arthur, *When This Bloody War Is Over*, 123.

26 Epstein, *Political Folk Music*, 25.

27 John F. Kendrick, "Christians at War," *The IWW Little Red Songbook: To Fan the Flames of Discontent* (Chicago: IWW, 1916), at: http://www.scribd.com/doc/27808417/The-IWW-Little-Red-Song-Book, 23, accessed 26 May 2012.

28 Jones, *The Songs that Fought the War*, 62.

29 Lynskey, *33 Revolutions Per Minute*, 27.

30 Epstein, *Political Folk Music*, 87.

31 Jones, *The Songs that Fought the War*, 117.

32 Paul Fussell, *Wartime: Understanding and Behavior in the Second World War* (New York and Oxford: Oxford University Press, 1989), 185.

33 Fussell, *Wartime*, 266.

34 Les Cleveland, *Dark Laughter: War in Song and Popular Culture* (Westport, Connecticut: Praeger, 1994), 61.

35 Les Cleveland, "Soldiers' Songs: The Folklore of the Powerless," *New York Folklore*, Vol. 11 (1985): 79.

36 Samuel L. Hynes, *Flights of Passage: Reflections of a World War II Aviator* (New York and Annapolis: Naval Institute Press, 1988), 195.

37 Martin Page, *Kiss Me Goodnight Sergeant Major: The Songs and Ballads of World War II* (London: Hart-Davis, 1973), 6.

38 Ivan M. Tribe, "Purple Hearts, Heartbreak Ridge, and Korean Mud: Pain, Patriotism, and Faith in the 1950–53 'Police Action,'" in *Country Music Goes to War*, eds., Charles K. Wolfe and James E. Akenson (Lexington: The University Press of Kentucky, 2005), 128.

39 Plank, "A Survey of the U.S. Army Entertainment Program," 41.

40 Joseph F. Tuso, *Singing the Vietnam Blues: Songs of the Air Force in Southeast Asia* (College Station, Texas: Texas A & M University Press, 1990), 168.

41 Cleveland, "Soldiers' Songs," 80.

42 Television Academy Foundation, "TV History," in the Archive of American Television at: http://www.emmytvlegends.org/resources/tv-history, accessed 26 May 2012.

43 Epstein, *Political Folk Music*, 119.

44 Ron Eyerman and Scott Barretta, "From the 30s to the 60s: The Folk Music Revival in the United States," *Theory and Society*, Vol. 25, No. 4 (August 1996): 522.

45 Lynskey, *33 Revolutions Per Minute*, 58.

46 Andresen, *Battle Notes*, 134.

47 Rikard, "Patriotism," 138.

48 Tuso, *Singing the Vietnam Blues*, 39.

49 Lydia M. Fish, "General Edward G. Lansdale and the Folksongs of Americans in the Vietnam War," *Journal of American Folklore*, Vol. 102 (October–December 1989): 9.

50 Caroline Page, *U.S. Official Propaganda During the Vietnam War, 1965–1973: The Limits of Persuasion* (London and New York: Leicester University Press, 1996).

51 Peter Blecha, *Taboo Tunes: A History of Banned Bands and Censored Songs* (New York: Backbeat Books, 2004).

52 R. Serge Denisoff, "Protest Songs: Those on the Top Forty and Those on the Streets," *American Quarterly*, Vol. 22, No. 4 (Winter 1970): 807–823, and Denisoff, review of *Minstrels of the Dawn: The Folk-Protest Singer as a Cultural Hero*, by Jerome Rodnitzky, *Contemporary Sociology*, Vol. 6, No. 2 (March 1977): 269–270.

53 Dave Rabbitt, "Vietnam War Pirate DJ Has Finally Come Forward: His Story in His Own Words," 15 February 2006, at: http://vietnamresearch.com/media/termer/feb2006.html, accessed 25 May 2012.

54 Plank, "A Survey of the U.S. Army Entertainment Program," 51.

55 Adjutant General, United States Army, *Armed Forces Song Folios*, monthly 1951, United States Army Heritage and Education Center (hereafter, USAHEC), Carlisle, PA.

56 The Monks, *Black Monk Time*, LP, track 1, ©1966, International Polydor Production.

57 "2 GI Groups Tie for Top Show-Band Title," *The Stars and Stripes*, 30 November 1971, 9.

58 Ben Beaumont-Thomas, "Funk Songs from American GIs," *The Guardian*, 15 December 2011, at: http://www.guardian.co.uk/music/2011/dec/15/funk-songs-vietnam-us-gis, accessed 25 May 2012.

59 Beaumont-Thomas, "Funk Songs."

60 Kurt Loder, "The First Annual Original Magnificent Special Services Entertainment Showband Contest," *The Overseas Weekly—European Edition*, 19 December 1971, 6.

61 Loder, "The First Annual," 6.

62 "The U.S. Army's Rock 'N' Roll Past," National Public Radio, 30 October 2011, at: http://www.npr.org/2011/10/30/141827472/the-u-s-armys-rock-n-roll-past, accessed 26 May 2012.

63 Plank, "A Survey of the U.S. Army Entertainment Program," 50.

64 Beaumont-Thomas, "Funk Songs."

65 Field Manual 12–50, 1–1.

7

BOB DYLAN

An American Tragedian

Kile Jones

Figure 7.1 Joan Baez and Bob Dylan perform during a civil rights rally in Washington, D.C.

Tragedy has been an essential mode of representing the human condition throughout history. It has anchored various narratives and has involved such horrendous themes as families being torn apart, greed, war, torture, revenge, strife, and meaningless suffering. The Greek poets are the original patriarchs of tragedy—not only because of their interest in tragedy, but also because they constructed tragedy as a distinctive literary genre—and, as such, they are the beginning point for any study of tragedy. Aeschylus' *Oresteia*, Sophocles' *Oedipus the King*, and Euripides' *Alcestis* form the early canon of tragedy. Aristotle, who wrote on these early tragedians, distinguishes tragedy by its cathartic effect in soliciting pity and fear in the spectator.[1]

Centuries later, there was a German renaissance of tragedy in the writings of Georg Hegel, Arthur Schopenhauer, Friedrich Nietzsche, and Karl Jaspers. These four examined tragedy as a philosophical and existential concept. Arthur Schopenhauer's *magnum opus*, *The World as Will and Representation* (1818) elevates tragedy to "the summit of poetic art" as it expresses "the terrible side of life."[2] Georg Hegel's *Lectures on Fine Arts* (first published in 1835) reveal to us how tragedy is incorporated into his own dialectical method. Friedrich Nietzsche's early work, *The Birth of Tragedy from the Spirit of Music* (1872), argues for a Dionysian revelry in tragedy. Karl Jasper's *Tragedy Is Not Enough* (1962) finds tragedy as a condition for the experience of transcendence. Up to the present time, we are still discussing tragedy as a genre, a concept, a method, and a phenomenon. In this essay, I will assess the extent to which tragedy undergirded the worldview of an individual in the world of "low culture"—American singer/songwriter Bob Dylan.[3]

Tragedy in Dylan

Numerous threadlines, from folk, rock and roll, beat poetry, and social protest, have shaped Bob Dylan's body of work. In *Chronicles: Volume One* (2004), he mentions the influence of Woody Guthrie, Hank Williams, and Robert Johnson. His friendship with Allen Ginsburg introduced him to a whole spectrum of beat poets. On the beats, Dylan says, "It was Jack Kerouac, Ginsberg, Corso, Ferlinghetti … I got in at the tail end of that and it was magic … it has just as big an impact on me as Elvis Presley."[4] Dylan was also influenced by the civil rights movement and Martin Luther King, Jr., and he performed with Joan Baez at the Great March on Washington in 1963. Steeped in this cultural brew, Dylan has painted a uniquely critical picture of the world, drawing upon familiar archetypes, such as the saint, prophet, sage, sinner, joker, gambler, hero, and rambler to represent forces like religion, politics, media, revolution, law, and war. An explicit usage of these archetypes can be found in the movie *Masked and Anonymous* (2003), in which Dylan stars. In this movie, each of the characters represents a social force, and their interactions say something about how world-drama plays out.

In the recent movie *I'm Not There* (2007), we are reminded that Dylan plays out each of these roles in his person. Thus Dylan becomes what one wants him to be; he is a litmus test for our culture. Not to overemphasize Dylan as a tragic-hero, it must be remembered that Dylan, unlike the tragic-hero, is lacking in pretension, pride, and egoism. He lacks pretension because he never categorizes himself as only one of these archetypal figures. He is a simple songwriter. In reference to tragedy, Dylan is the fortuitous loner who walks down the tracks. This loner, condemned to isolation and wandering, walks until his feet bleed in search for something that unifies his diverse and often confusing experiences. He is constantly mindful of tragedy.

Dylan has also changed, personally and lyrically, throughout the last half-century. In a 2008 article, Cynthia Whissell analyzed Dylan's lyrics from 1962 to 2001 with the *Dictionary of Affect in Language*. Whissell looked at three "popular peaks" in Dylan's career—1963, 1974–1975, and 1992–1999—and noticed that the "acclaimed Dylan" wrote "lyrics which were more Active and more Concrete," whereas the "criticized Dylan" wrote "lyrics which were more Passive and more Abstract."[5] Twenty years earlier, Michael Roos and Don O'Meara identified four "life structures" (or "cells") to which Dylan's lyrics correspond, although "each life structure represented by these four cells is inherently unstable and temporary, since they represent opposing dialectical forces resulting in some degree of ambivalence for the person living each life structure."[6] These attempts at making sense of Dylan's changing lyrics can be helpful but, since Dylan is such a paradox, they are often very limited in their explanatory power.

Tragedy in General

I see tragedy as a voice in Dylan's head that will not go away. It can be avoided, even answered, but it will never go away. This is why one needs fortitude, because of the ubiquity of tragedy. Dylan is like Atlas with a burden to bear; consider his laments in "Not Dark Yet" (1997)[7] and "Every Grain of Sand" (1981).[8] In "Song to Woody," (1962), "Gotta Serve Somebody" (1979), the aptly titled "Trouble," also from 1981, and "Everything is Broken" (1989), tragedy is something that fills not only Dylan's soul, but also the entire world.[9] Trouble is the working-out of the broken nature of humanity. Like Karl Jaspers, Dylan finds this "brokenness" central to the tragic nature of existence. In our life, full of trouble and brokenness, we are condemned to serve and be abandoned. Like Jaspers' claim that "I cannot live without struggling and suffering,"[10] Dylan finds ways in which we are stuck, determined, and condemned to fate."[11]

Being controlled is out of one's control. It is equivalent to the Christian doctrine of original sin, whereby our will is in bondage to our corrupt nature. Martin Luther's famous *De Servo Arbitrio* (*On the Bondage of the Will*) says that our evil disposition is not due to God compelling us to sin, but arises "spontaneously and voluntarily. And this willingness or volition is something which he cannot in his own strength eliminate, restrain, or alter."[12] In the vernacular of American blues, B. B. King has described the situation of humanity as enchained.[13] For Dylan, the world is simply a prison.[14]

When faced with the "tragic sense of being trapped without escape," Dylan reminds us of the perpetual change taking place in this world. In "Going, Going, Gone," (1974), to be "gone" may mean "being gone from a place in which we are stuck," or it may mean to die.[15] Perpetual change and death are two themes Dylan repeatedly emphasizes. In "Man on the Street" (1962), Dylan explores the latter in a way that is detached and eerily "matter of fact."[16] It is eerie because it is indicative of the reality of death. When faced with this reality, and its tragic dimension, we desperately want to expand our time, to have it pushed back or extended forward. Like everyone else, Dylan has wished this. In "Highlands" (1997), Dylan echoes Arthur Schopenhauer, who said of time that it was "never letting us take breath, but always coming after us, like a taskmaster with a whip." [17] Dylan accepts the reality of death and desires to face it with dignity and composure. Alongside those panicking the threat of atomic war, he offers acceptance ("Let Me Die in My Footsteps," 1963).[18] To fear, accept, and desire to be delivered from death all at the same time is an outstanding feature of human existence. It shows us how complicated our responses to death are. All three of these responses to death oscillate throughout Dylan's lyrics.

Tragedy and Politics

Since the world in which we are "trapped" is broken and full of trouble, it seems inevitable that social interactions will mimic such a state. Politics, as the *exemplar* of social interactions, provides us with a macrocosmic picture of humanity. For Dylan, politics is all around us; consider "Political World" (1989), "License to Kill" (1983), and "Band of the Hand" (1986).[19] In the latter, Dylan tells political stories about police brutality, corrupt judges and courts, big government, racism and fascism."[20] One of his earliest and most cutting songs about judicial injustice is "The Death of Emmett Till" (1963). Till was a black boy who was, in 1955, beaten and tortured to death by local whites in Mississippi. Dylan's lyrics are an especially pained jeremiad against the insensitivity of the murderers. In the wake of the popular uproar over this act, "two brothers confessed that they had killed poor Emmett Till." The jury, who had men in it "who helped the brothers commit this crime," found them innocent and so set them free. Dylan calls this trial a "mockery" and "a crime that's so unjust."[21] Another theodicy, though less charged, is called "Percy's Song" (1964). It tells a story of a man who was driving in a storm and crashed in a field, killing four people in the car. The driver was given a prison sentence of "ninety-nine years." Dylan expressed outraged over the fact that an accident caused by rain and wind could condemn someone to life in jail.[22] To this, Dylan turns to the rain and the wind in frustration and sadness. Two years after this song was written, Dylan had his own motorcycle accident—except, this time, Dylan turned to God with his frustration and sadness.

On a larger scale, states and nations perpetrate similar injustices. Wars are fought in the name of group and special interests. There is no better depiction of tragedy than in war. In "Masters of War" (1963) Dylan takes the role of the biblical prophet and indicts arms manufacturers:[23] these "faceless" businessmen act like they are playing chess with the world, living as they do, off the fear of the McCarthy era. The individual soldiers on the ground are "Only a Pawn in Their Game" (1963), who were lied to by the American government and the military-industrial complex. Throughout history, in Dylan's assessment, leaders and politicians have given the population a false picture, propaganda, and simulacra, about war and its effects. We are never given the whole picture—the "Big Business" of the arms race, the special interests of the U.S., the brutality of war, the effect it has on families and cultures, and the effects it has on those fighting in it. Along this line, Dylan tells a story about a soldier who went off to war with high hopes. During war, this soldier realizes that his supposed enemy is just like him and that he is just a pawn in "their" game ("John Brown," 1963).[24] Of course, some of the most memorable antiwar lyrics in Dylan's body of work come from "Blowin' in the Wind" (1962).[25] Unfortunately, we must continually ask ourselves about the merits of war, in the hope that someday we will realize the tragedy of war. The compassionate response to the tragedy of war would be to refocus our energies on peacemaking and constructive, non-violent, strategies for international relations.

The irony is that, even though Dylan wants a more peaceful society, he intimates that it probably will never happen. Human beings are much too selfish and fickle for utopia. The question then becomes how a pessimist, like Dylan, can retain the optimism needed for social criticism. Or, better put, how can Dylan want change when he knows it might not happen? These questions reveal a paradox in Dylan's thought. There are times when Dylan speaks in fatalistic, deterministic, terms, and there are times when he uses a language of freedom and responsibility. What can be said is that Dylan indicates that the world in which we live is deterministic, and that people should be allowed to think they are free and responsible (even if they are not), and that people can escape this determinism, if only for a small time, by contemplation and lament. At the end of his article on Dylan and free will, Martin Van Hees makes a valid point: "But, just like the old blues singers did, there is the possibility of describing and lamenting our fate. This in itself equates to taking a stance."[26] If this is the case, then Dylan follows a long line of philosophers, from Socrates to Bertrand Russell, who believed that contemplation shows our ability to step outside of our psychological determinism and view our lives from the position of a spectator. This ability shows a certain, limited, form of freedom.

Tragedy and Relationships

Tragedy can also be seen in the fickle nature of human relationships. Dylan, as a folk singer, spends many of his songs describing the proverbial "one that got away." In "Heart of Mine" (1981), and "Hero Blues" (1963), he speaks with a broken heart. When one has lost love, or has been through a failed relationship, one realizes the confusing, mystifying, nature of love. Pain and regret linger far longer than anyone usually expects. Dylan simply concludes that "Love is Just a Four Letter Word" (1967). The words of the song remind me of John Clare's experience of heartbreak: "I loved, but woman fell away/I hid me from her faded flame/I snatched the sun's eternal ray and wrote till earth was but a name."[27]

It is almost as if one stops loving love once it is lost, and starts blaming love for causing pain: "I was all right 'til I fell in love with you" ("'Til I Fell in Love With You," 1997). This "loathing space" that opens up upon doomed love makes for nostalgia, reminiscence, and melancholy. In this sense, it is something "that opens," although it is an easy temptation to remain in this loathing space indefinitely. One of the tragic characteristics of relationships is that they seem to have a fleeting air about them. They can leave at any given notice. A song of Dylan's, which reminds me of Paul Simon's "Slip Sliding Away," is "Driftin' Too Far from Shore" (1986). In this song, Dylan expresses how relationships can "drift," and, at one point, he moves from worry to expectation.[28] It is as if one comes to expect loss once one has lost.

Tragedy and Religion

So how do these different manifestations of tragedy play on Dylan's religious views? Or, better put, how does tragedy play out in light of Dylan's various religious convictions? For one, it has never been easy to pin a label on Dylan, especially regarding religion. Of course, there is the obvious "evangelical phase" of Dylan's life (1979–81) during which his songs sound like a southern gospel preacher, but this does not tell us much. Even before this period, Dylan utilized religious language and metaphor to express his thought. As two scholars have noted, "Almost from the start, Dylan's criticism of American society worked in a prophetic vein. Envisioning a secular world characterized by wealth, privilege, and power, Dylan associated social status with corruption, speaking as a latter-day Jeremiah."[29] Yet, in his early period, this kind of religious enthusiasm was on par with a liberal, social, gospel of peace, equality, and freedom. There was nothing explicitly conservative or evangelical in this approach.

Similarly, his later years are marked with a certain tolerance and forbearance not found in those couple of evangelical years. His lyrics remain saturated with religious imagery, but with a certain moderation. So, when asking how tragedy interacts with Dylan's religious views, we have to first choose the Dylan about which we are speaking. We also have to determine the strokes with which to paint Dylan: Is he a leftist-liberal or evangelical Christian? Prophet of the social gospel or conservative, folk, Christian? Is he a moralist or a postmodernist? Answering any of these questions forces us to simplify Dylan. How we answer this also has an effect on the way we interpret Dylan's view of tragedy and religion. In *Dylan Redeemed*, Stephen Webb notes the very point I am making: "Dylan's Christian period was not an unlikely development in his musical and spiritual journey. It looks unnatural only to those who let a leftist political perspective dominate their interpretation of his work."[30] This also works conversely: it is tempting to write off his leftist philosophy as something premature, if one prefers to interpret Dylan as a conservative Christian songwriter.

I think the balanced interpretation is to see Dylan in fluidity. He, like everyone else, has changed his views over time. His work is fundamentally protean and mutable. In light of this, I prefer to accept certain paradoxes in Dylan's thought. The most obvious paradox concerns death and the afterlife. In certain songs Dylan expresses a straightforward belief in the soul's afterlife ("In the Summertime" [1981]),[31] and in "Are You Ready" (1980) Dylan asks the listener if he or she has made the decision to be in either hell or heaven.[32] Other times, as in "Going, Going, Gone," Dylan hints at the tragedy and finality of death.[33] Like the writer of Ecclesiastes who says, "For the living know that they will die, but the dead know nothing,"[34] Dylan hints that death is, in fact, the end ("Hero Blues" [1963]).[35] In the latter type of songs, Dylan acknowledges what Jaspers calls "absolute and radical tragedy," and in the former he holds a belief in Christian salvation, which, according to Jaspers, "opposes tragic knowledge."[36] In the 1990s, Dylan had this to say about religion:

> I find the religiosity and philosophy in the music. I don't find it anywhere else. Songs like "Let Me Rest on a Peaceful Mountain," or "I Saw the Light"— that's my religion. I don't adhere to rabbis, preachers, evangelists, all of that. I've learned more from the songs than I've learned from any of this kind of entity. The songs are my lexicon. I believe the songs.[37]

More recently, Dylan has developed an interest in the Jewish Hasidic movement Chabad Lubavitch. So the question really becomes, which Dylan do *we* prefer?

It may also be that Dylan goes against Jaspers' interpretation of Christian salvation and tragedy. Dylan may be telling us that Christian salvation does not oppose tragic knowledge, or, at least, the tragic sense of life. Just think of the inner torment felt by Christians such as Augustine and Luther, as well as the outer torment felt by the early martyrs and Jesus himself. Even if there was an afterlife, it would not negate the tragic nature of this life and this world. Sin, rebellion, Satan, demons, pain, hell, and judgment are all tragic, even though they are not entirely tragic. They are tragic *experientially*. But, does the fact that, in Christianity, nothing is completely or utterly tragic, negate the reality of experiential tragedy? I do not think so. Does the fact that God controls all things (in the traditional sense of omnipotence) erase radical tragedy? I am of the opinion that it does. I think Dylan is aware of this conundrum and responds to it with appropriate caution and agnosticism. He would not abandon radical tragedy for teleology or visa versa. If he did, he would not be the same paradoxical Dylan.

In conclusion, Bob Dylan's vision of tragedy is a lens through which one may view the world around us. It is a world saturated with the tragic sense of life. Like Nietzsche's idea of the "eternal return of the same," Dylan reminds us that the world is forever changing and yet condemned to repeat itself. His lyrics tell us of the pain and loss associated with politics, relationships, and religion. The central difficulty into which we are thrown involves our responses to death and tragedy. How we deal with death and tragedy reveals our basic values, our philosophy of life. It is this philosophy, our perspective on life, that Dylan pushes us to keep fresh and willing, with the hope that it will never become stagnant with bigotry and similarity.

Notes

1 Aristotle, *Poetics*, trans. Richard Janko (Cambridge, Massachusetts: Hackett Publishing Company, 1987), 7

2 Arthur Schopenhauer, *The World as Will and Representation*, trans. E. F .J. Payne (New York: Dover Publications, Vol. I, 1966), 252

3 One of the best takes on tragedy, though forty years old, is Walter Kaufman's *Tragedy and Philosophy* (Garden City, New York: Anchor Books, 1969). For what I mean by *sense*, see Miguel de Unamuno, *Tragic Sense of Life*, trans. J. E. Crawford Flitch (New York: Dover Publications, 1954). For a look at what the criteria for tragedy have been, as well as challenges to them, see Oscar Mandel, *A Definition of Tragedy* (Lanham, Maryland: University Press of America, 1982), 1–23.

4 Sean Wilentz, *Bob Dylan in America* (New York: Doubleday, 2010), 50.

5 Cynthia Whissell, "Emotional Fluctuations in Bob Dylan's Lyrics Measured By the Dictionary of Affect Accompany Events and Phases in His Life," *Psychological Reports* (2008): 102, 483.

6 Michael Roos and Don O'Meara, "Is Your Love in Vain?—Dialectical Dilemmas in Bob Dylan's Recent Love Songs," *Popular Music*, Vol. 7, No. 1 (January 1988): 39.

7 Bob Dylan, *Lyrics: 1962–2001* (New York: Simon & Schuster, 2004), 566.

8 Dylan, *Lyrics*, 451.

9 Dylan, *Lyrics*, 5, 450, 528.

10 Karl Jaspers, *Philosophy*, Vol. II, trans. E. B. Ashton (Chicago, Illinois: The University of Chicago Press, 1948), 178.

11 Dylan, *Lyrics*, 401.

12 Martin Luther, *On the Bondage of the Will*, trans. J. I. Packer and O. R. Johnston (London: James Clark & Co., 1957), 102

13 B. B. King, *Indianola Mississippi Seeds*, CD, track 7, "Chains and Things" © 1970 MCA.

14 Dylan, *Lyrics*, 273, 288.

15 Dylan, *Lyrics*, 318.

16 Dylan, *Lyrics*, 16.

17 Dylan, *Lyrics*, 1997, and Arthur Schopenhauer, *Studies in Pessimism*, trans. T. Bailey Saunders (St. Clair Shores, Michigan: Scholarly Press, 1893), 12.

18 Dylan, *Lyrics*, 20.

19 Dylan, *Lyrics*, 525.

20 Dylan, *Lyrics*, 469, 514.

21 Dylan, *Lyrics*, 19.

22 Dylan, *Lyrics*, 105.

23 Dylan, *Lyrics*, 55.

24 Dylan, *Lyrics*, 46.

25 Dylan, *Lyrics*, 53.

26 Martin Van Hees, "The Free Will in Bob Dylan," in Peter Vernezze and Carl J. Porter, eds., *Bob Dylan and Philosophy* (Chicago: Open Court, 2006), 123.

27 John Clare, "A Vision" in *English Romantic Verse* (New York: Penguin Books), 273.

28 Dylan, *Lyrics*, 507.

29 Clifton R. Spargo and Anne K. Ream, "Dylan and Religion," in *The Cambridge Companion to Bob Dylan* (Cambridge, U.K.: Cambridge University Press, 2009), 88.

30 Stephen H. Webb, *Dylan Redeemed* (New York: Continuum Books, 2006), 7.

31 Dylan, *Lyrics*, 449.

32 Dylan, *Lyrics*, 443.

33 Dylan, *Lyrics*, 318.

34 Ecclesiastes 9:5, Revised Standard Version.

35 Dylan, *Lyrics*, 40.

36 Karl Jaspers, *Tragedy Is Not Enough*, trans. Harald A. T. Reiche, Harry T. Moore, and Karl W. Deutsch (North Haven, Connecticut: Archon Books, 1969), 38. I would like to thank Sir Christopher Ricks for his helpful editorial and academic advice.

37 David Gates, "Dylan Revisited," *Newsweek*, 6 October 1997.

8

A SCREAMING COMES ACROSS THE DIAL

Country, Folk, and Atomic Protest Music[1]

John Cline and Robert G. Weiner

Figure 8.1   Teenagers taking part in a protest march against nuclear tests and the war in front of the White House.

When the United States dropped the two atomic bombs on Hiroshima and Nagasaki in 1945, the world entered a nuclear era—the age of the Bomb. Although much has been written about the political dimensions of life in the shadow of the Bomb, less attention has been paid to the way that its lingering presence infiltrated the larger cultural imagination. There are, of course, some well-known Bomb-themed

Hollywood films, such as *On the Beach* (1959) and *Dr. Strangelove* (1964). However, little scholarly focus has been placed on the manifestations of the Bomb mindset in music. In this chapter, we examine the surprisingly pervasive Bomb-themed songs released between (roughly) 1945 and 1965, primarily through the genres of commercial country music (and its gospel variant) and "folk" music, specifically of the type pioneered by Woody Guthrie that reached its apotheosis with Bob Dylan. This period corresponds to the span between Hiroshima and Nagasaki and the Cuban Missile Crisis, when concern regarding nuclear weapons was at its highest point. Using song lyrics as primary source material, with country and folk being the main topical styles, this chapter attempts to answer these questions: What kinds of responses to the Bomb do we find in song during that twenty-year span? How do country songs about the Bomb differ from folk songs about the Bomb? What, if any, other types of music took on the Bomb? And, finally, what became of atomic protest music in the era of *détente* and after the fall of the Berlin Wall?

In Context

Although this chapter focuses on country and folk music as specific genres, the distinction between the two is not always clear. When someone says "country music," we can understand this term as indicating what musicologist John Wheat describes as a "stylized and commercial" genre. Its lineage dates back to the early 1920s, insofar as it was a self-conscious marketing category created by the recording industry—though "hillbilly" was then the preferred nomenclature. By contrast, Wheat describes folk musicians as self-taught and non-commercial, adding his assertion that folk music has been a voice for political ideas and activism.[2] This is far more problematic than his definition of country music and is representative of the slipperiness of the idea of "folk" within much of the literature. Since there are no conservatories for country music, we can assume that the genre's participating musicians are self-taught, as well. It also is difficult to see how the ballads of Appalachia are political in any explicit way, and the mere fact of recording belies any absolute interpretation of folk's "non-commercial" character. Furthermore, on a strictly sonic level, country and folk would seem to share some common ancestors in the predominantly white, region-specific, pre-recording era musical cultures of the U.S.—especially those that utilized acoustic string instruments. So what's the difference?

Primarily, it's a matter of lyrical content. As John Greenway suggests, all songs are "affected by the times and circumstances, cultural changes and surroundings" of their moment of creation.[3] At the same time, since all music is imbedded in complex processes of exchange, financially lucrative or otherwise, songs, especially in the era of recorded music, are used to sell certain "traits, attitudes and remedies" back to the world from which they sprang.[4] In the case of country music, this has typically meant reaffirming pre-existing values within U.S. culture. In the 1920s and 1930s, there was a general trend toward "traditional" (or, really, conservative) ideas about gender roles, family dynamics, and religious beliefs. By the 1940s, however, country music began to include rather explicitly political songs whose ideology was akin to the "consensus history" being proffered by people like Richard Hofstadter in the same period. Included among these were the Bomb songs, to which the next section is devoted.

At the same time, the first recordings by artists like Woody Guthrie were being released, inaugurating "folk" as a coherent genre in the same way that the Carter Family and Jimmie Rodgers had for country in the 1920s. In contrast to country music's consensus politics, however, folk music under the definition established in the postwar period was premised on dissent from normative values, even when the lyrical themes were not topical. Dissent is, unsurprisingly, less profitable than consensus, which has led to the faulty assumption that folk music is "non-commercial." Both folk and country music are actively engaged with "selling" something: records, ideas, etc., with variable end-goals and emphases regarding each. This was especially true in the postwar period, including those songs from each genre that engaged with the idea of the Bomb, and the political poles that country and folk represent continue to be evident today.

However, immediately after the dropping of the bombs on Hiroshima and Nagasaki, many (if not most) Americans felt that Truman's decision was for the good of the United States, viewing atomic energy as something that would eventually transform it "for the better."[5] During the late 1940s, and into the 1950s, this kind of positive view of technological advances helped spawn a fad for all things "atomic." As historian H. Bruce Franklin points out, as early as 1946 American culture had also become so enamored of its own burgeoning "Atomic Age" that "scores of businesses and dozens of racehorses" had been named for the particle. There were "Atomic Cocktails, and Atomic Earrings [...] General Mills was offering an 'Atomic Bomb Ring'" as a prize in their cereal boxes.[6] There was even a jazz record label called Atomic Records, and new dances were named things like the "Atomic Boogie" and the "Atomic Polka." Jazz and early rock 'n' roll songs had titles like "Atomic Cocktail," "Atomic Love," "Atom Buster," and "Atomic Bomb Baby."[7] All of these examples reflect a kind of postwar "bomb craze" that exploited the power of the atom in the public's imagination as a positive metaphor for all manner of the quotidian. While the musical examples cited above have little to do with the way either country or folk songs dealt with the topic—since they actually considered the ramifications of the Bomb, positively or negatively—they are still worth mentioning as part of a wider cultural context in which the more relevant, topical, songs emerged.[8]

Country's Consensus

The first country song released that details the Bomb is "When the Atom Bomb Fell," (1946) by Karl Davis and Harty Taylor. In it, the Bomb is viewed as the means to end the war and the "answer to our fighting boys' prayers."[9] Lines like this are indicative of what sociologist R. Serge Denisoff refers to as "persuasion songs." These songs "reinforce the value structure of individuals who are active supporters of ingrained social movements or ideologies."[10] Ingrained ideologies are, by their very nature, conservative, and the desire to see WWII end was not necessarily pacifistic, especially when gauged against the triumphant sense of techno-centric military might that coincided, for many, with the bombing of Japan. Country music was especially suited to reflect and reinforce this attitude because, as Denisoff suggests, not only did the musicians themselves tend to be politically and culturally conservative, but also so did the radio stations that promoted the artists' songs.[11] Furthermore, U.S. officials were not averse to using these artists in a mutually beneficial way. In this, Bomb-themed country songs can best be understood as "anti-protest music."

Fred Kirby, who toured radio stations during the war as the government's "Victory Cowboy," also wrote one of the most important Bomb songs: "Atomic Power." Although written the morning after the Bomb was dropped on Hiroshima, the song was not released until 1946. Nevertheless, it was an immediate hit, and within three weeks was also recorded by additional artists: the Buchanan Brothers, Riley Shepard, Rex Allen, and Red River Dave, with several other covers coming later.[12] An ad for the song appeared in *Billboard* magazine, stating that the "Whole World Is Talking About ATOMIC POWER," and claimed that "Atomic Power" was one of the greatest songs to come along in twenty years.[13] Further ads, running under the title, "Atomic Power News," kept fans abreast of the song's success.[14] As musicologist Charles K. Wolfe points out, "Kirby, for his part, was working in a songwriting tradition that was conventionally moralistic."[15] "Atomic Power" asserts that the United States was right to bomb Japan: "Hiroshima and Nagasaki paid a big price for their sins."[16] Both "When the Atom Bomb Fell" and "Atomic Power" reflect this same anti-Japanese sentiment, with references to "cruel Japs" and making them pay "for their sins."[17]

Although allies during the war, relations between the U.S. and the Soviet Union turned hostile shortly after—the beginning of a "Cold War"—and country songs of the period reflected the anti-communist attitudes that led to the Korean War and gave clout to figures like Joseph McCarthy.[18] In these songs, the use of the Bomb became, according to A. Costandina D. Titus and Jerry Simich, "a political symbol of freedom almost equal to the eagle or the flag. It was a patriotic reminder throughout the Cold War of our efforts to protect the democratic way of life from evil Communist aggression."[19] This attitude was explicitly expressed in songs like Roy Acuff's "Advice to Joe" (1951) and Jackie Doll's "When They Drop the Atomic Bomb" (1951). Doll's song refers to "hardheaded Communists" running scared when MacArthur gets to drop the bomb. In "Advice To Joe," Acuff describes Communists in a similar vein and associates the Soviet dictator with Satan. The "Bomb," in this context, is clearly a tool that the "righteous" could use against the wicked.[20] Fred Kirby's follow-up to "Atomic Power," "When the Hell Bomb Falls" (1950), echoes this sentiment. All three songs assert the United States' moral and military superiority.

Nuclear Jeremiads

At the same time that secular-themed country songs were endorsing the Korean War—and using religious imagery to do it—more gospel-tinged artists were calling into question the consequences of the Bomb's existence. These songs operated as musical "jeremiads," a rhetorical style that has been ingrained into American culture since John Winthrop's famous "City on a Hill" sermon on the *Arbella* in 1630. In summary, the jeremiad follows a tripartite structure: promise, declension, redemption. We (Americans) are a chosen people, but we have fallen away from the duties that come with such a state, and only through a return to the old patterns of devotion to an ideal (God and/or country) will we be worthy of our role as a beacon to the rest of the world. Country music has included religious songs as a subgenre within itself since the larger genre emerged in the 1920s, and numerous country artists have been personally quite devout, often of an evangelical nature—hence, "country-gospel." Thus, it should come as no surprise that the rhetorical form of the jeremiad would find its way into the Bomb songs of the postwar period, since the splitting of the atom is, as many have seen it, "playing God."

However, many of the first country songs that used religious imagery to tackle the Bomb did not follow precisely the jeremiad form. Fred Kirby's "Atomic Power" (1946) tells us that a force such as the Bomb could only come from the "mighty hand of God." His later "When the Hell Bomb Falls" asks the Lord for a "helping hand" to preserve freedom in Korea (1950). Similarly, Hawkshaw Hawkins' "When They Found Atomic Power" (1947) suggests that atomic power came about "when the Lord held out his mighty hand," and praises the scientists who worked on the Manhattan Project. In a sense, these songs are thank-you letters to God for Americans' "reward" following their sacrifice in WWII—an extension of successfully following the path lain out by a jeremiad.

By contrast, Billy Hughes "Atomic Sermon" (1953) follows a more classical jeremiad structure. His song expresses fear of scientists who would use atomic power for evil and destroy mankind. The song goes on to admonish the scientists to be socially responsible and use atomic power for the good of man.

The consequences of not following such warnings were obviously dire, and the possibility of a nuclear holocaust was sometimes compared to the Christian "Judgment Day." As Charles K. Wolfe points out, songs in this vein could use "atomic power as a metaphor to illustrate God's power." He further states that "country music was able to assimilate the atomic metaphor into the values of traditional gospel music."[21] Examples of songs which illustrate this include Whitey and Hogan's "There Is a Power Greater Than Atomic" (1946), Louis Blanchard's "Jesus Hits Like an Atom Bomb" (1949), and The Louvin Brothers' "Great Atomic Power" (1952), which asks listeners if they're ready to meet their maker.[22]

While these "nuclear jeremiads" register a level of dissent regarding the Bomb not found elsewhere in country music, the supposedly greater power of God is always "on our side." Consequently, while such songs are not "anti-protest," they are not genuinely "protestant" either, since, as a "chosen people," Americans have a direct line to the deity either via the Bible or through prayer; in "Brush the Dust from That Old Bible" (1950), Bradley Kincaid expresses the apocalyptic sentiment that people should seek out their savior, and the Harlan County Four tell of speaking to God on an "Atomic Telephone" (1951).[23]

By the mid-fifties, both the pro-Bomb and "nuclear jeremiad" country songs had fallen out of vogue, though the consensus mindset continued to permeate the genre, often invoking—like their historian counterparts—a selectively remembered version of America's past in order to reinforce militaristic and anti-communist values in the present. Among these are Bill Hayes' "Ballad of Davy Crockett" (1955), Connie Francis' "God Bless America" (1959), and Johnny Horton's "Battle of New Orleans" and "Johnny Freedom" (1960).[24] Later songs, like the Spokesmen's "Dawn of Correction" (1965), Johnny Wright's "Hello Vietnam" (1965), Lt. Barry Sadler's "Ballad of the Green Berets" (1966), and Stonewall Jackson's "The Minute Men Are Turning in Their Graves" (1966), reflect not just country musicians' and audiences' approval of the ideas behind Cold War consensus, but actively support their manifestation in the form of the Vietnam War.[25]

Other songs, also written and performed during the Vietnam War, ironically invoked the religious imagery of the Bomb songs of the decade prior, like Dale and Boydon's "Prayer for Peace" (1967), which asks Jesus to bless the bombs we drop in Vietman, and the *Broadside* magazine-published "Are You Bombing Me with Jesus" (1968).[26] Although not nearly as well known, these two songs are of a piece with the folk-inspired rock of Pearls Before Swine's "Uncle John" (1967), Country Joe and the Fish's "I-Feel-Like-I'm-Fixin'-to-Die Rag" (1967), The Bob Seger System's "2+2=?" (1968), and Creedence Clearwater Revival's "Fortunate Son" (1969), each of which identify a fundamental hypocrisy in Mainstreet U.S.A.'s cocktail of "piety 'n' patriotism"—the very same ideology espoused by the aforementioned country songs—as it was deployed in the service of military goals whose horrific consequences were more and more apparent from the nightly news, and in the faraway looks and broken bodies of soldiers returning home.

Dissenting Opinions

The idea of folk music as we've chosen to define it in this chapter has roots that extend most obviously back to the "Popular Front" activities of the 1930s, when Communists and fellow travelers sought to establish a "people's culture" that ran counter to the capitalism that had resulted in a global Depression. Like its later instantiations, this proto-folk music was frequently topical in nature, decrying exploitive working conditions, unfair governmental policies, and politicians' complicity with the business sector. Looking back a little further, one can also see antecedents in the pro-union songs of the early 1900s from artists like the Wobbly Joe Hill, and from them to the earliest manifestations of labor movement culture in the nineteenth century.[27] Consequently, folk music could be said to have dissent in its DNA.

In contrast to the government endorsement bestowed on Fred Kirby, many folk singers (most famously Pete Seeger and the Weavers) were blacklisted, during the McCarthy era, from radio and television performances, which also adversely affected their ability to perform in concert venues. In many cases, the perception that folk musicians were radicals was correct; the legal and ethical justification for their persecution, however, was far more suspect. Still, by the late 1940s, folk music had established itself as a viable genre of commercially recorded music, even if the more financially successful artists were the less overtly political, such as Burl Ives. (The so-called "folk revival" a decade later repeated this hierarchy in its vaunting of the Kingston Trio.) By contrast, organizations such as *People's Songs*—which included Pete Seeger and Alan Lomax—had definite ties with the Communist Party, hindering their message from going out on a wider scale.

Folk musicians' widespread expressions of dissent, of course, extended to the Bomb, seeing it as a problem in need of a solution and not a thing to be celebrated, as was the case with their peers in country music; the rhetoric of such folk songs was very much in "opposition to the status quo."[28] A West Coast newspaperman named Vern Partlow wrote the first folk song about the Bomb. His "Old Man Atom" (1946)—sometimes called "Talking Atomic Blues"—reflects a definite fear of the Bomb and its potential power.[29] The Hollywood singing cowboy band Sons of the Pioneers later recorded this song, although it generated little interest. Even the stature of the group within the country music world could not overcome the fact that "Old Man Atom" was fundamentally an expression of dissent—however watered down—and that had (or has) no place in country music. Nevertheless, Columbia and RCA Victor, both somehow seeing a potential hit, bought the rights to record the song. The song itself was blacklisted in August of 1950:

> [T]he Joint Committee Against Communism [...] informed the record companies that it considered the song subversive [...] The song was immediately withdrawn by the two record companies and was banned from the airwaves.[30]

Apparently, there was strong opposition to a song that pointed out that "All men could be cremated equal!"[31] However, other folk singers did try to make this song part of their repertoire, with ultimately greater success. Historian Robbie Lieberman points out that certain folk music organizations, most famously the unapologetically left-wing *People's Songs* group, frequently performed "Old Man Atom" in the late forties, because they were concerned with

> [H]ow the atom bomb would affect the world's future. Yet the group received little response to songs that called for "peace or the world in pieces." As the cold war developed, speaking out for peace came to be viewed as being pro-Soviet [...] those who might have shared their desire [...] failed to join them.[32]

Because they were blacklisted, the *People's Songs* group only got their message out to a self-selecting few. Still, due in part to their performances, "Old Man Atom" made a comeback during the early 1960s, becoming a staple of the "folk revival."

While he was best known as the "Dust Bowl Balladeer," folk music elder statesman Woody Guthrie himself engaged with the Bomb in several of his compositions. In 1950's "I've Got to Know," he asked, "Why do these bombs drop down from the sky?"[33] Thirteen years later, in an obscure song called "One Little Thing the Atom Can't Do," Guthrie secularized the message of the "nuclear jeremiad," when he expressed his belief that no matter how technologically advanced human beings become, there is nothing greater than human love. Atoms, it seemed, were even less personal than a distant deity.[34]

Other folk songs take a post-apocalyptic view of the world and describe the very human issues affecting life after a nuclear holocaust. These include Bonnie Dobson's "Morning Dew" (1961) and Fred Hellerman and Fran Minkoff's "Come Away Melinda" (1963). According to Dobson, her song takes the "form of a conversation between the last man and woman, post-apocalypse, one trying to comfort the other while knowing there's absolutely nothing left."[35] She was inspired to write the song after seeing the film *On the Beach*.[36] "Come Away Melinda" (1963) depicts a similar situation: "The song is a conversation between a mother and daughter in which the mother answers [her child's questions with the] refrain, 'the answer lies in yesterday, before they had the war.'"[37] Other songs, such as Tom Lehrer's "We Will All Go Together When We Go," take a broader view, but exhibit the same concerns for what life would be like in the wake of the actualization of "mutually assured destruction."

Still other folk musicians addressed the Bomb in more explicitly political terms, calling outright for full disarmament by both the U.S. and the Soviet Union. Although there had been a widespread consensus about the Bomb and atomic power more generally in the immediate wake of Hiroshima and Nagasaki, as the 1950s drew to a close, warnings from scientists like Linus Pauling about the health hazards of nuclear fallout and books like Neville Shute's *On the Beach* (upon which the film was based), contributed to the fragmentation of the old consensus. According to

Douglas T. Miller and Marion Novak's *The Fifties: The Way We Really Were*, people began to feel that their "leaders were unconcerned about them ... [and] began to question the goodness of The Bomb."[38] They add that "nuclear bombs would appear more and more evil" in the years just prior to—and certainly after—the Cuban Missile Crisis.[39] Organizations such as the National Committee for a Sane Nuclear Policy (SANE) were instrumental in organizing anti-Bomb protests, and the "Ban the Bomb" demonstrators began to come "out of their holes ... before each series of nuclear tests." They "saw themselves as humanity's last stand against ultimate annihilation."[40] Folk singers such as Pete Seeger were active in SANE demonstrations, and songs like John Brunner's "H-Bomb's Thunder" (1958) became anthems for protesters of nuclear testing.[41]

Banning the Bomb was a consistent theme throughout many folk songs of the period. They include not only Brunner's "H-Bombs and Thunder," but also Alex Comfort's "First Things First" (1959), Peter Lafarge's "Take Back Your Atom Bomb" (1963), Peggy Seeger and Ewan MacColl's "That Bomb Has Got to Go" (1963), "Doomsday" by Karl Dallas (1966), and Comfort's "Ban, Ban, Ban the Bloody H-Bomb" (1971), who added "If you want to stay alive next year" to the verse containing the title.[42] Dallas concurred, suggesting that "We could have been happy and peaceful. The Bomb could have been banned so easily."[43] In "First Things First," Comfort was even more explicit about this imperative, writing, "We're going to stop the loonies and preserve the human race"; he continues that the banning of the Bomb should be our "highest priority."[44]

To the artists who wrote and sang these songs, the continued testing of bombs, indeed the very existence of them, meant that war was inevitable. They understood the eminent sociologist and incisive social critic C. Wright Mills' argument in the late 1950s that the "immediate cause of World War III is the preparation of it."[45] From this insight followed the quasi-religious understanding of the Bomb as "evil" due to its capabilities for total human annihilation, and the folk songs of the period reflect this attitude—not completely unlike the "nuclear jeremiads" of country music a decade earlier.[46] While the folk musicians and others who marched and sang for nuclear disarmament weren't necessarily "evangelicals" in terms of their religious affiliation, as with the concurrent (and sometimes overlapping) Civil Rights movement, they took full advantage of Christianity's pacifist elements as a means of legitimating their dissent within the rest of American culture. According to Pete Seeger, they saw themselves not just as *against* the Bomb, but also *for* its opposite: "marching and singing for peace."[47]

Seeger, like his mentor Woody Guthrie, was part of an older generation of left-wing dissenters. They had been adults (or, at least, young adults) during WWII. By the early 1960s, the demographic for folk music had changed considerably. As *San Francisco Chronicle* music critic Ralph J. Gleason put it in 1965, the individuals who now attended folk concerts:

[H]ave lived with The Bomb all of their lives. It has been part of their con-sciousness ever since they were aware of anything at all outside their home. They are the true fallout from the blast that changed the world, the real Bomb Babies.[48]

It's little wonder than this new generation of fans and performers would be so con-cerned with the Bomb. Younger musicians like Bob Dylan, Joan Baez, and Phil Ochs began to occupy the space that had been reserved for Seeger and Guthrie, whom they admired greatly. The consequences of this general shift were multi-faceted. On the one hand, some complained that, like a 1962 letter-writer to *Time*, songs about the H-Bomb were replacing songs about labor—the very origins of the topical folk song genre itself.[49] At the same time, a year earlier an article in *Newsweek* pointed out the increasingly diverse connections between the genre and political causes, especially among college students: "Find a campus that breeds Freedom Riders, anti-Birch demonstrators, and anti-bomb societies, and you'll find a folk group."[50] This genera-tional shift identified within the "dissenting class" is the very essence of what came to be understood as the "New Left." The younger group of singers saw themselves as both allied with the forebears and adapting to a changing world. Phil Ochs exempli-fied this straddling of "old" and "New Left" in his 1964 song "I Ain't Marchin' Any More," in which he writes about mushroom clouds and burning cities.[51]

The implied points of reference in this song are both WWII—which was ended by the bombing of Hiroshima and Nagasaki—and the burgeoning war in Vietnam. Vietnam and the ongoing Civil Rights movement began to supplant the Bomb as major topics within folk song in the mid-1960s. This shift was influenced by the signing of the Limited Test Ban Treaty of 1963, itself both a result of the Cuban Missile Crisis and the first step towards easing nuclear hostilities between the U.S. and the Soviet Union. The Limited Test Ban Treaty was followed by the Nuclear Non-Proliferation Treaty in 1968, which led to the period known as *détente* (lasting between 1971 and the Soviet invasion of Afghanistan in 1979), and finally, following an increase in hostilities during Ronald Reagan's tenure as president, the collapse of the Soviet Union and the end of the Cold War. As a consequence, Bomb-specific songs became less prevalent. In their stead were songs like Bob Dylan's "A Hard Rain's a-Gonna Fall" (1963) and Barry McGuire's "Eve of Destruction" (1965). While both of these songs mention the Bomb, they are not about atomic weapons *per se*; they also tackle issues such as the hate that breeds racism, and war more generally. Each conceives of Vietnam, segregation, and the threat of nuclear annihilation, as part of an interconnected complex of humanity's afflictions, control of which must be wrested from the power elite. Because, as Barry McGuire argues, "If the button is pushed there's no running away."[52]

In summary, folk songs written about the Bomb through the 1960s depicted it in a universally negative light, often going so far as to advocate its banishment. In doing so, these songs were the first to dissent from the consensus regarding nuclear weapons in the United States, and prefigured more widespread opposition within the culture at large—even if they didn't quite convince their more stalwartly conservative colleagues in country music

To the Present

The 1970s and 1980s saw concern for the Bomb extend to nuclear energy after the disasters at Three Mile Island and Chernobyl, and the 1980s, in particular, were a ripe decade for protest song—due in no small part to President Ronald Reagan's flippant attitude toward the use of nuclear weapons. The September 1979 *No Nukes: The Muse Concerts for a Non-Nuclear Future* at Madison Square Garden in New York, featuring such artists like Bruce Springsteen, Jackson Browne, Bonnie Raitt, the Doobie Brothers, Crosby, Stills, and Nash, Tom Petty, and many others, were, in a sense, a grand finale to the atomic protest folk songs of the 1960s. Although folk music has survived to the present day, by the early 1980s it was clear that emerging genres such as punk and metal would take up the mantle of protest.

Punk, or punk-inspired artists such as the Dead Kennedys, Billy Bragg, Orchestral Manoeuvres in the Dark, and Crass, all released anti-nuke songs in the decade, most following the rhetorical template established by their folk predecessors. Although heavy metal perhaps engaged even more fully with the Bomb, its relationship was far more complex, akin to the "nuclear jeremiads" of a preceding generation. Starting with genre pioneer Black Sabbath, and extending through Iron Maiden to Megadeth and many, many, others, metal artists seemed to revel in the chaotic imagery of a post-apocalyptic world at the same time that they decried the power that wielded such awesome weapons; the fundamental ambivalence in metal's response to the prospect of a nuclear holocaust is not far from that master of the jeremiad, Jonathan Edwards, and his 1741 sermon "Sinners in the Hands of an Angry God," which too could be understood as delighting in the details of destruction at the same time that it issued dire warnings. Country music has not taken up the topic of nuclear war in any sustained way for a long time, though songs like Toby Keith's "Courtesy of the Red, White, & Blue" are quick reminders that country's consensus past is its present, too.

Postscript

In 2004, the UK record label Chrome Dreams released *Like an Atom Bomb: Apocalyptic Songs from the Cold War Era*, featuring some of the songs discussed in this chapter on one CD. In 2005, this concept was expanded with the German Bear Family label's box set, titled *Atomic Platters: Cold War Music from the Golden Age of Homeland Security*, with five CDs (four featuring music and historical sound bites and one featuring 2 vintage spoken word albums), one DVD (of historical clips and public service announcements related to all things atomic), and a lavish hardback book annotating each of the tracks.[53] Also in 2005, the National Nuclear Security Administration released a short pamphlet called "Atomic Culture," featuring a listing of songs: *The Atomic Hit Parade*.[54] Prior to this, the types of Bomb songs mentioned here were available only on the original (and out of print) releases, and the LP and cassette versions of the soundtrack to the film *Atomic Café* (1982), also out of print. Consequently, greater awareness of the history and legacy of atomic protest music has become possible for a general audience.

Notes

1 This chapter is a major revision of Robert G. Weiner, "Atomic Music: Country Conservatism and Folk Discount," in Dennis Hall, ed., *On The Culture of the American South: Studies in Popular Culture*, Vol. 19, No. 2 (October 1996): 217–235.

2 John Wheat, Musicologist from the Baker Texas Historical Center. Notes taken from telephone interview, 1 May 1992.

3 John Greenway, *American Folksongs of Protest* (New York: Perpetua, 1960), 3.

4 Mike Reegen, "Pious Rhetoric of Country Music," *The Music Journal*, No. 27 (January 1969): 50.

5 Paul Boyer, *By the Bomb's Early Light: American Thought and Culture at the Dawn of the Atomic Age* (New York: Pantheon Books, 1985), 135–136.

6 H. Bruce Franklin. *War Stars: The Superweapon and the American Imagination* (New York: Oxford University Press, 1988), 157.

7 Richard Aquila, "Sh'Boom; or, How Early Rock & Roll Taught Us to Stop Worrying and Love the Bomb," in Alison M. Scott and Christopher D. Geist, eds., *The Writing on the Cloud: American Culture Confronts the Atomic Bomb* (Lanham, Maryland: University Press of America, 1997), 106–118.

8 A. Costandina D. Titus and Jerry Simich, "From 'Atomic Bomb Baby' To 'Nuclear Funeral,' Atomic Music comes of Age, 1945–1990," *Popular Music and Society*, Vol. 14, No. 4 (Winter 1990): 25; and Boyer, *By the Bomb's Early Light*, 10–11.

9 Karl David and Harty Taylor, "When the Atom Bomb Fell" from the *Atomic Café Soundtrack*, cassette, track 2, © 1982, Rounder 1034; and Titus, "From 'Atomic Bomb Baby,'" 13.

10 R. Serge Denisoff, *Sing a Song of Social Significance* (Bowling Green, Ohio: Popular Press 1983), 2; Irwin Stambler and Grelun Landon, *Encyclopedia of Folk, Country, and Western Music* (New York: St. Martin's Press 1969), 4, 129, 165, 181; and Boyer, *By the Bomb's Early Light*, 25.

11 Denisoff, *Sing a Song*, 136, and Mike Reegen, "The Pious Rhetoric of Country Music," *The Music Journal*, Vol. 27 (January 1969): 70.

12 Michael Scheibach, *Atomic Narratives and American Youth* (Jefferson, North Carolina: McFarland, 2003), 173.

13 *Billboard*, Vol. 18, No. 21 (25 May 1946): 38.

14 *Billboard*, Vol. 58, No. 23 (8 June 1946): 25.

15 Charles K. Wolfe, "Nuclear Country: The Atom Bomb in Country Music." *Journal of Country Music*, Vol. 4, No. 4 (January 1978): 12; and Wolfe, "Jesus Hits Like an Atom Bomb: Nuclear Warfare in Country Music 1944–56" in Charles K. Wolfe and James E. Akenson, eds., *Country Music Goes to War* (Lexington, Kentucky: University Press of Kentucky, 2005), 102–115. A different take on Atomic Music was also published by Joseph C. Ruff, "Are You Ready for the Great Atomic Power? The Bomb and Music 1945–1960," in Alison M. Scott and Christopher D. Geist, eds., *The Writing on the Cloud: American Culture Confronts the Atomic Bomb* (Lanham, Maryland: University Press of America, 1997), 119–138.

16 Fred Kirby, quoted in Wolfe, "Nuclear Country," 11–12.

17 Karl Davis, *Atomic Café Soundtrack*; Fred Kirby, quoted in Wolfe, "Nuclear Country," 11–12; and Boyer, *By the Bomb's Early Light*, 25.

18 Jens Lund, "Country Music Goes to War: Songs for the Red Blooded American," *Popular Music and Society*, Vol. 1, No. 4 (Summer 1972): 212.

19 Titus, "From 'Atomic Bomb Baby,'" 18.

20 Jackie Doll, "When They Drop the Atomic Bomb" from the *Atomic Café Soundtrack*, cassette, track 6, © 1982, Rounder 1034; and Roy Acuff quoted in Wolfe, "Nuclear County," 19.

21 Wolfe," Nuclear Country," 15.

22 C. Louvin, I. Louvin, and B. Bain, "Great Atomic Power," quoted in Wolfe, "Nuclear Country," 14–17.

23 Wolfe, "Nuclear Country," 15.

24 Richard Aquila, *That Old Time Rock & Roll: A Chronicle of an Era: 1953–1963* (New York: Schirmer Books, 1989), 23, 25, 137.

25 Reegen, "The Pious Rhetoric," 50, 68, 70; and Lund, "Country Music," 214, 218–220.

26 Ralph Dale, "Prayer for Peace" in Barbara Dale and Irwin Silber, eds., *The Vietnam Songbook* (New York: Guardian Books, 1969), 11; Timothy E. Scheurer, *Born in the USA: The Myth of America in Popular Music from Colonial Times to the Present* (Jackson, Mississippi: University of Mississippi Press, 1991), 175; and Sis Cunningham and Gordon Friese, eds., *Broadside Volume III* (New York: Oak Publications, 1970).

27 Phil Hood, ed., *Artists of American Folk Music* (New York: Quill, 1986), 6.

28 Denisoff, *Sing a Song*, 3, 25, 27; and Elizabeth J. Kizer, "Protest Songs as Rhetoric," *Popular Music and Society*, Vol. 9, No. 4 (Summer 1972): 3, 6.

29 Vern Partlow quoted in Wanda Wilson Whitman, ed., *Songs that Changed the World* (New York: Crown Publications, 1969), 144.

30 Oscar Brand, *The Ballad Mongers: Rise of the Modern Folk Song* (New York: Funk & Wagnalls, 1962), 134.

31 Brand, *The Ballad Mongers*, 134.

32 Robbie Lieberman, *My Song is My Weapon: People Songs, American Communism and The Politics of Culture 1930–1950* (Chicago: University of Illinois Press, 1989), 109.

33 Woody Guthrie, "I've Got to Know," in Pete Seeger, *Bells of Rhymney & Other Songs from the Singing of Pete Seeger* (New York: Oak Publications, 1964), 53.

34 Woody Guthrie, "One Little Thing the Atom Can't Do" in Pete Seeger, *The Incompleat Folksinger*, ed., Jo Metcalf Schwartz (New York: Simon and Schuster, 1972), 240.

35 *Golden Road*, Vol. 1, No. 1 (Spring 1983): 12.

36 Daniel Gonczy, "The Folk Music Movement of the 1960s: Its Rise and Fall," *Popular Music and Society*, Vol. 10, No. 1 (Spring 1985): 20.

37 Titus, "From 'Atomic Bomb,'" 21.

38 Douglas T. Miller and Marion Novak, *The Fifties: The Way We Really Were* (New York: Doubleday & Company Inc., 1977), 59, 61.

39 Miller and Marion Novak, *The Fifties*, 59, 61.

40 David Pichaske, *A Generation in Motion: Popular Music and Culture in the Sixties* (New York: Schirmer Books, 1979), 28, 30.

41 John Brunner, "The H-Bomb's Thunder," in Pete Seeger, "From Aldermaston to London: They Walked and Sang For Peace," *Sing Out* (December/January 1960/61): 14.

42 Alex Comfort, "Ban, Ban, Ban The Bloody H-Bomb," in Tom Glazer, ed., *Songs Of Peace, Freedom and Protest* (New York: David McKay Company, 1971), 16–18.

43 Karl Dallas "Doomsday," in Student Peace Union, eds., *Songs for Peace* (New York: Oak Publications, 1966), 60; Peggy Seeger's "There's Better Things to Do" (1960); Enoch Kent's "Man With the Knob" (1962); and Sheldon Harnick's "The Merry Minute" (1960).

44 Alex Comfort, "First Things First," in Pete Seeger, "From Aldermaston," 17.

45 C. Wright Mills quoted in Miller and Nowak, *The Fifties*, 56.

46 Kizer, "Protest Songs," 6.

47 Seeger, "From Aldermaston," 14–16.

48 Ralph Gleason, "The Times They Are a Changin'," *Ramparts*, Vol. 3, No. 7 (April 1965): 36–48.

49 Robert Juran, Letter in *Time*, Vol. 79, No. 3 (19 January 1962): 7.

50 *Newsweek*, Vol. 58, No. 22 (27 November 1961): 84.

51 Phil Ochs, "I Ain't Marchin' Any More," in Wanda Wilson Whiteman, ed., *Songs That Changed the World* (New York: Crown Publications, 1969), 153.

52 P. F. Sloan, "Eve of Destruction" in David Rosen, *Protest Songs in America* (Westlake Village, California: Aware Press, 1972), 126.

53 Various Artists, "Like an Atom Bomb: Apocalyptic Songs from the Cold War Era (BZCD 0003; Chrome Dreams, 2004); Various Artists, *Atomic Platters: Cold War Music from the Golden Age of Homeland Security*, Bear Family Records, 2005. BCD 16065. See the website http://www.atomicplatters.com/.

54 National Nuclear Security Administration: U.S. Department of Energy, *Atomic Culture* (2005), http://purl.access.gpo.gov/GPO/LPS100997, accessed 20 May 2012).

9

A SOUL MESSAGE

R & B, Soul, and the Black Freedom Struggle

James Smethurst

Figure 9.1 Curtis Mayfield.

One way of thinking about the evolution of R & B and Soul music in the civil rights and Black Power/Black Arts eras is as political and aesthetic convergence. On one end, you have R & B artists who become increasingly interested in the new politics of civil rights and Black Power and the new artistic forms of free jazz and the emerging Black Arts Movement. In part, you might say that they are responding to political changes in their core audience. Popular artists have a way of addressing the moment. So, for example, James Brown's "Say It Loud" can be seen, in part, as engaging tropes and sentiments of black pride (emerging out of Black Power/Black Arts) that were widely circulating among African Americans in the late 1960s. Moreover, this is not simply a smart career move on the part of the artists, but often also a deeply felt statement. After all, these artists are black, live in the black community, and were intensely affected by Jim Crow and racism—the problems of touring and performing in the South. As a result, many felt strongly moved by the efforts of the civil rights and Black Power Movements. For example, the civil rights movement, Malcolm X, and the success of Peter, Paul, and Mary's version of Bob Dylan's "Blowing in the Wind," had an enormous impact on Sam Cooke, who felt that, if they were taking that stand, so should he: he recorded "A Change Is Gonna Come" in 1963.[1] Similarly, the excitement of free jazz led many of these R & B artists, especially as they were encouraged by their backing musicians, to include avant-garde jazz elements in their work, to reference iconic jazz musicians (especially John Coltrane), and to assume the stance that their music was aesthetically serious and able to engage serious social issues, a stance significantly derived from post-bebop jazz artists.

At the other end, you have Black Arts and Black Power activists, especially in the Northeast and the South, seeing in R & B the voice and spirit of the people. Nearly all of these activists grew up in urban black communities listening to black popular music. Thus, Askia Touré writes about R & B as a cultural weapon in the freedom struggle. Amiri Baraka declares that black revolutionary artists should listen not only to politicized R & B musicians like Curtis Mayfield, but also to Major Lance, Martha and The Vandellas, and, of course, James Brown. This new respect for, and theorization of, R & B/soul as music of the black nation inspires Black Arts hybrids, drawing on the resources of R & B/soul, as well as the avant-garde and the black church, to create works that are formally and thematically radical, but also have the familiar sounds and tropes of R & B and soul. A prime example of such a hybrid can be heard in Amiri Baraka's 1972 recording of his poem "It's Nation Time," in which Baraka appears to be trying to answer the poet and critic Larry Neal's question, "Listen to *James Brown scream*. Ask yourself, then: Have you ever heard a Negro *poet* sing *like* that?"[2]

Sounding Soul: Spirit and Politics in the 1950s

Rhythm and blues was really a marketing approach rather than a musical genre or coherent set of genres. Quite simply, it replaced the terms "race records" and "Race Music," denoting popular, and generally secular, music marketed to African Americans, including popular jazz, blues, jump blues, vocal groups (eventually known as "doo wop"), and so on. Like the transformation of "hillbilly" into "country and western," "rhythm and blues" was seen as a more polite, less demeaning, locution than "race music," reflecting new political attitudes and the exponential growth of African Americans as urban consumers in the post-World War II era. Of course, there was a significant white audience for R & B (just as there was a considerable southern black audience for country and western), in large part because, with the growth of stations aimed at the black community, radio reception could not be segregated. This audience increased as the 1950s wore on and the category of rock 'n' roll (to a large extent a marketing term for different strains of R & B by black and white artists aimed at a white audience) emerged. Some black artists, such as Sam Cooke, Jackie Wilson, and Ray Charles became stars on both the R & B and pop music charts. Still, it is worth noting that even Sam Cooke's songs charted noticeably better in the R & B surveys than in pop music. In short, while early R & B significantly emerged out of the urban blues and the bluesier end of swing music, especially that associated with the "Territory Bands" of the Southwest, and was, as the name suggests, generally dance-oriented, as many critics have noted, early R & B is a very eclectic category.[3]

Early R & B was rarely political in any direct way, and R & B singers seldom expressed themselves on social issues, including the civil rights movement, in any direct manner. The nature of their careers made them extremely vulnerable to legal and extralegal political repression. After all, they had seen the career of Paul Robeson destroyed, and Robeson had a big overseas audience. A very large part of their audience was in the urban South; indeed, many of the leading R & B performers lived in the South and Jim Crow border states. At the same time, due to the fact that the average R & B artist was almost constantly on tour, they came into conflict with the most gross aspects of the segregation of public accommodations and with racist white law enforcement personnel and civilians (who often were extremely resentful of the success of better black popular performers) more often than almost any other group of African Americans, even in the South. While some, like Sam Cooke, personally resisted Jim Crow discrimination, generally they, like Cooke, were reluctant to risk their careers (and their lives) by public opposition to Jim Crow in their music. Having said that, it is worth noting that black pride, black community, and black oppression was thematized in the R & B songs of the 1950s, as in Chuck Berry's "Brown-Eyed Handsome Man," Cooke's "Chain Gang," and Howlin' Wolf's "Just My Kind" ("Just my color, oooh you're just my kind").

Of course, a black politics of pride, solidarity, and opposition to racism and Jim Crow was sounded in other ways. One much noted change in R & B that comes about in the 1950s is an increase of overt crossover between black secular and sacred music. Of course, such crossovers of styles, tropes, and personnel had occurred since the earliest days of gospel music. However, black secular performers, most notably Ray Charles, literally transformed gospel songs into secular love songs. Charles, for example, adapted the Silver Tones' "It Must Be Jesus" into "I've Got a Woman," keeping not only the tune but also the emotive feeling of the original gospel song. While many were outraged by such obvious and profane repurposings of the sonic forms and spirit of gospel, Charles sold a lot of records. This period also saw prominent gospel singers cross over into pop careers. No doubt the most prominent was Sam Cooke, who had been a huge gospel star with the Soul Stirrers before his entry into pop/R & B. Thus, one could argue that the sound of the spirit or soul, however altered for carnal purposes, becomes a notable formal feature of R & B.

It is notable that this increasing foregrounding of a secularized sacred sound and sensibility took place as a similar, but far more politicized phenomena, occurred in jazz, with the rise of hard bop or soul jazz in the late 1950s, with its various invocations of the blues and the black church in its sounds, instrumentation, and song and album titles (e.g., Charles Mingus's "Better Git It in Your Soul" on the 1959 *Mingus Ah Um*, and "Wednesday Night Prayer Meeting" on the 1960 *Blues & Roots*). In part, this was a response to what was seen as a move away from an African American musical and social foundation in cool jazz. While this move to regain a mass black audience for jazz had a commercial aspect, it was also a move toward black pride and black community, engendered in large part by the civil rights movement, resurgent black nationalism, and the rise of the new nations of Africa and Asia in what black radicals were increasingly calling the "Bandung World" after the Afro Asian Conference that took place in 1955.

Some jazz artists placed these movements front and center in their recorded music. One of the first was Sonny Rollins' 1958 *Freedom Suite*, which featured liner notes that clearly connected Rollins' music with political, as well as aesthetic, freedom. Charles Mingus' "Fables of Faubus" attacked the segregationist icon Governor Orville Faubus of Arkansas and the other prominent white supremacists who opposed the civil rights movement, first without lyrics on *Mingus Ah Um* and then with lyrics as "Original Faubus Fables" on *Charles Mingus Presents Charles Mingus* in 1960. Drummer Max Roach released *We Insist! Freedom Now Suite* in 1960. With lyrics by Oscar Brown, Jr. and vocals by Abbey Lincoln, *We Insist!* linked the black freedom movement in the United States with the Pan-African struggle for independence and against apartheid, as did Randy Weston's 1960 *Uhuru Africa* (which included "African Lady" with lyrics by Langston Hughes).

A new sort of black spiritualism with conscious political implications found its way into jazz in more personal ways during the 1950s. Quite a few musicians converted to Islam, especially the Ahmadiyya Muslim Community that is particularly strong in West Africa. Ahmadi converts included Art Blakey, Yusef Lateef, Ahmad Jamal, and McCoy Tyner, who generally linked their religious beliefs to an increased interest in Africa and who (with the exception of Jamal) significantly emerged from the hard bop musical idiom. In short, the politicized sound of soul—indeed "soul" as a term describing a music genre—emerged in jazz as the soul sound in R & B became a key feature of black popular culture; indeed a sort of soundtrack of secular black life. It is worth pointing out in this regard that many R & B singers were great admirers of bebop and post-bop jazz. Some, such as Ray Charles, Stevie Wonder, and Marvin Gaye, made jazz or jazz-pop hybrid singles and albums. Charles recorded with the great jazz vibraphonist Milt Jackson in 1958 and 1961 and the singer Betty Carter in 1961. Also, many R & B instrumentalists, such as Motown's Funk Brothers, leading session musician King Curtis, and James Brown's Famous Flames often had second lives as jazz musicians. These singers and their bands were well aware of the work of Mingus, Roach, and Weston. While there was no obvious "message" to most of the recordings of these R & B artists before the mid-1960s, as Brian Ward notes, this music was significantly about "affirming individual worth within the context of collective black identity and pride," much like the civil rights movement and, indeed, the more Black Power/Black Arts oriented work of the high soul era.[4]

"Keep on Pushin'": The Emergence of the Black Liberation Struggle in R & B

A confluence of events allowed the emergence of a distinct civil rights strain in R & B/soul in the early 1960s. Some of these developments include the previously mentioned overtly political jazz, such as *We Insist* and "Fables of Faubus"; the burgeoning of civil rights sit-ins all across the South, and the formation of the black student movement with significant white support (especially among young people); the 1963 March on Washington; the increasing circulation of black nationalism, especially that of the Nation of Islam and Malcolm X (who was personally acquainted with a number of leading R & B musicians, notably Sam Cooke); increasing dissatisfaction and unrest in urban black communities that would explode in major uprisings in 1964 and 1965 (most famously, but not only, in Harlem in 1964 and Watts in 1965); and the entrance of the more political side of the folk music revival onto the pop music charts, especially Peter, Paul, and Mary's version of Bob Dylan's civil rights anthem "Blowin' in the Wind," which reached number two on the *Billboard* pop music chart in 1963. Dylan's song and its success despite its politics had a big impact on R & B/soul musicians, including Sam Cooke and Stevie Wonder, whose cover of the song reached number one on the R & B charts and number nine on the pop charts in 1966. One might say that both black popular artists and audiences were increasingly politicized, and even, to some extent, radicalized (at least when considered within the relatively narrow political spectrum of Cold War U.S. politics), not only motivating black popular musicians (and white composers and lyricists who wrote for black artists) to create songs with overt (or only slightly coded) civil rights "messages,"—such as the Crystals' 1962 "Uptown," Sam Cooke's 1964 "A Change Is Gonna Come," and The Impressions' 1964 "Keep On Pushin'" and "People Get Ready,"—but giving them the popular support necessary to allow these songs to circulate through the music and broadcast industries.

Cooke's "A Change Is Gonna Come" and The Impressions' "Keep On Pushin'" (written by the group's lead singer and guitarist Curtis Mayfield) are paradigmatic examples of the R & B/emergent soul civil rights songs. One thing they share with Dylan's "Blowin' in the Wind" is a penchant for figurative, often allegorical, language that rarely refers specifically to the particulars of the civil rights struggle—unlike the work of Mingus and Roach, in which actual people, such as Orville Faubus, actual places, such as Johannesburg, and actual historical events, such as slavery and Jim Crow segregation, appear. The closest Cooke gets to such specificity is in the third verse of "A Change," where he touches on segregated movie theaters and public accommodations, albeit still a bit obliquely. However, the audience clearly understood the song to be about the black freedom struggle. Both Cooke's and Mayfield's songs differ sharply from the plaintive "Blowin' in the Wind" in their emphatic gospel inflection—in other words, in their sounding of soul. They also are quite different from Dylan's piece, and in fact almost all of his "protest" *oeuvre*, in that they put the singer/speaker of the song right at the center of the action and, explicitly or implicitly, at the center of a collective "we," whereas Dylan's singer/speaker is more of an observer or commentator. As a result, Cooke and Mayfield put far more emphasis on collective struggle, a new pride, a refusal (to paraphrase Langston Hughes) to defer black dreams any longer, and inevitable—and more or less imminent—triumph.

"Listen to James Brown Scream": Soul, Black Power, and Black Arts

The convergence of the popular and the radical in black music and politics formally and thematically becomes most obvious in the overlapping soul/Black Arts eras from about 1965 to about 1975—though in many respects, this convergence has continued to be standard operating procedure in black popular music ever since, certainly from the rise of hip hop in the late 1970s.[5] As with any musical genre, especially in the African American popular tradition, it is difficult to date the beginning of "soul" as a category precisely. As noted above, the term "soul"—as denoting a politicized return to a distinctly African American sonic, experiential, and spiritual form—goes back to, at least, jazz in the 1950s. Certainly, the use of "soul" in African American popular music to comprehend, though not definitively describe, a positive experiential, emotional, spiritual, and moral quality (growing out of the perseverance over oppression that distinguished black people from white Americans) antedated the common usage of the term "soul music" after 1965, as heard in The Impressions' 1964 "The Woman's Got Soul." By 1967, "soul music" had circulated through popular audiences and the music industry in the United States to appear frequently in song titles on both the soul/R & B and pop music charts. One iconic example is Arthur Conley's "Sweet Soul Music" (written by Conley and Otis Redding), which pays tribute to leading performers and styles of soul, including Lou Rawls, Sam and Dave (whose "Soul Man" was released the same year), Wilson Pickett, Otis Redding, and James Brown. (Interestingly enough, the song does not mention any women, even Aretha Franklin, whose work was, along with that of James Brown, considered the epitome of the soul genre.)

As Black Power and Black Arts grew into increasingly coherent and interlocking movements in the mid-1960s, radical black nationalist artists and intellectuals, long attached to jazz, especially the "free" or "new thing" jazz of such musicians as John Coltrane, Ornette Coleman, Cecil Taylor, Archie Shepp, Milford Graves, and Sun Ra, increasingly linked the jazz avant-garde to R & B/soul, posing R & B/soul as the music of an increasingly militant black nation. Amiri Baraka (then LeRoi Jones) was one of the first black cultural critics (other than Langston Hughes) to make these connections in print, even before his 1965 move from the downtown bohemia of New York's lower east side to Harlem, where he was among the principal founders of the Black Arts Repertory Theater and School (BARTS). In his seminal study of the historical development and meaning of African American music, *Blues People* (1963), Baraka posited a "blues continuum" (a forerunner of his later concept of the "changing same") stretching from the earliest work songs and hollers through the blues, early jazz, swing, bebop, hard bop, and R & B to free jazz. He made a sort of class and nation argument that suggested black music was propelled by a dialectical opposition between the black working class ("blues people"), whose music was marked by a formal and thematic engagement with freedom and rebellion against white domination, and the black middle class who were drawn toward musical assimilation and accommodation in such genres as swing, cool jazz, and "third-stream" hybrids of jazz and European art music. (Baraka also severely criticized hard bop and soul jazz for what he saw as a formal and clichéd use of blues and gospel idioms without the sort of formal freedom that he takes to mark the blues tradition.)

Baraka further developed this notion of R & B/soul as the bedrock of the national culture of the black masses, suggesting that the jazz avant-garde must pay attention to R & B/soul:

> I say this as one way to get into another thing: namely, that even the avant-garde American music suffers when it moves too far from the blues experience. All the young players now should make sure they are listening to The Supremes, Dionne Warwick, Martha and The Vandellas, The Impressions, Mary Wells, James Brown, Major Lance, Marvin Gaye, Four Tops, Bobby Bland, etc., just to see where contemporary blues is; all the really nasty ideas are right there, and these young players are still connected with that reality, whether they understand why or not. Otherwise, jazz, no matter the intellectual bias, moved too far away from its most meaningful sources and resources is weakened and becomes, little by little, just the music of another emerging middle class.[6]

In perhaps the most influential essay about the meaning of African American popular music, and the significance of that music to the work of radical black artists-activists from the Black Arts/Black Power era—"The Changing Same (R & B and New

Black Music)," first published in 1968—Baraka similarly posits R & B as doing much of what the jazz avant-garde was attempting to do in a more self-consciously radical way:

> The songs of R&B, for instance, what are they about? What are the people, for the most part, singing about? Their lives. That's what the New Musicians are playing about, and the projection of forms for those lives.[7]

Music becomes a metonym for black culture generally. Consequently, Baraka declares R & B to be an essential part of revolutionary black culture, of a liberated black nation in the making:

> That what will come will be a *Unity Music*. The Black Music which is jazz and blues, religious and secular. Which is New Thing and Rhythm and Blues. The consciousness of social reevaluation and rise, a social spiritualism. A mystical walk up the street to a new neighborhood where all the risen will live.[8]

Other leading Black Arts activists made much the same point, often anticipating and helping inspire what Baraka would articulate in "The Changing Same." The poet, another BARTS founder, Askia Touré (then Rolland Snellings), himself an R & B singer as a young man, saw R & B as an essential part of a new black politics and a new black consciousness, particularly in the already socially engaged work of such artists as Curtis Mayfield and Sam Cooke. Like Baraka, Touré argued that it was necessary for any serious black radical to see the rebellious impulses and revolutionary potential in R & B and other forms of black popular culture:

> Somewhere along the line, the "Keep On Pushin'" in song, in Rhythm and Blues is merging with the Revolutionary Dynamism of COLTRANE of ERIC DOLPHY of BROTHER MALCOLM of YOUNG BLACK GUERILLAS STRIKING DEEP INTO THE HEARTLAND OF THE WESTERN EMPIRE.[9]

The poet, playwright, and critic Larry Neal, who coined the term "Black Arts Movement," further suggested that Black Arts writers look to the soul performers for a model of the relationship of the revolutionary black artist to the people in "And Shine Swam On," the Afterword to *Black Fire* (1968), undoubtedly the most important Black Arts anthology. The relationship, in Neal's view, encompasses the poetics of performance, style, voice, embodiment, and text:

> What this has all been leading us to say is that the poet must become a performer, the way James Brown is a performer—loud, gaudy and racy. He

must take his work where his people are: Harlem, Watts, Philadelphia, Chicago and the rural south. He must learn to embellish the context in which the work is executed; and, where possible, link the work to all usable aspects of the music. For the context of the work is as important as the work itself. Poets must learn to sing, dance and chant their works, tearing into the substance of their individual and collective experiences. We must make literature move people to a deeper understanding of what this thing is all about, be a kind of priest, a black magician, working juju with the word on the world.[10]

This is all to say that Black Arts critics and cultural theorists not only noted the appearance of a new strain of socially conscious R & B/soul as a marker of the radicalization of the black masses that was seen most dramatically in the urban uprisings of the 1960s, but also provided interpretations of R & B/soul as sounding the new spirit, sacred and profane, and social basis of the emerging black nation that helped open spaces for soul artists to release even more radical and far less figurative records of social protest and black affirmation. There was, perhaps, some irony in this theorization of R & B/soul since, as Craig Werner points out, soul, at least in its early incarnation, was very significantly an interracial affair, with black and white producers, arrangers, songwriters, and studio bands at Motown, Stax, Muscle Shoals, and Atlantic—though these white musicians and music industry workers clearly understood that they were working in a black idiom for a largely black audience—even at Motown.[11] Of course, the black masses themselves understood the music as theirs, reinterpreting and repurposing the sounds, words, and tropes of R & B/soul in moments of sharp rebellion and racial conflict. The cry of "Burn, Baby, Burn" on the streets of Watts in 1965 was drawn from the trademark call of the Magnificent Montague, a leading R & B DJ in Los Angeles, without any prompting, as far as is known, by any organized black radical group. Similarly, Martha Reeves and The Vandellas' 1964 "Dancing in the Street" was widely taken or appropriated by activists, and black people generally, to refer to the uprising that broke out that year as well as to African American protest generally, a connection that Martha Reeves would later deny.

The soul artists themselves became increasingly radicalized as their urban audience became increasingly restless and revolutionary nationalism grew into a major strain in the black community. If revolutionary politics of one kind or another never became the predominant view of the black masses, it certainly was seen as a plausible and sensible position with which the majority of black people felt at least *some* sympathy. Looking back, it is often hard to grasp how touch and go the civil rights movement, challenged by massive Southern (and, often, Northern) resistance, seemed in the mid-1960s. While much of what went on might be thought of as petty Jim Crow in public accommodations (restaurants, buses, hotels, stores, and so on), larger questions, particularly the segregation of public education and voter rights, remained unsettled despite various court decisions and newly enacted laws—most Southern public schools systems (and some Northern systems, as in Boston) would not be effectively desegregated until the 1970s. Civil rights leaders and rank and file workers were arrested, beaten, fire-hosed, bitten by police dogs, bombed, shot, and murdered with shocking frequency. The 1963 bombing of the 16th Street Baptist Church in Birmingham, which killed four girls at choir practice, served as an iconic instance of this massive and ongoing racist violence. Court decisions and laws also seemed unable to touch the hyper-segregation, discrimination, and police violence of the urban ghetto, north and south, east and west. Dr. Martin Luther King, Jr., the Southern Christian Leadership Council, and the Coordinating Council of Community Organizations encountered some of the worst incidents of racist mob violence against the civil rights movement when they marched against slum conditions and for open housing in white neighborhoods during the Chicago Freedom Movement campaign of 1966. The murder of King in 1968 seemed to symbolically foreclose any great further advance of civil rights, prompting urban uprisings across the United States. In short, while we know now that civil rights and the Black Freedom Movement fundamentally changed U.S. society, especially with the growth of affirmative action programs and court-ordered desegregation remedies during the Nixon Administration, the successful implementation of such advances were far from clear in the mid-to-late 1960s.

Consequently, soul artists increasingly spoke directly and concretely to black social existence, black history, black pride, black anger, and black self-determination. Curtis Mayfield, already known for his social engagement, identified closely with Black Power and Black Arts, even as critics from those movements identified Mayfield as an inspiration and, effectively, a brother and comrade. The 1968 "This Is My Country" laid direct claim to a place in the United States based on the oppression, labors, and struggles of African Americans from slavery to the present. The 1970 "Move On Up" was a cry for black self-determination and a revolutionary break from the past; for black people to take their leading place in history. The musical soundtrack that intentionally undercut the visual images, plot, and dialogue of the classic blaxploitation film *Super Fly* (1972) provided a counter-story to plot, undercutting the glorification of the gangster in the figure of the cocaine kingpin, Priest. Like most blaxploitation films, *Super Fly* invoked the anger of the soul/Black Power/Black Arts era, but pointedly elevated the heroic individual/gangster/bad man (or sometimes bad woman, as in the Pam Grier movies) over the movement, which is often represented as somewhat villainous, removed from the masses, or inept. Mayfield's music, to some considerable degree, humanizes *and* deromanticizes the gangster-hero, and restores a sense of the movement and collective action as a positive thing.

James Brown's move to a more radicalized politics and sound was sharper and more abrupt in the Soul era than that of Mayfield, who was already heading in that direction. As seen in Larry Neal's comments, Brown's stripped down, hypnotic, polyrhythms, chant-like songs, deeply meaningful, if not verbal, vocalizations, and dynamic and theatrical visual presentations made him the epitome of an African-descended soul for Black Arts and Black Power. Black avant-gardists like Baraka saw Brown as a resource and model for establishing a vanguard black art that was meaningful to the broader African American community, as seen in the Brown-like vocalizations in Baraka's 1972 recording of "It's Nation Time." In response to this ideological framing of his music, and the movement of his black audience toward active sympathy with revolutionary black nationalist politics, Brown's music took on an increasingly activist tenor, so to speak, breaking with the patriotic sentiments of the 1967 "America Is My Home," which was, in many respects, a rejection of the new nationalism. The 1968 "Say It Loud (I'm Black and I'm Proud)," of course, is the most anthemic and iconic of Brown's Black Power-inflected songs. However, it is only one of many of Brown's socially engaged songs of this era, including "Down and Out in New York City," "Soul Power" (a call for self-determination that is almost diametrically opposed to "America Is My Home"), "Hey America," "Funky President," and "King Heroin."

In addition, if Brown moved into a significantly Black Power/Black Arts modality in his lyrics, he also referenced and incorporated the sounds of the jazz avant-garde so beloved by the new black radicalism. If new jazz players heeded the call of Baraka, Neal, Touré, Sonia Sanchez, and others, to study the R &B/soul artists carefully (and they did, for the most part), Brown's call to "blow me some Trane, brother" on the hit single "Super Bad, Part II" shows an increased and public acknowledgment of the new jazz. Brown's call was answered by Famous Flames saxophonist Robert "Chopper" McCollough, who, like many R & B instrumentalists, doubled as a jazz player with what was, in fact, a free jazz solo.

Aretha Franklin was the only artist who could challenge Brown as the epitome of the soul artist. Her work was more based in the sounds and tropes of gospel music, out of which Franklin came—her father, C.L. Franklin, was one of the most prominent black preachers in the United States, as well as an outstanding singer and supporter of the civil rights movement in Detroit. For the most part, Franklin's music did not move in the direction of overt political statement that Brown's did—one of the exceptions being her 1972 recording of Nina Simone's "To Be Young, Gifted, and Black." (Simone, who was more of a jazz and cabaret singer, and was known as the "grand priestess of soul" for her militant songs, including "Mississippi Goddam," "Four Women," and "To Be Young, Gifted, and Black," served as an example of the engaged artist for black women popular singers.) However, Franklin specialized in giving romantic songs a black feminist cast that resembled the sort of intersectional radicalism of Toni Cade Bambara's 1970 anthology *The Black Woman*. As many critics have noted, in 1967 Franklin transformed Otis Redding's "Respect" from a song of sexual satisfaction to one of black women's empowerment (including sexual empowerment), pushing the movement toward an increased awareness of gender, much like the work of Bambara. Franklin's 1967 take on "Do Right Woman, Do Right Man" (written by two white males, Chips Moman and Dan Penn) was also in much the same vein.

From 1966, or so, onwards, the soul/R & B artists who take on social issues in a direct way are almost too numerous to count. Most of Stevie Wonder's albums from 1966 on featured some sort of political commentary and vignettes of black social life; maybe the most pointed was "Big Brother" from the 1972 album *Talking Book*, which, among other things, highlighted the assassination of black political leaders during the Nixon Administration and predicted the fall of the United States. Many songs of The Isley Brothers ("Freedom," "Harvest," "Fight the Power"), Labelle (covering Thunderclap Newman's "Something in the Air" and Gil Scott Heron's "The Revolution Will Not Be Televised"), George Perkins ("Cryin' in the Streets"), The Chi-Lites ("Give More Power to the People"), Freda Payne ("Bring the Boys Home"), and The Staples Singers ("If You're Ready" and "Respect Yourself") were infused with a Black Power/Black Arts revolutionary spirit and ethos in the early 1970s. Motown artists who (other than Stevie Wonder) showed little inclination in that direction released similar songs, including The Supremes' "Love Child," The Temptations' "Cloud Nine" and "Ball of Confusion," and Marvin Gaye's "What's Going On," "Inner City Blues," and "Mercy Mercy Me."

Even with the decline of soul in the 1970s, with the rise of funk, disco and hip hop, the notion of black popular music as both socially and aesthetically serious—a notion that would have been practically laughable in most critical circles prior to 1964—became commonplace. The idea that popular music should be "real"— should express the social, emotional, and spiritual realities of African Americans, as well as their aspirations—was so widely held that it became almost cliché in the hip hop era, which began, in many respects, as a sort of marriage of R & B, soul, and funk (many of whose leading artists, such as Earth, Wind, and Fire and Chaka Khan emerged directly out of Black Arts institutions) with Jamaican Sound System and toasting. Even in the earliest days of rap, before the birth of consciousness hip hop as a recognized sub-genre, quite a few of the DJs and rappers, such as DJ Afrika Bombaataa, saw rap and its subculture in terms of a sort of black (and Puerto Rican) unity derived largely from the Black Power/Black Arts/soul era.

This convergence of the radical and the popular can also be seen in the continuing engagement of the black visual arts, art dance, music, theater, and literature with the sounds, tropes, and styles of black popular music. Even the notion of "post-soul" art and thought grows out of the Black Power/soul moment in much the same manner that post-Marxism comes out of Marxism and postmodernism out of modernism. This is particularly true of the more politically engaged of these artists, who not only draw on current black popular music, but pay homage to the Black Power/Black Arts/soul era, looking back as they look forward. One of the most impressive projects in this regard is *The Inside Songs of Curtis Mayfield*, a collaboration of younger neo-free jazz bassist William Parker, and his band, with Amiri Baraka, that, among other things, mixes new jazz, spoken word, soul, and gospel, and was released on a live 2007 recording.

To sum up: R & B/soul had an enormous impact on the shape of the political and cultural moment of the 1960s and 1970s and vice versa. Black Arts activists and theorists helped shape how R & B artists thought of their art, and one might even say that, by the 1970s, certain R & B artists, such as Curtis Mayfield, Stevie Wonder, and (perhaps) Marvin Gaye, thought of themselves as part of the movement. In turn, the entrance of radical black thought into black popular music ultimately had an enormous and transformative impact on how African Americans (and ultimately all Americans) understood the work of popular music, popular culture, and art.

Notes

1 Peter Guralnick, *Dream Boogie: The Triumph of Sam Cooke* (Boston: Little, Brown, 2005), 537–554.

2 LeRoi Jones (Amiri Baraka) and Larry Neal, eds., *Black Fire: An Anthology of Afro-American Writing* (New York: Morrow, 1968), 653.

3 Portia Maultsby, "Rhythm and Blues" in *African American Music*, ed., Mellone V. Burnim and Portia K. Maultsby (London: Routledge, 2006), 245.

4 Brian Ward, *Just My Soul Responding: Rhythm and Blues, Black Consciousness, and Race Relations* (Berkeley, California: University of California Press, 1998), 185.

5 For a different take on R & B/soul, black consciousness, and black politics that posits a disjuncture between the Black Arts Movement and African American popular music during the Black Power/Black Arts era, see Ward, *Just My Soul*.

6 Amiri Baraka (LeRoi Jones), *Black Music* (New York: Morrow, 1967), 125.

7 Baraka, *Black Music*, 190–191.

8 Baraka, *Black Music*, 240.

9 Askia Touré, "Keep On Pushin': Rhythm & Blues as a Weapon," *Liberator*, Vol. 5 (October 1965): 8.

10 Jones and Neal, *Black Fire*, 655.

11 Peter Guralnick's *Sweet Soul Music* is a path-breaking account of the interracial genesis of Southern soul music, albeit one that argues, contrary to my claims here, that the rise of Black Power/Black Arts, especially after the murder of Martin Luther King, Jr., signaled the death of soul. See, Guralnick, *Sweet Soul Music: Rhythm and Blues and the Southern Dream of Freedom* (New York: HarperCollins, 1986).

Part II

CONTEMPORARY SOCIAL PROTEST IN ROCK MUSIC

10

THE MUSIC'S NOT ALL THAT MATTERS, AFTER ALL

British Progressive Rock as Social Criticism

Edward Macan

Figure 10.1 Genesis performing on stage in support of their album *Foxtrot*.

> *Progressive rock* (n): A pretentious, effete, stylistic dead-end
> that evinces no social conscience, or even awareness,
> whatsoever.

If your only acquaintance with progressive rock is through canonical rock historiography or (even worse) rock journalism,[1] then the invented definition given above may very possibly reflect your understanding of it. You will have been told that progressive rock drew on elements of European classical music merely to bask in the reflected glory of the Great Tradition; that its fusion of classical, jazz, and British

123

folk in a rock matrix represented the worst type of dilettantism; that its complexity was nothing more than a sophomoric attempt at artistic respectability; and that its monumentality was mere bombast. Above all, you will have been made to understand that no style of rock music ever evinced less social conscience than progressive rock. Indeed, its primary goal was to siphon off rock's rebellious energy and give it a thin veneer of cultural respectability.

I have addressed these assertions elsewhere;[2] here, I must confine myself to demonstrating that, both through its music and through its lyrics and album cover art, progressive rock proved itself more than equal to the task of social criticism. To maintain focus, I will confine myself to progressive rock's first decade, from 1969 to 1979—that is, I will consider it as a phenomenon of the 1970s—and concentrate on the British bands who were its founders.

The Music's All That Matters: Reading the Progressive Rock Musical Style

The first wave of progressive rock scholarship produced three major studies: my *Rocking the Classics: English Progressive Rock and the Counterculture* (1996),[3] Paul Stump's *The Music's All That Matters: A History of Progressive Rock* (1997),[4] and Bill Martin's *Listening to the Future: The Time of Progressive Rock, 1968–1978* (1998).[5] While each book's title says something crucial about the genre, here I would like to focus on the title of the Stump book, *The Music's All That Matters*. Of course, this wasn't literally true: the words of the songs, the album cover art, the fashion sense of the musicians, and the stage show mattered too. Nonetheless, the musical style itself, as a set of semiotic codes, played such an important role in conveying the ideology of the music that I would assert if one wants to understand in what sense progressive rock was "protest music," one must begin by considering progressive rock strictly as a musical style.

What was progressive rock, *as a style*, protesting?

Above all, progressive rock positioned itself against philistinism, which it blamed especially on the music industry, with its assembly line-like approach to the creation of musical "product." This critique is not new: it originates with nineteenth-century Romanticism. It was formally articulated by Robert Schumann, today remembered as a major composer, but primarily known to his contemporaries as the iconoclastic editor of the journal *Neue Zeitschrift für Musik*, and who championed the music of such progressives as Berlioz, Chopin, and Brahms, and relentlessly assailed what he regarded as the insipid salon music and shallow virtuoso showpieces churned out, cookie-cutter like, by the nineteenth-century music industry. Schumann was the first modern music critic to explicitly link progressivism in musical style and politics:

> Like the political present, one can divide the musical into liberals, centrists, and reactionaries, or romanticists, moderns, and classicists ... on the right sit

the elderly—the contrapuntists, the anti-chromaticists; on the left the youth-ful—the revolutionaries in the Phrygian caps, the anti-formalists, the genially impudent … the center, the just milieu, is the mediocre mainstream.[6]

One could easily transpose this characterization to the late sixties, with "the elderly" representing the dwindling audience for the music of high culture, "the youthful" the hippie counterculture and the new rock music, and "the center" Schumann's "medi-ocre mainstream" who, sheep-like, accept whatever new "product" the music indus-try serves up. It is the latter for whom both Schumann and sixties hippies reserved the greatest contempt.

Schumann's conception of the commercial music machine as hopelessly philistine and reactionary was further developed in the twentieth century by musicologist and neo-Marxist cultural theorist Theodor Adorno. His still controversial "On Popu-lar Music" (1941) takes Schumann's critique several steps further.[7] The fundamen-tal characteristic of popular music, Adorno argues, is standardized structure. Even when a popular song contains seemingly individualistic details—unusual substitute chords, "dirty" notes, and so on—listeners will always hear such seeming gestures of individuality in the context of the standardized structure. Therefore, as Adorno put it, "The composition hears for the listener. This is how popular music divests the listener of his spontaneity and promotes conditioned reflexes."[8] In Adorno's view, listening to popular music involves manipulation by "a system of response mecha-nisms wholly antagonistic to the ideal of individuality in a free, liberal society."[9] Commercial music promises two things people desire from their leisure time: novelty and "relaxation which does not involve the effort of concentration."[10] It appears to grant them both: the standardized structures reassure, while the pseudo-individual features offer the promise of novelty. However, ultimately, "to escape boredom and avoid effort are incompatible."[11] Adorno's view of popular music should be under-stood in the context of his theories about Western capitalist society. He sees popular culture (particularly the popular music, movie, and television industries) as the prin-cipal forum through which the government-corporate-media complex pacifies the masses—to put it in explicitly Marxist terms, as a purveyor of false consciousness.

Like Schumann, Adorno links musical and political-cultural progressivism. While he firmly believes in the superiority of high over popular culture and of European classical over American popular music, he does not uncritically accept all classical music as "great." For Adorno, "greatness" is a function of historical and cultural rel-evance. In *Philosophy of Modern Music* (1948),[12] he argues that a musical style can only exert its full expressive and communicative power in its own time. "Nothing in art is successfully binding except that which can be totally filled by the historical state of consciousness which determines its own substance."[13] Therefore, a socially conscious composer can compose neither according to the dictates of the popular music indus-try, with its insistence on standardized structures and clichés, nor according to the norms of "great music" of previous historical eras. For Adorno, the only truly modern and socially relevant music of his day was the atonal, so-called twelve-tone music of Arnold Schoenberg and his followers. Adorno admits that this music doesn't make for pleasant listening: it "enchains music by liberating it,"[14] is "infinitely static,"[15] and relies on crudely obvious contrasts of register, dynamics, and timbre to make any expressive impact. Nonetheless, Adorno defends twelve-tone music as the most truly modern form of music, inasmuch as it honestly reflects modern cultural conditions: "It points out the ills of society, rather than sublimating those ills into a deceptive humanitarianism which would pretend that humanitarianism had already been achieved in the present."[16] It exemplifies Adorno's notion of "negative dialectics." "Only the utmost dissonance found in modernist art ... has the capacity to suggest by negation something other than the counterfeit status quo."[17]

It should be understood that British progressive rock bands of the 1970s never took Adorno's critique of popular music as far as Adorno himself. If they had operated on the assumption that there was no possibility of a popular/vernacular avant-garde, they would never have been active at all. Nor did they adopt Adorno's doctrinaire view that only atonal music could transcend the "pacifying" role of modern commercial music and fulfill a "truth telling" function. On the other hand, once one understands the congruence between the aesthetic ideologies of progressive rock, on the one hand, and Schumann and Adorno, on the other, one perceives the so-called "bombast," "pretention," and "obscurity" of progressive rock in a different light.

For instance, a characteristic feature of progressive rock is its suite-like structures, drawn from nineteenth- and early twentieth-century classical music. These consist of distinct sections set apart by tempo, meter, key, instrumentation (particularly juxtapositions between primarily electric and acoustic passages), and mood. For the rock critic, the use of such structures was a matter of pretentiousness, of trying to bask in the reflected glory of high culture, and the juxtaposition of seemingly unrelated sections, a matter of willful obscurity. For the progressive rocker, though, the use of such structures had nothing to do with winning the approbation of high culture apparatchiks, and, while the charge of willful obscurity has validity (see below), it was not the primary goal of its sectional alternations. To the contrary, in the best progressive rock, the contrasting sections interact dialectically in the Hegelian sense, and the structure develops, with the disjunctions, contradictions, and uncertainties between the different sections ultimately being reconciled, or at least clarified. Progressive rockers intended this type of structural progressivism to model, or mirror, cultural progress through struggle. It is idealistic.[18]

One can explain all other unconventional aspects of the progressive rock style through the prism of the Schumann/Adorno critique as well. For instance, a defining feature of seventies progressive rock is its fusion of European classical, British folk, and modern jazz in a rock matrix. For the rock critic, this was mere dilettantism. For the progressive rocker, it was a critique of the prevailing dichotomies of high culture/low culture and European art/African American entertainment, as well as a utopian model of a new culture in which the best elements of disparate cultures are harmoniously blended. Another defining feature of seventies progressive rock is its emphasis on keyboards, particularly the Hammond organ, Moog synthesizer, and Mellotron. For the critic, this emphasis results in a "bloated" sound; for the musicians, it is a means of bringing a sense of depth, both sonic and cultural, to a popular music that had been trivialized and desacralized under the deadening weight of corporatism.

Finally, despite the claims of critics like Lester Bangs that the progressive rock style was hopelessly effete, "a contamination of all that was gutter pure in rock,"[19] one can, in fact, identify subversive undercurrents in the progressive rock style. Many of these derive from late-sixties psychedelic rock, progressive rock's single most important lineal ancestor. Michael Hicks has identified three fundamental effects of the LSD experience: dechronization (the breaking down of conventional perceptions of time), depersonalization (the breaking down of the ego's ordinary barriers and resulting awareness of undifferentiated unity), and dynamization (whereby static physical forms appear to dissolve into molten, dripping, objects).[20] All three impacted the development of the psychedelic rock style, and, less directly, progressive rock.

Dechronization is reflected by songs being lengthened and slowed down, with open-ended forms becoming the rule; compare both the tempos and the forms of pre-countercultural and countercultural rock, and the difference is immediately apparent. Progressive rock derives its modal harmony and fondness for long instrumental solos over an ostinato from psychedelic rock. Modal harmony's weak, "floating" sense of progression, and the sense of stasis created by ostinati, also mirrors dechronization.[21] Depersonalization is reflected in progressive rock's insistence on collective virtuosity against the pre-countercultural model of "front man" and "backing band." The distinction between lead and accompaniment dissolves into a democratic counterpoint that is denser and more complex than any pre-countercultural rock music. Dynamization, though not as important to progressive rock as to psychedelic rock, is still evident through the use of ample reverberation, echo, and stereo panning to suggest enormous interior spaces, the Hammond and Mellotron to create a sense of (respectively) "cathedral-like" and "symphonic" spaciousness, and effects devices to render "molten" otherwise stable timbres. To be sure, progressive rock is not, strictly speaking, "drug music." While its 1970s audiences often partook, the music was too complex and demanding for the performers to safely indulge themselves while performing. Nonetheless, it is undeniable that progressive rock as a style was shaped to some extent by late-1960s hallucinogenic drug culture.

There is notable congruence between progressive rock and hermeticism, in which a complex network of fantastic visual and literary symbols conveys deep truths. As with hermeticism, progressive rock's tendency towards complex music, arcane lyrics, and surreal cover art masks skepticism about mainstream society's confidence in the communicative capacities of literal language.[22] Again like the hermeticists, progressive rock's tendency towards obscurity suggests a desire to "keep out the squares" and force those who want to be part of the "scene" to make a real effort to come to grips with its ideology and values system. Here, one notes the similarity in sensibility between progressive rock and modernism, which brings us full circle, since Theodor Adorno was musical modernism's most persuasive philosophical exponent. Even though it's likely the founders of progressive rock never heard of Adorno, they saw in their difficult, knotty, music a kind of negative dialectics set against the puerile, clichéd, mass-produced swill of the corporate music machine.

The Music's Not All That Matters, After All: Progressive Rock as "Protest" Music

In other words, even if progressive rock had been entirely instrumental music, it could still be read as a criticism of late-1960s/1970s Western capitalist culture: its philistinism, materialism, conformism, lack of spiritual depth, and stifling and limiting cultural categories ("high culture"/"low culture," "art"/"entertainment," etc.). Of course, progressive rock is not an entirely instrumental style. Therefore, the music's not all that matters, after all. Lyrics and album cover art also contribute to, indeed, bring specificity to, its social criticism.

Setting the Parameters: In the Court of the Crimson King

King Crimson's debut album of October 1969, *In the Court of the Crimson King: An Observation by King Crimson*, is generally recognized as the first full-blown progressive rock album. Elsewhere I have discussed it as a stylistic template for the nascent progressive rock style.[23] Here I will confine myself to addressing the album's societal vision as conveyed through Peter Sinfield's lyrics. Its songs are grouped intentionally, with the two tracks on side two of the LP elaborating, via parable, topics that were addressed in a more-or-less straightforward manner in the three songs of side one.

The album's first song, the abrasive "21st Century Schizoid Man," paints a bleak picture of a dystopic society whose violence is driven by the hyper-materialism of the "schizoid man" who's visually represented by Barry Godber's expressionistic illustration on the front album cover. "Schizoid Man" is followed by the gentle "I Talk to the Wind," which traces a conversation between a "straight man" (an Establishment man, to use the word in its late-sixties sense) and a "late man" (a hippie). The late man says he's been on the outside looking inside (very much how the hippies viewed their relationship with mainstream society), and has seen much disillusionment, adding that he's talked to the wind, but his words have been carried away—that is, his attempt to speak truth to the straight man has been futile. The tragic, portentous, "Epitaph," which unites the heaviness of "Schizoid Man" and the melancholy of "I Talk to the Wind,"[24] describes Western culture as "the wall on which the prophets wrote," but adds that this wall is "cracking at the seams," and the fate of humanity now rests in the hands of fools, upon whose instruments of death "the sunlight brightly gleams." The fact that this weaponry is openly exhibited, rather than hidden away, suggests it has become the West's proudest achievement: technology has been spectacularly corrupted into a Frankenstein's monster that threatens all life on earth. In sum, side one of *Crimson King* depicts a society whose materialism is shored up by systematic violence, exposes this society's hypocrisy, then turns to a science gone apocalyptically awry under the influence of Cold War paranoia.

Side two of the LP shifts from essentially straightforward social criticism to parable. Its first song, "Moonchild," is a kind of nocturne, portraying an elfin girl who plays in the shadows of the moonlight, waiting for the appearance of a "sun child." The short song proper is followed by an instrumental improvisation in which pointillist flecks of sound alternate with near silence, suggesting a shadowy world whose denizens await the coming of day, in not only a literal, but in a symbolic (that is, spiritual), sense. And, sure enough, the album's final song, "In the Court of the Crimson King," begins with Greg Lake's description of a Sun King whose reign promises to bring light to a benighted world; he is pictured, in the album's inner gatefold, smiling, with sad, expressive eyes. Although the lyric weaves a tale of a luxurious and cultured court, we gradually come to understand something is amiss, and, near the end of the tale, our narrator, who has come to the court as a pilgrim, finds himself obliged to "run and grasp divining signs to satisfy the hoax"—that is, to resort to hypocrisy in explaining away the distance between the court's appearance and its reality. The final lyric is a stroke of genius. As the yellow jester makes his puppets dance, we realize that it is he, and not the Crimson King, who is the real power in this court, and we are involuntarily reminded of the key lyric of "Epitaph," that the "fate of all mankind" is in the hands of fools.

Although Peter Sinfield was lyricist for the next three King Crimson albums, none of them quite recaptured the power and immediacy of *In the Court of the Crimson King*. Its approach to social criticism through fantasy/science fiction parable made a lasting imprint on progressive rock, as did its topoi: the spiritual malaise of philistinism, the folly of militarism, the apocalyptic danger of technology corrupted by greed and paranoia. We will, therefore, turn our attention to how the British progressive rock bands that emerged in the wake of this album developed these topics.

Emerson, Lake, and Palmer: Technology Gone Awry

It can be argued that no band of the 1970s was more dependent on new music technology than Emerson, Lake, and Palmer. It is, therefore, paradoxical that no one took the subject of technology gone awry as seriously as ELP: two of their major albums, *Tarkus* (1971) and *Brain Salad Surgery* (1973), address this subject. While *Tarkus* succeeds brilliantly on a purely musical level, conceptually it never quite gels: Carl Palmer later opined that William Neal's art for the inner gatefold was made to bear too much of the album's conceptual premise.[25] Two years later, the band approached the same general theme again, but now, working with lyricist Peter Sinfield, they tied their conceptual strands together more tightly. H. R. Giger's cover art posits the ambiguous relationship between humanity and technology as the album's central concern. While the outside cover shows a human skull imbedded in a horrific mechanical device, when the two halves of the cover are opened, the device disappears, replaced by the face of a sleeping woman with the infinity sign on her forehead.

The album opens with the band's arrangement of "Jerusalem," Britain's equivalent to the American "Battle Hymn of the Republic." Written at the dawn of the industrial revolution, William Blake's poem "Jerusalem" decries the "dark satanic mills" of early industrial capitalism, holds up agrarian England as a lost Eden, and calls for the overturning of the new order. The poem was unambiguously anti-establishment when it was written, but its history was complicated when composer Hubert Parry set it as a patriotic hymn honoring the fallen British soldiers of World War I. ELP's arrangement, denied airplay by the BBC, recaptures the anti-establishment resonance the poem held for its original audience. It also introduces both the idea of technological progress as a "worm in the apple" of Western civilization, and the musical motifs—hymn-like melodies, march rhythms, fanfare figures, military drum cadences—which are developed across the album.

The next track, the abrasive "Toccata," is a free arrangement of the final movement of Alberto Ginastera's Piano Concerto No. 1. It's music of, and for, the "dark satanic mills" inveighed against in "Jerusalem," diabolically distorting the latter's heroic fanfare figures. The nexus of the track is Carl Palmer's synthesized percussion solo, which evokes the paranoia and alienation of contemporary society, paradoxically through the auspices of the technological advances that the album appears to excoriate. Following two shorter tracks that are only tangentially tied to the album's concept is the thirty-minute, three-movement "Karn Evil 9" suite, the album's musical and conceptual center of gravity.

The storyline of "Karn Evil 9" conflates two distinct ideas. The lyric of 1st Impression stems from a Keith Emerson concept, originally titled "Ganton 9," concerning a planet to which all manner of evil has been banished. The storyline of 3rd Impression is a Sinfield inspiration—a monumental battle between Man and Computer, waged in the future in the depths of outer space—that was indebted to the Arthur C. Clarke/Stanley Kubrick movie *2001: A Space Odyssey*. Eventually, the two concepts were loosely woven together, with the lyrics alternating between the viewpoints of three dramatic personae—a Narrator who stands outside the action, a Carnival

Barker who represents computer technology gone apocalyptically wrong, and a Liberator, a heroic individual who has vowed to liberate oppressed humans from their electronic overlord(s).

The beginning of 1st Impression presents a manipulative totalitarian world of the not-so-distant future as the logical fulfillment of Blake's dire prophesies about "Satanic mills," with the individual who describes this dystopic society presenting himself as a potential Liberator. The viewpoint then shifts, and the remainder of the 1st Impression unfolds from the perspective of a Carnival Barker (hence the "Karn Evil" pun), who assures us that his is a "show that never ends." Its attractions include violence, human tragedy, sexual titillation, sports, what's left of the environment, and popular music.[26]

The 2nd Impression is instrumental, alternately frantic and mystical, and functions as a turning point in the unfolding of the concept. The lyric of the climactic 3rd Impression unfolds from two viewpoints. The first two verses are in the voice of a narrator who stands outside the action: we are taken back to the dawn of human history, and then far into the future (although not necessarily far into our own future), when computers have attained God-like powers, and a "man of steel" wields a blade "kissed by countless kings." From this point on, the 3rd Impression increasingly recalls the martial musical imagery of "Jerusalem," as the viewpoint shifts to the "Liberator"—presumably the character whose voice we heard at the opening of the 1st Impression—as he engages in his life-and-death struggle with the Computer, the "Man of Steel," who emerges victorious in the album's surreal closing section. Whether this Computer is the "Carnival Barker" who guided us through the 1st Impression's "show that never ends" is essentially immaterial to the album's concept as a whole: one of the masterstrokes of the lyrics of the 1st and 3rd Impression is that although each is self-contained, when combined they cohere into a more or less unified storyline.

Brain Salad Surgery is a remarkable and, in many ways, prophetic album. Granted, one of its two major subtexts, the possibility of the computer somehow becoming an ensouled organism, is much harder to take seriously now than in the heady days of the late sixties, when the idea of "progress" seemed so much more self-evident. On the other hand, it's hard to argue that the central conceit of 1st Impression—the emergence of a softly oppressive corporate-government-media complex that manipulates and pacifies its populace through a never-ending flood of essentially trivial "news" and entertainment (the two having become more or less synonymous)—has not come true. Like the neo-Marxist Adorno, ELP undertake a sophisticated criticism of the role of media in the contemporary West that's (paradoxically) anti-collectivist and libertarian in its bent, suggesting that the emergence of the modern corporate-government-media complex is likely to be inimical to existing definitions of freedom, liberty, and individuality. Indeed, today we essentially live in the world of 1st Impression, and nobody seems to mind.

Yes: Redemption through Gnosis

If ELP developed one particular strand of the *Crimson King* critique—the dangers of technology, especially in the hands of a potentially malign military-industrial-government-media complex—then Yes develops different aspects: the search for *gnosis* (presumably the underlying motive of the pilgrim/narrator's journey to the Crimson King's court) and the futility of militarism. Indeed, in their epic "The Gates of Delirium," the two topics are counterpoised.

Much of Yes's most representative output involves the quest for enlightenment (in the Eastern sense) or *gnosis* (in the esoteric Western sense). The entirety of *Close to the Edge* (1972, inspired by Hermann Hesse's novel *Siddhartha*), *Tales from Topographic Oceans* (1973, based on the four-fold division of Shastric scripture outlined in Paramahansa Yoganda's *Autobiography of a Yogi*), and the epic "Awaken," from *Going for the One* (1977), can be read in this context. "Close to the Edge" and "And You and I" (both from *Close to the Edge*) convey *gnosis* as a flash of spiritual illumination that brings a Hegelian "end of history," opening up higher levels of consciousness not just at a personal but a social level; thus the climactic lyrics of "Close to the Edge," and "And You and I," which refer to higher planes of existence.

It's easy to criticize this line of thought as "escapist" or "apolitical," but notice the underlying subtext. When a critical mass of people have attained genuine spiritual awakening, there will be real "revolution." This was a pervasive line of thought amongst a segment of the late-sixties/early-seventies counterculture that was much disliked by the counterculture's Marxist wing, who saw it as utopian in an unrealizable sense. It has a history in twentieth-century esoteric circles: George Gurdjieff, for instance, argued that without a critical mass of spiritually awakened people, it is illogical to speak of genuine political revolution. While the type of mysticism commended by Gurdjieff (or Yes) has traditionally been the concern of the few, rather than the many, the potential relationship between religious belief and political revolution is undeniable, even in our supposedly secular modern world: think of the intimate connection between Islamic fundamentalism and the Iranian Revolution.

While "Yours Is No Disgrace" from *The Yes Album* (1971) is generally recognized as Yes's first "antiwar song," it's only with "The Gates of Delirium" from *Relayer* (1974) that the band makes its definitive statement about the futility of militarism. The song begins with a call to arms, invoking the traditional justifications for going to war, while the second section begins in a more pensive tone, linking fear to the impulse to fight. Finally, the ugliness underlying any war effort emerges with images of immolated children. What follows is one of prog rock's great extemporaneous improvisations, "battle music" that seems to reference the martial passages of ELP's "Karn Evil 9, 3rd Impression," released the year before. The "battle music" climaxes with a transcendent "cosmic" synthesizer theme, and is followed by a gentle, hymn-like finale whose peace represents the attainment of cosmic awareness, expressed (as *gnosis* often is in vocalist Jon Anderson's lyrics) in solar imagery. "The Gates of

Delirium" was inspired by Tolstoy's *War and Peace*. One can see why Anderson was drawn to this novel: it presents a "God" that is similar to Hegel's "World Spirit," a force that produces a history that is not just a repeating circle, but a progressively ascending spiral. Such a view mirrors Anderson's own optimistic view of the cosmos struggling towards redemption through *gnosis*, as well as his belief that militarism belongs to a lower, earlier, cycle.

Jethro Tull: The Danger of Groupthink

Aqualung (1971) is Jethro Tull's most famous album, and the central text for understanding lyricist Ian Anderson's sociopolitical perspective. However, someone who only knows *Aqualung* may believe that Anderson's central concern is the failure of institutional Christianity. This would be an incomplete view. The key song for contextualizing Anderson's social vision is "The Teacher," from *Benefit* (1970).

"The Teacher" exemplifies the manner in which progressive rock is post-1960s music. It is unlikely this song would have been written at the height of the Summer of Love: it is a critique of the manner in which earnest hippies cast off traditional authority only to give the same blind allegiance to new authorities. Anderson may have had in mind The Beatles' falling out with the Maharishi Mahesh Yogi, their one-time "spiritual advisor"; however, there was a host of other self-styled gurus who may just as easily have been his target.[27] Anderson's "Teacher" is essentially a huckster who profits off the gullibility of his students. Besides criticizing sixties faddishness, "The Teacher" lambastes credulity (as Anderson later does in "Backdoor Angels," from 1974's *Warchild*) and blind loyalty to authority of any kind.

The two sides of the *Aqualung* LP are titled "Aqualung" and "My God," respectively. Side one presents a series of character sketches. The two most sharply etched are "Aqualung" (a homeless man who may be a pedophile, since he eyes little girls with "bad intent") and "Cross-Eyed Mary" (a teenage girl who prefers the company of older men to boys her own age). Both are presented unsentimentally, yet with a sense of underlying humanity. The other principal song on side one, "Mother Goose," suggests that the divine is to be found in the ordinary moment-to-moment interactions of daily life: for just a moment, a walk through Hampstead Fair and Piccadilly Circus becomes a fairy tale.

The songs of side two mainly constitute a theological and sociopolitical critique of institutional Christianity. "My God" develops Ian Anderson's view that God is immanent, not transcendent, and that orthodox Christianity, in its obsession with sin, salvation, and exterior observance, has lost sight of the fact that "He's a part of you and me"—with the result that we don't see the divine spark in each other. The Church as a social institution comes in for some rough treatment in "Hymn 43," in which it is depicted as the justifier of whatever crimes the government of the moment pursues as social policy—Anderson specifically cites the slaughter of Native

Americans—and in "Wind Up," where it becomes the enforcer of social custom, and Jesus a wind-up toy who mouths whatever platitudes the Church wants to hear. Although the two sides of the album are never explicitly linked, they loosely cohere, and one infers Anderson's point is that, if the Church were to change its emphasis from external ritual to honoring the immanent spirit, then every moment could be a "Mother Goose" moment, we could see Aqualung and Cross-Eyed Mary as God's children rather than social castoffs, and the social dysfunction they exemplify could be reversed. In recent decades, this critique has become fairly mainstream, but in popular culture ca. 1971 it was still new enough to pack a punch.

Anderson was amused that *Aqualung* was received as a concept album—that had not been his intention—and decided that its follow-up, *Thick as a Brick* (1972), would be an *über*-concept album. Indeed, it became both a satire of, and a notable artifact of, the burgeoning progressive rock movement. The album consists of one enormous "song" split across two sides of the LP; the arrangements are denser, the metric shifts more intricate, and electric keyboards more prominent than on any previous Tull album. The lyrics are intentionally obscure, and the album "cover," a complete *faux* "newspaper" (the January 7, 1972 edition of the *St. Cleve Chronicle*), bears the primary burden of conveying the album's conceptual content. The cover story of the "newspaper" involves a local eight-year-old prodigy, Gerald Bostock, who has written an epic poem titled "Thick as a Brick" which was awarded first place in a national literary competition for children. However, he was stripped of the award in the wake of protests generated when he read his poem over the BBC. A panel of psychiatrists recommended him for immediate treatment due to his "extremely unwholesome attitude towards life, his God and Country," and the prize was awarded to runner-up Mary Whiteyard for her poem "He Died to Save the Little Children." We learn that "major beat group" Jethro Tull were so impressed by Gerald's poem that they agreed to set it to music on their upcoming album.

Here we have Anderson's principal preoccupations—herd mentality, the triumph of religiosity over true religion—as well as a new theme, the difficulties of precocity in a philistine society, which becomes the one (more or less) clear thread in the otherwise obscure lyrics. The "newspaper" is a fascinating cultural relic in its own right, with its affectionate satire of the provincialism and amateurism of small-town newspapers and its Monty Python-like stories. Among the silliness, however, is seriousness. An article about a lecture by Andrew Jorgensen on society's future at St. Cleve's Church Hall elegantly sums up Ian Anderson's entire social philosophy:

> Man must learn to assume individual identity as opposed to the collective super-society style of life. To some extent Jorgensen said this had already taken place with the emergence of subcults which attempt to break away from the social consciousness of the collective group, but man must learn to function as an independent observer of mass-behavior and develop the right

of each individual to intellectual freedom on the particular level of which he is personally capable.[28]

Apparently, Anderson believed that the masses were not yet ready to accept his libertarian gospel. The article notes "Unfortunately the lecture was terminated by flying bottles which hit Mr. Jorgensen below the left eye."

Genesis, Gentle Giant: Minstrels for the 1970s

ELP, Yes, and Jethro Tull were bands whose most representative work develops one or two key ideas; in this sense, it was philosophical. Genesis and Gentle Giant, on the other hand, are more like medieval minstrels, spinning stories out of news events of the day and interweaving social commentary into their tales; indeed, Gentle Giant explicitly portray themselves this way in "Raconteur, Troubadour" on their 1973 album *Octopus*. One might expect that this approach would give rise to sententious philosophizing: however, there was no more canny social critic in British progressive rock than Peter Gabriel during his 1969–1974 tenure with Genesis as the band's lyricist and lead vocalist.

Genesis's first great song is "The Knife" from *Trespass* (1970), a none-too-subtle warning against the Demagogue, who convinces his followers that they have been duped, nakedly appeals to their worst instincts, and promises them a martyr's death in service of a greater good. After persuading them of the righteousness of their cause, he sets them on their bloody course of action. Significantly, Gabriel gives no clue as to the Demagogue's politics. Like virtually all major progressive rockers, Gabriel was born in the eight-year period between the deaths of Hitler and Stalin; his generation feared the reemergence of such men regardless of political stripe. Contrary to popular belief, the counterculture generally did not favor violent revolution, and Genesis's "The Knife" gives a cogent description of the scenario many expected a violent revolution to produce. Indeed, the 1970s proved an exceptionally fertile time for the emergence of genocidal demagogues across the Third World.

"Harold the Barrel," from *Nursery Cryme* (1971), is a brilliant little song in the style of late Beatles *faux* music hall numbers like "Maxwell's Silver Hammer," although Gabriel's wit and social criticism cuts deeper. Harold is a restaurant owner who (in one of the bizarre flights of violence that Gabriel delighted in) cuts off his toes and serves them to his patrons in a fit of depression. We follow Harold's flight from the scene of the crime to the ledge of a building, outside which a self-serving politician bellows for justice, reporters drum up their story to a hysterical pitch, a well-meaning but clueless expert ("Mr. Plod") offers platitudes, and a mob gathers to enjoy the spectacle. Finally, Harold's mother arrives, and—in a brilliant jab at the English obsession with appearances—begs him not to jump, since his shirt is dirty and the BBC is filming him. Suddenly, slow, somber, piano chords cut off the song's frantic rhythm: Harold's story does not have a happy ending. Here Gabriel presciently skewers the emerging phenomenon of reality TV—its tendency to turn "news" into "entertainment," its lack of concern for the human cost of its success in creating spectacle, its instantaneous creation of an unthinking herd hungry for entertainment. The parallels with the concerns expressed by ELP in *Brain Salad Surgery* and Jethro Tull in *Thick as a Brick* are obvious.

Foxtrot (1972) includes Gabriel's most ambitious forays yet into social criticism, with the epic 23-minute "Supper's Ready," an invective against class, religion, and war that culminates in Armageddon, and the quasi-operetta "Get 'Em Out by Friday." This song is an indictment of both capitalist greed and the British council housing system, which by the early 1970s was in serious decline; it also forecasts developments of the Thatcher era, specifically the contradictions inherent in a marriage of convenience between two systems, the Welfare State and private enterprise, which have starkly differing agendas. Again, concern about the emergence of a government-corporate complex is paramount.

Selling England by the Pound (1973), which addresses Britain's socioeconomic decline of the early 1970s, marks the apogee of Genesis's social commentary. The opening song, "Dancing with the Moonlit Knight," makes much use of Grail imagery, and initially appears to involve an ill-defined Grail Quest with odd interspersions of contemporary imagery. To someone who is familiar with English life of the 1970s, however, the intent is clear. The lyrics address the acquiescence of the English people to the corporatization of their country (indeed, we're told that "for her merchandise" the protagonist has "traded in his prize"), and the lyric's medievalism contrasts the authenticity of the old with the crassness of the new. Gabriel specifically criticizes the dissolution of local culture and homogenization of national culture under the onslaught of "big box" stores and national chains; thus the "wimpy dreams" the people chew on is a pun on Wimpy, a British fast-food chain that predated McDonald's by some years, and the Knights of the Green Shield are not heroes of the days of yore, but consumers who hoard Green Shield stamps in the hopes of saving a few pennies on their big box purchases. The reference to credit cards is a reminder that credit, formerly local, personal, and based on mutual trust, had become impersonal and corporatized.

Most of the album's remaining songs evoke some aspect of social decline. "I Know What I Like" highlights the stultifying effect of the British class system. "The Battle of Epping Forest" sketches the ferocious battle between two gangs for control of the protection racket in a tiny slice of London's East End: the interspersion of "The Reverend's Song" here illustrates the frailty of sixties idealism in such an environment, and again points up that progressive rock is a post-sixties music. The climactic point of the album is the penultimate "Cinema Show," based on the section of T. S. Eliot's epic poem *The Waste Land* in which the seer Tiresias observes and comments on the seduction of a young woman by a young man in a shabby apartment in London. Eliot intended the scene to illustrate the difficulty of meaningful human relationships in modern life, but the band casts the episode in a more positive light, with the brilliant instrumental section evoking the transcendence symbolized by Tiresias' androgyny. However, the final track, "Aisle of Plenty," reprises music from the opening song; an old woman named Tess cries out "I don't belong here," but she's reassured "there's the Safe Way home," and, after hearing this, "Tess Co-operates." Safeway and TessCo (Tesco) were two of the rising big box behemoths of Britain during the 1970s. The suggestion is that they and their ilk are Britain's new overlords, and the album fades with a "sales boy" crying out the prices of sales items. Gabriel left the band after the subsequent *The Lamb Lies Down on Broadway* (1974), and Genesis never achieved this kind of incisiveness again.

Gentle Giant are remembered today primarily for the intricacy of their music, forbidding even by the standards of progressive rock. The band's lyrics never attracted a lot of attention, even though their output includes two concept albums, *Three Friends* (1972) and *The Power and the Glory* (1974), which engage in social criticism. The former is the closest thing progressive rock produced to a comprehensive critique of the British class system, tracing the progress of three childhood friends from their schooldays to their adult lives. One becomes a manual laborer, one, an artist, one, a successful businessman. Each man is sketched objectively. Thus, we become aware both of the manual laborer's sense of being exploited and his limited outlook, and of the artist's insecurity at the fringes of society and his egocentrism. The least sympathetic character is the businessman, dubbed "Mr. Class and Quality." His wife, like his car and house, is a "prize," his friends a means to an end, and he himself "a steady man" whose greatest strength is his ability to "give and take the orders." This caustic portrait lays bare a number of major countercultural concerns—the dangers of materialism, acquisitiveness, and philistinism—and exposes capitalism not only as a form of economic exploitation, but an agent of spiritual barrenness.

The Power and the Glory is more sophisticated yet, paradoxically, less successful. Released just after the Watergate scandal had ended the presidency of Richard Nixon, the album explores the mechanisms through which politicians either survive or fall in modern Western governments: the P.R. machines that craft images far removed from reality and spin negative publicity via "sincere" but meaningless statements, and the ritualistic expression of public sorrow that errant politicians are expected to undergo to gain absolution. The lyrics are often witty and sophisticated, but the album suffers from a central difficulty: the concept and music are so complex (this is probably Gentle Giant's most musically knotty album, which is saying a lot) that it is difficult to digest both word and sound. During the mid-1970s, Pink Floyd's Roger Waters began to argue that the more developed the concept, the simpler the music should be.[29] While this approach was not unproblematic for Pink Floyd and progressive rock generally (see below), *The Power and the Glory* suggests Waters' sentiment was not without merit.

The Pink Floyd "Problem": When the Composition Hears for the Listener

Here we come to a pervasive tension underlying 1970s progressive rock. It was committed to two types of critique. One was aesthetic, akin to the modernism of high culture, involving the cultivation of a difficult, "hermetic," musical style against the philistinism of mainstream culture. The second was a more straightforward social criticism, undertaken mainly through the lyrics. This approach was in line with the protest music tradition of popular music, and relied on comprehensibility. The peculiar tension of the best progressive rock results from a delicate equilibrium between the two approaches. As is evident in an album like *The Power and the Glory*, this was not easily achieved. The lyrics, which often used fantasy or science fiction imagery to express social criticism as parable, had to simultaneously convey the concept more or less clearly, and create a sense of correspondence with the aesthetic values of the music. Album cover art was relied on to further tie music and lyrics together. From 1969 to 1974, the major progressive rock bands achieved this balance more often than not. After 1974, it became rarer.

Musically, much progressive rock ca. 1975–80 shed its "prickly," outwardly difficult aspect. Ironically, for the most part this simplification was not undertaken to throw challenging lyrics into bold relief. Lyrics also increasingly lost their critical bite. The case of Pink Floyd is somewhat different. While their music of ca. 1975–80 underwent the same process of simplification as the other bands discussed here, their lyrics became increasingly confrontational. Nonetheless, it can be argued that Pink Floyd's move towards musical simplification ultimately weakened the power of their social critique.

Pink Floyd's output always grappled with the subject of alienation. On their early albums, though, the band evoked alienation primarily through the music itself— through unfamiliar, disorienting, uses of timbre, texture, and structure. Beginning with *Dark Side of the Moon* (1973), their musical syntax becomes more conventional, and the increasingly prosaic lyrics of Roger Waters bear an ever-growing burden in conveying the band's (and, increasingly, Waters' personal) conception of alienation. By *The Wall* (1979), the music is thoroughly conventional, often little more than a backdrop to the words. In other words, Pink Floyd's later music lost the power of unfamiliarity of their early classics. Pink Floyd's early fans did not conform to Adorno's stereotypical popular music listener, who listens for reassurance and relaxation: it took commitment to absorb the genuinely radical "Interstellar Overdrive," the disturbing "Careful with that Axe, Eugene," and the starkly beautiful "Echoes." On the other hand, Waters' ever-growing contempt for Pink Floyd's enormous post-*Meddle* fan base is well known. As the 1970s wore on, he became increasingly frustrated with what he perceived as the audience's indifference to his sophisticated analyses of alienation.

I suspect Adorno's retort to Waters would have been that this state of affairs was the result of Waters' paradoxical effort to address alienation through music that is not, in itself, alienating. He would have argued that Waters was mistaken to insist that the band's music become ever more conventional during the second half of the 1970s, since conventional song forms and stock musical syntax are the death knell of any kind of "progressive" music. And he would note that, at the point when "the composition hears for the listener," the listener is probably not paying much attention to the lyrics that are intended to challenge or stimulate, either.

As suggested above, progressive rock stood in a unique relationship to the sixties. Although it was a step removed from late-sixties consciousness, and could comment on it in quotation marks, it grew out of, and was energized by, late-sixties utopianism. Progressive rock's golden age existed in a narrow historical window when the sixties were "past," but sixties utopianism still resonated culturally. Progressive rock's expansive structures and virtuosity were reflections of sixties' utopianism, as was the delicate balance between hermeticism and comprehensibility that gave it its peculiar tension. When this utopianism began to wane in the mid-1970s, so did progressive rock's faith in itself. But, in smoothing out its challenging musical style, progressive rock lost its inner tension, and much of its dynamism as a form of social critique.

Progressive Rock as Political Philosophy

Clearly, progressive rock had a political dimension, with a consistent core of central themes—fear of a coercive and manipulative government-corporate-media complex; contempt for herd mentality and blind conformity; rejection of militarism; concern over the atomization and commoditization of society; and, above all, scorn of philistinism and materialism. Such themes were addressed from a multiplicity of perspectives including Romantic and modernistic aesthetics, a plethora of "religious" and "spiritual" currents (in which both Eastern and esoteric Western perspectives were prominent) that defy easy political categorization, and various strains of Marxism, anarchism, and libertarianism. Therefore, we need not ask if progressive rock articulated a rigorous, self-contained, political philosophy. It did not. Nor should we expect it to: these were musicians, not cultural theorists, mostly in their twenties when they created their best work. Nonetheless, as Bill Martin notes in *Listening to the Future*,[30] their best music is prophetic. It denounces the wrongs and follies of their society, and lays out a vision of what will likely result if these are not abandoned. In its time, progressive rock was, to quote Adorno, "totally filled by the historical state of consciousness which determines its own substance." One could ask for no more.

Notes

1 Unfortunately, rock journalism has had a disproportionate influence in the formation of rock historiography. Obviously, this issue falls well beyond the scope of this chapter.

2 See, especially, Edward Macan, *Endless Enigma: A Musical Biography of Emerson, Lake and Palmer* (Chicago: Open Court, 2006), 164–168, 189–196, 336–349.

3 Edward Macan, *Rocking the Classics: English Progressive Rock and the Counterculture* (New York: Oxford University Press, 1997).

4 Paul Stump, *The Music's All That Matters: A History of Progressive Rock* (London: Quartet Books, 1997).

5 Bill Martin, *Listening to the Future: The Time of Progressive Rock, 1968–1978* (Chicago: Open Court, 1998).

6 Quoted by Michael Chanan, *From Handel to Hendrix: The Composer in the Public Sphere* (London: Verso, 1999), 98.

7 Theodor Adorno (with the assistance of George Simpson), "On Popular Music." Reprinted in *On Record: Rock, Pop, and the Written Word* (New York: Pantheon, 1990), 301–314. Excerpted from *Studies in Philosophy and Social Science* 9 (Frankfurt: Surhkamp, 1941).

8 Adorno, *On Popular Music*, 306.

9 Adorno, *On Popular Music*, 302.

10 Adorno, *On Popular Music*, 310.

11 Adorno, *On Popular Music*, 310.

12 Theodor Adorno, *Philosophy of Modern Music* (New York: Continuum, 2004).

13 Adorno, *Philosophy of Modern Music*, 213.

14 Adorno, *Philosophy of Modern Music*, 68.

15 Adorno, *Philosophy of Modern Music*, 65.

16 Adorno, *Philosophy of Modern Music*, 131.

17 Kirsten Grimstad, *The Modern Revival of Gnosticism and Thomas Mann's 'Doktor Faustus'* (Rochester, New York: Camden House, 2002), 237.

18 It is only with The Beatles, post-1965, some of the psychedelic rock bands of the late 1960s that followed in their wake, and (above all) progressive rock of the 1970s that popular music was opened up to teleological structures. The music that Adorno inveighed against in "On Popular Music," Broadway songs and big band jazz (the two most popular styles of music in America ca. 1940), is unremittingly cyclical in its structure.

19 Lester Bangs, "Exposed! The Brutal Energy Atrocities of Emerson, Lake and Palmer," *Creem* (March 1974), 44.

20 Michael Hicks, *Sixties Rock: Garage, Psychedelic, and Other Satisfactions* (Urbana, Illinois: University of Illinois Press, 1999). See Chapter 5, "Getting Psyched," 58–74.

21 Progressive rock's extensive use of modal harmony and ostinato patterns can be read as a reaction against the regular harmonic rhythm of common-practice harmony, which encapsulates industrial society's obsession with the passing of a quantifiable, objectively measured, chronological time. Progressive rock's fondness for asymmetrical and shifting meters can be similarly interpreted.

22 In the case of progressive rock, the skepticism toward the communicative capacities of literal language undoubtedly stem from late-1960s hallucinogenic drug culture.

23 Edward Macan, *Endless Enigma*, 67–74.

24 "Epitaph" is therefore an excellent example of the dialectic nature of progressive rock structure, seeming to emerge out of the dialectic succession of the abrasive "Schizoid Man" with the gentle but melancholy "I Talk to the Wind."

25 Here's Palmer: "I thought it was an interesting concept, but ... I couldn't understand the [inner gatefold's] armadillo with the tank tracks disappearing into the sea. It didn't have

the adult flavor that I wanted that, say, Pink Floyd had done ..."Tarkus" was meant to be about dealing with chemical warfare and weapons of mass destruction. It could have been a film, but we dealt with it as a cartoon. The music is incredible, though." Quoted by Ken Micallef, "Carl Palmer: From the Beginning," *Modern Drummer* (June 2005), 121.

26 The attractions of the Carnival Barker's show in 1st Impression obviously foreshadow modern cable television and reality TV. Note the reference to rock and roll, which prefigures Roger Waters' concern with rock's potential for totalitarian misuse, especially in regards to mob manipulation, which was such an important aspect of Pink Floyd's *The Wall.*

27 Anderson also may have had in mind Timothy Leary and/or Richard Alpert, a.k.a. Ram Dass. Both were apostles of the late sixties' hallucinogenic drug culture. Anderson was one of a very few rock stars of the era who were outspokenly anti-drug.

28 Jethro Tull, *Thick as a Brick*, LP, "newspaper," page 5, © 1972 Chrysalis.

29 Nicholas Schaffner, *Saucerful of Secrets: The Pink Floyd Odyssey* (New York: Harmony, 1991), 199.

30 Bill Martin, *Listening to the Future*, 121.

11

RADICAL PROTEST IN ROCK
Zappa, Lennon, and Garcia

Jacqueline Edmondson and Robert G. Weiner

Figure 11.1 Frank Zappa.

The word "radical" has its origins in the Latin word *radicalis*, meaning "of roots" or "root." In social and political circles, something radical is seen as revolutionary and as an attempt to change existing social structures. Radical protest thus begins at the grassroots, with people (rather than the authorities) who attempt to change norms by raising objections to the status quo.

Musicians have long engaged in radical protest against social and political injustices. These protests can take many forms: protest through lyrics or the form music takes, protest through the delivery of a song and message (i.e., how and where a message is conveyed), or protest through other overt statements against industry or societal norms, where the platform an artist has allows him or her to make public statements (i.e., at a concert venue, press conference or other public forum). The three musicians featured in this chapter—Frank Zappa, John Lennon, and Jerry Garcia—engaged in radical protest in rock music in impactful and unique ways that were aimed in several directions.

Frank Zappa

Frank Zappa (1940–1993)[1] was one of the most iconic figures in popular music history. In his short but creative life, he released more than sixty albums and made several films (both concert releases and feature films). There are many more unauthorized recordings in circulation. Although Zappa lacked formal musical training and wrote some songs in traditional rock and pop styles, he didn't consider himself a rock artist *per se*, but rather a composer. He wrote symphonic music that one might consider "high-brow" for a writer of rock songs, but Zappa hated to be pigeon-holed and wrote music, to satisfy his own musical cravings, in many musical styles. Moreover, he developed a reputation for becoming "one of the finest lead guitarists to emerge in the mid-60s."[2] From an early age, Zappa was fascinated with music of all kinds, from blues to the experimental pieces of French composer Edgard Varèse, and he performed his compositions in unexpected ways and often in ironic settings.[3] In 1963, for instance, he found his way onto the *Steve Allen Television Show*, where he played a bicycle as a musical instrument, much to Allen's bewilderment.[4] Above all, Zappa framed his musical career as a challenge to a number of establishments—the music industry, the general public, high culture, and politics—crafting music that engaged this challenge through off-putting humor, parody, and sarcasm. In 1985, he moved from music to direct political action with testimony before Congress in protest against the labeling of record albums with the now infamous "parental advisory."

John Lennon

John Lennon (1940–1980) had an irreverent streak from the time he was a young boy growing up in his Aunt Mimi's house in Liverpool, England. He was known to purposely find ways to subvert the system, which often created problems for him in school, and he took great pleasure in authors like Edward Lear and Lewis Carroll who knowingly twisted taken-for-granted norms. Lennon's early books, *In His Own Write* (1964) and *A Spaniard in the Works* (1965), demonstrate how he enjoyed subverting language and text structures to create humorous effects. Much to his middle-class Aunt Mimi's dismay, he adopted the Scouse accent of working class Liverpool when he was a teen and just breaking into the music scene with the Quarrymen and The Beatles.

Lennon's first political opinions began to seep out in the mid-1960s, although he was advised not to be publicly political because it could have negatively impacted the image and commercial success of The Beatles. The album cover for *Yesterday … and Today* (1966), with photos of The Beatles in butchers' clothes with raw meat and beheaded dolls, combined with Lennon's comment that The Beatles were more popular than Jesus Christ, stirred some of the first negative controversy for the band. Lennon said the photo was "as relevant as Vietnam" and, in a press conference in New York City in August 1966, he told reporters he didn't like war and thought it was wrong, a sentiment he repeated at the movie premiere of the dark comedy he appeared in called *How I Won The War*.

Critics did not typically phase Lennon, and he did not appear to take positions based on what the general population or his fans would think. Instead, he seemed to find some pleasure in pushing boundaries and causing people to see the world differently whether through his music, art, films, or public statements. But when John Hoyland wrote in the radical London newspaper the *Black Dwarf* that Lennon's song "Revolution" was an inadequate response to repressive authoritarian structures, Lennon lashed back. In his 1969 response, Lennon wrote that he did not care what "[Hoyland], the left, the middle, the right or any fucking boys club think."[5] He challenged Hoyland's call to destroy the system by explaining that the problem was really people, and, until "sick heads" are changed, there was no chance for humanity. Lennon's solution to the problem of the world clearly resided with individuals, rather than social structures and systems of both the left and right.

Lennon's protest not only had an ideology, but it also had a particular form, conflating performance art and politics. While some saw publicity stunts, others connected with the theatricality of his numerous "events"—those such as the honeymoon "bed-in" with Yoko Ono in the Amsterdam Hilton in May 1969, the couple's follow-up "bed-in" in Montreal, the mailing of acorns to world leaders to promote peace, and the "bagism" press conference in Vienna. Following the break-up of The Beatles, Lennon took up permanent residence in New York City, but he spent years fending off deportation efforts because of his politics, doing so again in a way that incorporated performance art. Few might remember the details of the various cases brought against Lennon, but they might remember the press conference he and Yoko held on April Fools' Day in 1973, inaugurating their "conceptual country" of Nutopia, a state with no land, boundaries, passports or laws (except for cosmic ones). Lennon later said that his political passion almost ruined his music,[6] yet one could argue that, like Zappa, the way he expressed his ideology was just as problematic, risking the alienation of those who wanted his message amplified in a more accessible way.

Jerry Garcia

Jerry Garcia (1942–1995)[7] found plenty of trouble as a young boy growing up on Harrington Street in San Francisco, California. After dropping out of high school and a short, unsuccessful stint in the U.S. Army, Garcia began to hang out at Kepler's Book Store in Menlo Park, California, where he engaged with the counterculture, read books by Beat intellectuals, wrote songs, and played his guitar. Around this time, he met Phil Lesh, Ron "Pigpen" McKernan, Bob Weir, and Bill Kreutzmann, forming the Warlocks. The group played for Ken Kesey's Acid Tests, changed their name to the Grateful Dead, and, in a short amount of time, had a following of loyal fans that compared to no other music group in the United States.

Garcia was known to be an anarchist who did not tell other people how to live their lives (nor did he want anyone to tell him how to live), and so the question of how he engaged in social protest is an interesting and complex one. With the exception of "New Speedway Boogie," which was a protest against the violence at the Altamont concert in December 1969 during which a concert-goer was killed by a member of the Hell's Angels, Garcia's protests were typically more subtle in nature. He did not conform to social or music industry norms, preferring music that involved lengthy jams. He encouraged fans to tape concerts and freely share and enjoy music, rather than requiring everyone to pay to listen to the Grateful Dead. (Of course, if one wanted the Grateful Dead "live experience," one still had to pay to see the band.) As de facto leader of the Grateful Dead, a position Garcia renounced, he was reluctant to make too many public statements about social issues and events, due in part to his concern that fans might uncritically adopt his views solely based on who they thought he was.

Later in his life, Garcia supported environmental causes to preserve the rainforest and he backed the establishment of the non-profit charitable Rex Foundation, which promotes creative endeavors in the arts, science, and education. Garcia clearly cared about what happened in the world and he wanted to see society become a more equitable and just place, but he did so more obliquely than either Zappa or Lennon.

Protest against Form

One way in which Zappa pushed boundaries in his music throughout his career was through his use of four-letter words and sexually explicit content (often in a humorous way). In the 1960s, this activity got him into trouble with the law; while running a small studio (Studio Z) in Cucamonga, California, in 1965, he was arrested by undercover police officers for allegedly making a pornographic audiotape, an event Zappa always considered to be entrapment.[8] Throughout his career, he made support for free and open inquiry a hallmark of his belief system, and he rejected religious and political movements that didn't encourage people to think. Songs that express this sentiment include "Dumb All Over," from the 1981 album *You Are What You Is*, and "The Meek Shall Inherit Nothing," from *Thing-Fish* (1984).

Zappa's first major band, the Mothers of Invention, formed in 1965, went through various personnel changes until Zappa retired the moniker in 1974. Their 1966 debut album, *Freak Out*, contained several songs that commented on the social unrest of the time, including "It Can't Happen Here," "Who are the Brain Police," and "Trouble Every Day," the latter being a commentary on the 1965 Los Angeles Watts race riots in which Zappa laments that "there's a whole lots of times I wish I could say I'm not white." "Plastic People" and "Brown Shoes Don't Make It," from the second album, *Absolutely Free*, poke fun at consumer culture and conformity. But it was really with the Mothers' third album, *We're Only in It for the Money* (1968), that Zappa took his social protest and satire to its extreme. The cover was a parody of one of the most popular albums at the time, The Beatles' *Sgt. Pepper's Lonely Hearts Club Band* (1967). The whole album is more or less a commentary on the silliness of hippie culture and its trappings. One critic argued the album is "a swing attack on the hypocrisy of adult America which drinks itself into oblivion ("Bow Tie Daddy"), sets up a disastrous system of sexual ignorance ("Harry You're a Beast"), or colludes with the proto-fascist goon squads of 'Concentration Moon.'"[9] Other albums with unique musical forms that Zappa released during his early days include a symphony (*Lumpy Gravy*, 1967), a doo-wop tribute (*Cruising with Ruben and the Jets*, 1968), and jazz-blues offerings (*Hot Rats*, 1969, and *The Grand Wazoo*, 1972).[10] Later, two live albums, *Filmore East* (1971) and *Just Another Band from LA* (1972), featured Flo and Eddie of The Turtles in one of the most beloved of Mothers' line-ups. Mothers' performances were interactive affairs, with audience participation and theater, but Flo and Eddie as front men took it another level, with epics such as "Billy the Mountain," a lengthy spoof of rock operas, which were prominent in the late 1960s and early 1970s (*Hair* and *Tommy* being two of the most famous). Zappa also directed and wrote the score for *200 Motels* (1971), his sardonic look at the life of a rock musician. During the 1970s, Zappa continued to release cutting-edge music. He pushed boundaries by releasing songs like "Don't You Eat the Yellow Snow" (which made it onto the *Billboard* charts, as the album it was taken from, *Apostrophe*, was number ten and one of his most recognizable "mainstream" songs), "Titties and Beer," "The Illinois Enema Bandit," "Jewish Princess," which angered the Anti-Defamation League, and "Inca Roads," the prog-rock-skewering classic which angered anyone who believed in UFOs.

Zappa's body of work in the 1970s focused on pushing compositional boundaries. This was something that was a priority to John Lennon as well. One could argue that these efforts were a form of protest against the commercialized music that typified the early days of the Beatles, something Lennon seemed to despise. While he was still with the Beatles, Lennon altered commonly accepted forms and expectations for songs. In some cases, Lennon challenged gender norms in songs like "Baby You

Can Drive My Car," which inverted traditional male/female roles, and he penned "Norwegian Wood" as a more sophisticated take on the modern woman.

Lennon also challenged commonly accepted music forms through his experimentation with sound. When The Beatles began recording, there were single-track recorders, and later four-track and more advanced options. They experimented with ways to get more and different sounds by taking heads off the recorders, using spinning speakers from inside Hammond organs, and experimenting with various sound effects and gadgets. Lennon claimed that his guitar playing in *Beatles for Sale* was the first intentional use of distortion in rock music. Lennon asked producer George Martin to make him sound like the Dalai Lama shouting from the top of a mountain for "Tomorrow Never Knows," and they put microphones in condoms under water to get the sound effects for "Yellow Submarine." This pushed boundaries in music in new and different ways, with historic results like "Strawberry Fields Forever," "A Day in the Life" and other classic songs.

Lennon also challenged music norms in his avant-garde creations with Yoko Ono, which provided often very personal glimpses of their lives (quite unusual for the time). Their debut album *Two Virgins* (1968) consisted of Lennon playing different musical instruments while trying out various sound effects. An unflattering picture of a naked Lennon and Ono was on the album cover, something Lennon explained as an effort to show they were just human. The film of the same name involved merging Lennon and Ono's faces into one image. Lennon and Ono's second album, *Unfinished Music No. 2—Life with the Lions*, included more experimental music, as well as a recording of the heartbeat of a baby they lost in a miscarriage several months before the album's release. *The Wedding Album* contained no music and instead consisted of Lennon and Ono calling out each other's names with heartbeats sounding in the background on one side, and sounds from the Amsterdam bed-in on the other. Film No. 5, also known as *Smile*, was a 52-minute close-up of Lennon's face as he made different expressions. *Up Your Legs Forever* was a 75-minute film of people's legs while they walked, with a closing shot of Lennon and Ono's bare buttocks.

Garcia challenged standard forms in ways that differed from Zappa and Lennon. He pushed against the idea that music was a singular thing, explaining:

> You have to get past the idea that music *has* to be *one* thing. To be alive in America is to hear all kinds of music constantly—radio, records, churches, cats on the street, everywhere music, man.[11]

Perhaps most obvious way in which Garcia pushed against norms was through the signature improvisations in which he engaged with members of the Grateful Dead. Garcia once explained, "I've always been a musician and into improvising and it's like I consider life to be a continuous series of improvisations."[12] These improvisations could last more than an hour as fans danced to songs like "Dark Star" and found pleasure in the variations they heard from one concert venue to the next. Sometimes, concerts stretched through the night into the early hours of the morning, something other bands of the era did not regularly do. The result of lengthy improvisations was that the band's music could not be easily recorded for albums or played on the radio. Instead, they encouraged fans to bring recording devices to concerts and to freely share the music they heard, a practice that was out of sync with other bands and the music industry as a whole.

Garcia and the other members of the Grateful Dead were largely distrustful of the music industry and believed, generally, that albums would not really benefit them. When the band began to work with music studios to record albums, they frustrated producers with their experimentation and suggestions of things that seemed far out, such as attempting to record the sound of air. Garcia compared studio work to trying to build a ship in a bottle,[13] and the group clearly missed the synergistic relationship they had with audiences in their live venues. Their second album, *Anthem of the Sun*, was a musical composition Garcia created with Lesh, but he was largely disappointed that the effects he thought were wonderful in the studio did not come across well on the album.[14] When the album was finished, Warner Brothers studio executive Joe Smith complained about the band's unprofessionalism, describing the Dead as the most undesirable group among Los Angeles recording studios. Garcia was not concerned. The band went on to form their own label in 1973, and produced several albums, including *Wake of the Flood* (1973), *From the Mars Hotel* (1974) and *Blues for Allah* (1975), among others. They ended up losing money, but the idea that a band would have its own label in the early 1970s was a clear effort to subvert the record industry, and was groundbreaking at the time. Zappa also started his own label, Zappa Records, in 1977.

While Garcia wrote original music, he was also interested in preserving and performing old-time music, including Appalachian songs such as "Shady Grove," an eighteenth-century folk song, and "The Wind and Rain," a murder ballad. Bluegrass music and old stories clearly influenced Garcia as well, as seen in songs like "Dire Wolf" and "Candyman." He played these songs up to the time of his death, well after the folk revival of the 1960s was out of fashion. Garcia's interests in chromaticism and atonalism, and the influences of jazz and bluegrass, contributed to his unique sound and approach to music. He played because he loved music, not because he wanted to sell records or please large audiences. In many ways, his protest against the forms common in his day was challenging the idea that music had to fit easily into a box. He once explained: "There's a lot of great music in the American experience, and I hope to be able to touch as much of it as I can. I feel that I can honestly contribute something."[15]

Garcia did contribute to American music in profound ways. After Garcia's death, Bob Dylan explained "There are a lot of spaces and advances between the Carter Family, Buddy Holly and, say, Ornette Coleman, a lot of universes, but he filled them all without being a member of any school. His playing was moody, awesome, sophisticated, hypnotic and subtle."[16]

Protests against Social and Cultural Problems

Zappa, Lennon, and Garcia engaged in protest against social and cultural problems through their music, social engagements, and public statements and commitments. Though they approached protests against problems in different ways, they each found ways to make their viewpoints known.

In the three-record set of *Joe's Garage* (1979), Zappa returned to the concept album and social protest in a really big way. Released on his own label, Zappa Records,[17] *Joe's Garage* "follows the adventures of Joe as he struggles and fails to become a musician in an oppressive future." All the while, the Central Scrutinizer (voiced by Zappa), "enforcer of all the laws that haven't been passed yet," is narrating the story.[18] This is one of Zappa's most complicated and creative works, which takes Joe on his journey throughout a dystopian society while also taking jabs at religion for profit, as one of the characters is L. Ron Hoover from the Church of Appliantology. In the liner notes to the album, Zappa discusses the danger of listening too closely to government mandates that call for blind obedience, in this case the "abolition of MUSIC." The album is a "stupid story about how the government is going to try and do away with music," which had recently happened in Iran.[19]

The early 1980s saw Frank Zappa release a string of albums containing his political and social comments. *You Are What You Is* (1981) contains Zappa's most vehement attack on religion with "Dumb All Over" and "Heavenly Bank Account." The songs on the album also deal with spoiled teenagers (in an increasingly yuppie society), the "stupidity of the privileged," and the "corruption of government."[20] The most overt social protest song on the album is the title track, "You Are What You Is," in which Zappa argues "for the relationship between freedom and responsibility … [and where] Zappa's main argument is about people and their refusal to accept themselves or others at face value."[21]

In 1982, Zappa, oddly, had an unexpected hit with a song he wrote with his daughter Moon, "Valley Girl," from *Ship Arriving Too Late to Save a Drowning Witch* (which charted at no. 32). The 1984 triple album *Thing-Fish* was Zappa's attempt at writing a Broadway musical featuring Ike Willis (imitating Kingfish from the 1950s television program *Amos and Andy*). Zappa himself referred to this album as "the weirdest one in my career."[22] This album features commentary on race, sexuality, and the concept of Broadway musicals. The 1984 concert film *Does Humor Belong in Music* contains one of Zappa's most sarcastic comments about the two major political parties in the U.S. In an interview he stated that it takes a lot of "pressure" to join either the Democratic or Republican parties. Zappa found the Republican Party particularly distasteful for what he saw as supporting, and selling out to, the religious right. When asked whether humor belongs in music, he responded with, "I think so. It belongs in everyday life unless the Republicans want to take it away."[23]

In 1985, Zappa became involved in the controversial discussion of rating rock records for transgressive content, spearheaded by the Parents' Music Resource Center (PMRC), a group of Washington wives. They were afraid that too many children were exposed to pornographic and violent content in popular music. Zappa testified during Congressional hearings against official government involvement in the record industry. He even wrote to President Ronald Reagan, stating, "Mr. President, if you are not serious about getting government off our backs, could you at least do something about getting it out of our nostrils."[24] In his testimony to Congress, Zappa explained how the schemes of the PMRC "infringes the civil liberties of people who are not children … [and that an organization such as the PMRC] seems intent on running the Constitution of the United States through the family paper-shredder."[25] Zappa saw government involvement in the music industry and in the personal lives of musicians as lunacy and against the rights of the individual.

Shortly after appearing before Congress, Zappa released *Frank Zappa Meets the Mothers of Prevention,* which contained the track "Porn Wars," featuring much of the Congressional testimony. It also featured his sly commentary on musicians' unions and the '60s revival "You Cats" and "We're Turning Again."[26] On the album was a big sticker-like warning notice that:

> This album contains material which a truly free society would neither fear nor suppress. In some socially retarded areas [certain groups] violate your First Amendment Rights by attempting to censor rock & roll albums. We feel that this is un-Constitutional and un-American.[27]

In 2010, the Zappa Family Trust released the spoken word CD of Zappa's congressional testimony, *Congress Shall Make No Law,* as a historical document and a reminder of the need to advocate for free speech without government intervention. The CD booklet reprinted Zappa's letter to the President and other articles related to Zappa's testimony, including his letter to the music industry publication *Cashbox* and the *Library Bill of Rights,* among other documents related to free speech.

On his short 1988 tour, Zappa did something unprecedented in the history of popular music. Tables were set up so that concert-goers could register to vote, and from the stage Zappa encouraged his fans to get their registrations in. He firmly believed in the principles of the Constitution and that democracy only works if you participate. One critic said that Zappa's tour document, *Broadway the Hard Way* (1988), represented his "most intellectually stimulating post '60s political efforts."[28] The album was filled with commentary on political and government lunacy ("Dickie's Such an Asshole," "When the Lie's So Big," "Promiscuous"), and how the country might look if televangelist Pat Robertson became president ("Jesus Thinks

You're a Jerk"). Zappa never toured again, but continued to release music from his personal archives and orchestral works like *The Yellow Shark* (1993) until shortly before his death.

In 1991, Zappa announced that he was considering running for president as an Independent. Part of his platform included getting rid of income tax but raising sales tax "twelve to fourteen percent on certain products."[29] He saw this as a way for the country to solve its deficit problems, reasoning that if people have more money in their pockets, they will end up spending it, which would help the U.S. economy. Zappa also became friends with Czech President Vaclav Havel and worked as a cultural advisor to the Czech nation (rare for a music personality). Zappa's attempt at a political career was cut short after he was diagnosed with prostate cancer.

Frank Zappa advocated for the separation of church and state, as stated in the Constitution.[30] He saw himself as a "practical conservative" who wanted a "smaller, less intrusive government."[31] His social protest included his unwavering advocacy of the principles of American liberty as outlined in the Constitution of the United States (which he read to his children). He was uncompromising in his belief that participatory democracy can, and does, work. Since Zappa's death in 1993, the Zappa Family Trust has continued to release his music and encourage his fans to vote and carry on Frank Zappa's legacy.

John Lennon's music contains a range of protests against social injustices as he advocated for peace and individuals to change. The song "Revolution" (1968) may have generated a great deal of controversy upon its release, but other versions of protest songs preceded this. "A Day in the Life" (1967), adapted from stories that were reported in the London newspaper *The Daily Mail*, turns newspaper writing on its head. "I Am the Walrus" (1967) criticizes education, art, religion, and more, in something scholar Ian MacDonald described as the most idiosyncratic protest song ever written.

Some of Lennon's songs are well known around the world, and have become anthems for demonstrators engaged in a range of social issues that span from the civil rights struggles of the 1960s to the Occupy movement that began in 2011. "Give Peace a Chance," famously sung by Pete Seeger, Brother Fred Kirkpatrick, Peter, Paul and Mary, and Mitch Miller at the March on Washington on 15 November 1969, was a pivotal song in the anti-war movement, although Lennon did not perform it at any Vietnam War protests. It has been described as "the only protest song that is literally self-congratulatory, ending with the sound of Lennon and his ad hoc band clapping themselves. It is less an end in itself than a launch pad for something bigger."[32]

Lennon was pleased to know this song had such appeal and its success inspired a flurry of activity. He returned his Member of the Most Excellent Order of the British Empire to the Queen of England with a note explaining that it was a gesture of protest against the Vietnam War, the atrocities in the African colony of Biafra, and his song "Cold Turkey" losing ground in the music charts. He pledged support to

James Hanratty, who was accused of murder and hanged in 1962 in spite of questions about his guilt. With Ono, he had billboards installed around the world that proclaimed "War is over if you want it. Happy Christmas from John and Yoko." After Lennon gave an interview with Tariq Ali and Robin Blackburn in *Red Mole* in 1971, famously telling them he would like to compose songs for the revolution, he wrote "Power to the People." Later Lennon admitted that the song was "written in the state of being asleep and wanting to be loved by Tariq and his ilk."[33] Some of his gestures seemed difficult for the public to understand and some ridiculed him, yet he continued on with this efforts.

In the early 1970s, Lennon became publicly involved in a number of social causes. He joined a demonstration in London "For the IRA, against British imperialism." He also marched to protest an obscenity charge against the magazine *OZ*, a psychedelic hippy magazine based in London. Lennon and Ono released "God Save Us" and "Do the Oz" to raise money for legal fees. Lennon also donated money to Scottish shipbuilders who held a work-in led by union leader Jimmy Reid. The action saved more than 8,000 jobs.

Lennon's song "Imagine" is considered to be among the greatest songs of all time. The film version includes footage of John sitting at a grand piano in his expansive mansion in the English countryside as he calls for people to join together as one, with no country, religious or other boundaries to divide them. The contradictions in his presentation of the song and the nihilism called for in the lyrics did not seem to bother fans, and the song remains to be viewed by many as a utopian anthem that will bring social change.

Once he settled in New York City, Lennon released the album *Some Time in New York City* (1972). The album included songs expressing Lennon's social interests, such as in negating sexism in "Woman is the Nigger of the World," which evoked a quite controversial reaction, "Attica State," intended as a statement against police brutality, and "The Luck of the Irish" and "Sunday Bloody Sunday," which addressed the many hardships in Northern Ireland. The album was originally released as a double album and contained live tracks, including a recording of Lennon and Ono performing with Frank Zappa and the Mothers of Invention in June 1971 at the Fillmore East. The inner sleeve included a photo of Lennon drawing on a cover of Zappa's album *Fillmore East—June 1971*. Zappa had issues with the recording because it did not include all the vocals and he did not receive writing credit for the song "King Kong."

Once in New York, Lennon and Ono met up with Yippies Jerry Rubin and Abbie Hoffman, as well as other members of the radical left that included Allen Ginsberg, Bobby Seale, and Huey Newton. Within months, he was under FBI surveillance and the U.S. government began a four-year unsuccessful effort to deport him. Lennon released the song "Gimme Some Truth" on the album *Imagine*, in which he sang "No short-haired, yellow-bellied, son of tricky dicky is gonna Mother Hubbard soft soap me" to express his frustration with deceptive politicians. Lennon and Ono participated, to mixed reviews, in the rally in Ann Arbor, Michigan, to free John Sinclair from prison for drug possession. They also appeared on a series of television talk shows (notably with Dick Cavett), expressing their views about any number of issues.

Whereas John Lennon was outspoken in the media, and not overly concerned whether people adopted his views or not, Garcia tended to avoid making explicit public statements about his position on social and political issues. People often sought him out to share their ideas or ask his views, but he avoided addressing large audiences on matters of social or political consequence. Instead, we can interpret his position based on a number of causes he supported over the years.

In October 1966, California had passed a law making LSD illegal, and protestors demonstrated in the Love Pageant Rally to express their disagreement and belief that they were not criminals because they chose to use drugs. Hundreds of people attended the event, and the Grateful Dead performed on the back of a flat bed truck, one of their first free outdoor concerts to show support for a particular cause. Other free concerts supported the Diggers, an anarchist group that combined street theater, art and political action and gave away free food on a daily basis. Once, after a riot on the Haight, the police shut down Haight Street, and the Dead took advantage of the moment to trick the authorities and play a free concert on a flat-bed truck bed parked on the street.[34]

The Human Be-In (14 January 1967) came a year after the Trips Festival. It was three days of rock music and psychedelic drugs that kicked off what many consider to be the era of the 1960s, and it continued the October 1966 protest. The Grateful Dead performed in front of a crowd that some estimated was as large as 30,000 people. Other bands that joined the scene included longtime friends Jefferson Airplane and Quicksilver Messenger Service. Several speakers addressed the crowd, including poet Allen Ginsberg and Timothy Leary. It was here that Leary famously uttered the line "Turn on, tune in, drop out."

While he eschewed speaking openly about political events, Garcia was well aware of what was going on in the world. The Grateful Dead did not support Nixon's hope to be re-elected to a second term as U.S. President in 1973, but they also would not publicly support McGovern in his bid for presidency. When McGovern asked them directly, telling them they would be invited to the White House if he won, the Dead explained that they could only do so if McGovern legalized marijuana.[35] Of course, he would not.

Garcia was clearly opposed to the war in Vietnam. During an interview after the release of *The Grateful Dead*, he uncharacteristically explained his position:

> The war is an effort on the part of the establishment to keep the economic situation in the United States comparatively stable ... [W]ould I go? I would

not go. I am totally against war … I could never kill anybody … I don't feel like I'm any kind of subversive force, you know; I feel like an American, and I'm really ashamed of it, lately.[36]

Garcia respected Al Gore's concern about the environment and future of the planet and, in September 1988, the Dead played a benefit concert with other artists including Suzanne Vega, Bruce Hornsby, and Hall and Oates at Madison Square in New York to raise money for, and awareness about, vanishing rainforests. While it was out of character for the Grateful Dead to support a political cause, they believed this was serious enough and life-threatening enough to warrant their support. After much research into various organizations, they decided the money would go to Greenpeace, Cultural Survival, and the Rainforest Action Network. This was the first time Garcia spoke out on a public issue at a large press conference, but he clearly felt strongly about the cause. He explained:

> We've never really called on our fans, the Deadheads, to align themselves one way or another as far as any political cause is concerned because of a basic paranoia about leading someone … But this is, we feel, an issue strong enough and life-threatening enough that inside the world of human games … there's the larger question of global survival.[37]

The benefit raised $600,000, and the *Blues from the Rainforest Album*, with Merl Saunders and Jerry Garcia, followed.

Conclusions

While Zappa, Lennon, and Garcia each engaged in subverting music forms and protesting social concerns, they approached the problems of their day in different ways. Zappa was perhaps the most strategic, getting audiences with Congress and using public forums in ways that generated respect. Lennon also used public forums, but his efforts were sometimes seen as quite fringe and inadequate. Garcia made most of his statements as non-statements, instead providing a living example of an alternative lifestyle and his objectives to the mainstream. All three, however, created music that has endured and inspired people to reconsider their own conditions and new possibilities, and they influenced musicians who followed them. Operation Ivy singer Jesse Michaels has written:

> Music is an indirect force for change, because it provides an anchor against human tragedy. In this sense, it works towards a reconciled world. It can also be the direct experience of change … The momentum is made of all the people who stay interested, and keep their sense of urgency and hope.[38]

Zappa, Lennon, and Garcia help us to consider a reconciled world, and their music, words, and actions provide us with a sense of the limits of human efforts to bring change—as well as the possibilities.

Notes

1 Zappa played with John Lennon at the Fillmore East in 1971, sequentially released on Lennon's 1972 *Sometime in New York City* album, much to Zappa's displeasure. He also was on a double bill with the Jerry Garcia Band August 18, 1984 at the UIC Pavilion Chicago, IL. Garcia opened and Zappa closed the show.

2 Kevin Crowley, *Surf Beat* (New York: Backbeat Books, 2011), 73.

3 A present for his fifteenth birthday—see Ben Watson, *Frank Zappa: Negative Dialectics of Poodle Play* (New York: St. Martin's Press, 1995), 7

4 Available at to be seen at the time of this writing on YouTube (accessed 5 April 2012), http://www.youtube.com/watch?v=y9P2V0_p6vE&feature=related.

5 John Lennon, "A Very Open Letter to John Hoyland from John Lennon," *Black Dwarf*, Vol. 13, No. 9 (10 January 1969).

6 Dorian Lynskey, *33 Revolutions Per Minute: A History of Protest Songs, from Billie Holiday to Green Day* (New York: HarperCollins, 2011).

7 The Grateful Dead performed at the Café au Go Go in NYC in the early 1960s. Frank Zappa's Mothers of Invention played upstairs, but Zappa was never a fan of the San Francisco music scene. Garcia was influenced by the Beatles and met John Lennon while touring with Legion of Mary in the fall of 1975. The group was playing at the trendy New York club called the Bottom Line.

8 Crowely, *Surf Beat*, 194–195. See also Frank Zappa, *The Real Frank Zappa Book* (New York: Poseidon Press, 1989), 55–60.

9 Jon Savage, "We're Only in It for the Money," in Mark Blake, ed., *Mojo Classic: Zappa* (Mojo, 2010): 30.

10 Martin Aston, "Hot Rats," *Mojo Classic: Zappa*, 48.

11 Garcia, as quoted in Holly George-Warren, *Garcia: By the Editors of Rolling Stone* (New York: Little, Brown and Company, 1995), 64.

12 Garcia, as quoted in Jerry Garcia, Charles Reich, and Jann Wenner, *Garcia: A Signpost to a New Space* (New York: De Capo Press, 1972), 20

13 Jeremy Marre, *The Grateful Dead: Anthem to Beauty* (New York: Eagle Rock Entertainment, 1997).

14 Marre, *The Grateful Dead*.

15 Garcia, quoted in George-Warren, *Garcia: By the Editors*, 196.

16 Dylan, as quoted in George-Warren, *Garcia: By the Editors*, 30.

17 Zappa, tired of the way record companies, specifically Warner Brothers, tried to control his product.

18 Chris Ingham, "Joe's Garage," in *Mojo Classic: Zappa*, 82.

19 Frank Zappa, "Liner notes," *Joe's Garage* (Salem, MA: Rykodisc, 1995), 5 (Originally released in 1979); Ingham, 82.

20 Kelley Fisher Lowe, *The Words and Music of Frank Zappa* (Westport, Connecticut: Praeger, 2006), 167–177.

21 Lowe, *The Words and Music*, 172.

22 Fabio Massari, "Talking with Frank," *Sonora* (Italy: Stampato pesos, April 1994), 62

23 Frank Zappa, quoted from Frank Zappa, *Does Humor Belong in Music*, DVD, © 1984, Virgin Records.

24 Zappa, *The Real Frank Zappa*, 267.

25 Zappa, *The Real Frank Zappa*, 268, 270.

26 Lowe, *The Words and Music*, 196.

27 Frank Zappa, cover, *Frank Zappa Meets the Mothers of Prevention*, CD, © 1985, Rykodisc. See Chapter 15 in Zappa, *The Real Frank Zappa*, 261–291.

28 Steve Huey quoted in Lowe, *The Words and Music*, 203.

29 Bob Guccione, Jr., "Sings of the Time," in Richard Kostelanetz, ed., *The Frank Zappa Companion* (New York: Schirmer Books, 1997), 230.

30 See chapter 16 in Zappa, *The Real Frank Zappa*, 293–313.

31 Zappa, *The Real Frank Zappa*, 315.

32 Lynskey, *33 Revolutions Per Minute*, 136.

33 Lynskey, *33 Revolutions Per Minute*, 141.

34 Phil Lesh, *Searching for the Sound: My Life with the Grateful Dead* (New York: Little Brown and Company, 2005), 124.

35 Dennis McNally, *A Long Strange Trip: The Inside History of the Grateful Dead* (New York: Random House, 2002), 442.

36 Garcia, as quoted in McNally, *A Long Strange Trip*, 186–187.

37 Garcia, as quoted in Blair Jackson, *Garcia: An American Life* (New York: Penguin Books, 1999), 380.

38 Jesse Michaels, at http://www.pinstand.com/pins/opiv.html , accessed 23 May 2012).

12

FALLING INTO FANCY FRAGMENTS

Punk, Protest, and Politics

Travis A. Jackson

Figure 12.1 Sex Pistols.

Since its emergence into public consciousness in the mid-1970s, punk has increasingly seemed, for self-selected and overlapping groups of scholars and fans, to be the apotheosis of protest music. In particular, those writers concerned with punk's initial manifestations in England have designated, as the targets of the musicians' protest, the pretentiousness and excesses of progressive rock, on one hand, and the depredations of 1970s working-class life, on the other. In the former case, the newer music was a generational antidote to the adaptations of European concert music, the concept albums, and the elaborate stage shows that characterized work by English groups such as Yes, Genesis, and Emerson, Lake, and Palmer. The southern English/London-based hippie subculture which nurtured this first target of punk protest primarily comprised college-educated youth from middle to upper-class families.[1] By the mid-1970s, however, whatever cozy, communal vibe had obtained at venues like The UFO Club or The Marquee in late 1960s London had given way to what some regarded as self-indulgent spectacle: rather than changing the world, those young people had merely succeeded in attracting derision and disdain. Indeed, "hippie" became perhaps the most venomous epithet writers and readers of publications like *New Musical Express* (*NME*) and *Melody Maker* (*MM*) could hurl at those they disliked.[2] This was especially true among those sympathetic to non-elite, working-class youth facing rampant unemployment and growing inequality who, the story goes, saw the lyrics, simplicity and sonic aggression of punk as outlets for their disaffection and disenfranchisement.

Among those expressing or endorsing this view of punk as protest a consensus of sorts has emerged, one that posits and celebrates at once the emancipatory, oppositional, anti-racist power of the music and its creators' do-it-yourself ethos.[3] Their collective, cumulative, pronouncements register as a set of variations on a "year zero" narrative of rock history with punk—or, more precisely, The Sex Pistols[4]—occupying the extended moment that separates the before and the after. That is, now many critics and fans write almost as though everything prior to the November 1976 release of "Anarchy in the UK" was a rehearsal for punk, while they measure everything since in terms of fealty to what they see as the core values of the music. A brilliant fictional parody of that conceit—or is it an endorsement?—is Neal Pollack's novel *Never Mind the Pollacks*.[5] Its protagonist, also named Neal Pollack, manages, in picaresque fashion, not only to move through the entirety of rock history over the narrative's arc—exerting a profound influence at each pivotal moment—but also to have understood and embodied its essential spirit over the same span. As some reviewers have observed,[6] Pollack the character is a thinly disguised proxy for the critic Lester Bangs, whose own writing for *Creem* and other publications rebranded sometimes amateurish 1960s garage rock as "punk" in its advocacy of three pillars of a now-taken-for-granted pop anti-aesthetic. As Bernard Gendron distills them from three essays published by Bangs in 1971 and 1972, these pillars raise punk above hippie, progressive music through negation: "Assaultiveness opposed itself to aesthetic edification and seriousness, minimalism to the worship of complexity, and, of course, that most anti-art of all these traits—ineptness and grunginess—to the false pretenses of instrumental virtuosity."[7]

Of course, the history of punk and punk's relationship to protest are more conflicted and complex than those narratives allow.[8] Most critically, the sonic field of popular music in the early 1970s was as densely populated as any, for critics in the British press were coining terms for or discovering rock sub-genres by the week.[9] Thus, alongside progressive rock, the landscape included the singer-songwriter fare of Joni

Mitchell, Carole King, Laura Nyro and James Taylor; the space rock of Hawkwind; the glam rock of T. Rex, David Bowie and New York Dolls; the jazz-funk, jazz-rock, and Latin fusions of Miles Davis, Herbie Hancock, Return to Forever, Santana, The Mahavishnu Orchestra and Blood, Sweat, and Tears; the soul music of Aretha Franklin, Donny Hathaway, Al Green, Curtis Mayfield and Marvin Gaye; the reggae of (Bob Marley and) The Wailers; the folk music of Fairport Convention and Pentangle; and the heavy rock of Led Zeppelin and Black Sabbath. Given evidence of such variety, there's no clear reason articulated in most retrospective assessments why only progressive musicians were the recipients of punk fans' and musicians' opprobrium. Moreover, as early as 1976, a number of putatively counter-cultural punk musicians were actively seeking conventional markers of success, such as major-label contracts and prime-time television appearances. Looking back at this period, commentators like Dave Laing have also questioned the degree to which independent labels altered the economic and ideological terrain of the recording industry[10] when signees and personnel at such labels seemed to revel in their imprints' status, as had been the case for other musicians and personnel in other eras, as stepping stones to larger, better-financed entities. Likewise, Simon Frith and Howard Horne argue that, rather than coming from the streets, "Punk rock was the ultimate art school music movement. It brought to a head fifteen years of questions about creativity in a mass medium, and tried to keep in play bohemian ideals of authenticity and Pop art ideals of artifice."[11]

Lingering in the background of each of those qualifications of the conventional punk narrative is the question of how (and how well) punk or any other music—as performed in public, as sounded on recordings and as lived by various social actors—might materially effect protest through expressive practices. Likewise, given the many different strains of punk that have emerged and the contexts in which they have appeared since the middle of the 1970s, one also needs to specify what punk musicians and their fans and supporters have protested and why, ever mindful that protest and politics—contrary to what appears, for example, in work by Street and essays collected by Garofalo—are not the sole province of those on the left or those involved in anti-hegemonic struggles.[12] In what follows, then, I want to explore some of the issues raised previously in more detail and, in so doing, to track both the means through which musical styles might register as protest and the discursive and ideological commitments that have encouraged punk commentators to read the music, often against the grain, as protest.

One might reasonably begin such exploration by asking what exactly punk is. Where Lester Bangs, Greg Shaw and Dave Marsh—with whom the term originated—were concerned, punk was first and foremost a style of music, but that style was more their retrospective creation than it was either the result of any self-consciously deployed practices and conventions, or of any easily aggregated ensembles of ideological commitments on the part of musicians. Disillusioned as each of these critics were with what they perceived as the bloated decadence of rock in the late 1960s, they sought a means to revitalize the music, to give it a new, revolutionary, charge. "In their search for 1960s rock 'n' rollers who were neither touched by decadence nor influential of it," Bernard Gendron explains:

> Bangs and his allies searched through different makeshift categories—the British Invasion, surf music, American bands influenced by the British Invasion, such as the 'San Jose groups.' Gradually, they settled upon a collection of not well-known 1960s bands, one-hit wonders previously neglected by critics, who combined rank amateurism with a certain pugnacity—bands such as Count Five ("Psychotic Reaction"), Question Mark and the Mysterians ("96 Tears"), The Seeds ("Pushing Too Hard"), and The Troggs ("Wild Thing"). Today we refer to them as "garage bands," but Shaw (or was it Marsh?) saw fit to name them "punk bands," a name that stuck.[13]

What those groups had in common, in the view of Bangs and his counterparts, was an expansive stance toward "art" that was also an implicit critique of a diverse array of rock styles:

> Being against art simply meant being against the unmediated appropriation of mainstream art notions and their pretensions into popular music—the pieties of singer-songwriters, the virtuosic convolutions of heavy metal, and the classical music quotationalism of British art rock. Yet at the same time, the punk aesthetic was clearly incorporating avant-garde notions that came from outside the rock 'n' roll ambit.[14]

Interestingly, at the same time that the critics were imputing certain ideas to the musicians, they were also more explicitly borrowing the discourse of scholars—such as Theodor Adorno and Herbert Marcuse—associated with the Institute for Social Research at the University of Frankfurt am Main in the 1930s. Those scholars, in turn, saw popular music as an ideological tool for pacifying social agents and inhibiting the development of mass critical consciousness.[15] As the original punk theoreticians understood it, rock music, like other cultural items produced in opposition to dominant modes of thought, was a necessary form of negation, standing at a critical remove from pop or classical music and, as a result, was most paradigmatically itself when challenging, rather than reinforcing, the status quo. Bangs, Shaw, Marsh and their followers, as Robert Tillman explains more generally, helped to assemble a foundational toolkit for rock criticism and appreciation: "when new styles of rock music emerge"—or are discursively constructed in this instance—"critics have a firm precedent for seeing the revolutionary or counter-cultural implications within them, particularly when those styles seem to accentuate the conflictual aspects traditionally associated with rock."[16]

The degree to which one might characterize punk sonically as a form of protest music, then, rests discursively and relationally on how the music resonates after and alongside other styles in a broader field of musical practice. When one examines what Dick Hebdige, in *Subculture*, calls punk's "dubious parentage," one gets the sense that those musicians who more or less claimed the label in the mid-1970s were defined less by the novelty or experimental nature of what they did sonically than by the circumscribed eclecticism of what they combined:

> Strands from David Bowie and glitter rock were woven together with elements from American proto-punk (the Ramones, the Heartbreakers, Iggy Pop, Richard Hell), from that faction within London pub-rock … inspired by the mod subculture of the 60s, from the Canvey Island 40s revival and the Southend R & B bands …, from northern soul and from reggae.[17]

Such a mix, Hebdige argues, was inherently unstable, with each of the elements threatening to "separate and return to their original sources." Whether or not they might have done so, those elements suggest that punk was less a break with the past than a particular kind of continuation—other musicians had played at fast tempos, at deafening and distorted dynamic levels, or with brashness and impudence, especially those canonized by Lester Bangs et al. Indeed, a Geoff Hunt review of an April 1976 show headlined by the 101'ers (before they became The Clash) with the Sex Pistols as an opening act, stresses, above all, how conventional both groups were. Of the latter, he writes:

> The trouble is that the Pistols are too good for anyone to really hate them. The occasionally-routed assertion that they "can't play" is far from the truth. They try nothing flash, but play hard and sharp within limitations which act as a positive discipline … Their own songs are intelligent punk rock … and they invest "Substitute" with more downright cynicism than the Who ever did.

And, of the former:

> The 101'ers are basically '60s r 'n' b, but are creating a more varied act by including more of their own songs. They are much less sloppy than the last time I saw them, and are no longer struggling against an inadequate sound system … The focus of their act is the self-styled Joe Strummer, lead singer and one of the few genuine rhythm guitarists around. He's everywhere at once, chopping out chords as if there is no tomorrow, and his nervous-energy vocal improvisations on the climactic "Gloria" are a treat.[18]

With musicians drawing from such a wide array of sources and seemingly invested in conventional, even professional, performance standards, it is perhaps not surprising that, among British and American critics, there was some disagreement about which musicians were really punk; at its most capacious, the grouping included ensembles ranging from The Clash, Sex Pistols, Slaughter and the Dogs, Buzzcocks and The Adverts to The Jam, The Ramones, The Damned, The Runaways, Ian Hunter, Bruce Springsteen and Patti Smith.[19] In fact, by the end of 1976, a number of fans were questioning punk in both stylistic and ideological terms, claiming in letters to *NME* that the music wasn't sonically radical enough and that its popularity was but a result of manipulative marketing.[20] At no point, in fact, did even the broadest reach of punk include musicians of a more experimental bent—such as Captain Beefheart, This Heat, Cabaret Voltaire or Throbbing Gristle; the latter's ties to the shock-oriented aesthetics of some performance art were clear in the performance/exhibition "Pornography" at London's Institute for Contemporary Art in October of 1976.[21] At least in terms of musical style, then, punk barely registered as even a challenge to what was already on offer.

There was also widespread concern over whether punk constituted a form of protest and, if so, of what kind. Neil Spencer, reflecting on the destruction of 200 seats at a May 1977 package show at the Rainbow Theatre that featured The Prefects, Subway Sect, Buzzocks, The Jam and, finally, The Clash, wrote:

> The prevailing impression I took away was one of nihilism, of anti-life as opposed to life-affirmation, of a perverse and slightly sick communal spirit, of a movement that glorifies hopelessness and has nothing positive to offer beyond the mere fact of its existence … So far the New Wave have been largely incapable of saying exactly what they're fighting for rather than who they're fighting against. We know they're not fighting to defend love and peace, what then?[22]

Near the article's end, especially, Spencer was defending the hippies derided by punks and partly suggesting that reggae performers (and black musicians more generally) socially and lyrically had a stronger claim to being engaged in protest. In fact, Dave Laing's content analysis of punk lyrics revealed that, while slightly more "political" than those produced by musicians in other styles at the time, they were hardly unprecedented or any more effective.[23] Likewise, Dick Hebdige had convincingly argued earlier that as much as subcultural groups, like punks, contested prevailing social orders through their very existence, they also reinforced those orders through accepting "dominant definitions of who and what they are," even as they attempted to resignify them.[24] He would later have even more disparaging things to say about the comparative weakness of punk as protest music compared to reggae, as we'll see below.

Even in early pieces that valorized punk, however, the emphasis was decidedly on the generational/stylistic valence of the music and musicians, rather than any articulated social or political messages. Caroline Coon, writing for *Melody Maker* in August of 1976, argued the music's significance through its affordances for a generation unable to forge affective alliances with distant millionaire rock musicians playing complicated music through expensive instruments and equipment. Beyond there, though, the terms in which she couched her assertions were openly indebted to those used a few years earlier by Bangs, Shaw and Marsh. Citing a "grassroots disenchantment with the present state of mainstream rock" evident in letters written to the newspaper, she wrote that "[T]here is a growing, almost desperate feeling that rock music should be stripped down to its bare bones again. It needs to be taken by the scruff of its bloated neck and given a good shaking."[25] Although she positioned herself as rhetorically channeling the sentiments of British punk fans, she nonetheless seemed to be projecting rather than reporting when she stated as fact the belief that, "The arrogant, aggressive, rebellious stance that characterizes the musicians who have played the most vital rock and roll [e.g., Elvis, Gene Vincent, Mick Jagger, Keith Richard, Jimi Hendrix] has always been glamorised" and that 1976's punks were an updated version of those previous eras' rebels. If punk was going to foment a revolution, she suggested, it would be a stylistic one leading to a "fourth generation" of musicians carrying the rock banner.[26] For a time in 1977 and '78, Coon's projection seemed apt, as a number of major label executives thought punk might be the "next big thing" and started signing any artists who might remotely have been described as punk.[27] Still, there was nothing in that activity, or in the discourse that preceded it, to suggest a connection between protest, especially of the kind associated with folk musicians from the 1950s and '60s, for example.

If neither from its earliest advocates or detractors, from where, then, does the idea that punk equates with protest come? There is abundant evidence to suggest that the equating of punk with protest was indeed an after-the-fact form of justification for the style. In one major sense, punk became annexed to protest because *journalists and public officials* politicized it through their creation of, and responses to, an outcry occasioned by the real (and imagined) actions of the Sex Pistols and groups of fans. The alleged behavior of both at shows led event promoters and local councils in England to be wary of booking punk musicians.[28] In response to what he saw as a manufactured crisis, Charles Shaar Murray wrote a long thought-piece in the *NME* suggesting that punk, with Johnny Rotten as its most prominent figure, was neither a societal problem nor a solution to one. If anything, it was a symptom of a malaise whose victims included all those duped into believing something valuable might emerge from eliminating whatever punk musicians and their fans stood for:

Hippies rejected society; society has rejected the punks. And society has always hated, suppressed and tried to destroy the people who bear most blatantly the scars inflicted upon them by the system under which they have to live because those scars remind the authorities of their own guilt and failure … [S]tardom '77 style means being set up, and Johnny Rotten—more than anyone else—has been set up. Not—as used to be opined—by Malcolm McLaren, but by all the hysterical Punk Rock Shock Horror Youth Cult Probe shit that's been peddled by media fools who love nothing better than to create a new target out of the nearest available human material, stir up hatred for and fear of it and then lead the attack … This country is up shit creek at the moment—and it's more the fault of Jim Callaghan and Maggie Thatcher than John Rotten. And the fact that everyone's feeling pressure right now means that they turn to the nearest available target in the vain and ugly hope that by destroying an irritant they'll somehow make things better and obtain some satisfaction. It's this blind, maimed rage that made the occupants of black America's urban ghettoes burn down their own turf rather than razing Wall Street to the ground. It's this same thing that makes disenfranchised teds bottle Kid Reed of The Boys in a bus queue.[29]

A couple of weeks later, in a letter to *NME*, Dick Hebdige asserted that, whatever value there was in arguments like Murray's, punk's supporters in the press were overlooking the obvious:

> As I'm sure you know, reggae is exiled from the airwaves not only because it's the music of a racial minority but because it doesn't compromise—it experiments with sound, it alludes to ganja, police, politics and black identity … As far as the mainstream media is concerned, reggae is quite literally Beyond the Pale … Punk shocks within strictly defined limits—it pogos for posterity, knocks the Queen (David Frost used to do that in T.W.3 and look where he is now), and turns the flag upside down. Reggae is rather more subversive … it speaks a different language, looks in large part towards Africa (and a different flag) and occasionally provides the soundtrack for real riots (the Carib Club confrontation, the Notting Hill Carnival) … As a result, reggae continues to pursue its course largely underground within the black community (which after all keeps it strong, healthy and unacceptable) whilst Punk rock poses its way up the charts and on to Radio One's turntables.[30]

Indeed, UK punk's most prominent resonance as politics and protest came less from the sound or lyrics of any groups associated with the music than they did from the music's association with reggae through the concerts and activist work of Rock Against Racism (RAR), a group formed in response to Eric Clapton's drunken exhortation to "Keep Britain White" and his stated support of Enoch Powell from a stage in Birmingham in August of 1976.[31]

In a letter sent simultaneously to *NME, Melody Maker* and *Sounds*, RAR's founders, like rock critics, understood the power of popular music with regard to protest/politics in aspirational terms:

> Rock was and still can be a real progressive culture not a package mail order stick-on nightmare of mediocre garbage. Keep the faith, black and white unite and fight. We want to organise a rank and file movement against the racist poison in rock music—we urge support—all those interested please write to: ROCK AGAINST RACISM, Box M, 8 Cottons Gardens, London E2 8DN. P.S. 'Who Shot The Sheriff', Eric? It sure as hell wasn't you![32]

In the rallies and concerts RAR mounted over the next several years, often in collaboration with the Anti-Nazi League, its connection to punk seemed less important *per se* than the symbolic gesture of bringing together black and white musicians regardless of their stylistic leanings. Artists such as Steel Pulse and Aswad shared bills with X-Ray Spex, Stiff Little Fingers, Tom Robinson and Elvis Costello, and the organization used them not only to "reach youth and publicize particular local struggles," in the most general sense, but also to mobilize people in "a series of instant responses to local racial incidents," such as attacks on Pakistani-English residents of Coventry.[33] Beyond the work of The Clash, in fact, one would hard-pressed to find, in most canonic punk, anything resembling the directly targeted forms of protest that characterized music from before (Bob Dylan's "With God on Our Side," for example) and after (Gang of Four's "Not Great Men").

Indeed, even the independent labels that proliferated during the era, sometimes created by performers, sometimes by record shop owners or other music enthusiasts, did not constitute serious threats to the existing order of the recording industry. They had as models, after all, a number of independent jazz[34] and, more directly, contemporary labels like Chiswick and Stiff, whose releases featured pub-rock artists like Eddie and the Hot Rods and Nick Lowe.[35] The new "indies" rapidly became little more than scouts for larger commercial concerns. They were supported by a range of fanzines which likewise duplicated models dating back to 1941[36] and only retrospectively came to present punk as a radical break from the past. Indeed, alongside a feature on the Ramones and reviews of recordings by the Flamin' Groovies, Eddie and The Hot Rods, The Runaways, Todd Rundgren, and Captain Beefheart, Mark Perry devoted a quarter of the 1976 inaugural issue of *Sniffin' Glue ... and Other Rock 'n' Roll Habits* to a critical guide to the recordings of Blue Öyster Cult.[37] Perry's choices, if nothing else, revealed him to be equally interested in styles of music—like heavy metal and experimental rock—that would soon become anathema in the punk world. Moreover, despite the historical significance accorded punk fanzines, pronouncements about their vanguardism are undercut by the political broadsheets of activists and the (pre-punk) underground press in and outside the United Kingdom.

The publishers of those latter works pioneered most of what punk's supporters and apologists have attributed to 'zine producers.[38] In other words, the institutions associated with punk's putative DIY aesthetic, as well as the bands like Buzzcocks, The Desperate Bicycles and Scritti Politti, who tried to demystify recording and distribution through their lyrics and record sleeves,[39] were in many ways extending, rather than inventing, such strategies. When critics and musicians started pronouncing punk dead in 1978, then, on nearly every front it remained unclear, or insufficiently demonstrated, what exactly its links to protest were.

By 1982, when only a few of the original punk groups were still making music, they and some of their followers, such as Gang of Four, started to devote more concentrated attention to the exploration of single styles of music, and a few formerly experimental groups such as The Human League, competing with a host of "New Pop" and "New Romantic" artists, set their sights even more explicitly on chart success and vaguely articulated notions of "subversive consumption."[40] With that locution, Simon Frith and Howard Horne gestured toward the "incoherent" positions taken by "theoretical artists," like Marc Almond of the punningly-named Soft Cell and Green Gartside of Scritti Politti, who wanted to celebrate consumption as a liberating, equalizing, act partially through sneaking into their lyrics what they'd learned from reading Barthes and Derrida. Part of the problem with their strategy, of course, was that they relied on hierarchies of consumption: "If creativity came into play only at the moment of market choice, then superior creativity must be indicated by superior market choices."[41] For consumption to be subversive, in other words, consumers had to choose subversive material over the other fare offered in clothing shops, record stores and other outlets. And, perhaps somewhat reductively, subversion became a matter of taste, of discrimination.

The seemingly weak protest that, in Frith and Horne's assessment, characterized 1980s New Pop and New Romanticism in the United Kingdom powerfully resembles the sketch of punk presented here. That is, punk was not a music whose adherents were allied in any long-term fashion with any political or social causes. Its musicians were not making recordings or deploying performance strategies that departed in any significant ways from what had preceded them, and the lyrics of their songs were only slightly more political or protest-oriented than some of the pub and progressive rock extant when the music emerged. The conceit that punk was and is a music of protest persists, nonetheless, and I'll move toward my conclusion by suggesting that those who valorize the challenges—sonic and social—offered by punk do so because it distinguishes them from fans of other music. While they themselves might not be subversive in ways that draw legal or political scrutiny, they nonetheless challenge orthodoxies of various kinds because their tastes are superior to others' tastes—even if the criteria for determining superiority are self-serving—as was the case with Bangs and Coon, (or with Spencer and Hebdige, who argued against Bangs and Coon in favor of other music).

It is in that spirit, in fact, that a number of commentators on punk have seemed unwilling to separate their aspirations for punk and, thus, for themselves, from what a critical consideration of the relationship between protest and music might require. As Michelle Phillipov argues:

> Much contemporary analysis of punk frequently identifies a self-consciously political band or scene (e.g. Fugazi or the D.C. Scene) and then works backwards to determine the relationship between music and politics: that is, given that we already know that this scene/band/etc. is politically inclined, how are their political dispositions expressed in the music?[42]

How different might the resulting commentaries be, however, were their writers to do things in reverse, methodologically: start with the broad corpus of music in a particular style and then work through it—analytically, historically, ethnographically—to determine its ranges and means of signification? Someone working in that way would have to acknowledge, for example, the musical conservatism of punk; the ambiguity and idiosyncrasy—and not in a coded sense—of much of its lyrical content; the ephemerality of the argument that punk is an anti-commercial "attitude" rather than a musical style; and, most damagingly, the degree to which the music has appealed to and been championed by right-wing reactionary groups from the National Front in 1970s England to neo-Nazi and white power groups from then until now. That person or those people would see that the collage-like edifice of punk had, from its inception, been "falling into fancy fragments,"[43] which a few generations have seen fit to reassemble for a wide range of constituencies. Until such time as the dominant discourse on punk recedes into residual status (to borrow Raymond Williams' terms), it will be difficult to hear emergent critical voices. Just as elements of Spencer's in-the-moment critique and the subtleties of Hebdige and Laing's near contemporaneous positions seem to have been submerged in the din of the preceding years, so too does that din threaten to mask Phillipov's and other latter-day interventions. For those carrying on the conversation that started with Lester Bangs, punk needs to be a music of protest because, in the end, that's what makes it (and them) better.

Notes

1 Edward L. Macan, *Rocking the Classics: English Progressive Rock and the Counterculture* (New York: Oxford University Press, 1997), 146–51.

2 Charles Shaar Murray, "'We Didn't Know It Was Loaded:' Panic on the Titanic (Part 77)," *New Musical Express*, 9 July 1977, and Neil Spencer, "Is This What We Ordered?" *New Musical Express*, 21 May 1977, 7–8.

3 Dave Laing, *One Chord Wonders: Power and Meaning in Punk Rock* (Milton Keynes, UK: Open University Press, 1985), 14.

4 Caroline Coon suggests that bands at the time of her writing were already making distinctions among themselves with regard to a BSP/ASP—before/after—Sex Pistols axis: Caroline Coon, "Punk Rock: Rebels against the System," *Melody Maker*, 7 August 1976, 24–25.

5 Neil Pollack, *Never Mind the Pollacks: A Rock and Roll Novel* (New York: HarperCollins, 2003).

6 See, for example, David Kamp, "Reelin' and Rockin'," *The New York Times*, 9 November 2003, sec. B, 34.

7 Bernard Gendron, *Between Montmartre and the Mudd Club: Popular Music and the Avant-Garde* (Chicago: University of Chicago Press, 2002), 236.

8 Roger Sabin, "Introduction," 1–13, Andy Medhurst, "What Did I Get? Punk, Memory and Autobiography," 219–31, and Roger Sabin, "'I Won't Let That Dago By': Rethinking Punk and Racism," 199–218, in *Punk Rock: So What? The Cultural Legacy of Punk*, ed., Roger Sabin (London: Routledge, 1999).

9 For a representative sample from the early 1970s, see Nick Johnstone, *Melody Maker History of Twentieth Century Popular Music* (London: Bloomsbury Publishing, 1999), 174–85.

10 Laing, *One Chord Wonders*, 19–21, 32.

11 Simon Frith and Howard Horne, *Art into Pop* (London: Routledge, 1989), 124.

12 John Street, *Rebel Rock: The Politics of Popular Music* (Oxford: Basil Blackwell, 1986), and Reebee Garofalo, ed., *Rockin' the Boat: Mass Music and Mass Movements* (Boston: South End Press, 1992). For a persuasive (and long overdue) perspective on these issues, see Michelle Phillipov, "Haunted by the Spirit of '77: Punk Studies and the Persistence of Politics," *Continuum: Journal of Media and Cultural Studies*, Vol. 20, No. 3 (2006): 391.

13 Gendron, *Between Montmartre*, 232.

14 Gendron, *Between Montmartre*, 237.

15 See, for example, Theodor Adorno's essays "On Popular Music" and "On Jazz," in Theodor W. Adorno and Richard Leppert, *Essays on Music*, trans. Susan H. Gillespie (Berkeley, California: University of California Press, 2002), 437–69.

16 Robert H. Tillman, "Punk Rock and the Construction of 'Pseudo-Political' Movements," *Popular Music and Society*, Vol. 7, No. 3 (1980): 166. At least one *New Musical Express* reader, "Jane," took matters further, suggesting, in a letter printed in the 3 January 1976 edition of the paper, that rock critics were projecting their own ideological and psychological desire for rebellion onto fans, rather than providing reporting on what fans thought: "*NME* gives the impression of being written by middle-class rebels determined not to conform to the pattern of settling down with their responsibilities at about 35. But their 'bourgeois' natures show in their pathetic worship of 'true' punkdom e.g. the (short-lived) joy some writers showed over Springsteen—like Bernard Shaw's indiscriminate admiration of 'the working man' … I don't suggest that rock is unworthy of analysis and should be classified only by its danceability or tunefulness, as some of your readers do, but you seem to me too anxious to find someone to believe in—although you always infer that this is a trait of the public" (34). For more critical information about the history and ideological dimensions of rock criticism, see Gestur Guðmundsson et al., "Brit Crit: Turning Points in British Rock Criticism, 1960–1990," 41–64, Kembrew McLeod, "Between a Rock and a Hard Place: Gender and Rock Criticism," 93–113, and Steve Jones and

Kevin Featherly, "Re-Viewing Rock Writing: Narratives of Popular Music Criticism," 19–40, in *Pop Music and the Press*, ed., Steve Jones (Philadelphia: Temple University Press, 2002); Kembrew McLeod, "'★½': A Critique of Rock Criticism in North America," *Popular Music*, Vol. 20, No. 1 (2001), 47–60; and Paul Gorman, *In Their Own Write: Adventures in the Music Press* (London: Sanctuary, 2001).

17 Dick Hebdige, *Subculture: The Meaning of Style* (London: Routledge, 1979), 25. See also Laing, *One Chord Wonders*, 101–05.

18 Geoff Hunt, "Punks' Progress Report: 101'ers/Sex Pistols: Nashville, Kensington," *New Musical Express*, 17 April 1976, 43.

19 Charles Shaar Murray, "Rebel Fun Page: Sex Pistols, Screen on the Green," *New Musical Express*, 11 September 1976, 41.

20 "P**KBAG," *New Musical Express*, 11 December 1976, 42. See also, "Sex Bag," *New Musical Express*, 11 September 1976, 50.

21 Tony Parsons, "'But Darling, Mutilation Is So Passe …,'" *New Musical Express*, 30 October 1976, 47, and Simon Ford, *Wreckers of Civilisation: The Story of COUM Transmissions and Throbbing Gristle* (London: Black Dog Publishing, 1999), 6.19–6.30. Nor did the term's ambit include, at least in the long term, the work of somewhat contemporary musicians like The Shaggs, Jandek or Daniel Johnston, whose amateurism was a function of an apparently guileless belief that what they did was correct, rather than of self-consciously held, maverick, stances on tuning, song form, subject matter or the like. For more information on the just-mentioned artists, see Irwin Chusid, *Songs in the Key of Z: The Curious Universe of Outsider Music* (Chicago: A Cappella Books, 2000), 1–11, 56–78.

22 Spencer, "Is This What We Ordered?" 7–8.

23 Laing, *One Chord Wonders*, 31.

24 Hebdige, *Subculture*, 86.

25 Coon, "Punk Rock: Rebels against the System," 24.

26 Coon, "Punk Rock: Rebels against the System," 25. For more on Coon's position *vis a vis* punk, see Gorman, *In Their Own Write*, 210, 12–13.

27 Laing, *One Chord Wonders*, 32.

28 Tony Stewart, "Move Over, Sid Vicious," *New Musical Express*, 9 July 1977, 11–12.

29 Murray, "We Didn't Know" 28–29. Indeed, the cover of that issue of *NME* featured the headline "This *Definitely* Ain't the Summer of Love," and articles detailed incidents in which members of other English youth subcultures sought violent confrontations with punk fans and musicians, including The Stranglers, The Boomtown Rats, The Damned and The Boys. See, for example, Phil McNeill, "Pistols, Thunders Jubilee Elbow," *New Musical Express*, 9 July 1977, and Phil McNeill and Chris Salewicz, "Summer Punk Toll Mounts," *New Musical Express*, 9 July 1977, 5.

30 "Punk Threads," *New Musical Express*, 30 July 1977, 46.

31 Simon Frith and John Street, "Rock Against Racism and Red Wedge: From Music to Politics, from Politics to Music," in *Rockin' the Boat*, 67–69.

32 "Sex Bag," 50.

33 Frith and Street, "Rock Against Racism," 70.

34 Gilles Peterson and Stuart Baker, eds., *Freedom, Rhythm and Sound: Revolutionary Jazz Original Cover Art* (London: SJR Publishing, 2009).

35 Laing, *One Chord Wonders*, 9–10.

36 Teal Triggs, "Scissors and Glue: Punk Fanzines and the Creation of a DIY Aesthetic," *Journal of Design History*, Vol. 19, No. 1 (2006): 81, n. 1.

37 For a facsimile reproduction, see the beginning of Mark Perry, *Sniffin' Glue and Other Rock 'n' Roll Habits: The Essential Punk Accessory* (London: Omnibus Press, 2009). Unfortunately, the volume is not paginated.

38 Stephen Duncombe, *Notes from the Underground: Zines and the Politics of Alternative Culture*, 2nd ed. (Bloomington, Indiana: Microcosm Publishing, 2008), 19, 32, 54–55. For a more orthodox, celebratory history of fanzines, from a design perspective, see Teal Triggs, *Fanzines: The DIY Revolution* (San Francisco: Chronicle Books, 2010).

39 Pete Dale, "It Was Easy, It Was Cheap, So What?: Reconsidering the DIY Principle of Punk and Indie Music," *Popular Music History*, Vol. 3, No. 2 (2008): 174–75.

40 Frith and Horne, *Art into Pop*, 136–45.

41 Frith and Horne, *Art into Pop*, 144.

42 Phillipov, "Haunted by the Spirit," 388.

43 That phrase taken from the Buzzcocks' song "Breakdown," from the EP *Spiral Scratch* (New Hormones ORG 1, 1977).

13

WOMEN, RAP, AND HIP-HOP

The Challenge of Image

Gail Hilson Woldu

Figure 13.1 Nicki Minaj.

Queen Latifah, rap's first diva, has long understood her anomalous presence in the world of hip-hop culture. Over the course of her ascension, Latifah battled stereotypes about women's place in the male-dominated genre as she sought to create a space for women that at once acknowledged their femaleness and observed the conventions of hip-hop performance. Her earliest performances, which date from the early 1990s, show a woman solidly secure in her domain, commanding the stage with the aggression ascribed to male MCs while introducing an unmistakably womanly presence. Missy Elliott, known for her humorous raps, which often poke fun at herself and at hip-hop's practices, ushered in a distinctly female interpretation of urban attire. Wearing the oversize pants, jackets, and baseball caps that were hip-hop's staples in the early 2000s, Elliott added a new twist: athletic gear in soft colors, often shades of pink and light blue, accompanied by fluffy or feathery accessories. Lil' Kim, rap's leopard-print-thong-wearing, self-proclaimed queen bitch, proved that women could be as vulgar and profane as men. And Nicki Minaj, hip-hop's human blow-up doll in yellow lipstick and pink wigs, forces us to reconsider the challenges of image in popular culture. Each woman pushed limits. Their presence alone constituted de facto protest as it confronted the status quo, broke barriers, and addressed concerns of an underrepresented group. Moreover, the women's infiltration into the male domain of hip-hop required us to understand more fully the multiple manifestations of protest music in popular culture.

The feminization of rap "brought wreck" to hip-hop's' male hegemony. By challenging its precepts, namely, that rap be the product of the black, male, urban underclass, women altered the music's raison d'être by insinuating their distinctive worldview. Women's rap chronicled women's experiences, addressing the quotidian angst of kindred souls. As such, the music, at once collective and individual, as witnessed in black women's blues of the 1920s and 1930s, filled a void in black women's creative expression in the 1990s and early 2000s while also serving as a counterpoint to an omnipresent male voice. Indeed, as cultural historian Gwendolyn Pough asserts, the rhetorical practices of black women in hip-hop culture bring wreck when they "disrupt dominant masculine discourses, break into the public sphere, and in some way impact or influence the U.S. imaginary," whether that influence endures or not.[1] And, as did the great blues women several decades earlier, hip-hop's women attacked stereotypes about women's presence and image in the public mainstream, as they simultaneously challenged representations of black womanhood.[2]

Nevertheless, female performers in hip-hop walk a slippery slope. As back-up dancers in rap videos, women clad in scanty attire for eye appeal are castigated as being ass-shaking hoochies; as MCs, women who, like Latifah, are confident, and assume a swagger gendered as masculine, have had their sexuality questioned. Other women have been masculinized to conform to the image and marketing standards of a particular company, including Lady of Rage, who had a short-lived career with Suge Knight's Death Row Records and whose image paralleled that of the label's headliner male rappers in the 1990s, among them Dr. Dre, Snoop Dogg, and Tupac. The dilemma of image is not confined to women in hip-hop, nor, for that matter, do issues of wardrobe and image belong to women only. Across decades, performers as disparate as Bessie Smith, Gene Simmons, Elvis Presley, Alice Cooper, and Motown's Supremes have been identified by an image conceived intentionally and linked to a stage persona based on it.

In the sections that follow, I consider image among women in hip-hop by exploring the music and performance practices of Queen Latifah, Missy Elliott, Lil' Kim, and Nicki Minaj. To establish a historical context, I look briefly at the roles black women have played in popular music across decades, looking, in particular, at the music of the blues women of the 1920s and Motown's Supremes. Image in popular performance culture has at least two goals: to make a statement and to attract attention. For women, this often centers on sex appeal and the verity that sex sells, no matter how noxious or debasing the marketing. We remember, and are drawn to, the visual image of a female performer's full lips, ample bosom, long legs, and shapely rear end. Admittedly, there has been no single recipe for conjuring the perfect mix of these aspects; indeed, we can point to contradictory images of women in popular culture: the animalistic sensuality of Tina Turner and the garishness of Lady Gaga; the monochromatic Tracy Chapman and the outré Nicki Minaj; the schoolgirl appeal of Britney Spears and the dowdiness of Britain's Susan Boyle. The contradictions are confounding. Although we know that image panders to popular taste, and in so doing often nurtures gender (as well as ethnic and racial) stereotypes, we are nonetheless flummoxed by images of women that are variously misogynistic, tasteful, and, on occasion, socially progressive.

Hip-Hop in the Continuum of Popular Culture Expression

Like other forms of contemporary popular culture, hip-hop has its tacit requirements: it is youth-centered, it is market-driven, and its trends are ephemeral. It also draws on previous traditions, and, as such, is part of a continuum of performance conceits and convention. In particular, black women have played myriad roles in this continuum: as gin-drinking blues women in the 1920s; as mammy characters in minstrelsy and on screen in the 1930s and 1940s; as temptresses on screen in the 1950s and 1960s; as Motown's sensual but respectable "dreamgirls" in the 1960s; and, more recently, as studio hoes in hip-hop videos of the late twentieth and early twenty-first centuries. Although women of color have been icons of popular culture outside the United States—witness, for example, the celebrity of Josephine Baker, whose bare breasts and banana skirts had wealthy Parisians, hungry for "exotic Negroes" to relieve their ennui, drooling in the 1930s—the omnipresence of black women in American popular culture is compelling.

The black blues women of the 1920s set the standard for popular performance in the early decades of the twentieth century, establishing a cultural imperative in the race record market and wowing audiences with their sassiness and distinctive sense of female bravado. A host of performers with the surname Smith (Bessie Smith, Clara Smith, Mamie Smith, Trixie Smith) moaned and groaned their way through the period, singing of no-good men, the joys of drinking, and proclaiming an unabashed delight in their own sexuality. They wore the fringed chemises of the era and shimmied across stages throughout Georgia, Alabama, and Mississippi. Gertrude "Ma" Rainey, by any account exceptional among these performers, was a unique spectacle, even by the standards of black minstrelsy. She was reputed for her flamboyant garb, which included flashy jewelry and spangled dresses. Jazz pianist Mary Lou Williams remembered Rainey as being "loaded with real diamonds—in her ears, around her neck, in a tiara on her head. Both hands were full of rocks, too; her hair was wild and she had gold teeth."[3] Rainey was a total performer, and her appearance mattered as much as the music she performed. If she was attired in sequins, beads, rhinestones, and ostrich feathers, the choice of wardrobe was at once a nod to the performance conventions of her trade and era and a public affirmation of her own physical beauty. In rejecting early twentieth-century standards of comeliness and decorum by adorning herself as might a more traditionally attractive showgirl, Rainey, as ordinary looking a black woman who ever lived in the Deep South in the early 1900s, became minstrelsy's black diva, a tangible symbol of beauty for every ordinary looking black woman who attended her shows and dreamed about a different life. Rainey transfixed audiences every time she stepped onstage bedecked in a queen's regalia of glimmer and shine, a visual feast to patrons who were delighted to see one of their own transformed into a showgirl.[4] More important, she defied contemporaneous mores that frowned on "colored entertainers" who wore white people's clothes in performance. Although Rainey and, in her footsteps, Bessie Smith, held sway in popular entertainment in the years leading up to the Great Depression, they could not compete with the new breed of upbeat and glamorous performers who emerged in the post-Depression era. In a country desperate for optimism and the illusion of prosperity, the urbane style of Hollywood's movie stars was the perfect remedy. Dancers Fred Astaire and Ginger Rogers set the tone for these fantasies in films that included *Top Hat* and *Shall We Dance*, in which the duo delighted audiences with stylish costumes and happy endings.

Several decades later, the women of Berry Gordy's Motown captivated national audiences. Rivaled only by The Beatles, Gordy's groups pervaded the airwaves and were headliners throughout the 1960s. The Supremes, in particular, became household names, and their elegant wardrobe raised the fashion bar for black women in popular entertainment. Under the watchful eye of Maxine Powell, proprietor of the eponymous finishing school in Detroit, the women of The Supremes were taught proper manners and deportment. They learned not to slouch or hunch over while singing; not to stand with their legs spread apart; and not to protrude their rear ends on stage.[5] More important, however, were the lessons in the relationship between wardrobe and respectability. Understated glamour was the look of choice. Mary Wilson, one of the original members of The Supremes, recalls that the women of Motown "wore little jewelry except chic custom made pieces, and everyone wore hats."[6] The group eschewed the loud clothing that was often associated with the lower classes, preferring instead the fashions of the day: the trendy "mod" style of designer Mary Quant and French couture designer Coco Chanel. Quant, whose youthful designs were synonymous with pop culture in 1960s London, attracted international attention for her miniskirts, hot pants, and brightly colored plastic raincoats. Chanel, best known for her "little black dress," established a reputation in high fashion for women's clothing that was simple and timeless. The Supremes were equally at home in both fashion worlds, wearing, as the occasion dictated, the laced white boots, miniskirts, bright colors and bold patterns of Carnaby Street, and the refined look of the designers whose houses lined the Rue du Faubourg Saint-Honoré in Paris.

That The Supremes dared to adorn themselves in such attire flew in the face of contemporaneous standards and contradicted established depictions of black women. "Within racist iconography," says feminist cultural critic bell hooks, "black females are most often represented as mammies, whores, or sluts."[7] Although there was certainly precedent for an alternate view of black women in the public eye, particularly in the classiness of jazz performers Sarah Vaughan and Dinah Washington, as well as in the unique beauty and grace of Lena Horne, The Supremes' image was nonetheless counterhegemonic. Their stated rejection of garishness is, at first blush, contradictory, given the glitter and glitz of their concert wardrobe. Whether in red sleeveless spaghetti-strap dresses with tons of fringe or a designer suit adorned with a single strand of pearls, the *recherché* Supremes were cognizant of the image they projected in public, fully aware that they tantalized audiences in clothes that were alternately fashionably outré or runway chic. The group's shifting images as women to the manor born and sensuous but untouchable "dreamgirls" collided with stereotypes of black women as "hard, low down, mean, nasty, and bitchified."[8] In this sense, The Supremes' image—and attendant seduction—was particularly provocative, as it forced a new, popular, vision of black femaleness.

Queen Latifah: The Intersection of Trousers and Glam

Latifah has always been a curiosity in popular culture, if for no other reason than her multiple personae make her difficult to pigeonhole. Do we buy into Latifah's hip-hop images, those in which she is attired in "men's clothing" and makes "masculine gestures" as she struts across a stage, dropping the f-bomb with insouciance? Do we accept the flawlessly gorgeous and very "girlie" image of Latifah as spokesperson for Cover Girl cosmetics? Or, more likely, do we attribute the kaleidoscope of Latifah's images to her business savvy, recognizing, as surely she has, the ephemeral nature of popular culture and its demands for variety and novelty?

In a video of a concert given in 1991, Latifah is dressed solemnly in nondescript black trousers, a boxy brownish blazer with shoulder pads, and a black turtleneck.[9] Every strand of hair is covered by a black cap, and sunglasses cover her eyes. We understand this attire to be the female replication of male hip-hop fashion of the period, a necessity, almost, for pioneering women in a field gendered throughout the 1980s and 1990s as male, with masculine ideals and masculine aesthetics.[10] Not only was there pressure for female MCs in the mid-1990s to look "mannish," but early female rappers often adopted performance behaviors "coded as male in the world of hip hop" in order to secure the respect of male peers.[11] Latifah's demeanor in this concert is accordingly severe, and, when she pumps her fist in the air to energize her audience, we again look to the period and genre and accept the gestures as stylistic conceits.

By contrast, much of the music Latifah performed is about being a woman—how women respond to men and what it takes to be treated as an equal in the male-dominated world of hip-hop. Her live performance of "Nature of a Sista" is classic early Latifah. She owns the stage, strutting back and forth, mike gripped tightly in a fist as she touts her skills as a rapper in the rapid-fire delivery characteristic of the period. Latifah belittles other rappers for not being able to compete with her, and, drawing on African history, tells everyone that she sees herself as a queen. Her trio of lissome male backup dancers provides a dichotomous counterpoint to her own aggressive movement. They are almost irrelevant to Latifah's performance, but perhaps that is just the point: our attention is poised on Latifah, who commands center stage. In this live performance before an audience of hip-hop's early aficionados, a woman, with all the outward trappings and inner confidence of a male performer, is in charge.[12]

By 2001, Latifah had found another calling: as a model for Cover Girl products and chief spokesperson for the Cover Girl Queen Collection. Her being chosen by Cover Girl was significant in at least two important regards. A full-figured woman, Latifah signaled to other plus-sized female consumers that their body types and round faces could be considered desirable by a leader in the beauty industry. Moreover, Cover Girl's selection of Latifah was a nod to urban culture. This was a smart business move that considered a demographic—women of color, and particularly black women—known for being big purchasers of beauty products. Latifah's image in this realm was the antithesis of her image in hip-hop. With her glowing skin, perfect eyebrows, straight, white teeth, and well-groomed locks, Latifah's headshot ads for Cover Girl are paradigms of female pulchritude. Her full-length shots in razzle-dazzle evening gowns reveal a glamorous woman, secure in her Rubenesque body, ushering in a new standard of beauty to mainstream popular culture. Because she understands that all women want to look beautiful, her clothing and cosmetics lines cater to every woman.[13] Indeed, a large part of her appeal, according to business partner Shakim Compere, is that "Every woman can relate to her."[14]

By any standard, Latifah's accomplishments are noteworthy. Understood in the context of popular culture, they assume even greater significance. If, according to cultural historian Imani Perry, the "visual image of black women in hip hop rapidly deteriorated into one of widespread sexual objectification and degradation" in the years immediately before the turn of the twenty-first century, Latifah was the antithesis of that image.[15] Commodified neither as a sexual object nor the acquisition, much like an expensive car or watch, of a superstar male rapper, she defied the stereotyped role of black woman as scenery: mute, anonymous, and half-naked, lounging poolside or dancing at a club.[16] In her videos, Latifah is portrayed on her own terms, and she is always the focal point. Her songs often portray a sense of her own identity as an independent black woman. In "U.N.I.T.Y.," for example, Latifah asks "who you calling a bitch?" and rails against men who demean women in order to make themselves feel superior. Interestingly, despite the decided feminist tenor of this piece, Latifah has never identified as a feminist. Instead, she has championed civil rights causes for both black men and women, rejecting association with feminist issues:

> I don't adhere to that [feminist] shit. All that shit is bullshit. I know that at the end of the day, I'm a Black woman in this world and I gotta get mine. I want to see the rise of the Black male in personal strength and power. I wanna see the creation of a new Black community for ourselves and respect from others.[17]

The piece is a "protest song," broadly construed, as it addresses an undesirable behavior and exhorts an oppressed group—young black women—to take action; in this case, to love and respect themselves enough to reject abusive behavior. She challenges romanticized images of "gangsta bitches" popularized in the lyrics of some male rappers, and she berates the wannabes for succumbing to peer pressure.[18]

Missy Elliott: Hip-Hop in Pastels and Hoop Earrings

On the front cover of the CD *Under Construction* (Elektra Records, 2002), Missy Elliott sits on a metal can, enormous boom box to her right. She is wearing pink and white Adidas sneakers, relaxed-fit jeans, bubble jacket in soft pink with a white, fur-trimmed hood, and a soft, white, cloche-style hat. As accessories, she sports huge hoop earrings with the initial M inside, a massive chain necklace with a gigantic pendant, and an oversize ring on her index finger with her initials, MSE. Her nails are meticulously manicured and her skin is radiant and dewy soft under flawless makeup. The back cover features Elliott in a white fur jacket with white pompoms and furry white beret. Photos inside the CD cover show Elliott in similar attire: wearing white and gold Adidas and a white jogging suit trimmed in gold; a green and black athletic jacket; and a white athletic jersey trimmed in blue and orange with matching baseball cap, visor turned sideways. In each she wears her trademark hoop earrings encircling the letter M and the gold chain.

Elliott's choice of attire is all about intentionality. This is no surprise, of course, as every aspect of popular culture is, in large measure, controlled and contrived, intended to reach a particular audience or strike a particular chord. Elliott's wardrobe yells to her audience, "I'm hip-hop. I'm a female, and I'm hip-hop." In an industry dominated by men and images of "thugsta" rappers in the late 1990s and early 2000s with gold grills, tattoos, platinum chains, and dark clothing, bubblegum-chewing Elliott popularized a hip-hop wardrobe for urban women that included contemporaneously fashionable unisex athletic gear and oversize clothing in soft, "girlie" colors, as well as *de rigueur* enormous monogrammed hoop earrings and perfectly manicured fingernails. There is a certain incongruity in this, however, that challenges us to question the image. Despite the femininity of her attire and the heavy makeup, complete with false eyelashes, Elliott has never been defined as a sexy MC; indeed, she has been called hip-hop's "anti-sex object role model."[19] And yet, we wonder whether Elliott's nod to "glam beauty" is an articulation of her own personality or a concession to hip-hop's tacit demands that its women—all of them—make an attempt to look pretty.

In "Work It," one of the most popular tracks from *Under Construction*, Elliott tells fly girl listeners to get their nails and hair done. Her emphasis on women and things women do is a hallmark of Elliott's raps. She establishes a sisterly rapport with women in her music, encouraging others through her presence, and showing that hip-hop culture can have a feminine side. We are reminded, here, of her forebears in the 1920s and 1930s, where black blues women spoke to other black women through their music and exhorted them to take control of their lives.[20] Elliott also reminds us that her music—indeed, all hip-hop culture, in her eyes—is about having a good time. In the prelude to "Back in the Day," Elliott tells listeners to have fun; in this light, she is not above poking fun at herself, as she does in "Work It," when she asks, ridiculously, if she looks like a poster of Halle Berry. Although the song contains text that is sexually explicit, it is not vulgar. Whatever the nature of Elliott's lyrics, we are not struck by its prurience. Perhaps this is because we understand that Elliott has not been marketed as a sexy rapper. She is every woman: big-boned, full-figured, ordinary looking, the hip-hop equivalent of Ma Rainey. Her attire is the perfect complement for her hip-hop worldview. Whereas Latifah's "queenly" stage persona demands a reserved and quasi-stately wardrobe, Elliott's laidback homegirl image, outfitted in hoodies, sweats, and sneakers, is casual. Her approachable demeanor makes her easily relatable to a wide cohort base of urban women and, as such, a realistic role model for hip-hop's female aspirants.

Lil Kim: Rap's Queen Bitch in a Thong and Pasties

"Queen bitch" Lil Kim built an image and reputation on the vulgarity of her music and the raunchiness of her attire. In photo after photo, we see Kim clad scantily in seductive—and in some instances, pornographic—poses. Whether squatting with legs wide apart in a leopard-print bikini thong, sucking a strawberry while reclining on a polar bear rug, sitting on a Harley-Davidson wearing a policeman's hat and black leather thong, crotch in full view, or dressed like a blow-up doll with blonde ponytails, blue eyes, penciled in lower eyelashes, and wide open mouth, the image is sexual. Her music is similarly dominated by erotic themes. In fact, Kim's music is a vehicle for talking about sex and flaunting her own lurid sexuality. Her place in hip-hop culture has been widely discussed, with most cultural historians contextualizing her provocative behavior in terms of the ways black women rappers "work within and against dominant sexual and racial narratives" in American culture and the hip-hop community.[21] Much of this conversation has centered on black women's body images in rap, and the inevitable—and omnipresent—dialogue about sexual objectification and the distribution of power in hip-hop culture between women and men.[22] According to historian Tricia Rose, works by black women rappers "affirm black female beauty and yet often preserve the logic of female sexual objectification."[23] In Kim, we find music that is obscene, coupled with a visual image that forces us to consider, as does Rose, notions of femininity, black female sexuality, and black women's complicity in their objectification.[24]

The point of Kim's music and her wardrobe is to shock. In both, she pushes the limits of acceptability, even in hip-hop culture. If hip-hop's aficionados begrudgingly accepted profanity and vulgarity from its male rappers, they were less inclined to do so from women. In her aptly titled first CD, *Hard Core* (Big Beat Records, 1996), Kim is alternately a hardened gangsta and a vulgar, acquisitive, hussy. Kim delivers an explicit how-to manual for her would-be lovers, filled with instructions that detail how she wants to be handled sexually. In "Not Tonight," Kim chides inept lovers and enumerates the quid pro quo nature of her relationships, saying she has sex for cars and money. In "We Don't Need It," Kim goes toe-to-toe with 2 Live Crew and Snoop Doggy Dogg, both known for prurient lyrics. She admonishes men who do not know how to please women, and she lists her demands for oral sex, insisting that it be given properly and reciprocally. More important is the way Kim defines herself as a sexually empowered woman. In 1999, she created an especially sensational stir at MTV's Video Music Awards ceremony by appearing in a lavender wig and matching skintight cat suit that exposed her left breast, covered only by a matching lavender pastie. Presenter Diana Ross added to the spectacle by grabbing Kim's breast on stage and bouncing it up and down. Later, Kim paraded along the red carpet and conducted interviews, noting that she chose the outfit because, she said, "I wanted people to say 'look at her.'"[25] To be certain, Kim is not the only female in hip-hop culture known for impropriety of dress and language: Da Brat, Trina, and Foxy Brown also forged identities as foul-mouthed icons of sexual lewdness.

And yet Kim stands alone. With her wardrobe of platinum blonde wigs and minks and boas dyed in a rainbow of pinks, blues, and greens, Kim confounds the hip-hop world and stupefies the cultural mainstream. Her shape-shifter image as a black girl/white girl is particularly knotty, according to *Vanity Fair* photographer Annie Leibovitz, because she is "not only dressing up to be a woman, but she's dressing up to be a white woman, with that blonde wig."[26] Kim's choice of blonde wigs and blue contact lenses as accessories is significant. In the days immediately before her conviction for conspiracy and perjury, Kim appeared on the front page of the *New York Post* (3 March 2005). In both photos she is shown as a blonde; in the larger photo, exceptionally long eyelashes frame intensely blue contact lenses. To be considered beautiful in a culture in which blue eyes and blonde hair are the barometers of beauty, it is little wonder that Kim—who as a young girl wanted to look like Jada Pinkett Smith and Halle Berry—and other women born with neither barometer would emulate these standards of desirability.[27] We are reminded of a Clairol jingle from the 1960s, long before Kim's arrival as hip-hop's queen bitch, that glorified blondness: "Is it true blondes have more fun? A Lady Clairol blonde, a silky, shiny blonde?" Ironically, in "becoming a blonde," Kim removed the allure and mystique, in much the same way that buying a designer bag for $20 from a garbage bag on a street corner in New York does. Once we realize that every woman can own a designer bag (or at least one that looks like one to the untrained eye) or "be a blonde," those symbols of beauty and desirability become less special. Those paradigms become less prized when they can belong to everyone. It matters not, either, whether the image or product is natural or fake. In racialized terms, if white women routinely dye their dark hair blonde, wear hair extensions, and then shake their fake, long, locks, proud to be a blonde, why would this not be similarly acceptable for black and other nonwhite women? In this sense, Kim—and, before her, R & B singer Etta James—is not dressing up to be a white woman, as Leibovitz alleges. She is dressing up to be a beautiful woman—at least in terms of American popular culture.

Nicki Minaj: Pure Fantasy in Bubblegum Pink

In her video "Stupid Hoe" (from the album *Pink Friday: Roman Reloaded*, 2011/12), Minaj appears in a mélange of colors and outfits. By turns big girl sexual and little girl demure, Minaj is a paradox in pastel-colored wigs and lipstick. The video is a rant directed at Lil' Kim, in which Minaj belittles Kim's status as rap's "queen bitch"; in fact, the chorus derides Kim, while other lines reference Angelina Jolie without malice. In "Right by My Side" (also from *Pink Friday*), performed with rapper Chris Brown, Minaj wears a long, flaxen wig that is alternately straight and slightly curly and attire that shows off her amply endowed figure. The music is a fusion of R & B and hip-hop, and the lyrics, with the exception of Minaj's explicit and sexual rapping near the end, tell a fatuous, too-cute tale of urban romance.

Not surprisingly, the words matter far less in these songs (the world of hip-hop has heard far more clever diss raps than "Stupid Hoe," and "Right By My Side" pales in comparison to Motown's love songs) than the visual spectacle of Minaj. In "Stupid Hoe" we are transfixed by the shifting images of Minaj: wearing vibrant turquoise lipstick, eye shadow, and exaggerated eyeliner, with her back arched and leg extended high over her head; in a short flirty pink-and-blonde wig with bangs; lying inside a cage, buttocks exposed, wearing fishnet stockings and a long blonde wig;

with huge eyes, yellow lipstick, painted on freckles, and long pink locks, doll-like and eerily innocent on an oversize red chair and holding a colorful lollipop; shaking her voluptuous derrière while squatting and wearing high heels—animagus-like, to coin a term from the popular Harry Potter series, transforming from a human into some species of large cat. And therein lies the appeal of Nicki Minaj. Everything about her is quixotic and pure fantasy. We struggle with Minaj because her performance persona is so mercurial, by turns a cartoon character with huge, creepy, anime eyes, an obscenity-spewing gangsta, and a cute, vulnerable, coquette.[28] Because no single component of this unlikely trio dominates, the three intersect seamlessly in her performances, cementing Minaj's appeal across a wide and diverse demographic. She acknowledges the variety of her audiences, stating, "I started off rapping, and then I've been transitioning into so many different genres of music. So it's like I pick up new people along the way."[29] Minaj finds particular favor among little girls because this cohort group sees in her a life-size doll with fake hair in fanciful colors, lips that can be painted creatively, and poofy fairytale princess skirts in shades of pink. Her "Barbz," as Minaj calls her young fans, like her because "I play dress-up. I also can put on a very cartoonish voice. So sometimes children may not know what I'm saying, but they like the sound of it, and they think I sound like some weird character."[30] Adults are often drawn to the music itself, she says, with its spicy lyrics delivered in the quick style of rapper Da Brat. They are also drawn, no doubt, to the sexual element of her performances. Her "behind-centered" dances, like those of Josephine Baker, Salt-n-Pepa, and countless anonymous dancers in hip-hop videos, invert the "aesthetic hierarchy that renders black women's bodies inadequate and sexually unattractive," and, as such, remind of us the complex history of black sexual expression in the public sphere.[31] Still, the music is never, ever, the focal point. Indeed, Minaj has been entangled in a debate with rapper and producer DJ Funkmaster Flex, who has criticized her music for not being "real hip-hop."[32] Because Minaj has created a performance personality that is based on the spectacle of her appearance, we are drawn to that spectacle. We anticipate outlandish attire and we focus on it.

It is tempting to lump all women in hip-hop into one convenient group, considering their music as issuing from a single, or similar, fount, regardless of their multiple perspectives. If some women rappers have bemoaned their status as women in the male-dominated world of hip-hop, we call women who rap "feminist home girls making some noise."[33] If others rap about their own sexuality and wear provocative clothing, we label them hip-hop's hoes and lament their objectification. The reality, of course, is rather more complicated, making any generic discussion of a protest culture in the women's music untenable. Queen Latifah, despite her bold style, formidable demeanor, and the powerful messages of "Ladies First" and "U.N.I.T.Y.," has steadfastly rejected association with feminist issues, preferring instead to be considered pro-woman.[34] Missy Elliott, for whom hip-hop is all about having a good time, defies any sort of facile classification. Lil' Kim, by contrast, has been both chastened as the "embodiment of immorality" and lauded for infiltrating areas of the hip-hop business that few women before her had dared.[35] As such, she is alternately praised and damned for her obscene music and vulgar deportment. And Nicki Minaj, who is making a career out of fantasy, exhorts us to think twice before we casually assign a label to women in hip-hop based on the illusion of an image.

Notes

1 Gwendolyn Pough, *Check It While I Wreck It: Black Womanhood, Hip-Hop Culture, and the Public Sphere* (Boston: Northeastern University Press, 2004), 76.

2 Pough, *Check It*, 87–88.

3 Cited in Nat Shapiro and Nat Hentoff, *Hear Me Talkin' To Ya: The Story of Jazz as Told by the Men Who Made It* (New York: Dover, 1966), 248.

4 For a discussion of the cultural hierarchy of wardrobe among blues and vaudeville performers, see M. Alison Kibler, *Rank Ladies: Gender and Cultural Hierarchy in American Vaudeville* (Chapel Hill, North Carolina: The University of North Carolina Press, 1999).

5 See Nelson George, *Where Did Our Love Go? The Rise and Fall of the Motown Sound* (New York: St. Martin's Press, 1985), 88.

6 Mary Wilson, *Dreamgirl and Supreme Faith: My Life as a Supreme* (New York: Cooper Square Press, 1999), 129.

7 bell hooks, *Art on My Mind* (New York: The New Press, 1995), 97.

8 hooks, *Art on My Mind*, 98.

9 See www.youtube.com/watch?v=PaZbL7KYdos

10 See Imani Perry, *Prophets of the Hood: Politics and Poetics in Hip Hop* (Durham, North Carolina: Duke University Press, 2004), 156.

11 See Pough, *Check It*, 86, and Perry, *Prophets of the Hood*, 257.

12 Any discussion of Latifah must also mention her counterparts, Salt-n-Pepa and MC Lyte. Cf. Tricia Rose, "Bad Sistas: Black Women Rappers and Sexual Politics in Rap Music," *Black Noise: Rap Music and Black Culture in Contemporary America* (Hanover, New Hampshire: Wesleyan University Press, 1994), 146–182.

13 Donna Freydkin, "For Queen Latifah, there's a renewed vigor," *USA Today*, 26 May 2011, 6D.

14 Freydkin, "For Queen Latifah."

15 Perry, *Prophets of the Hood*, 174.

16 Perry, *Prophets of the Hood*, 174.

17 Quoted in Pough, *Check It*, 89.

18 Pough, *Check It*, 89.

19 *Prophets of the Hood*, 156.

20 See Angela Y. Davis, *Blues Legacies and Black Feminism: Gertrude "Ma" Rainey, Bessie Smith, and Billie Holiday* (New York: Pantheon Books, 1998).

21 Rose, "Bad Sistas," 147.

22 Rose, "Bad Sistas," 147.

23 Rose, "Bad Sistas," 147.

24 Rose, "Bad Sistas," 148.

25 See www.youtube.com/watch?v=iF5IWXzTCJo

26 Quoted in Robert Marriott, "Blowin' Up," *Vibe*, June–July 2000, 132.

27 See Pough, *Check It*, 184.

28 Judith Newman, "Just Try to Look Away," *Allure*, April 2012, 234.

29 Quoted in Newman, "Just Try," 236.

30 Newman, "Just Try," 236.

31 Rose, "Bad Sistas," 168.

32 Dave Itzkoff, "Hip-Hop Beef, Round 2, on the Radio," *The New York Times*, 6 June 2012, C3.

33 Gwendolyn Pough, ed., *Home Girls Make Some Noise: Hip Hop Feminism Anthology* (New York: New York University Press, 2007).

34 Rose, "Bad Sistas," 177.

35 Cf. Elaine Richardson, "Lil' Kim, Hip-Hop Womanhood, and the Naked Truuf," in *Home Girls Make Some Noise*, 191.

14

I PREDICT A RIOT

Riot Grrrls and the Contradictions of Feminism

Shayna Maskell

Figure 14.1   Tobi Vail and Kathleen Hanna of Bikini Kill performing with Joan Jett on stage at Irving Plaza.

Notoriously difficult to categorize as both a genre of music and as a social movement, Riot Grrrl has come to be acknowledged as one of the most significant crossovers between politics and sound: feminism as music, music as feminism. Its roots stem from two Washingtons—Washington, D.C., and Olympia, Washington. In D.C., during the early 1990s, a group of girls set out to abolish the males-only club of the punk rock scene, in which they were relegated to second-class subcultural citizens. Across the country in Washington state, Kathleen Hanna, lead singer of the classic (soon-to-be known as Riot Grrrl) female band Bikini Kill, and her bandmates, created a two-page manifesto, demanding a feminist revolution under the banner of rock 'n' roll. With their slogan, the title of their demo album, "Revolution Girl Style Now," these women sought to expand the reach of women in the rock arena, and promote the social and political emancipation of females. Originally the title of a 1991 self-made 'zine made by Hanna, fellow all-girl band Bratmobile's Molly Neuman and Alison Wolfe, as well as friend Jen Smith, Riot Grrrl became the rallying call for girls across the country. The social and musical movement solidified at K Record's five-day festival in Olympia in 1991, designated as The International Pop Underground Convention. The first night was labeled Love Rock Revolution Girl Style Now and highlighted future Riot Grrrl royalty Bratmobile, Bikini Kill and Heavens to Betsy. Exploding from that festival, and from its sister network in Washington, D.C., Riot Grrrl 'zines, conventions, and bands popped up across the country.

On the one hand, Riot Grrrl embraced and propagated feminism through its music, lyrics, performances, 'zines and everyday activities. It complicated the notion of gender-based aesthetics in both music and in fashion, demanding attention and pointing out the hypocrisies present in our social norms. In addition, the music and movement worked to expose the social and personal concerns of girls that were habitually excluded from the mainstream—notions of sexual abuse, anorexia, and body image. Riot Grrrl, through its incorporation of feminism, attempted to give voice to girls, allowing for a self-representation that had never been accessible before. Yet, their efforts at reappropriation also led to some alarming contradictions in their feminism. Riot Grrrl's use of irony and reworking of traditional gender roles and mores in some cases actually acted to reinforce those culturally sexist ideas of women. These complications deepened the political and social implications of a group of women trying to re-seize control over how gender played out in our cultural landscape.

Music as Gender: The Reclamation of Rock

The history of popular music is largely punctuated by its surreptitious assignation of gender roles. Specifically, such a historical musical accounting consistently and nearly unfailingly designates males as the producers of rock, conveying onto their gender the cultural implications of that position: powerful, sexually potent, creative, and independent. Women, on the other hand, were relegated to a small niche of music. Theirs was to be a confidential, private discourse, and any hint of sexuality was to be sublimated into an intangible yearning, rather than an overt musical expression.[1] Consistently, males were considered the bearers of musical prowess, as both technical musicians and as passionate performers, and females, when at long last included into mainstream music, were situated as sweet songbirds, whose role was limited to expressing emotion about love and relationships.

Indeed, as rock emerged in the 1950s, it was feared for not just its racial implications—its African American roots and the ensuing racism surrounding such a sound—but also for its implicit sexualization. The budding rock revolution, while promising a challenge to the traditional function of race in both music and popular society, had no such effect on gender roles, some might argue, for decades. The sexual energy so feared by adults was a *male* sexuality. Rock almost single-handedly eliminated women from the ranks of bestselling musicians. Often lacking the access to musical equipment, and excluded in part to maintain rock 'n' roll's adolescent obsession with masculinity, young women were constrained from any role except for that of lyrical subject or adoring fan.[2] Women did not sing; instead, they were sung about. As objects of these male lyrics, they were the musical victims of young male rock 'n' roll singers caught between macho bluster and teenage passionate vulnerability. They were referred to as babies, as wild heartbreakers or as heavenly goddesses, either totally dependent on their males, totally manipulative of their males, or totally atop a pedestal. The cultural diversity of rock 'n' roll stopped short when it arrived at gender.

This narrow and confining construction of women in music is evident in the evolving forms of rock. Teenybop, as it came to be known, became a nonthreatening genre of rock music with which girls could identify. These girls were buying a representation of male sexuality, usually in the form of teen idols. These young men were portrayed as the boy-next-door—sad, thoughtful, pretty, and in need.[3] Without any strong female rock role models, these somewhat androgynous teens became the next best thing. Furthermore, such teenybop music was essential in the socialization of women within the realm of love and sex. Girls were told to interpret their sexuality in terms of romance, and falling in love with posters could be a way of excluding real males and hanging onto that version of "true love."[4] This music, and these idols, was a safe focus for the newly discovered sexual energy of these young women.

In the early 1960s, black female vocal groups or "girl groups" arrived in the popular music spotlight, taking a musical page from the emotional influence of rock 'n' roll. Yet, despite the massive success of groups such as The Chiffons, The Crystals, and The Ronettes, girl group music was most often associated not with the almost-exclusively black and female singers, but with the white male producers who created their sound.[5] These groups were often marketed as much for their sex appeal as they were for their musical capabilities, and, because gender roles had yet to be significantly altered, these groups were chiefly limited to singing about their relationship with men, rather than singing about themselves or women as a whole. The songs' ideological messages ("Be My Baby," "Chapel of Love," "He's a Rebel"), as well as the audience who consumed the songs, helped to reproduce the social definitions of female sexuality and social roles. Even the developing folk scene of the 1960s, which slightly altered the lyrical content from the personal to the political, and boasted female artists such as Joan Baez, Mary Travers, and Odetta, were most frequently only the voice of protest songs, covering tunes already penned by white males.

By the 1970s, women were clearly central to the music scene—that of soft rock— but they failed to emerge from the gender-constructed boundaries of the previous musical decades. Like girl groups before them, these female artists sang about being a woman, a wife or a mother, and continued to reinforce the wrong-headed idea that women in rock were performers and interpreters, rather than musical innovators.

Men, on the other hand, were given reign in the realm of music to perform their version of masculinity. This construction of gender was based, in part, in the exclusivity of rock itself. As a male-dominated mode of music, men could achieve a particular status, solidarity with his fellow male, and control over both music and his sexuality.[6] This can be seen most relevantly within in the punk rock scene of the 1980s, the scene from which Riot Grrrl was born. While punk originated as an expression of rebellion against the cultural and social norms that dominated mainstream society, it quickly devolved into reinforcing the structural inequalities of gender. Nearly uniformly, the punk scene was dominated by males. Indeed, the culture, and, therefore, identity, of early punk rock was "embedded with latent male-oriented bias" and even overt sexism.[7] In creating a collective identity, tensions arise as to exclusivity and inclusivity. In this case, having females diluted the identity meaning for punks.[8] While there was a place for women within the fashion or promotions side of punk, the musicians and audiences were primarily male and unfriendly to females. This also included live performances, in which violence was becoming a central tenet, in the form of both slam-dancing and fistfights; such insistence on the centrality of the masculine body as dominating force within the scene tended to act as a threat and, eventually, a barrier, to female participation.[9] Whether these were intentional attempts to prevent a female presence in punk or not, the result was the same: alienation and elimination of women in the punk scene.

The development of Riot Grrrl music as a female-centric genre, therefore, was itself an overt and meaningful expression of feminism within the landscape of a historically misogynistic music narrative. More specifically, its creation speaks to a feminist reaction to the male-controlled musical world of punk. By its appropriation of a typically gendered type of music, the women of Riot Grrrl questioned, subverted, and ultimately upset the boundaries as to what sounds could be categorized as male.

From the sonic underpinnings of punk, Riot Grrrl incorporated the musical ideology of simplicity. The three-chords basis of almost all punk music initially served as a democratization of sound, a way to destabilize the authority implicit in music as art. However, the utilization of this basic form remained in the purview of men; Riot Grrrl borrowed this system in order to galvanize women as musicians. As Molly Neuman, drummer for Riot Grrrl band Bratmobile explains, "We may not have been able to play perfectly, but we did play ... our impetus was, 'If that guy can do it, why can't we?'"[10] The simple act of picking up a guitar, of learning the fundamentals of chords, of forming a band, was an emancipatory act. If mastery of music had been not only a male domain, but also a mandate of both popular music and punk, then the formation of technically unskilled female bands served to challenge the boundaries of who could play. No longer were females merely within their traditional role of consumers of music (as fans, or, more disturbingly, as "groupies"). They were now the producers, the creators, of music.

But the rebellion of Riot Grrrl went beyond the mere formation of bands, and the aforementioned accompanying social implications. The music they produced— the aesthetics of sound they created—was itself a confrontation of the conventional norms of gendered sound. Taking their sonic cues from punk rock, bands like Bikini Kill, Bratmobile, 7 Year Bitch, and others, employed thrashing electric guitars, hard-driving drums, and sound progressions that were in direct defiance to both standard musical structure and tonality and the acceptable boundaries of what "feminine" music should be. The music prided itself on discontinuities and fragmentation and rejected the formula of the day, crafting songs that lasted usually less than three minutes and featured bursts of aggressive, intense, and often atonal, eruptions of sound. Indeed, the prominent use of the electric guitar in Riot Grrrl music resists the traditional understanding of the electric guitar as a primarily male instrument, often viewed as a phallic symbol, as an extension of the male body.[11] By assuming jurisdiction in the conventional sphere of the definition of masculinity and male sexuality (think of the overt guitar-based sexuality of Jimi Hendrix, Jimmy Page, Keith Richards), the women of Riot Grrrl struggled to redefine the music-based gender code. The electric guitar and its power, as both actual noise and as a symbol of masculinity, were harnessed by these females to topple the stereotypical image of a woman musician who is meek or dainty.

Similarly, the aggressive nature of the music, in its rhythm, timbre, and loudness, denoted a shift in the cultural acceptability of rage and antagonism for females. For Riot Grrrls, their sound acted as an expression of taste, which, in turn, acted as a tool for the development, maintenance, and expression of the self—a self that disregarded the prescribed conventions of womanhood. The sweet melodies of the 1970s singer/songwriter, à la Carole King or Carly Simon, were shredded by pounding drums and screeching bass; the dance-friendly female pop sounds of the 1980s were decimated by an ocean of dissonant noise of proudly amateurish female musicians. The narrative of rock music, and its offspring punk, as crude, as vulgarity of sound, was no longer ceded as the purview of men. It was a legitimate expression of, for, and by, women. Conventional constructions of female sentiment and sentimentality, represented sonically by the soft strumming of an acoustic guitar, or the nurturing sound of harmonies, gave way to the intense, almost violent, musicality of Riot Grrrl's instrumentation. This "out of control" 4/4 beat, and its accompanying timbre of low, dense, sounds, produced an aural assault on the senses, a musical insurgence heretofore associated with men (who were, and are, according to social mores, unable or not required to contain their feelings).[12] Importantly, this musical articulation of emotion was not an attempt to appropriate a male sound. Instead, it served as a redefinition of what emotions were acceptable for women to have. As Tribe 8's lead singer, Lynn Breedlove, asserts, "a lot of people say, 'You're just trying to be like men,' … [but] I'm a woman and I feel agro, and that means my aggression is not male."[13]

Similarly, the vocal stylings of Riot Grrrl, as epitomized by Bikini Kill's Kathleen Hanna and Heavens to Betsy's Corin Tucker, paralleled the rage of their music, confounding the stereotypes of what women "should" sound like. Analogous to the male-centered punk style of singing, Riot Grrrl vocalists shouted, growled, and snarled their lyrics, expressing an anger at not just the musical expectations of the time, but gender expectations as well. Archetypically, women did not yell; they were to be compliant and comforting. Those who deviated from that emotional neutrality were burdened by the derogatory labels of bitch, shrew, or hysteric.[14] Young women were to be silent or, at best, a songbird mouthpiece for the ideas written by others. Riot Grrrl invited them to scream.[15] These physical cries of pain, of frustration, and of ire, not only served to question the restrictions on female musician's vocal expression of negative emotions, but also reinforced a new representation of what a woman should be—bold, strong, and sure of herself, agonizing sentiments and all.

Riot Grrrl's Feminisms: Gender, Sexuality, Self, and Culture

But perceiving Riot Grrrl as only a musical genre vastly undermines the political and social implications that made this music, and its corresponding scene, a movement. Embracing many of the tenets of third-wave feminism, Riot Grrrl, as a social movement, worked to reclaim the voice and power of, and for, women. By producing a new form of culture, from music and lyrics, and by setting a new standard for female performance in rock, the Riot Grrrl scene not only redefined who and what was permitted to be represented in popular culture, but it also helped re-mold the representation of the modern-day female.

In the most basic sense, the naming of this music-based movement was a feminist act, aiding as a semiotic reclamation of a culturally patronizing term—"girl." Commonly attributed to Bikini Kill's Hanna, the term Riot Grrrl contains a multiplicity of meanings, all in an effort to subvert the customary condescension associated with calling a female a "girl." Notions of submissiveness, naiveté, and childishness that were typically suggested by referring to an adult woman as a girl simultaneously carried an underlying message of weakness, powerlessness, and diminutiveness. By reappropriating this term, and subverting it to Grrrl, the movement, and its female members, formed a new meaning and subtext. "Grrrl" indicated a growl, a belligerence, a threat of the violence to come if goaded. And the word "Riot," as a descriptor of this new female, is a nod to the political and social turbulence of the time, both literally—referring to the bands' temporary summer home of D.C., which saw actual riots in the city[16]—and metaphorically, suggesting the outcome of a movement of women demanding change. In doing so, the women of Riot Grrrl pushed the fight for feminism into the arena of intellectual discourse, where words are contested terrain, sites of struggle for meaning.

This acknowledgment of words, and their denotative and connotative meanings, as a space of struggle and a source of power remained a fundamental tool of Riot Grrrl. Using their lyrics, performances, and even conventions, the bands and scene members were able focus on largely ignored but critically important issues of women and teens. This musical and everyday documentation provided crucial agency and, therefore, legitimacy and validation, to women's personal, emotional, and social issues, ranging from eating disorders to lesbianism to idealization of the female body to serious sexual crises such as rape and incest. Lyrics in Bikini Kill's "Statement of Vindication,"[17] Bratmobile's "Do You Like Me Like That?,"[18] and 7 Year Bitch's "Dead Men Don't Rape,"[19] acted to galvanize females by destabilizing the cultural internalization of female issues and helping them externalize the traumas they suffered. In fact, Bikini Kill's ritual of passing around the microphone at concerts to allow girls to share their own stories of sexual abuse allowed for both a literal and figurative voice to girls who were too often ignored. Additionally, it created a community, showing girls that they were not alone in their hurting. As one Riot Grrrl fan expressed, "It's about speaking out, not keeping quiet … not buying into that whole put up or shut up."[20]

Indeed, it was this sense of community, of the creation of a space where girls and women were not only safe but also heard and valued, that was central to their attempt at a transformation of the culturally-mandated way that women relate to one another. Rather than perpetuating the chronic configuration of girl against girl (for the attentions of the opposite sex, for the best musician, for the prettiest), Riot Grrrl advanced the notion of the relationships of girls standing *with* girls, cultivating a unified gender structure. By "encouraging female support of one another,"[21] Riot Grrrl members hope to promulgate their motto: "Revolution Girl Style Now." Such a revolution had, at its heart, emotional validation of women and a rejection of patriarchal norms of womanhood. As the Riot Grrrl Manifesto (written by Bikini Kill's Hanna) states, the movement exists "BECAUSE we are interested in creating non-hierarchical ways of being AND making music, friends, and scenes based on communication + understanding, instead of competition + good/bad categorizations."[22] Creating this all-girl culture, including friendships, music, and sociopolitical opposition to the male-dominated mainstream, girls were able to develop their own identity, independent of the forces in their daily lives. This basis of and for communication and communal understanding was developed at concerts, conventions, and by the creation and distribution of fan-made 'zines. Despite the seemingly solitary nature of writing, the massive influx of audience-produced 'zines actually provided a community in which subcultural or "resistant identities" were formed in conjunction with other girls and women.[23] Building a community with similar values reinvigorated these girls, whose political and social concerns had strayed from their mothers' prototypical first wave feminist needs and anxieties.

Nowhere were these complex new wave feminist ideals more epitomized, or controversial, than in Riot Grrrl's performance of gender and sexuality. Growing up in a culture that demanded women be the impossibly perfect (and contradictory) version of thin, beautiful, smart, and nonthreatening to the male hegemonic structure, often left girls unsure of their worth outside of the male-appreciated gaze of their bodies. Riot Grrrls attempted to, much like their feminist sisters of the 1960s, reclaim their gender and their sexuality by embracing and performing both. In forming Bikini Kill, in fact, Hanna and Tobi Vail intentionally tried to have both "a strong feminist punk vision and also be sexy … more Madonna than Andrea Dworkin."[24] This incorporation and demonstration of gender and sexuality in the Riot Grrrl movement most overtly took the form of fashion and dress. Most frequently exemplified as a sort of hypersexuality, Riot Grrrl style included the seeming paradoxes of "little-girl dresses with Fredericks of Hollywood tacky glamour, rugged boots … and prominent tattoos or piercings."[25] Sunglasses, knee-high boots, dark lipstick, cropped tops, skirts, and babydoll dresses, were all a part of Riot Grrrls' struggle to redefine the stereotypical construction of girliness and womanhood, as well as own their sexuality, as creation of self, rather than of a patriarchal society. It served, then, as a way to reclaim the power to define what female was and what sexuality was. In one sense, the traditional "female dress" of skirts, dresses, and makeup adhered to conventional standards of beauty; however, this compliance to societal norms acted merely as a foot in the door—a way of demanding attention from the mainstream. In a nod to the standard role of females (and female musicians), Riot Grrrls resisted the marginalization of being labeled as overtly radical. Then, the women were able to display the inherent contradictions involved in the established constructions of femininity and sexuality. By juxtaposing the hard with the soft, the punk with the girly nostalgia, the "ugly" with the "sexy," the movement tried to confuse and confound the easy category of what beautiful was, of what women should be and look like. Instead of inhabiting a space of powerlessness, Riot Grrrl's use of confrontational sexuality pushed the boundaries of acceptability, regaining some of the control lost by the patriarchal norms of gender and sexuality.[26]

This challenge to culturally-constructed gender and sexuality often took a much more aggressive and provocative route. Often, during performances, Riot Grrrl band members would use their bodies themselves as sites of performance. Tribe

8's Lynn Breedlove would often dress in "masculine" clothes—baggy jeans and a baseball cap—with her back to the audience, until she turned around, flashing her breasts, nipple rings and all, as well as a dildo attached to her crotch.[27] As a lesbian singer, Breedlove used her body to blur the boundaries of gender (Is she a man? A woman?) and shock audience members into questioning their own assumptions about sexuality. In a similar vein, Bikini Kill's Hanna was also known to frequently bare her breasts during a show but, instead of a dildo, she presented the word "slut" drawn in thick black marker on her stomach; in doing so, the singer inspired other teen girls to make their own homemade t-shirts with "slut" or "bitch" crawled across the breasts. Much like the bra-burning methods of the 1960s feminists,[28] these acts served to reclaim a word that had a culturally negative connotation towards women. Moreover, the terms were regularly used as a technique to socially shame women's freedom to engage in liberated sexual acts (sluts) or express their anger or frustration (bitches). By taking ownership of the words, particularly on the space of one's own body, Riot Grrrls tried to resignify the words, to say "my body belongs to me … I sleep with who I want,"[29] thereby disavowing the patriarchal norms of acceptable female sexuality.

The cumulative effect of these feminist-based actions was greater than the individual acts. It was the creation of a female-centered culture, with its accompanying self-empowerment and ability to self-represent. The refashioning of traditional gender codes, through music, fashion, and lyrics, was a way of defining girlhood and womanhood *by* girls and women, *for* girls and women. This creation of culture was itself a shift from the typical role of women; no more were they epitomized as passive consumers (of music, of culture); now, they were producers. Promulgating an ethos of "girl power," women, for the first time, owned their own record labels and gained recognition as a viable market segment. In this subculture, music was imbued with politics, and those politics propagated the radical idea that women should represent themselves, and take proprietorship over their bodies, their sexuality, and the way they viewed themselves and each other.

The Contradictions of Feminism in Riot Grrrl

Despite the enormous strides the music and culture of Riot Grrrl generated in both the political and socio-cultural arenas, particularly within third-wave feminism, there were glaring incongruities in the way this particular subculture attempted to transform the cultural understanding of female gender and sexuality. Most glaringly, these paradoxes are found in the expression and reception of Riot Grrrl sexuality. While contradiction was a catalyst with which this subculture endeavored to muddy the waters of sexuality, this tool ultimately led to a conspicuous rift between the intent behind the performance of sexuality and the reception and interpretation of it by the general public.

These sexuality-based contradictions are overly pronounced, in part, because of the persistent, pervasive, and far-reaching socially constructed notions of female sexuality, and the opposing dominance of male sexuality. Historically, women gained power through their appearance.[30] However, this position is based primarily on the positionality of men's authority and sexual control. As Laura Mulvey, feminist film theorist, famously explains in her theory of the "male gaze":

> In their traditional exhibitionist role women are simultaneously looked at and displayed, with their appearance coded for strong visual and erotic impact so that they can be said to connote *to-be-looked-at-ness*. Woman displayed as sexual object is the leitmotif of erotic spectacle: from pin-ups to striptease, from Ziegfeld to Busby Berkeley, she holds the look, plays to and signifies male desire.[31]

Indeed, this objectification of women as bodies to be seen, as sexual objects to be admired, has become entrenched in the psychology and sociology of men and women alike. Permeating nearly every facet of culture, the record industry was no exception. Women in the business were eroticized and often valued for their sex appeal, rather than their talent. The problem then becomes: can Riot Grrrls, disavowing the traditional male gaze by caustically embracing it, actually subvert the patriarchal lens?

The answer is not clear-cut. The quandary lies, in large part, with the difficulty in using irony as an instrument of social change and the complexity of recoding dominant meanings. The understanding of irony must be based on a shared set of connotations, a communal acceptance of meanings; Riot Grrrl's irony failed because its performance of sexuality went outside of the small subculture and into the main stream. Although the women's sexuality was clearly presented in an exaggerated, overstated way, "because these communities sometimes conflict or at least do not overlap, audiences 'inevitably' interpret potentially ironic material in un-ironic ways."[32] The impenetrability of irony lies in the rigidity of dominantly coded ideas. As Hanna explains:

> I sort of anticipated guys thinking, 'Oh she's showing skin, therefore she's a slut.' So I wrote 'slut' on myself as a way to beat them to the punch ... Now it seems sort of sad in a way, like if I thought someone was gonna punch me in the face, would I beat them to it by punching myself? ... [T]here's a really fine line between 'reclaiming' derogatory slang and glamorizing it.[33]

Intentionality, or what performers and participants *meant* to represent with their subversions of female sexuality, was often obfuscated by audience reception or what the consumers (both Riot Grrrl and non-Riot Grrrl) understood the symbol(s) to mean. Meaning is highly dependent on social location and political ideologies (among other factors), and, given Riot Grrrl's position as a *sub*culture, its rebellious message was interpreted by the mainstream merely as a buttressing of its conventional view of female sexuality. Hanna's baring of her breasts might, in her mind, and the minds of the Riot Grrrl movement, signify a reclamation of the self, a de-objectification of female sexuality by men, but, to the outside world, Hanna acknowledges that "people want to stare at my tits"[34] and not understand the nuanced irony of her display.

In addition to failed ironic transmutation of female sexuality, Riot Grrrl's presentation of gender and sexuality also served to perpetuate the male-dominated and male gaze-influenced world of the music industry. Performing the sexualized stereotype of female musician, Riot Grrrl performers were dangerously close to being popular *"because of* their transgressions,"[35] rather than for their attempts to undermine them. In doing so, their bodies, music and culture could problematically be seen as commodities themselves. The new crop of mid-1990s female musicians (à la Gwen Stefani, Alanis Morissette, and Courtney Love) were packaged as a way to sell their music (and their accompanying image) to young girls. What's more, these women were still the product of "male-owned companies,"[36] and girls were viewed more as a market, thereby homogenizing and stereotyping them, once again, by gender—albeit a new more assertive, angry, type of gender label. In addition, this perpetuated the familiar structure of a top-down industry in which managers and label owners, who were primarily male, knew best, and made the executive decisions about product design and marketability. In this way, feminism was not just a political or social statement, but a commercial or market-based one. This is not to dispute that commercial buying power, or the attention paid to the wants and desires of a female-based audience, did not indicate a significant advance in an industry that had traditionally ignored or marginalized women; however, the political and revolutionary implications of Riot Grrrl were weakened and squandered by the pursuit of market share and profits.

Not only was the female body commodified in an attempt to simultaneously encompass both the traditional male gaze and the Riot Grrrl feminist subversion of that, but also the revolutionary spirit of female empowerment, or "girl power," was appropriated. This corporate takeover of female empowerment started with the music industry, cranking out groups, such as the hyper-sexualized Spice Girls, who literally seized the slogan "girl power," and Britney Spears, who tagged themselves with the superficial label of female liberation while retaining none of the radical spirit of Riot Grrrl feminism. Other industries followed the money trail—television (*Buffy the Vampire Slayer*), magazines (*Sassy* and *Seventeen* with their "Cute Band Alerts" and "'Zine of the Month") and corporate sponsorship of music festivals (such as Tommy Hilfiger's underwriting of the Lilith Fair). What all these different commercial incarnations and mutations of Riot Grrrl feminism have in common is the patina of female empowerment coupled with the unadulterated regression to the conventionally-based notions of women's sexuality. Britney dressed in a school-girl uniform, Buffy kicked ass as a blonde, skinny, Californian in leather pants and cropped tees, and the Spice Girls perpetuated every female stereotype (Sporty! Scary! Posh! Baby!) while still wearing revealing clothing.

Even more problematic than the subversion of Riot Grrrl for capitalistic success, were the sociopolitical repercussions, if not intentions, of this cultural appropriation. Historically, subcultures and social movements, or large portions of them, have been "adopted" by the mainstream in order to negate the power or threat such marginal-ized communities held. For instance, civil rights were integrated into the platform of the Democratic Party, while the Tea Party has been subsumed by the Republicans. This is no less true within the realm of music. Jazz, originally thought to be the pur-view of uncivilized barbarians, came to represent the best of American culture; R & B and early rock 'n' roll were transformed from "race" music to family-friendly teen idols; punk was remade from an anarchistic menace to a fashion trend. Each of these instances epitomize the lifecycle of an impending threat to the dominant socio-political world: a grassroots formulation of rebellion, then social unrest via cultural action, then a widespread fear that comes with the struggle against social norms, and, finally, the appropriation and integration of the most threatening principles into the mainstream. This, in turn, guarantees the retention of the conventional social order. Changes are small enough to not rock the proverbial cultural boat, while simultane-ously deflating the momentum of the subculture or social movement. The story of the Riot Grrrls follows a similar trajectory. Whether or not the reasons for appropriation were commercial or sociopolitical (which are, of course, intertwined), the outcome of their commodification was the same—the neutralization of female empowerment. Their incendiary feminist rhetoric was subsumed by the mainstream, neutering their rebellion and taming their voices.

The Riot Grrrl Legacy

Despite the contradictions that were played out, within the ethos and performance of feminism, Riot Grrrl ideas and music have had a profound impact on the cul-tural landscape of today. No longer is it strange to have women center stage, singing and playing instruments; no longer are their songs constrained to love songs and pretty harmonies. And no longer are girls and women unrepresented in popular culture. Clearly, these representations sometimes still cling to the traditionalist view of women as objects, as sexual beings, but Riot Grrrl opened the door for alternative representations—for self-representation, complicated and messy as that is. Similarly, Riot Grrrls continued the tradition of intertwining art with politics, music with social change. They used their voices, their instruments, and their bodies, as platforms for advancing their social cause—feminism.

Notes

1 Simon Frith, *Sound Effects: Leisure and the Politics of Rock 'n' Roll* (New York: Pantheon Books, 1981), 228.

2 Mavis Bayton, "Women Making Music: Some Material Constraints," in Andy Bennett, Barry Shank and Jason Toynbee, eds., *The Popular Music Studies Reader* (London: Routledge Press, 2006), 346–349.

3 Simon Frith and Anglea McRobbie, "Rock and Sexuality," *Screen Education*, No. 29 (1978): 13.

4 Sheryl Garratt, "Teenage Dreams," from *Signed, Sealed, Delivered* (London: Pluto Press, 1984), 409.

5 David P. Szatmary, *Rockin' in Time: A Social History of Rock-and-Roll* (Upper Saddle River, New Jersey: Prentice Hall, 1996), 133–136.

6 Angela Wilson, "After the Riot: Taking New Feminist Youth Subcultures Seriously" (Master's thesis, McGill University, 2004), 49.

7 Ross Haenfler, "Straight Edge: The Newest Face of Social Movements" (Ph.D. dissertation, University of Colorado, 2003), 45.

8 Haenfler, "Straight Edge," 52.

9 Mark Andersen and Mark Jenkins, *Dance of Days: Two Decades of Punk in the Nation's Capital* (New York: Soft Skull Press, 2001), 314–316.

10 Rachel Smith, "Revolution Girl Style, 20 Years Later," NPR.com, September 2011, accessed at www.npr.org/blogs/therecord/2011/09/20.

11 Steve Waksman, "Black Sound, Black Body: Jimi Hendrix, the Electric Guitar and the Meaning of Blackness," in *Instruments of Desire: The Electric Guitar and the Shaping of Musical Experience* (Cambridge: Harvard University Press, 1999), 154.

12 Vera Caisip Gamboa, "Revolution Girl Style Now: Popular Music, Feminism, and Revolution" (Ph.D. dissertation, Simon Fraser University, 1996), 80.

13 Andrea Juno, *Angry Women in Rock* (New York: Juno Books, 1996), 41.

14 Vera Caisip Gamboa, "Revolution Girl Style Now," 91.

15 Jessica Rosenberg and Gitana Garofalo, "Riot Grrrl: Revolutions from Within," *Signs*, Vol. 23, No. 3 (1998): 810.

16 Rachel Smith, "Revolution Girl Style, 20 Years Later."

17 Bikini Kill, "Statement of Vindication," *Reject All American*, LP, © 1996 Kill Rock Stars.

18 Bratmobile, "Do You Like Me Like That?" *Ladies, Women & Girls* CD © 2000 Lookout! Records.

19 7 Year Bitch, "Dead Men Don't Rape," *Sick 'Em*, LP, © 1992 C/Z.

20 Rosenberg and Garofalo, "Riot Grrrl," 818.

21 Catherine Strong, "Grunge, Riot Grrrl and the Forgetting of Women In Popular Culture," *Pop Culture*, Vol. 44, No. 2 (2011): 398–416.

22 *Bikini Kill*, Olympia Washington, n.d., no. 2.

23 Elke Zobl, "Revolution Grrrl and Lady Style Now!" *Peace Review*, Vol. 16, No. 4 (2004): 452.

24 Mark Anderson and Mark Jenkins, *Dance of Days*, 310.

25 Ted Polhemus, *Street Style: From Sidewalk to Catwalk* (London: Thames and Hudson, 1994), 123.

26 Feona Attwood, "Sluts and Riot Grrrls: Female Identity and Sexual Agency," *Journal of Gender Studies*, Vol. 16, No. 3 (November 2007): 241.

27 Cynthia Fuchs, "If I Had a Dick: Queers, Punks, and Alternative Acts," *Mapping the Beat* (Reading, Massachusetts: Blackwell Publishers, 1998), 107.

28 Feona Attwood, "Sluts and Riot Grrrls," 236.

29 S. Reynolds and J. Press, *The Sex Revolts: Gender, Rebellion, and Rock n Roll* (London: Serpent's Tail Press, 1995), 325.

30 Ellen Riordan, "Commodified Agents and Empowered Girls: Consuming and Producing Feminism," *Journal of Communication Inquiry* (2001): 282–284.

31 Laura Mulvey, "Visual Pleasure and Narrative Cinema," *Screen*, Vol. 16, No. 3 (Autumn 1975): 6–18.

32 Melissa Campbell, "Go White Girl: Hip Hop Booty Dancing and the White Female Body," *Continuum: Journal of Media & Cultural Studies* (December 2004).

33 Betty Boob, "Interview with Kathleen Hanna," *Bust* (Issue 12, Spring 1991), 61.

34 Mark Anderson and Mark Jenkins, *Dance of Days*, 344.

35 Vera Caisip Gamboa, "Revolution Girl Style Now."

36 Jennifer Baumgardner and Amy Richards, *Manifesta: Young Women, Feminism, and the Future* (New York: Farrar, Straus, and Giroux, 2000).

15

ANGER IS A GIFT

Post-Cold War Rock and the Anti-Capitalist Movement

David Alexander Robinson

Figure 15.1 Tom Morello of Rage Against the Machine marching with Occupy Wall Street demonstrators during May Day rally.

On 30 November 1999, a new social movement debuted on the world stage, with more than 40,000 demonstrators disrupting the World Trade Organisation (WTO) meeting in Seattle. "The numbers and militancy of the protestors, and the innovative methods of organizing they used, took the authorities by surprise,"[1] and the public opposition helped ensure the meeting's collapse. The transnational movement launched an important pattern of political struggle, regularly challenging meetings of neoliberal institutions through "boisterous and well-attended protest events,"[2] particularly over the following two years. Known as the "Anti-Globalization

Movement," this outburst of activity was the early twenty-first century's most significant social campaign,[3] and presaged the contemporary Occupy Wall St. movement.

The "Anti-Globalization" moniker was always questioned by activists as unsuitable "for a movement that revels precisely in its international character."[4] As David Graeber asserts, "Insofar as this is a movement against anything, it's against neoliberalism … a kind of market fundamentalism … wielded largely through unelected treaty organizations like the IMF [International Monetary Fund], WTO or NAFTA [North American Free Trade Agreement]."[5] Thus, activists later adopted such titles as the "Alter-Globalization Movement" and "Global Justice Movement." Though neoliberals echo Margaret Thatcher's dictum that "There Is No Alternative," this movement reinvigorated debate about creating more socially, economically, and ecologically just global processes.[6]

At one level, this movement was anti-capitalist in *nature*, not because all its members embraced explicitly anti-capitalist politics, but because it opposed core elements of the global capitalist system.[7] However, significant sections of the movement were also *self-consciously* anti-capitalist, drawing on Marxist and anarchist traditions— Ronaldo Munck describing "an anarchism that takes on board much of the Marxist analysis of the nature of global capitalism and the anti-corporate movement's emphasis on consumerism."[8] The movement's explicitly anti-capitalist faction also advanced the most incisive critique of neoliberalism, and a meaningful program for social change.

T. V. Reed writes, "culture is always involved dialectically with the goings-on at the level of economics and politics, contesting for the meanings that can be made from … economic and political event-texts,"[9] and, indeed, various musicians prefigured or later interpreted the movement's anti-capitalist politics. This is particularly true of rock music, always popular among youth counterculture because of its "undeniably antagonistic impulse."[10] This chapter explores the anti-capitalist movement's politics through predominantly American and British post-Cold War rock music—the definition of 'rock' liberally spanning from folk rock to hip hop and electronica. Some thinkers periodize the post-Cold War era as ending with the 2008 Global Financial Crisis; thus, this study takes 1991–2008 as its scope.[11] Relevant artists from post-Cold War music are discussed to explore key elements of anti-capitalist politics and demonstrate their expression. This examination begins with the protest movement's evolution, then surveys its perspectives on environmentalism, marginalized social groups, exploitation of the developing world (the Global South), war and domestic securitization, and, finally, anti-capitalist systemic critique. The term "Anti-Globalization" is used when describing the diverse protest movement, and "anti-capitalist" when discussing the anti-systemic faction on which this study focuses.

The Music

Robin Ballinger argues music is important politically because, "through its complex system of signification … [it shapes] awareness, individual subjectivity, and social formations … [it] is a powerful site of struggle in the organization of meaning and lived experience."[12] Music encourages individuals' activity by helping them feel part of a coherent group, and reinforcing "movement values, ideas, and tactics … provid[ing] information in compact, often highly memorable and emotionally charged ways, both to educate new recruits and to refocus veterans."[13] Political songs also work as propaganda for "potential recruits, opponents, and undecided bystanders."[14] This study examines anti-capitalist lyrics on the basis that, regardless of whether musicians identify completely with anti-capitalist politics, anti-capitalist activists are buoyed by political memes reflecting their core beliefs.

Cultural theorist Lawrence Grossberg differentiates between "oppositional rock … [that] presents itself as a direct challenge or threat to the dominant culture … [and alternative rock, which] mounts only an implicit attack."[15] This study surveys oppositional rock explicitly expressing politics congruent with anti-capitalist beliefs. While many songs voice a general social *ennui*, or vague rage against authority, countercultural revolt has been so highly commercialized that "rebellion" and "revolution" are "catchphrases of the new standard marketing strategy."[16] Indeed, neoliberalism itself is a rebellion by capital against government impositions. So, artists transmitting unambiguous anti-capitalist memes are identified here, to demonstrate core elements of that radical social critique. The extreme concentration of music industry ownership with a handful of corporations forces musicians to accept "the advertising, marketing, styling, and engineering techniques of increasingly uniform and narrow profit-driven criteria."[17] However, this study addresses radical messages that *have* entered popular circulation—corporations still cannot (completely) control "the meanings, practices, and pleasures of listening, dancing, and partying at the site of consumption."[18] As Vladimir Lenin remarked, "the capitalists will sell us the rope with which we will hang them."

The Movement

The Anti-Globalization Movement originated in the late 1980s as neoliberal advocates pushed to create regional free trade blocs in North America and Europe, limiting government regulation of national economies. Ronald Reagan and Margaret Thatcher "successfully pioneered free-market policies … [and by] the end of the decade the world scene had become highly favourable to the generalization of these innovations."[19] The Canada–US Free Trade Agreement provoked Canadian opposition from 1988, and from the early 1990s European protest grew against the Maastricht Treaty's fiscal austerity and social cutbacks—the massive 1995 French general strike being the most dramatic example of this. Radiohead's lyrics later embodied these popular doubts in the song "Electioneering."[20] Civil society campaigns continued to grow in Canada, the US, and Mexico, with NAFTA's signing in 1992, though they would not prevent the treaty's ratification—Rage Against the Machine (RATM) warning of its impact in "Wind Below" from 1996.[21]

Parallel to these campaigns, a guerrilla uprising in Chiapas, southern Mexico, coincided with NAFTA's implementation on 1 January 1994. Led by the enigmatic Subcomandante Marcos, the "Zapatista Army of National Liberation" denounced NAFTA's neoliberal agenda on behalf of Chiapas' poor indigenous people.[22] Geoff Eley writes that the rise of the Zapatistas was the "founding event of recharged anti-capitalist political formation."[23] Various RATM songs later celebrated the Zapatistas.[24] The WTO's creation in 1995, and Multilateral Agreement on Investment negotiations to reduce international investment barriers, spurred campaigns against the WTO, World Bank and IMF. Activists, recognizing that neoliberal policies reinforced global corporate privilege and threatened established human rights, labor and environmental standards, successfully coordinated through new internet and email technology.[25] (Bands such as Anti-Flag and System of a Down (SOAD) would go on to rail against the IMF and globalization with particular fervor).[26] Amidst this activity, the Zapatistas helped shape the anti-capitalist movement from 1996 by inviting to Mexico "over 3,000 activists and intellectuals from 42 countries on 5 continents … to enhance the global struggle against neoliberalism."[27] Networks originating from those meetings, "which took place knee-deep in the jungle mud of rainy-season Chiapas,"[28] eventually organized the 1999 WTO protests. Successful protests at the Birmingham G8 Meeting in May 1998 and the Global Carnival Against Capitalism in June 1999, attracting tens of thousands of participants, established the context for the Seattle events.[29]

The Seattle protest coalition was extremely diverse, including anti-corporate groups; environmental organizations; farm, sustainable agriculture, and anti-GMO groups; labor unions; development/world hunger groups; animal rights groups; religious organizations; and government representatives from developing nations.[30] They were united by growing awareness that the international financial institutions threatened their causes, and they demanded the institutions balance "economic growth with considerations of the social and environmental consequences of trade and investment promotion."[31] Most activists were young, well-educated and involved in informal networks, while those in important logistical roles were predominantly older representatives of NGOs or labor unions.[32] Propagandhi reflected those young people's perspective that, despite their relatively comfortable, middle class backgrounds, they had a moral obligation to speak up for the poor and powerless.[33] SOAD describes them as "peaceful loving youth against the brutality/Of plastic existence."[34]

Activists' commitment to non-hierarchical, consensus-based, decision-making produced the organizational model of "affinity groups" sending delegates to larger "spokes councils" to discuss wider strategies. They had no over-arching leaders and operated through participatory democracy, allowing coordination without decision-enforcement mechanisms.[35] The WTO protest involved political marches and speeches, and the pre-coordinated blockading of roads and conference venues using knowledge of the downtown layout and cell-phone communication.[36] Meanwhile, the anarchist "Black Bloc" donned black clothes and masks, smashing windows of symbolic capitalist targets such as McDonald's, Nike, and Gap.[37]

Overnight, the "Battle of Seattle" launched the Anti-Globalization Movement as a well-known political force, and numerous bands later invoked the imagery of that protest and others in calls for social resistance. Anti-Flag railed against the suppression of free speech,[38] while Ani DiFranco, Tom Morello, and SOAD sang about protesters being shot by police.[39] Asian Dub Foundation (ADF)'s song "Basta" ("Enough," in Spanish) praises later G8 protests[40] and elsewhere they portentously link free markets with slavery.[41]

Over the next two years, dozens of such protests targeted national and international institutions representing neoliberal orthodoxy. Alongside global May Day demonstrations, and protests against the US Republican and Democratic National Conventions, prominent anti-globalization protests occurred in Washington, D.C.; Chiang Mai, Thailand; Melbourne, Australia; Prague, Czech Republic; Seoul, South Korea; Nice, France; Davos, Switzerland; Quebec City, Canada; Gothenburg, Sweden; and in Genoa, Italy, for the 2001 G8 Summit which drew 250,000 protestors.[42] From January 2001, the Anti-Globalization Movement also forged a more coherent counter-organization, with 12,000 activists attending the first World Social Forum in Porto Allegre, Brazil—Naomi Klein writing, "If Seattle was ... the coming-out party of a resistance movement, then ... Porto Alegre [was] the coming-out party for ... serious thinking about alternatives."[43]

The 9/11 terrorist attacks on the United States dramatically undercut the movement, dampening enthusiasm for large-scale protest and empowering governments to respond more aggressively and criminalize dissent. However, in subsequent years, less-frequent protests returned to encouraging sizes across Europe and North America, and were joined by larger demonstrations against war in Iraq and Afghanistan.[44] Almost half a million participants protested "Against a Europe of Capital and War" outside the Barcelona EU summit in March 2002.[45] World and Regional Social Forums have since attracted more than 50,000 delegates a year,[46] building what the second World Social Forum announced would be an "alliance from our struggles and resistance against a system based on sexism, racism and violence, which privileges the interests of capital and patriarchy over the needs and aspirations of people."[47] Despite the changing context, anti-capitalists maintained that, as SOAD and Faithless sing, greed, war, and turning away from those in need continue to determine individual and collective behavior.[48]

Environmentalism

Environmentalist beliefs are by no means the preserve of the anti-capitalist movement. Many today are stirred by Tracy Chapman's lament that we are witnessing a world being raped by corporations.[49] Nevertheless, environmentalism is a core anti-capitalist value, and one that motivated action against international institutions in the 1990s. Buttel and Gould argue that, from 1990, decisions by the General Agreement on Tariffs and Trade (GATT) and the WTO shocked environmentalists, beginning with a ruling against a US Marine Mammal Protection Act clause prohibiting import of tuna caught using methods resulting in numerous dolphin deaths.[50] Early WTO rulings prevented the US imposing higher environmental standards on imported gasoline than domestic production, and later a US law "banning shrimp imports from countries whose shrimp harvesters kill sea turtles" was struck down.[51] Europeans feared the WTO would force them to accept genetically-modified goods, which later occurred in 2006. These rulings disturbed mainstream environmental groups previously unopposed to free trade, demonstrating how liberalization could overturn hard-fought-for environmental legislation. This drew them into the coalition against the WTO meeting in Seattle.[52]

Anti-capitalists also recognized that free trade regimes endangered citizens of developing countries by "eliminating already inadequate environmental laws … turning the environment into a product to be bought and sold."[53] Morrissey and Immortal Technique have warned of the consequences of unbridled, unregulated, capitalism, with references to pollution and toxic dumping, while others, like Propagandhi, interject vegetarianism and animal rights into their broader ecological critique.[54] Generally, the interconnectedness of environmental and social struggles is recognized, whether in the corporate strategy of playing workers against environmentalists to degrade both labor and environmental protections,[55] or the wider understanding that the anti-capitalist movement thus views the capitalist compulsion to profit as the key driver of environmental destruction and commodification of the biological world.[56] As Propagandhi say, "You can tell by the smiles on the CEOs that the environmental restraints are about to go."[57]

The Marginalized

Anti-capitalist activists are generally extremely aware of social marginalization due to race, class, sexuality or gender, their intersectionality, and how these forms of oppression are overdetermined by capitalism. Robert Ross writes that the movement has "identity consciousness in which inherited characteristics—race, ethnicity, gender … are taken to be political building blocks."[58] Margaret Thatcher denied structural discrimination with her slogan "There is no such thing as society. There are [only] individual men and women, and there are families."[59] Neoliberals assert that a "level-playing field" exists within nations, and individuals bear full responsibility for their social circumstances. In contrast, anti-capitalists recognise that neoliberalism's "systematic and calculated process of human impoverishment is decidedly gendered with women and children comprising the vast majority of the world's poor ... Neoliberalism has meant fewer state services ... while the burden of care has fallen to communities, households and, ultimately, women."[60] Both Tracy Chapman and Ani DiFranco capture this gendered disadvantage with their songs "Woman's Work," and "Make Them Apologize."[61]

Today, Western feminist struggles often take place around identity. "Girl Power" is promoted as an empowered discourse, but is really a neoliberal phenomenon emphasising "the idealized form of the self-determining individual ... direct[ing] attention from structural explanations for inequality toward ... personal circumstances and personality traits."[62] Some female bands attack this sanitized feminist form by enacting 'ugliness' and violating feminine expectations. Bikini Kill drummer Tobi Vail states that "For girls to pick up guitars and scream their heads off in a totally oppressive, fucked-up male-dominated culture is to seize power ... a political act."[63] Patriarchal oppression is often embedded in interpersonal relations and, in songs like "Face Up and Sing," DiFranco bemoans both sexual harassment and the silence that perpetuates violence against women.[64] Propagandhi emphasize that the gender-binary also constrains men and they must be part of the solution,[65] while DiFranco welcomes men to the feminist cause.[66] Indeed, in interview, DiFranco asserts, "there is simply no such thing as peace within patriarchy," and that she "would like to see men and women embracing ... [Feminism] as a road out of here, this daily crisis that we live of perpetual war, of destruction of the environment, of racism etc."[67]

Racism has often gained more, and angrier, attention in rock music. In "The Only Good Fascist Is a Very Dead Fascist," Propagandhi characteristically confront the subject with no-holds-barred slamming of white privilege.[68] Michael Franti's songs also often reference discrimination against the poor and people of color, linking those trends to American capitalism and overseas imperialism.[69] Although exaggerating statistics, Franti captures the essence of racial inequality with his references to a quarter of all African-Americans being in prison and fifty percent in poverty.[70] RATM also highlight the intersection of race and class, emphasizing, in "Down Rodeo," that the only interaction the residents of Beverley Hills have with people of color is if they employ (or enslave) them.[71] RATM have also invoked the imprisoned activist and former Black Panther member Mumia Abu Jamal as a symbol of resistance to racist police oppression.[72]

Right-wing politicians often employ racism to mobilize public support; in the British context, directing this towards immigrant communities. Both Pop Will Eat Itself, in "Ich bin Ein Auslander," and the ethnically-Indian ADF, in "Free Satpal Ram," call out both hate speech and the persecution of ethnic minorities.[73] (Ram is a British-Bengali man who was jailed for life after killing a racially-motivated attacker; he was released from prison in 2002 following protests from individuals and groups like ADF).[74] ADF also calls for Europe-wide struggle against racism towards immigrants and asylum-seekers in songs such as "Fortress Europe."[75]

There is increasing concern over "the human rights abuses embodied in the 'prison-industrial complex', the vast growth of prisons ... filled disproportionately by men and women of color."[76] KRS-One likens modern law-enforcement to past slave-masters,[77] SOAD highlight the scale of incarcerations for drug offences in the United States,[78] and RATM references the interconnection of social decay and crime,[79] while DiFranco assigns ultimate responsibility to government policymakers for the racial disparity in American prisons.[80] Pointing to the correlation of rates of imprisonment and poverty, Immortal Technique describes the grinding life of the poor under capitalism.[81] Poverty's structural reality puts the lie to neoliberalism's assumed "level-playing field."[82] Anti-capitalists highlight increasing poverty under neoliberalism, which has attacked organized labor's power and created a "pattern of jobless growth," as semi-skilled positions give way to a combination of casualized "McJobs" and a well-remunerated but intensively overworked technological intelligentsia."[83] Free Trade agreements have "harmonized conditions downward" in other countries such as Canada, "hollowing-out ... the Keynesian welfare state in each participating country."[84] Chapman, RATM, and DiFranco go further, and insist that sexism, racism, and poverty are, at bottom, imbedded within capitalist economics.[85]

Systemic Change

Anti-capitalists have targeted corporations, global financial institutions, and the governments supporting them. The movement's key values illustrated herein have been environmentalism, advancing rights of the marginalized, ending the global disparity in wealth and power, and opposing war and the securitization of society. However, central to the anti-capitalist analysis is the interconnection of these issues and their roots in the global social and economic system that is capitalism. The capitalist system imposes "economic imperatives, introducing the compulsions of the market ... creating and maintaining a class of propertyless workers, who ... are obliged to enter the market to sell their labour power."[86] The meme of the "one percent" dominates current political discourse, and bands like Propagandhi sing about the increasing power of the rich.[87] It seems, in fact, that today, more than ever, "public values, dominant ideas, and [the] range of accessible politics are all ... [tied] to an overriding logic of capital accumulation."[88] Thus, the solution is systemic change—as one London May Day slogan read, "Get Rid of Capitalism and Replace it with Something Nicer."[89]

Precisely what the solution *is* has been debated for hundreds of years in Marxist and anarchist circles, but the consensus seems: first, as ADF expresses in

"Hypocrite,"[90] widespread redistribution of global wealth; second, this can only occur through revolution (see RATM's "Down Rodeo,"[91] Propagandhi's, "Rio De San Atlanta, Manitoba,"[92] Anti-Flag's "Got the Numbers,"[93] and Tracy Chapman's "Talkin' 'bout a Revolution"[94]). There's nothing easier in rock music than talking about revolution, but anti-capitalists take heart from those calls. There is also the tendency to casually emphasize violence, RATM frequently using the motif in songs such as "Calm Like a Bomb,"[95] "New Millennium Homes,"[96] and "Down Rodeo."[97] However, beneath rhetoric is the call for the economic pillars of society—the "means of production"—to be brought under popular control.[98] Rather than Soviet-style nationalization, the anti-capitalist movement generally has "consensus that participatory democracy at the local level—whether through unions, neighbourhoods, farms, villages, anarchist collectives or aboriginal self-government—is where to start building alternatives."[99] Graber argues it "is a movement about reinventing democracy … creating and enacting horizontal networks instead of top-down structures like states, parties or corporations; networks based on principles of decentralized, non-hierarchical consensus democracy."[100] Thus, the anti-capitalist movement of the early twenty-first century, and its successor movements today, call for a radical yet participatory change to the social and economic order.[101]

Notes

1 Alex Callinicos, *An Anti-Capitalist Manifesto* (Cambridge: Polity Press 2003), 4.

2 Jeffrey M. Ayres, "Framing Collective Action against Neoliberalism: The Case of the 'Anti-Globalization' Movement," *Journal of World-Systems Research*, Vol. X, No. 1 (Winter 2004): 11.

3 Frederick H. Buttel and Kenneth A. Gould, "Global Social Movement(s) at the Crossroads: Some Observations on the Trajectory of the Anti-Corporate Globalization Movement," *Journal of World-Systems Research*, Vol. X, No. 1 (Winter 2004): 38.

4 Callinicos, *An Anti-Capitalist Manifesto*, 13.

5 David Graeber, "The New Anarchists," in Tom Merte, ed., *A Movement of Movements: Is Another World Really Possible?* (London: Verso, 2004), 203.

6 Ayres, "Framing Collective Action," 12–13.

7 Callinicos, *An Anti-Capitalist Manifesto*, 15.

8 Ronaldo Munck, *Globalization and Contestation: The New Great Counter-Movement* (London: Routledge, 2007), 70–71.

9 T.V. Reed, *The Art of Protest: Culture and Activism from the Civil Rights Movement to the Streets of Seattle* (Minneapolis: University of Minnesota Press, 2005), 292.

10 Katrina Irving, "Rock Music and the State: Dissonance or Counterpoint?" *Cultural Critique*, No. 10 (Autumn, 1988): 151.

11 Alex Callinicos, *Bonfire of Illusions: The Twin Crises of the Liberal World* (Cambridge: Polity Press, 2010).

12 Robin Ballinger, "Sounds of Resistance," in Louise Amoore, ed., *The Global Resistance Reader* (London: Routledge, 2005), 430.

13 Reed, *The Art of Protest*, 299.

14 Reed, *The Art of Protest*, 299.

15 Brian Longhurst, *Popular Music & Society* (Cambridge: Polity Press, 2007), 108.

16 Karen Bettez Halnon, "Heavy Metal Carnival and Dis-alienation: The Politics of Grotesque Realism," *Symbolic Interaction*, Vol. 29, No. 1 (Winter 2006): 45.

17 Martin Scherzinger, "Music, Corporate Power, and Unending War," *Cultural Critique*, No. 60 (Spring 2005): 24.

18 Martin Stokes, "Music and the Global Order," *Annual Review of Anthropology*, Vol. 33 (2004): 54–55.

19 Callinicos, *An Anti-Capitalist Manifesto*, 2–3.

20 Radiohead, *OK Computer*, CD, track 8, "Electioneering," © 1997 Capitol/EMI Records.

21 Rage Against the Machine, *Evil Empire*, CD, track 9, "Wind Below," © 1996 Epic Associated Records.

22 Ayres, "Framing Collective Action," 15–16.

23 Geoff Eley, "Historicizing the Global, Politicizing Capital: Giving the Present a Name," *History Workshop Journal*, No. 63 (Spring 2007): 174–175.

24 Rage Against the Machine, *The Battle of Los Angeles*, CD, track 12, "War Within a Breath," © 1999 Epic Associated Records.

25 Duncan Green and Matthew Griffith, "Globalization and Its Discontents," *International Affairs*, Vol. 78, No. 1 (January 2002): 54.

26 Anti-Flag, *For Blood and Empire*, CD, track 11, "The W.T.O. Kills Farmers," © 2006 RCA Records; and System of a Down, *Mezmerize*, CD, track 4, "Cigaro," © 2005 American Recordings.

27 David E. Lowes, *The Anti-Capitalist Dictionary: Movements, Histories and Motivations* (London: Zed Books, 2006), 295–296.

28 Graeber, "The New Anarchists," 204.

29 Green and Griffith, "Globalization and Its Discontents," 50.

30 Buttel and Gould, "Global Social Movement," 48.

31 Ayres, "Framing Collective Action," 22.

32 Buttel and Gould, "Global Social Movement," 45.

33 Propagandhi, *Less Talk, More Rock*, CD, track 9, "Resisting Tyrannical Government," © 1996 Fat Wreck Chords.

34 System of a Down, *Toxicity*, CD, track 3, "Deer Dance," © 2001 American Recordings.

35 Buttel and Gould, "Global Social Movement," 39.

36 Ayres, "Framing Collective Action," 21.

37 Francis Dupuis-Déri, "The Black Blocs Ten Years after Seattle: Anarchism, Direct Action, and Deliberative Practices," *Journal for the Study of Radicalism*, Vol. 4, No. 2 (2010): 46.

38 Anti-Flag, *Mobilize*, CD, track 3, "What's the Difference?" © 2002 A-F Records.

39 Ani DiFranco, *Evolve*, CD track 11, "Serpentine," © 2003 Righteous Babe Records; System of a Down, "Deer Dance"; and The Nightwatchman, *One Man Revolution*, CD track 10, "Union Song," © 2007 Epic Records.

40 Asian Dub Foundation, *Enemy of the Enemy*, CD, track 10, "Basta," © 2003 Ffrr Records.

41 Asian Dub Foundation, *Community Music*, CD, track 7, "Crash," © 2000 Ffrr Records.

42 Callinicos, *An Anti-Capitalist Manifesto*, 5; Ayres, "Framing Collective Action," 23; and Buttel and Gould, "Global Social Movement," 43, 48–49.

43 Naomi Klein, "Farewell to the 'End of History:' Organization and Vision in Anti-Corporate Movements," in *The Global Resistance Reader*, 158.

44 Ayres, "Framing Collective Action," 25.

45 Callinicos, *An Anti-Capitalist Manifesto*, 18.

46 Ayres, "Framing Collective Action," 28.

47 Callinicos, *An Anti-Capitalist Manifesto*, 15.

48 System of a Down, *Steal This Album*, CD, track 4, "Boom," © 2002 American Recordings; and Faithless, *No Roots*, CD, track 2, "Mass Destruction," © 2004 Cheeky Records/BMG.

49 Tracy Chapman, *New Beginning*, CD, track 7, "The Rape of the World," © 1995 Elektra.

50 Buttel and Gould, "Global Social Movements," 46–47.

51 Buttel and Gould, "Global Social Movements," 46–47.

52 Buttel and Gould, "Global Social Movements," 46–47, and NOFX, *War On Errorism*, CD, track 3, "Franco Un-American," © 2003 Fat Wreck Chords.

53 Reed, *The Art of Protest*, 251.

54 Robert J. S. Ross, "From Antisweatshop to Global Justice to Antiwar: How the New New Left is the Same and Different from the Old New Left," *Journal of World-Systems Research*, Vol. X, No. 1 (Winter 2004): 310–311. See Morrissey, *You Are the Quarry (Deluxe Edition)*, CD, disc 2, track 9, "Mexico," © 2004 Sanctuary/Attack Records; Immortal Technique, *The 3rd World*, CD, track 7, "The 3rd World," © 2008 Viper Records; and Propagandhi, *Less Talk, More Rock*, CD, track 2, "Nailing Descartes to the Wall," © 1996 Fat Wreck Chords.

55 Reed, *The Art of Protest*, 253.

56 Propagandhi, *Less Talk, More Rock*, CD, track 1, "Apparently, I'm a P.C. Fascist," © 1996 Fat Wreck Chords.

57 Propagandhi, *Less Talk, More Rock*, CD, track 7, "And We Thought That Nation-States Were a Bad Idea," © 1996 Fat Wreck Chords.

58 Robert J. S. Ross, "From Antisweatshop to Global Justice," 310–311.

59 William K. Carroll and William Little, "Neoliberal Transformation and Antiglobalization Politics in Canada: Transition, Consolidation, Resistance," *International Journal of Political Economy*, Vol. 31, No. 3 (Fall 2001): 48.

60 Janine Brodie, "Globalization, Governance and Gender: Rethinking the Agenda for the Twenty-First Century" in *The Global Resistance Reader*, 250–251.

61 Tracy Chapman, *Matters of the Heart*, CD, track 5, "Woman's Work," © 1992, Elektra; and Ani DiFranco, *Imperfectly*, CD, track 10, "Make Them Apologize," © 1992 Righteous Babe Records.

62 Marnina Gonick, "Between 'Girl Power' and 'Reviving Ophelia': Constituting the Neoliberal Girl Subject," *NWSA Journal*, Vol. 18, No. 2 (Summer 2006): 2.

63 Karina Eileraas, "Witches, Bitches & Fluids: Girl Bands Performing Ugliness as Resistance," *TDR/The Drama Journal*, Vol. 41, No. 3 (Autumn 1997): 124–125.

64 Ani DiFranco, *Out Of Range*, CD, track 7, "Face Up and Sing," © 1994 Righteous Babe Records.

65 Propagandhi, *Less Talk, More Rock*, CD, track 14, "Refusing To Be a Man," © 1996 Fat Wreck Chords.

66 Ani DiFranco, *Educated Guess*, CD, track 10, "Grand Canyon," © 2004 Righteous Babe Records.

67 Megan Haines and Ani DiFranco, "Interview with Ani DiFranco," *Off Our Backs*, Vol. 37, No. 4 (2007): 23–24.

68 Propagandhi, *Less Talk, More Rock*, CD, track 11, "The Only Good Fascist Is a Very Dead Fascist," © 1996 Fat Wreck Chords.

69 Derrick P. Alridge, "From Civil Rights to Hip Hop: Toward a Nexus of Ideas," *The Journal of African American History*, Vol. 90, No. 3 (Summer 2005): 226–227.

70 Michael Franti, *Home*, CD, track 10, "Crime To Be Broke in America," © 1994 Capitol Records.

71 Rage Against the Machine, *Evil Empire*, CD, track 7, "Down Rodeo," © 1996 Epic Associated Records, and Rage Against the Machine, *Evil Empire*, CD, track 8, "Without a Face," © 1996 Epic Associated Records.

72 Rage Against the Machine, *Battle of Los Angeles*, CD, track 9, "Voice of the Voiceless," © 1999 Epic Associated Records.

73 Pop Will Eat Itself, *Dos Dedos Mis Amigos*, CD, track 1, "Ich bin ein Auslander," © 1994 Infectious Records; and Asian Dub Foundation, *Facts and Fictions*, CD, track 2, "PKNB," © 1995 Virgin France.

74 Tariq Jazeel, "The World Is Sound? Geography, Musicology and British-Asian Soundscapes," *Area*, Vol. 37, No. 3 (Sept 2005): 235; and Asian Dub Foundation, *RAFI's Revenge*, CD, track 7, "Free Satpal Ram," © 1998 London Records.

75 Asian Dub Foundation, *Enemy of the Enemy*, CD, track 1, "Fortress Europe," © 2003 Ffrr Records.

76 Reed, *The Art of Protest*, 252.

77 KRS-One, *Return Of The Boom Bap*, CD, track 7, "Sound of da Police," © 1993 Jive Records.

78 System of a Down, *Toxicity*, CD, track 1, "Prison Song," © 2001 American Recordings.

79 Rage Against the Machine, *Battle of Los Angeles*, CD, track 11, "Ashes in the Fall," © 1999 Epic Associated Records; and Rage Against the Machine, *Evil Empire*, CD, track 11, "Year of tha Boomerang," © 1996 Epic Associated Records.

80 Ani DiFranco, *Up Up Up Up Up Up*, CD, track 1, "'Tis of Thee," © 1999 Righteous Babe Records.

81 Immortal Technique, *Revolutionary, Vol. 2*, CD, track 4, "Harlem Streets," © 2003, Viper Records.

82 Faithless, *No Roots*, CD, track 14, "In the End," © 2004 Cheeky Records/BMG.

83 Carroll and Little, "Neoliberal Transformation," 45.

84 Carroll and Little, "Neoliberal Transformation," 38.

85 Tracy Chapman, *Matters of the Heart*, CD, track 2, "So," © 1992 Elektra; Tracy Chapman, *Where You Live*, CD, track 7, "America," © 2005 Elektra; Rage Against the Machine, *Evil Empire*, CD, track 11, "Year of tha Boomerang," © 1996 Epic Associated Records; and Ani DiFranco, *Not So Soft*, CD, track 5, "On Every Corner," © 1991 Righteous Babe Records.

86 Ellen Meiksins Wood, *Empire of Capital* (London: Verso, 2003): 20–21.

87 Propagandhi, *Less Talk, More Rock*, CD, track 7, "And We Thought That Nation-States Were A Bad Idea," © 1996 Fat Wreck Chords; and Propagandhi, *Less Talk, More Rock*, CD, track 9, "Resisting Tyrannical Government," © 1996 Fat Wreck Chords.

88 Geoff Eley, "Historicizing the Global," 163.

89 Callinicos, *An Anti-Capitalist Manifesto*, 106.

90 Asian Dub Foundation, *RAFI's Revenge*, CD, track 5, "Hypocrite," © 1998 London Records.

91 Rage Against the Machine, "Down Rodeo."

92 Propagandhi, *Less Talk, More Rock*, CD, track 5, "Rio De San Atlanta, Manitoba," © 1996 Fat Wreck Chords.

93 Anti-Flag, *A New Kind Of Army*, CD, track 6, "Got the Numbers," © 1999 Go-Kart Records.

94 Tracy Chapman, *Tracy Chapman*, CD, track 8, "Talkin' 'bout a Revolution," © 1988 Elektra.

95 Rage Against the Machine, *The Battle of Los Angeles*, CD, track 3, "Calm Like a Bomb," © 1999 Epic Associated Records.

96 Rage Against the Machine, *The Battle of Los Angeles*, CD, track 10, "New Millennium Homes," © 1999 Epic Associated Records.

97 Rage Against the Machine, "Down Rodeo."

98 Rage Against the Machine, "Down Rodeo"; and Immortal Technique, *The 3rd World*, CD, track 7, "The 3rd World," © 2008 Viper Records.

99 Naomi Klein, "Farewell to the 'End of History,'" 160.

100 David Graeber, "The New Anarchists," 212.

101 Rise Against, *Siren Song of the Counter Culture*, CD, track 2, "The First Drop," © 2004 Geffen Records; Rage Against the Machine, *The Battle of Los Angeles*, CD, track 12, "War within a Breath," © 1999 Epic Associated Records; Rage Against the Machine, *The Battle of Los Angeles*, CD, track 2, "Guerrilla Radio," © 1999 Epic Associated Records.

16

CONCERTS FOR A CAUSE (OR, 'CAUSE WE CAN?)

H. Louise Davis

Figure 16.1   Press conference at Live Aid, 1985.

When he addressed the Live Aid crowd at Wembley on 13 July 1985, benefit concert organizer come recent Africa activist Bob Geldof not only urged crowds to "Just give us the fucking money,"[1] but also ushered in a new culture of consumer activism centered around the highly visible and undeniably profitable mega-event.[2] In stating:

> You can be absolutely sure, on the day you die, somebody is alive in Africa because one day you bought a record or a book or watched a pop concert. And that, at once, is a compliment and a triumph, and on the other hand, it is the ultimate indictment of us all.

Geldof hailed every concert-goer, every television viewer, as a consumer-donor, as an active subject capable of effecting change on a global scale.[3] His words acknowledged the power of music and music entertainment to rally crowds around a cause, to transform ordinary consumers into participatory actors and global agents. But, while commending their participation, his statement also condemned the very system that enabled the concert's success. In mentioning that participation would be an "ultimate indictment" of consumer-donors, Geldof highlights the ridiculousness of a Western cultural logic that equates mainstream music entertainment with charitable aid.

In *Rockin' the Boat: Mass Music and Mass Movements*, Reebee Garofalo explains the roots of such logic, stating that:

> Since the 1980s, music—that is to say, culture—has taken the lead in the relative absence of … movements. With the decline of participation in grassroots political movements, popular music itself has come to serve as a catalyst for raising issues and organizing masses of people.[4]

Indeed, the mega-event firmly situates music at the center of social movement culture. The concert did nothing if not illustrate the power of music to unite diverse communities around the globe and showcase to the world the power of compassionate consumer activism as audible, visible, and impossible to ignore.[5] Given its success in raising funds (and to a lesser extent awareness) it is no surprise that, since 1985, numerous charities have been inspired to organize live benefit concert events in aid of a range of political, social, and cultural causes. Using the tried and tested Live Aid format, relying on a combination of media hype and consumer desire, such benefit concerts have proven effective in their awareness-raising aims time and time again. Their success can be attributed to the media spectacle that surrounds such events,[6] good planning,[7] and the fact that charity rock texts and mega-events provide some of the few appropriate venues within which ordinary members of society can overtly express compassion and enact protest within the compassionate conservative cultures in the West.[8] As a result of their emphasis upon purchasing and pleasure, benefit concerts are often criticized for supporting compassionate conservative ideologies that have permeated the West since the Thatcher-Reagan era. However, as a number of music scholars have noted, such concerts should not be simply read as the commercial usurping the political; on the contrary, they have also shown the potential to rupture dominant hegemonic processes.[9] This potential arises from the benefit concerts' ability to hail mass, diverse audiences and provide them—if only temporarily—with new sites of cultural expression, and alternative opportunities to enact agency on local, national, and global levels.

Neil Ullestad hints to the production of new sites at Live Aid when he suggests that the mega-event:

structurally emphasised charity and philanthropy (for others not so much like us), as well as global cooperation, at a time when the narrow dominant views have atomised and deadened the majority of the pop audience and locked us in our lonely rooms. Live Aid opened windows from our rooms to the world and made it legitimate to care, and called us to *act* ... The effects were not oppositional; the events spoke for internal alternatives, for action *within* the system.[10]

In opening windows, Live Aid enabled diverse groups of consumer-activists to commune, interact, to produce as well as consume social movement artifacts, and to effect global change. Since Live Aid, a vibrant and active music-centered movement culture has continued to grow and evolve, a movement culture that—as I shall illustrate—has had an enormous impact on Western cultural consciousness regarding the Global South, charity, and aid.

This paper examines the performance, format, and ideological underpinnings of Live Aid and its twentieth anniversary concert, Live 8, in order to illustrate how music-centered consumer activism, such as that enacted at live global benefit concerts, has the potential to simultaneously support and undermine, suture and rupture, conservative hegemonic processes from within. My analyses of performances, and the flexible roles of participants, indicate how mass mega-events have the ability to empower diverse groups of peoples in such a way that they not only affect government policy,[11] but also have the potential to alter the Western cultural imaginary with regards to the Global South, victimhood, philanthropy, and aid.

Live Aid

The Live Aid benefit concert was the culminating event of the celebrity-inspired, consumer-driven 1984–5 famine relief movement.[12] Broadcast live via seven telecommunications satellites from two separate locations, London's Wembley Stadium and Philadelphia's Kennedy Stadium, Live Aid was heralded as a global extravaganza the likes of which had never before been seen.[13] The concert boasted 162,000 audience members (70,000 at Wembley and 92,000 in Philadelphia) and was distributed to an estimated one billion television viewers in over one hundred and fifty countries worldwide.[14] Engineered by Geldof and the Band Aid charity, in collaboration with USA for Africa artists, the mega-event was designed to raise both funds and awareness for sufferers of famine in the Horn of Africa.[15]

Throughout the concert, emphasis was placed on the performers, with the most popular gaining prime spots in the line-up, and the celebrity supporters who introduced the acts. Stadium crowds and city landscapes also gained a great deal of visibility as telescreens in the stadiums and television screens at home provided a multitude of ground level and overhead shots of the concert crowds and the London and Philadelphia skylines. Telescreens enabled viewers in both stadiums access to performances across the pond, just as at home viewers were also treated to performances from both locations.[16] Throughout the concert, posters and product placement referenced the concerts' multiple sponsors. And, during intermissions, interviews with celebrities were aired for the pleasure of viewers worldwide.

From its moment of conception, the Live Aid concert reeked of extravagance that often seemed to overshadow, if not completely elide, the famine relief cause. Such focus on extravagance was not only evident throughout the concert performances, but was made apparent even during early planning discussions in which members of the organizing team discussed the simultaneous launch of rockets from Wembley and Kennedy, the former to shoot David Bowie, and the latter Mick Jagger, into the sky above the stadiums.[17] Although the rocket idea was eventually nixed (it being too expensive), and Bowie and Jagger instead co-recorded "Dancing in the Streets," organizers did not abandon the idea of combining satellite transmission with supersonic transportation. Instead of the rocket spectacle, they arranged with British Airways for Phil Collins to fly between concert venues via Concorde. After performing in London, Collins boarded the supersonic jet bound for Philadelphia, where he performed for a second time. Interviews with Collins prior to boarding and throughout the journey were interspersed with concert footage from both sides of the Atlantic. When asked why he was undertaking the journey, Collins responded thus: "We thought that if it could be done, wouldn't it be good to do it. And then we went into the logistics and we found out it was possible... Eric Clapton's on tour out there, so is Robert Plant, and so I rang them up to see if I could play with them so it would give me something to go for" Collins' rationale here could be applied to the concert as a whole.[18] Live Aid was done, not because it necessarily needed to be done, but because it could be done.

The Concorde journey and, indeed, Collins' comments as a whole, serve as prime examples of the misguided and misguiding focal points of the concert. During Live Aid, emphasis was almost always placed, if not upon celebrities and their exploits, then upon the needs and desires of consumer-donors. Rarely were actual famine sufferers or intended recipients of aid referenced, as organizers and performers preferred instead—and perhaps most pragmatically—to focus attention upon the compassionate donor impulses of mega-event audiences in the stadium and at home. This focus demonstrates a privileging of the audience over intended recipients and illustrates concert organizers' reliance on audience members to make connections between the concert spectacle and the famine relief movement. Such elision of the intended recipient of famine aid unfortunately indicates a clear-cut ideological divide between consumer donors and victims: as Ullestad mentions, the concert was in aid of "others not so much like us." That being said—given the line-up, rhetoric, and format—audiences could be forgiven for forgetting, at times, that such others actually existed.

David Bowie was one of few performers that attempted to challenge the dominant narrative of the concert, when he requested that a CBC report on famine relief be aired during some of his allotted stage time (a request that perhaps only a well-respected superstar with an extremely solid career could make).[19] Having sung a number of songs including the hits "Rebel, Rebel" and "We Could Be Heroes"—songs that, while not directly applicable to famine relief, certainly interpellated potential donors as rebellious and/or heroic actors (if only for the one day)—Bowie introduced the bizarre Canadian news short depicting a refugee camp in Ethiopia, a short that appeared vaguely reminiscent of a bad music video, set to the strangely inappropriate tune "Who's Gonne Drive You Home" by the Cars."[20] Notwithstanding the problematic nature of the representation chosen,[21] Bowie's request resulted in a rupturing of the concert narrative. With the exception of the CBC report, the sixteen-hour long event catered to, and focused solely upon, celebrities and consumers. The report, while still providing viewers and listeners with a consumable product (a set of African experiences to consume and appropriate), momentarily shifted attention away from the mega-event, and asked audiences to refocus on the intended recipient. Unfortunately, however, Bowie sutured the rupture he created when he addressed the crowd as heroes. In stating "God bless you. You're the heroes of this concert," he re-established the consumer-activist as the central figure of the famine relief movement.[22] His statement serves as a prime example of the neo-imperialist overtones of the concert, serving—as did most of the concert's narrative—to locate the Western concert participant at the epicenter of famine relief, as global consumer-savior, as the only hope for starving Africans. His actions overall, well-intentioned as one assumes they were, illustrate clearly the contradictions inherent in mega-events. While, on one hand, Bowie supports neo-imperialist notions of the Western savior, he also requires said saviors to reconsider their own position as subjects by changing the mode of their "entertainment" and momentarily exposing them to the experiences of the Other. If nothing else, the contradictory nature of his actions shows how dominant narratives are consistently in a state of flux, and that no one event can be decoded in a simple or single-minded manner.

Criticisms of the concert have rightly focused on the elision of famine sufferers and the fact that organizers and the media chose to emphasize consumer desires and gratuitous extravagance in a way that shifted emphasis away from the famine relief movement agenda.[23] Some have argued that the event pandered to consumer narcissism, as opposed to exposing the issues at hand,[24] and that, as a result, any social engagement of Live Aid audiences should be read as vacuous.[25] In addition, various critics have expressed concern about the motivations, not just of audience members, but more so of those celebrities and sponsors involved, often questioning why celebrities and sponsors would choose to participate in "global" spectacle.[26] The Western location of the mega-event, and the media hype that surrounded both the cities and the stadiums that housed them,[27] alongside the lack of representation of non-Western (and, in the U.K., non-white) artists throughout the course of the "global" spectacle,[28] proved even further cause for concern. Such an ethnocentric and paternalistic focus may not have been so problematic were it not supported by ethnocentric assumptions, and neo-imperialist rhetoric such as that espoused by Bowie's call to heroes.

While, like Bowie's comments, the concert functioned within and relied upon a neo-imperialist framework, its overall cultural impact should not be underestimated. First of all, the concert was nothing that it did not claim to be: an entertainment event designed to grab attention and raise a great deal of money for famine relief. It was successful in it aims, raising almost seventy million dollars to "feed the world."[29] As Reebee Garofalo suggests, this is a phenomenal amount raised simply by one event.[30] Second, the concert—like the charity rock singles that preceded it—inspired unprecedented corporate philanthropy.[31] And third, its very existence showcased how consumer activism was—by 1985—a force with which to be reckoned. Even though both U.S. and U.K. governments had reduced famine aid to countries in the Horn, particularly Ethiopia, with whose Marxist government both Thatcher and Reagan had expressed ideological disagreements, neither the U.S. or U.K. governments chose to ignore the demands of the masses when it came to Live Aid. On the contrary, the mega-event and the message of compassion expressed by participants affected changes in U.S. and U.K. governmental policies on foreign aid to famine-struck provinces in the Horn of Africa.[32] Government figures have chosen to be even more involved with mega-events since Live Aid and while, at times, such government involvement appears to do little more than emphasize dominant logic of neo-imperialist development, this participation does illustrate that even the most conservative of governments are willing to listen to and support the voices of the masses when expressed during mega-events (within certain limitations, granted).[33] Finally, Live Aid was most effective in opening not just spaces for expression and sites for the enactment of social movement cultures, but also new philanthropic and political trajectories. As Reebee Garofalo and T. V. Reed have noted, the mega-event inspired more politicized events after the fact. Garofalo states: "there is scarcely a social issue in the eighties and early nineties which has not been associated in a highly visible way with music and musicians.[34] Reed supports this assertion, pointing out that "[h]undreds of subsequent musical benefits and mega-benefits in dozens of countries attest to the ongoing impact of Live Aid."[35] I would expand on this point by noting that the concert was also significant in setting the scene for spin-off events to develop a new politic of suffering by providing both actual and representative sites within which the blurring of concert participant and intended aid recipient could, and can, occur.[36]

Live 8

One such spin-off event occurred in July 2005. In honor of the twentieth anniversary of Live Aid, Geldof helped arrange the Live 8 concerts, the last of which was timed to coincide with the G8 summit focusing on development and debt in Africa. As an off-shoot of Jubilee 2000, and in coordination with Make Poverty History,[37] the anniversary concerts were held in ten different locations around the globe, in London, Cornwall, Paris, Berlin, Rome, Philadelphia, Barrie, Tokyo, Johannesburg, Moscow, and lastly, in Edinburgh, over a three-day period. The concerts were distributed to an estimated three billion audience members, arguably as diverse as the genres of music represented at the mega-events.[38]

Each concert followed a format similar to that of Live Aid, with celebrities providing introductions to acts and referencing the purpose of the events, the most popular bands and musicians playing at prime time, and the linking of multiple concert sites via satellite at various points throughout the simultaneous broadcast. Performances were interspersed with interviews and, at times, complemented by simultaneously broadcast shorts not dissimilar to the CBC report that Bowie introduced. For instance, Travis performed their hit "Why Does It Always Rain on Me?" at Edinburgh, with footage juxtaposing gratuitous spending in the West with the lifestyles of Africans being projected on a screen behind the musicians. Coverage for at-home viewers consisted—as did much of the telescreen footage at each stadium—of shots of artists performing on stage, ground and air shots of stadium crowds, and occasional visual references to the technology being used.

Despite the occasional short film, the focus on intended recipients was, yet again, extremely limited. While the concerts were designed to make a public statement about debt relief in Africa and challenge the G8 to "make poverty history" on the African continent as a result, only one concert was held in Africa (in Johannesburg), and there was a notable absence of African artists in the mainstream concert line-ups. This absence was, in large part, due to Geldof's institution of a policy that excluded any artist without $4.5 million in sales from performing on any of the urban center stages.[39] In addition, as with its predecessor, Live 8 included only limited references to actual sufferers of poverty and almost no clear definitions of the poverty that was to become history. Such elision of supposed victims of poverty and representatives of the most impoverished of nations in the developing south also resulted, unsurprisingly, in Live 8 being assaulted with similar, yet equally valid, criticisms to Live Aid. Journalists and scholars alike again questioned the narcissistic motives of both consumers and celebrities,[40] not to mention the motives of corporate sponsors and beneficiaries.[41] The event's unsustainability,[42] and the concert's ultimate reinforcement of neo-liberalism, proved to be the largest cause of concern for critics.[43]

But, as with Live Aid, to assume that the concerts were united in one aim, or could be decoded in one way only, is too simple. In its totality, the Live 8 mega-event was as paradoxical and contradictory as the 1985 concert. Inasmuch as the Live 8 events supported or avoided challenging the status quo, they also simultaneously served to subvert dominant ideologies, despite Geldof's intent to avoid ideology altogether.[44] While, on one hand, the dominant rhetoric espoused at the events may have seemed to homogenize issues of poverty, packaging them neatly into neo-liberal frameworks, the events themselves also allowed for the creation of heterogenous cultural sites within which new rhetorics and modes of cultural expression emerged. As with Live Aid, ruptures in the dominant concert narratives and resistant cultural practices consistently emerged throughout the course of the Live 8 events. Two of the concerts held in the U.K., "Live Aid at Eden: Africa Calling" and the Live 8 concert in Edinburgh, serve as extremely effective examples of the contradictory and diverse nature of the Live 8 events. The concerts held at both locations produced heterogenic sites within which organizers, performers, and consumer-activists produced counter-hegemonic cultural messages.

Despite Geldof's position as both organizer of the mega-events and supposed expert on debt relief and Africa,[45] various other artists and organizers expressed discomfort and disagreement with his decision to deliberately exclude artists from the Global South, and actively chose to disregard his decision to exclude lesser-known African artists. In collaboration with music industry expert and activist Tim Smit, and a diverse range of African artists including Senegalese activist Youssou N'Dour, Peter Gabriel (musician and founder of WOMAD) worked to organize Africa Calling, a concert that highlighted musicians from all over the continent.[46] Held at the Eden Project in Cornwall, southwest England, Africa Calling provided African artists with a venue in which to perform.[47] In an interview leading up to the concert, Gabriel stated the "African artists needed to be really present here" and, at a press conference, noted that it was necessary to "allow some of these extraordinary artists to sing and to speak for themselves."[48] Later, in direct disagreement with Geldof's notion that only world renowned performers could hold audience attention, Gabriel stated his belief that "as long as the music is good, you hold the viewers" implying a respect for African artists that Geldof lacks, despite his role as spokesperson for Africa in the eyes of the British government and press.[49] Obviously of like mind to Gabriel, Midge Ure (Geldof's less visible partner and organizer of the "Do They Know It's Christmas" single and the Live Aid concert), later solicited Gabriel's help in arranging for African artists to play at the final concert in Edinburgh, where many performed on stage alongside Scottish acts.[50] Gabriel and Ure's decisions are proof again that visions and aims for the concert were multiple and, at times, opposed and contradictory.

Africa Calling allowed for the creation of multiple and occasionally unexpected social movement sites within which consumer-activists challenged, if not functioned beyond, the neo-liberal frameworks that critics such as April Biccum, James R. Compton, and Edward Comor identify. Analysis of this concert, alongside the Edinburgh concert in which the audience took participation to a new level of interactivity, illustrates that—despite their validity—such critical conclusions can often be too simplistic. In failing to focus on aspects of performance, and in assuming a moral consensus among the organizers and audiences, critics not only ignore the potential for both performers and performance to rupture dominant modes of meaning-making, but also mistakenly accept that musical codes maintain the same meaning across time and space. The concerts at Eden and Edinburgh prove this not to be the case.

Live 8 at Eden: Africa Calling

Africa Calling was separated both geographically and ideologically from the other concerts. While it provided global audiences the opportunity to see and hear a diverse range of African music performed by artists from all over the continent, its location outside of an urban center, and the fact that it received less media attention and traditional media coverage than the other concerts, led to a marginalization of the event.[51] Unlike those at the other Live Aid venues, charities, crews, organizers, and performers only had three weeks to arrange Live 8 at Eden. That being said, the event proved to be a success. The live event was well attended in Cornwall, it effectively showcased diverse African music and cultures to millions of television audiences and Internet users worldwide, and it proved that good African music can hold global audiences' attention. At the same time, the concert proved that Africans have both the ability and desire to act on their own behalf.[52]

The concert opened with introductions from British musician Peter Gabriel and British Indian dhol drum musician Johnny Kalsi. In his opening Kalsi asserted that—at that moment—Africa was located at Eden, stating that "The heart of Africa is right here at Eden, right in front of you all."[53] But the heart of Africa portrayed was a far cry from any imperialist or neo-liberal vision. Artists ranging from the global pop icons Youssou N'Dour and Angélique Kidjo performed at the same venue as artists lesser known in the West, such as Maryam Mursal, a singer from (and first female taxi driver in) Somalia.[54] The image of African artists presented was in direct opposition to images that dominate the Western cultural imaginary. Performers presented themselves as anything but impoverished, particularly in terms of culture, as they presented a range of music that drew on rich traditions and vibrant contemporary African music scenes. The rhetoric of the event was also distinct, with artists asking for support of both local and national political causes (such as the liberation of the Zimbabwean people),[55] describing activist successes (such as girls' education through UNICEF programs),[56] and celebrating music and culture in a range of African and European languages.[57]

In addition to showcasing African musicians, the concert provided a venue to showcase a wide range of local causes and charities working in Africa (ranging from the global NGO UNICEF to the more locally-based Green Futures, connected to the Eden Project). Any profits raised by Africa Calling were donated to charities chosen by the performers.[58] In providing a platform for such a broad range of interests and local and national causes, the concert at Eden proved that collaboration among NGOs and mass audiences need not result in the homogenization of ideology or a moral consensus. In enabling Africans and African artists to illustrate how they are active agents, making choices about the future of Africa, and calling for support for political change, Africa Calling also showed itself to be an event clearly distinct in terms of format and ideology to Live 8's predecessor, Live 8, where Western audience members were interpellated as the heroes of African aid while Africans were reduced to worn-out symbols of infertile land and dying babies.[59] In addition, the concert moved beyond what performer and Senegalese rapper Faada Freddy described as the "Nuremberg style of the other concerts"[60] which, in appearing non-partisan, also lacked the energy and diversity of the concert at Eden.

Africa Calling effectively illustrated to billions of audience members worldwide that Africans are not simply victims of systemic poverty but active agents in their own recovery. Like the consumer-activists of Live Aid, African artists at Eden demonstrated a willingness and an ability to participate in global events as conscious and active agents. Eden perhaps proves, more than any of the other concerts, that music can both unite and educate diverse audiences about cultures outside of their own experiences. The concert also proved, as Garofalo states, that music is central to expression within social movement culture.

Live 8 at Murrayfield: Scotland Calling

While certainly of more central focus than Africa Calling, the final Edinburgh concert also proved distinct to the other Live 8 events, in part because of its timing, and in part because it took the notion of audience participation to a new level, blurring the boundary between audience and performer in a way atypical of global mega-events. It was held on the final day of the mega-event in order to coincide with the G8 meeting at Gleneagles, only a few miles away. While the Edinburgh concert serves as a prime example of a Live 8 event occluding debates on neo-liberal trade policies—it being arranged to coincide with (and arguably overshadow) the largest protest in the history of Scotland—the event illustrated the power of audiences to appropriate mass events and sites and to take control over meaning-making.[61]

For all intents and purposes, the concert at first appeared very similar to the others, with a couple of distinctions—principally, the inclusion of African artists. But such inclusion was not all that marked Live 8 at Murrayfield as unique. Despite the global nature of the event, the concert had a uniquely nationalist flavor: it was distinctly Scottish. And this Scottishness was consistently emphasized throughout the event by musical and aesthetic choices made by performers, the rhetoric espoused by organizers, and the actions and attitudes of the crowd. West coast band Wet Wet Wet, for instance, referenced traditional Scottish songs—"Scotland the Brave" and "Loch Lomond," to be precise—during the instrumental segments of their hit single, the crowd sang the words to their national (anti-English) tunes along with lead singer Marti Pellow,[62] Annie Lennox appeared on stage in a tartan scarf,[63] Glasgow band Travis hailed the audience as "Scotland,"[64] and the crowd raised Scottish flags throughout the concert.

The event concluded with Ure, Bono, and Geldof on stage addressing the crowd. Geldof ended with the statement that he and fellow organizers would make the G8 leaders hear the crowd, keeping them awake, calling for "hope, and optimism, and joy, and life," and the "denial of the carnival of death that we see paraded across our television screens live."[65] Bono ended on a very different note. His speech noted not only the location of the event, the nation in which he was standing, but also made reference to a rich Scottish cultural heritage and to the ancestry of the crowd stood before him: "This is Scotland. This is a gathering of the clans, a tribal gathering. It is also a gathering of the global clans. It is time to think bigger than nations and longer than election cycles."[66] In his use of the word "clans," Bono implicitly referenced a pre-colonial Scotland in which Scottish clans had control over their own local cultures and governance, as well as the legacy of English colonialism that has since denied the Scottish full control over their own decision-making policies. His use of the word "tribes" suggested (rightly or wrongly) a vision of pre-colonial Africa, and the specific and diverse cultures and heritages located on that continent. But, while evoking the past (no matter how romantically), Bono also implied a vision of the future. He asked for a shift of focus from local place-bound concerns to an emphasis on global unity and action, as well as for a move beyond the concerns of national leaders. In doing so, he empowered people on a local level, and acknowledged the strength of unifying communities under one global umbrella. Such a vision of global unification is problematic, as Biccum indicates. But the vision also proved to be fragile and contradictory, as became clear moments after Bono's speech when, as a result of his own actions, the global scene was spontaneously appropriated for a nationalist cause by the audience at Murrayfield.

The concert ended with Midge Ure—at the behest of Bono—asking the crowd at Murrayfield to participate, not in a globally unifying act, but in the singing the unofficial Scottish national anthem "Flower of Scotland."[67] In immediately and wholeheartedly obliging Bono's request, the audience spontaneously crossed the boundary from consumer to performer. While this is not unusual at pop concerts—singers often encourage audience participation, as did a considerable number of performers at Murrayfield—the nature of the audience's performance was arguably layered with overtones of resistance. "Flower of Scotland" is a nationalist song that, in recalling the victory of Robert the Bruce over the English King Edward II and his army, evokes a romantic image of an independent Scotland that once existed and—as the song claims—could exist once again. Coming from an audience representative of people who, like many in former colonies throughout Africa and the Global South, had suffered economic hardships and cultural negations under the rule of the English for hundreds of years, the song functions as nationalist defiance, perhaps even an implicit call for independence (a call that many in Scotland support). The song allowed the audience, if only momentarily, to appropriate a global event for a national cause. It was not only a symbolic nod toward a history of poverty and legacy of colonialism within the Western hemisphere, but also an illustration that the Scottish, too, have a voice and are willing to express themselves within the global arena. The largest Scottish protest in history may have been overshadowed by the Live 8 concert at Murrayfield, but Live 8, in turn, provided at least one Scottish audience the largest ever venue (both actual and virtual) within which to express a sense of national pride and unity. In essence, the event became "Scotland Calling."

The audience performance at Murrayfield can be read as a hegemonic rupture in which consumer-activists altered modes of participation in the course of one concert, shifting the focus from global neo-liberal politics to a nationalist call for equality and independence. Although initiated by Bono, the pop star controlled neither the meaning nor the performance of "Flower of Scotland."[68] The audience's willingness to sing, to unite to make such a nationalist statement, serves as a prime example of mass audiences claiming celebrity, commercial, and charity spaces to create political statements and sites. Together, the crowd at Murrayfield and the performers at Eden showed the power of music activism to blur, to appropriate, to transmit, multiple meaning throughout the course of one, seemingly ideologically homogenous, global charity event. While the Eden concert allowed for an African appropriation of local space within the southwest of England (an ironic appropriation given the history of English colonialism throughout Africa), the concert at Edinburgh illustrated how nationalist appropriations of global events can occur even at the moment when celebrity organizers call for global unity and the end of national pride.

The Live 8 concerts at Eden and Edinburgh function as counterpoints to the rhetoric of global citizenship and call into question homogeneous neo-liberal approaches. Both show dissention among organizers, alternate concerns of participants, and the potential of performers and audiences alike to appropriate global space to showcase local cultural artifacts and express national political concerns. They illustrate a tension between the local, national, and global, and this tension ruptures the neo-liberal rhetoric of global moral consensus. It is through the ruptures and slippages in such events that history can and does change. Both concerts served as evidence that—as Neal Ullestad suggests—an alteration of Western hegemonic processes can occur within, and as a result of, mass music philanthropy and consumer activism.[69] They also illustrate how benefit concerts provide consumer movement participants a politicized voice with which to question, appropriate, and reconfigure (if only temporarily) the intersections between the local, national, and global.

Conclusion

The most recent celebrity-inspired benefit concert, Hope for Haiti Now, which aired in 2010, shares a number of similarities with the Live Aid and Live 8 concerts, in that it too has allowed for a reconfiguration of roles of participants and performers. Using the telethon model that has become particularly popular in the U.S. since the America: A Tribute to Heroes telethon was aired in 2001 in aid of victims of the 9/11 catastrophe, the Hope for Haiti Now concert moved one step even further than the Live 8 concerts by effectively blurring the boundaries between benefit concert participant and intended recipient of aid. The telethon accomplished this, not only by representing actual victims of the earthquake as figures captured on camera and projected on backdrops throughout the concert, but by also providing space for Haitians in Port Au Prince to participate in the music celebration, to sing and dance alongside the celebrity performers. Unlike with Live Aid, where participant and victim remained physically and ideologically distinct, and consumer-activists performed the role of global agent, Hope for Haiti Now provided sites and opportunities for all involved to act as global agents. Performers, virtually located audiences, and intended recipients alike all functioned as *participants* throughout the Hope concert. While Haitian artists were not given the coverage that African artists received at Eden (perhaps because, given the enormity of the earthquake, the amount of people afflicted, and the confusion left in the quake's wake, it would have been too difficult to arrange for Haitian musicians to perform), the concert ended with a similar emphasis on the country that was in need, as world renowned Haitian singer Wyclef Jean performed with his sister and cousin "Haitian style."

Singing in Haitian and English, the band illustrated, as did the African performers at Eden, that people of the Global South can speak for themselves. They are equally capable of activism, of functioning as agents on their own behalf. In showing themselves as global agents, Haitians blurred both the representational and ideological boundaries between aid activist and intended aid recipient, and helped to create social movement sites in which diverse groups with diverse interests can interact and produce alternate or counter-hegemonic cultural artifacts. This blurring of roles, of participants (which occurs all the more frequently as consumers, intended recipients, and performers alike have gained more control over modes of producing, disseminating, and consuming charity texts and events), is important to note, because it has the potential to alter, in the Western cultural imaginary, assumptions about aid, aid recipients, and victimhood. Such blurring at mass movement events has, in addition, helped precipitate the emergence of a new politic of suffering and victimhood within twenty-first-century concert texts and events. Hope for Haiti, like the concerts at Eden and Edinburgh, effectively challenged the Western cultural imaginary that positions people of the Global South as silent victims in need of Western aid, and thus clearly illustrated that such benefit concerts really do serve a necessary cause, and should not be thought of as events that occur simply 'cause they can.

Notes

1 Alex de Waal, "The Humanitarian Carnival: A Celebrity Vogue," *World Affairs Journal*, Vol. 171, No. 2 (2008): 51.

2 Reebee Garofalo, *Rockin' the Boat: Mass Music and Mass Movements* (Cambridge, Massachusetts: South End Press, 1992), 15–35.

3 *Live Aid*, DVD, directed by Vincent Scarza (Burbank, California: Warner Home Video, 2004).

4 Garofalo, *Rockin' the Boat*, 16–17.

5 Lauren Berlant, *Compassion* (New York: Routledge, 2004), 1–14.

6 James R. Compton and Edward Comor, "The Integrated News Spectacle, Live 8, and the Annihilation of Time," *Canadian Journal of Communication*, Vol. 32, No. 1 (2007): 29–53.

7 Frances Westley, "Bob Geldof and Live Aid: The Affective Side of Global Innovation," *Human Relations*, Vol. 44, No. 10 (1991): 1011–1036.

8 Berlant, *Compassion*, 1–14.

9 T.V. Reed, *The Art of Protest: Culture and Activism from the Civil Rights Movement to the Streets of Seattle* (Minneapolis, Minnesota: University of Minnesota Press, 2005), 165; and Neal Ullestad, "Rock Rebellion: Subversive Effects of Live Aid and 'Sun City,'" *Popular Music*, Vol. 6, No. 1 (1987): 69–71.

10 Ullestad, "Rock Rebellion," 72.

11 Kurt Jansson, Michael Harris, and Angela Penrose, *The Ethiopian Famine* (London: Zed Books, 1987), 154.

12 Jenny Edkins, *Whose Hunger? Concepts of Famine, Practices of Aid* (Minneapolis: University of Minnesota Press, 2001), 121.

13 "The Greatest Show on Earth, Tomorrow: 'Beatles' May Reunite for the Global Concert," *The Washington Post*, 12 July 1985, D1.

14 Roy Shuker, *Understanding Popular Music* (New York: Routledge, 2001), 237.

15 For discussion of Geldof's skills as a leader and organizer of mega-events, see Westley, "Bob Geldof."

16 Jean-Manuel Esnault, "The Definitive Live Aid Site." Last modified 2002. Accessed July 31, 2012. http://liveaid.free.fr/.

17 *Food and Trucks and Rock 'n' Roll: The Band Aid Story*, DVD, directed by Ian McMillan (Burbank, California: Warner Home Video, 2004).

18 Scarza, *Live Aid*.

19 David Rowe, "Rock Today: From Love-Ins to Live Aid," *The Australian Quarterly*, Vol. 59, No. 1 (1987): 24–33.

20 Scarza, *Live Aid*.

21 Susan Moeller, *Compassion Fatigue: How the Media Sells Disease, Famine, War, and Death* (New York: Routledge, 1999), 7–54, 97–153. See also, H. Louise Davis, "Watch Them Suffer, Watch Them Die: Depictions of African Mothers and Motherhood in Famine Footage and Fernando Meirelles' *The Constant Gardner*," in Elizabeth Podnieks, ed., *Mediating Moms in Popular Culture* (Toronto: McGill Queens University Press, 2012), 236–252.

22 Scarza, *Live Aid*.

23 Stan Rijven, "Rock for Ethiopia," *World Music, Politics, and Social Change: Papers from*

the International Association for the Study of Popular Music, ed., Simon Frith (Manchester: Manchester University Press 1989), 199–201.

24 E. Ann Kaplan, *Rocking Around the Clock: Music Television, Postmodenism, and Consumer Culture* (New York: Methuen, 1988), 149–151.

25 Michael C. Elavsky, "United as ONE: Live 8 and the Politics of the Global Media Spectacle," *Journal of Popular Music*, Vol. 21, No. 4 (2009): 389–394.

26 Garofalo, *Rockin' the Boat*, 29.

27 H. Louise Davis, "Feeding the World a Line?: Celebrity Activism and Ethical Consumer Practices From Live Aid to Product Red," *Nordic Journal of English Studies*, Vol. 9, No. 3 (2010): 89–118.

28 Reed, *The Art of Protest*, 159.

29 Roy Shuker, *Understanding Popular Music* (London: Routledge, 2001), 237.

30 Garofalo, *Rockin' the Boat*, 27.

31 Will Straw, "Rock for Ethiopia," *World Music, Politics, and Social Change: Papers from the International Association for the Study of Popular Music*, ed., Simon Frith (Manchester: Manchester University Press 1989), 204.

32 Jansson et al., *The Ethiopian Famine*, 154.

33 Garofalo, *Rockin' the Boat*, 27. See also, de Waal. "The Humanitarian Carnival," 49–53.

34 Garofalo, *Rockin' the Boat*, 16.

35 Reed, *The Art of Protest*, 165.

36 Belinda Smaill, *The Documentary: Politics, Emotion, Culture* (New York: Palgrave Macmillan, 2010), 70.

37 John Street, Seth Hague, and Heather Savigny, "Playing to the Crowd: The Role of Music and Musicians in Political Participation," *British Journal of Politics & International Relations*, Vol. 10, No. 2 (2008): 269–285.

38 Elavsky, "United as ONE," 388.

39 Street et al., "Playing to the Crowd," 283

40 Compton and Comor, "The Integrated News Spectacle," 46.

41 April Biccum, "Marketing Development: Live 8 and the Production of the Global Citizen," *Development & Change*, Vol. 38, No. 6 (2007): 1121.

42 Elavsky, "United as ONE," 390.

43 Compton and Comor, "The Integrated News Spectacle," 44.

44 Compton and Comor, "The Integrated News Spectacle," 39.

45 Street et al., "Playing to the Crowd."

46 WOMAD stands for World of Music, Arts, and Dance.

47 *Live 8 at Eden: Africa Calling*, DVD, directed by Bruce Gowers et al. (New York: Rhino, 2005).

48 "Africa Calling at Eden," *Live 8 at Eden: Africa Calling*.

49 Street et al., "Playing to the Crowd."

50 Street et al., "Playing to the Crowd."

51 Elavsky, "United as ONE," 388.

52 "Africa Calling at Eden," *Live 8 at Eden: Africa Calling*.

53 *Live 8 at Eden: Africa Calling*.

54 Like Collins at Live Aid, N'Dour performed in two locations during the Live 8 event, both in Eden and in Paris.

55 At the end of their set, Thomas Mapfamon and the Blacks Unlimited asked the crowd to support of people of Zimbabwe in their fight for liberation. *Live 8 at Eden: Africa Calling.*

56 Angélique Kidjo is a UNICEF representative focusing on the education of girls in Africa.

57 *Live 8 at Eden: Africa Calling.*

58 *Live 8 at Eden: Africa Calling.*

59 Moeller, *Compassion Fatigue*, 7–54, 97–153; and Davis, "Watch Them Suffer," 236–252.

60 *Live 8 At Eden: Africa Calling.*

61 Biccum, "Marketing Development," 1121.

62 *Live 8*, DVD, directed by Bruce Gowers et al. (Los Angeles: Capitol Records, 2005).

63 *Live 8.*

64 *Live 8.*

65 *Live 8.*

66 *Live 8.*

67 *Live 8.*

68 Lawrence Grossberg, "Another Boring Day in Paradise: Rock and Roll and the Empowerment of Everyday Life," *Popular Music*, Vol. 4 (1984): 225–258.

69 Ullestad, "Rock Rebellion," 72.

Part III

INTERNATIONAL PROTEST

17

WHAT EVERY REVOLUTIONARY SHOULD KNOW

A Musical Model of Global Protest

Ingrid Bianca Byerly

> Musical innovation is full of danger to the State, for when modes of music change, the laws of the State always change with them.
>
> Plato's *Republic*

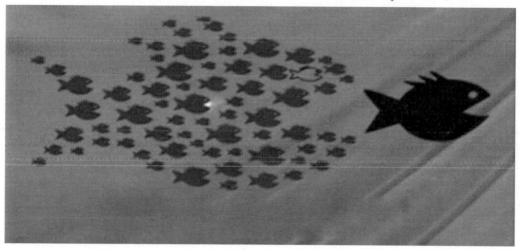

Figure 17.1 Banner over Syntagma Square in front of the Greek Parliament buildings in Athens in 2011.

In the summer 2011,[1] an imposing banner hung over Syntagma Square in front of the Greek Parliament buildings in Athens. It depicted an image of innumerable small red fish organized into the shape of a massive red fish, intent on capturing and devouring the large black fish swimming ahead of them. The lone black fish, enormous by comparison to the diminutive individual ones, had been reduced to being smaller than the fish formation of the collaborating group, and it seemed unclear whether he was still leading the group, or trying to escape from the group. The central message the protesters were attempting to communicate through the banner was simple—that the strategic goal of a revolutionary movement is to organize, and in so doing form a coalition (albeit even in the guise of the oppressor) that is large enough to devour it. What had been the "Arab Spring" had burst into full bloom around the Mediterranean, and as the banner wafted in the wind, its creases and folds suggested some striking metaphors. It revealed the importance of revolutionaries swimming together tactically against the tide, of organizing effectively enough that the resulting profile presents a movement with attributes and momentum sufficient to both outwit and outspeed the oppressor. If one looked closely enough, an interesting detail could be seen. The solitary outline of a single small black fish swam inconspicuously among the school of red ones, suggesting the integration of a single member of the powerful opposition. If one looked even closer, it became apparent that the appropriated member of the opposition was strategically placed to represent the eye of the populist fish. The only thing more striking than the message that lay in the metaphorical banner was the sound of music filling the square. Both the protests for political change in the Arab world, and the demonstrations against austerity as a solution to Europe's fiscal problems, have shared a musical dimension. Whether they have been angry lyrical rock songs, or confrontational spoken rap vocalizations, protest songs filled the air—from acoustic guitar music in the chaotic clutter of tents and tree-houses on the Place de Catalunya in Barcelona, to traditional songs in Egyptian sing-alongs on Tahrir Square in Cairo.

The Power of Music

Plato's observation, made some 2,500 years earlier, in the same city in which the Syntagma Square banner hung, held as much weight during the warring volatility in the Athens of Ancient Greece as it does during the political instability in the Athens of contemporary Greece. Revolutionaries know the power of music, and rulers fear the influence of music. Music is a double-edged sword, holding both influence for protesters with dire grievances, and menace for those against whom the grievances are held. Music arms and strengthens revolutionaries, and it confounds and weakens rulers. The complex attributes of music are a powerful weapon against the comparatively simple motivations of authoritarian rule. Music is the ultimate local and international communicator, transcending language barriers and undermining censorship unlike any other medium of protest. Fanon famously wrote how "the native is disturbed" when his art forms are colonized and exoticism replaces the national culture.[2] He stressed the importance of reviving traditional art forms to reassert cultural identity in the process of the decolonization of consciousness. According to Nabokov, Russian Tsars Nicholas I and II were both cognizant of the threatening influence of music in the conceptualization of rebellions, and "remained aware that anything outstanding and original in the way of creative thought was a jarring note and a stride towards revolution."[3] Musical censorship in modern rebellions and

230

revolutions has become increasingly forceful across time, and the strategies invoked by authorities are matched only by the creative initiative of musicians who outwit these strategies with the intricate components of music itself.

Music as Negotiator

Non-violent negotiations typically arrive at more enduring and successful social resolutions than forceful political overthrows. Collaborated transitions issue in democratic reform through the gradual dissemination and osmosis of ideals and ideologies, and the systematic inclusions or alliances of individuals previously marginalized from the movement. Simultaneously, the national psyche, consciousness and means of communication are transformed, until a consensus is met. Through attentive and unrelenting negotiations, which include all voices (whether in agreement or opposition), the inevitability of casualties is replaced by a groundswell of cooperation towards diplomatic change. By contrast, unmeasured and brutal depositions of power invariably bring with them the danger of simply substituting one form of tyranny with a variation on the theme, instead of negotiating an ideological and strategic alternative. In the area of popular negotiation, no communication medium compares to music, with its potential for intricate complexity, and its ability to initiate, motivate, collaborate, communicate, instigate, nurture, dispute, repulse, and reconcile. It is an unparalleled site for creativity and expression—containing infinite options for the configuration of melody, harmony, lyrics, languages, code-switching, rhythms, style, genres and forms. It is malleable and transposable, and can transform itself with chameleon-like agility, from being militaristic and confrontational to progressive and inclusive, jarring and accusatory to serene and conciliatory, discordant and dissonant to melodious and harmonious. It can reflect political tensions and suggest social compromises, and through the use of traditional instrumentation, folk themes and communal anthems on the one hand, and novel styles, experimental genres and unsuspected compositional collaborations, on the other hand it can individualize as effectively as nationalize, and unite as effectively as divide. It can use irony and humor to appease and amuse, and it can employ cynicism and criticism to inform and condemn. It can craft cunning and complex mixed messages through poetry and prose that outwits censors, and, increasingly, it can reach its audiences sooner than it can be silenced. Importantly, it can further trends in syncretic forms and collaborative styles that reflect the growing tendencies towards democratic inclusiveness, and it can give voice to the voiceless in oppressive transitions towards democracy.

Historically, and increasingly so in contemporary society, it is not only activists recognizing the unparalleled power of music in revolutions, but governments as well. Music is therefore a vehicle for both protest and propaganda, and its goal is to shift the relationship between rulers and ruled. Ian Peddie puts it simply when he asserts, "Music affects a relationship," and it does so through its unique ability to present a site for complex communication.[4] Interactions can be between like-minded members of a small community (like the ties music upholds in religious rituals and inclusive anthems), or between revolutionary forces of a global society (like the contentions music reveals in world wars, or the Arab Spring).

The strategies of revolution have evolved and refined themselves as history has unfolded more visibly, place has become more connected, and social media have made communication more accessible, widespread and immediate. No matter what the circumstance or era, however, revolutions remain distinctly situational and, as such, always unique. The idiosyncrasies that define any two revolutions may or may not be present in one another, whether they erupted abruptly and violently a thousand years apart, or occurred simultaneously, more gradually and strategically, continents apart. What they share is the inevitable incorporation of elements of history particular to the circumstances that mobilized them, and peculiar to the people who activated them. Importantly, music has been used throughout history as the highly-strung, tightly-tuned string in a tug-of-war between authorities and activists—the imposition of official propaganda weighing against the assertion of unofficial protest. In some revolutions, state-driven musical forms have drowned out or smothered the dispute of protesters, and, in others, the activists' songs of dissent have outwitted or outrun the vigilance of the state. The organized precision of mass events like the Nuremberg rallies are varied in style, but comparable in effectiveness to the spontaneous fervor of mass protests like those of the Arab Spring. Similarly, the stark austerity of Socialist Realism in the Soviet era is strikingly different from the creative leniency of the impulsive anti-colonial protest movements in Africa. In most, the waves of protest and propaganda have taken turns, because "with music is born power and its opposite: subversion," until the weight of the one sways in favor of the rebellious, and a tipping point is reached.[5] At that climactic moment, the revolutionaries have effectively accumulated a large enough chorus to drown out the tirades, and subverted the tactics of tyrants.

The Historical Role of Music in Revolutions

A sweeping overview of revolutionary characteristics across the ages reveals both the distinguishing dissent and the musical muscle that lies at the base of every revolution—whether causing empires and regimes to crumble slowly and inevitably, or ideologies and administrations to shift focus suddenly and dramatically. The era of empires was punctuated by the diluted western and eastern Roman Empires declining gradually through numerous wars, until the Ottoman dynasty rose to power. Its own dissolution following the Turkish War of Independence (1919–1922) eventually brought Mustafa Kemal (Ataturk) to the helm of the new Republic of Turkey. While the Turkish Jannisary bands were an important musical weapon in times of war, the Young Turk revolutionary movement placed large stress on the distribution of music and poetry to promote their causes during the revolution. The

British Empire, the largest in history at its height, granted gradual independence to its territories, but numerous countries that were dissatisfied by the speed or nature of the process engaged in dramatic rebellions against the authorities in the latter part of the twentieth century. Most notable were the Mau Mau uprising in 1952, which resulted in Kenyan independence from Britain in 1963, and the Algerian uprising of 1954, which resulted in independence from France in 1962. During the former, the Kikuyu produced a wealth of anti-colonial songs[6] criticizing their subservience to Britain, and, during the latter, the use of the traditional musical form *rai* was used as a weapon of criticism against the French regime by popular musicians, such as Ahmed Saber, who supported Le Front de Libération Nationale. Assertive attempts at decolonization in Africa were, of course, never achieved through isolated incidents of activism, but rather through persistent waves of progressively more effective rebellions, always accompanied by creative initiatives such as traditional music, poetry, song and dance. Musicians like Thomas Mapfumo, a member of the increasingly influential makers of isolated "rebel musics" toiled through numerous challenges in the anti-colonial music movement towards Zimbabwean independence in 1980.[7] The escalating stages through which autonomy in colonial countries was achieved were invariably slow, painful, and recurrent, yet they moved through increasingly effective rebellions to eventually attain first the voting or advisory representatives from the colonized population and, eventually, independence. Through this measured process, continuity could be found in the increasingly audible inclusiveness of the voices of the colonized themselves, until independence was secured. The expression "the sun never sets on the British Empire" eventually became obsolete in 1997, when Hong Kong was finally reunified with China in a transfer of sovereignty, and, symbolically, "The Last Post" was played one final time, on the bugle, as the British Flag was lowered.

Music played a seminal role in each of the great modern revolutions, characterized by their dramatic and overarching transformation of political, economic and social structures. Influential songs from the American Revolution of 1776 are known and sung to this day,[8] while activists in the French Revolution of 1789 were so aware of the power of music that it became a "muse for the masses"[9] and they used it as a primary vehicle through which to mobilize their cause.[10] Republican hymns were sung before operas, composers like Mehul[11] received incentives to write revolutionary songs and, for the first time in history, patronage, whether state-inspired or individually organized, had a profound effect on political developments.[12] Anthems like the patriotic "La Marseillaise" were to become unifying revolutionary forces, while, ironically, the national anthem of imperial Russia, "God Save the Tsar," was the rousing spur for picketers on the Bloody Sunday of the 1917 Russian Revolution against the imperial House of Romanov. It was soon to be replaced by the "Worker's Marseillaise" as the new anthem, and following that, it was the tension between musicians and Soviet leaders that molded the distinct musical culture of Stalinism.[13]

Seminal works by composers of Western art-music pursued political ideals; whether Beethoven's political commentary in *Fidelio*,[14] Mozart's visionary ideals in his opera *The Magic Flute*,[15] Chopin's expression of political affiliation in his *Revolutionary Étude*,[16] Liszt's *Revolutionary Symphony*, inspired by the 1830 revolution in Paris when he was 18 years old,[17] Verdi's profound musical influence during the *Risorgimento* (Italian Unification),[18] and Shostakovitch's controversial works reflecting the turmoil and tragedy of Stalin's Russia.[19]

During the Chinese Revolution of 1949, mass songs were a powerful means of propaganda through which to glorify the exploits of the Chinese Red Army in attempts to present a united front between the many factions in China.[20] In Castro's Cuban Revolution of 1959, the troubadours Silvio Rodriguez and Pablo Milanes, known as "The New Cuban Balladry" ("La Nueva Trova Cubana") traveled extensively, including to Soviet forces in Angola, to promote Castro's vision of communist ideals through song. In post-independence Angola itself, "the historical narrative of Angolan musicians parted ways with the official historical narrative of Angolan nationalism."[21] There was ruthless censorship on all forms of popular music during the Iranian Revolution of 1979, and yet a great deal of it was smuggled into the country on cassette tapes. During the anti-Soviet era, singer-songwriters musicians, known as "bards," would be heavily censored and persecuted in their attempts to criticize the Soviet regime,[22] especially through the use of allegories, satire, humor, irony, symbolism and clever play on words. A master of all these skills, Boris Grebenshchikov (with his band Aquarium) became a spokesman for counter-culture in underground music, and rose to be considered Russia's first rock star. The story of rock in Russia is, in fact, the story of the demise of the Soviet Union.[23] Extending the pursuits of activists during the cold war, music targeting the ominous presence of the Berlin Wall reached an international audience with the release of Nena's "99 Luftballons" in 1983 (translated into the English as "99 Red Balloons" in 1984), Sandra Kim's "Berlin" (1988) and eventually Neil Young's optimistic "Rockin' in the Free World" (1989). While the developments surrounding this area came as a surprise to many, music had served as a mediator and prophet throughout the struggle. Garofalo states that, "In this way, rock music contributed to the erosion of totalitarian regimes throughout Eastern Europe long before the cracks of the system became apparent and resulted in its unexpected demise."[24] Counter-cultural movements that championed anti-establishment dissent were led by groups such as the Sex Pistols in Britain (from 1975 to 1979), and the Ramones in the United States (1976–1996), but where there wasn't a singular agenda and clear, sustained, grievances, they were forerunners of sensational "popcorn-protests," rather than serious revolutions that runs their course to arrive at a desired agenda.

The watershed years of 1989–91 produced what some might dub "the triple-crown" for democracy. Three seminal developments changed the face and future of the world forever: the collapse of communism in eastern Europe, the demise of the Soviet Union, and the end of Apartheid with President de Klerk's announcement of Nelson Mandela's release with the legitimization of the African National Congress (ANC) as an official opposition party to the Nationalist government in South Africa. In all three cases, music was central and pivotal to the struggle. International music events have also targeted specific causes, whether the Rock against Racism series between 1976 and 1981,[25] or singular mega-events such as the 1976 *Graceland* concerts in Harare, and the 1988 Nelson Mandela concert at Wembley stadium. Unexpected music genres have developed in countries historically viewed as traditional in musical style, such as the trend towards heavy metal in Nepal to illuminate human rights violations,[26] and the unanticipated success of the revived Buena Vista Social Club in readdressing both struggle and identity in Cuba.[27]

Critical Criteria of Coordination and Unity

While every conflict in history, to date, has revealed its own idiosyncratic path and strategy for successful resolution, one thing all revolutions reveal is the undeniable reality that no political goal is achieved without the methodical and persistent coordination between activists in a movement. While factions and disparities invariably exist between protesters, their eyes are often on the same prize, thereby presenting either an advantage or an impediment to its achievement. It is widely recognized that opposing riptides in currents of contention can be both an obstacle to, and source of energy for, a revolutionary movement. Conflict between factions moving towards the same goal can result in one of two paths: either the purging of those perceived as obstructionist to the cause (the reason behind the adage that "revolutions devour their own children"), or eventual compromises and affiliations between protesters with varying or contrary *modus operandi*. Disagreements in strategy can therefore both hider and help the momentum of a movement, either by retarding its pace through obstructions, or accelerating its pace through the friction caused by attraction and repulsion. Approaches of moderation or radicalism vary greatly in revolutions where the stakes are high, and, for that reason, great danger can lie in attaching one's carriage to the wrong horse in a rebellion, or choosing a volatile resistance group with which to affiliate. This is why music also serves as both an optimally creative, and a potentially protected, site through which to negotiate social transformation, political transition or the expression of affiliation. Music's complexity allows for innumerable blatant or subtle messages or tracks to be laid, like polyphonic themes of commentary within a single composition, and its audiences (whether in solidarity, or in opposition) are in the position to interpret innumerable meanings from the works, whether the musicians want to explicitly commit their intention or not. So, while individual ideologies and group strategies towards overthrowing a common enemy may not be identical at the outset, communication and compromise between advocates of change is central to the successful initiation, sustained mobilization and successful conclusion of a revolution. This is never more the case than when there is a complex configuration of players with potentially conflicting agendas in the arena, and where music can serve as both explosive catalyst, and calm unifier in the fray.

Dangers and Pitfalls

While the incentive is to build on waves of contention until a resolution is achieved, there is also the danger of music, like any protest medium, presenting an obstacle to the mobilization of a cause. "Musicking harms movements" when it works against the central interest,[28] especially when it perpetuates the very cause it fights against through lyrics that (even inadvertently) reinforce a problem. Most dangerously, music can alienate those they are protesting against, especially if they adopt a style so confrontational, or an approach so disrespectful towards certain values of the common "enemy," that there is little chance that they will be heard, and even less that a negotiation can take place.[29] In fact, "many human habits, sentiments, dispositions, cannot be changed at all rapidly, that the attempt made by the extremists to change them by law, terror, and extortion fails, that the convalescence brings them back not greatly altered."[30]

An added threat to any movement is the inability to discern, at any given time, exactly how successful its efforts are in the big scheme of things (especially after a setback or a suppression). This lack of clarity in progress constantly presents the temptation for revolutionaries to weaken or abandon their efforts. But, while they may not know which wave they are riding, their contribution to a movement is seldom futile. Shostakovitch may not have seen his anti-Soviet compositions reach their goals in 1939 Stalinist Russia, but his compatriot Grebenshchikov did exactly 50 years later, when the final protest wave crested in 1989, causing the demise of the Soviet Union. Similarly, the participants at the musical rallies marking the 1944 founding of the anti-Apartheid ANC Youth League in South Africa would have no way of knowing that it would also take exactly 50 years, and many more waves of dissent, before the official end of Apartheid in 1994.

Of course, successful revolutions may also beget a new regime which simply replaces the jackboot with the gumboot—where the new order re-collars the neck of the ones who ensured freedom. The most notorious of these developments are cases in which the overthrow of a vilified monarchy resulted in authoritarian rule under leaders like Napoleon, Stalin, and Mao. Revolutionary musicians are cautioned to be careful what they wish for, because they may well achieve it. Numerous instances of destructive consequences follow revolutions: the fragmentation of the Kikuya tribe following their successful uprising against their colonial powers, singer Fela Kuti's persecution after longed-for independence in Nigeria, or the renewed autocracy under Mugabe's post-colonial Zimbabwean government, against which musician Thomas Mapfumo targeted a revised struggle.

The Formation of a Protest Wave

While the mission of protest music is often to thaw frozen prejudices, or to sway solid convictions, effective artistic endeavors take on an ever-accelerating and expanding snowball effect: collecting partisans as it moves across time and space. Remaining mindful that adversaries and allies change constantly, and that affiliations are both unpredictable and fickle, the resolve of protest musicians is not to preach to the converted, but to unremittingly convert. They understand that their art requires constant modification of focus and strategy to make provision for the political fluidity of a society in transition, or, as Pielke puts it, revolutionaries "may or may not know all of the right paths to take—or all the wrong ones either—but ... surely can notice what's happening along the way and make adjustments as necessary."[31] The methods of innovation in attempts of ideological conversion are chronically precarious, as some appeal to an audience while others don't. Styles or genres may lose their effectiveness unexpectedly when considered hostile, over-used, inappropriate, offensive, unappealing or out-dated. Activist musicians that are adaptable and persistent, however, create gradual networks of revelation and contention which continuously broaden their field of assimilation. Every autonomous pocket of initiative, or genre of mutiny, becomes part of a greater whole, which, in turn, forms the most powerful force of all—the single, integrated wave of dissent which crests, and breaks through the sound barrier, enforced until that point by authoritarian censorship. Threatened by the power of the protest wave, the authoritarian regime strengthens its hold, and subdues the dissent through more ruthless suppression (whether through violence, persecution or renewed censorship), or an imposition of propaganda (whether through news media, or tactically-commissioned art). And so the rise and fall of waves begins, in a series of ever-growing strategic and spontaneous surges and suppressions.

While the participants in the reactionary waves of suppression are all members of either the authoritarian ruling party, or unofficial dictatorship, the allegiance of the participants in the protest movements become increasingly inclusive as the snowball effect gains momentum.

The first wave of dissent in a revolution usually comprises those burdened most by the consequences of authoritarian policies—the oppressed and the disenfranchised. While expressing sentiments of frustration and anger, and informing the public of their suffering, the often-strident tone of this wave can alienate as much as engage. The second wave adds already-sympathizing members of the empowered or elite: the lone trailblazing troubadours and bards who risk persecution by revealing a dilemma they feel needs the support of the more privileged in vocalizing injustice. With increasing exposure, and escalating awareness, the subsequent waves bring on board those who were not originally champions of the cause, but whose gradual conversion (or sudden "change of heart") solidifies their affiliation to the movement. Each wave adds activists from further afield, to strengthen the movement as it grows. A tipping point occurs when protest ideologies penetrate the stronghold of the autocrats, or those in indirect service of a ruling party, and their conversion causes them to defect to the "other side." Those that "jump ship" are the final frontier, as they have seen and heard strategic information from inside the ruling body, and therefore hold an advantaged insight into the inner workings of the revolutionaries' opposing camp. They have the ability to become the eyes and the ears for their new comrades-in-arms who have previously been working in the dark, and to assist in promoting new and unexpected plans or policies, propelling the last wave to its resolution. The final wave, then, consists of a polyphony of voices; "dynamic interactions among a multitude of contenders, including not only challenging protestors, but also their allies and adversaries—elite and non-elite—as well as the whole range of forms of claims-making from the most conventional and institutionalized, to the most provocative and disruptive."[32] The climactic moment of a revolution is reached when the balance of conviction leans in favor of the revolutionary causes, and when, as the Jamaican motto goes in the pursuits of reggae and rasta, "Out of many, One people."[33]

The South African Music *Indaba*

One of the most celebrated cases of such a music movement, driven largely by ideological negotiations through influential creative enterprises, is the South African music *indaba*,[34] a relentless initiative that positioned itself, for more than four decades, against the Apartheid regime. Few movements of creative ingenuity in recent political history have involved more factions, or met with more challenges. Yet the success of the enterprise serves as a seminal blueprint in the question of what makes for a successful revolution. Across the decades, it moved through numerous anti-establishment musical initiatives of counter-culture, which were consistently suppressed by not only brutal censorship,[35] but also the persistent reassertion of official art forms to silence the unofficial forms of dissent.[36] It was the classic paradigm of relentless propaganda pitted against unrelenting protest, until the goal of democracy was achieved.

The music *indaba* contained a musical soundtrack in which the history of a revolution can be traced and analyzed, in which all the voices are included across time, and in which the important musical markers[37] of the movement remain as influential anthems, even after a successful resolution to the struggle. It contained all the attributes necessary for a successful revolution driven by creative initiative.

Primarily, protest musicians were united in a clear and simple mission—to end apartheid. They acknowledged the existence of influential voices across time, each initiating a seminal wave of protest with a suitable, alternative genre or style. Starting from within the camp of the disenfranchised (whether "exiles"[38] like Miriam Makeba and Hugh Masekela, or "inziles"[39] like Dolly Rathebe and the bands Sakhile and

Bayete), these dissenting voices were joined by troubadours and folk musicians of the more progressive elite, such as the Lindberg-duo, Jeremy Taylor, and later, the highly-censored Roger Lucey.

These creative guides make provision for side-stepping previous suppressions or failures, that are, in turn, adjusted to mold into more appropriate forms of dissent, and set the tone for the burgeoning growth of each wave with a welcoming inclusiveness of all voices. There will also be those renegades, like Laurika Rauch and Coenie de Villiers, who champion revivals and integrations of traditional styles or speech, to draw in those who are attracted to nostalgic or conventional communication as a means of persuasion, or who answer to the invocation of their belief system or cultural ethos.

As awareness among white South Africans of the plight of the disenfranchised increased, musicians from a broader spectrum of the population joined the call to arts, creating an ever-widening movement from increasingly-remote groups who had initially distanced themselves (or benefited) from the political plight of others. A critical moment was reached with the rise of cabaret performances, where searing social commentary from artists such as Nataniel, and Casper de Vries, used irony, sarcasm, humor and symbolism to effectively outwit censors, and shed light on certain absurdities. The musical outreach culminated in the emergence of the strong *Alternatiewe Afrikaner* movement, a massive defection of members whose ancestry lay in the ruling Apartheid government, and the burgeoning protest movement had reached its tipping point. It took only the final battle-cry of Nationalist President de Klerk himself, who announced his intention to free Mandela and un-ban the vilified

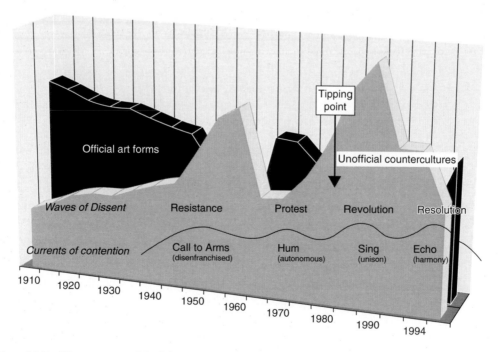

Figure 17.2   The wave model of the anti-Apartheid movement.[40]

ANC (African National Congress), making it the legitimate opposition party. The final wave of protest had crested, and broken the last hold of the Apartheid regime.

What Every Revolutionary Should Know

With historical case studies in mind, activists would benefit from recognizing eight primary components of a successful revolution, and the criteria necessary to realize them:

1) Clarity of Intent

   - An unambiguous mission
   - Clearly-stated grievances.

2) An expanding spectrum of players drawn into the movement

   - A dominant leader or figurehead: an ideological hero representing either present strategic leadership, or future visionary leadership[41]
   - A series of influential organizers or musical spokespeople spearheading each wave of dissent through their representation of specific genres, styles or statements of intent at each critical point in the revolution[42]
   - The creative commentary of the community "clown," court jester or insightful "fool"[43]
   - Counter-cultural "deviants" and political trailblazers and who break "sound barriers" that previously kept oppressive regimes in place
   - Individuals holding office who use their official voices to redefine the linguistic (and, consequently, the political) landscape[44]
   - Dissent which moves from the disenfranchised/oppressed and expands across the spectrum of the community to reach the powerful.

3) A concerted strategy of co-ordination towards a united movement

   - Individual techniques of civil disobedience and creative initiative which become shared visions
   - A communal awareness that oppressive systems of government reproduce themselves, that methods of oppression are increasingly predictable and follow conventional patterns, and that, in so doing, they offer repeated prospects for their own annihilation
   - A collective knowledge that, by contrast, artistic endeavors are chameleon-like in their adaptability and unpredictability, and consequently have the potential and the attributes to outwit and outrun the authorities.

4) A wide spectrum of musical techniques, styles and genres employed to draw in activists

- Martial music and military bands
- Anthemic pieces which serve as counter-cultural genres against the reigning military forms, in recognition that the style tends to unite certain sectors[45]
- Nostalgic style which appeals to cultural memory, and popular forms which suggest a connection with current trends
- Creative initiatives which utilize sophisticated or subtle cerebral tactics of artistic expression, such as the use of allegory, satire, humor, irony and symbolism.

5) The effective use of technology

- A sense of urgency in the use of state-of-the-art distribution processes
- The sensible and creative use of social media to communicate, organize, warn of impending state repression, and raise awareness of internet censorship.

6) The development of the resistance movement through waves

- A sustained awareness of inevitable waves of protest and suppression
- A relentless determination to form an effective counter-movement in opposition to the suppression, by official forces, of any waves of resistance
- A shared knowledge that each resistance wave gains increased affiliations
- A shared knowledge that the movement gains momentum with each wave
- A shared knowledge that each wave increases the strength of the revolution.

7) The presence of friction within the waves

- Dissenting voices rely on each other's strategies and ideologies as they gradually connect to become part of a collaborating whole
- Vying voices in the struggle oscillate between contention and conciliation until a common ideal is agreed upon
- Obstacles are seen as lessons and roadmaps from which to learn, rather than defeats from which to shy away.

8) The eventuality of a tipping point in the last wave

- Determination to persist through the suppression of each protest wave until the tipping point is reached
- Coordinated mobilization that is geared towards a tipping point, when the final protest wave outweighs the presence of the authoritarian foothold, and ruling insiders "jump ship" to the opposing cause
- With the defection of the authoritarian figures to the revolutionary camp, the balance hangs in the favor of the revolution
- The seal of the ruling party is broken, causing the final demise of the autocratic stronghold, and the securing, or reinstatement, of rights to the revolutionaries.

Present Revolutions

The Arab Spring of 2011 issued in a new model of dissent—not only in terms of strategy, but also in terms of reach. While revolutions have often been confined to dissent against more localized causes, in more isolated countries or regions (whether in a fight for independence, or for the demise of an autocrat) the Arabic Revolution was the first initiative that so widely involved revolutionary waves of influence, protest and demonstration, with such immediacy, across so large a territory, spanning continents. It was closely followed by the Occupy movement of anti-capitalist protesters later that year, and, although targeting different issues, both used similar means of social media to communicate the motives behind the movement, and the organizational details necessary for effective mobilization. The strategy of the Arab Spring and the Occupy movement it inspired were not dissimilar, and, halfway across the world from the Syntagma Square banner, a small tent community of students on Franklin Street in Chapel Hill, North Carolina, hoisted a banner echoing similar sentiments (see Figure 17.3).

What separates the success of the Arab Spring and the Occupy movements, however, can largely be found in the extent to which they conform to the criteria for an effective revolution. The Arab Spring had a clear and simple mission: to eradicate dictators and their ruthless agendas. They employed unprecedented organizational skills through social media, and relentless perseverance through brutal and violent obstacles. Numerous sites of contention provided fruitful ground for efforts towards the demise of the rulers of Tunisian, Libya, Egypt, and Libya. Importantly, music was a central form of communication throughout the riots, and a central anthem has been an adaptation of Pink Floyd's "Another Brick in the Wall," in which the lyrics were changed to addressing a targeted dictator, as in "*Hey, Mubarak (Ayatollah/Gadhafi/Saleh) Leave Those Kids Alone!*"

The Occupy movement, by contrast, eroded within the first wave of rebellion, falling short of even a clear stance on the mission of the movement. No doubt there

Figure 17.3 Banner by small tent community of students on Franklin Street in Chapel Hill.

will be consequent waves in the future, and the appropriation of seminal criteria to maintain momentum and move the cause forward, but, until that time, activists flounder in both their agenda and their strategy, and oppressive forces have effectively managed to silence the rise of a second wave.

Messages relayed through music in revolutionary circumstances have benefited immeasurably from gradual advances in technology across the centuries. The presence of early fife-and-drum bands on battlefields were reflected in the existence of live vocalizations and instrumentations of protest songs on the homefront of rebellions and counter-revolutions. World War I saw a great leap in the accessibility of recorded music, when the hand-cranked Victrola became present in households, and governments could use music to instill patriotism and national pride in citizens during wartimes. By World War II, electricity and mass-distribution of sound recordings and radio broadcasts enabled an even wider accessibility of songs, from the dedications of Vera Lynn to British troops, the more controversial offerings of Edith Piaf to German troops. The sophistication of distribution trends also allowed governments to censor music from a centralized position through recording studios. With the dawn of the digital age and the advent of social media, the comparatively slow reproduction and distribution of analogue recordings became replaced by lightning-fast digital technology that could instantly transmit music, and thereby messages, through miniature memory drives and virtual cloudspace into powerful loudspeakers and undetectable earphones. It also presented a substantial alteration of this acoustic environment, enabling the effortless transmission of sound, from drumbeats across faraway vistas, to vocals across vast arenas. Local protests could become global revolutions that would sweep across continents within hours.[46] Facebook, Twitter and YouTube could transport ideologies through music, visuals and speech instantaneously and, in serious attempts at pan-continental activism, technologies like the Internet Relay Chat (IRC),[47] MeetUp and Skype have been assisted by operations such as Indymedia[48] and MayFirst/Peoplelink[49] to play seminal roles in mobilizing and expediting communications between activists. Of course, the existence of pervasive social media has presented all sectors involved in a revolutionary movement with unprecedented access to both amplified communication opportunities and more effective censorship strategies. Novel modes of social interaction and sophisticated methods of surveillance create an ever-refined challenge in the game of wits and outwits and, for this reason, music still remains at the forefront of social communication.

In 1972, the Council of Europe adopted the *Ode to Joy* from Beethoven's *Ninth Symphony* as its anthem. The selection stemmed from the conviction that the anthem expresses the ideals of the Council, and of humanity everywhere: freedom, peace and solidarity. Beethoven chose Schiller's poem to set to music because it promoted the ideal of universal brotherhood through reconciliation and the "embrace of millions." While an ideology espousing the principles of liberation, harmony and unity is being strived towards, every day, through countless revolutions, in innumerable languages globally, the banners hanging over both Syntagma Square in Athens, and Franklin Street, North Carolina, reflects these ideals silently and visually, while Beethoven's revolutionary anthem echoes them audibly and powerfully.

> Where the Speech of Man stops short,
> There Music's reign begins.
> Richard Wagner (1813–1883)

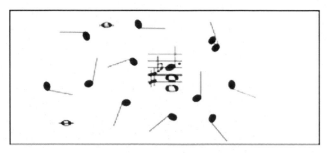

Don't tyrannize...

HARMONIZE!

Figure 17.4 Protest musician's banner serves as a clear call to arms.

Notes

1 This piece was conceptualized in the summer 2011 "Semester at Sea" voyage around the Mediterranean Basin. The author would like to acknowledge the insights of colleagues and fellow-travelers Professor Lawrence Butler, Professor Matthew Davis and Professor Roy Campbell, as well as the ideas of students in the 'Music and Social Revolutions' class.

2 Frantz Fanon, *The Wretched of the Earth*, trans., Richard Philcox (New York: Grove Press, 2004), 179.

3 Vladimir Nabokov, *Lectures on Russian Literature*, ed., Fredson Bowers (New York: Harcourt, 1982), 13, 14.

4 Ian Peddie et al., eds., *Music and Human Rights* (Burlington, Vermont: Ashgate, 2011), xvi.

5 Jacques Attali, *Noise: The Political Economy of Music* (Minneapolis Minnesota: University of Minnesota Press, 1985), 6.

6 Songs like *Maikariite Kaloleni* by Wanjiru was Kabuagara encourage the Kikuya revolutionaries to drive their own education system through lyrics such as *"Let us work hard and build the sharpener/We should not be sharpened by White people."*

7 Daniel Fischlin and Ajay Heble, *Rebel Musics: Human Rights, Resistant Sounds, and the Politics of Music Making* (Montreal: Black Rose Books, 2003).

8 Richard Schuckburg's "Yankee Doodle," John Warren's "Free America," John Dickenson's "Liberty Son," and Peter St. John's "American Taxation" were composed with anti-British sentiment.

9 Conrad Donakowski, *A Muse for the Masses: Ritual and Music in an Age of Democratic Revolution, 1770–1870* (Chicago: University of Chicago Press, 1977).

10 David Whitwell, *Band Music of the French Revolution* (Tutzing: Schneider, 1979).

11 *"The Chant du Depart"* was one of Méhul's most influential works of patriotism and propaganda during the French revolution.

12 Malcolm Boyd, ed., *Music and the French Revolution* (New York: Cambridge University Press, 1992).

13 Amy Nelson, *Music for the Revolution: Musicians and Power in Early Soviet Russia* (University Park, Pennsylvania: Pennsylvania State University Press, 2004), xiv.

14 Beethoven's story centers on the liberation of a political prisoner.

15 Mozart's opera traces a journey from oppression to freedom, and glorifies the passage from ignorance to enlightenment.

16 Chopin's étude was his contribution to the people's uprising when Russia occupied Poland in 1831. His own frailty prevented him from "soldiering," and music was therefore his offering to the cause.

17 Liszt expressed his commitment to social justice at an early age, and the idea of the demise of the autocrat Charles X was a source of great inspiration to him, even though his *Revolutionary Symphony* remained unfinished.

18 Verdi's *Nabucco* contains the chorus *Va, Pensiero*, in which exiled Hebrew slaves lament their lost homeland, as well as the hymn *Immenso Jehova*, in which they thank God for rescuing them. When the opera was performed in Milan (at the time of Austrian domination), the audience was moved by the nationalistic fervor of the work, and called for an encore. Verdi's works, including the chorus from *Ernani* (which alludes to amnesty granted to political prisoners), became closely identified with the Risorgimento, popularizing the slogan Viva VERDI.

19 Shostakovitch's performance of his *Fifth Symphony* in 1937 was historic for its impact on its Soviet audience, causing them to both weep through the third movement and rise to their feet in the triumphant finale. His *Piano Trio no. 2* of 1944 was composed during the genocide of Jews by Stalin and Hitler, and themes from Jewish music were threaded through the works to express the tragedy and injustice of the times. (The piece was banned until after Stalin's death.)

20 Two of the best known examples are "Sky over the Liberated Zone," and "Osmanthus Flowers Blooming Everywhere in August."

21 Jean Marissa Moorman, *Intonations: A Social History of Music and Nation in Luanda, Angola, from 1945 to Recent Times* (Athens, Ohio: Ohio University Press, 2008), 166.

22 Examples of this forum included Bulat Okudzhava, Alexander Galich, and Evgeny Kliachkin.

23 Artemiĭ Troitskiĭ, *Back in the USSR: The True Story of Rock in Russia* (Boston: Faber and Faber, 1987).

24 Reebee Garofalo, ed., *Rockin' the Boat: Mass Music and Mass Movements* (Boston: South End Press, 1992), 81.

25 Ian Goodyer, *Crisis Music: The Cultural Politics of Rock Against Racism* (New York: Palgrave Macmillan, 2009).

26 Ian Peddie, ed., *The Resisting Muse: Popular Music and Social Protest* (Burlington, Vermont: Ashgate, 2006).

27 Geoffrey Baker, *Buena Vista in the Club: Rap, Reggaetón, and Revolution in Havana* (Durham, North Carolina: Duke University Press, 2011).

28 Richard Flacks, ed., *Playing for Change: Music and Musicians in the Service of Social Movements* (Boulder, Colorado: Paradigm Publishers, 2011).

29 Examples are the counter-productive effects of some anti-Apartheid marches, where differing cultural approaches impeded communication between activists and audiences in 1984, and the disastrous effects of activists 'breaking order' on Tiananmen Square in 1989.

30 Crane Brinton, *The Anatomy of Revolution* (New York: Vintage Books, 1957).

31 Robert Pielke, *Rock Music in American Culture: The Sounds of Revolution* (Jefferson, North Carolina: McFarland, 2012), 231.

32 Ruud Koopmans, "Protest in Time and Space: The Evolution of Waves of Contention," in *The Blackwell Companion to Social Movements*, eds., David A. Snow, Sarah A. Soule, and Hanspeter Kriesi (Oxford: Blackwell, 2004), 21.

33 Chris Potash, ed., *Reggae, Rasta, Revolution: Jamaican Music from Ska to Dub* (London: Schirmer Books, 1997), xxix.

34 An *Indaba* is the Zulu for a meeting-place or conference where a consensus is arrived at.

35 Michael Drewitt and Martin Cloonan, eds., *Popular Music Censorship in Africa* (Burlington, Vermont: Ashgate, 2006).

36 Ingrid Bianca Byerly, *Composing Apartheid: Music for and Against Apartheid* (Johannesburg: Wits University Press, 2008).

37 The significance of musical markers is discussed more fully in Ingrid Bianca Byerly, "Peter Gabriel, from Genesis to Growing Up," in Michael Drewett, Sarah Hill, and Kimi Kärki, eds., *Musical Markers as Catalysts in Social Revolutions* (Burlington, Vermont: Ashgate, 2010).

38 The term "exile" is often debated in the case of these two musicians, whose initial departure from South Africa to perform abroad were personal choices, not official enforcements.

39 Dolly Rathebe considered herself an "inzile": one of the disenfranchised remaining by choice in the country that denies some sectors of the population certain human rights.

40 The wave model was first presented in Byerly (2008).

41 The desired leader may not be physically present in the everyday of the movement, as was the case of Nelson Mandela, who was imprisoned throughout the late-anti-apartheid movement, but whose future leadership was both anticipated, and achieved.

42 Touveres, golliards and jongleurs have adapted news since the Middle Ages to suit their own agendas, while troubadours, folk singers and bards of more contemporary social movements have reconfigured information to disseminate their revolutionary ideals.

43 Many dissenting musicians play the proverbial fool or village idiot to camouflage serious messages in humorous or ridiculous images which confound censors or mislead audiences selectively. Revealing and insightful social commentary has long been given by the likes of Shakespeare's comedic characters and court jesters, such as Touchstone, Yorick, Falstaff, and Feste. Similarly, music can intentionally reveal hidden knowledge or social insights, as found in the "yoridivy" (holy fool) Shostakovitch's creativity to outwit Stalinist critique.

44 Cases include the ruling deKlerks and Gorbachevs of history, a phenomenon described in Alexei Yurchak's *Everything Was Forever, Until It Was No More: The Last Soviet Generation* (Princeton, New Jersey: Princeton University Press, 2006).

45 Examples range from compositions taking on anthemic importance, like Dollar Brand's *Mannenburg* during Aparheid South Africa, to the cutting-edge "New Russian Anthem NOM," a stylistic take-off (anthemic commentary) of the controversial Russian group Pussy Riot's protest against Putin.

46 An example of this phenomenon is Rodriguez's 1970 album *Cold Fact*, which found a receptive audience not in the poverty of Rodriguez's ancestry in Mexico, or in the squalor of the Detroit it describes, but in the desperation of apartheid South Africa, an ocean away.

47 Internet Relay Chat is an open protocol used for real-time synchronous conferencing or personal text messaging. Its effectiveness is optimal throughout media blackouts, as was the case when it was used to communicate developments during the Persian Gulf War of 1990 and the 1991 Soviet coup d'état.

48 The Independent Media Center (IMC) consists of international journalists who report on topical social and political issues, while allowing anyone to contribute towards the forum of ideas, through a democratic media outlet not restricted by corporate affiliations.

49 MayFirst is a web hosting service that operates as a cooperative and provides internet services to organizations and individuals with a progressive and democratic agenda.

18

REVOLUTIONARY WORDS

Reggae's Evolution from Protest to Mainstream

Stephen A. King and P. Renee Foster

Figure 18.1 Bob Marley performing on stage at the New York Academy of Music.

> It doesn't matter what language you speak. When you
> hear that [reggae] beat, there's something in that beat,
> that everyone identifies and understands.
>
> Bunny Wailer, reggae musician[1]

Jamaica *is* reggae music. For some tourists, who know little about the country and its people, this is often the case. The international popularity of reggae music and the superstar profile of Bob Marley have, in many ways, come to define this Caribbean island. From splashy websites to tourist guides to advertisements, reggae music is an inescapable part of an overall heritage tourism campaign to draw foreigners to the island to "soak up glorious sun and splash in gentle surf" while the hypnotic beat of reggae music "soak[s] into your very bones."[2] Showcasing Jamaica's scenic beauty and hedonistic resorts, a Jamaica Tourist Board (JTB) commercial reframes Bob Marley's 1977 protest song "One Love/People Get Ready" as an exotic endorsement of Jamaica's visual allure, a land of peace, racial harmony, and tranquillity.[3] Indeed, the JTB champions the "thumping, infectious and passionate sounds" of reggae, "Jamaica's most internationally recognised music and the heartbeat of our people."[4] In Jamaica, some reggae musicians have been elevated to national icon status. Before Bob Marley died in 1981 from cancer, reggae's greatest star received The Order of Merit (OM) Award—the third highest honor in Jamaica—and there is a concerted effort to make Marley Jamaica's next National Hero, the highest honor a Jamaican can receive.[5] In all, reggae music is a significant part of Jamaica's national identity.

With all the celebratory discourse and national pride that has accompanied reggae music in recent years, it is easy to forget that at one time Jamaica's dominant classes viewed reggae as a source of real embarrassment and national concern. In a letter published in the *Daily Gleaner*, Jamaica's national newspaper, on September 9, 1968, one concerned citizen characterized indigenous music like reggae as "vulgar" and "imbecilic."[6] This letter was in response to reggae's emergence in 1968, a music born out of the suffering and hopes of Jamaica's poorest black communities. Reggae artists railed against perceived injustices, from poverty to police persecution, and song titles ("Beat Down Babylon," "Blood and Fire," "Dem Ha Fe Get a Beatin'") signified reggae's revolutionary tone. Reggae musicians were jailed (mostly for drug-related offenses) and government officials played a role in banning some of the more politically-oriented songs on Jamaican radio.[7] Reggae music was *not* something to be celebrated. It was something to be disarmed.

It is virtually impossible to analyze reggae music without referencing the Rastafarians, a socio-religious movement that employed reggae music as its main form of protest. Emerging from Jamaica's poorest black communities in the early 1930s, and influenced by Marcus Garvey, a Jamaican black nationalist, Rastafarian theology and goals included the belief in the divinity of Haile Selassie (former Emperor of Ethiopia) and calls for repatriation to Africa. Although early forms of Jamaican popular music—ska (1959–1965) and rocksteady (1966–1967)—contained elements of Rastafarian ideology, reggae music expressed the Rastafarian worldview to an unprecedented degree, leading one observer to note that reggae served as a "gateway to the Rastafarian world."[8] Many reggae musicians were members of the movement or, at the very least, expressed sympathy for Rastafari. For example, Bob Marley converted to Rastafari in 1966 and, until his death, served as a kind of global reggae ambassador, spreading the Rastafarian message to the international community.

While scholars have examined the Rastafarian movement's transformation from a "cult of outcasts" to a widely recognized and accepted part of Jamaican life, there has been relatively little scholarly attention paid to reggae's parallel metamorphosis from "protest" to the "mainstream."[9] The title of this essay is not intended to suggest that reggae's protest themes disappeared as the music became more acceptable to the wider Jamaican society. Reggae musicians continued to sing about poverty, unemployment, racial discrimination, crime, police harassment and political violence. Even today, reggae music can still be considered a type of protest music. In this essay, we examine how reggae music moved from "out there," the margins of Jamaican society, to "in here," an important symbol of Jamaica's national identity. Reggae's transformation occurred during a roughly ten-year period from the early 1970s to the early 1980s and, in this essay, we identify and discuss four reasons why this transformation occurred: (1) the use of reggae music in national politics, (2) the internationalization of reggae music, (3) middle-class "embracement" of blackness and Africa, and (4) the use of reggae music in tourism promotion.

Politics/Politricks

In her landmark study on Jamaican popular music and political campaigns, *Race, Class, and Political Symbols: Rastafari and Reggae in Jamaican Politics*, sociologist Anita M. Waters discovered that Jamaica's two mainstream political parties, the Jamaica Labour Party (JLP) and the People's National Party (PNP), did not fully understand the power of popular music to expand political support among the young and poor until the early 1970s. For example, during the 1967 political campaigns for Jamaica's first post-colonial national election, "no popular music slogans or Rastafarian symbols appeared in the parties' national advertising, but some were used in advertisements targeted toward specific constituencies."[10] The JLP, which had been in power since 1962, barely won re-election in 1967, beating its PNP rival by little more than one percent of the popular vote.[11]

However, the 1972 national political campaign changed all that. The PNP, and to a lesser extent the JLP, used reggae music and Rastafarian symbols in their respective campaigns. Targeting disaffected youth and exploiting the rising popularity of Rastafari, the political consciousness of Black Power, and the nation's deep Christian tradition, PNP contender Michael Manley used Rastafarian "talk" and catch phrases ("peace and love"), dubbed himself "Joshua" (a Biblical figure viewed with favor by Rastafarians), and brandished a staff he called the "Rod of Correction," allegedly given to him by Haile Selassie.[12] The PNP used a number of reggae songs (e.g., "Better Must Come") as political slogans and campaign songs.[13] It should be noted that the appropriation of song titles and lyrics by politicians is made easier by the fact that most (protest) music, principally because of its form, contains lyrics that are rooted in ambiguity rather than specific issues.[14] For example, Delroy Wilson, the composer of "Better Must Come," did not write the song for the Manley campaign (the song does not mention Manley, the PNP, or politics in general). It was reportedly written in reaction to Wilson's frustration with his music career.[15] However, some reggae artists, including Ken Boothe, Clancy Eccles, and Max Romeo, did write songs (e.g., "Power for the People," "Let the Power Fall on I") for the campaign.[16] The PNP also sponsored musical "bandwagons," free concerts (that involved some political speeches) featuring leading members of the original Wailers (Bob Marley, Peter Tosh, Bunny Wailer), Ken Boothe, Max Romeo, and many others.[17]

At one level, reggae's protest themes were suited perfectly to a political party out of power. Reggae musicians challenged the "system": race and class privilege, epidemic poverty, high unemployment, police brutality, and other socio-political woes. At the same time, reggae music was quickly becoming an important political tool to perpetuate the system itself. In the end, Manley won the election in a landslide and continued to mouth support for both reggae music and Rastafari during his eight-year reign as Prime Minister.

While Jamaica's two mainstream political parties understood the value of popular music and the Rastafarian movement as political currency, the Rastafarian position on politics wavered between hostility and ambivalence. Historically, the Rastafarian movement was, as a whole, decidedly apolitical. Rastafari sought emancipation from Jamaica in the form of repatriation to Africa (Ethiopia) rather than involving and immersing itself in Jamaica's often highly charged and sometimes violent political culture. By the late 1960s, however, a division between "religious" and "political" groups emerged.[18] The politicization of Rastafari was largely a result of the influence of U.S. and Jamaican Black Power movements and Haile Selassie's own dictum that Rastafarians should seek the liberation of Jamaica before repatriation to Africa.[19] Despite the "political awakening" of Rastafari and the increased militant and political themes in reggae music, many musicians openly expressed a deep cynical distrust of Jamaica's political system. Reflecting Rastafari's inventive use of language, politics became "politricks," a clever and creative play on words that evokes the image of a charismatic demagogue hoodwinking a gullible electorate. For example, although Bob Marley supported Manley during the 1972 campaign and became a friend to the Prime Minister, his criticism of politicians and Jamaica's political system was blunt and stinging, as revealed in songs such as "Revolution" and "Rat Race."

During the 1976 campaign, both political parties continued to use reggae music and Rastafari symbols to garner votes. JLP leader Edward Seaga, Manley's political rival, argued that politics and music have a symbiotic relationship in Jamaica: "Every public meeting begins and ends with music, and music is interspersed right throughout … So, you wouldn't be able to separate politics and music in terms of the extent they are interwoven as a form of message."[20] The JLP made quick use of reggae songs such as Ernie Smith's "Jah Kingdom Gone to Waste" to protest perceived

PNP's social and economic failures, including high unemployment and a decline in the standard of living of many Jamaicans.[21] While some reggae songs ("Promises, Promises") were critical of the Manley government, other songs reflected support for the PNP. In 1976, the PNP's campaign song was "The Message."[22] Manley's "message" won him re-election in 1976. However, the socio-economic problems his administration encountered during its first four years only intensified during the Prime Minister's second term. Although the PNP used two of Bob Marley's songs, "Coming in from the Cold" and "Bad Card" as political slogans during the 1980 campaign, not even the reggae star could save Manley's re-election bid.[23] Seaga won a decisive victory in October 1980, and the JLP remained in power until 1989. Interestingly, by the 1983 campaign, the use of reggae music and Rastafari in political campaigns had declined precipitously.[24] This decline can be attributed to a number of factors, including the fact that Jamaica's youth were becoming less interested in Rastafari's message of repatriation and reggae's "hypnotic" sound and "conscious" message. Competing forms of popular music, including dancehall, with its up-tempo beat and "slack" lyrics (girls and guns) were quickly on the ascent.[25]

In all, between 1972 and 1980, Jamaican politicians transformed certain elements of reggae's protest message into valuable political discourse. To be sure, reggae musicians continued to protest Jamaica's political system. During the 1978 One Love concert, for example, Peter Tosh publicly lambasted both Manley and Seaga for perpetuating a colonial, imperialistic, "shit-stem." However, the use of reggae music and Rastafarian symbols in politics played an important role in reggae's shift from the cultural margins to the mainstream.

Internationalization of Reggae Music

While Michael Manley explored the political potentialities of reggae music and Rastafari during the 1972 campaign, reggae music was in a *slow process* of transforming itself from more or less a regional style to a global phenomenon. To be clear, Jamaican music had already gone "international" at this point. For example, Jamaican ska had its equivalent in Great Britain, "blue beat." This cross-cultural fertilization was a result of Jamaican musicians touring England, as well as the need for Jamaican emigrants to use music to recreate their homeland as a defense against social isolation.[26] English record label Trojan Records played a key role in disseminating Jamaican music to its former colonial master. The record label outdistanced its rivals (e.g., Pama Records) by releasing hundreds of new titles (singles and albums combined) every year.[27] By the end of the 1960s, according to music journalist Lloyd Bradley, the "United Kingdom was the single biggest market for Jamaican music."[28]

However, by 1972, reggae music had yet to make a major breakthrough in the United States. Because the U.S. is the largest popular music market, "successfully penetrating the U.S. market is the goal of every artist aspiring to international recognition."[29] Island Records founder and President Chris Blackwell believed that The Wailers possessed the talent, experience, and charisma to significantly widen reggae's audience.[30] Prior to the release of The Wailers' *Catch a Fire* in 1973, most rock fans in England and the U.S. viewed reggae music as novelty music, "crude, cheap, not be taken seriously on any level."[31] Although the *Catch a Fire* story is generally well-known, a brief summary is warranted. The Wailers recorded the songs for what would become their major-label debut in Kingston, and then Marley flew (with master tapes in hand) to England to complete the second part of the recording and re-mixing process. Blackwell "beefed-up" the basic tracks by inviting American and British studio musicians to add synthesizer, clavinet, rock guitar, and other instruments to the mix.[32] Fearing reggae's hypnotic pulse and heavy bass sound would diminish reggae's potential cross-cultural appeal, Blackwell increased the music's tempo and produced a "lighter" reggae sound by emphasizing the guitar and keyboards and downplaying reggae's heavy bottom end, the bass and drums.[33] "This record had the most overdubs on it," recalled Blackwell. "This record was the most ... I don't want to say softened, but more enhanced to try to reach the rock market because this was the first record and they wanted to reach into that market."[34]

Targeting the U.S. rock market, Blackwell and Island Records promoted The Wailers as a "black rock group,[35] and *Catch a Fire* was packaged as a unified album rather than a collection of singles.[36] Rather than downplaying the music's rebellious themes, Blackwell emphasized the music's voice of dissent with the hopes of attracting converts among rock fans. This strategy worked. Within a few years, an increasing number of white middle-class rock fans in the U.S. had "accepted" reggae music, and some had even constructed their own Rasta identity.[37] Although *Catch a Fire* sold poorly at the time, the album's release proved to be a watershed event. After *Catch a Fire*, Island and other record labels, including Virgin Records, employed basically the same marketing strategy to promote artists ranging from Burning Spear to the Heptones, Inner Circle to Third World.[38] It should be pointed out that, despite predictions that reggae would be the "new sound in pop music for America in the 1970s," the music never achieved a mass audience in the U.S.[39]

The rock world did take notice, though. Eric Clapton's 1974 pop version of The Wailers' "I Shot the Sheriff" shot to the top of the charts and, in the process, expanded Bob Marley's profile.[40] Diverse artists from the Rolling Stones to Barbara Streisand flirted with the new reggae sound. Rock critics took notice, as well. In a 1977 article, "How to Learn to Love Reggae," Lester Bangs argued that reggae is

> fascinating, hypnotic, multifaceted (contrary to the claims of its critics), and startlingly beautiful *once you get it*. It is not the laid-back, coconut-clonk, ricky-tick redundancy it might at first seem; it brims over with passion, love, rage, pain, anguish, and joy, just like the best of all music.[41]

By the mid-1970s, reggae had entered its "golden era" with the release of now classic reggae albums, including those of Bob Marley and The Wailers (*Natty Dread*), Peter Tosh (*Legalize It*), Bunny Wailer (*Blackheart Man*), Burning Spear (*Marcus Garvey*), and the Mighty Diamonds (*Right Time*). *The New York Times, Newsweek, Time*, and other mainstream publications, reported on Jamaica's growing musical export and the careers of Toots and The Maytals, Jimmy Cliff, and other popular reggae acts. Yet, it was Bob Marley who became the public "face" of reggae. Marley received the most press, the most adulation, and "did more than any other person or group to introduce Rastafari, reggae, and Jamaica to the rest of the world."[42] Claiming The Wailers are the "real article," a *Rolling Stone* reporter characterized Marley as a reggae "master."[43] A *Time* magazine writer proclaimed him "Jamaica's superstar."[44] Marley was soon anointed with the title "King of Reggae."

Reggae's growing international popularity impacted how Jamaican institutions and ordinary Jamaicans viewed the music. In 1973, journalist and poet Carl Gayle, a native Jamaican, encouraged his nation to "be proud of reggae."[45] His nation started to listen. The *Daily Gleaner*, which had historically ignored or dismissed Jamaican popular music as "crude," warmed to the reggae sound and followed the careers of Bob Marley and The Wailers and other prominent reggae groups.[46] Jamaican radio stations, which had historically privileged foreign music over indigenous music, added more reggae to their playlist rotation.[47] Even academic scholars started to study the music.[48] Reframing the music as a symbol of cultural pride, more and more Jamaicans, especially the middle-class youth, embraced the music and the symbols of Rastafari. Dermot Hussey, a well-known Jamaican radio personality and journalist, argued that it was Marley's critically acclaimed 1975 album *Natty Dread*, and the accompanying U.S. and European tours, which had a tremendous impact on changing attitudes about reggae music in Jamaica:

> I think the turning point in terms of the middle-class, especially for the middle-class [Jamaican] youth latching onto reggae was 1975 and *Natty Dread* … That's where you found a lot of middle-class kids beginning to identify with Rasta, growing locks and you know smoking weed and that kind of thing—it was 1975. *Catch a Fire* was not an album that was especially popular here.[49]

Writing for the *Jamaican Daily News*, journalist Trevor Fearon's observations about reggae's new acceptance in Jamaica place the cause on external acceptance, rather than "internal" revelation:

> For whatever reason, many Jamaicans didn't start "appreciating" reggae until it started catching on overseas. It is amusing to hear people who a year ago were asking "Bob [Marley] who? of [sic] "Ken [Boothe] who?" suddenly speaking about them as their long-time brethren. This "cultural nationalism," like so many other things, seem[s] to be motivated by external forces.[50]

Fearon's accurate assessment of the changing attitudes in Jamaica about reggae music begs the question: Why did external acceptance of reggae music play an important role in a new-found appreciation of reggae at home? Communication scholar Humphrey A. Regis answers this question by conceptualizing a theory of cultural imperialism by re-exportation. His re-exportation model is a five stage process that includes the exportation of cultural artifacts from "less developed" countries to "developed" countries, the "endorsement" (and subsequent redefinition) of these cultural artifacts by developed countries, and the re-exportation of these "new" cultural artifacts back to the originating countries. Set against the history of colonialism, dependency relationships exist between developed and less developed countries where the former are perceived as "leaders," the latter "followers." This model is based on the perception that "more developed countries are superior and the less developed countries are inferior, and the more developed countries are sources of referents for living and the less developed countries are seekers and recipients of these referents."[51] In his analysis of reggae music, Regis argued that there is a "tendency of Caribbean people to evaluate the quality of their output of their culture partly on the basis of how much that output has been endorsed by the dominators" or dominant countries.[52] Reggae's endorsement—its international popularity and its relative acceptance by extra-regional reference groups (e.g., Great Britain, the United States)—convinced a growing number of Jamaicans that reggae is not "artless monotony," but rather a music that possessed quality and worth.[53] In turn, more and more Jamaicans viewed reggae with a real sense of cultural pride.

Middle-Class "Embracement" of Blackness and Africa

The international "endorsement" of a "re-exported" reggae certainly affected Jamaica's middle-class perception of the music. At the same time, Jamaica's "brown" middle-class was experiencing its own metamorphosis. During the 1970s, more and more black Jamaicans moved into the middle-class and the "brown" middle-class (and the whole nation) had started to shift from a Eurocentric "ideology of racism" toward an "embracement" of blackness as a racial category and Africa as a spiritual homeland. This revolutionary change made it possible for the wider Jamaican society to accept reggae music and, to a lesser extent, the Rastafarian movement. In our analysis of the "mainstreaming" of reggae, it is important to briefly consider this transformational change in Jamaica's class system as well as the changing consciousness regarding blackness and Africa. To do this, it is necessary to understand the role colonialism played in structuring Jamaica's social stratification system.

For nearly 500 years, Jamaica was subjugated under colonial rule, first by Spain (1494–1655), then by Great Britain (1655–1962). Reflecting colonial rule, Jamaica's social stratification system has been historically framed on the twin axis of class and color. From the end of slavery (1834) to the early twentieth century, a tiny white minority dominated the country's poorest and largest class, black and of African descent.[54] The brown middle-class, a product of miscegenation (often as a result of rape between white slave masters and female slaves), was encouraged to emulate European values and ideals as well as support white hegemony.[55] During the period from 1938 to 1962, the colonial social stratification system started to change as black Jamaicans started to achieve middle-class status, largely a result of obtaining higher levels of education as well as an "undaunting will for social advancement."[56] Nevertheless, according to Rastafarian expert Barry Chevannes, Jamaica's colonial system indoctrinated the entire population in a white racist ideology:

> Along with the denigration of Africa, her children and all things black, racism preached the exaltation of Europe, its peoples and culture. White skin and body attributes were idealised as the norms for purity, innocence and beauty. Europe's civilisation became the model for Blacks.[57]

During the post-colonial period, Jamaica's ruling classes constructed the myth of "Jamaican Exceptionalism."[58] Using the national motto "Out of Many, One People" as an ideological slogan, Jamaican Exceptionalism preached that Jamaica was a classless society in which different racial groups worked in harmony.[59] Writing in 1976, the Rastafarian Movement Association, one of the more politically-oriented Rastafarian organizations, dismissed this national myth, claiming instead that Jamaica "indulges in an inferior[ity] complex—a pretentious Class System, so it becomes a hypocritical, segregated society."[60] When Jamaica gained its independence in 1962, European hegemony did not disappear overnight, but continued to persist in one form or another. As one Rastafarian noted in 1968: "English customs and laws and English instructions still lead us. The white queen still rules ... Thus, Jamaica's independence mean a well without water, a treasury without money."[61]

Although the Rastafarian movement had, until the 1960s, remained apolitical, the movement "challenged and sought to reverse the dominant [Eurocentric] values and ethos in the society" through "a total rejection of the contemporary Jamaican society as a bastard product of white oppression and injustice."[62] Viewed as a threat to Jamaica's stability, Jamaican authorities employed social control strategies (e.g., harassment, arrest) to quell the movement's agitation and dissent. Despite public persecution of Rastafari, the movement continued to flourish during the 1960s and 1970s. Rastafari's growing popularity, the emergence of a black power movement in Jamaica, liberation movements in Africa and Asia, and other wide-sweeping socio-political changes, all played a role in changing attitudes about blackness as a racial category and Africa as a spiritual homeland. Reggae music played a crucial role in disseminating the Rastafarian worldview to an increasing number of middle-class listeners. In an analysis of 100 reggae songs, recorded from 1968 to 1981, King found that reggae music served to articulate a distinctive positive (black) African identity, attack Jamaica's neo-colonial state, and condemn "Babylon" for enslaving "Africans" in "mental slavery."[63] Erna Brodber, a Jamaican scholar, noted that reggae music was a "penetrative tool," allowing an Afro-orientated philosophy to embed itself within the consciousness of the brown middle-class.[64] The end result, according to Jamaican political scientist Anthony Payne, resulted in significant changes in Jamaica:

> During the 1970s many black Jamaicans did come to feel for the first time that they were full members of a national community, entitled to be treated as citizens on an equal basis with others of a lighter skin … Even the Rastafarian community, vilified and excluded from normal social intercourse in the 1960s, has been legitimised as an accepted part of society. Indeed for a while, the cultural characteristics of the movement, if not all its religious connotations, became a feature of youthful middle-class rebelliousness. Social values have changed and the social structure of the country has been loosened up.[65]

Despite these transformative changes to Jamaican society, it should be clear that Jamaica's middle-class did not convert to Rastafari. Relatively few did and, in fact, Rastafarians were still considered "dangerous criminals" in some sectors of Jamaican society. However, according to Chevannes, the middle-class was "defining themselves closer to the Rasta than to the white reference point."[66] Moreover, by the 1970s, Rastafarians had started to enter the middle-class. Rastafarians became doctors, lawyers, university professors, and pursued other occupations of the professional class.[67] The end result, according to a number of scholars and observers, was that by the early 1980s more and more Jamaicans viewed "blackness" as a positive racial category.[68] This trend has continued into the twenty-first century.[69]

Reggae Sunsplash and Cultural/Heritage Tourism

In Mutabaruka's 1986 song, "Revolutionary Words," the Jamaican dub poet lambasts reggae artists for mouthing words of revolution while leading comfortable and hedonistic lives, and mourns how "revolutionary words have become entertainment."[70] While there is no doubt that reggae music has been a great source of entertainment (e.g., dancing, parties) for ordinary Jamaicans, the use of reggae music in tourism advertisements has converted reggae's protest themes into entertainment for tourists visiting the island-nation. In effect, tourism has dislocated reggae from its origins in the ghetto to upscale inclusive resorts such as Sandals and Hedonism. For example, Sandals' list of entertainment theme nights includes a "Reggae Sandfest Irie Experience."[71] The melding of tourism and reggae music first occurred in the late 1970s, and tourism appears to be the last stage of reggae's integration into mainstream Jamaican life.

Interestingly, the Jamaica Tourist Board (JTB) initially balked at employing reggae music and Rastafari as part of its marketing campaign.[72] It was Reggae Sunsplash which portended the successful fusion of reggae music and tourism. In 1978, four Jamaicans (Tony Johnson, John Wakeling, Don Green and Ronnie Burke) organized Sunsplash via their Synergy Productions Limited company, and the event was held at Jarrett Park in the resort city of Montego Bay.[73] Bob Marley headlined the 1979 festival and, by 1982, attendance had swelled to 40,000.[74] With the success of Sunsplash, other festivals have emerged, including Reggae Sumfest, Air Jamaica Jazz and Blues Festival, Jamaica Ska and Rocksteady Festival, Jamcka Fest, and Rastafest Jamaica.[75]

After Bob Marley's death in 1981, elements of the reggae star's life were turned into tourist attractions. Marley's home on Hope Road in Kingston is now the Bob Marley Museum. Tourists can visit the Bob Marley Experience and Theatre in Montego Bay. Nine Mile, Marley's birthplace and burial ground, features a Bob Marley mausoleum. A Jamaica travel agency includes the mausoleum on its web site:

> The Bob Marley Mausoleum tour takes you through the house Bob lived in as a young boy, and your Rastafarian guide will share with you little known insights into Bob Marley's childhood and musical career. You will get to stand on "Mount Zion Rock" where Bob used to meditate and rest his head on "the pillow" made famous in the song "Talking Blues." Finally, walk through the mausoleum, which is the final resting place of the Reggae King.[76]

Today, most Jamaican tourism narratives make reference to reggae music. The penetration of reggae music into Jamaica's tourism industry cannot be overstated. Tourism professionals weave narratives that highlight a location's strengths, its virtues and values, while sublimating "undesirable" elements. Reggae and Rastafari were once undesirable elements. Today, the use of reggae to lure tourists to Jamaica signifies not only the global reach and popularity of the music, but the extent to which the music has penetrated Jamaican society.

From attempts by governmental officials to ban its airplay on radio, to its use in political campaigns, to being highlighted by the JTB in the country's international tourism advertising, reggae music has traveled the road from "out there"—the shunned protest music of a relatively small group of poor black Jamaicans—to "in here"—a source of national cultural pride and economic development for Jamaica. In the process, reggae helped create a "new" Jamaica in the 1970s, and its socially conscious lyrics and hypnotic beat still continue to exert a powerful social and cultural influence on this Caribbean nation. In this sense, then, reggae music *is* Jamaica.

Notes

1 *Rock & Roll*, "Volume 7: The Wild Side," Public Broadcast Corporation, September 2005.

2 *Jamaica-Jamaica* (Runaway Bay, Jamaica: Jamaica-Jamaica, n.d.).

3 Jamaica Tourist Board, "Jamaica—One Love," Youtube.com, uploaded on October 24, 2007, at http://www.youtube.com/watch?v=3DyVoXaBKEI, accessed March 22, 2012.

4 Jamaica Tourist Board, "About Jamaica: Culture," at http://www.visitjamaica.com/about-jamaica/culture-folk-music-mainpage.aspx, accessed March 22, 2012.

5 "Grange for Marley Becoming National Hero," *Jamaica Observer*, February 7, 2011, accessed March 22, 2012, http://www.jamaicaobserver.com/entertainment/Grange-for-Marley-becoming-national-hero_8339810.

6 Ted Dwyer, "Vulgar and Imbicilic [sic]," Letter to Editor, *Daily Gleaner*, September 9, 1968, 15.

7 Dermot Hussey, conversation with the author, Kingston, Jamaica, July 18, 1994.

8 Yoshiko S. Nagashima, *Rastafarian Music in Contemporary Jamaica: A Study of Socioreligious Music of the Rastafarian Movement in Jamaica* (Tokyo, Japan: Institute for the Study of Languages and Cultures of Asia and Africa, 1984), 3.

9 Orlando Patterson, "Ras Tafari: The Cult of Outcasts," *New Society*, November 12, 1964, 15–17. See, for example, Leonard E. Barrett, *The Rastafarians: Sounds of Cultural Dissonance*, revised edition (Boston: Beacon Press, 1988); and Ennis Barrington Edmonds, *Rastafari: From Outcasts to Culture Bearers* (Oxford, New York: Oxford University Press, 2003).

10 Anita M. Waters, *Race, Class, and Political Symbols: Rastafari and Reggae in Jamaican Politics* (New Brunswick, New Jersey: Transaction Publishers, 1985), 89.

11 Waters, *Race*, 61.

12 Waters, *Race*, 124–125. Rasta Talk is a sublanguage or argot.

13 Waters, *Race*, 130–132.

14 Ralph E. Knupp, "A Time for Every Purpose under Heaven: Rhetorical Dimensions of Protest Music," *Southern Speech Communication Journal*, Vol. 46, No. 4 (Summer 1981): 384–385.

15 Waters, *Race*, 130.

16 Waters, *Race*, 133.

17 Waters, *Race*, 131.

18 Stephen A. King (with contributions by Barry T. Bays III and P. Renee Foster), *Reggae, Rastafari, and the Rhetoric of Social Control* (Jackson, Mississippi: University Press of Mississippi, 2002), 34.

19 King, *Reggae*, 83.

20 *Bob Marley—Rebel Music: An American Masters Special*, Public Broadcasting Corporation, February 14, 2001.

21 Waters, *Race*, 185.

22 Waters, *Race*, 186–187.

23 Waters, *Race*, 238–239.

24 Waters, *Race*, 287.

25 Waters, *Race*, 287.

26 Lloyd Bradley, *Reggae on CD: The Essential Guide* (London, UK: Kyle Cathie Limited, 1996), 11.

27 Chris Prete, liner notes, *History of Trojan Records 1968–1971, Volume I* (London, UK: Trojan Records, 1995), 33, 43.

28 Bradley, *Reggae*, 101.

29 Barry Chevannes, *Rastafari: Roots and Ideology* (New York: Syracuse University Press, 1994), 270.

30 Timothy White, *Catch a Fire: The Life of Bob Marley*, revised edition (New York: Henry Holt and Company, 1992), 239.

31 "Classic Albums: The Wailers—*Catch a Fire* (Part One)," 1999, Youtube.com, uploaded on March 28, 2007, at http://www.youtube.com/watch?v=WzV6jhA77G4& feature= relmfu, accessed April 15, 2012.

32 White, *Catch*, 234–235.

33 Linton Kwesi Johnson, "Some Thoughts on Reggae by Linton Kwesi Johnson," *Race Today Review*, December 1980/January 1981, 58.

34 "Classic Albums: The Wailers—*Catch a Fire* (Part Two)."

35 *Bob Marley—Rebel Music*.

36 Simon Jones, *Black Culture, White Youth: The Reggae Tradition from Jamaica to the United Kingdom* (Houndmills, UK: Macmillan Education, 1988), 62–63. As Jones reminds us, before *Catch a Fire*, reggae albums were typically packaged as compilations ("various artists" or "greatest hits").

37 Jorge L. Giovannetti, "Popular Music and Culture in Puerto Rico: Jamaican and Rap Music as Cross-Cultural Symbols" in Frances R. Aparicio and Candida F. Jaquez, eds., *Musical Migrations: Transnationalism and Cultural Hybridity in Latin/o America, Volume I* (New York: Palgrave Macmillan, 2003), 84.

38 Jones, *Black Culture*, 64, 69. The soundtrack to the 1972 movie *The Harder They Come*, featuring Jimmy Cliff, as well as Toots and the Maytals' 1973 album *Funky Kingston*, also played a role in introducing the reggae sound to the American market.

39 Ed Ward, Geoffrey Stokes, and Ken Tucker, *Rock of Ages: The Rolling Stone History of Rock and Roll* (New York: Penguin Books, 1986), 537, 544.

40 By 1974, Peter Tosh and Bunny Wailer had left The Wailers to pursue solo careers.

41 Lester Bangs, "How to Learn to Love Reggae," in Chris Potash, ed., *Reggae, Rasta, Revolution: Jamaican Music from Ska to Dub* (New York: Schirmer Books, 1997), 76.

42 Chevannes, *Rastafari*, 270.

43 Michael Goodwin, "Marley, the Maytals and the Reggae Armageddon," *Rolling Stone*, September 11, 1975, 9.

44 "Singing Them a Message," *Time*, March 22, 1976, 84.

45 Carl Gayle, "This is Reggae Music …," *Black Music*, Vol. 3, No. 28 (March 1976): 40.

46 "The World Discovers Reggae," *Sunday Gleaner*, December 2, 1975, 4.

47 During the 1970s, reggae was still marginalized on Jamaican radio. Most reggae music was played at night from 1 am to 5 am. "Merry Go Around," Editorial, *Daily Gleaner*, August 14, 1976, 4, 9.

48 See, Pamela O'Gorman, "An Approach to the Study of Jamaican Popular Music," *Jamaica Journal*, Vol. 6, No. 4 (December 1972): 50–54.

49 Hussey, interview.

50 Trevor Fearon, "Where's the Rip-Off?" *Jamaican Daily News*, November 13, 1974, 21.

51 Humphrey A. Regis, "Calypso, Reggae and Cultural Imperialism by Reexportation," *Popular Music and Society*, Vol. 12, No. 1 (Spring 1988): 69.

52 Humphrey A. Regis, "Orientation and Interest in Popularity of the Works of Caribbean Musicians," *Howard Journal of Communications*, Vol. 5, No. 3 (Spring 1995): 185–186.

53 Barry Chevannes, "Healing the Nation: Rastafari Exorcism of the Ideology of Racism in Jamaica," *Caribbean Quarterly*, Vol. 36, No. 1–2 (June 1990): 79.

54 George Beckford and Michael Witter, *Small Garden ... Bitter Weed: The Political Economy of Struggle and Change in Jamaica*, 2nd edition (Morant Bay, Jamaica: Maroon Publishing House, 1982), 48.

55 Waters, *Race*, 30–31.

56 Beckford and Witter, *Small Garden*, 70.

57 Barry Chevannes, "Race and Culture in Jamaica," *World Marxist Review*, Vol. 31, No. 5 (May 1988): 139.

58 Obika Gray, *Radicalism and Social Change in Jamaica, 1960–1972* (Knoxville, Tennessee: University of Tennessee Press, 1991), 82.

59 See, for example, Alexander Bustamante, "This Menace to Our Future," Editorial, *Daily Gleaner*, October 10, 1960, 10.

60 Rastafarian Movement Association, *Rasta: A Modern Antique* (Kingston, Jamaica: Rastafarian Movement Association, 1976), 2.

61 Bongo Dizzy, "The Voice of the Interpreter: Bongo Dizzy," *Bongo-Man*, December 1968, 15.

62 Carl Stone, *Class, Race, and Political Behaviour in Urban Jamaica* (University of the West Indies, Jamaica: Institute of Social and Economic Research, 1973), 154.

63 Stephen A. King, "Protest Music as 'Ego-Enhancement': Reggae Music, the Rastafarian Movement and the Re-examination of Race and Identity in Jamaica," in Ian Peddie, ed., *The Resisting Muse: Popular Music and Social Protest* (Aldershot, UK: Ashgate Publishing Limited, 2006), 111–117. "Babylon" is a term Rastafarians use to describe various oppressors (e.g., Jamaican government, police).

64 Erna Brodber, "Black Consciousness and Popular Music in Jamaica in the 1960s and 1970s," *Caribbean Quarterly*, Vol. 31, No. 2 (1985): 54.

65 Anthony J. Payne, *Politics in Jamaica* (London, UK: C. Hurst and Company, 1988), 6.

66 Chevannes, "Healing," 79.

67 Arthur Kitchin, "Rastafari Movement on Trial," Editorial, *Daily Gleaner*, November 29, 1982, 8.

68 Mary F. Richardson, "'Out of Many, One People'—Aspiration or Reality? An Examination of the Attitudes to the Various Racial and Ethnic Groups within the Jamaican Society," *Social and Economic Studies*, Vol. 32, No. 3 (September 1983): 143–167.

69 Rivke Jaffe, "Ital Chic: Rastafari, Resistance, and the Politics of Consumption in Jamaica," *Small Axe: A Caribbean Journal of Criticism*, No. 31 (2012): 34.

70 Mutabaruka, *The Mystery Unfolds*, CD, track 3, © 1996 Shanachie.

71 Sandals, "The Sandals Difference," at http://www.sandals.com/difference/, accessed March 24, 2012.

72 It was not until the early 1990s that the JTB utilized reggae music in its advertising campaign. See T. Boots Harris, "Reggae's Growth in the '90s," *Jamaican Record*, August 4, 1991, 5C.

73 Nelson George and Isaac Fergusson, "Jamming in Jamaica," *Black Enterprise*, May 1983, 62.

74 Howard Campbell, "Remembering Good-Old Reggae Sunsplash Days," *Jamaica Gleaner*, June 13, 2010, at http://jamaica-gleaner.com/gleaner/20100613/arts/arts4.html, accessed March 22, 2012.

75 *Reggae Festival Guide 2012*, at http://reggaefestivalguide.com/, accessed March 22, 2012.

76 Jamaica Scene, "Jamaica Travel Guide," at http://www.jamaicascene.com/, accessed March 22, 2012.

"WE NEED MORE THAN LOVE"

Three Generations of North American Indigenous Protest Singers

Elyse Carter Vosen

Figure 19.1 A young Buffy Sainte-Marie performing on stage.

> In the darkest hour .../In the heart of this reservation
> I saw your light on .../I knew if I came and told you
> You'd surely paint what I said: I was mistaken
> We need more than love.
>
> —Annie Humphrey[1]

On her 2008 album *The Sound of Ribbons*, NAMA-winning Leech Lake Ojibwe singer-songwriter Annie Humphrey includes a prophetic song wherein an artist friend, painting in the middle of the night in purple and red, is visited in a dream by quintessential singer-songwriter John Lennon. She doesn't recognize him at first without his glasses, but he explains he no longer needs them. After flying over the hills of Hollywood and finding no one ready to listen, he comes upon her, ready to impart his message. His pronouncement in the dream encompasses what each artist discussed here intimately knows: the work of an indigenous artist and activist is complex. It demands tireless dedication and sacrifice. It often means saying things no one else has the courage to say. It requires becoming the ultimate translator in order to help others hear. Above all, it asks for constant reinvention of self and community.

The five artists I have chosen to highlight span the 1960s to the present, representing rock, country, folk, and hip hop genres.[2] Cree artist Buffy Sainte-Marie and Floyd Red Crow Westerman could easily be named the founders of indigenous protest music, their albums and honors too numerous to mention. Annie Humphrey won national recognition in the U.S. as Female Artist of the Year and Best Folk Recording with her first album *The Heron Smiled* at the 2000 Native American Music Awards. Her 2008 album was nominated for the same honors. Wab Kinew, a Winnipeg-based artist of Ojibwe and Lakota heritage, won an Aboriginal People's Choice Best Hip Hop album award for his 2009 album, *Live by the Drum*. Ta'Kaiya Blaney of Sliammon First Nation is just beginning, but already carries the entire earth on her small shoulders. In addressing these artists' work, I explore three intersecting themes: each artist's possession of an intellectual elasticity which motivates him or her to be both activist and ambassador; a multifaceted creativity which drives the artist to constantly create not in one medium but in many; and a driving responsibility to advocate for the next generation.

A Way of Our Own: Anger and Advocacy

Buffy Sainte-Marie's 2008 album *Running for the Drum*, the first in thirteen years, leads off with a song called "No No Keshagesh" about the consequences of pervasive greed for land and resources. The mocking lyrics are a critique of environmental destruction and corporate misogyny, packaged in the powwow rock style Sainte-Marie invented, with a tambourine pattern like the bells on a fancy dancer's regalia, a driving rhythm track, and a soaring electric guitar line accompanying her wry, cutting vocals:

> These old men they make their dirty deals/Go in the back room and see what they can steal/Talk about your beautiful and spacious skies/It's about uranium; it's about the water rights […] No no Keshagesh, you can't do that no more.[3]

A protest song must be more than angry. No matter how incisive it is, it must expose its humanity to draw in listeners. This song supplies a touch of prickly mirth that makes the listener a partner in the tirade. The recipient of this verbal lashing, *kes-hagesh*, is a Cree name for someone Sainte-Marie describes as "the puppy," she says, "who eats his own and wants everyone else's besides." Using the term contributes to her sardonic tone by adding just the right touch of condescension and allowing her to address The Man as though talking to a child: "old, old story boys; that's how you do it boys ..."[4]

Sainte-Marie's voice and persona, sure and direct, critical and playful, have been honed through five decades of conscious effort. The coffee-house scene in Toronto and New York she inhabited as a singer-songwriter in the 1960s, with its free flow of ideas, provided an open and supportive framework for her process of hardening raw emotion into forceful messages. In a 2009 interview with *Democracy Now*, she sketches the arc of iconic songs such as "Universal Soldier" and "Bury My Heart at Wounded Knee":

> As an artist, sometimes you can artfully say something in a three-minute song that it would take somebody else a 400-page book to write. And as a songwriter, I just really admire the art of the three-minute song. [...] If you put your head to editing it and working on it, sometimes you can come up with something that really there's no argument against it. [...] I wrote those songs kind of like I was writing for a professor who didn't want me to get an A, and I was determined.[5]

The audience was tough. The period 1965–1973 was arguably the most volatile in recent American history and, for indigenous people, a time of suffering the disastrous consequences of government termination and relocation policies. Sainte-Marie and the most well-known indigenous male artist of that time, Floyd Red Crow Westerman, used their prominence to explicate the concerns of American Indian Movement activists: crippling discrimination against indigenous men, women, and children, on the part of the social welfare, justice, health care, and educational systems, and the historical circumstances which led to these impasses.

An effective protest song holds the reality of a group of people up to the light. It cannot stop at simple catharsis, nor be satisfied with adroit analysis; it must expose the institutional frameworks which sustain injustice. Sainte-Marie's and Westerman's most poetic songs unfurl a vast emotional and political fabric for the listener's consideration, but do so a detail at a time. Two songs about cultural genocide, Sainte-Marie's "My Country 'Tis of Thy People You're Dying" (1965), and Westerman's "Missionary" (1969) walk the listener through grand sweeps of suffering with subtle imagery and clever turns of phrase. "My Country" is the first of its kind, a bold epic first performed on Pete Seeger's 1965 television show *Rainbow Quest*. It strikes a conversational tone, with chords strummed simply on the downbeat of each phrase and pauses between lines, allowing the listener time to digest each thought as it comes.

Such care both offsets and hammers home its directness, and capitalizes on elements of rhetorical questioning, anticipation, and surprise.

> Now that your big eyes are finally opened/Now that you're wondering, "How must they feel?"/Meaning them that you've chased cross America's movie screens/Now that you're wondering, "How can it be real?"/That the ones you've called colorful, noble and proud/in your school propaganda/They starve in their splendor/[...] My country 'tis of thy people you're dying.[6]

Sainte-Marie's referral to her own people as "they" and "them" allows for an ironic commentary on the dehumanizing impulse usually inflicted through such language. Phrases such as "big eyes," "school propaganda," and a sardonic contrast in the second verse between "nation of leeches" and "nation of patriots," twist the knife a bit deeper with each line. Her trademark vibrato brings a gravitas to the scenes she starkly presents: the voyeuristic fascination of dominant culture, and the evisceration caused by the residential schools' hypocrisy.

In 2006, Floyd Red Crow Westerman rerecorded his iconic song "Missionaries" with Jamaican artist Tevy Felix for Henhouse Records. Written thirty-six years earlier as a country song, the acoustic reggae framework even more strongly contrasts the deceptively soothing melody with the unflinching sarcasm of the message. In the video performance, Felix plays a gentle lullaby on his guitar while Westerman intently and whimsically shakes a set of maracas to underscore the ska upbeat. Despite the lilting melody, there could not possibly be a more scathing critique. The lyrics ruthlessly pull back the curtain to expose the Church as a predator.

> Spread the word of your religions/Convert the whole world if you can/Kill and slaughter those who oppose you/It's worth it to save one man [...].[7]

The language of these lyrics is neither subtle nor conciliatory. All but a few lines take the form of commands. The bitter, provocative tone rings out almost instantly in the word "slaughter." Wry twists on familiar aphorisms, such as "spoil the child, spare the rod," and imagery like "ever-circling vulture" make it impossible for the listener to remain at a distance. The lyrics capture the corporate nature of the Christianizing effort, connecting personal experience to institutional structure in a process that is part seduction, part rape. The confrontational and condescending narrative moves from a grand scale to an intimate one and back again.

"Missionaries" appeared first on the legendary album *Custer Died for Your Sins* (1969), a namesake of the book authored by Westerman's close friend, and one of the greatest public thinkers of that time period, Vine Deloria, Jr. Each made his own contribution to that tumultuous era's intellectual awakening; Lakota poet and novelist Elizabeth Cook-Lynn observes it was "no accident" that both men emerged at a time when so many oppressive ideologies, institutions, and laws were put in place to ensure "our subjugation and disappearance."[8] In particular, each drew attention to the potent combination of church and state that had caused such cataclysmic misfortune for American Indian people, and the bitterly ironic contradiction between its purported aims and outcomes.

> Europeans came here in part seeking religious freedom, but did not believe in religious freedom for [Indians], though our religion is far older than theirs. Indians the [early Christian] missionaries couldn't convert were killed and there are still missionaries out there after us. It's time they stopped trying to convert us, and listen to what our religion can teach them.[9]

> If Christianity saves the individual, and the evidence that it does appears to be increasing, it must certainly be determined a failure where societies or even large numbers of human beings are concerned.[10]

Vine Deloria was an intellectual giant who wove the critical web that held so many creative and intellectual strands of American Indian Movement activism together. Political scientist David Wilkins describes Deloria's endeavor as "an unrelenting, prodigious, and largely successful effort to provide those most grounded of Native individuals and their governments with the intellectual, theoretical, philosophical, and substantive arguments necessary to support their personal and national sovereignty."[11]

The singers of the AIM era cleared political paths for those who followed, courageously raising consciousness that led to action. The bold efforts of artists such as Tom Bee and XIT, John Trudell, Sainte-Marie, and Westerman undergirded those of activists like Dennis Banks, Clyde Bellecourt, and Russell Means. Their work, and that of countless others, resulted in legislation such as the Indian Self-Determination and Education Assistance Act (1975) promoting tribal infrastructure, the Indian Child Welfare Act (1978) keeping children with Native caregivers, and the powerful American Indian Freedom of Religion Act (1978), reversing one hundred years of bans on ceremonial practice.[12] These laws were the result of two decades of grassroots political participation, sculpted in part by the kind of discourse generated around this music.

Westerman remarks, in an interview from Sainte-Marie's 2009 documentary *A Multi-Media Life*, that the artists' work at this formative time completely agitated U.S. government officials. Sainte-Marie was more visible because of her commercial success, and he noted how terrified these powerful men seemed of "a girl with a guitar." He continues, "There was a Holocaust that Indians were stepping out of. She took the first step … and she took a hit for it. […] And I think that makes her a warrior of an unusual kind." And, indeed, the U.S. government did not want to hear such songs. Like poet and activist John Trudell, who lost five family members in a shocking fire 12 hours after he burned a flag in front of FBI headquarters, Sainte-Marie was ultimately silenced, as her songs were quietly banned from the airwaves.[13] In 1976, she left the public spotlight in favor of raising her son, and did not make an album for 16 years.

Annie Humphrey, born a generation after these AIM greats, attributes her political teeth to their influence. Her father taught her guitar at age 10, and mother imparted to her a 1970s activist sensibility, often playing tapes of John Trudell's oral poetry and, "scatterbrained poet that she is," sharing her gift for language.[14] As an adult, Annie eagerly followed Trudell around at a powwow in order to introduce herself for the first time. When she gathered the courage to ask if he would allow her to set some of his poetry to music, he was pleased with what she did. "I was always fascinated with the famous Indians," she told him.

Thirty-five years after Sainte-Marie's "My Country 'Tis of Thy People," Annie Humphrey revisits many of the same still-raw concerns in her expansive "500 Years" (2000). It is a litany of destruction, much like "My Country," but delivered in a dramatically different voice. Compared to the spare and definitive chording of Sainte-Marie, a great match to her haughty lyrics, Humphrey's guitar accompaniment is an assortment of plucked notes and sprinkled thirds against a warm background of string noise. In contrast to Buffy's chilling, plaintive, vocal technique, Annie's lyrical, even uplifting, melody utilizes a different kind of delivery.

> Christophoros' hungry eyes/Conquistadors' golden lies
>> So many ways to steal the prize/Who cares if one more Native dies?
>> Kings decreed across the waves/Antoniano makes us slaves
>> The Holy Church, the blood that saves/One hundred million unmarked
> Native graves/Our relatives are watching/Our spirit helpers near
>> 500 years of genocide/Who's left to hear? (2x)[15]

This song is epic, lasting eight minutes and five centuries, chronicling disease, removal, treaties, residential schools, relocation, termination, and both physical and cultural genocide. It bears the marked influence of Annie's mother, respected Anishinaabe storyteller Anne Dunn. In fact, Annie recalls standing in the sound booth with her mother passing scraps of paper to her with the final two verses, as Annie sang on and on.

Wab Kinew followed a parallel political path. As a teen, he became radicalized by Native and Black civil rights activists, on the one hand, and socially-conscious rap artists on the other: "I started reading the autobiography of Malcolm X, [...] *God Is Red* by Vine Deloria, *Bury My Heart at Wounded Knee* by Dee Brown. And I started to realize that [rap artists] like Nas were putting their knowledge into words, and they were speaking with passion."[16] Kinew's song "Heroes," from his 2009 album *Live by the Drum*, pays specific homage to two AIM-era figures, acknowledging the endurance required to maintain not just a lifelong, but multiple generation, fight against injustice:

> How does Leonard Peltier get out of bed each day? [...]
>
> How did Buffy Sainte-Marie keep on singin'?[17]

The song as a whole, while it differs dramatically from Humphrey's in musical style, bears a strong resemblance in tone and form: it traces the history of indigenous peoples' encounters with government, church, and popular culture, this time focusing almost entirely on individual figures in Canada through the song's collection of queries and responses:

> How did Fontaine get the apology?/He told the story then said "Come on, follow me" That's the gift: I guess I'll pass it on/Like the teachings passed at the Sun Dance before dawn.[18]

Kinew's voice, clear and forceful, holds the right amount of swagger. His drawling vowels and clear consonants articulate the names, past and present. He finds a balance between rhythm and lyricism on the mic, sliding into a calmer sound when he reaches the chorus. His gentle wordplay underscores a message of humility, as he recognizes his place in an ancestral narrative and finds a foothold amid the challenges of his own experience:

> And any man who knows a thing
> Knows he knows not a damn, damn thing at all
> And every time I felt the hurt and I felt the giving
> Gettin' me up off the wall.[19]

Bolstered by the determined example of his contemporaries and predecessors, Kinew exhibits hard-won patience, reining in some of the anger which comes out more strongly in other songs, such as "Stand 'n' Fight" and "Fuck John Wayne." The conclusion to the song underscores the responsibility he feels to give voice to a driving and seemingly endless flood of painful inspiration: "And this is just the beginning. This could be a five hundred bar song: one bar for every year of oppression. One bar for every rhyme I've got to make an impression ... on today's youth."[20]

Like a Bird in a Cage: Artistry

A common thread among indigenous protest artists of all generations is a relentless creativity. Such a drive to create results in agility, resourcefulness, an enormous sense of initiative, a knack for capturing the attention of extremely diverse audiences, and a refusal to be confined to one channel of expression. Westerman studied theater in college, had a prominent career in television and film, and later in his life turned to sculpture. Humphrey creates exquisite beadwork and has overseen public art projects with young people. Kinew is a CBC television producer and reporter, and Sainte-Marie has worked in a variety of media as a visual and graphic artist. She describes the creative impulse that permeates her work, regardless of the outlet:

> The real Art occurs in the imagination: then the Work begins. The tools are whatever we can get, beads or pixels, hunting bows or a computer. I began music in my head. [...] Throughout my crayon days, my watercolors and oils days, and my eventual falling in love with digital painting on the Macintosh, one fact has made itself clear: an artist will make music on pots and pans, or an orchestra, and we'll make images in the sand with a finger, or whatever else is available, including the computer.[21]

An impressionist aethestic characterizes Sainte-Marie's music videos. Much like her vibrant visual art—which often uses photographs enhanced with an array of digital processing techniques that play with color and light—they have a photographic quality, like a series of stopped-motion shots, with images overlaid upon each other. Some of her videos have a watery or iridescent sheen, like the ethereal folk song "Fallen Angels," while powwow rock tunes such as "No No Keshagesh" and "Darlin' Don't Cry" utilize blurs of bright color. A constant flow of movement juxtaposes Sainte-Marie, or, in two cases, fancy dancers, with more abstract background images. Light shines through water, through stars, through spotlights. She herself is frequently dressed in black and white, creating a dramatic set of contrasts. Sainte-Marie speaks of her most recent album *Running for the Drum* as "thematic with how I am, since as a songwriter I'm kind of like a camera, and I just take pictures of whatever is interesting to me."[22]

Wab Kinew is a storyteller. He began this craft as a young boy testifying before the Royal Commission on Aboriginal Peoples about his Ojibwe language immersion pre-school, coached by his father beforehand on ways to win over his audience. He did a piece for CBC radio as a young adult, then transitioned into work as a CBC television reporter and producer. He won acclaim for covering the Canadian Truth and Reconciliation Commission's first national event, telling the stories of residential school survivors, including his father, and of his family's numerous losses to suicides, drugs, and alcohol. He writes expressively of his father's momentous audience with the Pope as part of a delegation of chiefs to receive a statement of regret in 2009:

> That he stuck around long enough to see the Holy Father tremble in his presence and appear visibly upset as he tried to make amends is, for me, monumental. To me, it says that, in spite of the concerted efforts of the government of Canada and five churches to destroy our culture, it has survived.[23]

270

Kinew views his verbal art, in all of its forms, as a continuation of indigenous oral tradition. The Sun Dance, hand drum, rap music, and his televised storytelling all harness language as a means to convey cultural values and address political concerns. The lyrics of his song "Fly" (2011), co-written by Leonard Sumner (Lorenzo), offer commentary on his process:

> Feelin' like a bird in a cage, burdened with a rage/I picked up my pen and started hurtin' the page/With each line the writin' starts easin' the pain/D3s [Ha ha] You know what I mean/Yes, my therapy, the flow, started to take me away, feelin' pretty damn good to be Anishinaabe.[24]

His most noteworthy battle recently came in the area of language and representation, as he successfully convinced the CBC to change its terminology for those swallowed up by boarding schools from "former students" to "survivors." He fiercely objected to the media outlet's implication that these elders "didn't know their own experience." "You don't understand your own story. Here's the language to describe what happened to you," Kinew intoned in an interview with George Stroumboupolous. He took a stand, tendering his resignation and thus putting a hard-won admiration for his reporting to the test:

> Is the CBC gonna be a place that is diverse in the fact that we put brown people on the air but everybody just has to act white, or are we truly diverse in that we change our reality to encompass other Canadians' experience?[25]

Instead of waiting for someone else to make it happen, Kinew has taken it into his own hands. His most ambitious project to date is the CBC television and radio series *8th Fire*, named for an Anishinaabe prophecy declaring now the time for Native and non-Native peoples to join forces, "a provocative, high-energy journey through Aboriginal country," which introduces "emerging leaders, artists, activists and thinkers" and explores possibilities for change.[26] The program represents an impressive breadth of personal stories and professional skills encompassed by Aboriginal people across Canada. Episodes highlight the work of a surgeon in rural Quebec, a T.V. producer in Edmonton, an NHL player in Toronto, and a professor of indigenous governance from University of Victoria, all of whom translate indigenous knowledge and experience to non-Native society. Wab Kinew notes his process of convincing CBC to pick up the programming mirrors the show itself, namely "engaged native people helping to shed light on some important issues to a mainly non-native audience."[27]

Media and technology have dramatically impacted indigenous artists' ability to transmit their ideas. The informal networks which have long brought indigenous individuals and communities together are set afire by the Internet, an electronic "moccasin telegraph." Concerts and powwows are advertised on Facebook, announcements about ceremonies are sent via text and email, and creativity flourishes on websites sharing film, song, poetry, language, and cultural learning. Buffy Sainte-Marie played a groundbreaking role with her appearances on PBS's *Sesame Street* from 1976 to 1980, where she strove to impart to mainstream children a simple message, "Indians exist: we are not all dead and stuffed in museums like the dinosaurs."[28] In 1995, she established Nihewan, an educational foundation which gave rise to the Cradleboard project, a multimedia, multidiscipline, curriculum that pairs Native and non-Native classrooms to create cross-cultural learning partnerships.

Floyd Westerman was also deeply concerned with issues of media representation for indigenous people:

> In a world where we need to build on mutual respect, we first have to get rid of racism in sports ... mascots. So I think the objective of AIM is to stay on the front line of that issue, even while there are many other issues that are very pressing, and seemingly more important. Our children have to live under the kind of racist attitudes that are expressed through mascot racism in sports. Movies do it the same way.[29]

He played a series of droll film and television roles which reinforced some stereotypes and broke others, but always expressed his whimsical personality: a trucker's voice on the CB in *Powwow Highway* (1989), Chief Ten Bears in *Dances with Wolves* (1990), "One Who Waits" on *Northern Exposure*, and Uncle Ray on *Walker, Texas Ranger*. In the late 1990s, he launched a film, television and music production company in Los Angeles, the nonprofit Eyapaha Institute, which provides seminars and conferences for young indigenous people in media production.

8th Fire: Community

Unique to indigenous protest music—throughout the world—is the intensity of the drive toward protecting and strengthening young people. North American indigenous artists who have achieved prominence have an unquestioned priority of acting as role models and mentors. In order to secure a future for indigenous youth, these artists pursue two complementary impulses: channeling their resources into indigenous communities, on the one hand, and translating indigenous concerns for non-Native people, on the other.

Each artist discussed here has utilized his or her multidimensional personality and skills to be an emissary, with the ultimate goal of securing the future for future generations. Floyd Westerman has been called "the American Indian Movement Minister of Culture," and Wab Kinew "an ambassador for Native people" who proudly displays a photo on his website of himself with President Obama. Annie Humphrey's thoughts in this vein are stated on her Makoché Records website:

> We need to care for children wherever they are in the world. [...] People everywhere need healing. [...] I consider anyone who walks in a sacred way and honors the earth to be indigenous to our planet.[30]

Buffy Sainte-Marie says her happiness lies in putting Native children and teachers "in the driver's seat of delivering our self-identity" by connecting Native and non-Native people, "whoever our nations are, to anybody who wants to know about it."[31]

Sainte-Marie set the stage for such bridge-building efforts even in the earliest years of her career. She began mobilizing a wide range of indigenous audiences in the 1960s, connecting urban concerns to those of the reservation communities while, at the same time, taking every opportunity she could to educate non-Native audiences. She speaks of how her mainstream success fueled her activist efforts, and how her multifaceted style made her a conduit:

> So I used my show business airplane tickets to—you know, I'd have a concert in Paris, and then I'd go up to the Arctic and spend time with the indigenous people there, or a concert in New York, because I was living in Greenwich Village then, I'd go up to Akwesasne, the Mohawk reservation, you know, at the top of New York on the Canadian border. And it kind of became the paradigm of my life. I wasn't intentionally trying to become a bridge for anything, but I did see that people in the cities, they wanted to know.[32]

Solidarity was one of the major outcomes of the American Indian Movement. Artists like Sainte-Marie, Westerman, and XIT helped create a pan-tribal identity through their performances just as surely as activists such as Dennis Banks, Clyde and Vernon Bellecourt, and John Trudell. Sharing knowledge and seeing collaboration among tribes provided the undergirding for the cultural revitalization movement which has gathered increasing momentum during the past three decades.

A savvy generation was born out of this struggle, bruised and battered from their families' battles with boarding school trauma, but with the skills and self-awareness to move forward. A focus on reclaiming education—from language immersion preschools all the way up to the dramatic increase in graduate degrees—has empowered those born in the 1970s and 80s, often called "the seventh generation," to confront their demons and go on.[33] Annie Humphrey's "Spirit Horses," which won the 2003 NAMA award for Best Music Video, captures this sense of intergenerational rebirth. She is joined by John Trudell and, accompanied by Annie's rhythm guitar, piano, and the soaring voice of a solo electric, they make a powerful duo as they express the turmoil loosed by colonization and embody the turning of generations toward each other, of young indigenous people leading the way back and finding a way forward.

Hunger, need and fear/Slavery, grief, confusion
Freedom waiting near [...]
The sound of spirit horses/Dancing on a storm
Old ways, new dreams reborn.[34]

Annie devotes herself selflessly to nurturing young people's creativity and strength. She founded Turtle Heart, an organization promoting "positive lifestyle choices" for indigenous youth, and has received Smithsonian grants to engage them in the arts.[35] She has worked as a cultural instructor in a treatment center for Native youth and in numerous tribal and public schools, creating public art and teaching song-writing skills. As her teenaged son has begun to work in the area of rap and spoken word, she has collaborated with him, creating melodic components to complement his rhythmic ones. Listening to old recordings of Buffy Sainte-Marie, Annie admitted she sometimes feels the pull of the stage and misses the opportunity to voice her concerns. She muses,

> I think about myself and how I've mellowed into this person who is at home and working with these kids ... and then I hear something like this and I think, 'There's more that needs to be said.' But then, maybe I can teach those kids to say it themselves.[36]

Wab Kinew's work reverberates with the dreams and fears he has for his young sons, and with stories of dead young men. "Last Word," nominated for an Aboriginal People's Choice Award in 2009, captures a tension between gritty realism and buoyant optimism in his own life story. Constructed as a musical last will and testament, Wab expresses gratitude to his Creator and family, admits to his struggles, celebrates his intellectual accomplishments, and pledges his dedication:

> I hit the lessons hard, the hard knocks I did learn/The pride made me suffer, my ego made me burn/[...] I never stop runnin' for my demons might catch me.

> I am my own man with the means to more, a Native/[...] Original, creative, successful, I made it [...] Hope I did you proud and gave my boys the elements/That they need to succeed and didn't leave impediments.[37]

Like so many indigenous artist-activists, Kinew embraces both dominant culture and traditional indigenous notions of success. His publicity describes both his economics degree and his knowledge of traditional medicine. He consciously sets a hybrid example, aspiring to serve in the Canadian government and sprinkling his lyrics with the Ojibwe language. He believes the challenges in indigenous communities—"domestic violence, poor scholastic achievement, unemployment, and suicide"—have a common solution: "to build a new generation of active, passionate, and engaged citizens."[38]

Enter Ta'Kaiya Blaney, an eleven-year-old from the Sliammon Nation in British Columbia who is gaining recognition for using her creative voice in several dimensions. Her work as an actress focuses entirely on cultural activism. She has played leading roles in three short films about the residential school experience: *Shi-Shi-Etko* (2009), *Savage* (2010), and *Nooka Rose* (2011). *Savage*, made by Vancouver filmmaker Lisa Jackson, won a Genie award in 2010 for Best Short Film. *Shi-Shi-Etko* follows a six-year-old Aboriginal girl four days before she is taken to residential school, and is filmed in Halq'emelem, the language of the Stó:lō Nation. Another of her films, *Spelling Bee* (2010), is part of a series celebrating First Nations languages. In it, Ta'Kaiya plays a little girl who dreams she is in a Spelling Bee which requires its young contestants to spell words from over 30 distinct First Nation languages and dialects.

But Blaney has received equal attention for her activism as a singer. She has co-written several songs concerned with environmental destruction, and has performed them at a number of public protests. A broad appeal to young people of all nations, "Earth Revolution" convicts developed nations, "poisoned by pollution, greed and war," and exorts "Generation Now, children of the future" to abandon talk and take action.[39] Her own actions speak loudly, as she sings and speaks again and again at rallies in her traditional woven cedar hat, foregoing typical eleven-year-old pursuits to proclaim her dedication: "Creation's crying out, […] can't walk away/I'll do my part to fix what's broken, give back what we've taken, hope for the dawn of a new day."[40]

Her lyrics echo both the urgency and determination that characterize the environmental songs of other indigenous singers. On the one hand, her songs ring with somber pronouncements, like Floyd Westerman's in his "Day without Tomorrow" (1969), when he sang "And the trees are dead and buried, and the grass has turned to stone, and only man has caused it all, a victim of his greed and profit, now he stands alone." On the other, they resonate with Annie Humphrey's poignant yet hopeful reflections in "Justice Hunters" (2004): "Some say we'll be forever alive, and some say only the rocks will survive […] the new warriors are here to […] make the water pure […]we all pray that justice for all is on the way."[41]

Blaney's "Shallow Waters" was written in 2010, and focuses specifically on the implications of the proposed Keystone XL oil pipeline from the tar sands in northern Alberta through the pristine Great Bear Rainforest to the rugged British Columbia coast. It vividly captures the ongoing impact of the 1989 Exxon Valdez oil spill, compelling listeners to consider the potential consequences of allowing supertankers into the Port of Kitimat and into the dangerous waters beyond.[42] Ta'Kaiya's voice, mature yet innocent, traces a lilting melancholy melody, paired with simple piano accompaniment. The music video includes footage of Ta'Kaiya in cedar bark regalia, being paddled in a traditional Squamish ocean-going canoe interspersed with scenes of her playing on the beach with an oil refinery in the background. The song was a semi-finalist in the 2010 David Suzuki Songwriting Contest, Playlist for the Planet.

> The lifeless ocean, black not blue/I didn't help, deep down I knew[…]
> Splashing around in the summer heat/Now it's just oil up to our knees.[43]

In 2011, Ta'Kaiya and her mother went to the Enbridge Oil corporate office in Vancouver to hand-deliver a copy of her music video and a letter asking them to stop their plans. Security guards stopped her from entering the building, and the office refused to send someone down to the street to accept her letter. A commentator from Greenpeace remarked, "Apparently Enbridge, who has touted their willingness to listen and work with First Nations, is afraid of a ten-year-old First Nations girl."[44] She went on to send the music video, along with an open letter, to the members of the Canadian Parliament, asking them to "replace jobs that destroy the environment with jobs that help the environment," and urging them not to repeat the mistakes of the past.[45]

Indigenous protest singers are a bold and brilliant, tough and caring lot. Powered by unrelenting creativity and grounded in stalwart community, their passion and probing intellect are balanced by a gift for diplomacy. The resourcefulness and resiliency of Ta'Kaiya Blaney and her entire generationhave not appeared out of thin air; they were built on the stubborn shoulders of her parents' generation: attendees of tribal schools who went on to battle institutional racism in order to earn college degrees. They, in turn, rest on the strong backs of the marchers and agitators of the American Indian Movement, mentors and grandparents to all who raise their voices today.

> Lightning Woman, Thunder Child/Star soldiers
> one and all/Oh, sisters, brothers, all together/Aim
> straight, stand tall.
> —Buffy Sainte-Marie, "Starwalker" (1973)

Notes

1 Annie Humphrey, "We Need More Than Love," *The Sound of Ribbons*, CD, © 2008 Red Cedar Music.

2 This range of genres, while broad, obviously does not represent the entirety of those encompassed by socially-conscious indigenous artists of the U.S. and Canada. The brother–sister band Blackfire, with NAMA-winning albums such as *One Nation Under* (Canyon, 2002) and *Silence Is Weapon* (CD Baby, 2007), produces what has been called "fire-ball alternative punk," addressing themes of genocide, ecocide, and government oppression, while Bay-area thrash metal Testament have been active since 1983. Their most recent album, *Dark Roots of Earth* (Nuclear Blast America, 2012) includes the notable single "Native Blood," focused on the personal and communal impact of racism.

3 Buffy Sainte-Marie, "No No Keshagesh," *Running for the Drum*, CD, © 2009 Appleseed Records.

4 Buffy Sainte-Marie, "No No Keshagesh."

5 Buffy Sainte-Marie, *Democracy Now! Special: An Hour of Music and Conversation with Legendary Native American Singer-Songwriter Buffy Sainte-Marie*, interview by Amy Goodman, video, October 12, 2009.

6 Buffy Sainte-Marie, "My Country 'Tis of Thy People You're Dying," *Little Wheel Spin and Spin Little Wheel Spin and Spin*, CD, © 1966 Vanguard.

7 Floyd Red Crow Westerman, "Missionaries," *Custer Died for Your Sins / The Earth Is Your Mother*, CD, © 1993 Trikont (re-recording of 1969 vinyl album).

8 Elizabeth Cook-Lynn, "Comments for Vine Deloria Jr. upon his Early and Untimely Death, 2005," in *Wicazo Sa Review*, Vol. 21, No. 2 (Fall 2006): 149–150.

9 Floyd Red Crow Westerman, *Salt Lake Tribune*, April 26, 1996.

10 Vine Deloria, *God Is Red: A Native View of Religion* (Golden, Colorado: Fulcrum Publishing, 2003 [1972], 30th anniversary edition), 294.

11 David Wilkins, "Vine Deloria Jr. and Indigenous Americans," *Wicazo Sa Review*, Vol. 21, No. 2 (Fall 2006): 151.

12 Laura Waterman Wittsock and Elaine J. Salinas, "A Brief History of the American Indian Movement" at http://www.aimovement.org/ggc/history.html, accessed July 18, 2012.

13 Colin Irwin, "Buffy Sainte-Marie on a Rollercoaster Career That Even the FBI Kept an Eye On," *The Guardian*, July 30, 2009, at http://www.guardian.co.uk/music/2009/jul/31/buffy-sainte-marie, accessed July 30, 2012.

14 Interview by Elyse Carter Vosen, October 3, 2009.

15 AnnieHumphrey "500 Years," *The Heron Smiled*, CD, © 2000 Makoché Records.

16 Wab Kinew, interview by George Stroumboupoulous, *George Stroumboupoulous Tonight*, Candian Broadcasting Company, video, June 19, 2012.

17 Wab Kinew, "Heroes," *Live by the Drum*, CD, © 2009 Strongfront Productions and Indie Ends.

18 Wab Kinew, "Heroes."

19 Wab Kinew, "Heroes."

20 Wab Kinew, "Heroes."

21 Buffy Sainte-Marie, "Painting with Light, Playing with Sound," excerpted from a speech given at the Institute for American Indian Arts, Santa Fe, NM, at http://www.creative-native.com/artwork-speech.php, accessed June 30, 2012.

22 Buffy Sainte-Marie, *A Multi-Media Life*, DVD, EMI, 2009.

23 Wab Kinew, "The Day the Pope Said Sorry," CBC News, May 11, 2009 at http://www.cbc.ca/news/canada/story/2009/05/11/f-vp-kinew.html, accessed August 7, 2012.

24 "Fly," Lorenzo and Wab Kinew (2011), Hip-Hop Summit Special. Aboriginals podcast, CBC News at http://music.cbc.ca/#/blogs/2011/3/Brave-New-World-Wab-Kinew-and-Lorenzo-Present-Fly, accessed August 3, 2012.

25 Wab Kinew, interview by George Stroumboupoulous, *George Stroumboupoulous Tonight*, Candian Broadcasting Company, video, June 19, 2012.

26 *8th Fire: Aboriginal Peoples, Canada, and the Way Forward*, Canadian Broadcasting Company at http://www.cbc.ca/doczone/8thfire/, accessed August 4, 2012.

27 *8th Fire.*

28 Buffy Sainte-Marie, "Cradleboard History" at http://www.cradleboard.org/2000/history.html accessed July 30, 2012.

29 Floyd Red Crow Westerman, interview by Roibeard O'Ceallaigh (2004). http://www.youtube.com/watch?v=qa5xwjE4T9k

30 Makoche Records artist page for Annie Humphrey at http://www.makoche.com/artists/viewarticle.asp?id=101, accessed July 3, 2012.

31 Sainte-Marie, "Cradleboard History."

32 Buffy Sainte-Marie, *Democracy Now!*

33 For analysis of the history of American Indian education and its particular impact from the 1970s to the present, see Amy Bergstrom, Linda Miller Cleary, and Thomas Peacock, *The Seventh Generation: Native Students Speak about Finding the Good Path* (Denver, Colorado: Eric Clearinghouse, 2003); and Jon Reyhner and Jeanne Eder, *American Indian Education: A History* (Norman: University of Oklahoma Press, 2006).

34 Annie Humphrey "Spirit Horses," *The Heron Smiled*, CD, © 2000 Makoché Records.

35 Humphrey is also co-founder, along with her mother, Anne Dunn, of the Sister Brave Heart Lodge, a nonprofit cooperative with a goal of assisting women and their children in their efforts to provide for themselves. Mendota Mdewaketon Dakota Community website, July 8, 2008 at http://mendotadakota.com/mn/tag/national-museum-of-the-american-indian-native-arts-program/, accessed August 3, 2012.

36 Annie Humphrey, interview by Elyse Carter Vosen, October 3, 2009.

37 Wab Kinew, "Last Word," *Live by the Drum*, CD, © 2009 Strongfront Productions and Indie Ends.

38 Wab Kinew, interview by Elyse Carter Vosen, November 5, 2011. In 2009, Kinew put that notion into practice, teaching youth from the Immigrant and Refugee Community of Manitoba (IRCOM) from places as far flung as Kyrgyzstan, Pakistan, the Sudan, Burundi, and Somalia to express themselves through rap music and video art.

39 Ta'Kaiya Blaney website, lyrics page at http://www.takaiyablaney.com/kids-page-2/

40 Ta'Kaiya Blaney website.

41 Annie Humphrey, "Justice Hunters," *Edge of America*, CD, © 2004 Red Cedar Music. Environmental concerns have been a major theme in indigenous protest music. Other notable contributions: XIT in 1973 with "Color Nature Gone," Walela in 1997 with "Muddy Road," and Robbie Robertson in 1998 with "In the Blood."

42 Ian Austen, "A Squabble Over Moving Oil and Sharing Royalties," *The New York Times*, July 25, 2012.

43 Ta'Kaiya Blaney website, lyrics page at http://www.takaiyablaney.com/kids-page-2/

44 Stephanie Goodwin, "Why Enbridge is Afraid of Ta'Kaiya Blaney," Greenpeace Blog, March 24, 2011 at http://www.greenpeace.org/canada/en/Blog/why-enbridge-is-afraid-of-takaiya-blaney/blog/33920/, accessed August 10, 2012.

45 Goodwin, "Why Enbridge."

20

EUROPEAN POP MUSIC AND THE NOTION OF PROTEST

Anna G. Piotrowska

Figure 20.1   Russian president Dmitry Medvedev speaks with rock musicians AndreyMakarevich and Boris Grebenshchikov during a visit to Beat-Blues Café in Moscow.

The fraught relationship between European popular music and various kinds of power has stimulated intensive scholarship and encouraged heated discussions. Of special interest seems the multifaceted character of that interrelationship. It is generally agreed that artistic expression in popular music is influenced by political power, and that the two mutually inform and shape each other. However, it needs to be stressed that in this approach, under the general and rather imprecisely used notion of "popular music," one must consider not only the actual sounds but also a complex variety of actions. These involve, among others, the production of music, performances, and the audience's reception, as well as the support of sponsors. Specified by their own aesthetics and carrying their own history, these factors play an important role in the processes taking place outside purely musical reality. In this understanding of music, the structures of the sound alone do not stand for the multitude of meanings attributed to popular music; the significance of music is related to a number of elements including (but not confined to) aesthetic values, social interest and, finally, political regulations.

Hence, while analyzing European (and, as a matter of fact, any other) popular music in the context of protest, the multitude of these extra-musical factors is usually brought to the fore. It can even be claimed that authors, often implicitly, agree that popular music defines itself through opposition. There seems to be a growing agreement that the notion of pop music is "inherently oppositional."[1] Songs are thought to be vehicles for the expression of the oppressed or those opposing. However, the question arises: oppositional to what? Possible answers usually refer to the "powers-that-be," whether they are political, religious, social, or economic. The list seems far-reaching, yet the prevailing tendency is to view pop music as politically indebted.[2] This entails discussing popular music as a means of resisting or undermining power relations of various kinds, or as a pivotal element in shaping the expression of politically relevant identities. Hence, popular music and its political involvement are usually entwined within the public sphere, and its communicative and transformative potential has been subject to control by those in position of power. Direct limiting by banning songs from official broadcasting, declaring them ideologically unsuitable, or harnessing such musical events as rock festivals for authorities' own ends—these are just a few methods used to control the pop music production or discourage the dissemination of songs considered too dangerous for a given political or social system.

What Is Meant by "Protest in Popular Music?"

Two important questions appear at this stage of consideration: what is meant by protest and what is actually discussed under the heading "popular music and protest." Protest in popular music is associated with opposition, contestation, revolt and resistance. However, as sociologists Jocelyn A. Hollander and Rachel L. Einwoher point out, "there is little consensus on the definition of resistance"[3] let alone resistance in music, or popular music, which in itself is a difficult to define concept. Nevertheless, they suggest their own typology and singled out the following modes of resistance:[4]

1 Overt resistance—characterised by visible actions easily identified as of resistant nature by targets and observers.
2 Covert resistance—intentional acts of resistance that go unnoticed by their targets, although classified as resistance by the observers/listeners.
3 Unwitting resistance—unintended resistance that is recognised by both the target and observers.

4 Target-defined resistance—identified solely by the target, without the actor and the observers/listeners and fans even realizing the resistant character of the action.

5 Externally-defined resistance—actions described as resistance only by the onlookers and listeners.

6 Missed-resistance—intended acts of resistance that go unnoticed by the observers.

7 Attempted resistance—acts which neither the target nor the third party seem to interpret as resistance.

This detailed typology illustrates to the best extent the diversity of phenomena that can be described as resistance. Furthermore, they can be interpreted according to the above-mentioned typology at various levels: collective (bands) or individual (solo performers), referring to constant actions and permanent behaviors, as well as one-off acts. The richness of musical life presents several possibilities to investigate further the phenomenon of resistance, especially in the context of complicated situations such as that of post-WWII Europe, with its division between the communist East and capitalist West—with all ideological and economic consequences of the split. It should be stressed that the diversity among what is hailed as resistance stems from three factors identified by Hollander and Einwoher as modes of resistance (under-stood literally as acts of physical resistance or as a type of, usually protesting, behav-iour with symbolic meaning), the scale of resistance and its directions or aims.[5] The inevitable element of resistance is action, broadly defined, targeted against certain goals. The opposition requires then at least two parties—an opposing one and one being opposed. However, in the case of performance art such as pop music, apart from the two indispensable actors (opposing creators and opposed addressees) there is still room for the third factor—the element of recognition by the public, critics, and musicologists. Although some theoreticians of resistance, such as James Scott, claim that there is no need for recognition in the case of resistance,[6] there is a general consensus among other authors that, in order to call an opposing behavior an act of resistance, it should be recognized as such by others.[7]

There are issues that immediately come to mind when thinking about pop music and protest actions. For one, who gets to decide what constitutes undesirable musical practices (and therefore musical protest), and on what basis and in which historical, social, or political circumstances? What role is attributed to the censorship? How is popular music employed in resistance towards various forms of control? Does popular music oppose political ambitions, and, if yes, how? How do musical expressions support or undermine the political and social structures?

Several authors have attempted to address these important questions. Barbara Lebrun, for example, highlights such notions as protest identities, nostalgia, multicul-turalism, hybridity, Arabness, anti-globalization, and post-colonialism. She discusses "protest music" in the context of politics, arguing that protest music in France refers "to various ways in which chart music and political conservatism are connected."[8] One of the most often debated instances of the interrelation between pop music and power is hip-hop youth culture, which articulates local conflicts via rap music.

In French cities, in particular, the amalgamation of ethnic minorities enables the creation of new cultural codes. African communities have adapted American gansta rap patterns to their own political and social status, influenced by their post-colonial legacy. Via music, these often impoverished minorities are able to demonstrate their African descendancy, incorporating sounds of such instruments as derbuka, kora, balafon, and ngoni or bèlè drums.[9] French rap proliferated in Parisian neighborhoods (with such DJs as MC Solaar, Dee Nasty, and Doc Gyneco), and Marseille (e.g. the trio Al Iman Staff, or the El Matador, a DJ of Algerian origin). In French cities, rap is mainly associated with suburbia, whereas in Hungarian Budapest the Roma community—present in the heart of the city, in its 8th district, Józsefváros—cultivates its own rap music influenced both by external and internal sources. The first Hungarian Roma rap band established in late 1990s, Fekete Vonat, decisively referred to their ethnic background in their lyrics. Pride, equality, and integrity, slogans inherited from the USA hip-hop culture, found their ultimate place in rap lyrics by ethnic minorities in Europe. However, this is not always the case. In Polish rap, ethnic differences are of no importance; here the conflict is based on an urban-village demarcation. Polish rap has become an outlet for young people living in apartments in medium-sized cities (such as, for example, the first Polish rapper from the early 1990s, Liroy), while its rival on the national musical scene, disco polo, is more associated with country dwellers.[10]

How Is Protest Expressed in Popular Music?

When pondering the relationship between popular music and protest, most discuss the lyrics of songs and the broadly-defined context within which pop music is functioning, with stress laid on the attitudes of musicians and the reception of their conduct and songs by the audience. It is arguable that the Adornian tradition of explaining popular music by examining the surrounding socio-musical world is still influencing discussion on protest in popular music.[11] One could add to this the idea of the Birmingham Centre of Contemporary Cultural Studies that youth subcultures and their music can be characterised as oppositional, i.e. anti-status-quo and anti-capitalist.

Content analysis prevails in research on forms of protest expression in European pop music. Many authors have defined the "protest song" through reference to its lyrics, treating song words as manifestos contesting social conditions.[12] Some authors claim that rock music is able to fuel revolutionary movements, with protest songs serving as their anthems.[13] Rebellion is marked in songs by the choice of words, by putting emphasis on such issues as intellectual prostitution, lack of freedom and tolerance, dishonesty, low morals, ideological slogans, dissatisfaction with reality, etc. Pop lyrics occasionally center around a hero—most often, a young white male not only trying to figure out his own fate, but also attempting to understand the rules governing the world, violently reacting to injustices that may meet him or those dear to his heart, and expressing his disagreement with the system. Yet the *criteria* for assessing lyrics as authentic expressions of anger and rebellion are vague and lacking uniformity.[14]

Moreover, in focusing on lyrics, scholars all too often overlook the importance of music and the choice of musical devices; for the lyrically-minded, music in protest song merely serves as a background for the lyrics.[15] For example, in the Russian bard tradition, whose representatives include Bulat Okudzhava (1924–1997) and Vladimir Vysotsky (1938–1980), the lyrics played the critical role of political commentary in Soviet Russia. Texts were full of innuendos, often written in a humorous way, sometimes metaphorical, sometimes down to earth, resembling street jargon. Musical accompaniments—usually played on the guitar by the bard himself—were uncomplicated, comprising a few basic chords (C major, C minor, E flat major, etc.), and the style of playing was classical, requiring finger-picking the strings in ascending or descending arpeggios. Most bards could not even play their instruments very well, let alone read music, since the emphasis was not on their music-making but, rather, the lyrics. Other European protest songs are sometimes discussed in reference to the long tradition of revolutionary songs performed in Europe during political upheavals. David Robb, for example, sees the German protest songs of the 1980s as a continuation and legacy of European revolutionary song.[16]

The choice of topics is clearly a crucial element distinguishing protest songs from "pop" songs.[17] Some authors[18] assert that protest songs depend directly on the authorities to which they are referring; this type of resistance may be classified as target-defined. Even in "covert" protest music, content matters. Drawing on the works of Iron Maiden or Black Sabbath, scholar Sean Kelly sees the choice of themes in heavy metal (a genre not typically associated with protest) as oppositional to social norms and values.[19] However, not only does a focus on libretto or "the text" potentially neglect music, it can also overshadow an assessment of the communities for which various musical pieces are intended.

It seems that, since "the position of pop music is negotiated within historical, social and political context,"[20] this aspect of pop music has been most widely underlined. In discussing resistance, as already observed by Hollander and Einwoher, actors are also important, e.g. musicians undertaking various actions which could be labelled as resistance. The other crucial element in the concept of resistance is the presence of the audience—the group able (or unable) to decipher the coded message of contestation.

Protesting musicians may be assigned—for the clarity of this argument—to two categories: those seriously involved in protesting actions, sometimes even becoming "proper" politicians, and those ridiculing and mocking the power relations who take the opposite role—the role of contemporary jokers. Musicians then adopt two strategies inherited from the European court tradition, embodying either the role of the "king" (as a ruler, politician) or the "jester."

The importance of musicians, their image, and behavior in creating the world of popular music is axiomatic. For Robert Burnett, music-making as a profession is linked to representation,[21] the public domain, and market demands. The star system[22] enables musicians to reach a wide range of listeners. Songs with protest messages may reach those already interested, as well as those who are still neutral. Such charitable actions as Live Aid at Wembley Stadium in 1985 (initiated by Irish rock musician Bob Geldof, in order to help Africa) show the impact of rock stars and their ability to contest reality. It may also be argued that the star system helps to multiply the effect of such integrated actions[23] by gathering in one place artists considered as the top performers of the decade (e.g. Queen, Alison Moyet, etc.).

Music performances bound to political activism are often seen as cyclical.[24] Their characteristic trait is agitation against an entire set of miseries, and their efforts are spearheaded by committed idealists who often leave the purely musical world for the realm of politics.[25] John Street dubs these personalities "musician-politicians."[26] Bono from U2 could serve as an archetype here. The activities of the "musician-politician" range from civil rights advocacy[27] to even religious and ecological concerns.[28] For a discussion of continental Europe, one could include the numerous folk musicians who took part in the political upheaval that led to the disappearance of the former GDR.

It can be claimed, though, that European pop musicians have often adapted a completely different position: that of a joker. This, as I see it, is a continuation of the medieval court jester who ridiculed reality and, by means of satire and mockery, represented the world through a distorted mirror. Today's "foolosophers"[29] are also heirs to the continent's bard and minstrel traditions.[30] They are people who do not conform to general rules and who express themselves freely while opening themselves up to ridicule. Some in the world of pop culture have attained almost mythical status as prophets and visionaries.[31] Two aspects of the "musician-jester's" activities seem important: what they want to communicate (in their lyrics) and how (the performative element of their profile). Contemporary European jokers of, say, the 1970s, like glam musicians such as David Bowie and Peter Gabriel, often created distinct stage "personas" whose performances operated on a level of bizarre and absurd social commentary.

Boris Grebenshchikov can be cited as an example of a "musician-jester" in Soviet Russia. Grebenshchikov (born in 1953) is an intertextual performer whose "closest kin are Russian poets from the beginning of the twentieth century, especially the symbolists,"[32] and he has admitted to the influence of "8th century Celtic bards."[33] Tomi Huttunen discusses Grebenshchikov in relation to Jim Morrison and Bob

Dylan, in terms of text and message, asserting that the "Russian rock-lyric must be seen against its historical background and intertextual sources." Russian rock is, for Huttunen, "not only ... a cultural-historical subject, but also ... a powerfully semioti-cised concept, which has abundant, mutually diverging connotations."[34]

Peter Wicke argues that subversive political content requires a "knowledgeable" audience that has to recognize what singers want to imply. It is up to the audience to determine the meaning of the lyrics and the behavior of rock stars.[35] Listeners may inter-pret or assume more than there is to see or hear; such externally-defined resistance was characteristic of the Polish musical scene in the 1980s, when even the names of punk bands, for example Brygada Kryzys (Crisis Brigade), were treated as opposition to the political establishment. To co-opt and channel the frustrations of younger Poles, authorities allowed, in 1980, a tightly controlled punk festival to be staged in Jarocin, one of the first punk festivals in a communist country. Officials carefully monitored the event, which was during the period of martial law, treating it as a controlled means of letting young people "blow off steam."[36]

Contesting Musical Devices?

In addition to lyrics and audience reception, we need to discuss music and the choice of musical devices and how they can convey protest content. A useful beginning here is Allan Moore's question—what sort of meaning does music have?[37]—and how can it express contestation? One assumption is that the musical genre most associ-ated with protest is folk music. Both Mark Willhard and Reebee Garofalo stress the role of protest song in folk traditions.[38] But it is clear that protest content is not confined to just one genre. Most European bands active by the 1980s were "difficult to categorize stylistically," and the blending of genres was typical of many musical practices at that time.[39] A second assumption relates to the homological relation of music and musical devices to content.[40] Sean Cubitt suggests that music, as a non-referential entity, only generates meaning rather than possesses any inherently.[41] Yet music is able to tap into and unleash emotions,[42] and there is general agreement on the social character of the musical communication process and an acknowledgment of the fact that musical sound structures are socially constructed. Cognitive musicol-ogy as a discipline (which has developed since the 1980s) rejects the concept of an abstract and autonomous musical work and the idea of the objective and impersonal character of commenting on music phenomena, stressing instead the fact that music is conceived by human minds and, thus, reflection on it should concentrate on audi-ence's perceptions.

My claim is that, in regard to the musical layering of songs, contestation in Euro-pean popular music has taken the form of rejection. On the one hand, it has rejected European concepts of musical work, and on the other, at least in certain genres, it has rejected (or absorbed only to a limited degree) American patterns.

Cases: Breaking Up with Tradition as Observed in European Punk Music

Understanding music as *opus perfectum* was initiated as early as the fifteenth century, and was deeply rooted in a European tradition. The minds of theoreticians of music, especially in the second half of the nineteenth century, were also captured by the idea of biological evolution and progress. Some intellectuals even used terms such as *Keim* (grain) and *Entwicklungsmotive* (evolutionary motif), while others discussed music in reference to the notion of *cellule-motif* (cell-motif). And yet, punk consciously defied these rules, cutting off the ideas of progress so characteristic of nineteenth and early twentieth-century definitions of music.

Despite its usage of strange visual imagery, and its coverage of provocative, political subjects, punk rejected the rich arsenal of elaborate musical devices. Primitivism and crudeness formed the basis of its aesthetic. Shortening the length of compositions, increasing the tempo of their deliverance, sustaining one level of dynamics without using any shades of piano, employing simple harmonic progressions, and sticking to a purely electric guitar format are all manifestations of punk's rejection of modern European musical conventions. Also, the manner of performance, with shrieking and aggressive vocals, represented the negation of the *bel canto* tradition. By stressing the ability to become a self-made musician, simply by playing two or three chords (without years of practice) and singing out of tune, punk performers undermined the whole tradition of European music-making seen as a profession. The Sex Pistols, for instance, used, in the words of Alan Moore, the "most normative organizational pattern in rock," relying on a simple riff, based on three major chords: C, F, and E.[43] Its harmony may not only be described as "poor" but also as predictable, reaching the function of Dominant in the middle of the verse. In other words, "insulting" the audience took place on two levels: not only in terms of the vocabulary used in the lyrics but also in terms of the musical offense to listener expectations. It is important to note that in "this pure form punk lasted only a couple of years,"[44] but post-punk failed to find adequate means of expressing protest. Early punk's limited musical palette gave way to a broader range of instrumentals, more advanced harmony, and a wider spectrum of topics (not so much politically charged), which, in turn, made the second wave of punk (post-punk and new wave) less rebellious.

The rejection of certain musical patterns interpreted as a sign of protest in popular music can be mirrored in other forms of rejection—for example, rejection of the English language.[45] I do not consider this in terms of preferring national languages over English so that the message of lyrics can be better understood by the local public. It is, in my opinion, often connected with a choice of specific sonoristic qualities. Let us take as an example the Slovenian band Laibach. They use German, not only because it is the language of supremacy and power that they try to convey in their artistic performances, but also because it has a very distinguished and identifiable "hard" timbre:

The widespread use of the German language and terminology ... is based on the specific evocative quality of the language which, to non-German speakers, sounds decisive, curt, domineering and frightening, and automatically activates traumas buried deep in sub-consciousness and history. The activation of the Germanic trauma in turn activates the undifferentiated, unidentified, passive, nightmare-filled Slavic dream.[46]

"De-anglicization" is certainly a way to convey content better to non-English speakers, but the sound of the language is just as crucial as a way of expressing liberation from Anglo-American "cultural imperialism."[47]

On the other hand, adaptation of Western musical patterns may be understood as a form of protest. In communist Bulgaria, Gypsy bands playing during wedding ceremonies often incorporated Western instruments and imported Western melodies, thus smuggling into ethnic Bulgarian music elements frowned upon by socialistic authorities.

Continuing European Tradition, as Against American Tendencies

Contesting and limiting the absorption of American pop music's legacy in performers' choice of musical devices can be also understood as a sign of (musical) protest. Richard Middleton says that American music was considered in Europe as exotic, a symbol of modernity, a manifestation of barbarian tendencies, or all three and more.[48] Hence, incorporating European traditions in the music of The Beatles, for instance, could merit consideration as externally-defined resistance. Musicologists decode resemblances of early songs by the Liverpool band with the tunefulness and folksiness so characteristic of German *Lieder* of the nineteenth century, represented by Robert Schumann or Johannes Brahms (whose songs were also described as "quasi–*volkstümlich*"[49]), among others. Aeolian cadences or modal flavor are undeniably typical of The Beatles, even if used unintentionally. Ian MacDonald claims that this influence comes from Anglo-Celtic folk music, as seen in harmonization in 4th and 5ths and verse-refrain organization. Although MacDonald criticizes what he calls "inapposite parallels with, for example, Schubert,"[50] he also talks about the romantic-sentimental qualities of McCartney tunes. The Beatles represented, after all, the tradition of Beat Music, which, at least in part, derives from late Romantic chromaticisms and triadic parallelism. Consequently, their songs are full of natural melodies and classical cadential patterns, often commencing with the chorus. Their cultivation of European traditions can be also deduced in their self-presentation, modelled as it was upon Romantic instrumentalists and professional musicians (with their neat outfits and on-stage behavior).

Continuing European traditions may take other forms. In electronic music, such groups as Tangerine Dream or Kraftwerk cherished the European legacy and fascination with machines and urbanization. Noise effects and the dehumanizing of voice are reminiscent of the decadent tendencies observed throughout the continent in the late nineteenth century, especially in the literature and painting of that period. The manner of performance adopted in industrial music (Cabaret Voltaire, Borghesia) is then the reflection of European sensitivity towards sound qualities and sonoristic effects. Thus, subversively, these singers "use lyrics, music and techniques of vocal delivery" to create a narrative that could be associated with protest[51] (attesting that "it is not just what is sung that is important,"[52] but also how).

In Lieu of an Ending

By identifying semantic conventions in reviews, Kembrew McLeod has analyzed how critics valorize pop music.[53] Of the various categories he identifies, "protest" does not appear, although notions that can be associated with contestation and opposition show up: aggressive intensity, violence, rawness, slickness, simplicity, personal expression, seriousness, authenticity, originality. Others, such as softness, simplicity, traditionalism, formulaic unoriginality or sweet sentimentalism, can also be employed while still manifesting signs of protest in popular music. In other words, all semantic dimensions used to describe popular music seem to fit the idea of how protest may be expressed. Perhaps it is so because the potential of rock lies in its ability to liberate. Its free use of the body and the voice,[54] its free application of instruments and harmonic logic, melodic patterns, etc., on top of politically-charged lyrics and the accompaniment of free behavior may always be decoded and deciphered by anybody as a form of protest.

Notes

1 Ian Peddie, ed., *The Resisting Muse: Popular Music and Social Protest* (Burlington, Vermont: Ashgate, 2006), xvii.

2 Neal Ullestad, "Diverse Rock Rebellions Subvert Mass Media Hegemony," in Reebee Garofalo, ed., *Rockin' the Boat: Mass Music and Mass Movements* (Boston, Massachusetts: South End Press, 1992), 44.

3 Jocelyn A. Hollander and Rachel L. Einwoher, "Conceptualizing Resistance," *Sociological Forum*, Vol. 19, No. 4 (2004): 545.

4 Einwoher, "Conceptualizing Resistance," 545.

5 Einwoher, "Conceptualizing Resistance," 536.

6 James, C. Scott, *Weapons of the Weak: Everyday Forms of Peasant Resistance* (New Haven, Connecticut: Yale University Press, 1985).

7 Einwoher, "Conceptualizing Resistance," 541.

8 Barbara Lebrun, ed., *Protest Music in France: Production, Identity and Audiences* (Burlington, Vermont: Ashgate, 2009), 3.

9 Veronique Helenon, "Africa on Their Mind: Rap, Blackness, and Citizenship in France,"

in *The Vinyl Ain't Final: Hip Hop and the Globalization of Black Popular Culture*, ed., Dipannita Basu and Sidney J. Lemelle (Ann Arbor, Michigan: Pluto Press, 2006), 151–166.

10 Anna G. Piotrowska, "Kategoria alternatywności w polskiej muzyce popularnej drugiej połowy XX wieku—próba typologii (The Phenomenon of Alternativeness in Polish Popular Music in the Second Half of the 20th Century—an Attempt at Typology)," in Małgorzata Woźna-Stankiewicz and Andrzej Sitarz, eds., *Muzyka jest zawsze współczesna. Studia dedykowane Profesor Alicji Jarzębskiej (Music is Always Contemporary)* (Kraków: Musica Iagiellonia, 2011), 321–333.

11 Robert Burnett, *The Global Jukebox: The International Music Industry* (London and New York: Routledge, 1996), 41.

12 Allan Moore, *Rock: The Primary Text: Developing a Musicology of Rock* (Burlington, Vermont: Ashgate, 2001), 194.

13 Peter Doggett, *There's A Riot Going On: Revolutionaries, Rock Stars, and the Rise and Fall of the 60s Counter-Culture* (New York: Canongate, 2007).

14 Brian Longhurst, *Popular Music and Society* (Cambridge: Polity Press, 1995), 172.

15 Deena Weinstein, "Rock Protest Songs: So Many and So Few," in *The Resisting Muse*, 10.

16 David Robb, ed., *Protest Song in East and West Germany since the 1960s* (New York: Camden House, 2007), 2.

17 Peddie, *The Resisting Muse*, xviii.

18 Weinstein, "Rock Protest Songs," 3.

19 Sean K. Kelly, "Communities of Resistance: Heavy Metal as a Reinvention of Social Technology," in Peddie, *The Resisting Muse*, 149–162.

20 Peddie, *The Resisting Muse*, xxiv.

21 Jacque Attali, *Noise: The Political Economy of Music* (Minneapolis, Minnesota: University of Minnesota Press, 1985), 19.

22 Attali, *Noise*, 21.

23 Neal Ullestad, "Diverse Rock Rebellions Subvert Mass Media Hegemony," in Garofalo, *Rockin' the Boat*, 45.

24 Peddie, *The Resisting Muse*, xxiv.

25 Ullestad, "Diverse Rock Rebellions," 34.

26 John Street, "The Pop Star as Politician: From Belafonte to Bono, from Creativity to Conscience," in Peddie, *The Resisting Muse*, 49–61.

27 Weinstein, "Rock Protest Songs," 5.

28 Weinstein, "Rock Protest Songs," 7.

29 Beatrice K. Otto, *Fools Are Everywhere: The Court Jester around the World* (Chicago: Chicago University Press, 2001), 35.

30 Otto, *Fools Are Everywhere*, 13.

31 Otto, *Fools Are Everywhere*, 33.

32 Tomi Huttunen, "Russian Rock: Boris grebenschikov, intertextualist," http://www.helsinki.fi/venaja/e-materiaali/mosaiikki/en1/th1_en.pdf, 1, accessed April 12, 2012.

33 Ilja Smirnov, *Prekrasnyj diletant: Boris Grebenshtshikov v sovremennoj istorii Rossii* (Moscow: Lean, 1999).

34 Huttunen, "Russian Rock," 1.

35 Garofalo, "Understanding Mega Events," in Garofalo, *Rockin' the Boat*, 18–19.

36 Krzysztof Lesiakowski, *Jarocin w obiektywie bezpieki* (*Jarocin in the Eyes of Security Police*) (Warszawa: Instytut Pamięci Narodowej. Komisja Ścigania Zbrodni przeciwko Narodowi Polskiemu, 2004).

37 Moore, *Rock: The Primary Text*, 195.

38 Garofalo, *Rockin' the Boat*, 2.

39 Richard Middleton, "Pop (IV, 1)," in Stanley Sadie, ed., *The New Grove Dictionary of Music and Musicians*, Vol. 20 (London: Macmillan, 2001), 114.

40 Alicja Jarzębska, "Model dyskursu o muzyce w ujęciu Philipa Tagga (Tagg's Model of Discourse on Music)," *Res Facta Nova*, Vol. 12, No. 21 (2011): 79, 81.

41 Sean Cubitt, "Maybellene: Meaning and the Listening Subject," *Popular Music*, Vol. 2 (1984): 215.

42 Lucy Green, *Music on Deaf Ears* (Manchester: Manchester University Press, 1988), 33–34.

43 Moore, *Rock: The Primary Text*, 194.

44 Middleton, "Pop (IV, 1)," 114.

45 Dave Laing, "Pop (IV, 2)," in *The New Grove Dictionary of Music*, 117.

46 Eda Čufer et al., "Concepts and Relations," in *Zemljopis Vremena / Geography of Time* (Umag: Galerija Dante Marino Cettina, 1994).

47 Edward Larkey, "Popular Music and National Identity in Austria," *Popular Music*, Vol. 11, No. 2 (1992): 151.

48 Middleton, "Pop (IV, 1)," 111

49 Susan Youens, "Words and Music in Germany and France," in Jim Samson, ed., *Nineteenth-Century Music* (Cambridge: Cambridge University Press, 2002), 467.

50 Ian MacDonald, "The Beatles," in *The New Grove Dictionary of Music*, 23.

51 Robb, *Protest Song in East and West Germany*, 2.

52 Longhurst, *Popular Music and Society*, 173.

53 Kembrew McLeod, "Between Rock and a Hard Place," in Steve Jones, ed., *Pop Music and the Press* (Philadelphia: Temple University Press, 2002), 96–107.

54 Middleton, "Pop (IV, 1)," 112.

21

FLOWERS MADE OF LEAD

Paths, Times, and Emotions of Protest Music in Brazil

Ricardo Santhiago

Figure 21.1 Fan of Brazilian rock group Sepultura holds a sign reading "We Refuse Resist" during an outdoor performance in Havana.

An Immersive Atmosphere

In 1972, Alaíde Costa, a Brazilian singer who has cultivated an essentially romantic repertoire and played a pioneering role in establishing the soft singing style that was the basis for bossa nova, participated in the Seventh International Song Festival sponsored by TV Globo, the largest television station in Brazil. Amid the so-called Years of Lead (1968–74; the most violent and repressive phase of the military dictatorship), Costa performed "Serearei," a song written by experimentalist musician Hermeto Pascoal. It was ranked high by the jury, despite the preference of the audience, unaccustomed to that sort of hermetic, puzzling, music. The presentation in the final show was a fiasco, eliciting massive booing. Moreover, the artists faced alleged "technical problems" and were removed from the stage during their presentation. The order had come from the police officers on duty, who had been told that Pascoal would include dozens of pigs in the onstage performance, which was considered a "subversive" act.[1] After clarifying the falseness of that information, the artists were allowed to return to the stage, once again being greeted with torrential boos. Costa decided to intervene, and took the microphone to explain the song's sound: "People, people ..." But before she even completed the phrase, her microphone was turned off and Costa, all nervous, threw it down and walked off the stage. The audience, surprisingly, gave her a loud, standing ovation. In the following days, the newspapers would explain that unexpected response: rumors held that Alaíde Costa had been "censored" because she had planned to read a "subversive manifesto" against the dictatorship. The myth of the politically committed artist (a role she had never played) replaced the facts.

This episode speaks volumes about the intertwining of music and politics during a particular period in Brazilian history—the military dictatorship that lasted from 1964 to 1985. In a repressive atmosphere, an uncommon ensemble of musical creations was lionized under the label of "protest music." The generation that carried out this laborious task has become legendary and to this day occupies the highest echelon of the music scene, with internationally renowned composer Chico Buarque de Hollanda as its most powerful symbol. However, this does not mean that music served as a vehicle for protests only during the military dictatorship. In a country historically marked by a high level of illiteracy, popular music has always been seen as a utilitarian device, as a social field able to shelter and also disseminate insurgent voices. Literary critic, composer and musician José Miguel Wisnik provides a key for understanding this phenomenon: he argues that the direct passage from an oral to a technological culture has made popular music, rather than print culture, a privileged path for discussing matters of public interest.[2]

On the long path traversed by Brazilian protest music, we might run into "Fala meu louro" ("Speak Out, My Parrot"), a 1920s samba written by composer Sinhô, which mocked Rui Barbosa's defeat in the previous year's presidential election; Lamartine Babo's biting comments on those adopting English-language words and expressions in his 1932 "Canção para inglês ver" ("A Song to Impress the English"); or Noel Rosa's magnificent sambas, such as the 1933 "Onde está a honestidade?" ("Where Do We Find Honesty?"), which questioned the upper classes about their morality. We can also find criticisms of racial prejudice in Wilson Batista and Marino Pinto's 1941 "Preconceito" ("Prejudice"). We meet Geraldo Pereira and Arnaldo Passos' samba "Ministério da Economia" ("Ministry of the Economy"), bashing the ministry created during President Getúlio Vargas' second term (1951–1954), on the basis of the dual meaning of the word ("economia") in Portuguese, meaning both "economy" and "savings." We might also encounter Billy Blanco's 1957 protest song against the moving of the federal capital from Rio de Janeiro to Brasília, in "Não vou pra Brasília" ("I'm Not Going to Brasília"). We notice that even bossa nova, usually deemed a lighthearted, frivolous genre, gave birth to songs such as Sérgio Ricardo's "Zelão," a dramatic description of the personal tragedy of a man who lost all his meager belongings during a flood in a favela. The use of art for political protest is not limited to popular music. A detailed inquiry[3] has demonstrated the loud voice of protest within the avant-garde, erudite, generation called Música Nova. Composer and performer Gilberto Mendes, who played a leading role in this heterogeneous scene, for example, created in 1984 one of his most famous protest pieces: "Mamãe, eu quero votar" ("Mommy, I Wanna Vote"), taking part in the broader campaign for the restoration of direct elections in Brazil, which was known as "Diretas Já" ("Direct Elections Now!").

Even if a researcher's sole task were to map the numerous incidences of protest music in Brazil, such an enterprise would prove virtually impossible. Thus, this essay is limited to a small number of these events. I am dealing with a highly uneven mass of works that could not be collected under a common aesthetic sign. Moreover, in my view, socio-political commitments do not help us in judging a work of art, although many supporters of protest music readily dismiss any other type of song as being "decadent," "mechanical," "apathetic," "numbed," "futile" and "selling out" (to the cultural industry).[4] Even protests against this sort of ideological policing of music have had their place in the sun, as in Adriana Calcanhotto's "Minha música" ("My Music").

The Slum's Got No Chance (Not Even in Protest Music)

In the early 1960s, after Sérgio Ricardo composed "Zelão," established artists opened their eyes to the theme brought to light by that song: poverty and difficult living conditions in slums, many times through the perspective of its inhabitants' emotions. Vinicius de Moraes and Tom Jobim, for instance, would compose "O morro não tem vez" ("The Slum's Got No Chance"), first recorded by Jair Rodrigues on his album *O samba como ele é* (*Samba as It Really Is*). But the main outlet for the great mass of people to express their demands was not bossa nova, but samba.

In fact, it was in the previous decade that the "critical samba" (*samba crítico*) arose, using as raw material the "tensions between populist, clientelist habits, and people's demands for better living conditions."[5] Luis Antônio and Jota Júnior in 1952 composed "Lata d'Água" ("Water Can"), describing the everyday life of Maria, who "does the laundry up there (in the slum)/struggling to earn her daily bread." Antônio is also the co-author of the classic "Barracão" ("Big Hut"), with Oldemar Magalhães. Ismael Silva's "Antonico," Geraldo Pereira's "Escurinho" ("Darky"), and Zé Keti's "A voz do morro" ("The Voice of the Slum") are other exemplary pieces of this tradition. Surprisingly, historical reviews of Brazilian protest music rarely mention this fruitful branch, nor similar ones such as the songs dealing with the severe droughts (*secas*) in Brazil's Northeast. Luiz Vieira protested against the government's blindness to this situation in "Se eu pudesse falar" ("If I Could Speak Out"), recorded in 1953.

The musical play authored by Tom Jobim and Vinicius de Moraes, *Orfeu da Conceição*, which premiered in 1956 in the Theatro Municipal do Rio de Janeiro, is often deemed Brazilian protest music's groundbreaking mark due to its setting in a favela, but its romantic melodies were far from foreshadowing the radicalization that was about to come. Theaters in the 1950s would present the play *Eles não usam black-tie* (*They Don't Wear Black-Tie*, 1958), by Gianfrancesco Guarnieri, and the *Missa Agrária* (*Agrarian Mass*) by the same author and the former bossa nova composer Carlos Lyra. Singers and musicians were converted into portrait painters of subjects such as the insurgent new nationalism, social justice, human suffering, and, particularly, agrarian reform—an old claim which by that time was considered imperative if Brazil was to solve problems in its economy, the exclusion of a large part of the population from the markets, and the rising level of rural–urban migrations.

At the dawn of the 1960s, one could observe Juca Chaves succeeding as a "*sui generis* artist, a witty, sarcastic critic of the Brazilian way of life"[6] in frisky songs such as "Presidente bossa nova" ("The Bossa Nova President") and "Tô duro" ("I'm Penniless"), mocking President Juscelino Kubitschek's developmentalist goals. Protest sounds, though, would shortly become gloomy, stodgy, following the tune of national politics. With Jânio Quadros' election to the presidency in 1960, and his inauguration and subsequent abdication in 1961, a major crisis unfolded. A significant part of society (particularly the Army) wanted to block the inauguration of leftist vice president João Goulart, but his supporters created a national campaign entitled Cadeia da Legalidade (Legality Chain), which succeeded in assuring his ascent to the presidency. Composers Carlos Lyra and Zé Keti created the "Samba da Legalidade" ("Legality Samba"), which proclaimed that their movement would not be silenced. In those turbulent times, local student councils, and regional and national student unions, closely connected to the Brazilian Communist Party, were in upheaval. In September 1961, the Center for Popular Culture (CPC) was created as a division inside the National Student Union (UNE), by leftist, committed, artists who believed it would be possible to enlighten and transform Brazilian society through artistic expression: music, theater, and cinema. Within the CPC, artists would express their idealism toward achieving a fair, egalitarian, society.

Carlos Lyra figured among the founders of the CPC. In 1963, he met poet Vinicius de Moraes and composed the "Hino da UNE" ("Ode to UNE"). That same day they also produced the memorable song "Marcha da Quarta-Feira de Cinzas" ("Ash Wednesday March"), a premonitory work that envisaged the destruction of personal liberties. Indeed, from 31 March to 1 April 1964, military dictatorship was introduced. Forbidden to speak out, people would look to music as the form par excellence which would engender and disseminate major questions about Brazil.

Politically Leaden Years as Musical Golden Years

Reasons abound to understand why the expression "protest music" has become an instant synonym for those songs that defied the Brazilian military dictatorship. That was probably the most critical moment of our modern history, but their temporal proximity also acts in another way: most of the major artists from that era are still alive and active. They are currently considered the greatest of our times.

The decade of 1960 is indeed a time shared by the establishment and persistence of the dictatorship and the prestigious, sophisticated, popular music scene in Brazil—a coincidence that contributed to "consolidate the popular song [canção] as a major vehicle of cultural and ideological agendas."[7] During that period, the field of popular music flourished thanks to new possibilities offered by the advent of television, especially through the musical competitions known as the Festivais de MPB. MPB, the acronym for "música popular brasileira" ("Brazilian Popular Music"), is not merely a word, but also a concept "that everyone knows what it means, but no one succeeds in explaining."[8] MPB refers to a selected set of works, singers, and authors; it does not evoke folk songs, but urban and commercial ones; it relates to a "set of aesthetic and ideological positions."[9]

The capstone of this process is the musical show *Opinião* (*Opinion*), written by Oduvaldo Vianna Filho, Armando Costa, Paulo Pontes, and Ferreira Gullar, and directed by Augusto Boal, an internationally renowned drama theorist and activist who died in 2009. The concert took place in 1964 and aimed to protest against the still-young dictatorship, and it brought together an urban composer (Zé Keti), a migrant from the Northeast (João do Vale), and an intellectualized upper-middle-class woman (Nara Leão) who shared the same "opinion." To paraphrase a pivotal song composed by Zé Keti, one may be subjected to all manner of physical abuse and privation, but that will not change the spirit.

Armed struggles, political actions, demonstrations: all were possible activities and, indeed, were carried out. But, starting with *Opinião*, music and protest became a united entity. The arts showed their ability to voice protests or to unload psychological oppression; popular songs had an advantage in that they (unlike cinema or theater, for example) did not demand huge investments, and could not be created or destroyed physically. Moreover, they had an enormous communicative power, as shown in 1965 during the First Festival of Brazilian Popular Music, supported by TV Excelsior, in which Elis Regina sang "Arrastão," composed by Edu Lobo and Vinícius de Moraes, a nationalist samba urging listeners to join together and act. Also in 1965, Augusto Boal and Gianfrancesco Guarnieri staged the musical show *Arena conta Zumbi*, with songs by Edu Lobo, featuring "Upa Neguinho" (also recorded definitively by Elis Regina), which told the story of a black boy urged to grow up in order to fight for liberty. Also at this time, Chico Buarque debuted with his first extended play, which included the lyrical "Pedro Pedreiro" ("Peter [the] Builder"), recounting the despair of a construction worker.

Still in his lyrical phase, Chico Buarque presented "A banda" ("The band") in the Second Brazilian Popular Music Festival, sponsored by TV Record—and reached first place, sharing the central podium with "Disparada," the most compelling protest song heard up to that time, performed by Jair Rodrigues. Composers Théo de Barros and Geraldo Vandré used the image of a knight to convey steadfastness and integrity in the face of censorship. In the same year, Vandré created another song, co-authored with Fernando Lona, and submitted it for the TV Excelsior festival. It was "Porta Estandarte" ("Standard Bearer"), then performed by Tuca and Airto Moreira, which exhorted the "people" to stand strong, offering "praise for people's union, for the collective singing, for the hope that 'the day' will come and bring happiness and peace for everyone—three elements construed as *topoi* of 1960s protest songs."[10]

Vandré was not a newcomer on the *festivais* scene.[11] He had already participated in the 1965 TV Excelsior festival as a singer, performing Chico Buarque's "Sonho de um carnival" ("Dream of Carnival"). With "Disparada," he reached new heights but his most glorious moment was yet to come—not without competition. In 1966, for example, Gilberto Gil and Torquato Neto released "Louvação" ("Worship"), which harshly criticized religion as a stultifying and blinding practice. Even Wilson Simonal, a showman mostly devoted to entertainment, recorded, in 1967, songs such as "Tributo a Martin Luther King" written by him and Ronaldo Bôscoli, and "Balada do Vietnã," composed by Elizabeth Sanches and David Nasser.[12] Chico Buarque de Hollanda would write, and debut in early 1968, his musical play *Roda viva* (*Wheel of Life*), which became notorious because its theater group was repeatedly assaulted by extremist right-wing groups who could not tolerate a play whose main song insisted: "we want to have a voice/to control our own destinies." But, from 1968 on, there would be no competition for Vandré: he would become the first icon of protest music.

Vandré's crowning moment came in September 1968 during the Third International Popular Music Festival, considered the most politicized of these events, for which Geraldo Vandré submitted his work "Pra não dizer que eu não falei das flores" ("Not to Say I Didn't Speak of Flowers"), known as "Caminhando" ("Strolling"), a leading symbol of the opposition to the military dictatorship. Performed by the composer himself, accompanied only by his guitar, the "most radical protest song, with a strong revolutionary plea"[13] immediately gained an audience. Against the predictions of TV Globo, which thought it had no chance of qualifying, the song reached the finals. But, with a three-point advantage, the winner was Tom Jobim and Chico Buarque's "Sabiá" ("Thrush"), which approached the theme of exile but had no explicit political overtones. When replayed by Cynara and Cybele, the song was strongly booed. Then Vandré, a long-time admirer and colleague of Jobim and Buarque, uttered his famous phrase: "Life is not just about festivals." Indeed Vandré himself was not confined to huge stages—he used to tour throughout Brazil, seeking to raise the consciousness of the population with his music, particularly "Caminhando," which summed up the national feeling: "The one who can make it happen/ Doesn't wait for an accident."

An Accident Halfway There

The military dictatorship would not tolerate, for long, the music of political and social protest. In a hyper-ideological scene, artists would soon lose the *carte blanche* they had been offered. The first persecutions were directed toward politicians and unionists, but singers would no longer be the owners of their own voices. Music was a nuisance not only for its critical contents, but also because it used to encourage popular gatherings, seen as potentially dangerous. The "festivals era," which allowed for a creative flow and presented to a broad audience previously unknown artists, would not end soon—but it would be deprived of its provocative impulse.

On December 13, 1968, Institutional Act Number 5 (AI-5) was issued, suspending democratic rights in Brazil. Blatantly targeting the arts, the AI-5 de-politicized the musical scene. Disruptive artists were banned from festivals, and their songs had to be subjected to censorship's prior approval. Leading artists would leave Brazil, either forcibly exiled or travelling voluntarily. Chico Buarque would go to Italy; Caetano Veloso and Gilberto Gil, to London; Edu Lobo, to the United States. Even Geraldo Vandré, who had quickly become an outstanding artist, went to Chile and France. He was probably the most reclusive of them all: he renounced his own songs, refused to give interviews, started to work as a lawyer, and rarely appeared in public. Furthermore, he would write a song in tribute to the Brazilian Air Force, an episode that kick-started a conspiracy theory that he had been co-opted by the U.S. Central Intelligence Agency (CIA).

The newly-installed authoritarian regime put an end to political energies that spread nationwide—but social criticism did not cease.[14] Here and there, fine pieces of protest music appeared. And, more important still, the censorship system inspired creativity on the part of composers, eager to outsmart the overseers. The repressive structure itself reinforced the need to explore words' and sounds' creative resources. Within the Tropicália movement,[15] Capinam and Gilberto Gil would compose the rumba "Soy loco por ti América" ("I'm Crazy about You, America"), a hidden homage to Che Guevara, recently murdered. Caetano Veloso would juxtapose images and symbols into a critical description of Brazilian social reality in his legendary "Tropicália." Before going into exile in London, Gilberto Gil would compose "Aquele abraço" ("Cheers"), saying goodbye to his country.

Other musicians would engage in protest through their music. Sidney Miller would sound hopeless in "Cicatrizes" ("Scars"). In "Nada será como antes" ("Nothing Will Be as It Was"), Milton Nascimento and Ronaldo Bastos were concerned with the "tomorrow to come," alluding to the unpredictable fate of Brazilian exiles abroad. This song would gain a sequel in "Fé cega, faca amolada" ("Blind Faith, Sharpened Knife"). Marcos Vale and Paulo Sérgio Vale, bossa nova heirs, would compose "Viola enluarada" ("Moonlight Guitar"), whose lyrics evoked armed struggle. One of the most inventive artists was probably the most systematically pursued by the dictatorship: Chico Buarque. After his 1969 exile in Italy, he came back to Brazil in the next year hoping to find a better situation. When Buarque realized that he had acted in haste, he injected into his work a highly critical, less lyrical, aspect. His song "Agora falando sério" ("Now I'm Serious") is emblematic of this transition, but it was "Apesar de você" ("In Spite of You") that changed the composer's path. Disguised as a note to an overbearing woman, the song was addressed to then-President Médici. Surprisingly, the lyrics were approved by the censors and allowed to be released. Its resounding success (more than 100,000 records were sold) caused an intensification of the political persecution aimed at Chico Buarque. He faced a difficult situation: almost each and every composition would be vetoed. Buarque started to use nicknames, such as Julinho da Adelaide, to register his songs, but he was quickly exposed. He had to record a number of his songs in instrumental versions, as happened with "Vence na vida quem diz sim" ("Successful Is the One Who Says Yes"), a daring song co-written with Ruy Guerra that evoked the tortures conducted under the military government. In 1973, Buarque and Gilberto Gil would have their microphones turned off during a show in which they were to present the song "Cálice" ("Chalice"), a word that has the same pronunciation as *cale-se* (shut up), in an episode that ironically evoked the lyrics themselves. Finally, in 1975, Chico Buarque had no choice but to record an LP with songs written by other composers. Its provocative title came from a Paulinho da Viola samba: *Sinal fechado* (*Red Light*).

The "disciplinary action" aimed at Chico Buarque did not succeed in silencing him or his contemporaries. Belchior would write a cry against passivity in "Como nossos pais" ("Like Our Parents"). Ivan Lins and Vitor Martins would express hope for the future in "Abre alas" ("Heralds") and "Começar de novo" ("Make a Fresh Start"). João Bosco and Aldir Blanc would warn people of the uncertainty of political liberalization, initiated with amnesty in 1978, in the song "O bêbado e a equilibrista" ("The Drunk Man and the Tightrope Walker"). Later on, Taiguara released an album entitled *Canções de amor e liberdade* (*Songs of Love and Freedom*). Milton Nascimento and Wagner Tiso composed "Coração de estudante" ("Student's Heart"), dedicated to a student killed by the regime. Caetano Veloso created his defiant song "Podres poderes" ("Putrid Powers"). Even after its termination, in 1985, the dictatorial regime left its mark. In 1987's "Carta à República" ("Letter to the Republic"), Milton Nascimento and Fernando Brandt created a moving, poignant song with imagery of a better future for the children of Brazil.

All at Once: Voices for the Culture, Voices against Globalization

The question asked in the song "Carta à República" would be answered by the disenchanted and disillusioned generation of Brazilian rock—the BRock,[16] a strongly politicized movement. Their songs, critical and negative, were directed toward a broad range of themes. The "tomorrow" long awaited by the 1960s generation was afflicted with a deep disenchantment, reinforced by the harsh economic recession of the early 1980s. Born in the federal capital Brasília, BRock members mostly came from educated upper-middle-class families. They criticized the bourgeoisie, while being themselves bourgeois. Renato Russo writes in "Geração Coca Cola" ("The Coke Generation") of the junk that his peers consume, while Cazuza in "Burguesia" ("Bourgeoisie") distances himself from the decadent middle class.

Many rock bands had protest songs in their repertoire—such as Titãs, with "Televisão" ("TV") or "Comida" ("Food"), or Ultraje a Rigor, with "Inútil" ("Useless"). The most acerbic group was Legião Urbana, mainly due to its vocalist, Renato Russo. Notable amongst their songs are "Que país é este?" ("What Country Is This?"), "Descobrimento do Brasil" ("Discovery of Brazil"), "Ainda é cedo" ("It's Still Early"), and "Soldados" ("Soldiers"). But, from the mid-1980s, BRock drank their own poison; protest was exhausted and became trivialized. Successful formulas were exploited ad nauseam, and replaced by the lightweight pop rock of bands such as Kid Abelha, Paralamas do Sucesso, and RPM.

Contemporary to BRock, the Vanguarda Paulista movement developed a predominantly cultural form of protest. Its artists were victims of a new situation in terms of the cultural industry; they were despised by major music companies, which had became increasingly conservative and used to focusing on the reproduction of pretested patterns rather than investing in rising artists. Vanguarda Paulista had to create its own structure for producing and circulating its work,[17] for which it depended on the falling costs of producing records. In its wake, myriad protests took place. The outstanding singer Tetê Espíndola used to literally scream against the destruction of nature on albums such as *Gaiola* (*Cage*) and *Birds*. Group Tarancón sang for social justice and was closely connected to the Nueva Canción, a folk-music movement that took place in the 1970s and 1980s in a number of Latin American countries.[18]

Moreover, a substantial number of protest songs were produced by Vanguarda Paulista's leading artists: the group Língua de Trapo approached the subject of unionism in "Xote bandeiroso" and the standardization of culture in "Xingu disco"; Arrigo Barnabé criticized consumerism in "Kid Supérfluo, consumidor implacável"; the group Premeditando o Breque pointed out the problems of the city of São Paulo in the ironic "São Paulo, São Paulo" (parodying Sinatra's "New York, New York").[19] Beyond these, the main exponent of Vanguarda Paulista, Itamar Assumpção, was frequently characterized as "acursed artist." And there was no lack of reasons: he was strongly combative in his cultural protest, which led him to stay outside the mainstream. Until his death in 2002, he was considered "marginal," though more recently his talent has been acknowledged. Fenerick mentions the song "Cultura Lira Paulistana" as a superb protest piece, for it openly criticizes the decline of taste and the poverty of contemporary artistic creations. "Help us, Elis Regina," Assumpção invoked.[20]

Since the 1980s, once in a while an eminent MPB personality has appeared, giving protest music a shot. In 1993, Caetano Veloso and Gilberto Gil composed "Haiti," comparing Brazil's situation to that impoverished country. Chico Buarque in 1997 recorded his compositions "Levantados do chão" ("Raised from the Floor") (along with Milton Nascimento) and "Assentamento"[21] ("Settlement") for a CD enclosed in a book authored by photographer Sebastião Salgado,[22] devoted to the struggles of the landless movement.

Strangely, the most important political event of that decade (the impeachment of President Fernando Collor de Mello, in 1992) did not inspire a particular soundtrack. It is true that the group Legião Urbana released the 8-minute song "Metal contra as nuvens" ("Metal Against the Clouds"), written by Renato Russo, symbolizing the disappointment of those who believed in Collor's promise of a modern country, and also "Reggae," protesting against the confiscation of saving accounts (poupanças) ordered by Collor. Local groups released songs and got minor appreciation, as happened with Skank and its song "In(dig)nação"[23] ("In[dig]na[c]tion"), and with Garotos Podres and its "Fernandinho Viadinho" ("Fernandinho Little Fag"). Nonetheless, there is no doubt that the hymn of Collor's impeachment was "Alegria, alegria" ("Happiness, Happiness"), a song by Caetano Veloso released in the late 1960s.

Themes for protest music proliferated, drawing on current issues and trends such as globalization, multiculturalism, human rights, diversity, as well as the political arena. A Vanguarda Paulista heir, composer Chico César stands out as the greatest lyricist broaching themes such as migrations and racial prejudice. One of his best CDs is *Respeitem meus cabelos, brancos* (*Respect My Hair, You White People!*)—the name is a pun on the popular expression "respect my white hair," that calls for respect for older people. Like Chico César, the Mangue Beat movement emerged in Northeast Brazil, led by Chico Science, addressing poverty in urban peripheries, and even mentioning as their inspiration revolutionary icons such as Zapata, Sandino, the Black Panthers, and the Brazilian figures Lampião and Antonio Conselheiro.[24]

However, the scepter of protest music belongs, since the 1990s, to rap, which deals with the concrete results of poverty and criminality exacerbated in the 1980s. The Brazilian face of the universal hip hop movement was enhanced particularly in the city of São Paulo, where it still offers firsthand testimony on the miserable and violent life in the *favelas*. Rap became the spokesman for criticisms of education, racial prejudice, unemployment, social inequalities, mass media culture, and lack of opportunities. In the form of acerbic chronicles or life stories, rap lyrics employ the vocabulary and diction of the poorest classes, and its sonority is disturbing, aggressive, intended to cause discomfort.

Racionais MCs is the most emblematic group of this trend. Their extremely famous rap "Diário de um detento" ("A Prisoner's Journal") recounts the life of a prisoner inside the legendary, now destroyed, Carandiru prison. Criticizing the culture industry, they sold at least one million copies of the CD *Sobrevivendo no inferno*

(*Surviving in Hell*), putting themselves in a dilemma, given that rappers "try to ignore the culture industry, while aiming to preserve the 'purity' of political, social, cultural claims."[25] In addition to Racionais MCs, prominent rap artists are DJ Hum, Thaíde, and groups Clã Nordestino, Facção Central, and Planet Hemp. The former vocalist of Planet Hemp, Marcelo D2, now has a successful national solo career. Like him, Gabriel O Pensador reaches the entire Brazilian population with famous protest songs such as "Lôraburra" ("Miss Stupidblondwoman"), against the opportunistic behavior of "gold-digger" women; "Indecência military" ("Military Indecency"), against compulsory conscription in the armed forces; and "Lavagem cerebral" ("Brainwashing"), against prejudice directed toward migrants and racial minorities, as well as a number of songs defending the use of marijuana.

Demands and Feelings Persist

Protest proved to be an integral part of twentieth-century Brazilian music, not limited to what was sung under the military dictatorship. It has often been favored where inflamed political emotions are shared by its authors and listeners, who understand music as a connection between those two poles and even between a current, unpleasant, situation and a positive, utopian, future. Protest music remains viable because of the predisposition of artists, musicians, and singers to use music as a way of voicing criticism, and because there is an audience that embraces it.

We find protest in affective memories of people who think "the really good songs were those of the 1960s, 1970s," reinforcing the magnetism of that generation and calling into question the very inventiveness of an artist in the absence of a clear enemy. Protest is also found today in memorable presentations of the group Capital Inicial during the 2011 Rock in Rio festival, performing Renato Russo's "Que país é este?" and speaking out against "oligarchs that still maintain major newspapers under censorship," addressing their performance to the politician José Sarney and the Congress. We find protest as pastiche in *axé* music (a musical genre made for dancing, linked to Bahian carnival); As Meninas (The Girls) claim that they invented "protest *axé* music" with a song named "Xibom bom bom." Anyone who watches its video clip on YouTube will notice that the lyrics, discussing the oppression of the poor by the rich, are an absolutely secondary element, subordinated to the sex dance performed by As Meninas.

We also find Zélia Duncan singing against postmodern buzzwords in "Pré-pós-tudo-bossa-band" ("Pre-post-everything-bossa-band"), co-written with Lenine, and the group Os PoETs commenting on the politics of personalism in Alexandre Brito, Ricardo Silvestrin, and Ronald Augusto's "O Brasil Não É" ("Brazil Is Not"): "[Brazil is not the property of] any marshall/of the short Getúlio [Vargas]/of the stud [Juscelino] Kubitschek (…)/of FHC [Fernando Henrique Cardoso] (…) of Luiz Inácio [Lula]." We also find Madan and Frei Betto's tribute to the militant priest Frei

Tito, tortured under the dictatorship; Zeca Baleiro's "As meninas dos Jardins" ("The Girls from Jardins") and its lethargic criticism of the lack of personal and cultural exchanges in the contemporary city; and group O Rappa's cry in "Minha alma (A paz que eu não quero)" ("My Soul [The Peace I Don't Wanna Have]"), against security measures that promote isolation and fear.

In the end, why are so many artists invested in protest music? Songs and their lyrics have not put an end to hunger, brought down military dictators, or eradicated racial prejudice. Not even the "triste Bahia" sung by baroque poet Gregório de Mattos in the seventeenth century has been completely overcome. We do not learn enough from history, as composer Moisés Santana puts it in the lyrics to "Compromisso" ("Commitment"), one of his combative, humanist songs. He may admit that "not even music has a point," in his "Terra em trânsito" ("Earth in Transit"), but the message of his "Do mesmo lugar" ("From the Same Place") is unmistakable: anything can be achieved, but a collective awakening—a rise above the chaos—has to happen first.

Notes

1 As told by Alaíde Costa in her oral history interviews with the writer, which are published in the book *Alaíde Costa: Faria tudo de novo* (São Paulo: Imprensa Oficial, 2013).
2 José Miguel Wisnik, "Algumas Questões de Música e Política no Brasil," in Alfredo Bosi, ed., *Cultura Brasileira: Temas e Questões* (São Paulo: Ática, 1987), 114–123, and José Miguel Wisnik, "The Gay Science: Literature and Popular Music in Brazil," *Journal of Latin American Cultural Studies*, Vol. 5, No. 2 (1996): 191–202.
3 Teresinha Prada, *Vanguarda e Utopia nos Mares do Sul* (São Paulo: Terceira Margem, 2010).
4 Terms employed in discussion groups on Brazilian music in the social network *Orkut*. See: www.orkut.com.br.
5 Marcos Napolitano, "A Música Brasileira na Década de 1950," *Revista USP*, No. 87 (2010): 56–73.
6 Jairo Severiano and Zuza Homem de Mello, *A Canção no Tempo: 85 anos de musicas brasileiras, Vol. II: 1958–1985* (São Paulo: Ed. 34, 1998), 40.
7 Marcos Napolitano, *História & Música* (Belo Horizonte: Autêntica, 2005). See, by the same author, Marcos Napolitano, *"Seguindo a Canção": Engajamento Político e Indústria Cultural na MPB (1959–1969)* (São Paulo: Annablume/Fapesp, 2001). See also the concept of "critical song" developed in Santuza Cambraia Naves, *Canção Popular no Brasil* (Rio de Janeiro: Civilização Brasileira, 2010).
8 Marcos Napolitano, "A Canção Engajada nos Anos 60," in Paulo Sérgio Duarte and Santuza Cambraia Naves, eds., *Do samba-canção à tropicália* (Rio de Janeiro: Relume Dumará/Fapesp, 2003), 127.
9 Carlos Sandroni, "Adeus à MPB," in Berenice Cavalcante, Heloisa Starling, and José Eisenberg, eds., *Decantando a República v. 1: Outras Conversas sobre o Jeito da Canção* (Rio de Janeiro/São Paulo: Nova Fronteira/Fundação Perseu Abramo, 2004), 23–35.
10 Napolitano, "A Música Brasileira," 56–73.

11 For a comprehensive analysis on Geraldo Vandré's work, see Dalva Silveira, *Geraldo Vandré: A Vida Não se Resume em Festivais* (Belo Horizonte: Fino Traço, 2011).

12 Yet, for a long time, Wilson Simonal was marginalized in Brazilian music and history, given the suspicions that he had cooperated with the military regime by informing on his colleagues. Starting in the year 2000, his image has been rehabilitated, but he is still controversial. For more information, see the biography Ricardo Alexandre, *Nem Vem que Não Tem: A Vida e o Veneno de Wilson Simonal* (São Paulo: Globo, 2009).

13 Jairo Severiano, *Uma história da música popular brasileira* (São Paulo: Ed. 34, 2008).

14 In a lengthy book, Paulo Cesar de Araújo showed that other musical styles, less prestigious than the MPB, such as the *música brega* (kitschy, cheesy music), also engaged and had problems with the military regime in the 1960s and 1970s. See Paulo Cesar de Araújo, *Eu Não Sou Cachorro, Não: Música Popular Cafona e Ditadura Militar* (Rio de Janeiro: Record, 2002).

15 On the tropicalist movement, see, Christopher Dunn, *Brutality Garden: Tropicalia and the Emergence of a Brazilian Counterculture* (Chapel Hill, North Carolina: The University of North Carolina Press, 2000).

16 On BRock, see Arthur Dapieve, *BRock, o Rock Brasileiro dos Anos 80* (São Paulo: Ed. 34, 1995) and Ricardo Alexandre, *Dias de Luta: O Rock e o Brasil dos Anos 80* (São Paulo: DBA, 2002).

17 On the aspects of "independent music" developed by Vanguarda Paulista, see Gil Nuno Vaz, *História da música independente* (São Paulo: Brasiliense, 1988) and Laerte Fernandes de Oliveira, *Em um porão de São Paulo: O Lira Paulistana e a produção alternativa* (São Paulo: Annablume/Fapesp, 2002).

18 Tânia da Costa Garcia, "Tarancón: Invenção Sonora de um Brasil Latino-Americano," *ArtCultura*, Vol. 8, No. 13 (2006): 175–188.

19 José Adriano Fenerick, *Façanhas às próprias custas: A produção musical da Vanguarda Paulista (1979–2000)* (São Paulo: Annablume/Fapesp, 2007).

20 There would be myriad other possible examples, as analyzed in my work: Ricardo Santhiago, "Com quantos nãos se fez um som: Itamar Assumpção e a indústria fonográfica" (unpublished research report available for consultation at Comissão de Pesquisa, Pontifícia Universidade Católica, São Paulo, 2005).

21 Adélia Bezerra de Menezes, "Utopia Renitente: Levantados do Chão/Assentamento," in *Decantando a República v. 3: A cidade não mora mais em mim*, eds., Berenice Cavalcante, Heloisa Starling, and José Eisenberg (Rio de Janeiro/São Paulo: Nova Fronteira/Fundação Perseu Abramo, 2004), 115–122.

22 Sebastião Salgado, *Terra* (São Paulo: Companhia das Letras, 1997).

23 Graziela Vianna, "Os vários sentidos da música," in *Proceedings of the V Congresso da Seção Latinoamericana da Associação Internacional para o Estudo da Música Popular* (Rio de Janeiro: IASPM-LA, 2004).

24 Maria Rita Kehl, "Da Lama ao Caos: A Invasão da Privacidade na Música do Grupo Nação Zumbi," in *Decantando a República v. 3*, 141–156; and Herom Vargas, *Hibridismos musicais de Chico Science e Nação Zumbi* (Cotia, SP: Ateliê, 2007).

25 Arnaldo Daraya Contier, "O rap brasileiro e os Racionais MC's," *Proceedings of the First Simpósio Internacional do Adolescente* (São Paulo: Scielo Proceedings, 2005).

22

SONGS FOR FREEDOM

Music and the Struggle against Apartheid

Mark Malisa and Nandipha Malange

Figure 22.1 Peter Gabriel performing "Biko" at the "Give One Minute of Your Life to AIDS" concert in Cape Town.

Perhaps one of the realities that points to the significance and power of anti-apartheid music is the way musicians and artists were treated by the apartheid government. Many, like Miriam Makeba, Hugh Masekela, and Abdullah Ibrahim were exiled. Others were imprisoned, while some, like Vuyisile Mini were hanged. Their words were deemed dangerous because they were a critique of the injustice of apartheid at a time when the project of modernity was consolidating itself. In many respects, anti-apartheid songs were a call to revolutionary cultural, psychological and political combat. At the same time, it was a music that affirmed a different form of life as compared to the official government version.

One of the distinguishing characteristics of anti-apartheid songs is that they owe their existence or composition to "traditional composers." That is, most of them belonged to "the people." As such, even though apartheid was experienced at a personal level, it was also a public/collective dehumanization and discrimination against nonwhites. Anti-apartheid songs were often a collective response to the circumstances of the day. However, there are differences among music from South Africa, Europe, and the Caribbean.

Most of the current literature on South African music focuses on the dancing style and structure of the music, often in an effort to draw comparisons with African American soul or jazz.[1] Even in instances where and when connections are made to African American music, the literature misses out on the radical protest inherent in jazz.[2] Indeed, much like jazz, anti-apartheid music was an invitation to fight against a system which dehumanized blacks globally. The role of reggae, for example, is rarely studied in connection with the struggle against apartheid.

There could be a variety of reasons for the dearth of such literature. Among these include the possibility that most of the literature is by scholars who do not speak or understand the African languages in which most of the songs are sung.[3] But it is also true that African languages are marginalized when it comes to scholarship, and in the process, African life is also made invisible.[4] The rush to draw comparisons and similarities with European styles of music is reflective of a scholarship that also sees the genesis of African philosophy with the encounter or arrival of the Anglos.[5] It was not unheard of for European philosophers to write that Africa had no viable philosophy,[6] and that Africa indeed was outside history.[7]

However, the absence of significant scholarship on anti-apartheid music also contributes to making the role of the armed struggle in South Africa invisible, or making it easier to gloss over the violence so characteristic of apartheid. Indeed, some of the writers give a silent nod to such a trend. Coplan[8] barely makes reference to revolutionary songs (although he alludes to his being a victim of apartheid). Even Charles Hamm, in his monograph, *Afro-American Music, South Africa, and Apartheid*, sees in African music a "basis for non-violent struggle against a society determined to crush African aspirations."[9] Both understate the armed nature of the effort to throw off apartheid, begun in 1961 with the African National Congress' decision to do just that. Apartheid's end came through the barrel of a gun, with many battles waged by uMkhonto weSizwe. Likewise, many of the "Frontline States" were victims of military aggression by South Africa's armed forces, often backed by NATO.

It is also true that post-apartheid discourses of reconciliation[10] make it difficult for many to talk frankly about the nature of apartheid itself, as well as the songs for freedom. "Dubul' ibhunu," made popular during the height of the guerrilla warfare, for example, has been recently associated with hate speech, and likely played a role in the fall of ANCYL president, Julius Malema. Likewise, "Umshini Wami," a song that President Zuma used as a rallying call for his presidency, has almost been taken off the airwaves in South Africa. There seems to be a deliberate and systematic silencing of the songs of freedom, all in the interest of national healing and reconciliation. It is as if to have reconciliation and healing, those who fought apartheid have to forget their story, their songs. Indeed, at the birth of the post-apartheid dispensation, intellectuals like Njabulo Ndebele and Albie Sachs began to critique the role of art and culture in national struggle and debate, concluding that "our members should be banned from saying that culture is a weapon of struggle."[11] Even Ndebele observed that the new task was to "free the entire social imagination of the oppressed from the laws of perception that have characterized apartheid society."[12] The philosophy of the oppressed was equated with sloganeering. What could be the motivation for silencing the songs that fueled the struggle against apartheid? There is a stark contrast with the views of Amilcar Cabral[13] and Aime Cesair[14] on the role of culture in political struggles for liberation.

In contrast to Albie Sachs and Njabulo Ndebele, Nadine Gordimer views music as central to the struggle (against apartheid) and the reconstruction efforts subsequent to the legal abolition of apartheid. For Gordimer, music cannot be reduced to sloganeering or unreflective thought since it is a form that is based on a concrete awareness of the historical conditions of the people.[15] As such, the call to "forget" about the songs for freedom is not universal in South Africa, especially since economic apartheid remains largely unchanged.

Even for former South African President, Nelson Mandela, songs were an essential component of the struggle, often bridging the gap between theory and motivation by capturing the emotions through the use of reason. After the Defiance Campaign, Mandela called for armed engagement with the apartheid government:

> At the end of the day, I said, violence was the only weapon that would destroy apartheid …. At that point I began to sing a freedom song, the lyrics of which say, 'There are the enemies, let us take our weapons and attack them.' I sang this song and the crowd joined in.[16]

But this was not the only occasion when Mandela highlighted the importance of songs in the struggle. During the Congress of the People's meeting at Kliptown when the Freedom Charter was adopted, songs helped the occasion go smoothly. When the government soldiers surrounded those congregated and threatened them with guns, "the people responded … by singing Nkosi Sikelel' iAfrika."[17] During the early part of the treason trials, the captured prisoners continued to sing "Nans' indod' emnyama Strijdom, Bhasobha nans' indod' emnyama Strijdom."[18] Of course, with each new apartheid head of state, the song changed. For example, it later became "Nans' indod' emnyama Verwoerd."[19] Music, as such, gave those who were fighting apartheid something they could hold on to in the face of a common enemy. According to Mandela:

> The curious beauty of African music is that it uplifts even as it tells a sad tale. You may be poor, you may only have a ramshackle house, you may have lost your job, but that song gives you hope. African music is often about the aspirations of the African people, and it can ignite the political resolve of those who might otherwise be indifferent to politics. One merely has to witness the infectious singing at African rallies. Politics can be strengthened by music, but music has a potency that defies politics.[20]

At the same time, many who see connections between African American music and anti-apartheid musicians seem to be unaware of the fact that when the two joined forces to protest the nature of global apartheid, they were punished. For example, when Miriam Makeba married Stokley Carmichael, Makeba's shows in the United States got cancelled.[21] In the end, both had to leave the United States. In other words, those who collaborated in opposing global apartheid were not welcome in South Africa and/or the United States.

In the following sections I describe the nature of apartheid, analyze a selection of anti-apartheid songs, and give an outline of the vision of freedom in post-apartheid music. Some of the songs make reference to individuals who were fighting against apartheid, while others point out those who were enforcing apartheid. Although, to a certain extent, apartheid was unique to South Africa, the practice of racism was near global in so far as encounters between Europeans and nonwhites were concerned. As a result, some of the songs allude to the global reach of apartheid as well as the ill-effects of colonialism across the African continent. A close reading and analysis of the songs/lyrics reveals the extent to which Africans were perceptive of the extent to which Europe and Europeans had declared the destruction of Africans as central to the colonial enterprise, a fact substantiated by the practices and policies of the apartheid government.

Apartheid

Descriptions of apartheid vary and reflect a broad response to the nature of racism and imperialism, or the spread of white civilization in South Africa. Legal apartheid ended in 1994. In brief, apartheid was legalized racism or institutional white supremacy. It reflected the most perfect form of capitalism by refusing to conceal its dependence on the exploitation of black labor and resources while simultaneously seeking to destroy black life and culture. Morrow describes apartheid as:

A form of oppression which has 'disempowered' its victims. By persistently treating them as objects of policy, by refusing to see them as wholly and rightfully 'human', as beings who have moral titles and standing, Apartheid has dehumanized its victims; their dignity and self-esteem as persons, and their intellectual and moral confidence and autonomy, have been damagingly undermined.[22]

Apartheid was built on the myth of a superior European civilization and the belief that European ways were the best with regards to creating a truly better world for all of humankind (even as blacks were being dislocated and robbed of their land and natural resources). Descendants of Europe were entitled to the privileges that came with their heritage, and non-Europeans were bound to minister to whites. The purity of whites would be best preserved by minimizing or eradicating contact with nonwhites while educating them on the role of European civilization.

As an ideology of white supremacy, apartheid constructed a hierarchy of what it meant to be human based on race. People who originated from European countries or Western Europe were deemed to be the best and most civilized. Next to the Europeans were Indians or people from Asian countries. After the Indians came Coloreds or all bi-racial people. At the bottom were blacks or Africans. Under apartheid, each group had to live separate from others.

Songs of Freedom: Pan-Africanism

Almost every phase of the struggle against apartheid had its song. However, throughout the struggle, "Nkosi Sikelel' iAfrika" was the rallying song against apartheid. But "Nkosi Sikelel' iAfrika" was also a recognition of the shared experience that Africans faced with regard to the colonial encounter. That is, apartheid and its problems were experienced across the continent. It is perhaps significant that "Nkosi Sikelel' iAfrika" was composed in 1897, less than two decades after the Berlin Conference where various European countries parceled out Africa as if the humanity of the Africans did not matter.

"Nkosi Sikelel' iAfrika," in many respects, tugged at the pan-African nature of the challenges faced by the continent, and in many ways made a mockery of the partitioning of Africa. While the continent had been divided by Europeans into different European colonies, for many Africans, Africa was one, with a number of artificial borders created by the Europeans. "Nkosi Sikelel' iAfrika" was a prayer for God to bless the whole continent, rather than single colonial creations. As such, at the birth of the anti-apartheid struggle was also a realization that the colonial problem in South Africa was something that affected the rest of the continent. Consequently it is of little surprise that at least four countries adopted the song as their national anthem. Among them included Zambia, Zimbabwe, and Tanzania. Originally composed by

Mqhayi and Sontonga of South Africa, the song resonated with the experiences of other African nations during the colonial period.

Although some colonial powers tolerated the singing of "Nkosi Sikelel' iAfrika," not many might have been aware of the fact that by the nature of its invocation, Africans had given up on using European developed institutional or democratic practices for ending apartheid/racism. What Europeans thought of and saw as the project of modernity/enlightenment, or bringing civilization to the 'dark continent' was, in fact, the destruction of Africa. The prayer/plea in "Nkosi Sikelel iAfrika" implied that there could be no faith invested in systems developed by Europeans, since none of the systems/institutions were designed with the wellbeing of Africans at heart. The redemption and salvation of Africa would come from the mercy of God, rather than European intervention. "Woza Moya, Sikelela" was a plea for God to intervene on behalf of Africans, and as such an invitation for judgment. "Nkosi Sikelel' iAfrika" captures the complexity and depth of African languages and their ability to "philosophize" about the human condition from an African perspective. It simultaneously veils and unveils the callous nature of the colonial experience without sacrificing the historical content and context or the emotions associated with said encounter. Because it was composed and sung in different African languages even within the context of South Africa, the song made a mockery of the European claim that tribalism was the scourge of Africa.

n unsophisticated listener might read or misread "Nkosi Sikelel' iAfrika" as a call for nonviolent opposition to apartheid. South Africans had taken up arms against European invaders in 1879 and 1896. On both occasions, the Europeans had prevailed on the strength of superior weapons (guns against spears, or umkhonto).[23] South Africans had fought the Boers, and the British. But when the Dutch and the British united under the banner of whiteness, a military uprising by South Africans seemed doomed to fail. The defeat of the Zulus had a lasting impression on many, including Mahatma Gandhi[24] who began to question the nature of western/European civilization, especially in light of the massacre of defenseless African women and children in 1896. For a significant period of time, South Africans refrained from armed engagement and resorted to, among other strategies: civil disobedience and strikes. As an appeal for God to intervene, "Nkosi Sikelel' iAfrika" also points to the dehumanization of Africans by Europeans as well as the theft of land and material resources by European settlers.

Armed Engagement

With the legal adoption of apartheid as a national policy in 1948, it became apparent that peaceful protest had run its course. By 1961 the African National Congress (ANC) had started taking measures toward using military violence to counter the violence of apartheid. In February 1962 the ANC presented its case to the Pan African

Freedom Movement for East, Central and Southern Africa. MK (*uMkhonto weSizwe*) cadres began training in Tanzania, Zambia, Mozambique, Russia, Cuba, and various Warsaw Pact countries. Needless to say, most of the countries that gave support for military training believed in the political philosophy of socialism.

The nature of the armed struggle waged by the ANC was understood within the context of a quest for freedom. Although the struggle took place within a well-defined pan-African context, some of the songs made it clear that there was a sense of "exile." "Sangena kwamanye amazwe, laph' okungela, baba lomama silandel' inkululeko" was an indication of the cost of the war in terms of familial ties as well as living together with parents and extended families. The desire and need for freedom far outweighed the comfort of witnessing parents being ill-treated by the apartheid regime.

Perhaps two of the songs that highlight the urgency of the call for armed engagement are "Dubuli iBhunu" and "Umshini Wami. Dubuli iBhunu" ("Shoot the Boer") was not just a call to shoot Boers. In fact, the song makes it clear that phenotype/melanin was not always an indicator of one's attitude toward the struggle. The reader, however, has to understand and deconstruct the use and meaning of "iBhunu." Umkhonto weSizwe cadres were well aware of the organizational structures and personnel in the African National Congress. Indeed, one of the field commanders of the armed struggle was Joel Slovo, originally from Eastern Europe. A few Afrikaners, including Bram Fischer, where committed to the armed struggle. As such, "Dubuli iBhunu" was a call to shoot racist people since for the most part, racism and apartheid were one and the same thing. Many were aware that some Europeans were committed to destroying racism. But "Dubli iBhunu" was also a direct command to shoot racists.

"Umshini Wami" ("My Machine Gun") pointed out the weapon of choice in the anti-apartheid struggle. But the struggle was born of the realization that the apartheid regime had no conscience when it came to blacks in South Africa (and the sub-region). Victims of apartheid were aware that South African armed forces had no qualms with shooting unarmed black civilians or enforcing apartheid laws. The murders of black children during the Soweto Uprising as well as the Sharpeville Massacre were evidence of the ways such soldiers were committed to apartheid policies. The militarization of the state machinery also made it easier justify the use of violence against blacks. But South African soldiers also invaded and bombed neighboring countries they suspected of providing refuge for victims of apartheid, including Mozambique, Zambia, Angola, and Namibia. "Umshini Wami" was thus a call to defend through armed engagement.

Race and Racism

Race and racism have played, and continue to play an important role in South Africa. South Africans also had many encounters with Europeans and as such were in a position to know *that no one is born white: one becomes white.* As such, within the context of South Africa, whiteness was a political and economic union formed by Europeans on the basis of oppressing non-Europeans. Under apartheid, the Dutch, the British, the German and other European invaders decided to become white, and declared themselves as different from, and better than all the others. The creation and use of separate amenities for whites, including accommodation, hospitals, transportation, and schools has to be understood in the context of race and racism.

For most South Africans, in the process of creating whiteness, Europeans lost part of what made them human beings since whiteness itself was based on a rejection of the full humanity of non-Europeans. Many of the anti-apartheid songs reified the abstraction of dehumanized whites, often equating them with dogs. "Amabhunu azizinja" in "Senzeni na" reflected the extent to which racists did not care about the humanity of nonwhites. It was not uncommon to come across signs reading 'no blacks and no dogs allowed' during the days of apartheid. Because racists were not willing to acknowledge the humanity of black people, black people in turn were forced to suspend their belief in the humanity of racists. *Senzeni na* juxtaposed the humanity of blacks with the undeserved oppression and violence visited upon blacks by whites. Like "Nkosi Sikelel' iAfrika," "Senzeni na" does not hide the issue of race in understanding the problem of apartheid, or the solution to the problem. Briefly stated, the issue was racism. And race became the lens through which almost everything was ordered. But the arrangements were such as to advantage whites, leaving blacks with very few alternatives for redress.

The two songs ("Nkosi Sikelel' iAfrika" and "Senzeni na") hint at what could be described as political theology as well as a theology of African or black liberation. Apartheid, as well as Europeanized Christianity had colluded to describe blacks as cursed by God and destined to be hewers of wood for whites. The religious beliefs and practices of whites were in harmony with regard to the treatment of blacks. South African blacks were quick to understand that whites had used religion or a perverted version of Christianity to oppress blacks. "Isono sethu kubamnyama" was a call for blacks to realize that they had been decreed as less than human by whites, not because of anything they had done or not done, but by virtue of being born black. How were blacks to reconcile themselves to such a theology?

However, blacks were cognizant of the fact that the encounter with God antedated the encounter with modernity. In "Senzeni na" and "Nkosi Sikelel' iAfrika," blacks expressed their humanity in ways that challenged the theology in apartheid Christianity. Because generally presented as cursed and sinful by white Christianity, under apartheid, the humanity of blacks was of no value, especially to whites. "Isono sethu kubamnyama" was also a call for black unity. As long as one was black, they were at the mercy whites and had no rights. One could easily argue that race did not care about class divisions when it came to blacks. In other words, it did not really matter what one had acquired or learned, or not acquired and not learned: one was condemned because they were black. Whiteness and apartheid theology were grounded on the dehumanization and destruction of blacks, spiritually, physically, and economically.

In its various manifestations and ways of operating, apartheid was very clear on the choice of its victims and its beneficiaries. The deliberate and systematic destruction of black life occurring in South Africa under apartheid did not differ much from the general world-wide disposition of whites toward blacks. Under apartheid or a system based on white supremacy, it was sinful to be a black person. "Isono sethu kubamnyama."

Women

An oversimplified (mis)reading of the history of the armed struggle might gloss over the role played by women. In addition, the divorce between Winnie and Nelson Mandela has led to the marginalization of Winnie (and African women) in post-apartheid narratives. However, a close reading of stories about women reveals the revolutionary power held by women, which they used for the common good. The saying, "wathinta umfazi, wathinta imbokodo" captured the strength and unity of women, particularly black women.

Even within the context of the struggle for national liberation, Nelson Mandela saw women as more perceptive than men with regards to what was needed to remove oppression. Reflecting on the role of the Federation of South African Women, he observed that it "was way ahead of the thinking of even the ANC at the time, because it brought together women of all races, classes and religious affiliation."[25] With regard to protesting the discriminatory laws passed by the apartheid government, Mandela observes that in general, "women were courageous, persistent, enthusiastic, indefatigable, and their protest against passes set a standard for antigovernment protest that was never equaled."[26] Their protest was non-violent and trans-racial at a time when the ANC was still addressing the issue of the role of Europeans in the liberation struggle. There are numerous instances when and where women display their independence from men, and on occasions even Mandela found he had to step aside. When he tried to intervene during one of the protest marches he recollects being "told in no uncertain terms that the matter was the women's affair and that the ANC-as well as husbands-should not meddle."[27]

Many Africans were aware of the suffering that black women faced in South Africa, and this was captured in song. In "Thula Mama," Vusi Mahlasela sings about African women who stood against state brutality while protecting their children and grandchildren. In many ways, children witnessed the suffering of their parents and sought to comfort them. Instead of parents soothing their parents, it was the children who had to convince the elders that a better tomorrow would come. According to Mahlasela, the apartheid state machinery routinely imprisoned African children and adolescents, especially towards the anniversary of the Soweto Uprising.[28] Women, including pregnant women were not spared. "Thula Mama," as it were, reflects the ways in which even children were conscious and cognizant of the brutal nature of apartheid, and had to quickly 'grow up' and assume the role of comforters to their mothers and parents.

Although, in general, African women raised their children to be peaceful and respectful of elders, there was an unambiguous militant resistance to racism/apartheid. "Umam' uyajabula masishay' amabhunu" was an acknowledgement of the explicit approval that women had in seeing the youths resist the violence of apartheid with their own violence as well.[29] While "Thula Mama" offered comfort and solace to mothers, "umam' uyajabula masishay' amabhunu" was a pointer to what made mothers/women happy—violent resistance to apartheid. According to Mahlasela, it was possible to hear a "voice more powerful than the enemy bombs/ the song that washed our lives and the rains of our blood."[30]

Composed and sung by mostly African women who worked as domestic servants and maids, "Shonamelanga" ("Sheila's Day") implored white women to consider the needs of black children who were "abandoned" by their mothers who were working for the white women.[31] In essence, black women "ran" the white households partly by raising white children, nursing white children, doing domestic labor (including cooking and laundry as well as yard-work and gardening). While white women seemed to care about the health and wellbeing of their children, they seemed to care very little, if at all, about black children

For many African women it was difficult to reconcile the suffering they endured with the comfort that the vast majority of white women enjoyed during the apartheid era. In other words, it was not easy to relate their concern for their own children with the brutality, murder, and dehumanization that was perpetuated and perpetrated by the system. It was almost impossible for white women to pretend they did not know about the evil of apartheid/racism.

Nelson Mandela and Steve Biko (Commercial Protest Music)

To a great extent, the anti-apartheid protests and the history/story of Nelson Mandela are intertwined. A significant number of the protest songs were also about Nelson Mandela, but most songs did not place a messianic aura on the prisoner of apartheid. Rather, most just called for his release, and the release of all political prisoners. As such, the personal and the collective blended, without one diminishing the other. What the apartheid government had done to Nelson Mandela and other political prisoners, it had done to most Africans in general. The same is true also with regard to Steve Biko.

Of significance in the song "Biko" by Peter Gabriel are the references to the systematic violence perpetrated by the apartheid government, as well as the nature of racism. Under apartheid, according to this song, the murder (legal/illegal) of blacks was part of business as usual. It was not rogue forces that murdered Biko, but part of the government agencies of maintaining law and order.[32] The slaughter of blacks by whites was not accidental; hence in a world with blacks and whites, it was mostly blacks who were being killed by whites. Granted that the murder of blacks was systematic, the immorality of the apartheid government is made explicit in the killing of Biko. The murder of blacks was an everyday occurrence (business as usual) for the apartheid government. Although it was only Blacks who were being murdered, Peter Gabriel implies that whites, even those outside South Africa, could not choose to ignore the plight of blacks in South Africa. Even if they opted to be silent, they were also witnesses to the slaughter of the innocent. Most of the songs performed and composed outside South Africa are generally in English (or other European languages). However, "Biko" by Peter Gabriel made it clear that sometimes non-Africans could also capture the apartheid experience (without distorting or appropriating it as their own). Without making it their own personal experiences, such artists were also able to give the victims of apartheid a name and a face. "Biko" is perhaps one of the few anti-apartheid protest songs that intimates at alternative political and economic systems/ideologies as a viable solution to apartheid. "I can only dream in red" can be easily read as an allusion to the socialism/communism with which the South African based anti-apartheid movements (whether African National Congress or Pan African Congress) identified. Consequently, the song can also be understood as a message to the West, whose government structures unequivocally supported apartheid: the murder of blacks by the apartheid government left South Africans with fewer options other than to embrace socialism/communism as one of the possible solutions.

There is a significant difference between the songs about Mandela performed and composed by South Africans, and those composed and performed outside South Africa (sometimes by those who happened to be sympathetic to the anti-apartheid protest). In "Nelson Mandela" by the Specials, the song appeals to the non-existent conscience of the apartheid government to "free Nelson Mandela, I'm begging you please to free Nelson Mandela," ("Nelson Mandela," by Specials). But, other than the amount of time that Nelson Mandela had spent in prison, the song rarely delves into the brutal nature of apartheid (other than political prisoners). Even "Mandela Day" by Simple Minds[33] makes little mention of the nature of apartheid/racism, but it calls for, and anticipates Mandela's release from prison.

It is possible to argue that the "pressing and specific" issues that one hears in the protest songs by black South Africans are glossed over or made inaudible and invisible in most protest songs composed by those simply sympathetic to the anti-apartheid struggle. Erased from such songs are issues of land and resources as well as race. An unintended (or perhaps intended) consequence of focusing on the imprisonment and release of Nelson Mandela was to equate/associate the release of Mandela from prison with the ending of apartheid. That is, the moment of his release, within such a framework, also marked the end of apartheid. Such songs, although they highlighted the plight of political prisoners, often neglected the economic nature of apartheid and racism.

In listening to the protest songs about Mandela by black South Africans, one hears more details and specifics about the problems in South Africa. In addition, the songs hint at the nature and spirit of ubuntu[34] by blending the collective with the personal. In "Bring Him Back Home," Hugh Masekela[35] ties the freedom/freeing of Nelson Mandela to political and economic independence. In addition, Masekela points out his wish to see Nelson Mandela reunited with his family (Winnie Mandela) and home (Soweto) and the nation in general. The imprisoning of political leaders did not affect only the prisoners: families were torn apart. In many respects prison and exile seemed to be interchangeable in the sense that families could not be together.

South African musicians who were not exiled also produced music to protest apartheid. But these musicians were also aware of the fact that the apartheid government had no qualms about killing/imprisoning/exiling anti-apartheid activists. Consequently such musicians often used coded verses to transmit their messages and the sentiments of the people. "We Miss You Manelo" by Chicco Sello Twala (1988)[36] expressed the people's longing for Nelson Mandela. Mandela had been in prison for over twenty years by that date. Could the apartheid government be trusted on its words regarding the whereabouts of Nelson Mandela? By 1989 there was no denying that the military conflict had escalated, whether between the apartheid government and uMkhonto We Sizwe, or the senseless slaughter by the Inkatha Freedom Party *impis*. "Papa Stop the War"[37] can be read as an indication of the belief that Nelson Mandela could intervene and stop the war. The unnamed "papa" is absent/missing, but he could heal the racial venom that was tearing the nation apart and was behind the war. Needless to write, the appeal could not have been to the apartheid government since its policies were based on the subjugation and dehumanization of blacks.

That most of commercial protest music focused on Mandela did not necessarily mean that musicians were blind to the general suffering of the 'nameless and faceless' victims of apartheid. Some musicians rarely made their political ideologies explicit, and yet their music had veiled criticism of apartheid. In "Bazobuya" ("They Will Return"), the Soul Brothers captured the many ways apartheid had destroyed part of the fabric that held African communities intact.[38] The arrest and imprisonment of politicians had left women and mothers abandoned, and children were suffering. However, those who were imprisoned were not in a position to contribute to the upkeep of their children or families, in contrast to those whose parents were free and working under the apartheid regime.

Although Ladysmith Black Mambazo is not often associated with protest music, some of their songs also point out the inhumanity of apartheid, especially with regard to causing problems related to crime and poverty. "Homeless" is one of the songs that protests the existing conditions even without mentioning apartheid by name.[39] To many South Africans familiar with forced removals and dispossession, migrant labor and the deliberate creation of shackles and squatter camps, the song reflected the extent to which apartheid had made many Africans homeless in the country of their birth. Even for commercial musicians, the need for survival and self-preservation led to taking a principled stand against apartheid, even if at times that stand was not apparent to the undiscerning eye. The terror brought by the apartheid government demanded silence and compliance from the victims. Instead, through music, the victims found a way to tell their story, to protest.

Notes

1 Carol Muller, *South African Music: A Century of Traditions in Transformation* (Santa Barbara, California: ABC-CLIO, 2004), 22–23, and Louise Meintjes, *Sound of Africa: Making Music Zulu in a South African Studio* (Durham, North Carolina: Duke University Press, 2003), 52–54.

2 Scott Saul, *Freedom Is, Freedom Ain't: Jazz and the Making of the Sixties* (Cambridge, Massachusetts: Harvard University Press, 2003), 123–145.

3 Mark Malisa, *(Anti) Narcissisms and (Anti) Capitalisms: Education and Human Nature in the Works of Mahatma Gandhi, Malcolm X, Nelson Mandela, and Jurgen Habermas* (Boston & Rotterdam: Sense Publishers, 2010).

4 Ngugi wa Thiongo. "Europhone or African Memory: The Challenge of the Pan-Africanist Intellectual in the Era of Globalization," in Thandika Mkandawire, ed., *African Intellectuals: Rethinking Politics, Language, Gender and Development* (Dakar, Senegal: CODESRIA Books, 2005).

5 Thiongo, "Europhone."

6 Ninian Smart, *The World's Religions* (Cambridge: Cambridge University Press, 1998).

7 Hegel, as quoted Enrique Dussel, "Eurocentrism and Modernity," in Jacques Derrida, *On Cosmopolitanism and Forgiveness* (London: Routledge, 2001).

8 David Coplan, *In the Time of Cannibals: The Word Music of South Africa's Basotho Migrants* (Chicago: University of Chicago Press, 1994), 1–30.

9 Charles Hamm, *Afro-American Music, South Africa, and Apartheid* (New York: Institute for Studies in American Music, 1988), 14.

10 See, Antjie Krog, "This Thing Called Reconciliation …' Forgiveness as Part of an Interconnectedness-Towards-Wholeness," *South African Journal of Philosophy*, Vol. 27, No. 4 (2008), 353–366.

11 Ulrike Ernst, *From Anti-Apartheid to African Renaissance: Interviews with South African Writers and Critics on Cultural Politics Beyond the Cultural Struggle* (New Brunswick & London: Transaction Publishers, 2002), 16.

12 Njabulo Ndebele, *South African Literature and Culture* (Manchester, United Kingdom: Manchester University Press, 1989), 65.

13 Amilcar Cabral, "National Liberation and Culture," February 1970, at http://historyisaweapon.com/defcon1/cabralnlac.html, accessed June 11, 2012.

14 Aime Cesaire, *Discourse on Colonialism* (New York: Monthly Review Press, 2000).

15 Nadine Gordimer, *Telling Tales* (New York: Picador, 2004).

16 Nelson Mandela, *Long Walk to Freedom: The Autobiography of Nelson Mandela* (Boston, Massachusetts: Back Bay Books, 1994), 157.

17 Mandela, *Long Walk*, 173.

18 Mandela, *Long Walk*, 202.

19 *Amandla! A Revolution in Four-Part Harmony*, DVD, directed by Lee Hirsch (New York: Artisan Entertainment, 2002).

20 Mandela, *Long Walk*, 178.

21 Hank Bordowitz, *Miriam Makeba: Noise of the World: Non-Western Musicians in Their Own Words* (Brooklyn, New York: Soft Skull, 2004), 245–260.

22 W. Morrow, "Aims of Education in South Africa," *International Review of Education*, Vol. 36, No. 2 (1990): 176.

23 John Laband, *Historical Dictionary of the Zulu Wars* (New York: Scarecrow Press, 2009), 5.

24 Mahatma Gandhi, *Gandhi: An Autobiography: The Story of My Experiments with Truth* (Boston, Massachusetts: Beacon Press, 1997).

25 Nelson Mandela, *In His Own Words* (Boston, Massachusetts: Little, Brown and Company, 2003), 474.

26 Mandela, *Long Walk*, 220.

27 Mandela, *Long Walk*, 222.

28 Vusi Mahlasela, "Thula Mama," © 2007 Mino wa Tswane Music.

29 *Amandla!* 2003.

30 Mahlasela, "Thula Mama."

31 *Amandla!*, 2003.

32 Peter Gabriel, "Biko" © 1980 Charisma Records.

33 Simple Minds, *Mandela Day* © 1988, Emi Music.

34 See, Praeg, Leonhard, "An Answer to the Question: What Is [ubuntu]?" *South African Journal of Philosophy*, Vol. 27, No. 4 (2008), 367–385.

35 Hugh Masekela, "Bring Him Back Home" © 1987 Warner Brothers.

36 Sello Chicco Twala, "We Miss You Manelo" © 1988 Philips Music.

37 Sello Chicco Twala, "Papa Stop the War" © 1988 Philips Music.

38 Soul Brothers, "Bazobuya" © 1996 Gallo Music.

39 Ladysmith Black Mambazo "Homeless" © 1990 Gallo Music.

Further Reading

Lucky Dube, "Together As One" © 1988 Gallo Music.

Michael Onyebuchi Eze, "What is African Communitarianism? Against Consensus as a Regulative Ideal," *South African Journal of Philosophy*, Vol. 27, No. 4 (2008), 386.

Paul Gready, "The Sophiatown Writers of the Fifties: The Unreal Reality of Their World" *Journal of South African Studies*, Vol. 16, No. 1 (March 1990), 4.

Ulf Hannerz, Sophiatown: The View from Afar, *Journal of Southern African Studies*, Vol. 20, No. 2 (June 1994).

Miriam Makeba, *Sophiatown* © 1959 RCA Records.

Hugh Masekela, *Stimela* © 1993 Triloka Records.

Junior Murvin, *Apartheid* © 1986 Greensleeves.

Steel Pulse, *Tribute to the Martyrs* © 1979 Island Records.

Pedro Alexis Tabensky, "The Postcolonial Heart of African Philosophy," *South African Journal of Philosophy*, Vol. 27, No. 4 (2008): 287.

The Congos, *Apartheid* © 1986 RAS.

Peter Tosh, *Apartheid* © 1977 Island Records.

Malcolm X, *By Any Means Necessary* (New York: Pathfinder, 1992).

23

"SORROW, TEARS, AND BLOOD"

Fela Anikulapo Kuti and Protest in Nigeria

Saheed Aderinto

Figure 23.1 FelaKuti with Africa '70.

This chapter examines the protest music of Fela Anikulapo Kuti (1938–1997), variously described as Africa's "most controversial musician" and "most challenging and charismatic popular music performer."[1] He assumed multiple and often contradictory identities, ranging from rebel, martyr, visionary, revolutionary, and hero, to playboy, rock star, social pervert, troublemaker, and trickster.[2] Scholars from the humanities and social science have adopted diverse approaches in studying his music and career. Indeed, he is arguably Africa's most studied musical artiste of the twentieth century.[3] Fela's protest music is grounded in the idiom and realities of Africa's post-colonial challenges of underdevelopment, corruption, military dictatorship, and abuse of rights—to mention but a few. A dogged fighter to the core, he spent the last twenty-five years of his musical career exposing—through music—the impact of neo-colonialism on Africa's development, while situating Africa and Africans within global politics and cultural production. In fact, he believed in the power of music in instilling political correctness and sparking a revolution.[4] Fela did not just criticize African leaders and Western collaborators for their leadership ineptitude: he launched an unsuccessful and unpopular bid to become Nigeria's president during the 1970s and 1980s.

Fela's musical career did not start in Nigeria. He formed his first band "Kola Lobitos" while studying at Trinity College of Music, London, between 1958 and 1963. His London clientele included African and West Indian students who enjoyed his uncommon blend of jazz and "highlife music," the latter being a genre that features a fusion of many different African traditional style, Latin guitar, jazz, and brass-band music. In 1963, he relocated his band to Lagos, Nigeria, but failed to impress audience who were reluctant to substitute the highly popular highlife music with Fela's awkward experimentation, which was neither jazz nor highlife.[5] Fela probably decided to blend jazz with highlife because he could not compete with well-established highlife artistes of the period, such as Victor Olaiya and Bobby Benson, among others. In addition, Fela's style could not favorably compete with Juju, another popular urban music with superstars such as King Sunny Ade and Ebenezer Obey.[6] However, a breakthrough came in the early 1970s, when he invented "Afrobeat," a style based on chant, call and response vocals, complex interactive rhythms, American styled funk, and traditional rhythms.[7]

Although most of his songs dealt specifically with political situation in Nigeria, his audience and imaginations transcended the physical and cultural geography of Africa's most populous country. He realized that Black people, regardless of where they live, experienced similar forms of institutionalized oppression, hence his message appealed to the sentiments of individuals and groups across the African continent and beyond. Fela committed his career to putting Africa on the world map by internationalizing the everyday social realities that people confronted. His resistance music operated at three interrelated levels. First, he perceived himself as a teacher/preacher, instructing and educating the public about issues around poverty, Western cultural implantation, neocolonialism, and underdevelopment.[8] Second, he channeled his artistic energy directly towards criticizing the Nigerian authorities for abuse of rights, maladministration, and corruption.[9] Lastly, he attempted to become Nigeria's president by floating an unregistered political party named Movement of the People (MOP) during Nigeria's Second Republic (1979–1983).[10] But this rough schematization of Fela's musical expression is inadequate. He also composed hit songs dealing with sex, love, gender, and the impact of foreign religions on indigenous lifestyle.[11] For the purposes of this chapter, we shall be dealing with the first two typologies since they boldly speak to his philosophy as a resistance artiste and his self-imposed responsibility as the "liberator of the masses."

Political and Sociocultural Context to Fela's Protest Music: Military Dictatorship, Underdevelopment, and Re-Discovering Africa

Fela's musical career was shaped by his family background, the political situation in Nigeria from the 1960s, and, lastly, his exposure to Black Power and the ideologies of the civil right movement during a trip to the United States in 1969. Fela's mother, Funmilayo Ransome Kuti (FRK, 1900–1978), was his earliest role model for "social protest, opposition to repressive authority, a distrust of the ruling class, and the use of ridicule and sexual innuendo as political tools."[12] She was a renowned women's right activist and one of Nigeria's most fearless anticolonial figures. She founded the Abeokuta Women's Union and led women to protest against several draconian policies of the colonial regime. Aside local politics and her campaign for the improvement of women's welfare, FRK was well known internationally for supporting labor movements. She travelled extensively in communist countries during the 1960s and 1970s, when the Cold War degenerated into large scale violence across the globe. In 1970, FRK was awarded the Lenin Peace Prize by the Supreme Soviet of the USSR in recognition of her "noble activities for many years in promoting friendship and mutual cooperation between Nigeria and the Soviet Union."[13] She died in 1978 from injuries she sustained when armed military men invaded Fela's home during one of the numerous violent attacks against his criticism of government ineptitude. Fela's father (Israel Oladotun Ransome Kuti) was a well-known labor leader and the pioneering president of the Nigerian Union of Teachers. In sum, Fela grew up learning about issues of social justice and state-sponsored violence against often defenseless citizens.

Fela's musical career was also shaped by the political situation in Nigeria and, indeed, Africa, from the 1960s. The immediate post-independence period in Africa was characterized by enormous crises of underdevelopment. Military dictatorship consumed legitimate democratic governments which were frequently accused of corruption and ethnic bigotry.[14] Illegitimate military regimes, civil wars, and political instability shattered the hope that the newly independent countries would use their enormous human and natural resources to launch sustainable development projects after political disengagement from European colonial rule.[15] With particular reference to Nigeria, the two successive military coups of 1966, which paved the way for the intervention of the military in politics, was followed by a thirty-month civil war between July 1967 and January 1970. Military dictatorship in Nigeria, as elsewhere in Africa, intensified the abuse of rights and violence against the citizenry. But, more importantly, the embezzlement of state resources and corruption impoverished the people, created a vicious cycle of social unrest, crime, and public disorder. As we shall see, Fela's main detractors were the military leaders, and their local and international collaborators who aided the looting of the nation's treasury. Unlike many African leaders, who used civil wars, military takeover of government, and guerilla warfare to seek justice from the state, Fela's only weapon was music.

Fela's visit to the US in 1969 left an indelible imprint on his ideology towards injustice and the common problems facing Black people, both in continental Africa and the diaspora. He attended several meetings with civil rights leaders and members of the Black Panthers, took part in protests, and witnessed the racial discrimination against Black people in America. He was also exposed to the works of leading African Americans, such as Malcolm X and Karenga Mualani. Although Fela was born and raised in Nigeria, Afrocentric consciousness did not mean much to him until he experienced how African Americans were reconnecting to their African roots. According to Niyi Coker, in one of the most detailed biographies of Fela, "It is right to say that Fela actually discovered Africa and all it had to offer from as far away as Los Angeles."[16] Through an African American lady, Sandra Izsadore (formerly Smith), who would later become his lover, Fela embarked on a re-Africanization which manifested in his attitude, music, and lifestyle.[17] Scholars have argues that his US trip significantly influenced his rebel posture after 1970.[18]

Fela returned from his US trip in 1970 and began a process that would completely change the face of his musical career and African popular culture. First, he invented Afrobeat, and changed the name of his band "Kola Lobitos" to "Nigeria 70" and, later, "Africa 70," in a bid to highlight the African component of his style.[19] At the same time, he began to raise the "clenched fist" of the Black Power salute. He also changed the name of the club in which he performed from "Afrospot" to "African Shrine." Before, during, and after performances, he would perform rituals eulogizing prominent African leaders and pan-Africanists like Kwame Nkrumah and Sekou Toure. The renaming of his band and site of performance transcended the desire to openly identify with African traditional religion and culture. He believed that resistance to all forms of state violence must start from self-reclamation of African dignity and pride. Hence, highlighting one's Africanness or a re-Africanization supplied the language and energy required to protest against underdevelopment and the de-Africanization caused by colonialism and the introduction of Christianity and Islam, the two most popular foreign religions. His first protest music, which was titled "Black Man's Cry" and composed in 1971, extolled the beauty of Black skin, while decrying modern slavery and servitude.[20]

"Sorrow Tears and Blood": The Abuse of Human Rights and the Military Dictatorship

Fela did not begin to have direct confrontations with the Nigerian government until 1974, when he criticized the military government for its policies.[21] The government of General Yakubu Gowon (1966–1975) was not only dictatorial, by not returning Nigeria to democratic rule, but it inflicted enormous pain on the people. It was not unusual for Nigerians to be harassed and assaulted on the streets by military personnel under the pretext of maintaining law and order. Fela found the government's violence against its own people disgusting. He granted critical interviews to both the print and electronic media, and was gradually gaining attention as a public "intellectual."

By 1974, the authorities were tired of accommodating Fela's public criticism. Checking or arresting him did not present them with significant problems. Fela and his band members openly used marijuana (a controlled substance) both on stage and in their private residence; the Nigerian Indian Hemp Decrees of 1966 provides for a fifteen year term of imprisonment for anyone convicted of using marijuana. In addition, Fela indulged in open and reckless sexual conduct with underage girls, most of whom were runaways.[22] Both the authorities and some of the educated elite saw his public sexuality as a threat to mainstream ideals of sexual morality and respectability. If the government and elite frowned at his commoditization of the female body and his almost naked appearance on stage, millions of Nigerians enjoyed his social deviance, the provocative sexual humor of his lyrics, and images such as those on the album "Expensive Shit" (1975), which featured photos of over two dozen breast-displaying women.[23] Fela's quest to "un-silence" sexuality through his sexually revealing appearance and lifestyle earned him an eccentric fame in a sexually conservative society that considered sex as a subject and performance reserved for the "private" space.

On 30 April 1974, Fela's residence on Agege Motor Road was invaded by over fifty policemen and soldiers under the pretext of enforcing marijuana and child protection laws. While adults and male residents were jailed, the underage girls were taken to the Welfare Department for rehabilitation. Fela was arrested, released, and rearrested several times between 1974 and 1976. So bad were the injuries he sustained during a November 1974 arrest that he had to be hospitalized before he was formally charged to court. The circumstances of his arrest and his experience under the Nigerian criminal justice system influenced the titles and lyrics of three songs, namely "Alagbon Close" (1975), "Expensive Shit" (1975), and "Kalakuta Show"

(1976). "Alagbon Close" was the location of the police station in which he was held, while Kalakuta was the name of the section of the jail in which he was kept. "Expensive Shit" euphemizes the desperation of the police in establishing Fela's use of marijuana by collecting and examining samples of his feces. These three songs detailed the conditions of Nigerian jails, the manner in which suspects were treated, and the violence perpetrated by the police and the criminal justice system in general. In "Alagbon Close," Fela sang about how taxpayers' money was used to procure equipment, such as guns, which were, in turn, employed in terrorizing them. Satirically and confrontationally, Fela sang about the unprofessional manner in which law enforcement officers handled often law abiding citizens.[24]

It is important to note that Fela did not introduce protest music into Nigerian popular culture. The hundreds of Nigerian cultures have diverse methods of criticizing the authorities, dating back centuries. Among the Yoruba, Fela's ethnic group, performances by such masquerades as Gelede helped check the excesses of community leaders.[25] Traditional Yoruba artistes enjoyed "poetic freedom" to criticize the chiefs and call their attention to issues of public importance. Fela borrowed elements of the Yoruba culture of artistic resistance and blended it with his own in order to create a distinctive vocabulary and performance appropriate to the audience and political landscape of the 1970s. However, unlike the Yoruba protest music, which was mostly satirical, Fela, in addition to satirical composition, adopted a boldly confrontation style. If Yoruba protest songs rarely mentioned names when criticizing authorities, and were mostly proverbial, Fela would mention the names of important law enforcement officers and leaders, and accuse them of corruption and hypocrisy.[26] He would call them such unprintable names as "thieves" and "rogues."[27]

"Alagbon Close," "Expensive Shit," and "Kalakuta Show" were all highly successful songs, aired in public places and college campuses across the country. In many obvious ways, he helped intensify the distrust for the military regime. Through music, Fela promoted his self-appointed role as the mouthpiece and representative of the Nigerian masses. He was among the few Nigerians that could confront the government overtly, while daring all anticipated backlash. For him, music was the weapon of choice to instill political "correctness" and get the authorities to implement citizen-centered development policies. By singing in Pidgin English—a corrupted version of the standard British English mixed with local dialects spoken in various parts of Africa and the Caribbean—Fela not only broke the barriers of Nigeria's rigid multi-linguistic existence, but also was able to effectively connect with the Nigerian masses who used this hybrid language in their everyday human communication. If the lyrics of Fela's protest music plainly revealed his philosophy as a resistance artiste, his appearance and stage performance added a subculture character to his iconic personality. On stage, "his lips pouted petulantly, his jaw was thrust out defiantly … his every gesture proclaimed a defiance and assertion of self."[28]

While Fela's rebel music and art increased his popularity among the Nigerian masses, they nevertheless intensified authorities' antipathy for him. In 1976, he released another song, "Zombie," which humorously described the rank and file of the Nigerian army as unintelligent individuals who would yield to the orders of their superiors because they had "no brake, no jam, no sense."[29] The song was so popular that it motivated civilians to ridicule and shout out "Zombie!" to soldiers on the streets. In addition, Fela's refusal to participate in the steering committee of the second world Festival of Black Arts and Culture (FESTAC), because the committee was headed by a military general—who was mainly interested in stealing public money by awarding contracts to his cronies—rather than an artiste, intensified his unpopularity among government officials. Although he refused to participate in the planning of FESTAC and in numerous events, international visitors (such as the American Stevie Wonder) came to see him play at the shrine. It was public knowledge that authorities were unhappy that Fela almost stole their show.[30]

However, as previously mentioned, Fela's "reckless" public persona, and the composition of his household (a majority of whom were runaways and homeless youths) gave the government leeway to violently attack him under the pretext of enforcing law and order. A disagreement between a member of his band and a soldier was all that about a thousand heavily armed soldiers needed to invade his residence on 18 February 1977. They raped the women and threw his seventy-seven year old mother out of the first floor window. She would later die of the injuries sustained during the rowdy attack. About sixty residents of the house were removed, paraded naked, and later incarcerated unjustly. Fela immortalized this attack in his song, "Sorrow, Tears, and Blood" (1977), and he detailed the manner in which the most violent government sponsored attack against him was executed in an interview published in 1982:

> The soldiers were everywhere! All in the yard, inside the house, in all the rooms on the ground floor. They beat up the girls, raped some of them and did horrors to them, man, they beat the boys. Then they stormed upstairs. They beat my brother, Dr. Beko, who was trying to protect my mother. They fractured his leg, his arm ... I could hear my own bones being broken by the blows! Then, the whole Kalakuta Republic [Fela's residence]—at 14A Agege Motor Road Surulere—went up in flames. The soldiers had set fire to the house ... First the hospital. Then prison. I stayed in jail for twenty-seven fuckin' days with wounds all over my body and several bone fractures ... I was told by my lawyer that all of my people who were in the house were either in hospitals or in jail ... I was taken to the court and charged. Imagine, I—not the army—was taken to court.[31,32]

Throughout the 1980s and 1990s, Fela continued to use his experience of state-sponsored violence to preach against the abuse of rights. After returning from jail in 1989, he released "Beats of No Nation," describing the outside world (life outside jail) as more brutal than the inside world (jail). He painted life outside jail as a "crazy world," inhabited by General Buhari (the military head of state), his lieutenant General Idiagbon, and corrupt law enforcement officers, whom he labeled "animals in human skin." Buhari's short-lived regime (1983–1985) continued the age-old practice of imposing social order by violently attacking citizens. He introduce a program "War against Indiscipline" which, like traffic regulations of the 1970s, sought to control people's public conduct by allowing military personnel to violently dispense "justice on the spot." Fela felt that a responsible government should not label its citizens as "useless, senseless and indiscipline[d]."

"Suffering and S[h]miling," Poverty, Underdevelopment, and the Culture of Corruption

There is a considerable overlap between Fela's protest songs on dictatorship and abuse of rights, and those that detailed the agony of everyday life for the Nigerian people. Indeed, extreme poverty—attributable to a deep-rooted culture of corruption at virtually all levels of society—created tension between the state and the citizenry. Crime and civil disobedience, which the military attempted to coercively contain, was precipitated by poverty and unemployment. Nigeria, like most countries in Africa, is an economic paradox: while it derived enormous wealth from oil, its citizens wallowed in untold hardship.[33] During the 1970s, a period that coincided with Fela's ascendancy as a rebel artiste *par excellence*, revenue from oil quadrupled,[34] rising from 196.4 million naira in 1970 to 15.234 billion naira in 1980.[35] Oil money was not channeled towards a large scale and sustainable program of poverty alleviation, job creation, and infrastructure development; rather it was siphoned into the private pockets of the ruling elite.

Fela's songs of poverty and corruption can be grouped into two overlapping categories, based on the audience. One set of songs was directed to the Nigerian masses, while the other addressed the authorities. While the first challenged the masses to stand for their rights in a revolutionary manner, the latter exposed the shady deals of the authorities. Put together, Fela intended to use his music to create political change by inciting the poor to challenge their oppressors. In a song titled, "No Bread," released in 1976, he unleashes a lyrical depiction of the physical appearance and mentality of a typical Nigerian who is completely emaciated due to lack of food. In another song, "Suffering and S[h]miling," released in 1978, he dissected the contradictory behavior of a Nigerian who resorted to smiling despite undergoing untold hardship and seeking refuge in Christianity and Islam. In his usual confrontational manner, he decried the unequal social and economic relations between the people and religious authorities: while the former encountered difficulties in meeting their daily needs, religious authorities enjoyed the splendor of life.

In three others songs, "Confusion" (1975), "Upside Down" (1976), and "Original Sufferhead" (1991), he painted gloomy pictures of public facilities—such as schools, prisons, and hospitals—chaotic traffic congestion, and the urban lifestyle, using such derogatory words as "pafuka" and "kwench" (broken and destroyed). In "Original Sufferhead," in particular, he condemned the inadequate supply of electricity, food, water, and accommodation for the "common man." While the poor were denied water and electricity, the rich (according to Fela) enjoyed an unlimited supply of these basic public amenities. He condemned both the failure of the government to implement a workable agriculture policy and the policy of food importation. Other components of the song included a swipe at inflation and the reliance on external agents, such as the World Bank, to solve the basic problems of development in Nigeria.

A couple of Fela's songs on poverty, corruption, and underdevelopment, as previously mentioned, were directed at the ruling elite. In "International Thief Thief" (1979), Fela sang about how the Nigerian elite collaborated with multinational corporations to divert wealth meant for local development into private coffers. He boldly called Chief M. K. O. Abiola (a civilian) and General Obasanjo (the military head of state between 1976 and 1979) thieves. Fela's critique of the discrepancies in the administration of justice is equally interesting. In "Authority Stealing" (1980), he sang that, while the elite who steal millions of naira (Nigerian currency) were usually not arrested or tried in court, common or "small" thieves could be incarcerated for months or even years. The real thieves, Fela maintained, were the rich elite whose greed was responsible for the underdevelopment of his country, not the "small" or petty thieves. He compared the theft *modus operandi* of both the authorities and an armed robber: while the armed robber needed a gun in order to steal, the authorities simply needed a pen—and the pen was capable of stealing far more money than the gun. "If gun steal eighty thousand naira," "pen will steal two billion naira," Fela maintained.

Conclusion

Fela was a rebel artiste *par excellence*. From the 1970s to 1997, he directed his artistic energy towards using music as a weapon against the myriad challenges facing the Nigerian state and its citizens. If Nigeria, like other countries in Africa, was underdeveloped, it was because of the violence and corruption of its leaders. The military dictatorship not only prevented Nigerians from choosing their own leaders, but also paved the way for abuse of rights of all kinds. In preaching against underdevelopment, Fela risked a number of consequences, including incarceration and even death. Between 1974, when he was first arrested and incarcerated, and August 1997, when he surrendered to death, he was arraigned in courts about three hundred and fifty-six times.[36] Fela died an unhappy man. In his final days, he confessed that all the problems he directed his music against still marred the Nigerian social and political landscape: Nigeria was still ruled by a dictator (General Sanni Abacha), and state-sanctioned violence against ordinary Nigerians, and Fela himself, remained a tragic fact of life. In fact, Fela was arrested in July 1997, just a month before he died of complications from HIV/AIDS.[37]

Fela created a counterculture that has favorably weathered decades of backward social and political transformation in Nigeria. The slang he created is still being used in everyday urban social interaction. His songs remain popular across social class, not only because of their deep artistic quality, but also because most, if not all, of the problems he preached against in the 1970s and 1980s remain largely unresolved. Indeed, more Nigerian live in poverty in 2013 than in the 1970s or 1980s. Corruption and embezzlement of public funds has reached an all-time high since the beginning of the new millennium, despite the fact that the country is under "democratic" governance. Fela's children (Femi and Seun) continue to propagate his message. Although not as eccentric, bold, confrontational, and controversial as their father, Femi and Seun have seen the need to keep the legacy of their father alive, while creating a unique artistic niche for themselves.[38]

Notes

1 Randall F. Grass, "Fela Anikulapo-Kuti: The Art of an Afrobeat Rebel," *The Drama Review*, Vol. 30, No. 1 (1986): 131–148.

2 Trevor Schoonmaker, "Introduction," in Trevor Schoonmaker, ed., *Fela: From West Africa to West Broadway* (New York: Palgrave Macmillan, 2003), 1.

3 See, among others, Sola Olorunyomi, *Afrobeat! Fela and the Imagined Continent* (Trenton, New Jersey: Africa World Press, 2003); Niyi Coker, Jr., *A Study of the Music and Social Criticism of African Musician Fela Anikulapo-Kuti* (Lewiston, New York: Edwin Mellen Press, 2004); Schoonmaker, ed., *Fela: From West Africa*; Trevor Schoonmaker, *Black President: The Art and Legacy of Fela Anikulapo-Kuti* (New York, New York: New Museum of Contemporary Art, 2003); Michael Veal, *Fela: The Life and Times of an African Musical Icon* (Philadelphia: Temple University Press, 2000); Tejumade Olaniyan, *Arrest the Music! Fela and His Rebel Art* (Bloomington, Indiana: Indiana University Press, 2004); Meghan Langley, "Peace Profile: Fela Kuti, An "Africa Man Original," *Peace Review: A Journal of Social Justice*, Vol. 22, No. 2 (2010): 199–204; Myke O. Olatunji, "Yabis Music: An Instrument of Social Change in Nigeria," *Journal of African Media Studies*, Vol. 1, No. 2 (2009): 309–328; Carlos Moore, *Fela: This Bitch of a Life* (London, UK: Omnibus Press, 2010), and Frank Tenaille, *Music is the Weapon of the Future: Fifty Years of African Popular Music* (Chicago, Illinois: Lawrence Hills Books, 2002), 69–76.

4 Joseph Shekwo, "Use of Music to Create Political Awareness and Mobilization: A Case Study of Two Nigerian Musicians: Fela Anikulapo-Kuti and Sonny Okosun," Paper presented at the American Culture Association and Popular Culture Association Conference, Atlanta, Georgia, April 1986.

5 For more on highlife, see, among others, Sonny Oti, *Highlife Music in West Africa* (Lagos, Nigeria: Malthouse Press, 2009).

6 On juju, see, Christopher Alan Waterman, *Juju: Social History and Ethnography of an African Popular Music* (Chicago, Illinois: Chicago University Press, 1990).

7 Grass, "Fela Anikulapo-Kuti," 134–135.

8 Songs in this category include the following, among others: "Confusion" (1975); "Upside Down" (1976); "No Bread/Unnecessary Begging" (1976); "Suffering and S[h]miling" (1978); "No Accommodation for Lagos" (1979); and "Colonial Mentality" (1977).

9 Examples include "Alagon Close" (1974); "Expensive Shit" (1975); "Everything Scatter/ Who No Know Go Know" (1975); "Sorrow, Tears, and Blood" (1977); "Vagabonds in Power" (1979); "Coffin for the Head of State" (1981); "Beast of No Nation" (1989); "Authority Stealing" (1980); "International Thief Thief" (1979); "Unknown Soldier" (1979); and "Army Arrangement" (1985).

10 Songs in this category include "Movement of the People" (1980) and "Movement of the People Political Statement 1" (1990).

11 Examples include "Lady" (1977); "Frustration of My Lady" (1970); "Na Poi" (1971); "Shakara Olojc" (1977); "Fefe Naa Efe" (1975); and "Yellow Fever" (1976).

12 LaRay Denzer, "Fela, Women, Wives," in *Fela: From West Africa*, 113.

13 Cheryl Johnson-Odim and Nina Emma Mba, *For Women and the Nation: Funmilayo Ransome-Kuti of Nigeria* (Urbana, Illinois: University of Illinois Press, 1997), 173.

14 Shekwo, "Use of Music to Create Political," 6.

15 Kwame Nkrumah, *Ghana: The Autobiography of Kwame Nkrumah* (New York: International Publishers, 1957), 164.

16 Coker, *A Study of the Music*, 29.

17 For more on how Sandra Izsadore influenced Fela, see Denzer, "Fela, Women, Wives," in *Fela: From West Africa*, 122–124.

18 Durotoye, "Roforofo Fight," 175.

19 Moore, *Fela*, 110.

20 Moore, *Fela*, 176–177.

21 Dorian Lynskey, *33 Revolutions Per Minute. A History of Protest Songs, from Billie Holiday to Green Day* (New York: HarperCollins, 2011), 237.

22 For more on Fela and his "wives," see, Derek Stanovsky "Fela and His Wives: The Import of a Postcolonial Masculinity," *Jouvert: A Journal of Postcolonial Studies*, Vol. 2, No. 1 (1998). Available at: http://english.chass.ncsu.edu/jouvert/v2i1/STAN.HTM.

23 For more on the making of Fela's album jacket, see, Ghariokwu Lemi, "Producing Fela's Album Jackets, in *Fela: From West Africa*, 51–54.

24 Durotoye, "Fela Anikulapo-Kuti," 181.

25 See Arinpe Adejumo, "Conflict Resolution in Oral Literature: A Review of Some Yoruba Satirical Songs," *Journal of African Poetry*, Vol. 5 (2008): 95–116.

26 Grass, *Great Spirit*, 67.

27 Example include calling Chief M. K. O. Abiola and General Obasanjo thieves, in "International Thief Thief" (1979).

28 Durotoye, "Roforofo Fight," 175.

29 Iyorchia D. Ayu, "Creativity and Protest in Popular Culture: The Political Music of Fela Anikulatpo Kuti" (Department of Sociology, University of Jos, Nigeria, 1989), 23–25.

30 Lynskey, *33 Revolutions Per Minute*, 239.

31 Moore, *Fela: This Bitch of a Life*, 140.

32 Olatunji, "Yabis Music," 314.

33 According to S. O. Osoba, a frontline neo-Marxist corruption "was the single most significant issue on which the Gowon regime became seriously embattled with the Nigerian public." See S. O. Osoba, "Corruption in Nigeria: Historical Perspectives," *Review of African Political Economy*, Vol. 23, No. 69 (1996): 377.

34 Shekwo, "Use of Music to Create Political," 7.

35 Durotoye, "The Political Contexts of Fela's Activism," in Schoonmaker, *Black President*, 45.

36 Moore, *Fela*, 283.

37 Moore, *Fela*, 283.

38 "Femi Kuti @ 50: 'My Pains, My Gains.'" Available at: http://saharareporters.com/interview/femi-kuti-50-%E2%80%98my-pains-my-gains%E2%80%99-vanguard.

24

TELLING THE TRUTH AND COMMENTING REALITY

"Harsh Criticism" in Guinea-Bissau's Intervention Music

Anne-Kristin Borszik

Figure 24.1 Manecas Costa performing on stage.

Within a few hours in March 2009, Guinea-Bissau's chief-of-staff Tagme na Waie and President "Nino" Vieira were killed in the capital city of Bissau; this was followed by the assassinations, three months later, of two additional high-ranking politicians.[1] Reacting to these incidents, various rappers recorded a mix-tape called "Big Up GB!—Nunde ke no na bai?" ("Where are we going?") Having received extensive media coverage, the tape mirrors the musicians' impressions and reflections in the face of impunity and political violence. Guinea-Bissau—a small country located on the west coast of Africa, and a former Portuguese colony—has struggled with a wide range of domestic problems for decades. Among them are low literacy and a weak education sector, various forms of (political) violence, corruption, and a marginal role in the regional and global economy. In becoming a center of the global drugs trade, Guinea-Bissau has recently won further notoriety.[2] The country's inhabitants include around 20 ethnic groups. Besides their mother tongue, most Bissau-Guineans speak Kriol, the country's lingua franca, which is derived from Portuguese and local languages. Portuguese, the official language, is spoken by a minority.

A popular and political music genre, *música de intervenção* ("intervention music") is the term used in Portuguese to denote music that addresses social and political problems. In Portugal, and in the country's former colonies, particularly Angola, Cape Verde, Guinea-Bissau and Mozambique, intervention music has been produced since the 1930s, with a culminating point during the 1960s and 1970s.[3]

Drawing on anthropological fieldwork,[4] this article discusses Guinea-Bissau's "intervention music." In their songs, intervention musicians convey harsh criticism by "telling the truth" (*konta bardadi*)[5] about "what is going on" and by singing about the "reality" (*realidadi*) of life in Guinea-Bissau. Musicians criticize corruption and violence, but also express hope for change and their desire for peace and unity.

As far back as the late 1940s, the group Ngola Ritmos promoted Angolan identity and raised political consciousness, and Ruy Mingas' "Monangambé" (1961) was among the most famous examples of social criticism during the Angolan independence struggle.[6] Since the 1990s, underground hip-hop musicians have commented on sensitive social issues such as homosexuality, racism, the drug trade and politicians' enrichment, and expressed their desire for freedom and justice.[7] Artists also address social problems via *kuduru*, a style of music popular in the suburbs of Luanda.[8] In Portugal, the songs of Sérgio Godinho, Zeca Afonso, Paulo do Carvalho, and José Mário Branco accompanied the dictatorial regime of António de Salazar and the 1974 Carnation Revolution. Now, hip-hop seems to have taken the role of political music.[9] In Mozambique, Azagaia is among the rappers who articulate the sentiments and interests of the "new generation," the "people who are daily confronted with the difficulties of life."[10] Azagaia's popularity stems from people's fear: while people prefer to remain silent in order to avoid confrontation, the musician's songs express their concerns.

Among the (about) 130 musicians and 20 groups living in Guinea-Bissau or abroad,[11] only a few are considered "intervention musicians." The first generation, which has performed since the late 1960s, featured artists such as José Carlos Schwarz,[12] Zé Manel Fortes, and Adriano "Atchutchi" Gomes Ferreira (who took charge of the group "Super Mama Djombo" in 1974). These artists accompanied, critically and enthusiastically, the independence struggle and the first years of socialist political rule in Guinea-Bissau. Justino Delgado and Manecas Costa are among the musicians who have performed since the mid-1980s. Since the 1990s, hip-hop groups such as F. M. B. J. and Baloberos, who identify themselves as the "new generation," have taken up the tradition of intervention music. Phrases like "Please, please, return us our flag/please, please, return us our country" in Naka B's "Colisensa" ("Please") are considered "harsh criticism" with regard to politicians' private appropriation of public means.[13]

Intervention music in Guinea-Bissau mainly offers criticism on politics, but it also "speaks about people's life, it entertains and narrates whether things go well or badly for the population. The musician explains everything."[14] Musicians "translate everyday experiences into living sound,"[15] and they aim to sensitize listeners by singing about "reality" and telling the "truth."

Since the 1970s, "singing everyday realities" has been an essential feature of Bissau-Guinean intervention music.[16] The term "reality" alludes both to national concerns like war, elections, and poverty, and to general characteristics of Guinea-Bissau, such as the beauty of its nature, its ethnic diversity, and its rich musical culture. However, "reality" does have negative connotations, and has become "an indigenous term, a word a kid would use when he explained to you why he'd rather leave the country than stay there and go to school."[17]

The term "truth" (bardadi) also features in many songs and in musicians' self-conception. Telling the truth means to uncover the allegedly hidden, the unsaid. At court, in parliament, but also in family life, people observe that, often, "the truth is not told, only lies" (bardadi ka ta kontadu, só mintida).[18] Intervention musicians are popular precisely because they articulate "what is really going on in Guinea-Bissau" (ke ku na pasa na Guiné), and they become examples for others to follow. "The truth must be told in this country," sing F. B. M. J., and Manecas Costa's appeal "there may only be truth, so that the country can rest," implies that telling the truth may relieve tension and anxiety.

While harsh criticism is reserved to intervention musicians, other artists indirectly criticize politics by speaking about the population's everyday life. Maio Coopé argues:

> Whoever speaks about society, actually also speaks about politics. These two things are connected. I am concerned with the whole society, and this also touches some aspects of politics—but political intervention in my songs?

No, no, no, no. Directly? No, no, no, no. I am more interested in the social aspects, people's everyday life.[19]

Musicians compose songs predominantly in the lingua franca, Kriol. While, during the independence struggle, composing in Kriol was intended to convey political messages beyond Portuguese reach, artists nowadays have recourse to this language to promote national identity and unity. Musicians conceal and reveal by using specific popular expressions, proverbs, and metaphors in Kriol (see below), arguing that such poetic means increase the artistic quality of songs and the probability that listeners understand the message.[20]

Metaphors or proverbs leave room for diverse interpretations and thus protect musicians from being persecuted. Though musicians like Justino Delgado maintain that, "nowadays, nobody in Guinea-Bissau has the power to prohibit a song,"[21] indirect forms of impeding the dissemination of criticism—for instance, by switching off the current during concerts—do occur. Journalists are regularly prevented from investigating[22] and, "if democracy would end today, it would be a reason to celebrate"[23] for those who wish to silence both musicians and journalists. Music censorship is a highly politicized phenomenon,[24] and hip-hop groups such as F. B. M. J. and Baloberos, who overtly criticize politicians, have become the target of censorship.[25] In addition to the use of metaphors, musicians' persecution is prevented by them "never singing about those who are alive" and criticizing retrospectively "actions and results, but never persons."[26]

The approach of avoiding criticism of individuals is impressively exemplified in Jovem Binham's song "Turpessa Dissabidu" ("Bitter Throne," 2011). The singer comments on corrupt, violent, and false politicians and generals; he proceeds to announce, repeatedly, that he will reveal their names (*n'na tchoma nomis*). The song appeals to listeners because it highlights the familiar fact that revealing the powerful people's names is unthinkable under the given political conditions and might result in Binham's killing; thus, it mirrors the "reality" of censorship. But this line also seems to have a catalytic effect (see below) on listeners; it unburdens them of publicly speaking out.

In order to convey their message, musicians adopt lyrics, instruments and rhythms familiar to people. Maio Coopé's lyrics, for instance, awaken people's childhood memories:

> Basically, the music always contains something that people recognize (...). Normally, people are surprised when they hear my music because it reminds them of something they have experienced in their childhood.[27]

Musicians take recourse to local instruments like the balafon, the tina[28] or the kora and to familiar music-styles like *mandjuandadi*[29] and *gumbé*, Africa's "earliest form of urban music."[30] Gumbé seems to have first emerged around 1900 among slaves in Jamaica (who later returned to Sierra Leone),[31] but Bissau-Guineans consider it to be specifically national.[32] In addition to these styles, intervention music also adopts *kizomba* from Cape Verde and *zouk* from the Antilles.

Intervention music is a popular genre. It is readily accessible, generally intelligible, and emotionally anchored.[33] It is particularly through the use of polysemic metaphors that have "points of relevance to a variety of readers in a variety of social contexts," that musicians manage to both mirror reality and be thought-provoking.[34] By addressing people's hopes, fears and aspirations, and by articulating the population's sentiments, musicians emotionally anchor their songs. Following Stäheli, I argue that the popular provides an imaginary, temporary home; a place of identification and belonging.[35] In this sense, intervention music allows people to feel "part of the whole" and to participate at an imaginary level in the musicians' criticism and their call for political change.

Reality and Truth: Criticism in Intervention Music

To understand a given society, Bender argues, "one cannot under any circumstances avoid the song texts of popular musicians."[36] Intervention music actually conveys a fair impression of what concerns Bissau-Guinean society. At the same time, the genre's name suggests that intervention music aims to "intervene" in society and politics. Looking exclusively at political song texts reduces songs, however, to pieces of lyrics, and ignores how melody, rhythm, and arrangement shape their social impact.[37] From the perspective of music theory, it is in fact difficult to establish a correlation between the structure of the music and socio-cultural phenomena. Generally speaking, political music reaches listeners if it is "popular."[38]

Bissau-Guinean listeners tend to listen attentively to song texts when the musical style of a song is "beautiful" (*bonitu*). Beauty implies familiar rhythms and instruments. Song texts are categorized either as "beautiful" or "interesting." While "beautiful" texts distract listeners from everyday life, and comfort them by conveying the hope for a better future, compositions that emphasize "reality" are considered "interesting."[39] In the following section, it is on these "interesting" compositions that I will particularly focus.

The "Truth" about Corruption and Impunity

Impunity and corruption are central themes in Guinea-Bissau's intervention music. Journalists and the public in Guinea-Bissau lament "absent justice" and corruption.[40] In a recent song, Masta Tito accuses traffic policemen of "robbing drivers' money in order to buy food at the market" (*roba dinheru di fera na mon di condutoris*); the Baloberos comment, in their song "7 Minutos de Bardadi" ("7 Minutes of Truth"), on impunity in the legal realm. With such songs, hip-hoppers now take up a tradition of intervention music that was established in the 1970s by artists like Zé Manel. His song "Ladrau di Tabanka" ("Village Thief," 1982) speaks of embezzlement by high-rank politicians, and contrasts this with petty thefts.

Musicians are frequently considered clairvoyants (*djambakus*) of future events. As early as 1982, Zé Manel called attention to the unfavorable consequences of the drug trade. Listeners may consider him a *djambakus*; the huge trade in cocaine, prevalent since 2006, has complicated Guinea-Bissau's current political and economic situation.[41] Interestingly, the drug trade is not among the most criticized topics in intervention songs. Though musicians comment on the existence of cocaine—referred to as *farinha branku* ("white flour") or *forsa dos* ("sweet power")—they remain fairly silent about its impact on society and politics.

While thieves in the village are ostracized and lose social recognition, "thieves of the people" may safely store their loot in foreign banks. The phenomenon of politicians "eating people's money" (*kume dinhero di povo*) has become commonplace; "eating" as a metaphor for embezzling is known in many African countries.[42] Besides legal actors' embezzlement and wrongdoers' social sanctioning, "development does not advance," as Zé Manel puts it, because legal institutions do not adequately settle local disputes. Many people denounce impunity, maintaining that "there is no justice in Guinea-Bissau" (*djustisa ka ten na Guinê*).[43] In his song "Pubis ka Burro" ("The People are not Stupid," 2001), Zé Manel comments on Bissau-Guineans' passivity in the face of large-scale private appropriation of public funds. "Pubis ka Burro" is one of the most important intervention songs, and Zé Manel's words are considered harsh criticism towards politicians who exhibit their unjustly acquired wealth while the population remains passive and poor. The short-term practice of corruption and other forms of "bad governance" feature in "Bissau kila Muda" ("Bissau is Changing," 1996) by Super Mama Djombo. Adriano Gomes Ferreira, who composed the lyrics, calls on people to stay calm in the face of unsatisfying politics, using the allegory of a monkey on a mountain. Since chimpanzees are common in rural Guinea-Bissau, the metaphor seems to work, particularly for people living in or coming from villages. By remaining vague about the criticized politicians, the song leaves room for interpretation:

> Whether dead or alive, the monkey must leave the mountain some day. The mountain will not move, so leave him alone. Whoever is in power, arrests people, and does many other things. But at some point he must cede power. Like this, I have illustrated my idea. One has to create beautiful metaphors in order to be audible and easily intelligible.[44]

Musicians are artists of language and songs are documents of the language in use.[45] But songs also document a country's political culture. In "Bissau kila Muda," the acceptability of short-term embezzlement and bad governance is presented as part

336

of Bissau-Guinean political culture.[46] The idea that the power of politicians must be limited is seemingly shared by many Bissau-Guineans, and the ways in which power can be circumscribed range from democratic elections to violent putsches and physical elimination.[47]

The Burden of Having Incompetent Politicians

Just as they criticise corruption, musicians also accuse "incompetent politicians" (*políticos incompetentis*) of their inability to rule the country.[48] The population is, in various songs, depicted as suffering from this incompetence.[49] In "Kaminhu Sukuru" ("Dark Road") F. B. M. J. address Guinea-Bissau's rulers, and the musicians even dare to call them, quite explicitly, stupid. In "Konbersa di Bardadi" ("Issue of Truth," 2008) N'pans quotes a phrase from José Carlos Schwarz's song "Si bu sta Dianti na Luta" ("When You Are Standing in the Fight on the Front Line," 1975) and uses the classical melody of Super Mama Djombo's "Julia." Employing these familiar musical references, N'pans appeals to the President's responsibility to build the nation, to be "a good father," and to contribute to peace and progress. In contrast to F. B. M. J.'s "harsh criticism," N'pans remains respectful of politicians. He, rather, "tells the truth" by referring to Guinea-Bissau as backward (*atrasadu*) in development, but he also emphasizes the country's potential to escape from poverty.

The "Reality" of Violence

Though to foreigners visiting the country (and even in Bissau-Guineans' self-conception) Guinea-Bissau appears to be a calm place, violence occurs on the most diverse occasions and to a surprisingly large extent. The beating of children by their parents is socially accepted, and police beating of suspects is an everyday practice. Parties in dispute may throw hot oil in their opponent's face, or injure him with knives or razorblades. Threatening to kill others (*n'na matau*: Kriol for "I will kill you") is a characteristic expression in conflicts where items of considerable value—such as cows or land—are involved.[50] Killing occurs at the highest state level, but also in everyday life.

One of the causes of violence seems to be the widespread impunity. In the context of "absent justice," people may refrain from seeking justice and remain passive (see above), but they may also take the law into their own hands.[51] A "culture of war"[52] shaped inter-ethnic relations in pre-colonial times, existed during the independence struggle (1959–1973), and still pervades present day society and politics.[53] While violence persists, music allies with those who long for peace: "On the long journey that Guinea-Bissau was on the path of war, music has rhymed with peace. Wounded in their sensitive souls, Bissau-Guinean artists have sung of peace during the war and of fatigue in times of carnage."[54]

Among the songs that represent this attitude is José Carlos Schwarz's "Ke ki Mininu na Tchora?" ("Why Is the Boy Crying?" 1972). Schwarz addresses the cruelty and horror of war, which makes innocent victims. "Ke ki Mininu na Tchora?" is, like "Pubis ka Burro," among the most famous and popular intervention songs of Guinea-Bissau's cultural history. The song's emotional charge and its representation of "reality" are appealing to listeners. By formulating a collective suffering, it creates a sense of community and belonging, and it increases people's identification with their country.

Back in the 1970s, José Carlos Schwarz had commented on violence at the societal micro-level, namely, the unequal relations between women and men.[55] In the tradition of Schwarz, Zé Manel's song "Mindjer i um Kumpanher" ("A Woman is a Companion," 2003) criticizes men's disrespect for women. Criticizing people's lack of respect towards one another at the individual level corresponds to harsh criticism of political violence at the state level. In "Ditadura" ("Dictatorship," 2003), F. B. M. J. comment on a long chain of political violence.[56] Armed violence is now common ("exchange of fire as usual"), the singers observe, and the most recent putsch on 12 April 2012 confirmed this. Zé Manel harshly criticizes such forms of violence in "Si Bala ten" ("As long as there are bullets," 2007). The bullets stand for all kinds of weapons, like knives, razorblades, machetes, pistols, guns and bombs. Guns and pistols circulate openly in the country and are also widely traded with Guinea-Bissau's neighbor, Senegal.[57] Many people keep a gun below their bed for defending themselves against thieves. In one of their songs, F. B. M. J. blame the military for providing weapons to young people who then "rob gold chains and mobile phones/ and carry out armed assaults."

In eastern Guinea-Bissau, the inefficiency of legal institutions means that disputing parties consider armed violence an appropriate option for safeguarding honor, restoring respect, and lowering anger. Killing as an option for reacting to unpunished offence is present in everyday life, and there are quite a number of people who are ready to die for their rights. The adopted all-or-nothing attitude is expressed in phrases like, "his body or my body, his cadaver or my cadaver" (own observations).

Interestingly, violence is also present in musicians' self-conception. Rappers, particularly, consider themselves "soldiers without guns," and speak of hip-hop as a "weapon without bullets," singing that "if rap is the pistol, we are its bullet" (F. B. M. J. in "Kaminhu Sukuru").[58] Such self-conceptions illustrate that musicians cannot escape the system they criticize. Seemingly, the association of music with weapons is frequent in Africa. The group Tinariwen, founded in Algeria, "decided to lay down their guns and fight with a different weapon—music."[59] In South Africa, music was a "weapon of struggle" during the 1960s, and Fela Kuti referred to music as the "weapon of the future."[60]

Zé Manel refers to the "master of the land" (*dunu di tera* in Kriol) as the owner of the bullets. While *dunu di tchon* ("master of the earth") denominates autochthonous ethnic groups, *dunu ti tera* seemingly alludes to the President, the late João Bernardo "Nino" Vieira. As long as violence is backed by high-ranking politicians ("bullets that come from the master of the land"), people will continue to die, and Manel's providence was fulfilled two years after the song had been released, when both General Tagme Na Waie and "Nino" Vieira himself became victims of political violence.

By singing "As long as there are enemies, there will be dead people," Manel comments on Guinea-Bissau's problem of national reconciliation. Centuries-old tensions between ethnic groups, executions during and after the struggle for independence, grievances from the 1998–99 conflict, as well as non-persecuted assassinations since the country's independence, persist in people's minds and fuel hatred at both the individual and societal level. The Bissau-Guinean League of Human Rights (*Liga Guineense de Direitos Humanos*) recurrently appeals to people to give up the "mentality of war and revenge" (*sintidu di guera ku vingansa*) in order to end violence and establish peace. Though reconciliation is difficult and "far more humanly exacting than vengeance," there is no peace without reconciliation, at least in the form of "non-lethal coexistence."[61]

"People have to die in this democracy of interests" is an expressive phrase in Zé Manel's song. The call for, and the promise of, "democracy" characterizes discourses of politicians and development workers, but this political concept tends to be little known among Bissau-Guineans.[62] Against this, the "interest-based" practice of exchanging favors (*troca de favores*) as "reciprocity" is a central feature of traditional social relations. Manel illustrates, with the term "democracy of interests," the ambivalence inherent in both traditionally and occidentally-shaped social and political relations which can claim many victims.

When confronted with corruption, violence, impunity, and poverty, people may either resort to violence or *sufri* (Kriol for "accepting an undesirable situation"). Though this latter attitude is very common, it is hardly mirrored in intervention songs. One of the few examples is José Carlos Schwarz's "Bu djubin" ("You Looked at Me," 1973). Composed during Schwarz's imprisonment at Ilha das Galinhas between 1972 and 1974, the song denunciates torture and humiliation and promotes an attitude of sufferance. This position—to accept undesirable situations of violence—can be coupled with the hope that things will ultimately change for the better.

Hope, Longing for Peace and the Tendency to Outward Orientation

Though musicians do, quite openly, accuse others of corruption and violence, a gleam of hope for a prospering Guinea-Bissau shines through many compositions. Without hope, Guinea-Bissau would be lost, and both musicians and listeners know this. Songs of hope offer both comfort and provide a space for relaxation from everyday struggle (*kansera*). Hope is expressed, for instance, by recalling Amílcar Cabral's visions that enlightened and motivated Bissau-Guineans to combat colonialism.[63] In the widespread saying, "Cabral has not died" (*Cabral ka muri*), Super Mama Djombo emphasize in "Alma" ("Soul," 2008) the topicality of Cabral's ideas. In times of putsches and assassinations, when hopes are ruined, radio stations broadcast classical songs like Super Mama Djombo's "Sol Maior para Comanda" (1979), remembering Cabral's achievements and suggesting that "looking ahead is the solution" (*só pa no pintcha*). Other songs that speak of hope for peace in the face of daily struggle are Manecas Costa's "Fidjus di Guiné Foronta" ("Guinea's Children Are Suffering," 1999) and "Guiné-Bissau—Terra di Bambara" ("Guinea-Bissau—Land of the Bambara," 1987),[64] in which Maio Coopé expresses his hope for joy and peace among his people, though this may be achieved only in the afterlife. In this song, Nelson Mandela is called upon to guide Bissau-Guineans to "heaven" (*gloria*). As mirrored subtly in this song, external support is one source of hope. At the individual level, *djambakus*, *murus* (Muslim marabouts) and *baloberos* (animist priests and sorcerers) foresee the future and advise people about their decisions on political careers, emigration, or marriage. At the broader societal level, people hand over their destiny to the government or the President, while politicians, for their part, rely on financial, political, and economic support by foreign institutions.[65]

Rhetoric and physical outward orientation are everyday phenomena and, as part of Guinea-Bissau's *realidadi*, they are reflected in songs. The appeal to the President as a father is a contemporary feature of intervention music. N'pans' "Konbersa di Bardadi" is representative in this respect. Bissau-Guineans refer to themselves as "children of Guinea" (*fidjus di Guiné*), thus imagining the country as a "family" and articulating their dependent status on their "father" (the President) or "mother Guinea" (as expressed by F. B. M. J.). Schatzberg describes this recurrent concept of the African state and society as a family as deriving "from a pervasive, yet largely unarticulated, conceptual understanding of the distribution of rights and responsibilities."[66] In "Big Up GB!—Nunde ke no na bai?" the rappers appeal to the United Nations to help the country, just as the government asks the UN to support security sector reform and help combat the drugs trade.

The appeal for help is associated with the musicians' conception of Bissau-Guineans as "poor" (*koitadis*) and pitiful. This mirrors the *realidadi* of political discourses, in which "the expression 'Guinea is poor' belongs to a repertoire of general expressions used by the country's leaders to mobilize people in support of development policies, to dissuade opponents who aspire to rule, to rebuke their critics, to ask for international assistance, and even to justify the misuse of such aid."[67]

The most recent album of Super Mama Djombo, "Ar puro" ("Fresh Air," 2008), presents an alternative, interesting perspective on outward orientation. The album was not only been recorded in Iceland's capital Reykjavik, and the recording financed by an Icelandic businessman, but one of its songs, "No Festa" ("Our Feast") also features some lines performed by the guest musician Egill Ólafsson in Icelandic. Here, outward orientation allows for the expression of the hope that Guinea-Bissau will prosper ("Despite difficulties we will find hope, freedom, and justice").

Conclusion

I have argued that Guinea-Bissau's intervention music addresses recurrently topical issues like violence, corruption, poverty, and the hope for change. Composed in the country's lingua franca, Kriol, it adopts familiar, "beautiful," music styles and instruments. Musicians sing about the *realidadi* of Guinea-Bissau, about impunity from criminal sanction, the drugs trade and unequal gender relations, and they tell the "truth" (*bardadi*), particularly about politicians' corruption and incompetence. Musicians and listeners agree that such references to *realidadi* and *bardadi* are harsh criticism.

The term "intervention music" alludes to the possible power of music to induce social and political change. While musicians limit themselves to commenting on the country's *realidadi*, the interest in identifying signs of political brisance and impact might, rather, belong to scholars, who consider calls for change more "relevant" than artistic descriptions of the status quo.[68]

Intervention music circulates in a rather closed communicative circle between musicians and listeners. "The nation" (referred to as Guiné, "my country" or Bissau) is the central object of musicians' expression. By speaking for the people and "giving a voice to the voiceless," musicians intend to artistically mediate between the population and those politicians who become more and more alienated from the people. Here, the Portuguese term *intervenção* can also be conceived of as "mediation." By allowing for imagined participation, musicians temper people's worries with regard to Guinea-Bissau's various social problems and nurture their hope for political change.

Notes

1 Lorenzo I. Bordonaro, "Introduction: Guinea-Bissau Today—The Irrelevance of the State and the Permanence of Change," *African Studies Review*, Vol. 52, No. 2 (2009): 35–45.

2 Some of the publications addressing history, politics, economy and religion in Guinea-Bissau are Eve Crowley, "Contracts with the Spirits: Religion, Asylum and Ethnic Identity in the Cacheu Region of Guinea-Bissau" (Ph.D. dissertation, Yale University, 1990); Carlos Lopes, *Kaabunké: Espaço, território e poder na Guiné-Bissau, Gâmbia e Casamance pré-coloniais* (Lisbon: Comissão Nacional para as Comemorações dos Descobrimentos Portugueses, 1999); Ulrich Schiefer, *Von allen guten Geistern verlassen? Guinea-Bissau: Entwicklungspolitik und der Zusammenbruch afrikanischer Gesellschaften* (Hamburg: Institut für Afrika-Kunde, 2002); Joshua Forrest, *Lineages of State Fragility: Rural Civil Society in Guinea-Bissau* (Oxford/Athens: Ohio University Press and James Currey, 2003); Henrik Vigh, *Navigating Terrains of War:*

Youth and Soldiering in Guinea-Bissau (New York and Oxford: Berghahn Books, 2006); Clara Carvalho, "Local Authorities or Local Power? The Ambiguity of Traditional Authorities From the Colonial to the Post-Colonial Period in Guinea-Bissau," *Soronda Especial: Experiências Locais de Gestão de Conflitos—Local Experiences of Conflict Management* (December 2008): 39–55; Georg Klute, Birgit Embaló, Anne-Kristin Borszik, and A. Idrissa Embaló, eds., *Soronda Especial: Experiências Locais de Gestão de Conflitos—Local Experiences of Conflict Management*, 2008, and Birgit Embaló, "Civil-Military Relations and Political Order in Guinea-Bissau," *Journal of Modern African Studies*, Vol. 50, No. 2 (2012): 253–281.

3   César Augusto Monteiro, *Manel d'Novas: Música, Vida, Caboverdianidade* (São Vicente: author's edition, 2003), 42.

4   Fieldwork was carried out in Portugal (2003 and 2004) and Guinea-Bissau (2002, 2007, 2008 and 2009). Interviews were held in Lisbon with the musicians Adriano "Atchutchi" Gomes Ferreira, Justino Delgado, and Maio Coopé. Research in eastern Guinea-Bissau (2007–2009) focused on strategies of handling disputes in a semi-urban setting.

5   Unless otherwise specified, expressions in italic are in Kriol.

6   Jorge Macedo, *Ngola Ritmos: Obreiros do Nacionalismo Angolano* (Luanda: União de Escritores Angolanos, 1989).

7   Marta Lança, "Luanda está a mexer! Hip Hop Underground em Angola," ntama," *Journal of African Music and Popular Culture* (2008). Available at: http://www.uni-hildesheim. de/ntama/index.php?option=com_content&view=article&id=201:luanda-esta-mexer-hip-hop-underground-em-angola&catid=79:african-hip-hop&Itemid=39, accessed 15 May 2012.

8   Nadine Siegert, "Kuduru—Musikmachen ohne Führerschein," *Bayreuth African Studies Working Papers*, Vol. 7 (2009): 9, 15.

9   Claudia Luís, "Hip-Hop é nova música de intervenção em Portugal?" *Jornal de Notícias* (2007). Available at: http://www.jn.pt/paginainicial/interior.aspx?content_id=668494&page=-1, accessed 15 May 2012.

10 Juliana Borges, "Quando a palavra fere mais que a lança, entrevista a Azagaia," *BUALA—cultura contemporânea africana*. Available at: http://www.buala.org/pt/cara-a-cara/quando-a-palavra-fere-mais-que-a-lanca-entrevista-a-azagaia, accessed 17 May 2012.

11 Many of Guinea-Bissau's musicians live abroad (in Portugal or the USA), particularly those considered intervention musicians.

12 José Carlos Schwarz is considered "the most fascinating personality of Guinea-Bissau's cultural life." Besides his activities as an artist, Schwarz also engaged in political activities, having been *chargé d'affaires* in Havana. Killed during an airplane accident in May 1977, the artist and his songs are remembered by Bissau-Guineans and performed by contemporary artists. See, Moema Parente Augel, *A nova literatura da Guiné-Bissau* (Bissau: INEP, 1998), 219.

13 Joana Sousa, "Rap guineense: a Guiné ouvida por todos," *BUALA—cultura contemporânea africana* (2012). Available at: http://www.buala.org/pt/palcos/rap-guineense-a-guine-ouvida-por-todos, accessed 17 May 2012.

14 Interview with Justino Delgado, 9 September 2003.

15 Francis Bebey, *African Music: A People's Art* (New York: Lawrence Hill, 1975), 122.

16 Augel, *A nova*, 397.

17 Eric Gable, "Conclusion: Guinea-Bissau Yesterday ... and Tomorrow," *African Studies Review*, Vol. 52, No. 2 (2009): 172

18 Statement by a woman from Gabú (Guinea-Bissau), 10 January 2009.

19 Interview held on 15 September 2003.

20 Anne-Kristin Borszik, *Die 'Interventionsmusik' aus Guinea-Bissau: Kommunikationsprozesse zwischen Produktion und Rezeption in der Lissabonner Diaspora* (Münster: LIT, 2007).

21 Interview held on 9 September 2003.

22 Cf., for instance, the case of António Aly Silva (https://guinebissaudocs.wordpress.com/2012/04/13/jornalista-antonio-aly-silva-preso-na-guine-bissau-ionline/; accessed 8 June 2012.

23 Interview with an anonymous journalist, 29 January 2009.

24 Martin Cloonan, "Popular Music Censorship in Africa: An Overview," in Michael Drewett and Martin Cloonan, eds., *Popular Music Censorship in Africa* (Hampshire: Ashgate, 2006), 10.

25 Sousa, "Rap guineense."

26 Interview with Adriano Gomes Ferreira, 10 September 2003.

27 Interview held on 15 September 2003.

28 The *tina* is a kind of drum. It is composed of half a calabash, which is placed on top of half a barrel filled with water.

29 *Mandjuandadi* is a group of people who grew up together and belong to the same ethnic group. There exist specific songs that are performed during *mandjuandadi* meetings called "songs of *mandjuandadi*." Like intervention songs, they have a "double sense" and some mystery to them. Hildo Honório do Couto and Filomena Embaló, "Literatura, língua e cultura na Guiné-Bissau. Um país da CPLP," *PAPIA—Revista Brasileira de Estudos Crioulos e Similares/Special Edition*, Vol. 20 (2010): 209–212.

30 Flemming Harrev, "Francophone West Africa and the Jali Experience," in John Collins, ed., *West African Pop Roots* (Philadelphia: Temple University Press, 1992), 229.

31 Interview with musicologist Lucy Duran, available at: www.guine-bissau.net/index.php?option=news&task=viewarticle&sid=31&Itemid=2; accessed 27 April 2004.

32 Augel, "A nova," 219f.

33 Urs Stäheli, "Das Populäre zwischen Cultural Studies und Systemtheorie," in Udo Göttlich and Rainer Winter, eds., *Politik des Vergnügens: Zur Diskussion der Populärkultur in den Cultural Studies* (Cologne: Herbert von Halem, 2000), 321–336.

34 John Fiske, *Understanding Popular Culture* (London and New York: Routledge, 1989), 141; and Niklas Luhmann, *Art as a Social System* (Stanford, California: Stanford University Press, 2000.

35 Stäheli, "Das Populäre," 331.

36 Wolfgang Bender, "Modern African Music—An Autonomous Music," in *Sounds of Change—Social and Political Features of Music in Africa*, ed., Stig-Magnus Thorsén (Stockholm: Sida, 2004), 88.

37 Birgit Englert, "Popular Music and Politics in Africa—Some Introductory Reflections," *STICHPROBEN—Vienna Journal of African Studies*, Vol. 14 (2008): 10.

38 Personal communication by Rainer Polak, 22 May 2012.

39 Borszik, *Die Interventionsmusik.'*

40 Birgit Embaló, "Civil-Military Relations and Political Order in Guinea-Bissau," *Journal of Modern African Studies*, Vol. 50, No. 2 (2012): 273.

41 Embaló, "Civil-Military Relations," 271, and Dirk Kohnert, "Democratization via Elections in an African 'Narco-state'? The Case of Guinea-Bissau," *GIGA Working Papers*, No. 123 (Hamburg: German Institute of Global and Area Studies/Leibniz-Institut für Globale und Regionale Studien, 2010).

42 Jean-François Bayart, *The State in Africa: The Politics of the Belly* (London: Longman, 1993); Michael Schatzberg, *Political Legitimacy in Middle Africa: Father, Family, Food* (Bloomington and Indianapolis: Indiana University Press, 2001).

43 Research results from fieldwork in eastern Guinea-Bissau will be published in 2013.

44 Interview with Adriano Gomes Ferreira, 10 September 2003.

45 Bender, "Modern African Music," 87.

46 Cf. also the interview with the member of a chief's family in Gabú on the chief's accepted inappropriate way of ruling, 17 January 2008.

47 Embaló, "Civil-Military Relations."

48 Embaló, "Civil-Military Relations," 272, 276.

49 Wilson Trajano Filho, "Narratives of national identity in the web," *Etnográfica*, Vol. 6, No. 1 (2002): 156.

50 Cf. the author's observations and conversations during fieldwork in Gabú (2007–2009).

51 Klute et al., eds., *Soronda Especial*.

52 Interview with a political observer in Gabú, 19 February 2009.

53 Cf., for instance, the blog of journalist António Aly Silva, available at: http://ditadurado-consenso.blogspot.pt/; accessed 8 June 2012.

54 Fafali Koudawo, ed., "'Paz é Cultura'—Especial Músicos Guineenses," *ECO da Voz di Paz—Boletim Informativo* (Bissau: Voz di Paz, 2011).

55 Augel, "A nova," 230.

56 Christoph Kohl, "Hiphop aus Guinea-Bissau—die Gruppe 'F. B. M. J.'" *ntama—Journal of African Music and Popular Culture* (2007). Available at: http://www.uni-hildesheim.de/ntama/index.php?option=com_content&view=article&id=198:hiphop-aus-guinea-bissau-die-gruppe-fbmj&catid=79:african-hip-hop&Itemid=39, accessed 15 May 2012.

57 Embaló, "Civil-Military Relations," 265, 273.

58 Sousa, "Rap guineense."

59 Personal communication by Georg Klute, 8 June 2012.

60 Michela Vershbow, "The Sounds of Resistance: The Role of Music in South Africa's Anti-Apartheid Movement," *Student Pulse*, Vol. 2, No. 6 (2010). Available at: http://www.studentpulse.com/articles/265/2/the-sounds-of-resistance-the-role-of-music-in-south-africas-anti-apartheid-movement, accessed 7 June 2012. See also Stefan Sereda, "Riffing on Resistance: Music in Chris Abani's Graceland," *ARIEL: A Review of International English Literature*, Vol. 39, No. 4 (November 2008): 31–47.

61 Wole Soyinka, *The Burden of Memory, the Muse of Forgiveness* (New York: Oxford University Press, 1999), 34.

62 Embaló, "Civil-Military Relations," 257; and Lars Rudebeck, "'To Seek Happiness': Development in a West-African Village in the Era of Democratisation," *Review of African Political Economy*, Vol. 71 (1997): 75–86.

63 Patrick Chabal, *Amílcar Cabral. Revolutionary Leadership and People's War* (London: Hurst, 2002).

64 *Bambara* is a Kriol term designating the cloth used in Guinea-Bissau—and many other African countries—to tie children to their mother's back.

65 Schiefer, *Von allen guten*.

66 Schatzberg, *Political Legitimacy*, 2.

67 Trajano Filho, "Narratives," 155.

68 Englert, "Popular Music," 1–15.

25

DEGLAMORIZING PROTEST

The Politics of "Song and Dance" in Popular Indian Cinema

Prakash Kona

Figure 25.1   Visually impaired persons playing music during a protest outside the Town Hall in Ahmedabad.

> To interpret language means to under-
> stand language; to interpret music means
> to make music.
> > Theodor Adorno, "Music Language,
> > Composition"[1]

Sustaining the Idea of Indianness through "Song and Dance"

The central theme of this chapter is that the "popular" cannot exist without an element of protest built into it. To glamorize protest is to take away the tenor of protest and replace it with a semblance of resistance that conforms where it must challenge the status quo. The deglamorizing of protest is to show resistance in its raw forms as an argument in support of social and political justice. This chapter deals with protest as embodied in music as much as it delves into the politics of "song and dance" that serve, to a large extent, as a vehicle to mainstream cultural hegemony that is embodied in discourses such as casteism, gender, and class inequalities. If reactionary attitudes are sustained through suppression of radical consciousness, nowhere is this more evident than in popular Indian cinema. I have taken the liberty of including regional language movies under the rubric of Indian cinema, given the "popular" dimension of it, which means that they are commercially produced with the intent of making profit through entertainment. The role of protest music in popular culture is an interesting one because, by its very nature, it goes against the grain of *popularity* and argues in less than popular terms. Protest goes against standardization which, to Adorno, characterizes popular music, as opposed to "serious" music which emerges from "concrete totality."[2] "The whole structure of popular music is standardized, even where the attempt is made to circumvent standardization."[3]

Interestingly, not all music that goes against standardization ends up being protest music. The popularity of the anti-standardization argument with reference to popular music hardly needs to be overemphasized, though Roy Shuker has no hesitation in "equating 'popular music' with commercially mass-produced music for a mass market."[4] This does not reduce the need to look at popular music in complex ways. Shuker notes that:

> the question of meaning in popular music cannot be read off purely at one level, be it that of the producers, the texts, or the audience. It can only be satisfactorily answered by considering the nature of the production context, including State cultural policy, the texts and their creators, and the consumers of the music and their spatial location. Most importantly, it is necessary to consider the interrelationship of these factors.[5]

Another possibility within the popular music discourse is that the *popular* becomes a base to argue in alternate terms. At the heart of the popular there are minority voices fighting for visibility and presence. "Popular" is a word meant to contain voices of protest and make them acceptable to a mainstream majoritarian audience. By protest music, I refer to arguments made through music which play a conscious role in "affecting the property structure which the masses strive to eliminate."[6] While going against standardization is an important element in protest music, we must identify how music becomes a basis from which to make political demands in terms of basic rights; how the "weak" are able to create "weapons" out of banal contexts in which "symbolic compliance is maximized *precisely* in order to minimize compliance at the level of actual behavior."[7] While the masses accept standardization as norm through a process of "symbolic compliance," at the level of "actual behavior" those elements within popular music which empower them to argue against standardization are relevant.

Throughout the chapter, I have broadly equated the idea of the "popular" with a notion of the "mass." The terms are used interchangeably, barring a minor distinction where the popular refers to "people," by which I mean members in an order who seek to find solutions to social and economic problems, while the term "masses" indicates the majority who are unwilling to raise serious political questions that could disturb the order. Benjamin points out that "the masses have a right to change property relations; Fascism seeks to give them an expression while preserving property. The logical result of Fascism is the introduction of aesthetics into political life."[8] In equating the masses with the majority, I intend to argue that standardization of music gives "expression while preserving property." Through the introduction of "musical aesthetics" into political life, which is the goal of standardization, the "right" of masses to "change property relations" is taken away from them. While popular music is music of the *people*, where a conscious effort is made to view music as a means to bring about change, mass music is music of the majority that preserve the status quo: commercial music that you get to hear on the streets, restaurants, tea shops, or wedding functions; music that does not require the effort of interpretation, responding instead to pre-given categories in one's consciousness. As Adorno and Eisler observe, commercial music composers "have had to deal with an illiterate, intolerant, and uncritical public taste, and they have had to bow to it if they wanted to remain true to their dubious maxim: give the public nothing but what the public wants."[9]

With this theoretical backdrop, I intend to examine protest music in its natural habitats and the protest that goes into mainstream music cultures, especially those composed for films. The primary assumption is that there is a protest music emerging directly from the masses and moving upwards, from the margins, to knock in an intimidating manner upon the cold, iron gates of a center which is safeguarded by instruments of state coercion—the army, the police and the judiciary—and promoted by ideological apparatuses, such as the family, religious institutions, and the media.

There are two arguments that the chapter uses to examine what protest means in the Indian musical context. The "culture industry" thesis that Adorno propounds, whereby the "commercial character of culture causes the difference between culture and practical life to disappear,"[10] is one facet of contextualizing song and dance in popular Indian cinema. The other argument is that of Raymond Williams, who notes that, "The conception of persons as masses springs, not from an inability to know them, but from an interpretation of them according to a formula."[11] As Williams argues, the problem with this view is that "contemporary historians of popular culture have tended to concentrate on what is bad and to neglect what is good."[12]

Both are equally significant points of view to situate the song and dance discourse within the larger nationalist framework; in attempts to *imagine* communities and to legitimize that which is imagined. While there is undoubtedly a culture industry whose role is to perpetuate colonial style exploitation through the national bourgeoisie, Frantz Fanon strikes at the heart of the issue of decolonization in what he says of the bourgeoisie:

> Because it is bereft of ideas, because it lives to itself and cuts itself off from the people, undermined by its hereditary incapacity to think in terms of all the problems of the nation as seen from the point of view of the whole of that nation, the national middle class will have nothing better to do than to take on the role of manager for Western enterprise, and it will in practice set up its country as the brothel of Europe.[13]

In its "role of manager for Western enterprise," a role that allows for the blatant exploitation of the poor through multi-national companies whose agenda is globalization of goods, rather than of labor, the native bourgeoisie needs the culture industry to play its part in subjugating protest through a retelling that dilutes the possibility of open insurrection and looks for solutions within the parameters defined by the corporate state. The culture industry argument is an important one by which to examine the possibility of decolonization, which directly challenges the commercialization of culture connected to a profit-based industry. The aesthetics of song and dance must be located both within the framework of decolonization and the attempts by the state to prevent decolonization from becoming a reality. Fanon's point ought to be given due consideration here:

> The national bourgeoisie turns its back more and more on the interior and on the real facts of its undeveloped country, and tends to look toward the former mother country and the foreign capitalists who count on its obliging compliance. As it does not share its profits with the people, and in no way allows them to enjoy any of the dues that are paid to it by the big foreign companies, it will discover the need for a popular leader to whom will fall the dual role of stabilizing the regime and of perpetuating the domination of the bourgeoisie.[14]

The protest in the Indian context is thus not only about addressing issues related to class, gender, and caste, but is also connected to decolonization, where neocolonial forms of exploitation, along with concomitant ideologies, need to be actively undermined in order to give the poor a chance to articulate their selfhood. Song and dance become the basis by which an idea of Indianness that is abstract, and not rooted in concrete lives of the masses, can be sustained. They are Indian to the extent that they consume the idea of belonging to a nation. In an article entitled, "The imagined community of *Maa Tujhe Salaam*," Rangan Chakrabarty, while offering an incisive analysis of the music video "Maa Tujhe Salaam" from the album *Vande Mataram* (*Hail Motherland*) by A. R. Rehman, points out that:

> The dominant imagination of an Indian nation, formulated at a moment of anti-colonial movement, did not include all the inhabitants as equal members of a national community within the geographic boundaries of the colonial territories increasingly conquered and unified as India. The processes of the rise of certain dominant social forces to take over the reins of anti-colonial movements and eventually succeed the coloniser to the throne of the nation-state were clearly mediated by power relations of class, caste, gender, religion, cultural capital and other social markers of privilege.[15]

Where the imagination actively participated in excluding the weak and the powerless in constructing a national community, decolonization responds through a simultaneous process of making an alternative nation that includes those left out of mainstream politics. We identify the role of protest at points where the idea of Indianness is either sustained to exclude non-consumers or compelled to include those who have made it a goal to resist exclusionary positions. The docile body ideal to manufacturing consent is built on illusions generated through the discourse of romantic love and the conflict-free family, both of which emerge owing to suppression of the bodies of women and dissenting men. This apolitical body can best be observed in the non-dialogical context of the song and dance where no explanation is necessary; the erotic speaks with forced innocence, disguising its consumerist intentions; the epiphany, which is usually a thinly-veiled orgasm, leaves little space for serious reflection; the community that is formed through the apolitical bodies is ideal to the making of a mass society filled with faces that look alike and which are without the names necessary to identify them individually.

What Indian Audiences Want

While the culture industry dictates what the audiences want through the song and dance equation, the masses are not silent partners to a vicious order dedicated to keeping them in a comatose state. Sudipto Chatterjee, in his article, "The Case of the Irritating Song: Suman Chatterjee and Modern Bengali Music," argues that the songs of Suman Chatterjee have successfully worked as an alternative to mainstream music. The article, while giving a social and political background to Suman Chatterjee's rise as an alternative voice in the domain of the popular song, notes that:

> Despite the fact that they are never released through any means of mass reproduction, these songs are on the lips of thousands in no time. These

songs do work, even in their small way, meta-textually against the other "industrialised" songs co-opted for regressive listening, creating a site for resistance close to the street, or even a site for an alternative history, the possibility of a paradigm shift.[16]

The popularity of Suman Chatterjee's songs is clear indication of the fact that the masses are willing to make choices that might go completely against standardized forms of musical entertainment. In a Brechtian manner, Suman Chatterjee combines intense emotion with a trenchant critique of the political order. More importantly, "Suman's diffidence to the system, however small, is exemplified by his conscious efforts at trying to reach his audience without help from his recording company, through direct communication from and off the stage, and on the streets."[17] In a heavily populated third world nation such as India, streets are political theaters with the potential to disrupt or arrest the lifelines of an entire system and bring it to a grinding halt. The ability to use streets as platforms to resist oppressive politics is important to any protester. The street is opposed to the recording company, because one does not have to pay anything to be standing on a street to watch a performance; the emotions that run on the street precede some of the most unexpected social changes. To the third world performer, the street, in itself, is an alternative argument to dominant ideologies that wish to occupy the spaces of the street, leaving no scope to reflect on serious change.

To enable the politicization of aesthetics, it is imperative to recognize that which is good in popular culture, as Raymond Williams points out. The culture industry argument is a wholesale dismissal of popular culture as a commodity manufactured for the indoctrinated *walking dead* consumer. Terming this view "elitist," Kotarba and Vannini say that "early critical thinkers like Adorno felt that capitalists marketed popular music to anesthetize the working class politically and to increasingly subjugate them economically."[18] If that is the avowed intention of a profit-seeking industry, its practical success has not been met without resistance. While noting that "musical choices are cultural choices,"[19] Kotarba and Vannini add that, "If we wish to understand the meanings of pop music and be critical of those cultural practices and values which result in the formation or recreation of cultural injustices, we need to follow an approach to the study of our subject matter which is interpretive and critical at the same time."[20] This, in fact, is the approach taken by Sangita Gopal and Sujata Moorti, editors of the groundbreaking book *Global Bollywood: Travels of Hindi Song and Dance*. They express the view that:

> song and dance has been tied to Indian cinema from its very start. Although a history of the media world in which Indian film arose is still an ongoing project, there is some consensus that the centrality of music, song, and dance in preexisting popular and folk traditions in India must partly account for the persistence of song-dance in Hindi film.[21]

Anustup Basu, in the article "The Music of Intolerable Love," on the 1998 Mani Ratnam Film *Dil Se* (*From the Heart*), writes of the song sequences as opening up "luminous intervals for the visual consolidation of an unremitted desire, a picture of ardor that is an otherworldly life without political status."[22] The inability to locate these scenes in "real" life, and the freezing of moments in fantasy sequences, is deeply colonial in character. The otherworldliness of desire and the politics of day-to-day life are clearly at odds with one another. The containment of protest takes place in preventing the political argument from entering the domains of desire. Freud notes, in his essay, "On the universal tendency to debasement in the sphere of love," that:

> The genitals themselves have not taken part in the development of the human body in the direction of beauty: they have remained animal, and thus love, too, has remained in essence just as animal as it ever was. The instincts of love are hard to educate; education of them achieves now too much, now too little.[23]

The discussion of "terror" that happens in the movie *Dil Se* is secondary to educating the "instincts of love." I merely replace what Freud calls "civilization"—an abstract idea—with the concrete reality of the nation state: "Thus we may perhaps be forced to become reconciled to the idea that it is quite impossible to adjust the claims of the sexual instinct to the demands of civilization."[24] The politics of curtailing the "sexual instinct" except in the free-floating void of non-belonging goes against the politics of protest; both the "politics" that articulates desire and the desire that rejects violent suppression are dangerous to existence of the nation state. To keep this contradiction alive is the objective of the neocolonial state; the song and dance demonstrates, through its own vacuity, that all attempts to fight social injustices and bring about political transformation are doomed to similar kind of vacuity. Basu notes that

> In the melodramatic dispensation of *Dil Se*, the song sequences do not just bring into a critical proximity the sublime and terrifying aspect of love and the tragic naïveté of a perpetually becoming metropolitan subjectivity. Their affective and intellectual dimensions also help us think about despair and boredom in themselves as political and historical categories.[25]

The despair is inevitable and the boredom is natural, because what we see in the third world is the absence of a "real" bourgeoisie. Fanon astutely observes that, "the bourgeoisie in underdeveloped countries is non-existent,"[26] precisely because we don't have those economic conditions that made the Western bourgeoisie a reality.

Now, in the colonies, the economic conditions are conditions of a foreign bourgeoisie. Through its agents, it is the bourgeoisie of the mother country that we find present in the colonial towns. The bourgeoisie in the colonies is, before independence, a Western bourgeoisie, a true branch of the bourgeoisie of the mother country that derives its legitimacy, its force, and its stability from the bourgeoisie of the homeland.[27]

The music of popular Indian film is not about India, but about the making of dominant versions of Indianness. It essentially defies the reality of anything remotely Indian, not merely because art transforms the details of life, but because commercialized art must reduce life to an object that could be consumed. To say that the ideal is what the real could possibly be is not the same thing as saying that the ideal is what the real will never be. When students from Iran or the Middle East tell me that the films gave them the impression of India being a singing and dancing nation, my response is that if it were so then we wouldn't be a third world nation. In a short article entitled "Notes on an Unpleasant Subject," Paul Bowles says: "The period of a quick cultural death exists particularly for those parts of the globe peopled by races other than the Caucasian, but where Western civilization enjoys more prestige than the indigenous."[28] This is what decolonization seeks to actively address, because there is no space for protest in an imitation. The national bourgeoisie which, as Fanon observes, is not a real bourgeoisie, but an agent of the West, refuses the portrayal of any serious encounter between unequal forces. The voices of protest populate the worlds outside the screen, and the music they make is barely audible to those engrossed in the song and dance sequence in the films. As Paul Bowles notes,

> now, wherever you may be in Latin America, you can hear the same pseudomusic, the same poisonous clichés of melody and harmony, the same empty purple lyrics. It has all been made digestible for the radio and film audiences of the Latin American republics, and presumably everyone is happy.[29]

This does not imply that the masses do not participate, in however brief a manner, in the making of the song and dance. Gregory D. Booth rightly observes that, "An enormous range of cultural behaviors and content owes its existence to the specific ways in which Indian popular music was produced exclusively (for much of the twentieth century) for commercial narrative films."[30] Likewise, the music owes its existence to the ways in which the Indian masses are able to produce a shared understanding of what constitutes a song and dance performance. David Davies makes that point that "the artist must consciously operate by reference to certain presumed shared understandings in order for her manipulations of a vehicular medium to count as the articulation of an artistic statement."[31] The artistic statement originates with reference to "shared understandings" that the audience created for the artist. "Because a focus of appreciation of an artwork can be specified only by one who so orients herself to a community of receivers, art is indeed essentially institutional in the broad sense."[32] In noting the institutional character of song and dance, it is easier to perceive what the audiences want, because they are consciously performing to create meanings for themselves through the music. As Stefan Fiol observes, at the conclusion of his fascinating study on the journey that Himalayan musicians make to East Delhi to record their songs, which then return back to the village in a reinterpreted form:

> One obvious point to take from this is that musical performance evolves unevenly and unpredictably across many arenas of social life; it is made up of many streams of influence, making it difficult if not impossible to determine a starting or ending point in the creative process. While it is commonly assumed that commercial studio recording encourages musical standardization and village festivals encourage musical vernacularization, it is more accurate to say that both of these processes are unfolding dialectically as songs are continuously refashioned across these contexts.[33]

Therefore, to accept, unreservedly, either the culture industry argument or the argument that views song and dance as representative of popular choice, would risk us arriving at generalizations divorced from reality. The relationship between "musical performance" and "social life" is a conflict-ridden one filled with paradoxes of every kind. Popular will exerts pressures of various kinds in demanding expression to what it deems as articulation of its artistic and political needs. Where the culture industry succeeds on the Indian landscape, is in depoliticizing social reality. The point is not that there is no space for protest in the song and dance discourse. The point is that the protest is glamorized to make it palatable to a bourgeoisie that produces cinema to suit its larger economic interests.

The Politics of Deglamorized Protest

The language of protest entails an awareness of the body as a vehicle of resistance. Where fantasy is the way out of repression, reality is the issue in popular versions of song and dance on the Indian screen. The reality of a dominant family that thrives on preserving the status quo through romantic love and marriage is central to our understanding of why the song and dance emerges out of nowhere. The discourse of realism that is vital to control the body in a narrative keeps class and gender relations intact without any scope for raising questions. Peter Brooks makes the following observation about realism in his chapter "The Body In the Field of Vision":

> To know, in realism, is to see, and to represent is to describe. To the extent that persons are the object of knowledge, they too must be described, not only in their psychological composition but also in their "objectal" form, as

bodies. While the bodies viewed are both male and female, vision is typically a male prerogative, and its object of fascination the woman's body.[34]

If knowing is about seeing, and representing is describing, realism in Indian cinema fulfills both these functions. The culture of song and dance is appropriate to the realist mode of storytelling because it creates a space in which the body can be described. The body—especially that of a woman, which is, until then, confined to the fetters of home and norms of public behavior—is released temporarily from the cage of convention and allowed to run free in the wilds of fantasy. It is *the* time, though, in which the body will be watched the most carefully. It is the time for the male audiences to *know* the body that they are seeing. It is a time when vision will assert itself as masculine; this does not mean female audiences will not experience the fantasized freedom of the body. (Interestingly, such a freedom is about the girl/woman who is in her virginal state and yet to be touched by a man.) The woman's role is not just about being a good homemaker, but also about being a sex partner because, apart from preserving the family honor, as a giving wife she must produce the male heir who will inherit the property. The song and dance interludes are times when the woman has the space to demonstrate that, apart from labor value, she also stands the test of desirableness. Her willingness to offer her labor in service of the patriarchal family is related to her making herself desirable to the male who defends the interests of the family with which he identifies himself. The need to make herself desirable to the "family" man is as critical as the labor itself, though never more than the latter.

In the article "The Cognitive Universality of the Hindi Musical," Patrick Colm Hogan points out that:

> One common use of the interlude is to suspend ordinary time constraints. A song sequence allows us to experience the elaborate development of a romantic relationship in the course of a few moments. For example, lovers sing to one another in a series of verses. Perhaps they change locations for each verse. Perhaps they change clothing. In any case, the development of the song communicates the development of their relationship. Interestingly, this need not be matched by a corresponding lapse in time in the actual story. Thus an interlude may begin and end at the same moment in story time.[35]

Ironically, the "development of their relationship" is never preceded by material discussions—relevant, especially, to the girl—with regard to sharing of work or finding a larger meaning to the relationship. The passive status of the woman character as worker and unconditional giver is taken for granted. Questions are never raised with regard to the psychological and ethical commitment that marriage might ideally demand. The song and dance is a vehicle for preserving monogamy in its most inhuman forms, which takes for granted the economic subservience of the woman in relation to the man. Hogan's detailed analysis of the song "Suraj Hua Maddham" ("The Sun Dims into Twilight") from the 2001 movie *Kabhi Khushi Kabhie Gham …* (*Through Smiles through Tears …*) delves into a series of interrelated questions:

> Are we to imagine that the lovers go through this sort of developing relation in a period stretching out after that moment at the fair? In other words, are we to imagine that this is a paradiegetic flash forward? Alternatively, did the brief touch of the lovers communicate so much; was there such intensity of understanding that it was equivalent to a developed relationship? Or should one completely accept the sexual implications and assume that there has indeed been a consummation? Or perhaps it was, after all, entirely a fantasy, with some parts merely indeterminate as to which one of the lovers was dreaming?[36]

Hogan views this "ambiguity" as essential to our "engagement" with the film as a whole. The ambiguity, however, is the ambiguity of a civil society in a state of crisis; it is as deliberate as in the song and dance itself because, on the one hand, to show that the man and the woman are really involved in a sexual relationship prior to marriage is unacceptable to the middle class audiences, since that is more choice given to the young than is officially permitted; on the other hand, to relegate it to the level of fantasy still leaves the stick of authority in the hands of parents and the social order. The authority is not challenged, and the young are given the illusion of choice. Either way, the aestheticizing of politics is achieved with remarkable success.

The glamorizing of protest is to disallow any serious discussion related to the body in its material condition. The idealized body is not worried about banal issues, such as finding a decent job, as a creative expression of oneself or about one's sense of selfhood. It's about keeping the order alive which, by default, is greater than the individual. Adorno's point that "the liquidation of the individual is the real signature of the new musical situation"[37] is not without basis in the context of Indian reality. The deglamorizing of protest is to change the parameters of discussion regarding the body; to evacuate it from the idealization and to bring it to the level of social and political reality. As Foucault says,

> it is the agency of sex that we must break away from, if we aim—through a tactical reversal of the various mechanisms of sexuality—to counter the grips of power with the claims of bodies, pleasures, and knowledges, in their multiplicity and their possibility of resistance. The rallying point for the counterattack against the deployment of sexuality ought not to be sex desire, but bodies and pleasures.[38]

Where "bodies" are able to articulate their "pleasures," an effective "counter attack" is formed against the "agency of sex." In the third world, social change cannot be imagined without a material reading of the body as part of the workforce, along with a process of decolonization that aims to dislodge the nationalist bourgeoisie, the producers of a pseudo-culture, and agents of the west, from positions of power. It is the latter who control the culture industry and who refuse the visualization of a multiple understanding of the body as an agent of transformation. The body has to be restrained within the format prescribed by the bourgeoisie. Lakshmi Subramanian, in her study on the social history of music in south India, speaks of the devadasis who stood on the "margins of the classical."[39] Traditionally viewed as women married to a god or a temple, these women who were artists in their own right became objects of interest at the peak of colonialism in the nineteenth century. Subramanian mentions that:

> Nineteenth-century social reform in south India was fixed firmly on the body of the devadasi who became the site of multiple definitions, imaginings and contestations ... Added to this was the legitimately and widely shared impression that the devadasi community was especially proficient in the arts.[40]

While nineteenth-century social reformers saw the devadasi as a "prostitute," a more complex view looks at:

> the devadasi as a legitimate custodian of traditional religion and of artistic skills and graces, who was permitted to express her sexuality in a space that was denied to the wife of the householder ... Law, social reform and the cultural project worked in unison from the late nineteenth century to create new standards of morality, new idioms of cultural expression and standards of aesthetics and performative practices. The combination was potent and served to dislodge the devadasi from the stage and push her into the wings as a relic.[41]

There is, however, no reason to believe that the artistic achievements of the devadasis were left to perish out in the cold. On the contrary, most of the artistic traditions were appropriated by upper caste elites and the song and dance tradition in Indian cinema owes an extensive debt to the devadasis. Davesh Soneji, in his study, says that "*Devadasi* dance is thus unhitched from the location of its emergence, only to be imported into diffuse systems of value when it is reinvented by Indian elites as "Bharatanatyam."[42] The latter is a more accepted mainstream dance with an air of respectability to it. The denigration of the body of the devadasi complemented the appropriation of the arts connected with these marginalized women artists. Protestant Christian morality, combined with Hindu casteism, successfully ostracized these women while making sure that much of their work was institutionalized in other ways without any official credit given to the devadasis. The subtext to Indian cinema in the song and dance discourse contains Derridean traces of an effectively marginalized text. The researcher into protest music uncovers the substructures of mainstream Hindi and regional cinema to examine the contributions of social groups such as the devadasis in the making of the social history of popular music.

Rachel Dwyer says that "Hindi cinema manifests what could be called postmodern love, in which consumerism and love are inextricably bound."[43] The deglamorizing of protest is not about saving love from the claws of consumerism. A subaltern reading is selective: it submits to what Shuker says about the media, which "operate as consciousness industries, shaping our perceptions, values and norms, and confirming or denying these."[44] The point is whether the subaltern reading submits to the *terms* set by the consciousness industries or whether it creates a reading based on its life-worlds and material conditions. An instance of deglamorized protest can be taken from the study by Jeffrey G. Snodgrass of the Bhat community of Rajasthan, who are narrators and genealogists of their community's past. Snodgrass observes that, as bards,

> the Bhats' discursive resistance is double—or perhaps once removed. That is, Bhats themselves overturn elite ideas about time and the future, be they traditional or modern. Equally, however, through their crafty control of images, they also strive to raise the consciousness of their audiences, thus providing others with the tools to recognize and resist the agendas of the powerful. Indeed, Bhats, through self-deprecating jokes and double-speak, even encourage their audiences to resist the Bhats' own messages.[45]

The politics of subversion is about the cunning with which the poor and the marginalized will select from the culture industry, especially the song and dance tradition, and use those messages as "modern" in order to serve their own economic and political goals. In doing so, they are not just interpreters, but also makers, of music.

Notes

1 Theodor W. Adorno, "Music, Language, Composition," *The Musical Quarterly*, Vol. 77, No. 3 (Autumn 1993): 403.
2 Theodor W. Adorno, "On Popular Music," *Studies in Philosophy and Social Science IX* (New York: Institute of Social Research, 1941), 18.
3 Adorno, "On Popular Music," 17.
4 Roy Shuker, *Understanding Popular Music* (London and New York: Routledge, 2001), x.
5 Shuker, *Understanding Popular Music*, x.
6 Walter Benjamin, "The Work of Art in the Age of Mechanical Reproduction," in *Illuminations* (New York: Schocken Books, 2007), 241.

7 James Scott, *Weapons of the Weak: Everyday Forms of Peasant Resistance* (New Haven: Yale University Press, 1985), 26.

8 Benjamin, *Illuminations*, 241.

9 Theodor Adorno and Hanns Eisler, *Composing for the Films* (London: Continuum, 2007), 38.

10 Theodor Adorno, *The Culture Industry: Selected Essays on Mass Culture* (London and New York: Routledge, 2001), 61.

11 Raymond Williams, *Culture and Society, 1780–1950* (New York: Anchor Books, 1960), 322.

12 Williams, *Culture and Society*, 327.

13 Frantz Fanon, *The Wretched of the Earth*, trans. Constance Farrington (New York: Grove Press, 1963), 154.

14 Fanon, *The Wretched of the Earth*, 165.

15 Rangan Chakravarty, "The Imagined Community of *Maa Tujhe Salaam*," in Allen Chun et al., eds., *Pop Music in Asia: Cosmopolitan Flows, Political Tempos, and Aesthetic Industries* (London and New York: Routledge Curzon, 2004), 65.

16 Sudipto Chatterjee, "The Case of the Irritating Song: Suman Chatterjee and Modern Bengali music," in Allen Chun et al., eds., *Refashioning Pop Music in Asia: Cosmopolitan Flows, Political Tempos, and Aesthetic Industries* (London and New York: Routledge Curzon, 2004), 108.

17 Chatterjee, "The Case of the Irritating Song," 105.

18 Joseph A. Kotarba and Phillip Vannini, *Understanding Society through Popular Music* (New York and London: Routledge, 2009), 10.

19 Kotarba and Vannini, *Understanding Society through Popular Music*, 7.

20 Kotarba and Vannini, *Understanding Society through Popular Music*, 13.

21 Sangita Gopal and Sujata Moorti, eds., *Global Bollywood: Travels of Hindi Song and Dance* (Minneapolis, Minnesota: University of Minnesota Press, 2008), 17–18.

22 Gopal and Moorti eds., *Global Bollywood*, 169.

23 Sigmund Freud, "On the Universal Tendency to Debasement in the Sphere of Love," *Complete Works* (New York: Ivan Smith, 2010), 2346.

24 Freud, "On the Universal Tendency," 2346.

25 Gopal and Moorti eds., *Global Bollywood*, 169.

26 Fanon, *The Wretched of the Earth*, 178.

27 Fanon, *The Wretched of the Earth*, 178.

28 Timothy Mangan and Irene Herrmann, eds., "Notes on an Unpleasant Subject," in *Paul Bowles on Music* (Berkeley, California: University of California Press, 2003), 235.

29 Mangan and Herrmann, "Notes on an Unpleasant Subject," 237.

30 Gregory D. Booth, *Behind the Curtain: Making Music in Mumbai's Film Studios* (Oxford: Oxford University Press, 2008), 27.

31 David Davies, *Art as Performance* (Malden, Massachusetts: Blackwell Publishing, 2004), 245.

32 Davies, *Art as Performance*, 246.

33 Stefan Fiol, "From Folk to Popular and Back: Musical Feedback between Studio Recordings and Festival Dance-Songs in Uttarkhand, North India," *Asian Music*, Vol. 42, No. 1 (Winter/Spring 2011): 46.

34 Peter Brooks, "The Body in the Field of Vision," in *Body Work: Objects of Desire in Modern Narrative* (Cambridge, Massachusetts: Harvard University Press, 1993), 88.

35 Patrick Colm Hogan, *Indian Movies: Culture, Cognition, and Cinematic Imagination* (Austin, Texas: University of Texas Press, 2008), 165.

36 Hogan, *Indian Movies*, 170.

37 Adorno, *The Culture Industry*, 35.

38 Michel Foucault, *The History of Sexuality: Volume One*, trans. Robert Hurley (New York: Pantheon Books, 1978), 157.

39 Lakshmi Subramanian, *From the Tanjore Court to the Madras Music Academy: A Social History of Music in South India* (New Delhi: Oxford University Press, 2011), 115.

40 Subramanian, *From the Tanjore Court*, 115.

41 Subramanian, *From the Tanjore Court*, 116.

42 Davesh Soneji, *Unfinished Gestures: Devadasis, Memory, and Modernity in South India* (Chicago: University of Chicago Press, 2012), 100.

43 Rachel Dwyer, "Kiss or Tell? Declaring Love in Hindi Films," in Francesca Orsini, ed., *Love in South Asia: A Cultural History* (Cambridge: Cambridge University Press, 2007), 290.

44 Shuker, *Understanding Popular Music*, 10.

45 Jeffrey G. Snodgrass, *Casting Kings: Bards and Indian Modernity* (Oxford: Oxford University Press, 2006), 159.

26

PROTESTING COLONIAL AUSTRALIA

Convict Theatre and Kelly Ballads

Stephen Gaunson

Figure 26.1   Australian bushranger and outlaw Ned Kelly.

The oral tradition insists on a direct performative participation with the text. As Benedict Anderson explains, "no matter how banal the words and mediocre the tunes, there is in this singing an experience of simultaneity. At precisely such moments, people wholly unknown to each other utter the same verses to the same melody. The image: unisonance."[1] Through colonial ballads, Australia's jocular mockery of the English and celebration of the under-class was ingrained into the Australian culture and character. Folklorist and Kelly expert Graham Seal understands the English as a target to be lampooned in popular song as stuffy, pompous, and unable to endure Australia's bucolic outdoors.[2] Briton Francis Adams in 1891 conceded that, in Australia, "the bush is the heart of the country, the real Australian Australia, and it is with the Bushman that the final fate of the nation and race will lie … the English cannot thrive far from the sea."[3]

Australia's history of protest began aboard the convict transport, *The Scarborough*, where a number of prisoners performed a political farce as it moored at Sydney town on 2 January 1788. Convict theatre became a hugely popular pastime for many, allowing the performance of not just convict and bushranger ballads but, deliciously, the spectacle of watching convict rogues performing these ballads.[4] The performance of protest ballads and protest plays, with which audience members were encouraged to "sing-along," rooted the theme of protest into the national popular entertainment culture. How audience members responded to the performances impacted and normalized attitudes and themes of Australian popular culture. Globally, the theatre, during the eighteenth and nineteenth centuries, became a haven for economically frustrated community members—the unemployed, laborers, shopkeepers—to sing protest ballads and interact with their content.[5] As Oliver Goldsmith opines, "It was they who called for the music, indulging every noisy freedom, and testifying all the insolence of beggary in exaltation."[6]

The controversy of the convict theatres, however, was not the songs performed by the actors (although it was often riotously provocative). Its real problem was the behavior of the audience members whose rowdiness resulted in arrests and plays having to be abandoned mid-way into the performances. Because convict theatres were seemingly fostering a culture of unruly conduct, many were outlawed, with barely any remaining by the 1840s. And, with hiked admission prices at theatres, Australia's downtrodden convict communities suddenly found themselves locked out of the auditoriums that once depended on their involvement. Instead, such community members had to manufacture their own entertainment through street vaudeville and in pubs and social rounds. These entertainments were then staged in "professional" theatres and, later, the moving pictures. Through these agencies, convictism and bushranging was commodified for the popular mainstream audience.

Moving Pictures

The early Australian cinema enjoyed two genre booms: convict films and bushranger films. The former was sparked by the rousing success of writer Marcus Clarke's *For the Term of His Natural Life*—initially published, between 1870–1872, in serialized form in *The Australian Journal* as *His Natural Life*. In 1908, Charles MacMahon adapted Clarke's text in what sparked an explosion of convict films including, among others, *It Is Never Too Late to Mend* (W. J. Lincoln, 1911), *The Assigned Servant* (John Gavin, 1911), *One Hundred Years Ago* (Gaston Mervale, 1911), *Sentenced for Life* (E. I. Cole, 1911), *The Life of Rufus Dawes* (Alfred Rolfe, 1911), *Mark of the Lash* (John Gavin, 1911) and *The Romantic Story of Margaret Catchpole* (Raymond Longford, 1911). Such films firmly placed the audience's sympathy on the side of the impoverished and bullied prisoners. Moreover, at such films, as part of the theatre spectacle, balladeers and musical troupes performed a variety of convict ballads to narrate the onscreen action. Such performances dovetailed the popular ballads to the images on the screen, something which would be taken up further once sound (talking pictures) took over.

The bushranger was a natural precursor to the convict. Most nineteenth-century bushrangers had convict history, either by their fathers being convicts or experiencing the convict life themselves. The cinema's bushranger genre was always going to be more successful than the convict genre, for it could narrate scenic adventure stories of rogues roaming the country while the convict, in comparison, is a hermetic fellow confined to the prison walls.[7] The film *The Story of the Kelly Gang* (Charles Tait, 1906) started an explosion of bushranger films that were stunted only by government censorship in 1911. The bushranger ban was certainly wider than just the Kelly films, but the very subject of Ned Kelly seemed to exacerbate the concern of bushrangers fetishizing social protest. There, indeed, was no figure of the bushranging tradition more lionized than Kelly. Appearing much later than the "golden days" of the bushranger epidemic of the 1850s, he would posthumously become the codified symbol of the classic Australian dissident—helped, of course, by his steel helmet, a symbol to represent all dissidents. Because of the cinema's profound impact, especially on minor and adolescent filmgoers, there was a concern about how Kelly was represented as a felonious binary to the police. Even before the bushranger ban, the Kelly films endured the most scrutiny of all the bushranger films.

As with convict films like *His Natural Life* (Norman, Dawn, 1927), bushranger cinema was an adaptation of popular stage plays. *The Story of the Kelly Gang* is said to have been adapted from one of the stage plays, *The Kelly Gang or the Career of Ned Kelly, the Iron-clad Bushranger of Australia* (1898) produced and written by Arnold Denham; or *Hands Up! Or Ned Kelly and His Gang or The Iron-Clad Bushranger* (1903) produced by E. I. Cole.[8] Denham's play inspired other vaudeville celebrating the subject of "lawlessness." William Routt summarizes the gang from *The Story of the Kelly Gang* in a way to liken them to Denham's play of social rebellion: "Vile fellows, not like heroes at all."[9]

Prior to their 1906 Kelly film, the Tait family was involved in the international exhibition of protest theatre. In addition to holding the rights to the Kelly "Flesh and Blood" Show, they toured David Burn's *The Bushrangers* around Britain.[10] As Graham Shirley and Brian Adams note, 1904 saw the Taits make their first substantial move into film exhibition. Their Melbourne Town Hall programs were generally divided between the entertainment of imported cinema newsreels and gramophone recordings—as performed by opera soprano extraordinaire Nellie Melba.[11] Then, from 29 March 1906, they had a very successful run with the documentary *Living London*. By the year's end, they had filmed *The Story of the Kelly Gang*.

Its astonishing box-office records prove the popularity of social protest and lawlessness. Playing for five weeks to capacity houses at the Athenaeum Hall in Melbourne, it soon moved to the spacious Town Hall. It further enjoyed successful tours across Australia, New Zealand, and London. As boasted in the updated editions of the program booklet: "The whole series of pictures were taken by Messrs J. and N. Tait, of Melbourne and London, and have been shown by them throughout Australasia and also England with phenomenal success."[12] Its producer, William Gibson, later alleged that the film had returned no less than £25,000.[13] If true, this makes it (by percentage) one of the highest ever grossing Australian productions.

The Jerilderie Ballad

"Moreton Bay" (also known as "The Convict's Lament on the Death of Captain Logan" and "The Convict's Arrival") is the convict ballad that is most associated with bushranger Ned Kelly. It is perhaps the most popular and widely circulated of all the convict ballads. It tells the story of an unnamed man overhearing a conversation between imprisoned felons. The "beastly treated" prisoners will undoubtedly perish under the watch of Captain Logan. The narrator—an innocent bystander—comes to champion and speak on behalf of the dead convicts. The song is a gripe at authorities who condone the "beastly treatment" of prisoners, and the lyrics are written as an internal monologue from an eavesdropping stranger, who is shocked to witness this hardship: "Like the Egyptians and ancient Hebrews, we were oppressed under Logan's yoke, till a native black lying there in ambush did give our tyrant his mortal stroke." The ballad forewarns "monsters such a death may find." A benchmark of future bush ballads, gleeful vengeance is unmistakeably foregrounded. More than celebrating the downtrodden battlers, however, is the villainous depiction of the rank-and-file as procrustean tyrants. Such a song establishes a clear divide between us and them—government and community. The performance of the song gave normally muted prisoners and ordinary people a chorus to protest against the Crown's penal system.

"Moreton Bay" became an anthem of defiance, and was most prominent within the Irish selector communities in which Kelly was immersed. More than any other group, the Irish Catholics were treated disdainfully and with great suspicion. Defined as a special class, they formed Australia's first white minority and, "from the outset, the Irish in Australia saw themselves as a doubly colonized people."[14] Not just Irish, however; songs about English convicts are also in abundance and seem just as vengeful towards their jailors. "Jim Jones," about the Englishman sent for "life" in Botany Bay, ends with the recurring TREAT ME RIGHT threat.

> And some dark night when everything is silent in the town
> I'll kill the tyrants one and all, I'll shoot the floggers down;
> I'll give the Law a little shock, remember what I say:
> They'll yet regret they sent Jim Jones in chains to Botany Bay

Folklorist Graham Seal describes "Moreton Bay" as a song about "the suffering of a transported Irishman."[15] This ballad had such a penetrating influence on the lore of Ned Kelly that many, such as Jack Bradshaw, identify it as a "Kelly Ballad"—despite it being in circulation since the 1830s, some fifty years before Kelly's hanging.[16] In the Jerilderie letter, Kelly not only poached one of the lines from "Moreton Bay"—"many a blooming Irish man rather than subdue to the Saxon yoke were flogged to death and bravely died in servile chains"— but further routed the ballad's lyrical and rhythmic style. The Jerilderie letter was written in response to the press's vilification of him and as a way to apotheosize his heroic qualities. Individualizing his own persecution and hounding, rather than discussing his role as the leader of the Kelly Gang, Ned posits the outbreak within the genealogy of the Irish convict ancestry that had endured generations of hardship at the hands of the procrustean police. More than any other historical account, Kelly's Jerilderie letter gave him a voice to respond directly to the public vitriol regarding his ambush and killing of three police officers at Stringybark Creek. Written when still at large—the outbreak ran from 1878 to 1880—the missive is punctuated with ominous threats and warnings: "I am a widows (sic) son outlawed and my orders must be obeyed."

Kelly's 5,200-word manifesto first appeared as a complete "unedited" document in Max Brown's *Australian Son* (1948) in which he coined it the "Jerilderie letter." Colonial newspapers had initially published edited excerpts before this time. The Jerilderie letter is the moment at which convict ballads and bushranger ballads converge, which is why the two accompany one another so fittingly in performance. On Graham Seal's musical LP record, *Game as Ned Kelly* (1980), the letter is read to the accompaniment of Irish bagpipes, playing the tune of "Moreton Bay." Discussing the song's effect on Kelly's missive, Seal explained:

> Poorly educated, poorly represented in Parliament, and just plain poor, the Kellys, and many like them, had no other means of expressing their anger than through the inherited images and clichés of Irish nationalism.[17]

In more recent times, the sentiment of the protest ballads is heard in voice as well as seen in on-screen action. In Jordan's 2003 film, *Ned Kelly*, the letter's composition is the response to a hostage—during the gang's raid of the New South Wales Bank—accusing them of being "a bunch of common criminals." Infuriated that his martyrdom is mistaken for thuggery, Ned (Heath Ledger) growls at his gang, "if we act like common criminals that's exactly what they will call us." He continues, to the hostages:

> My mother is rotting away in a prison cell because of the lies of a policeman named Fitzpatrick. She's an innocent woman and so are these boys here. My Irish brethren have been unlawfully imprisoned and blacklisted from their selections. How do you expect me to behave other than stand up against this treatment … if I can beg your patience, this is my statement to the Premier of Victoria, Graham Berry, and you are my witnesses … Joe get together your pen and paper.

The image of Ned dictating his words—a monologue of sorts—as he stands amongst his hostages, certainly denotes the letter as a performance of "community" grievances. Its composition becomes a ballad of public harmony.

Kelly Ballads

In Jordan's 2003 film, Irish music becomes a soundtrack by which to identify Kelly as a protest figure, and Bernard Fanning—lead singer of the now defunct Australian rock band Powderfinger—performs a mournful rendition of "Moreton Bay." Early on in the film, Aaron Sherritt (Joel Edgerton) uses music to shield Ned from a standoff with the contingent of police officers. "This one is a request for Ned Kelly," he hollers as the musical troupe erupts into a spirited rendition of "Kesh Jig." Dancing among his patrons, Ned is rhythmically placed in harmony with his community. And there, among his peers on the dance floor, he cheekily grins at Constable Lonigan—a grin of victory. "Nerve of the bloody knacker," the Constable retorts from the side. "Look at him. Acts as if he owns the joint." Despite this paradox of Lonigan (in reality) being Irish, such ancestry is ignored in this film in favor of giving the Victoria Police the label of "racist British thugs." Irish music, as a boundary between the sympathizers and resisters, is a staple amplified throughout the Australian folk protest tradition, so much so that, during the bans on the bushranging films, directors and exhibitors needed to be wary as to how the ballads fetishized Kelly as a noble and justified resister. In fear of a public ban, during *The Story of the Kelly Gang*'s Australian premiere tour in 1906, Sydney Monk sang popular bush ballads, prior to the feature's screening, but not during its presentation.[18]

Irish balladry also frames Kelly within the oral tradition of the Irish rebel-hero. William Brennan is one obvious example, for the opening lines of "Brennan on the

Moor" seem nascent to the sentiment echoed later in many of the Kelly ballads. As argued by Graham Seal, this Brennan ballad foregrounds the sentiment of "stressing the outlaw's bravery, courtesy, and his standing as a friend to the poor."[19]

Kelly ballads have continued to offend. George Wilson Hall's 1878 book, *The Kelly Gang or, the Outlaws of the Wombat Ranges*, even prefaced his readers to the affront that waits:

> We have limited our extracts to the most harmless portions to be selected from the mass of leprous distilments of the composer's perverted genius, such as it is, feeling confident that the majority of readers will join our estimate of the wretched and mischievous production, inductively judging what the character must be of the lines we have withheld from publication, as being outside the limits of decency and order. The following lines form a portion of a bad parody on "The Bould Sojer Boy"; this sample will be enough of the song to judge by. It refers, of course, to the Kelly Gang.[20]

McQuilton writes how "young toughs had taken to singing pro-Kelly ballads in 1879 to taunt the police."[21] Performance as social protest was reverberating around the country. In 1879, Hobart theatre broadsheets included the Kelly songs "Ballad of the Kelly Gang," and "Sticking up of the Euroa Bank." In this same year, *The Mansfield Guardian* distributed a pamphlet featuring the lyrics to four Kelly ballads.[22] The circulation of these ballads demonstrated Kelly's heroization amidst his outlawry. However, after his 1880 hanging, Kelly's oral musical tradition posthumously gained great momentum. In 1897, a successful magic lantern tour featured balladeer Joe Watson singing folk songs as Kelly magic lantern slides were shown.[23] Elizabeth Hartrick, in her Ph.D. thesis on the magic lantern phenomenon in Australia and New Zealand, outlines the common songs, canticles, recitations, hymns, and comic narratives that would have been performed at such presentations: "Singing aroused feelings of community and enjoyment, and the message of salvation was conveyed through 'modern' hymns and songs accompanied on the screen with text slides and illustrations."[24]

And as would be the case for popular music a century later, the global subgenre of "outlaw country" became a more modernized version of the protest folk ballad. In 1968, Bob Dylan wrote and recorded an entire album inspired by the Texan outlaw entitled, *John Wesley Harding* (sic) (1968) (This was Dylan's misspelling of Hardin, and pronunciation, on the title track). Not surprisingly, British director Tony Richardson had originally wanted Dylan to record his Kelly soundtrack for the 1970 film. In an interview he declared how "Dylan, like Jagger, can present the human reality of the rebel, the justifiably angry rebel that the historical Kelly really was."[25] Unable to obtain the services of Dylan—who would go on to score the social bandit film *Pat Garrett & Billy the Kid* (Peckinpah, 1973)—American country singers Waylon Jennings and Kris Kristofferson instead performed a number of folk ballads as written for the film by Shel Silverstein.

The metamorphosis of Kelly ballads are found in more contemporary genres of musical protest, including rock 'n' roll. The casting of Fanning in Jordan's film is evidence of this, as is Midnight Oil's song, "If Ned Kelly Were King" (Midnight Oil, 1981), and The Whitlam's song, "Kate Kelly" (Whitlams, 2002). Furthermore, beyond direct dovetails to the bushranger himself, the Kelly comedy film *Reckless Kelly* (Yahoo Serious, 1992), and *Ned* (Abe Forsythe, 2003), also include contemporary "outlaw" songs to demonstrate the universality of protest, and Kelly's identity as an international outlaw rebel. Reckless Kelly's "I Fought the Law" and "Wild Thing" (1993) or Ned's "The Fun Lovin' Criminals" and "Damn It Feels Good to Be a Gangsta" (2003), are not songs specifically written about Ned Kelly, but, in the context of his modern day status as an anti-authoritarian symbol, they suitably express the popularity of the Irish rebel hero.

The Wild Colonial Boy

Graham Seal asserts that the Kelly ballads echo "the man's own words, and in the words of the people who saw him as something more than a common criminal."[26] Kelly Gang member Joe Byrne was said to have written many Kelly ballads, including "Stringybark Creek," "Euroa," "Jerilderie," and "The Ballad of the Kelly Gang." In the miniseries *The Last Outlaw* (1980), Joe (Steve Bisley) performs a rendition of his "Ballad of the Kelly Gang." The claps from the intimate gathering keep rhythm.

> It was when they robbed Euroa bank you said they'd be run down
> But now they've robbed another one that's in Jerilderie town
> That's in Jerilderie town, my boys, and we're here to take their part
> And shout again "Long may they reign—the Kellys, Byrne and Hart".

At the conclusion of the performance, Ned (John Jarratt) praises its overriding theme of Irish-Australian protest: "You wrote a grand old song there … a proud old Irish tune in the words of a trueborn colonial son." Jones identifies this ballad as a reworking of "Wearing of the Green," a tune that dealt specifically with the theme of Irish oppression. Dubbed by a sympathizer as a "Hymn of Triumph," it was "sung to a clapping of hands and stamping of feet"; the performance from *The Last Outlaw* (1980) stages such a description.[27]

Following the pattern of *The Last Outlaw*, in Tony Richardson's 1970 *Ned Kelly*, with Mick Jagger cast as Ned, folk ballads are performed inside a pub, or an enclosed space (sometimes a sympathizer's home) where alcohol is plentiful. Before this 1970 film, seminal Australian troubadour Glen Tomasetti had been attached to the Kelly lore by interleafing a number of Kelly ballads into Jones's presentation of his paper,

"Kelly—The Folk Hero," at the 1968 Wangaratta Kelly symposium.[28] In the 1970 film, the patrons, spread throughout the pub, stop their chitchat to hear Tomasetti's quite poignant rendition of "She moved through the fair." In another scene, in another pub, Jagger sings, "The Wild Colonial Boy." This is the only ballad that he performs for the entire film, albeit in two very different renditions. For the first time, he sings it a cappella. Spitting the words with rebellious panache into the face of Constable Fitzpatrick, who enters mid-way into the performance, the gathering demonstrates its anti-authoritative unity by joining in the chorus.

This song's title ("Wild Colonial Boy") was in fact a famous description for outlaws who enjoyed the "help of a sympathetic network of friends, commonly known as the 'bush telegraph.'" John Molony understands "The Wild Colonial Boy" to be Kelly's most beloved ballad.[29] In Richardson's 1970 film, Ned sings it for a second time, inside the Glenrowan Inn, as the gang wait for their showdown with the police. Different from his earlier a cappella, this one—accompanied by a musical troupe and chorus from the hostages—is fast, roughhouse, and raucous. A colonial rock performance, one might say. To delineate these different editions, Helen O'Shea posits them to:

> convey characteristics associated with stereotypes of the Irish ... the first is the melancholy soprano wail that throughout the film gives voice to emotions of pain, loss, heartbreak, longing, and romantic love. The second is the lively, vigorous sound of Irish dance music that accompanies scenes of earthy celebration, pranks and high spirits ... these twin musical representations of Irishness, also employed in the music tracks to the Ned Kelly films, have a long history.[30]

Most certainly they do. The version of the ballad used in Richardson's film is about the Tasmanian-born Jack Doolan. Like Kelly, he never ventured to Ireland, despite his ancestry. Hence, Graham Seal claiming the "Wild Colonial Boy" to be anthemic of the Irish protest spirit:

> In the Anglophone context, it is also the Irish element that imparts a distinctive connotation of political dissent. The fact that "The Wild Colonial Boy" was often sung to the tune of the "The Wearing of the Green," a melodic icon of Irish revolt, is a further indication of the importance of the 'Celtic connection.'[31]

In reference of this, no narrative captures the essence of Eric Hobsbawm's social banditry code better than does the "Wild Colonial Boy."[32] In his paper, "The Wild Colonial Boy Rides Again," Seal deconstructs it to mirror Hobsbawm's nine enumerations of the noble robber:

The "Wild Colonial Boy" scores well in various versions of his song:

1) He is a member of a nationality that is widely represented as oppressed.
2) He is brave and defiant.
3) He robs the wealthy squatters or, in some versions, a judge. In an American/Irish version he is said to have 'helped the poor.'
4) He is adept at disguise, eluding pursuers and escaping from tricky situations.
5) He dies game.
6) While not betrayed in a direct sense, many versions of the song have him being deserted by his cowardly companions in the ultimate moment of need.

The "Wild Colonial Boy" therefore scores six out of nine, for those who like numbers. But as well as these considerations, it is arguably the very clearly articulated revolt of the Wild Colonial Boy against the powers of authority and law that make the song, in all variants, so internationally appealing.[33]

"Bandit," as defined by Hobsbawm, is a person "placed outside the law"; the term "bandito" or "Bandoleros" originated from the Catalan term for armed partisans in Catalonia during the fifteenth to seventeenth centuries.[34] Since the early 1970s, Hobsbawm's social bandit has been popular prototype for many historians of the oral tradition of protest. The "Wild Colonial Boy" as a symptom of this is ubiquitous. Appearing in many different accompaniments—despite the Irish-American version celebrating the Colonial Boy as a Robin Hood figure, robbing the rich to help the poor—in Australia, the ballad became popular during the gold rush era of the 1850s to1860s. Perhaps more suitable than any other example, it articulates how every outlaw would rather "die game" than surrender. Hence, Kelly Gang members Steve and Dan choosing death in a suicide pact, rather than be shot down by the hand of law. "'I'll fight but I won't surrender,' said the Wild Colonial Boy."

Conclusion

As this chapter has discussed, the first and second generation convicts were seminal in forming what is now the proud Australian national character. By drawing on the Irish tradition of cultural protest, Australian popular culture was never isolated or new. It was merely a continuum of generations of Irish protest balladry, which found its way onto the stage of convict theatre. Protest was commodified as a genre of popular entertainment and encouraged to be performed as a form of political opinion and unity. From the convict theatre stage, second generation sons of convicts continued the tradition by moving it into the bush and bushranger landscape. Indeed, no figure, it seems, embodied this notion of colonial Australian antipodean resistance more profoundly than Ned Kelly, who not only reworked Irish convict balladry into his own Jerilderie letter, but inspired many "original" Kelly protest ballads.

What these protest ballads share is a romantic nostalgia of loss—mourning the disappearance of community rituals and social customs in the context of modernity and nation-building. As Sventlana Boym writes, "Nostalgia is a sentiment of … displacement but also a romance of one's own fantasy."[35] Although rooted in an earlier historical time and faraway place, Australian protest ballads developed their own distinctive qualities and resilience beyond popular communication forms. From convict ships to convict theatres, these ballads were integrated into magic lantern shows and cinema performances. And now, with more lax censorship regulations, films are able to show how these daring ballads would have been performed in colonial times as a mode of political protest and community harmony.

Notes

1 Benedict Anderson, *Imagined Communities: Reflections on the Origin and Spread of Nationalism* (London: Verso, 2006), 145.

2 Seal's research around Kelly's identity as a recognized global bandit has been groundbreaking. Besides writing an illuminating book on Kelly's cultural tradition, with a predominate focus on the oral tradition, deliciously titled *Tell 'em I Died Game*, his most eloquent analysis of Kelly appears in *The Outlaw Legend* that essays the bushranger's homogenization in reference to other global outlaws including America's Jesse James and England's Robin Hood.

   Graham Seal, *Traditions of Prejudice* (Perth: The Antipodes Press, 1990).

3 Francis Adams, "The Labour Movement in Australia," in I. Turner, ed., *The Australian Dream* (Melbourne: Sun Books, 1968), 196–197.

4 The idea of the convict-as-a-stage-performer that Robert Jordan narrates in his groundbreaking book, *The Convict Theatres of Early Australia 1788–1840*, challenges a number of popular conceptions that Harold Love, in *The Australian Stage: A Documentary History*, posits, such as the tradition of Australian theatre being an activity of genteel society, and convict theatre as an essentially fragile and marginal activity. Harold Love, ed., *The Australian Stage: A Documentary History* (Sydney: New South Wales University Press, 1984).

5 One of the most staged plays, and the first to occur on Australian soil, was *The Recruiting Officer* by Irish writer George Farquhar, which follows the social and sexual exploits of two officers, the philandering Plume and the craven Brazen.

6 Oliver Goldsmith, *The Collected Works*, ed., Arthur Friedman (Oxford: Clarendon Press, 1966), 2.89.

7 The earliest known bushranger films include *Bushranging in North Queensland* (Joseph Perry, 1904) and *The Bushranger* (Fitzgerald 'family', 1904).

8 Richard Fotheringham, "The Man in the Iron Mask," *Cinema Papers*, Vol. 62 (1987): 32.

9 William Routt, "The Kelly Films," paper presented at Still Riding On: The Kelly Influence Conference, 7 May 2003.

10 Eric Reade, *Australian Silent Films* (Melbourne: Lansdowne Press, 1970), 28.

11 Graham Shirley, and Brian Adams, *Australian Cinema: The First Eighty Years* (Sydney: Angus and Robertson, 1983), 16.

12 John Tait, and Nevin Tait, *The Story of the Kelly Gang: Theatre Program* (Melbourne: Syd. Day, 1906), 22.

13 Andrew Pike, and Ross Cooper, *Australian Film 1900–1977* (Melbourne: Oxford University Press, 1980), 9.

14 Robert Hughes, *The Fatal Shore* (London: Vintage, 2003), 181.

15 Graham Seal, *Tell 'em I Died Game* (Melbourne: Hyland House, 2002), 90.

16 John Manifold, *The Penguin Australian Song Book* (Ringwood: Penguin, 1964), 27.

17 Seal, *Tell 'em I Died*, 90.

18 "News of the Day," *The Bulletin* (24 January 1907), 8.

19 Seal, *Tell 'em I Died*, 17.

20 George Wilson Hall, *The Kelly Gang Or, The Outlaws of the Wombat Ranges* (Sydney: Australian History Promotions, 1878), 60.

21 John McQuilton, *The Kelly Outbreak 1878–1880: The Geographical Dimension of Social Banditry* (Melbourne: Melbourne University Press, 1979), 144.

22 Seal, *Tell 'em I Died*, 3.

23 Warren Fahey, *Joe Watson Australian Traditional Folk Singer* (Sydney: Australian Folklore Unit, 1975), 3.

24 Elizabeth Hartrick, "Consuming Illustrations: The Magic Lantern in Australia and Aotearoa/New Zealand 1850–1910" (Ph.D. dissertation, The Australian Centre, The University of Melbourne, 2003), 100.

25 Adrian Rawlins, "Ned Kelly in Two Dimensions," *Go-Set* (1970): 9.

26 Seal, *Tell 'em I Died*, 10.

27 Ian Jones, *Ned Kelly: A Short Life* (Melbourne: Lothian Books, 2002), 201.

28 Ian Jones, and Glen Tomasetti, "Kelly—The Folk-Hero," in C. Cave, ed., *Ned Kelly: Man and Myth* (Melbourne: Cassell, 1968), 74–104.

29 John Molony, *Ned Kelly* (Melbourne: Melbourne University Press, 2001), 176.

30 Helen O'Shea, "New-Aged Ned: Scoring Irishness and Masculinity in Ned Kelly," in R. Coyle, ed., *Reel Tracks: Australian Feature Film Music and Cultural Identities* (Malaysia: John Libbey Publishing, 2005), 38–39.

31 Graham Seal, "The Wild Colonial Boy Rides Again and Again," *Australian Studies*, Vol. 7 (1993): 169.

32 Eric Hobsbawm, *Primitive Rebels: Studies in Archaic Forms of Social Movement in the 19th and 20th Centuries* (Manchester: Manchester University Press, 1959).

33 Seal, "The Wild Colonial Boy," 168.

34 Eric Hobsbawm, *Bandits* (London: Weidenfeld and Nicolson, 1969), 12.

35 Svetlana Boym, *The Future of Nostalgia* (New York: Basic Books, 2002), xiii.

27

AMBUSHED FROM ALL SIDES[1]

Rock Music as a Force for Change in China

Dennis Rea

Figure 27.1 Cui Jian performing during a concert in Beijing.

The early twentieth-century English novelist David Lindsay once wrote, of one of his fictional worlds, "If one sows an answer there, a rich crop of questions immediately springs up."[2] Lindsay may just as well have been speaking of China, a bewilderingly complex culture that stubbornly resists all attempts at reductionist analysis, especially where received notions of "protest music" are concerned. Upon being invited to contribute a chapter to this volume, with the suggested title "Contemporary Rock as an Agent of Change in China," I was immediately confronted with a bumper crop of thorny questions: Do Western notions of what constitutes protest music apply in the Chinese context? Must there be explicit textual content for music to be considered subversive? Is protest music inherently a force for the betterment of society, or can it also be deployed toward more sinister ends? And what exactly is meant by "China," a cultural sphere that includes such divergent polities as the communist People's Republic of China (PRC)—itself home to dozens of ethnic minority populations—the democratic Republic of China (ROC) on Taiwan, the erstwhile British and Portuguese colonial enclaves of Hong Kong and Macau, respectively, and the far-flung Chinese diaspora? It is imperative to consider these questions when examining the role that Chinese rock plays—if, in fact, it does play a significant role—in advancing social and political change in Chinese culture.

As the world's most populous nation, with all the attendant social strains and stark inequities, one might reasonably expect to find a strong anti-authoritarian streak running through mainland China's rock music subculture. Yet, apart from a generalized oppositional stance that superficially characterizes rock music anywhere, one finds surprisingly few examples of what could be termed "protest rock" in China. Underscoring this apparent scarcity of politically engaged Chinese rock musicians is the *Wikipedia* article on "Protest Song,"[3] which includes lengthy entries on the protest music of numerous countries and regions of the world, but just two sentences on China:

> Chinese-Korean Cui Jian's 1986 song "Nothing to My Name" was popular with protesters in Tiananmen Square. After the crackdown, he frequently played in public wearing a symbolic red blindfold when playing "A Piece of Red Cloth," a practice which led to censorship officials canceling concerts."

Period. Surely there is more to the story than this? There is, although it may not always take a form that outside observers would recognize as protest.

Rock Music vs. Chinese Cultural Norms

It is perhaps surprising that rock music, the epitome of the individualistic West, took root in Chinese soil at all, given the many ways in which it conflicts with traditional Chinese cultural values. Perhaps most importantly, the Chinese people historically have rarely challenged authority directly, instead employing devices such as allegory, metaphor, and wordplay to cleverly (and safely) express their grievances. The perils of being outspoken in an authoritarian society are exemplified by the well-known Asian proverb "The nail that sticks out gets hammered down." Among the more egregious examples of this in recent Chinese history is Mao Zedong's famous dictum "Let a hundred flowers bloom, let a hundred schools of thought contend"; ostensibly an official green light to Chinese intellectuals to freely and constructively debate their government's policies, the campaign instead resulted in the round-up, imprisonment and, in some cases, execution, of those who'd been lured into speaking out.[4]

One time-honored means of expressing dissent is to play on the multiple meanings inherent in many Chinese words. A case in point is former Chinese leader Deng Xiaoping's forename, Xiaoping, also a homonym for *xiao ping* ("little bottle"); fittingly, people who would never have dared to condemn his leadership verbally instead did so symbolically by smashing small bottles on the pavement. For this reason, one must carefully scrutinize any text, or rock song lyric, with an eye to whether it is subtly coded with hidden meaning, something that would very rarely be apparent to an outside observer, especially in translation.

Another important consideration is that rock music is, above all, about the individual, as shown by the preponderance of songs about personal relationships, self-gratification, and so on, and therefore cuts against the grain of a society that traditionally has been more collectivist than self-centered in its orientation.[5]

Taiwan: Deng Lijun, the Campus Folk Movement, and Hou Dejian

A strong argument can be made that rock and pop musicians from China's "renegade province" of Taiwan have had a much greater cumulative impact on cultural values on both sides of the Formosa Strait than any mainland music figure, apart from Cui Jian. Often held up by Western interests as a beacon of democracy in contrast to its colossal communist neighbor, what's much less well known is that under the exiled Kuomintang (KMT) regime of Chiang Kai-Shek, the Republic of China (ROC) on Taiwan endured oppressive martial law until as recently as 1987, when Chiang's son and successor Chiang Ching-Kuo initiated a period of gradual reform that culminated in Taiwan's first democratic national elections in 1996.[6]

In the 1970s, when Taiwan was still in the tight grip of martial law, the contested former province inadvertently "invaded" its vast neighbor, not through military force but through the unlikely vehicle of the angelic voice of charismatic Taiwanese songstress Deng Lijun (aka Teresa Teng), whose girlish bubblegum love songs fell like rain on an emotionally parched PRC populace. Surprisingly, Deng's innocuous and wholly apolitical music would prove to have a seismic impact on mainland culture, launching as it did the *tongsu* ("mass music") phenomenon that arose to fill the emotional void left by the Great Proletarian Cultural Revolution and its monotonous, sexless paeans to Chairman Mao, socialism, and the motherland. Before long, singers in the mold of Deng Lijun were dominating the public airspace with their glossy ballads and selling out huge arenas from Nanning to Harbin. Although state censors normally tolerated G-rated love songs, mild social criticism, and even lighthearted parodies of Cultural Revolution era anthems (pumping disco versions of Maoist slogans were all the rage in the late 1980s), watchful Chinese Communist Party (CCP) censors ensured that no *tongsu* performer crossed the line into political dissent.[7] While not "protest music" by any measure, *tongsu*'s most important achievements as a cultural phenomenon were to relax rigid public mores, restore the respectability of romantic (as opposed to filial or patriotic) love, and nurture a desire for personal fulfillment over collective self-sacrifice.

Back in Taiwan, the "campus folk" movement of the late 1970s did much to further the political liberalization of the ROC. A synthesis of contemporary Western soft rock and Chinese melodic sensibilities, modeled in part on the Greenwich Village folk scene of the 1960s, the movement's chief preoccupations included personal freedom, the resurrection of specifically Taiwanese cultural values, and Taiwanese political self-determination.[8] Among the scene's most influential figures was activist singer-songwriter Chen Ming-chang, who flouted KMT strictures by singing exclusively in the officially proscribed Taiwanese dialect. With their 1989 album *Songs of Madness*, Chen's notorious group Blacklist Studio raised the ire of KMT politicians with an irreverent rendition of the ROC anthem that was subsequently banned from Taiwanese media.

Another important figure to emerge from the campus folk movement was Luo Daiyou, whose fame, like Deng Lijun's, spread far beyond the island. Unlike Deng, however, Luo laced his music with biting social and political criticism; consequently, a number of his songs were banned in both Taiwan and mainland China. But it was Luo's contemporary, the Taiwanese songwriter, political activist, and all-around cause célèbre, Hou Dejian, who became the first significant catalyst for political dissent in Chinese rock music. The living embodiment of China's post-1949 split personality, Hou was catapulted onto a larger stage with the release of his massive 1979 hit, "Descendants of the Dragon," a ringing statement of pan-Chinese nationalism that placed Hou at the center of the maelstrom on the contentious issue of Chinese reunification.

Hou grabbed headlines and reversed a trend when he defected to the mainland in 1983 to reassert his Chinese roots. Welcomed at first by a PRC government that viewed him as a useful propaganda tool, Hou became a nationwide celebrity and important influence on China's nascent rock music scene. But he soon grew disenchanted with communist rule, and in 1989 he became a highly visible spokesperson for pro-democracy demonstrators in Tiananmen Square. While the putative avatar of Chinese protest rock, Cui Jian (see below), displayed admirable courage in performing for the demonstrators at Tiananmen in a show of solidarity, he stopped well short of explicitly denouncing the PRC government's policies, instead cloaking his critiques in elliptical double entendres. Hou, on the other hand, put himself at far greater personal risk on behalf of the pro-democracy movement by acting as a negotiator for the assembled protesters, as well as participating in their hunger strike. After the inevitable bloody crackdown, the PRC forcibly repatriated the disillusioned Hou to Taiwan, where authorities briefly placed him under house arrest. Although he would never again be an influential role model for young mainlanders, his imprint on China's subsequent rock scene remains indelible.[9]

Protest rock is very much alive in today's relatively open Taiwan, as exemplified by the environmentalist music collective Sheng Xiang and Water 3,[10] who were catalyzed by a grassroots movement to halt the construction of a dam in an environmentally sensitive region of Taiwan. Elder statesman Chen Ming-chang also continues to command a devoted following.

Cui Jian and the Advent of Chinese Rock

Ask anyone who's conversant with recent Chinese history to name a dissident musician and you'll hear one name: Cui Jian. The subject of hundreds of human interest stories in the foreign press, in post-Mao China Cui Jian was Bob Dylan, John Lennon, and Bruce Springsteen all rolled into one, a one man rock-and-roll revolution whose moving songs of alienation spoke volumes to a generation searching for meaning in a rapidly changing and increasingly globalized China. As the reluctant spokesperson for China's disenfranchised youth, Cui Jian will forever be linked in the public's mind to the democracy movement that was crushed by the tanks at Tiananmen Square.[11] The image of the rocker defiantly rallying hunger strikers with his stirring outsider anthems epitomized a generation's struggles and aspirations, and his artfully crafted songs possessed an undeniable gravitas that made a mockery of the flaccid *tongsu* pop tunes of the day.

Born in 1961 to musically inclined parents of ethnic Korean descent, by age 20 Cui Jian was already playing trumpet with the prestigious Beijing Philharmonic Orchestra, but, by that time, the young musician had already been smitten by the rock and roll he was hearing on cassettes spirited into the country by international tourists and students. Initially inspired by the likes of Simon and Garfunkel and the rough-hewn "Northwest Wind" genre of contemporary Chinese folk music, he learned to play guitar and started singing in public, at first covering tunes by well-known pop singers, then eventually writing his own material.

Cui Jian first attracted widespread attention with his 1985 appearance on a TV talent contest, where his impact on viewers was similar to that of seeing Elvis Presley gyrating on "The Ed Sullivan Show" in strait-laced 1950s America. Even at this early stage in his career, Cui Jian's songs showed a preoccupation with weightier issues than the usual gauzy romantic fantasies, touching on such sensitive themes as individualism, sexuality, blind adherence to tradition, and, by inference, the integrity of the Chinese Communist Party.[12] To a generation numbed by CCP propaganda, the honesty and realism of Cui Jian's lyrics was a resounding clarion call. Equally important, his tunes *rocked* with an authenticity that earlier Chinese musicians had never fully internalized.

Cui Jian was not entirely without antecedents in China. The aforementioned Northwest Wind genre that was popular in the early 1980s, and the subsequent "prison songs" craze, both gave voice to outsiders and the downtrodden, and are considered important precursors to Chinese rock music.[13] The mid-1980s saw the arrival of mainland China's first homegrown rock icon, Zhang Xing, a national sensation who became something of a tabloid character and earned the disapproval of a regime that viewed him as an unwholesome role model for Chinese youth, and the emergence of rock and roll in general as a threat to societal stability—a sort of Trojan Horse bearing contaminating foreign ideas. Although there was nothing politically controversial about Zhang's rather tame music—"rock" only in the sense that it deployed typical electric rock band instrumentation—the authorities eventually sentenced the libidinous singer to eight years in prison on trumped-up morality charges, a rite of symbolic public execution that the Chinese call "killing the chicken to scare the monkeys." Now a largely forgotten figure, Zhang Xing is nevertheless important for having set the stage for Cui Jian and others to come.

Where Zhang Xing represented the attainment of fairytale wealth and glamour unimaginable to generations of Chinese accustomed to drabness and privation, Cui Jian couldn't have been more different. With his deliberately scruffy appearance and rough, untrained, voice, he personified an emerging generation of alienated urban youth. Frustrated by lack of opportunity and weary of the CCP's increasingly bankrupt ideology, Cui Jian and those he influenced eschewed the glossy escapism of Zhang Xing and his ilk in favor of a gritty urban realism.

All too predictably, the rebel rocker's growing popularity set him on a collision course with Chinese government officials, who painted him as a bad element. He was expelled from the orchestra for his dalliance with rock and roll, and soon afterward was forbidden to perform in public for a year after angering a highly placed military officer with his mocking rendition of the hallowed revolutionary paean "Nanniwan" ("South Muddy Bay").

Cui Jian began honing his own material in ADO, an innovative Beijing band that included two foreign embassy staffers. Ever since China launched its own version of *glasnost* under paramount leader Deng Xiaoping, these and other foreign musicians had been introducing Beijing musicians to the forbidden delights of rock music. With ADO, Cui Jian released his 1986 opus *Rock and Roll on the New Long March*,[14] the defining statement of China's new lost generation. A solid collection of original tunes, the album raised the bar for all future Chinese rock music and provided a potent and timely anthem in Cui Jian's most enduringly beloved song, "Yi Wu Suo You"

("Nothing to My Name"), a poignant, poetic articulation of the sense of powerlessness felt by members of his generation.

"Yi Wu Suo You" resonated deeply with a youth culture grasping for meaning in a China afflicted by institutionalized corruption, Party cronyism, rampant materialism, widening social stratification, and an increasingly out-of-touch socialist ideology. Like Dylan, Woody Guthrie, and a handful of others, Cui Jian managed to distill a generation's fears and longings into a simple four-minute song. It's no wonder that "Yi Wu Suo You" was spontaneously adopted as the unofficial anthem of the demonstrators at Tiananmen Square.

Yet, while he is perpetually identified with the 1989 student movement, Cui Jian's involvement was, in reality, limited to a single concert with ADO in Tiananmen Square. The singer's reputation as a rebel is deceptive, for he has always taken great pains to avoid making direct political statements in his songs, instead employing suggestive imagery and innuendo that can be interpreted in numerous ways.[15] A prime example of Cui Jian's modus operandi is his early 1990s tune "The Last Shot," a mournful ballad written from the perspective of a dying soldier and peppered with recorded gunshots all too reminiscent of Tiananmen. Yet, when asked if the song referred to the events of June 4, he insisted that it was about the 1979 Sino-Vietnamese border clash, neatly shifting the subject from protest to patriotism, though, of course, the song can be construed either way. He has doggedly resisted discussing politics (even with friends) and maintains that his songs are concerned only with universal human issues. He has also complained that foreign journalists only increase his woes by trying to politicize his music. In a sense, given his refusal to unequivocally criticize authority, Cui Jian could be viewed as a consummate performance artist, enjoying all the notoriety of a political subversive without ever having leveled a substantive critique of his country's policies. Although viewed by many as the epitome of the rebel archetype, Cui Jian's customary ambiguity places him within a longstanding Chinese tradition that privileges circumspection and obliquity over confrontation.

Cui Jian managed to escape serious punishment in the aftermath of Tiananmen, presumably to avoid setting off a generational backlash, but, like most of his peers among China's contemporary arts scene, he was forced to keep a low profile in the wake of the government's crackdown on dissidents, and found even fewer opportunities to perform than before June 4. In 1990, however, Cui Jian cannily proposed to the government that if they would allow him to undertake a national concert tour, he would donate all profits to the upcoming Asian Games, to be held in Beijing. It was no secret that Deng's beleaguered regime viewed the Asian Games as an opportunity to restore its tarnished international image after the Tiananmen disgrace. Officials granted Cui Jian's request, and he set off on a "New Long March" tour that took him to arenas throughout the country. Enormous crowds attended his concerts and responded with a passion that alarmed authorities, dancing in the aisles and provocatively flashing "V for Victory" signs. It was on this tour that Cui Jian first made what is perhaps his most overtly political statement, wearing a bright red blindfold over his eyes while performing his song "A Piece of Red Cloth." While the song's lyrics remained characteristically ambiguous, the symbolism of the visual gesture was unmistakable. Fearing an outbreak of public disorder, officials in Beijing abruptly canceled the singer's remaining dates after an especially rousing concert in the city of Chengdu, still recovering from its own bloody crackdown in June 1989.[16] Cui Jian's road trip was nonetheless highly significant, as it inspired the formation of dozens of grassroots rock bands in China's hinterlands.

For the next few years, Cui Jian was restricted to playing surreptitious gigs at private gatherings in Beijing. He was expressly banned from any university campus, and his notoriety ensured that large-scale public concerts were out of the question. The 1991 release of his second album, *Solution*,[17] did little to improve relations with the authorities, containing as it did both the sacrilegious "Nanniwan" and the provocative "Last Shot." It would be several years before the PRC government allowed him to resume touring, by which time the Chinese public was more bent on making money than on fomenting revolution.

One lesser-known and less telegenic contemporary of Cui Jian who also merits attention here is He Yong, widely considered to be China's original punk rocker. He Yong gained notoriety in 1989 when he also played for the protesters in Tiananmen Square, with his group Mayday. His most controversial song, "Garbage Dump,"[18] is a furious indictment of China's deepening environmental, social, and spiritual decay. With its splintered, dissonant piano figures and He Yong's howls of indignation joined to a driving rock pulse, "Garbage Dump" ranks among the most militant statements of Chinese rock.

Words and Music: Rock Music as Implicit Social Protest

A cursory glance at this volume's table of contents reveals that almost all of the protest music discussed herein takes the form of *songs*, where the human voice is the focus of attention and more meaning is vested in the lyrics than in the actual music, which largely recycles shopworn idioms. This is obviously owing to the fact that singing, as a form of speech, explicitly articulates the music's intended message, in this case messages of protest against social, political, or economic injustice. Yet, for the same reasons that the Chinese typically avoid challenging authority directly, one very rarely encounters Chinese music that presents an unmistakable *vocalized* message of protest. In the arena of Chinese rock, one seldom hears politicized speech except in underground venues that are well out of sight of the broader Chinese populace. This raises the intriguing question of whether words and the human voice must be present for music to function as a vehicle for protest, or whether music that lacks textual content can also be an effective means to express dissent.

Music mirrors deep structures in our brains and physiology. Leaving aside any textual content, variations in musical characteristics such as tempo, timbre, register, and dynamics can produce a broad range of effects on listeners, from serene calm to intense agitation. In extreme cases, instrumental music has been known to provoke actual rioting, as in the infamous 1913 Paris premiere of Stravinsky's "The Rite of Spring." Perhaps what Chinese authorities find so threatening about rock music is not its verbal message, but its tremendous sonic power and foreign provenance. It may be that what is truly radical about Chinese rock is not its textual message, but the simple fact that anyone in China plays this type of music at all.

The key to understanding Chinese rock as protest music is to recognize that what's important is not necessarily what is said, but what is *not* said. For example, when Cui Jian performed his version of "Nanniwan," what scandalized his detractors was not the song's lyrics, which were exactly the same as the patriotic original, but the way in which they were *framed* by this "barbarian" music; that is, the musician's *attitude* is more objectionable than the actual words. Similarly, authorities are deeply offended when an artist like Cui Jian has the insolence to appropriate and thereby debase such sacred political emblems as the Long March by situating them within a foreign musical context.

The 1990s and Beyond: The Triumph of Self-Interest

In the early 1990s, as memories of Tiananmen began to fade, Chinese rock music—now branded as *yaogun*—moved into higher gear, fueled not by idealism but by the desire for fame and fortune. Seeking to deflect attention from the human-rights issues raised by Tiananmen, in 1992 Deng Xiaoping publicly reaffirmed his conviction that "to get rich is glorious," igniting a sweeping entrepreneurial revolution that quickly transformed China into the world's fastest-growing economy. Deng's strategy neatly defused a volatile political predicament, for with fortunes waiting to be made on China's surging economic roller coaster, most Chinese would rather get a piece of the action than risk their necks for democratic ideals.

Ironically, the perennially marginalized rock scene was also swept up in the boom-town mentality. China's recording industry, long a strictly controlled government monopoly, rapidly became an arena of capitalist enterprise. Homegrown rock crept out of its furtive subculture of secret parties and embassy events and onto the stages of commercial rock clubs and flashy international franchises like the Hard Rock Café. Lured by cash advances and the promise of international recognition, Beijing bands naïvely signed lopsided contracts with predatory record labels based in Taiwan and Hong Kong.[19] Not surprisingly, competition for these record deals sowed discord within a music community once distinguished by its solidarity, inciting jealousy and feuding between rival camps. Many of the newer bands enjoyed privileges that first-generation Chinese rockers never dreamed of, thanks to hefty transfusions of cash and state-of-the-art equipment from wealthy overseas sponsors. Corporate sponsorship of rock events became the norm.[20]

Leading the pack of second-generation Chinese rockers was Tang Dynasty, China's first prominent homegrown heavy metal act. Songs extolling the vanished splendor of their namesake dynasty were taken by some as a rebuke to the CCP leadership for squandering China's glorious birthright; others read the lyrics as an outpouring of xenophobic anger against China's perceived enemies abroad.[21] (One band member was reportedly cashiered by his bandmates for being Chinese-American.) But, with a very few exceptions, such as the provocatively named 1989, the second-generation *yaogun* bands steered well clear of politics.

Hard on the heels of the second-wave bands came the "Peking Punk" movement[22] of the later 1990s, typified by aggressive nihilistic bands with names like Underbaby, Catcher in the Rye, and Brain Failure. Disgusted at their country's headlong slide into materialism, China's punks possessed neither the intelligence and compassion of Cui Jian, the novelty shock value of the proto-punk He Yong, nor the musical prowess of Tang Dynasty. For the most part, the music of the Peking Punks was little more than an inarticulate and ultimately impotent tantrum, and remained strictly an underground phenomenon.

During this period, onetime bête noir Cui Jian was once again allowed to perform throughout the motherland, and even made multiple tours of Europe and the U.S.[23] Perhaps nothing better illustrates the "mainstreaming" of Cui Jian than his many recent appearances on stage with visiting foreign rock musicians. Back in 1991, police blocked the singer from performing a duet with Paul Simon at the latter's concert in Guangzhou; by 2006, evidently no longer considered a public threat, he did a triumphant cameo spot singing "Wild Horses" alongside the Rolling Stones in Shanghai. Lao Cui ("Old Cui," as he is affectionately known today) continues to enjoy an active career in music and film, and is widely revered by those who experienced the heady events of 1989, but his later music has been noncontroversial and anticlimactic. He is increasingly viewed as irrelevant by subsequent generations of Chinese youth, and no noteworthy musician has arisen to assume his place as the face of defiance.

In sad contrast to the communitarian spirit of early Beijing rock, by the turn of the millennium, the scene had become dispiritingly hierarchical and narcissistic. Reporting on the 2002 Snow Mountain Music Festival in Yunnan Province—dubbed "China's Woodstock" by the international press—onetime Tang Dynasty guitarist Kaiser Kuo observed in *Time* magazine that, "Instead of Woodstock innocence, [the festival was marked by] cynical commercialism—by now a defining Chinese characteristic."

Although the scene continued to grow and diversify into the new century, the music the new bands produced was largely non-polemical, apart from a predilection for extreme volume and abrasive textures. When asked to describe a typical gig on today's *yaogun* circuit, and whether any of the bands he'd recently seen could be termed protest rock, a longtime foreign observer of the Chinese rock scene offered the following:

Picture a bad Chinese Sonic Youth plus Siouxsie and the Banshees complete with a very skinny girl lead singer who almost without exception has to have hair in her face. She stands motionless in front of the microphone as if she's about to slit her wrists while the guitarists thrash out loud chords … No conversation or eye contact with the audience … Look like you're pissed off at society—protest rock! During the break, the band grabs a smoke and updates their Weibo on their iPhones.

Where things get really strange is when black-clad, dreadlocked Chinese rock bands can be found singing hardcore *pro-government* protest songs, as in a performance video that went viral on YouTube during the 2008 Beijing Olympics.[24] The footage shows the Beijing punk band Ordnance bellowing at a mixed Chinese and foreign audience, "The Olympics have brought a lot of people here from outside the country. We should tell them, TAIWAN IS OURS!!! TIBET IS OURS!!!" amid a welter of coruscating distortion. This raises the uncomfortable question of whether nationalistic rants like these are just as legitimate a form of protest music as that promoting more peaceful, humanistic ends. One suspects that right-wing screeds of this sort are not exactly the type of protest music that readers of this volume had in mind. In striking contrast, that same year, during her Chinese concert tour, Icelandic singer Björk set off a nationwide firestorm by chanting "Tibet, Tibet" during a performance of her song "Declare Independence"—a sentiment with which extremely few Han Chinese, rock musicians included, have any sympathy. However well-intentioned her gesture, its only result was to bring even heavier restrictions on visiting foreign musicians, and it may well have provoked Ordnance's outburst.

Conclusion

Roughly thirty years after rock music first gained a foothold in the unlikely ground of communist China, it is difficult to escape the conclusion that it has, thus far, largely failed to fulfill its promise as a significant force for articulating discontent and effecting meaningful change. During the early 1990s, considered by many to have been the "golden age" of Chinese rock, it was not unreasonable to hope that a vanguard of visionary rock musicians would help bring about a transformation of Chinese society. Conditions were ripe for change in a nation whose citizens were thoroughly jaded with hypocritical CCP rhetoric and outraged over entrenched corruption and the butchery at Tiananmen. Yet, despite its early promise, Chinese rock, to borrow a well-worn Chinese idiom, has largely proven to be a paper tiger.

Underlying Chinese rock's failure to galvanize the masses into political action is the plain fact that most Chinese simply don't care for rock music, which remains largely the province of a relatively tiny coterie of disaffected, educated, urban youth, most of whose peers disdain rock in favor of pop, rap, and dance music. Unlike the

West, where once-outré rock and roll was so rapidly coopted by the mainstream culture that it is now a constant presence in all our lives, the greater Chinese public still hasn't really warmed to *yaogun*, with its strident timbres, celebration of the individual, and suspect foreign ties. Untroubled by the relentless political pogroms of the recent past, and boasting more disposable income than any previous generation, China's new leisure class instead turns to reassuring pop music as a temporary escape from an increasingly competitive materialistic lifestyle, and a world in which technology and the global marketplace are radically uprooting concepts of nation, culture, and self. In a sense, indulging in soothing pop music represents a yearning for a mythical golden age in China's past, when poets composed verse leisurely in idyllic riverside pavilions. Seen in this light, it's no wonder that most Chinese listeners prefer the comforting fantasy of romantic pop music to the harsh rhythms of Beijing rock. While protest musicians in other world cultures, such as Woody Guthrie, Fela Anikulapo Kuti, and Violetta Parra, connected with and inspired millions of their fellow countrymen by embedding their political broadsides in broadly acceptable forms of popular music, it is highly unlikely that Chinese rock will ever mobilize the masses unless it becomes far more popular in China than it is today.

The search for a Chinese Bob Marley or Rage Against the Machine may well prove to be a snipe hunt in the end; that is, there's no "there" there, at least until the authoritarian and deeply tradition-bound PRC undergoes an improbable political metamorphosis and a majority of its inhabitants grow disillusioned with the comforts of materialism. Asked to identify a contemporary example of protest rock for this essay, half a dozen correspondents with close ties to the PRC rock scene failed to come up with more than a single candidate, the curiously named Beijing band Rebuilding the Rights of Statues, who, in any case, have a microscopic following within China. That's certainly not to say that today's China is lacking in dissident musicians; it's just that rock music may be the wrong place to look for a truly committed music of resistance. Indeed, one is far more likely to find voices of protest among China's ethnic minority musicians (Mongols, Uighurs, Tibetans, et al.), with their ancient grievances against the Han Chinese majority, than among Han Chinese rock musicians. (In what may be the supreme irony, Cui Jian himself is not ethnically Chinese.) But you won't read about musicians like these in *Spin* magazine,[25] bereft as they are of the glamorous trappings of the rock lifestyle. Perhaps all the hopes pinned on Chinese rock as a political force amount to no more than narcissism, for the West is flattered to see itself reflected in the image of bold Chinese rockers playing "our" music, a sort of reverse-image Cultural Revolution led by guitars and drums.

Today, as in other periods of Chinese history, it is typically the visual artists (e.g., Ai Weiwei) and literary figures (e.g., Liu Xiaobo)—and, more recently, bloggers such as Han Han—who form the vanguard of political protest, not musicians. Yet, with new bands forming by the hundreds, some of whom are skirting the limits of what is politically tolerable in the PRC, it is unwise to count out Chinese rock as a potential force for societal change. However, it is equally unwise for outside observers with a reformist agenda to expect too much from what is, in the end, a borrowed musical style. If music is ever to effect broad-based change in China, it will no doubt take the form of a truly indigenous music of resistance.

Notes

1 "Ambushed from All Sides" is the title of a classic work of Chinese traditional music that sonically depicts battle scenes.

2 David Lindsay, *A Voyage to Arcturus* (Lincoln, Nebraska: University of Nebraska Press, reprinted 2002), 105.

3 "Protest Songs," *Wikipedia*, April 2012, at http://en.wikipedia.org/wiki/Protest_song#China, accessed 18 April 2012.

4 Jonathan Spence, *The Search for Modern China* (New York: W. W. Norton & Company, 1991), 569.

5 Colin B. Cowles, "You Can't Always Get What You Want: Rock and Roll, New Cinema, and the Rise of the Individual in Post-Reform China" (Master's thesis, 1996).

6 Murray A. Rubinstein, *Taiwan: A New History* (Armonk, New York: East Gate Books, 2006), 377.

7 Andrew F. Jones, *Like a Knife: Ideology and Genre in Contemporary Chinese Music* (Ithaca, New York: Cornell University Press, 1992), 65.

8 Linda Jaivin, "Hou Dejian and the Rise of Pop Music in Taiwan in the Seventies," *CHIME: Journal of the European Foundation for Chinese Music Research*, No. 9 (1996): 118.

9 Jaivin, "Hou Dejian."

10 Sheng Xiang & Water 3, *Getting Dark*, CD, © 2004 Trees Music & Art TMCD-330.

11 Matt Peters, "Rock 'N' Revolt," *Far Eastern Economic Review*, 28 March 1991.

12 Jones, *Like a Knife*, 65

13 Peter Micic, "Notes on Pop/Rock Genres in the Eighties in China," *CHIME: Journal of the European Foundation for Chinese Music Research*, No. 8 (1995): 77.

14 Cui Jian, *Rock and Roll on the New Long March*, audiocassette, © 1989 China Tourism Audio Video Publishing TAV9-5.

15 S. L. Law, "Cui Belts Out a Message but Doesn't Rock the Boat," *South China Morning Post*, 1991.

16 Daniel Southerland, "Pop Star's 'Long March' Is Cut Short," *Washington Post Service*, 1991.

17 Cui Jian, *Solution*, audiocassette, © 1991, UFO Records UFO-91172.

18 He Yong, "Garbage Dump," audiocassette, © 1994, Rock Records/Magic Stone Y-1132.

19 Michael Wester, "PRC Invades Taiwan with Rock Music," *The China News*, Vol. 1, No. 60 (1994).

20 Robert Efird, "Rock in a Hard Place: Music and the Market in Nineties Beijing," in Nancy N. Chen and Constance D. Clark, eds., *China Urban: Ethnographies of Contemporary Culture* (Durham, North Carolina: Duke University Press, 2001), 67.

21 Tang Dynasty, *Tang Dynasty*, audiocassette, © 1992 Rock Records/Magic Stone RC-303.

22 Various artists, *Peking Punks: Beloved Party*, audiocassette, © 1997 Sickboy Productions.

23 Jon Pareles, "Chinese Rock Legend Sings of a Different Malaise," *The New York Times*, 28 August 1995.

24 "Beijing, on the 7th day of the 2008 Olympics near the Olympic Green Village," YouTube, November 2008, at http://www.youtube.com/watch?v=XJyW11B_008, accessed 18 April 2012.

25 Andrew F. Jones, "Poachers," *Spin Magazine*, 1995.

28

CONCLUSION

A Hermeneutics of Protest Music

Allan Moore

Alan Merriam's structural perspective on the social functions music fulfills would find no obvious place for protest music.[1] Merriam's universal schema identifies a series of roles, ever more inclusive. He notes that music is used to establish, and thence enforce, conformity to social norms. He argues that it is used to validate social institutions and thus contributes to the continuity and stability of culture. Thus, music crucially contributes to the integration of society. Merriam's perspective emphasizes order, conformity, integration, unity. It needs little thought to find examples of these functions in contemporary culture, from nursery rhymes to football chants to national anthems to the sedimentation of musical decisions within *X Factor*. Observing these, however, suggests a modification to Merriam's schema for, rather than pertaining to social norms, in class society the schema relates particularly to intrinsic groupings (whether unified by generation, class, ethnicity, lifestyle, or taste). Perhaps a circumscribed questioning of hegemonic norms (circumscribed by, for example, the genre conventions by means of which we recognise song as song) only ultimately reinforces the stability of those norms. Perhaps such questioning leads to new norms, i.e. does not contribute to the "integration of society," to the "stability of culture," and it is that possibility I take here. Where, then, in Merriam's outline schema, belongs music which either issues such a challenge, or acts at the interface between such groupings? It is here, surely, that protest music surfaces.

To protest a situation means, in some measure, to *express* opposition to it, but it also implies something less than to *oppose* it outright. To sing a song is not, in itself, to land a blow.[2] In this context, social protest implies opposition to a hegemonic grouping, opposition which necessarily accepts the reality of power relations involved. John Street identifies four schemata for the politicization of music.[3] He refers to the contrast drawn by Dave Laing between a "protest song [which] identifies a specific issue or enemy" and a "song of resistance [which] may have no such focus or narrative."[4] In this essay, I do not focus on music which is necessarily *used* as a means of protest, but music whose internal sonic relations lead a competent listener to entertain the possibility that such a use may have been *intended* by the music's originator(s). In so doing, I shall suggest that the distinction drawn by Laing may have limited usefulness.[5]

Performance

The chants of a protest march are direct in their expression. It requires a minimum of critical interpretation to understand the call-and-response texture, the rhythmic regularity and the initial plosives of the man with a megaphone at a march protesting police brutality[6] as oppositional expression, even if we cannot make out a single word he's using. Thus, at least a part of his message is contained in his articulation of it. This is a key theme I shall follow through this chapter. A particularly effective expression of such opposition is Martin Luther King's famous "I Have a Dream" speech, delivered from the steps of the Lincoln Memorial in Washington on 28 August 1963. One can find analyses aplenty of this speech, from the superficial[7] to the deeply considered.[8] In every case, though, it seems that the power of the speech is considered to derive purely from its content.[9] It was delivered, of course, but its delivery is always considered secondary, if at all. I want to draw attention to two features of the speech's forward-looking, positive, second half.[10] (Although, for instance, Bobbitt notes this part "does not move one nearly as much in the reading as in the hearing, unless one reads the text mentally employing King's famous cadence and rhythm,"[11] he does not begin to address these features.) King has a particular way of using both rhythm and pitch to structure the "I have a dream" section, as in Figure 28.1.[12] He uses a specific rhythmic motif to deliver the phrase "I have a dream" which, at an early appearance (at 12' of the video), continues over eight syllables. That "da did-dy da" pattern then underpins most other deliveries not only of that phrase, but of others of four syllables (e.g. "so e-ven though"), giving a strong sense of unity. But that unity is given direction by his pitching. Up until this point, many of his phrases fall at the end (as with so much spoken English), but do not usually rise at the start; King hits a high pitch to start a phrase and remains there, removing his words from the world of everyday speech. Once we reach this climactic portion, his pitching surprisingly becomes precise enough for me to notate much of its structure. Much of this "heightened speech" focuses on a pitch around C#, clearly reached at 12'. By 12'35" he has introduced an upper E (which had been reached once, about a minute earlier), and much of the next few minutes is organised in terms of an approximate oscillation between these two, the upper used for emphasis. So much is shared with many speeches, although King's pitching is unusually regular. But the tension implied in that upper pitch is stretched ever tauter—at 13'42" he reaches further ("*one* day"); further still in the following phrase ("*dream*"); again, nearly a minute later, on "dream" (note the rhythmic consistency); and even higher, fractionally, on "crooked" some twenty seconds later. It is my contention that these musical (rhythmic; pitched) elements of King's delivery are not only highly unusual, and unusually structured, but in their removal from the world of ordinary discourse contribute markedly to the effect of a speech which still resonates half a century after its delivery.

Figure 28.1 Martin Luther King's "I Have a Dream" speech.

So, I maintain that any analysis of *performed* words *must* take account of their performance in order properly to address their effect. While such analysis need not explicitly be musical,[13] it must at least be sonic.[14] I have suggested elsewhere that any assumption that the meaning of a song can be equated with the meaning of its lyrics, abstracted from their performance, is greatly misguided. In order to provide a vehicle for the contextualization of lyrics, I developed the concept of the persona/environment relation,[15] whereby a song's environment can be read to modify the assumed position of the song's persona[16] through consideration of three elements: the textural matters normally considered under the heading "accompaniment"; the harmonic setting; and the formal setting or narrative structure, i.e. the order in which its events take place, and the patterns of repetition within this order. Such an analysis demonstrates five possible levels of relationship between the persona and the environment. The environment can be *inert*, contributing nothing specific to the meaning of the song. It can be *quiescent*, merely setting up the (largely attitudinal, often genre) expectations through which a listener may listen. It can be *active*, supporting the position of the persona, frequently through devices related to word-painting. All environments are partially inert (in terms of communication theory, this is the conative function of the environmental "channel"). Quiescence and action are frequently encountered, although only inconsistently through any song. The final two levels, while rarer, are most interesting. An environment can be *interventionist*, going further than what is specified in the lyric by amplifying what it signifies, or even by enacting the lyric and, finally, an environment can be directly *oppositional*.[17]

The Impact of Personic Environment

P. F. Sloan was a Screen Gems staff writer when he penned "Eve of Destruction," the immense 1965 hit for ex-New Christy Minstrel Barry McGuire.[18] The record's rough-and-ready sound came, in part, from McGuire's guide vocal, which appears never to have been replaced by a polished vocal. That vocal is gruff and intense, contributing to its common reading as somehow authentic. The rough use of harmonica and seemingly irregular numbers of lines per stanza contribute quiescently to this, as intertextual references to Bob Dylan's then-current usages. Other elements of the environment are entirely inert, particularly the I, IV, V repeating harmonic pattern (which climaxes as the doo-wop changes—I, vi, IV, V—in the chorus) and the now-standardised playing of guitar, bass and drums. The only challenging feature, other than the lyrics themselves, is the presence of a registrally high, putatively otherworldly choral sound deep in the mix of the chorus. Here, then, it is the lyric and McGuire's delivery of it which are made to do all the work. The situation protested (a very generalized contemporary malaise resulting from different sorts of violence) is simply presented, and no action recommended.

The Beatles' "Taxman" (1966)[19] was George Harrison's biting response to the contemporary UK Labour government's imposition of a 95 percent income surtax rate. Harrison's counting in ("1, 2, 3, 4") and the initial throat-clearing serves to assure us of the "authenticity" of this recording, a diegetic move which hauls us into the studio. I want to focus on the role in the personic environment of Harrison's guitar and, in particular, on three aspects of how it sounds. First, note the timbre. Judged by today's standards, it is rather thin, but it has a piercing edge to it (a predominance of treble frequencies), an edginess, an uneasiness, which would have been far more marked for a contemporary listener. Second, note that it appears throughout on the offbeat, supporting Harrison's vocal, which constantly anticipates Ringo Starr's beat. It is, however, attacked with some ferocity. We can hear this because the sonic effect is of a single chord, despite the fact that the strings, being played with a single plectrum, must in reality be struck consecutively; they cannot be hit simultaneously. And yet, simultaneity is what we seem to hear. The only way to achieve this is to attack the strings with extreme speed, and the speed of action of the hand, working as a single entity (the hand must be clenched to achieve this), *embodies* the violence which we then "hear" in the offbeat chords. Third, note that after each line of verse, the guitar rhythm alters to almost call out the word "Taxman" before we ever hear it (at 19" for instance). The chord used at that point is the rich dissonant chord Jimi Hendrix was to make famous in "Purple Haze."[20] Here, while the lyric serves to anchor the anger of Harrison's persona (which is likely to have been shared by Harrison himself), to give it historical specificity, it is his action on the guitar, both in what/when he plays, and in how, which conveys to us, nearly half a century later, the force of that anger.

For a third example, I turn to Paul Weller's "Homebreakers."[21] The situation protested here is the politics of Margaret Thatcher's UK Tory government, and its effect on the British working classes, most particularly the policy requiring jobseekers to travel far to find work, at the expense of the stability of their families (a situation unresolved to this day). The soul style which Weller was exploring at this time usually carries connotations of social accommodation, although more precisely, perhaps, it recalls Marvin Gaye's more troubled post-1970 aspirational style.[22] The key line in Weller's song, I submit, is the final one; two sons are pictured, one looking for a job, the other looking for answers from the government.[23] It is here, specifically, that the song proposes action, in the form of a threat whose precise form is only to be guessed at. At first listening, there seems to be a lack of congruence between the style and the message of the song. However, I would suggest that the way this particular line is delivered, with no apparent anger (cf. "Taxman," above), and in the same voice as the narrative of the rest of the song, actually intensifies the threat. An attacker out of control through rage is surely less to be feared than one so completely in control that his voice betrays no emotion? That control is underpinned by the track's style.

Style as Environment

I now take this mode of analysis further by noting that the protest song can imply the presence of two distinguishable environments. Sometimes these two can both be found in the same song, sometimes not. Of the former, the track "Peace Loving Man,"[24] by the minor British band Blossom Toes, is a good example. This track activates the band's protest by working within then-accepted parameters of popular song. The Vietnam War spawned many protests for "peace," but few were as musically rich as this. It makes use of distinct textures, largely drawn from the band's psychedelic identity. We have sound sources like backwards taping, "Near Eastern" nasal-sounding strings and proto-prog mellotron. We also have a proto-heavy metal growl delivering the initial and some subsequent lyrics about dropping the "bomb." Remember, this is only 1969, and such vocalization did not become common for nearly two decades.[25] In this context, its identity as distortion of a "normal" sung voice is paramount. The melodic line is dissonant, emphasizing the interval of the tritone[26] (when prominent, this so often emblematic of the negative, in many tonal/modal styles), and is doubled by a distorted guitar riff. The subsequent guitar line also focuses, unequivocally, on the tritone. In contrast, the chorus which references peace is sung in a normal register, and is accompanied by a treble-rich guitar playing diatonic scales. The contrast between the musical environment of the verse, and that of the chorus, could hardly be stronger. Two environments are set up within a single track, each sonically representing the viewpoint explored in the relevant section of lyrics. The distinction between the verse and chorus is not simply one of semiotic difference, for the awkward harshness of the first guitar, and the smooth pleasantness of the second, are at root cross-modal[27] transferences of inter-subjective bodily sensations.

In "Homebreakers," there was a single sonic environment which could, potentially, be read as oppositional to the persona's identity as partially given by the lyrics (even though I have offered a different reading). In "Peace Loving Man" there were two, consecutive, environments, oppositional to each other, but each supporting the point of view put forward by a protagonist. What, though, where no such oppositional perspective occurs within the confines of the track? Does this mean that, notwithstanding the ostensible content of the lyrics, the environment has to be read as inert, as making no contribution at all to the meaning of the track? Not necessarily, and I want to develop this argument by developing an alternative take on the notion of environment.

Style as Absent Environment

We all exist, individually, in relation to our environment. Indeed, we could not exist separate from it. This profound relationship is always present in popular song. Our physical environment, however, is frequently more subtle and less obviously monolithic than this statement suggests. For instance, as I look out from my study window onto the adjoining field, I cannot fail to be aware of the large concrete university hall of residence which sits in the middle of it. And, as I walk the paving slabs to climb the stairs of that building, I remain aware of the field within which it sits (not least because of the grass growing between the individual slabs), even as I can no longer see it. I am not trying to draw a crude distinction here between "natural" and "built" elements to the environment, but to point out that the environment we inhabit is not seamless. It is analyzable, even if part of that analysis is stored in memory. I argue, here, that such analyzability is present, too, in our experience of popular song, but that one element of the environment is, precisely, found in memory; that element is formed of the historically-constituted style which a particular song performs.[28] This carries the implication of the music of protest, the musical environment of a particular protest song, opposing some more established musical language. Bob Dylan's "Masters of War"[29] is emblematic of so many protest songs. The lyrics deride the military-industrial complex and are delivered with that faux-Appalachian sneer so characteristic of early Dylan. The melody line, as is well known, does not originate with Dylan, but was "borrowed" from the English folksong "Nottamun Town," while Dylan provides a harmonic underpinning. Note its bareness, as the rather imprecise lower strings of the guitar contrast with the brighter, but almost entirely static, upper strings. Two aspects of this eight-line verse structure are notable. The first is that the melody for lines 3–4 is repeated in lines 5–6. Both these pairs of lines exist at the top of Dylan's range. Lines 1–2 begin low, but rise towards this point, while lines 7–8 drop down. The contour is thus roughly parabolic, with an extended plateau. The resultant α-β-β-χ form is highly unusual, particularly in the detail of internal repetition (where one would more likely expect α-β-α-χ). The second is that the melody implies no particular harmonisation (which might be testament to its possibly medieval origins), and Dylan observes this implication, furnishing it simply with an accompanimental drone (i.e. the harmony remains static throughout with the occasional ornamental aeolian VII). At this, inherent, level, his accompanimental environment carries no implicatory message for the persona Dylan is acting out. However, if we consider the wider musical context for Dylan's intervention, the same cannot be said. On one level, his accompaniment accords with an early 1960s practice. The US folk scene was replete with bare, acoustic guitar accompaniments for relatively unadorned vocal lines. But such extreme harmonic minimalism was not the way folk(-like) songs were being accompanied, not even if they were protest songs.[30] Indeed, it may be more useful to consider Dylan's practice here as demonstrating the influence of contemporary blues artists.[31] But, even when John Lee Hooker uses a single under-lying harmony for something like "Boogie Chillun," the prominent riff ensures a more active personic environment than the one Dylan provides. Starkness is the essential quality of this performance of "Masters of War," offsetting Dylan's hor-rific lyric (and hence foregrounding his persona) and challenging the richer, more seductive, harmonic frippery of his contemporaries (and of other items in his oeu-vre). Dylan's artistic strategy here may not have convinced all,[32] but, within the milieu of the 1960s music industry, it appeared effective. So, while the "protest" quality of the lyrics seems self-evident, the "protest" position of the music can also be attested.

I move forward, historically, to the protest which was felt to be embodied in the punk movement. What is contextually remarkable in the Sex Pistols' "God Save the Queen"[33] is the extreme regularity of John Lydon's accompaniment; it has what is almost a martial quality. The kit pattern is unyielding, the guitar and bass, while syncopating, do so in a perfectly regular manner, repeating the same synco-pation every time, clearly rehearsed and permitting no individual variation. This exemplifies an almost extreme level of control, extending to the thoroughly norma-tive approach to harmony (even, at the end of the solo, preparing the subsequent downbeat on chord I with an extended chord V; eighteenth-century classicism was no less subtle at this intraopus juncture). Lydon's delivery, however, is altogether different. Rhythmically, his vocal is no less marshaled by the regular beat, while those syllables which would be stressed were his lyric spoken, are equally stressed in his delivery. His pitching, however, tells a different story. Occasionally, he coin-cides with a consonance in relation to the harmony. Such coincidence, however, appears accidental. This disdain for melody, combined with a generally energetic manner, characterises his entire approach. What should be made of the disparity between Lydon's voice and his accompaniment? Two types of implied reading of an accompaniment can be discerned from the general literature. The first is that of a representation of the persona's external environment; the second is that of an aural representation of the persona's body language, or inner monologue.[34] In this case, the latter seems unlikely, for Lydon's actual body language while singing often appeared far more awkward, wayward, unregulated, than is suggested by the aural qualities of his accompaniment.[35] A more reasonable reading here, then, is of his accompaniment as his established environment, i.e. of one of constriction; it is that inter-musical distinction which conveys Lydon's protest.

A Broad Conception of Protest

More interesting examples appear on P. J. Harvey's recent album *Let England Shake*. While the lyrics to "The Words That Maketh Murder"[36] might encourage an identification as a "song of resistance" (Laing), I shall argue that the personic environment clearly identifies "a specific issue or enemy," thus defining it as a "protest song." Note first the strange dislocation introduced by the harmony. The verse is based on a simple, almost chthonic, sequence: A, G, F# minor, E minor. This downward pattern is very easy to play on the guitar (or the autoharp Harvey uses) but, right from the outset, seems to call for continuation to its logical outcome, D. I suspect this call comes from the fact that the chords do not change on the beat, but on the afterbeat. We eventually get a chord of D, as the "resolution" to the chorus, on the song's title words, but it's D minor, not major, and it has been introduced by a G and a G minor, a context closer to D minor than D major. That turn from an "expected" major to a minor is, I think, crucial to the way the song signifies. The outro returns to a downward sequence focused on D minor (i.e. D minor, C minor, B flat, G minor), in a sense drawing together both verse and chorus.

The lyrics seem fairly straightforward. As one posting has it, the song refers "to the act of documenting the atrocities, bringing them to light. The concept of justice, like a war tribunal that investigates 'war crimes,' judges them and calls them murder. Until this happens they are just acts committed in war."[37] With the first person address ("I've seen …"), one can certainly imagine such a tribunal, but what of the word "maketh"? This is an archaic form of "makes," i.e. third person singular.[38] It is thus grammatically incorrect, and yet the archaism is self-evident. Archaisms distance us from the action, so this suggests some heightened reality for the described body parts blown hither and thither. Rhythmically, the second syllable is crucial; "the words that ma—ke murder" would sound very awkward. "The words that make it murder" would work, but the "it" may be too specific for what Polly Harvey wants to convey. The grammatical inaccuracy, if uttered by the same protagonist who describes what he has seen, would convey a sense of his being unlettered, simply an ordinary soldier of perhaps a century ago ("corporal whose nerves were shot" implies a time before a diagnosis of post-traumatic stress was available). This perspective is reinforced by Polly Harvey's delivery, both uninvolved in the action (none of the horrific images are matched by any horror, fear, or disgust in the voice) but also almost hysterical (those strange leaps which begin in the first verse on "soldiers," for example). That her persona is female, and yet the protagonists are male, simply intensifies the distancing. Were this such a tribunal, presumably it is decision-makers at some level, and not the poor squaddie, who are answering for their actions.

This is all very well, but how does it relate to that strange, extended, repetitive outro? Co-copyright in the song is assigned to the estate of "Edward Cochran," acknowledging the intertextual reference to his "Summertime Blues."[39] That reference is multiplied if we take into account two textural features of Harvey's track.[40] First, the track, in general, is bathed in reverb at about 15ms[41] (the tail of the reverb on guitar chords is clearly audible in its own right), equivalent to that of a dance hall, a typical venue for Cochran's brand of rockabilly. However, a full dance hall would have soaked up the sound, so this is an empty dance hall. The song is therefore being sung to nobody specifically, Cochran's own physical absence (his accidental death on the A4 in Chippenham, Wiltshire, in April 1960) perhaps marked. Second, close listening reveals two strummed string signals in the mix, one on either side. One is mixed plain, with no reverb (as "authentically" played, perhaps), while the other is wet. Perhaps this signifies an ironic take on the guitar sound, also reminiscent of Cochran's Grech. In "Summertime Blues," Cochran's persona's taking of his problem to the UN is a useless gesture; the excessively repeated line here only intensifies that uselessness. The gesture of Cochran's persona, though, is effectively selfish, whereas that of Polly Harvey's persona is most assuredly not. Perhaps those repetitions also signify the effort that has to be made to get heard? And who is Polly Harvey's persona here? The fact that the outro is centred on D minor, rather than the E minor of the descriptive verses, indicates that the outro is spoken from the position of a different protagonist, perhaps Polly Harvey herself? This would mean that the verdict ("the words that maketh murder") is more likely her own than a soldier's (since that chorus is also based on D minor).

So, how does this bear on the difference between a "song of resistance" and a "protest song" wherein the "specific issue or enemy" is identified? The issue is specified by the Cochran intertextual references. It is only with recent conflicts[42] that the idea of a war crimes tribunal has taken root. The Cochran references take us back to the Cold War; the images in the lyrics imply earlier conflicts, perhaps of the late nineteenth or earlier twentieth century. This peppergun approach implies that all such conflicts are in scope here, but all potentially are ineffectual (the involvement of the UN, the testimony of the individual soldier, the error embodied in "maketh"). It is thus a profoundly pessimistic song, a protest which recognises its own ineffectuality.

The subject of the protest of Skunk Anansie's "On My Hotel TV"[43] is also not immediately obvious. An interested listener can certainly find out the reported intention of the singer, Skin, in discussing two aspects to the song. She claims that the offensive adjectives which constitute the majority of the lyrics have been directed at this multi-racial band, by persons unnamed, and that the title refers to her experience of being on tour, of her only access to the "real world" being through the images of her "hotel TV"[44] The song has no narrative, though, and it is as if it is left to the listener to construct sense from barely related elements. What are those distinct elements? The name-calling ("Skinny, kacky, para ... nigger," etc.) and title act as verse and chorus; there is a single pair of sung lines and brief instrumental which together act as a bridge, there is a short introduction, a post-chorus guitar hook, and a more extended coda. No obvious link is made between "verse" and "chorus." Does the name-calling take place on the TV? Again, I argue that the most effective aspect to the track is not the ostensible meaning of the lyrics, but how they are delivered, and two aspects of this dominate. Note, to begin, the dominant rhythmic profile of the guitar hook. We hear two busy beats, with internal syncopation, and then two beats of silence filled only by the time-keeping hi-hat. Against this regularity, note how Skin throws out her list of epithets. In the first line, these are each of two syllables, but the first is ejected so swiftly; there is a clear gap between each pair of syllables. Had this been a film scene, an actor could have spat out such a list with an equal degree of venom but, without a regular, constraining, track of beats, part of its force would have been lost. It is that constraint which is so powerful here, reining in some of the anger which we can feel, empathically, but do not hear. And how strong a warning that is, that there is emotive force still held back. In particular, note how the empty part of the hook (two beats at the end of the bar) reveals perhaps the most potent of these epithets—"nigger"—to be heard loud and clear. The second aspect appears in the chorus. In order to "top" this, to fulfil the proper function of a chorus, Skin has to unleash the force held back in the verse and, I would maintain, she achieves this. "On my hotel TV" is sung with immense power, and yet it is sung, not shouted; again, something is held in reserve. It is not until the ensuing short bridge (at 46"), when she finally shouts "turn it off," that the process set in motion by the beginning is completed, a process which also relies on the guitar now filling the entire rhythmic space, and with a gradually climbing chromatic line so perfectly emblematic of rising emotional tension.

So much, so strong. And yet, we are still not finished. Three remarkable events in the track are still to come. The first follows the second verse/chorus pair, in a short guitar break over which Skin does what I can only describe as whooping with joy (1'34"). While this might appear out of line with the interpretation I am mounting, it is a highly expressive response to the success with which the rising anger is portrayed earlier. At this point, perhaps we should recall that the persona through which a track is delivered is always fictional, no matter how autobiographical the narrative. The performance, even if constructed in the studio, is a performance. It results from specialized labor. And here, perhaps, Deborah Dyer (that individual who adopts the stage name Skin) briefly emerges. For the final two events I am indebted to my student Sam Heath. At 1'57", in the third verse, Skin opposes "black" with "white" (each sung six times). And yet, if you listen closely, there is something wrong with the way that latter word is enunciated, the "-t" encroaching on every subsequent "wh-". Reverse this through sound manipulation software, and the resultant word (which sounds something like "stew") appears a little more credible as a set of phonemes which can actually be performed. It is at least possible, then, that what we hear as "white" is, literally, a reversed form of what was actually sung, and the clue lies in the not-quite-right-sounding nature of the "white" we hear (particularly since it is followed by two lines of what literally sound as nonsense). This, then, is an intensely evocative realizing of the racial opposition which is, at least in part, the subject of the band's protest. In the track's long playout, a similar device is used. Immediately prior to the line "truth and reconciliation," presumably sampled from a speech, we hear a small excerpt of African traditional call-and-response singing but, again, reversed. The nature of the black/white opposition, with all that historically entails,[45] is thus foregrounded as something which, as a listener, one is encouraged (I might almost say *required*) to take on board.

Conclusion

So, how should I bring to an end this rather meandering discussion? What thoughts are brought to the fore? I hope there are sufficient examples here to convince you that to consider the meaning of a protest song to lie, simply, with its lyrics, is to completely misunderstand the cultural form that it is. A musical persona, from whom the protest comes, always exists within a musical environment, an environment which may consist, as in my Martin Luther King example, of no more that a hint of rhythmic identity and pitch profile. That environment sometimes intervenes in the relationship which persists between the persona's words and the listener's making of sense, sometimes supports such a relationship, and sometimes remains inert. It is, though, always there. Which is, surely, why we don't read protest songs, we listen to them.

Notes

1 Alan Merriam, *The Anthropology of Music* (Chicago, Illinois: Northwestern University Press, 1964), 219–227.

2 The protest of a protest song is not generally illocutionary. See J. L. Austin, *How To Do Things With Words* (Oxford: Oxford University Press, 1976).

3 John Street, *Music and Politics* (Cambridge: Polity, 2012), 44.

4 He also distinguishes between situations where "states—as censors—invest music with political significance, even where none is intended by the performer" and, finally, where "fans may use music to express political ideas that the performer never imagined." Street, *Music and Politics*, 44–45.

5 And, thus, that the circumscription Street draws around the *political* may be likewise unhelpful, in this circumstance.

6 Available at http://www.youtube.com/watch?v=t9e7j0CRd08, accessed 6 July 2011.

7 http://www.presentationmagazine.com/analysis-of-martin-luther-kings-i-have-a-dream-speech-8059.htm considers just its content, while http://sixminutes.dlugan.com/speech-analysis-dream-martin-luther-king/ at least considers its rhetoric.

8 For instance, Alexandra Alvarez, "Martin Luther King's 'I Have a Dream': The Speech

Event as Metaphor," *Journal of Black Studies*, Vol. 18 (1988): 337–357; David Bobbitt, *The Rhetoric of Redemption: Kenneth Burke's Redemption Drama and Martin Luther King Jr's I Have a Dream speech* (Lanham, Maryland: Rowman and Littlefield, 2004).

9 Even if, as Bobbitt notes, some have found "the speech as being empty of substance," and insisting that "Americans misuse the speech when they try to treat it as anything more than an inspirational sermon (albeit a great one) articulating an ideal vision." Bobbitt, *Rhetoric of Redemption*, 114, 115.

10 Available at http://www.youtube.com/watch?v=smEqnnklfYs, accessed 18 October 2011.

11 Bobbitt, *Rhetoric of Redemption*, 115.

12 The full text can be found at http://www.usconstitution.net/dream.html, accessed 6 July 2011.

13 The rhythmic analysis of conversation in Peter Auer, Elizabeth Couper-Kuhlen, and Frank Müller, *Language in Time* (New York: Oxford University Press, 1999) represents a useful starting-point.

14 Cf. the argument in Greg Goodale, *Sonic Persuasion* (Urbana, Illinois: University of Illinois Press, 2011).

15 "The Persona/Environment relation in recorded song," reprinted in Mark Spencer, *Rock Music* (Farnham: Ashgate 2012), 275–294; "Where is here? An issue of deictic projection in recorded song," *Journal of the Royal Musical Association* Vol. 135, No. 1 (2010): 145–182; and *Song Means* (Farnham: Ashgate, 2012), 188–207.

16 By no means necessarily coextensive with the real-life identity of the performer.

17 I discuss dozens of examples along these lines in the writings cited above.

18 Barry McGuire, *Eve of Destruction*, LP, © 1965 RCA Victor, RCA1469.

19 The Beatles, *Revolver*, LP, © 1966 Parlophone, PCS7009.

20 Jimi Hendrix, *Are You Experienced*, LP, © 1967 Experience Hendrix/MCA 612 001.

21 Style Council, *Our Favourite Shop*, LP, © 1985 Polydor, 825 700-1.

22 I particularly have in mind the album *What's Going On*, LP, © 1971 Tamla, STML 11190.

23 Available at http://www.marcogiunco.com/Testi/001585_01.htm, accessed 17 November 2012. Whitehall is the street/area in central London which houses most of the functions of UK central government.

24 Blossom Toes, *If Only for a Moment*, LP, © 1969 Marmalade 608 010.

25 My guess as to its source would be Captain Beefheart, probably as filtered through Edgar Broughton.

26 The interval between, for instance, the notes B and F, or C and F#.

27 For discussion of cross-modal meaning in popular song, see *Song Means*, 239, 256, and the references therein.

28 I develop this perspective on the concept of the performance of music style in my *Rock: The Primary Text* (Aldershot: Ashgate, 2001), 201ff.

29 Bob Dylan, *The Freewheelin' Bob Dylan*, LP, © 1963, Columbia CS 8786.

30 I have in mind the singing, particularly, of Pete Seeger, Phil Ochs, Fred Neil, Vince Martin, Tom Paxton, and Richard Farina.

31 A source of some of both his and Ochs' protest lyrics in "talking blues" mode. On Bob

Dylan and the blues, see Albin Zak III, "Bob Dylan and Jimi Hendrix: Juxtaposition and Transformation in 'All Along the Watchtower'," reprinted in Mark Spencer, ed., *Rock Music* (Farnham, Ashgate 2012), 373–418.

32 The words of Ewan MacColl in 1987: "Dylan is so self-conscious, so lugubrious, the kind of way he uses the theft from Garcia Lorca: it's Garcia Lorca reduced! If you're going to use somebody, you should enhance it not reduce it ... I think if Dylan really was such a revolutionary influence, or such a mirror of the revolutionary youth, why is it that within five years the whole of that revolution had been dissipated?" "The first interview," in Allan F. Moore and Giovanni Vacca, eds., *The Legacies of Ewan MacColl* (Farnham: Ashgate, forthcoming).

33 Sex Pistols, *Never Mind the Bollocks*, LP, © Virgin 202984.

34 And these readings are not necessarily mutually contradictory.

35 Note his complete lack of physical involvement with his performance at this gig from 1977: http://www.youtube.com/watch?v=YwXc-RFI-zk&feature=related, accessed 13 December 2011.

36 P. J. Harvey, *Let England Shake*, CD, © 2011 Island 2763025.

37 "Daphne84" at http://www.songmeanings.net/songs/view/3530822107858857371/ (accessed 17 Jan 2012). The song's lyrics can be found reproduced here, also.

38 In a phrase such as "manners maketh man," the "manners" acts as a singular, collective, noun. "Words," though, cannot act as a singular noun.

39 Eddie Cochran, "Summertime Blues," London 45HLU8702, single, 1958.

40 My thanks to my student Iain Campbell for alerting me to these.

41 That is, 15 milliseconds.

42 The establishment of the UN war crimes tribunal in 2002 after ad hoc tribunals had existed for a decade or so.

43 Skunk Anansie, *Post-orgasmic Chill*, CD, © 1999 Virgin 7243 8 47104 0 8.

44 The relevant interview can be found at http://www.youtube.com/watch?v=RMm4Om_i1pY, accessed 7 February 2012.

45 Surely, the sample refers, and may even be taken from an explicit reference, to the South African Truth & Reconciliation process which helped ease racial tension in the wake of the dismantling of apartheid, although its role here is in no way clarified by this realisation.

INDEX